SURVIVING THE GREAT INDOORS

Other Baby Blues® Books from Andrews McMeel Publishing

Guess Who Didn't Take a Nap?

I Thought Labor Ended When the Baby Was Born

We Are Experiencing Parental Difficulties . . . Please Stand By

Night of the Living Dad

I Saw Elvis in My Ultrasound

One More and We're Outnumbered!

Check, Please . . .

Threats, Bribes & Videotape

If I'm a Stay-at-Home Mom, Why Am I Always in the Car?

Lift and Separate

I Shouldn't Have to Scream More Than Once!

Motherhood Is Not for Wimps

Baby Blues®: Unplugged

Dad to the Bone

Never a Dry Moment

Two Plus One Is Enough

Playdate: Category 5

Our Server Is Down

Something Chocolate This Way Comes

Briefcase Full of Baby Blues®

Night Shift

The Day Phonics Kicked In

My Space

The Natural Disorder of Things

We Were Here First

Ambushed! In the Family Room

Cut!

Eat, Cry, Poop

Scribbles at an Exhibition

Bedlam

Wetter, Louder, Stickier

No Yelling!

Gross!

Binge Parenting

Adult Time

Treasuries

The Super-Absorbent, Biodegradable, Family-Size Baby Blues®

Baby Blues®: Ten Years and Still in Diapers

Butt-Naked Baby Blues®

Wall-to-Wall Baby Blues®

Driving Under the Influence of Children

Framed!

X-Treme Parenting

BBXX: Baby Blues: Decades 1 & 2

Gift Books

It's a Boy

It's a Girl

SURVIVING THE GREAT INDOORS

rick kirkman

jerry scott

Scrapbook

NO. 36

Andrews McMeel
PUBLISHING®

To John, Brittany, and baby Jane with friendship and gratitude.

—J.S.

To John Arnett, friend, master percussionist—
and always there with a laugh for a Hammie strip.

—R.K.

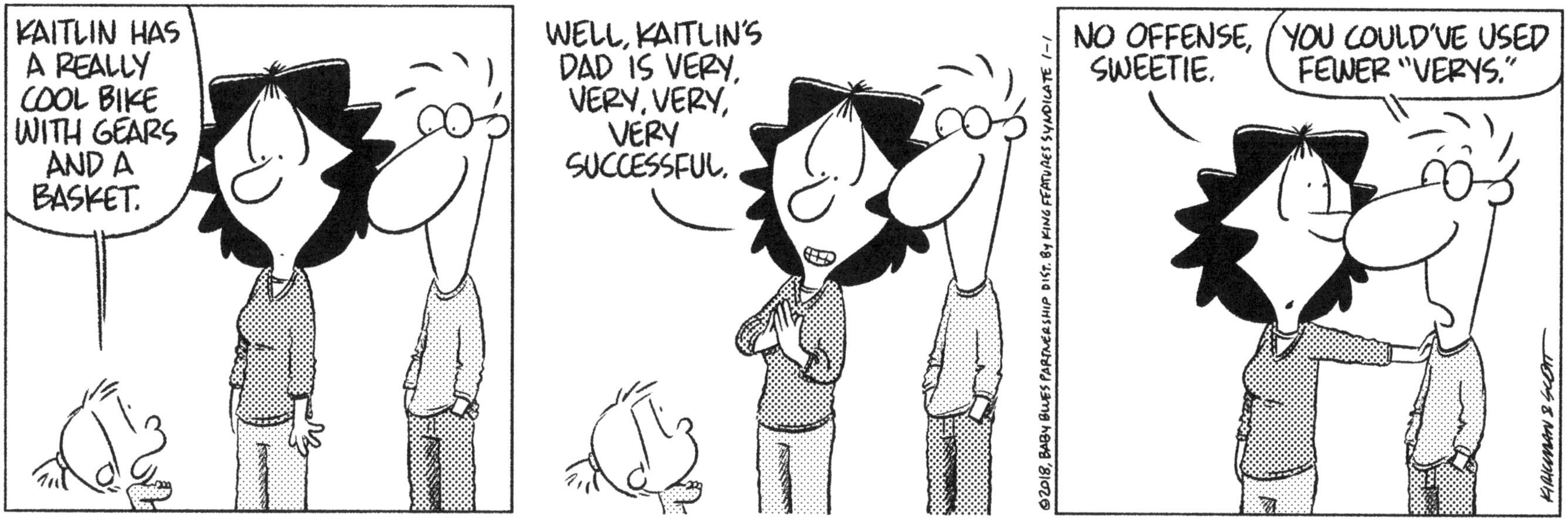
KAITLIN HAS A REALLY COOL BIKE WITH GEARS AND A BASKET.
WELL, KAITLIN'S DAD IS VERY, VERY, VERY, VERY SUCCESSFUL.
©2018, BABY BLUES PARTNERSHIP DIST. BY KING FEATURES SYNDICATE 1-1
NO OFFENSE, SWEETIE.
YOU COULD'VE USED FEWER "VERYS."
KIRKMAN & SCOTT

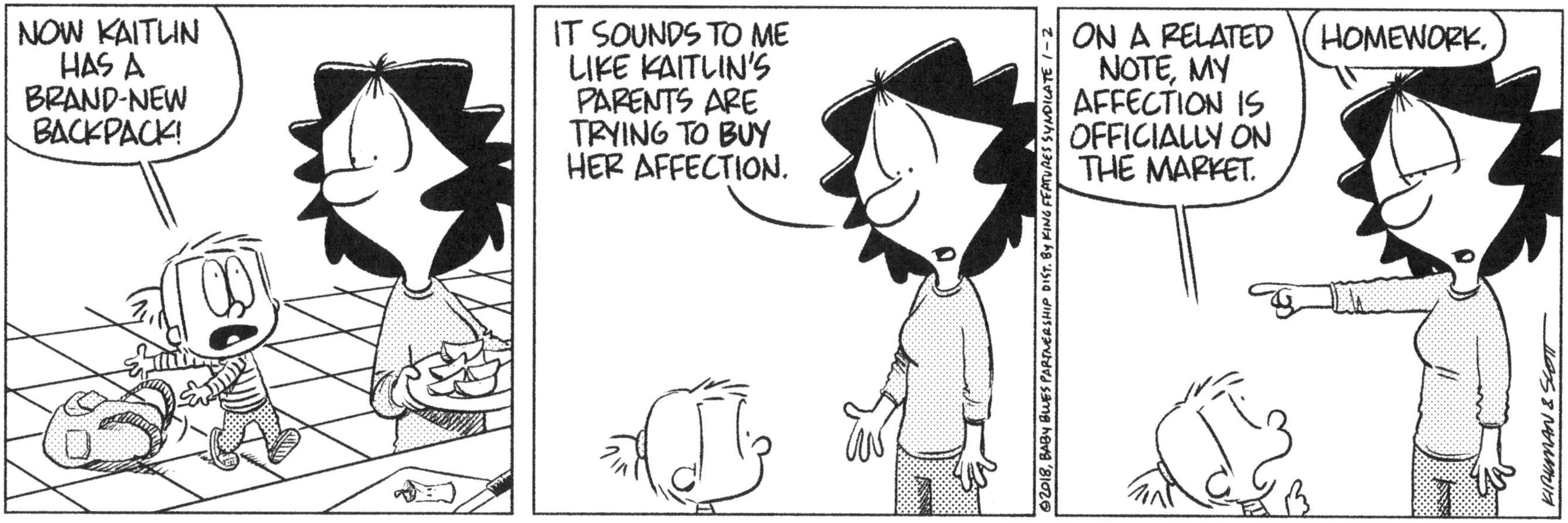
NOW KAITLIN HAS A BRAND-NEW BACKPACK!
IT SOUNDS TO ME LIKE KAITLIN'S PARENTS ARE TRYING TO BUY HER AFFECTION.
©2018, BABY BLUES PARTNERSHIP DIST. BY KING FEATURES SYNDICATE 1-2
ON A RELATED NOTE, MY AFFECTION IS OFFICIALLY ON THE MARKET.
HOMEWORK.
KIRKMAN & SCOTT

Rick: I feel like every parent struggles with this. I know we did. Instant, transient love from a kid vs. the delayed gratification of producing a great adult.

Jerry: This does not apply to all Kaitlins. Just the annoying ones. You know who you are.

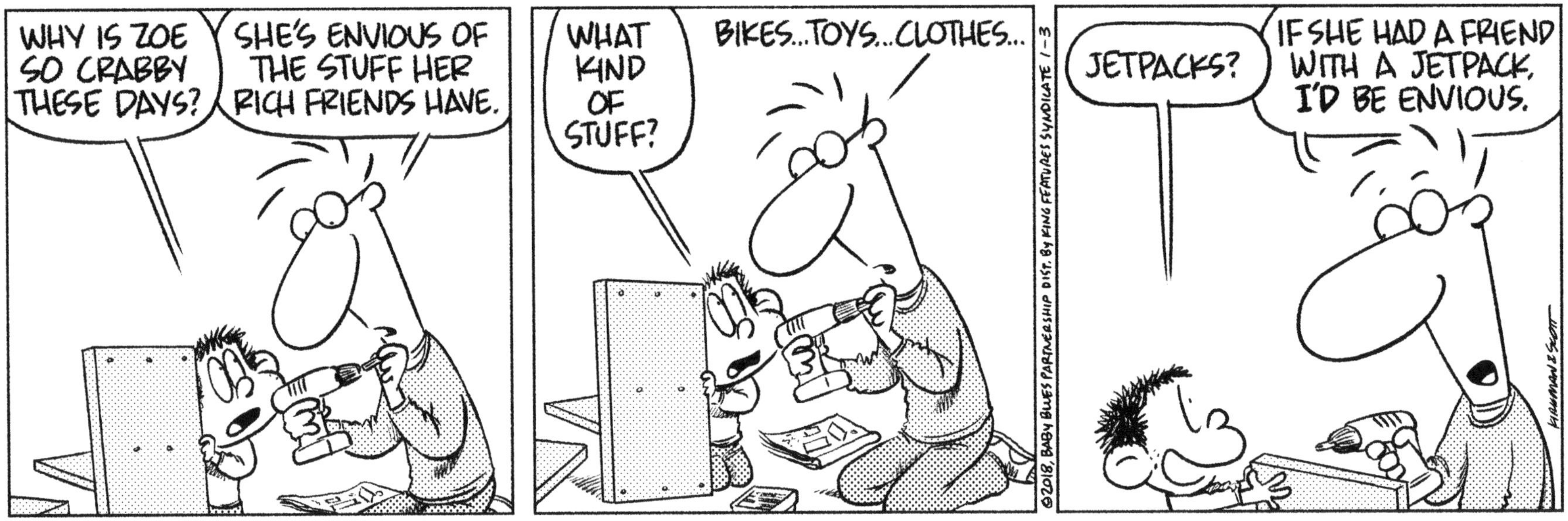
WHY IS ZOE SO CRABBY THESE DAYS?
SHE'S ENVIOUS OF THE STUFF HER RICH FRIENDS HAVE.
WHAT KIND OF STUFF?
BIKES...TOYS...CLOTHES...
©2018, BABY BLUES PARTNERSHIP DIST. BY KING FEATURES SYNDICATE 1-3
JETPACKS?
IF SHE HAD A FRIEND WITH A JETPACK, I'D BE ENVIOUS.
KIRKMAN & SCOTT

Rick: I have no idea what I have Darryl and Hammie assembling, but I'd put money on it that there will be at least one part left over.

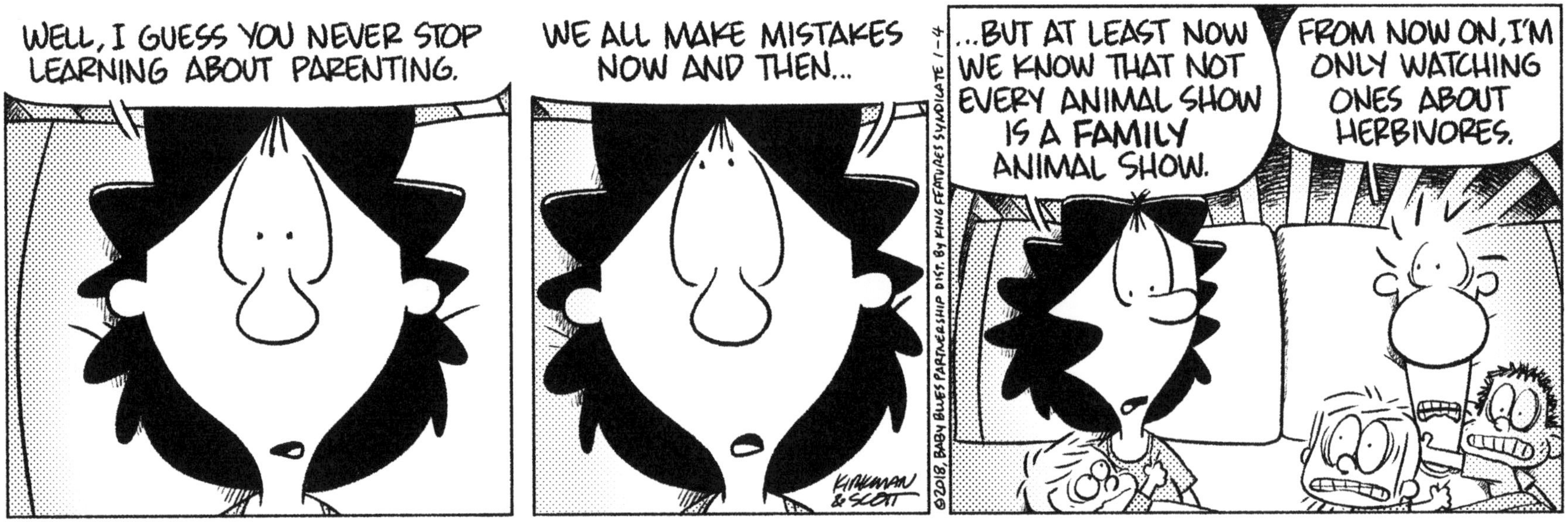
WELL, I GUESS YOU NEVER STOP LEARNING ABOUT PARENTING.
WE ALL MAKE MISTAKES NOW AND THEN...
KIRKMAN & SCOTT
©2018, BABY BLUES PARTNERSHIP DIST. BY KING FEATURES SYNDICATE 1-4
...BUT AT LEAST NOW WE KNOW THAT NOT EVERY ANIMAL SHOW IS A FAMILY ANIMAL SHOW.
FROM NOW ON, I'M ONLY WATCHING ONES ABOUT HERBIVORES.

Rick: Revisiting a lesson learned in an old strip about a meerkat documentary.

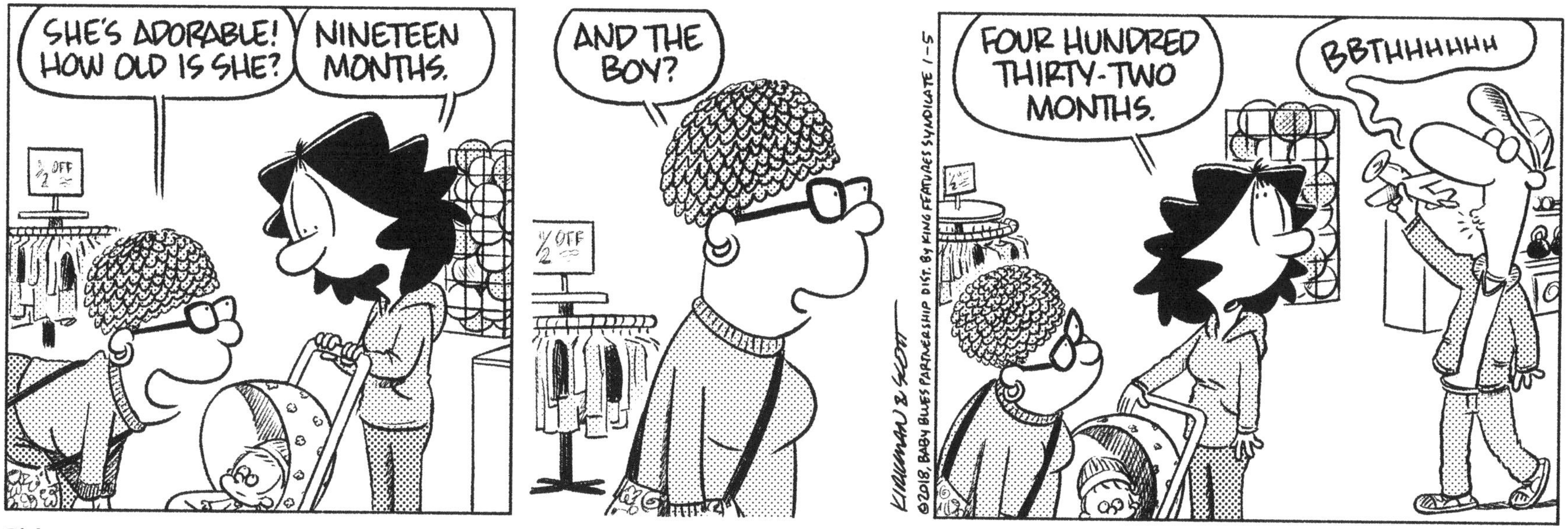
SHE'S ADORABLE! HOW OLD IS SHE?
NINETEEN MONTHS.
AND THE BOY?
FOUR HUNDRED THIRTY-TWO MONTHS.
BBTHHHHHH
½ OFF
KIRKMAN & SCOTT
©2018, BABY BLUES PARTNERSHIP DIST. BY KING FEATURES SYNDICATE 1-5

Rick: I had to use a calculator to see if Jerry just pulled that number out of his . . .

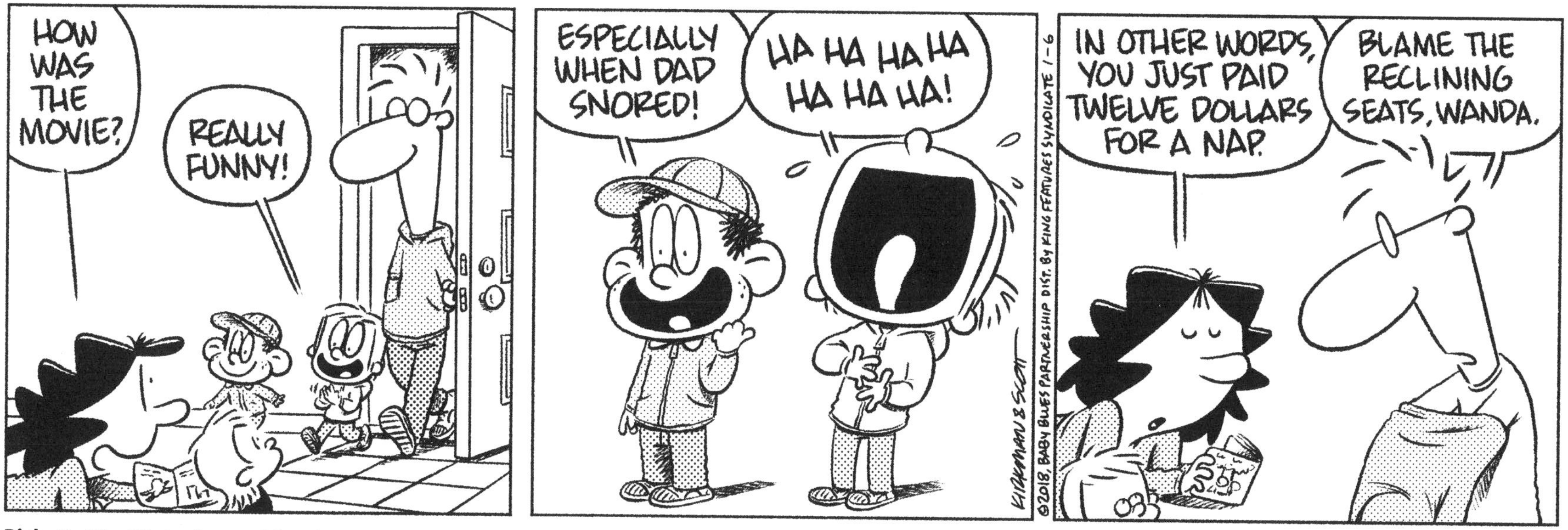
HOW WAS THE MOVIE?
REALLY FUNNY!
ESPECIALLY WHEN DAD SNORED!
HA HA HA HA HA HA HA!
IN OTHER WORDS, YOU JUST PAID TWELVE DOLLARS FOR A NAP.
BLAME THE RECLINING SEATS, WANDA.
KIRKMAN & SCOTT
©2018, BABY BLUES PARTNERSHIP DIST. BY KING FEATURES SYNDICATE 1-6

Rick: Guilty. We took my older daughter to see *Dick Tracy* to celebrate her graduation from kindergarten. You guessed it.

HAVE FUN!

WHO WANTS TO GO FOR A WALK WITH US?
NOT ME.
CAN WE STAY AT HOME ALONE?
WELL, I GUESS SO...
IF YOU'RE CAREFUL.
JUST DON'T ANSWER THE DOOR IF SOMEBODY KNOCKS.
OR THE PHONE... UNLESS IT'S ONE OF US.
KEEP THE DOORS AND WINDOWS LOCKED, AND DON'T GO OUTSIDE.
AND LEAVE THE BLINDS DOWN, IN CASE SOMEONE TRIES TO LOOK IN.
IF THERE'S A FIRE, A GAS LEAK, A BURST PIPE, EXPLOSION...
...BLEEDING INJURY, CHOKING OR BROKEN BONES, CALL 9-1-1.
©2018, BABY BLUES PARTNERSHIP DIST. BY KING FEATURES SYNDICATE
HAVE FUN!
KIRKMAN & SCOTT 1-7

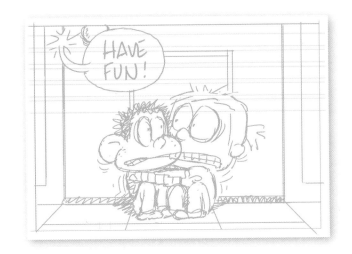

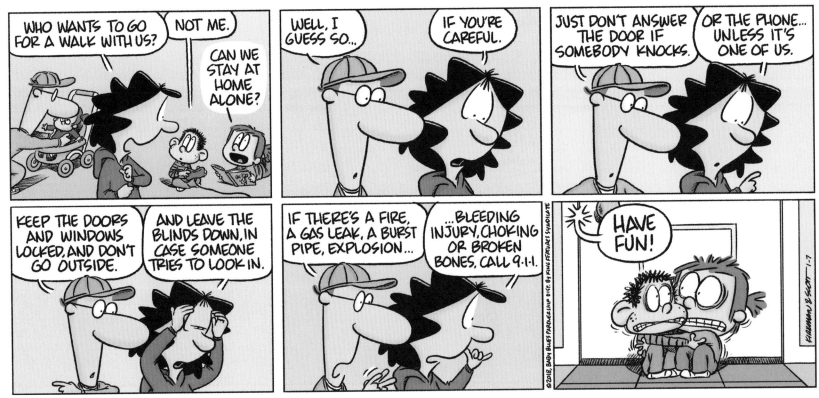

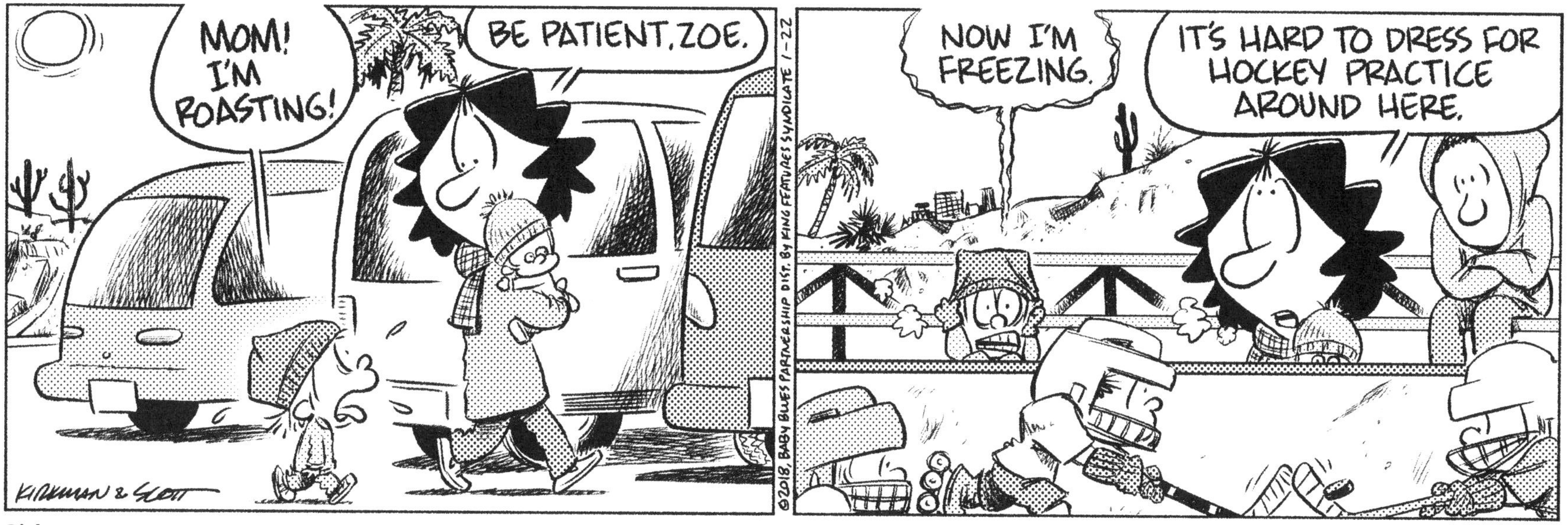
MOM! I'M ROASTING!
BE PATIENT, ZOE.
NOW I'M FREEZING.
IT'S HARD TO DRESS FOR HOCKEY PRACTICE AROUND HERE.
KIRKMAN & SCOTT
©2018, BABY BLUES PARTNERSHIP DIST. BY KING FEATURES SYNDICATE 1-22

Rick: That's Arizona in the winter for you.

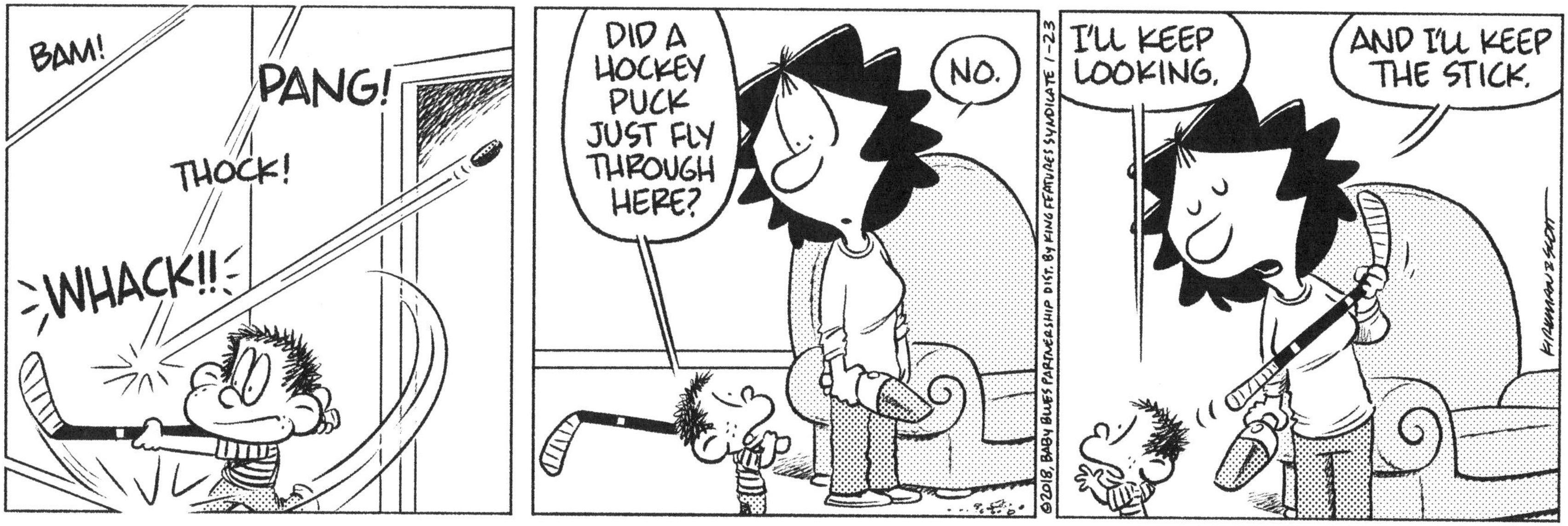
BAM!
PANG!
THOCK!
WHACK!!
DID A HOCKEY PUCK JUST FLY THROUGH HERE?
NO.
I'LL KEEP LOOKING.
AND I'LL KEEP THE STICK.
KIRKMAN & SCOTT
©2018, BABY BLUES PARTNERSHIP DIST. BY KING FEATURES SYNDICATE 1-23

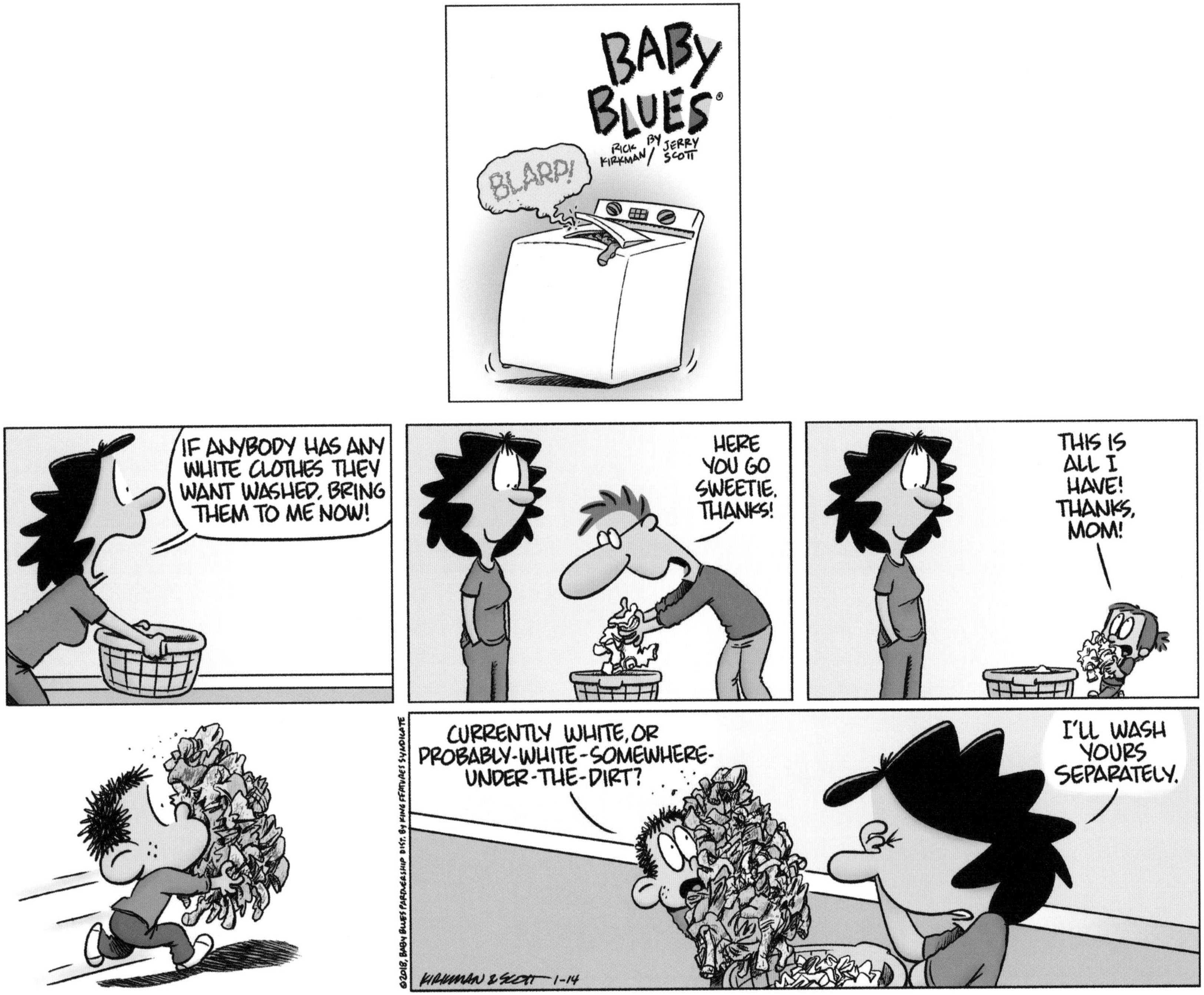
BABY BLUES®
RICK KIRKMAN / BY JERRY SCOTT
BLARP!
IF ANYBODY HAS ANY WHITE CLOTHES THEY WANT WASHED, BRING THEM TO ME NOW!
HERE YOU GO SWEETIE. THANKS!
THIS IS ALL I HAVE! THANKS, MOM!
CURRENTLY WHITE, OR PROBABLY-WHITE-SOMEWHERE-UNDER-THE-DIRT?
I'LL WASH YOURS SEPARATELY.
©2018, BABY BLUES PARTNERSHIP DIST. BY KING FEATURES SYNDICATE
KIRKMAN & SCOTT 1-14

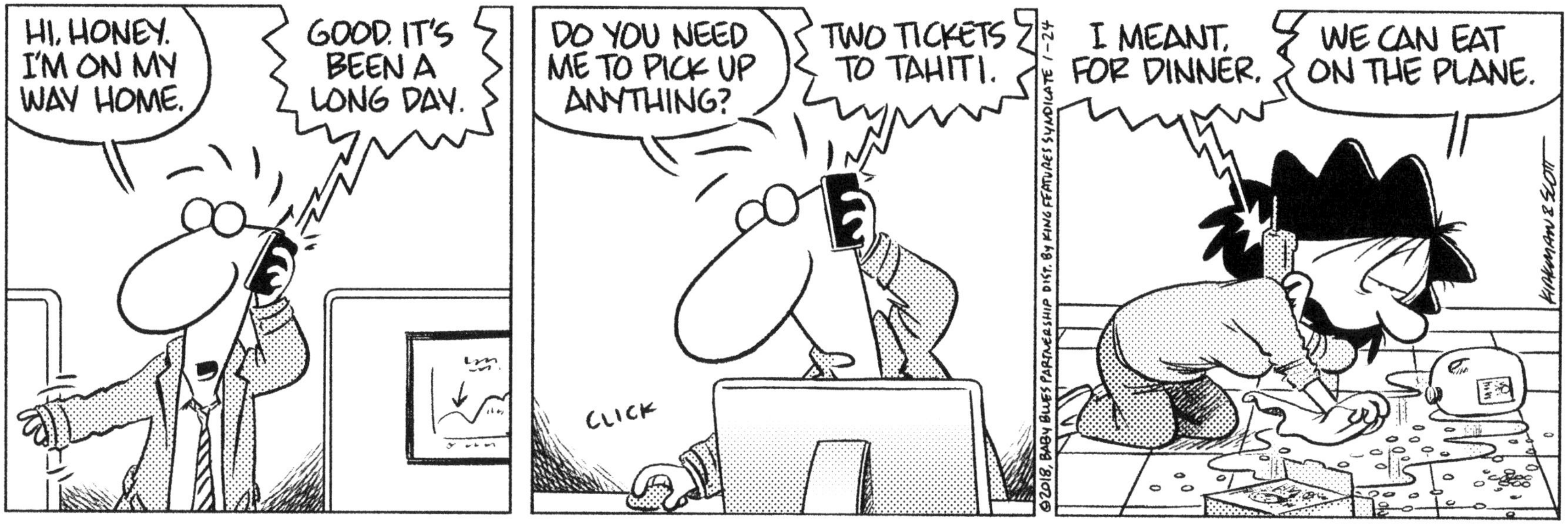
HI, HONEY. I'M ON MY WAY HOME.
GOOD. IT'S BEEN A LONG DAY.
DO YOU NEED ME TO PICK UP ANYTHING?
TWO TICKETS TO TAHITI.
CLICK
I MEANT, FOR DINNER.
WE CAN EAT ON THE PLANE.
©2018, BABY BLUES PARTNERSHIP DIST. BY KING FEATURES SYNDICATE 1-24
KIRKMAN & SCOTT

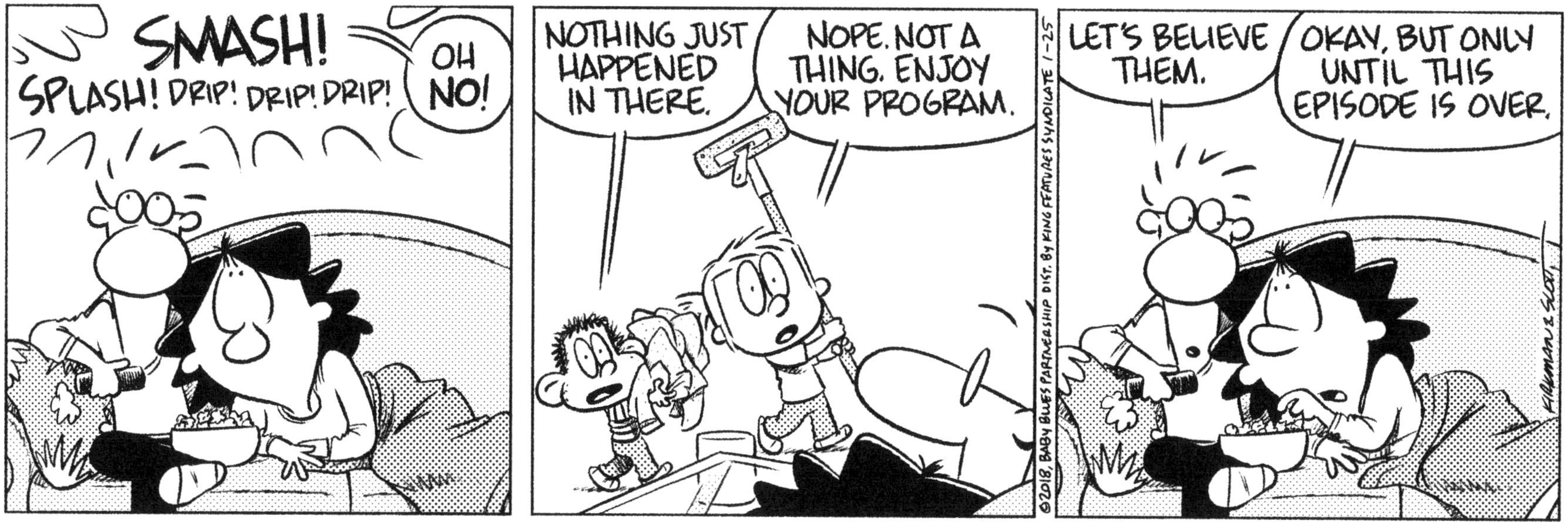
SMASH!
SPLASH! DRIP! DRIP! DRIP!
OH NO!
NOTHING JUST HAPPENED IN THERE.
NOPE. NOT A THING. ENJOY YOUR PROGRAM.
LET'S BELIEVE THEM.
OKAY, BUT ONLY UNTIL THIS EPISODE IS OVER.
©2018, BABY BLUES PARTNERSHIP DIST. BY KING FEATURES SYNDICATE 1-25
KIRKMAN & SCOTT

Rick: Binge-watching seems to take the urgency out of some things.

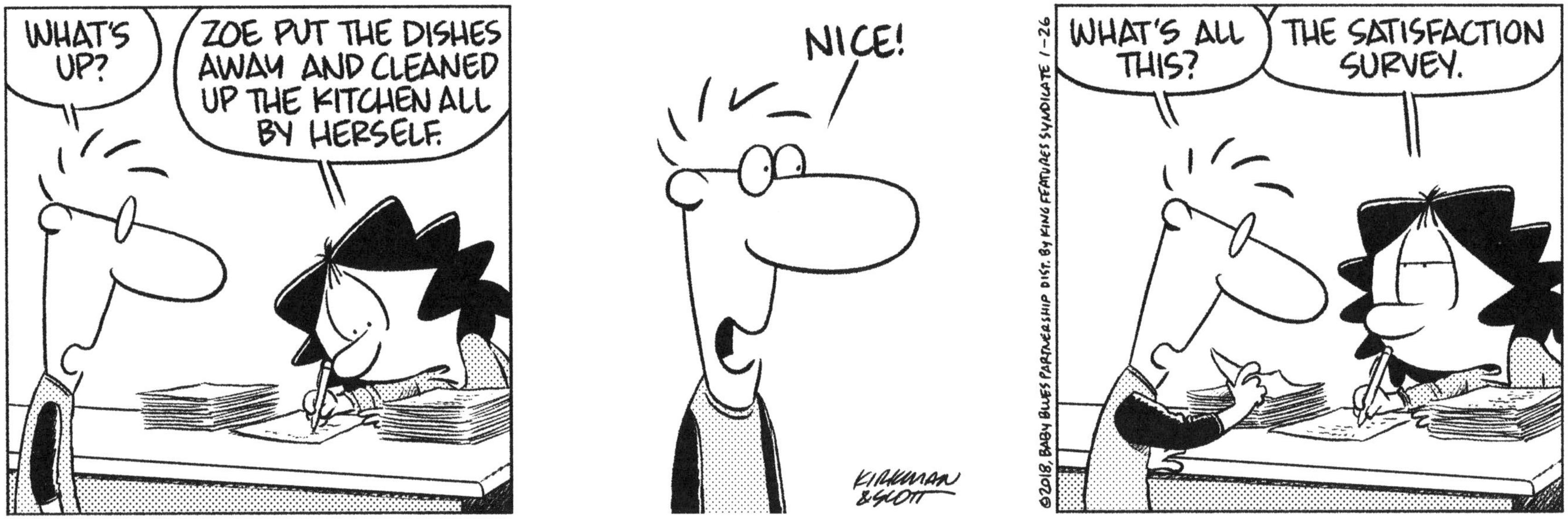
WHAT'S UP?
ZOE PUT THE DISHES AWAY AND CLEANED UP THE KITCHEN ALL BY HERSELF.
NICE!
WHAT'S ALL THIS?
THE SATISFACTION SURVEY.
KIRKMAN & SCOTT
©2018, BABY BLUES PARTNERSHIP DIST. BY KING FEATURES SYNDICATE 1-26

Rick: I hate those! They're everywhere these days!

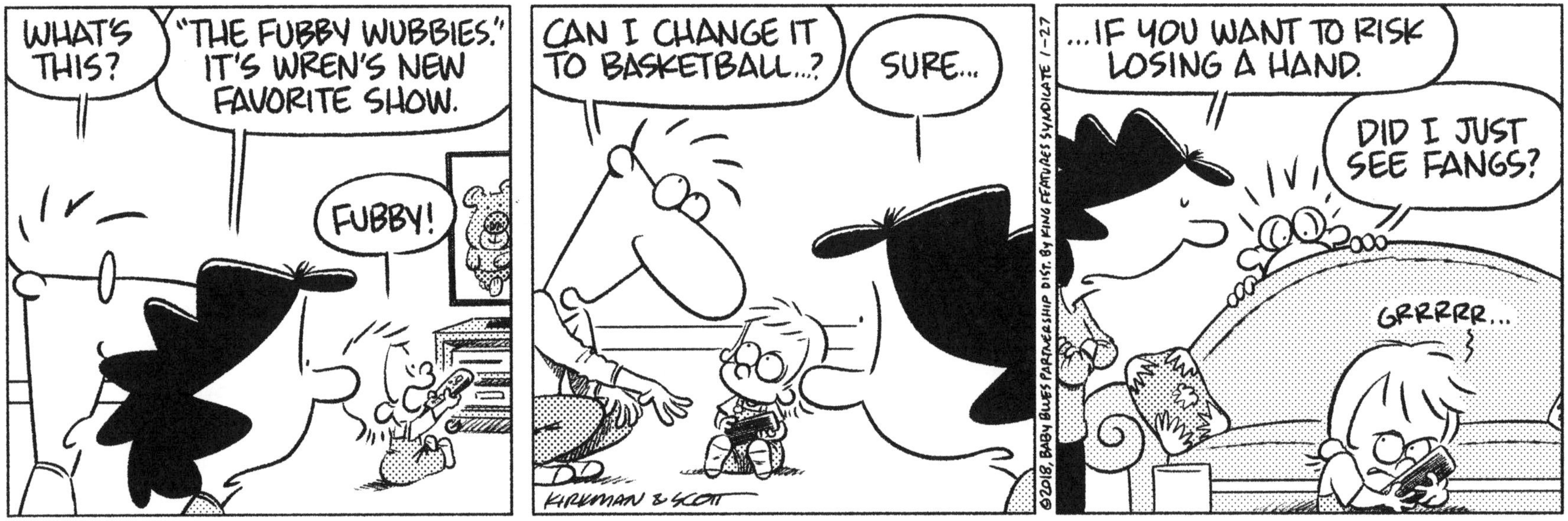
WHAT'S THIS?
"THE FUBBY WUBBIES." IT'S WREN'S NEW FAVORITE SHOW.
FUBBY!
CAN I CHANGE IT TO BASKETBALL...?
SURE...
KIRKMAN & SCOTT
©2018, BABY BLUES PARTNERSHIP DIST. BY KING FEATURES SYNDICATE 1-27
...IF YOU WANT TO RISK LOSING A HAND.
DID I JUST SEE FANGS?
GRRRRR...

Rick: "Fubby Wubby" was actually the way we told the old "Fuzzy Wuzzy" kids' rhyme, replacing all the *z* sounds with *b*'s. We were all in hysterics over it. Dibs on making a kids' book out of it.

Jerry: Don't disrespect the Fubby Wubbies.

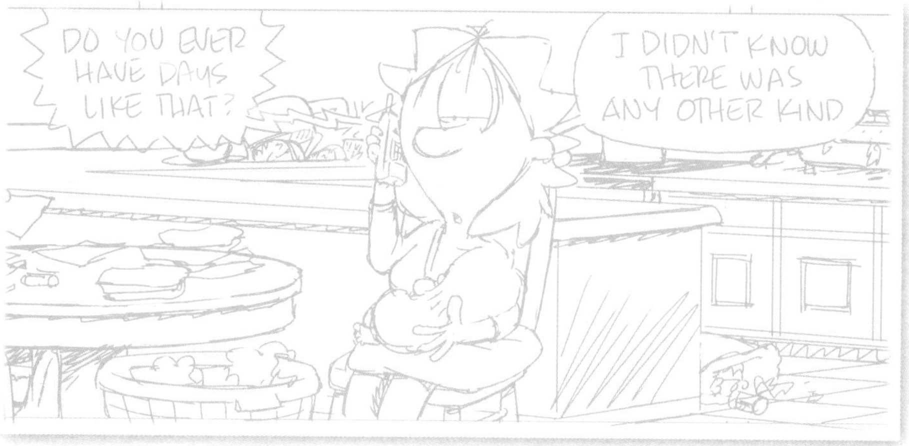
DO YOU EVER HAVE DAYS LIKE THAT?
I DIDN'T KNOW THERE WAS ANY OTHER KIND

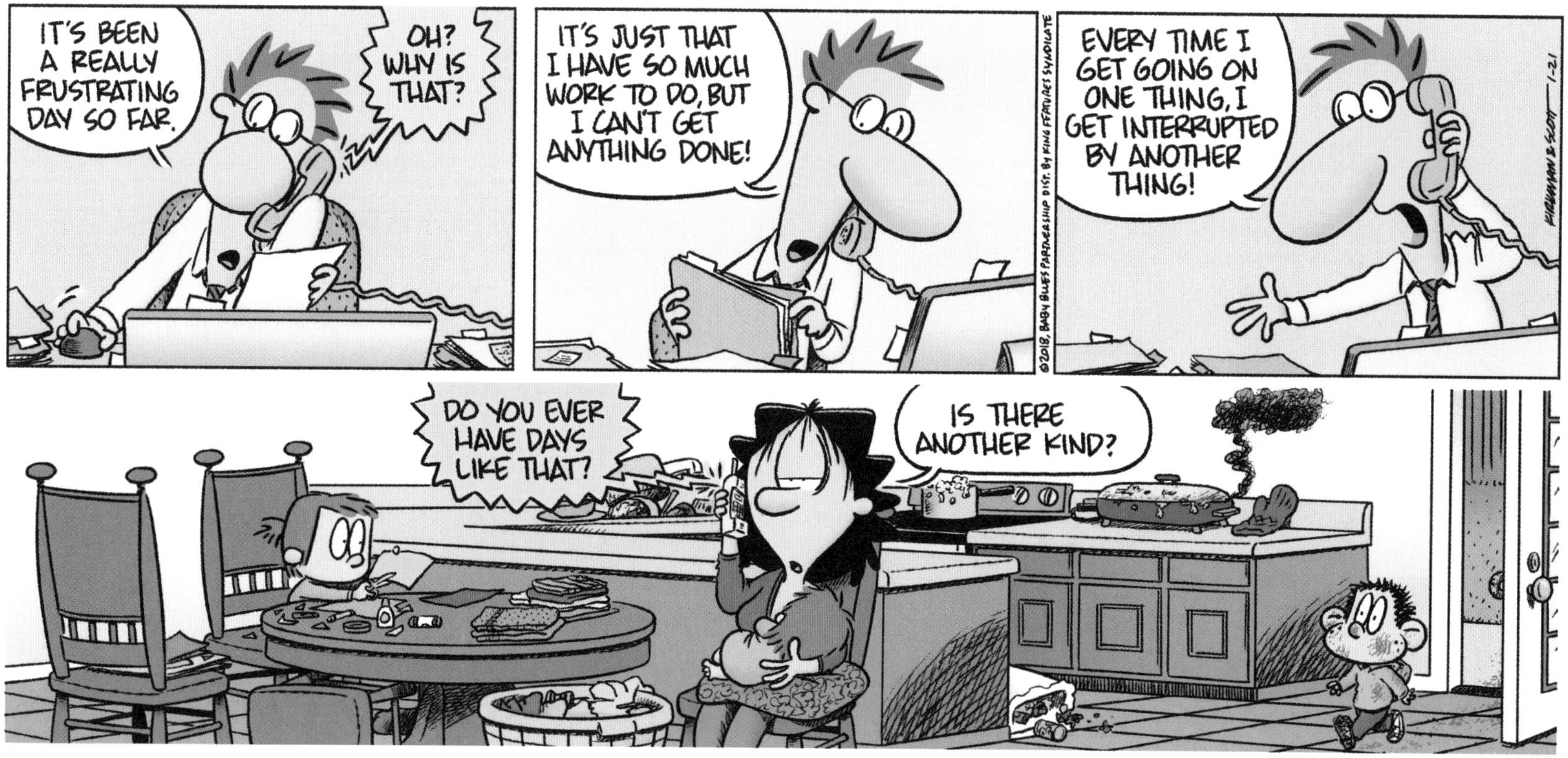
IT'S BEEN A REALLY FRUSTRATING DAY SO FAR.
OH? WHY IS THAT?
IT'S JUST THAT I HAVE SO MUCH WORK TO DO, BUT I CAN'T GET ANYTHING DONE!
©2018, BABY BLUES PARTNERSHIP DIST. BY KING FEATURES SYNDICATE
EVERY TIME I GET GOING ON ONE THING, I GET INTERRUPTED BY ANOTHER THING!
1-21
DO YOU EVER HAVE DAYS LIKE THAT?
IS THERE ANOTHER KIND?

Rick: Strips keep changing up until the last minute. Here, Jerry refined the last line to shorten it from the line you see in the rough sketch.

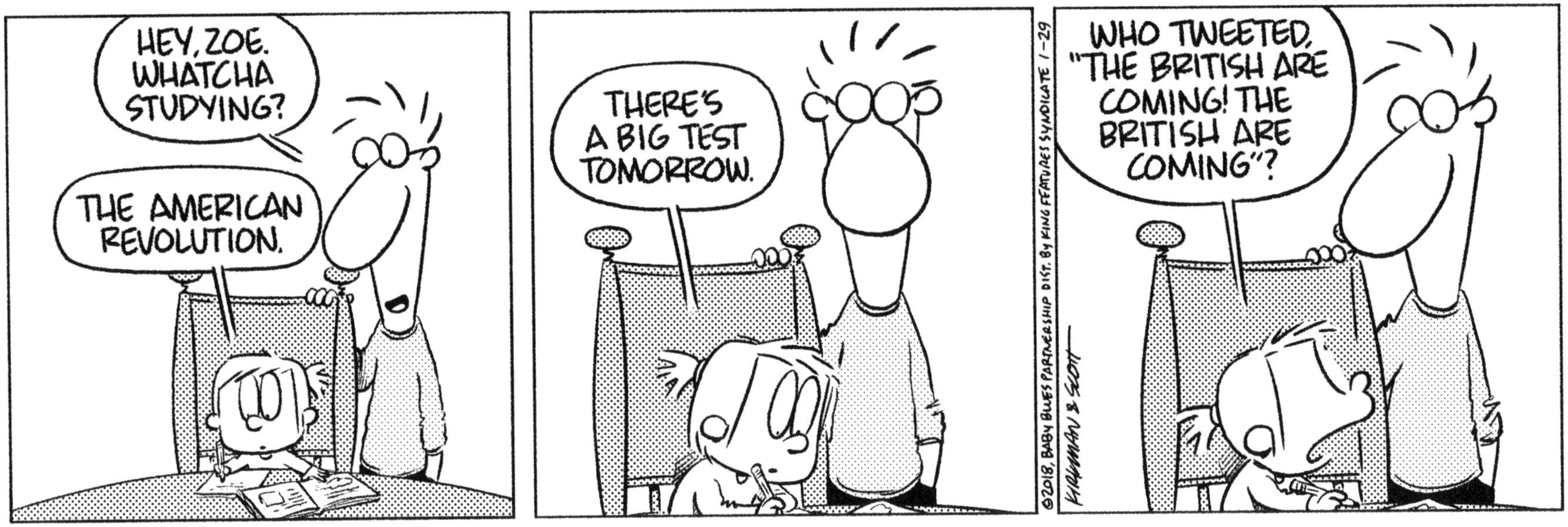
HEY, ZOE. WHATCHA STUDYING?
THE AMERICAN REVOLUTION.
THERE'S A BIG TEST TOMORROW.
WHO TWEETED, "THE BRITISH ARE COMING! THE BRITISH ARE COMING"?
©2018, BABY BLUES PARTNERSHIP DIST. BY KING FEATURES SYNDICATE 1-29
KIRKMAN & SCOTT

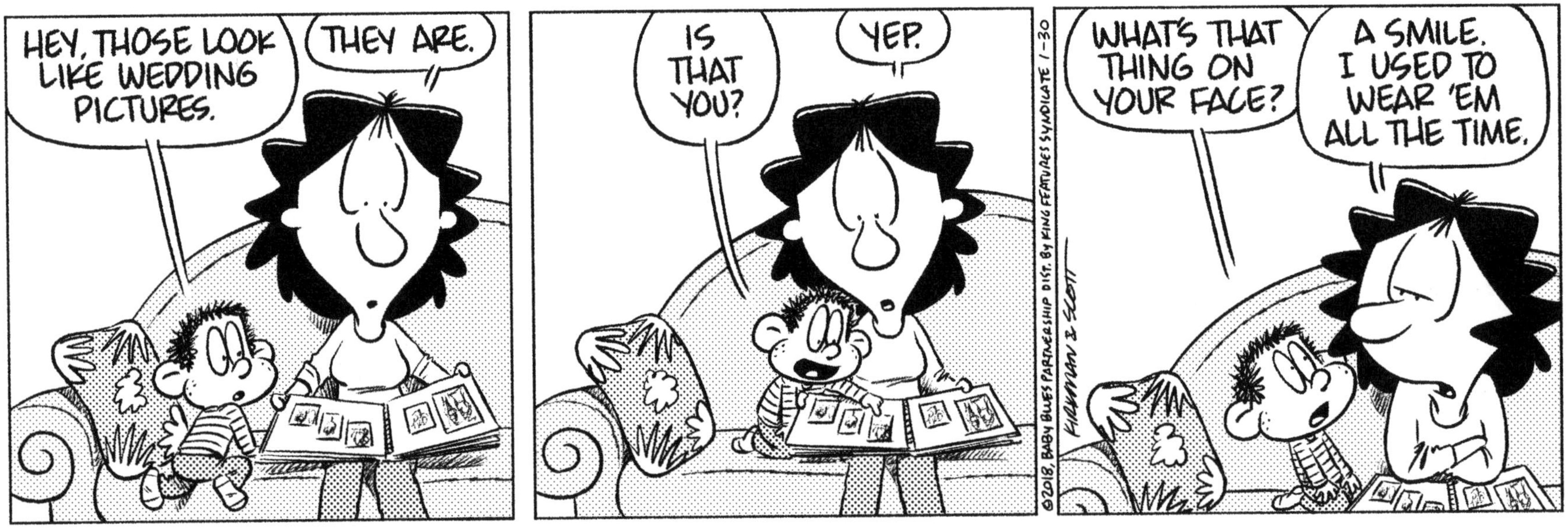
HEY, THOSE LOOK LIKE WEDDING PICTURES.
THEY ARE.
IS THAT YOU?
YEP.
WHAT'S THAT THING ON YOUR FACE?
A SMILE. I USED TO WEAR 'EM ALL THE TIME.
©2018, BABY BLUES PARTNERSHIP DIST. BY KING FEATURES SYNDICATE 1-30
KIRKMAN & SCOTT

Rick: So true.

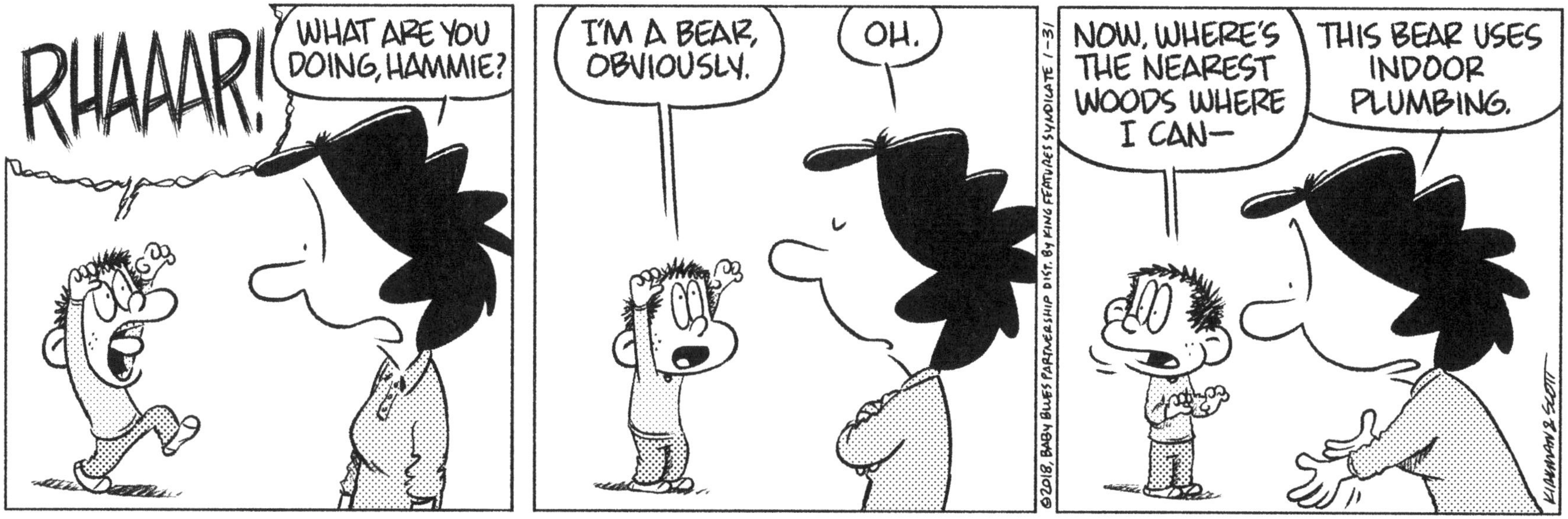
RHAAAR!
WHAT ARE YOU DOING, HAMMIE?
I'M A BEAR, OBVIOUSLY.
OH.
NOW, WHERE'S THE NEAREST WOODS WHERE I CAN—
THIS BEAR USES INDOOR PLUMBING.
©2018, BABY BLUES PARTNERSHIP DIST. BY KING FEATURES SYNDICATE 1-31
KIRKMAN & SCOTT

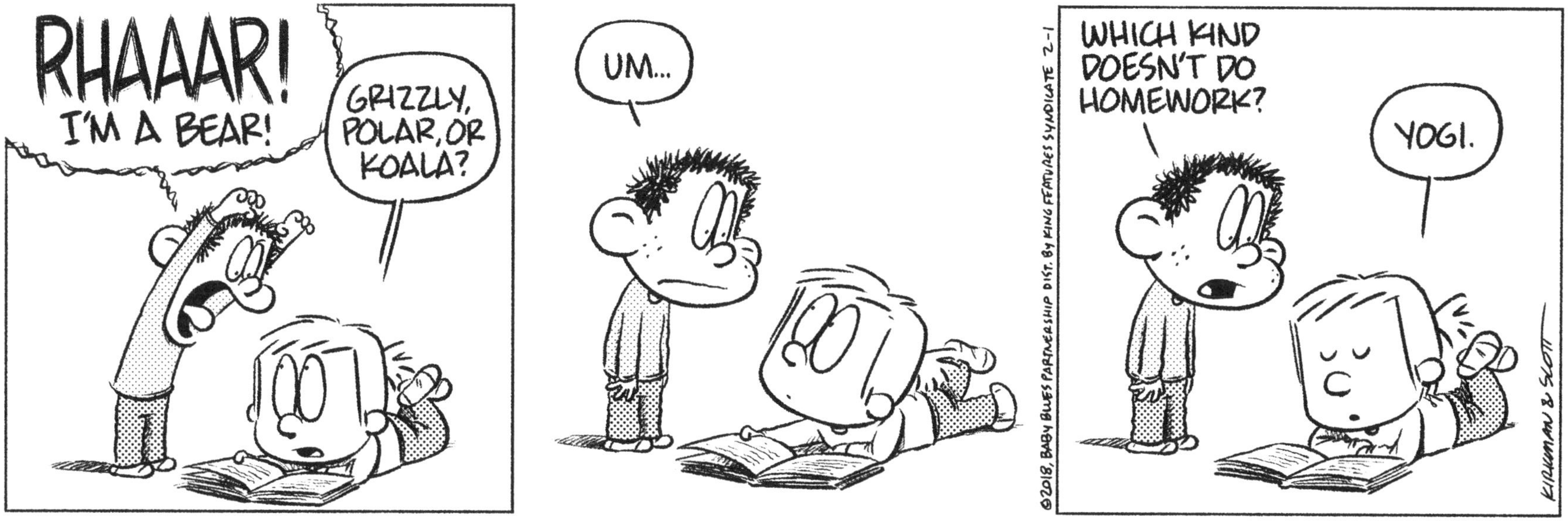
RHAAAR! I'M A BEAR!
GRIZZLY, POLAR, OR KOALA?
UM...
WHICH KIND DOESN'T DO HOMEWORK?
YOGI.
©2018, BABY BLUES PARTNERSHIP DIST. BY KING FEATURES SYNDICATE 2-1
KIRKMAN & SCOTT

Jerry: I doubt many kids Zoe's age would reference Yogi Bear, but he was right for the joke.

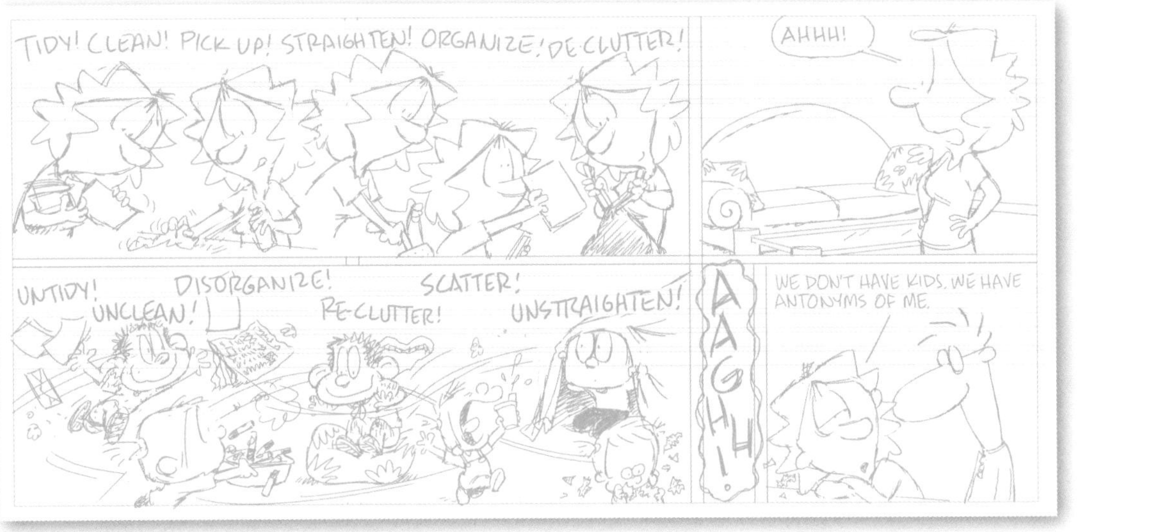
TIDY! CLEAN! PICK UP! STRAIGHTEN! ORGANIZE! DE-CLUTTER!
AHHH!
UNTIDY!
UNCLEAN!
DISORGANIZE!
RE-CLUTTER!
SCATTER!
UNSTRAIGHTEN!
AAGHH!
WE DON'T HAVE KIDS. WE HAVE ANTONYMS OF ME.

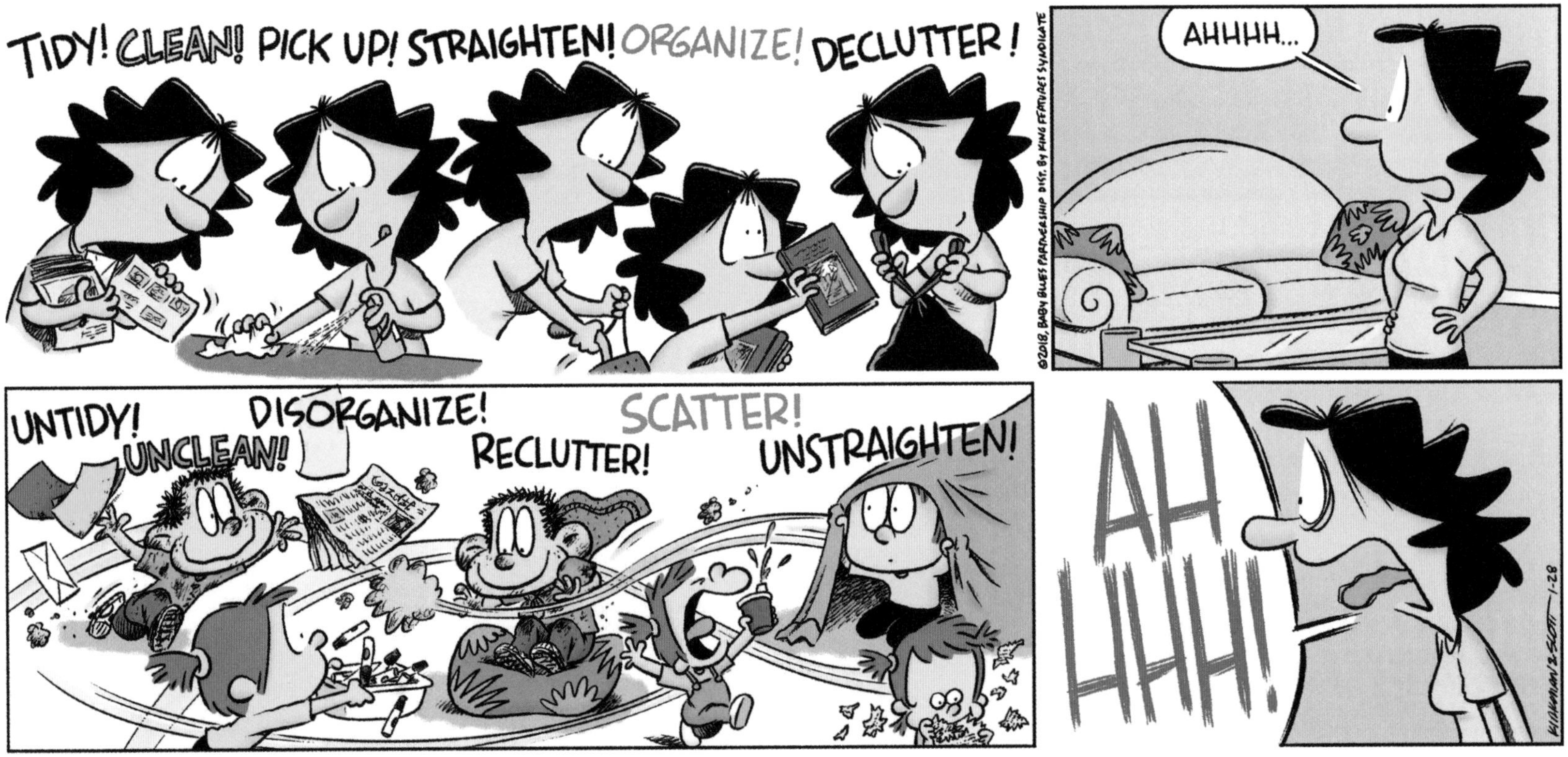
TIDY! CLEAN! PICK UP! STRAIGHTEN! ORGANIZE! DECLUTTER!
©2018, BABY BLUES PARTNERSHIP DIST. BY KING FEATURES SYNDICATE
AHHHH...
UNTIDY!
UNCLEAN!
DISORGANIZE!
RECLUTTER!
SCATTER!
UNSTRAIGHTEN!
AHHHHH!
KIRKMAN & SCOTT
1-28

Rick: The original ending of this gag was different, as you can see in the blue-line rough. We decided it would be better for the bottom to more closely mirror the top two panels so it created two tiers of opposites.

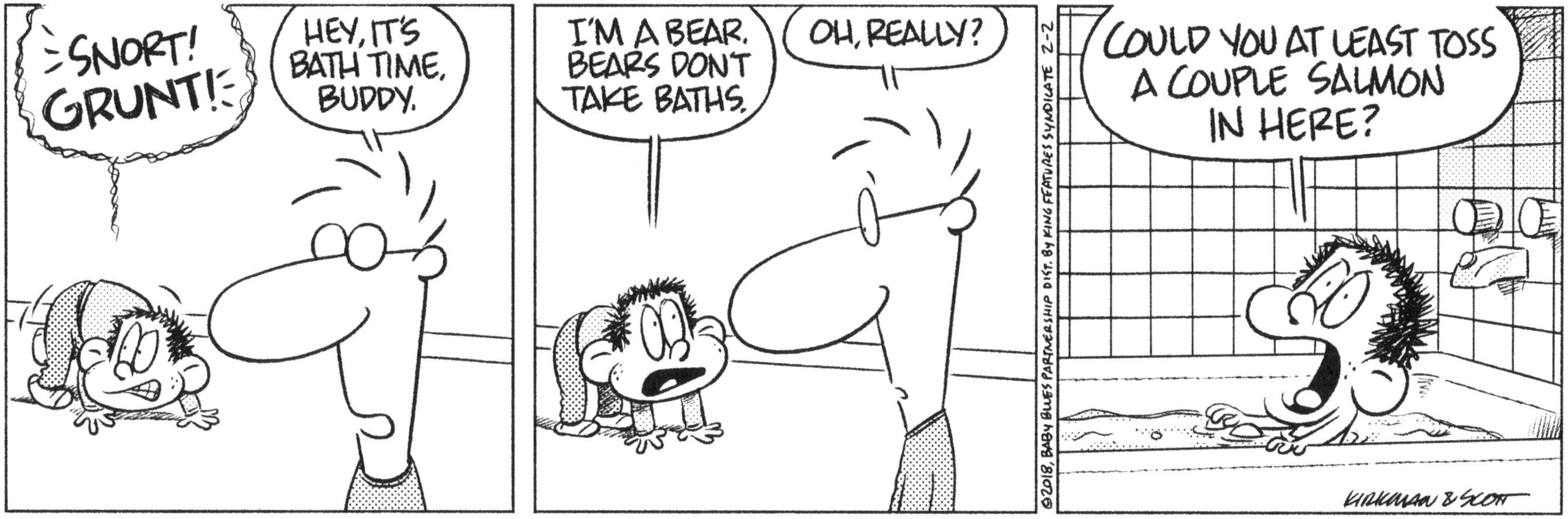
SNORT! GRUNT!
HEY, IT'S BATH TIME, BUDDY.
I'M A BEAR. BEARS DON'T TAKE BATHS.
OH, REALLY?
©2018, BABY BLUES PARTNERSHIP DIST. BY KING FEATURES SYNDICATE 2-2
COULD YOU AT LEAST TOSS A COUPLE SALMON IN HERE?
KIRKMAN & SCOTT

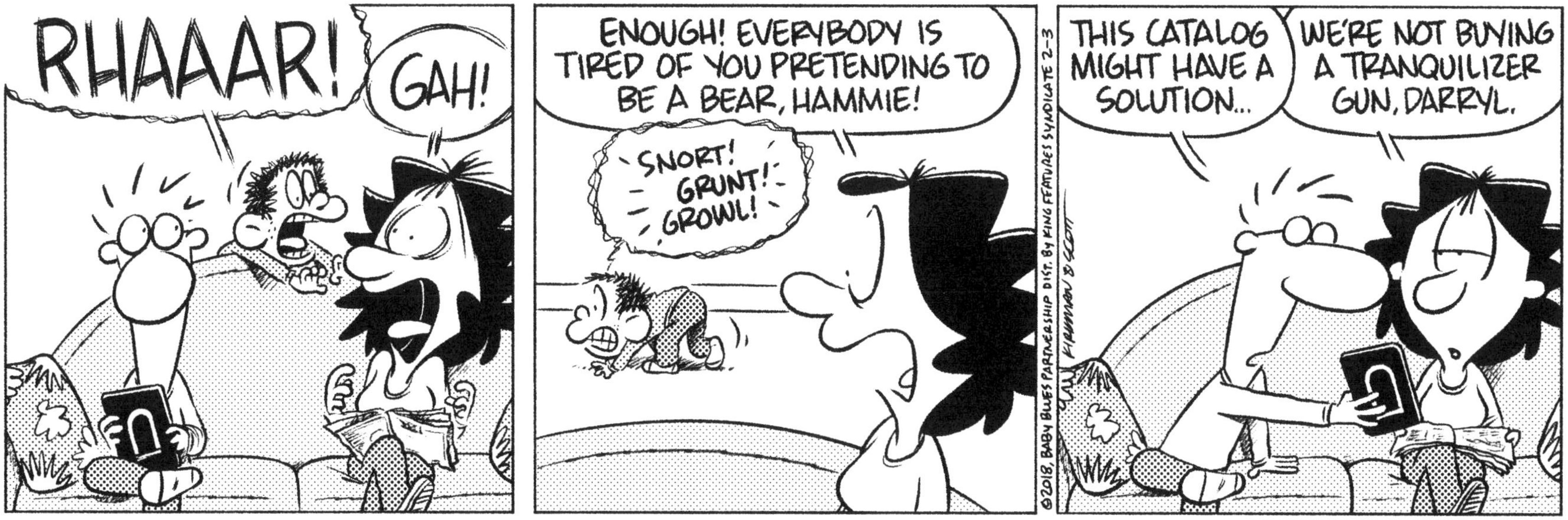
RHAAAR!
GAH!
ENOUGH! EVERYBODY IS TIRED OF YOU PRETENDING TO BE A BEAR, HAMMIE!
SNORT! GRUNT! GROWL!
©2018, BABY BLUES PARTNERSHIP DIST. BY KING FEATURES SYNDICATE 2-3
KIRKMAN & SCOTT
THIS CATALOG MIGHT HAVE A SOLUTION...
WE'RE NOT BUYING A TRANQUILIZER GUN, DARRYL.

Rick: By this time, I was becoming fond of Hammie as a bear. Then it turned dark.

Jerry: Family humor with just a touch of darkness. That's my sweet spot.

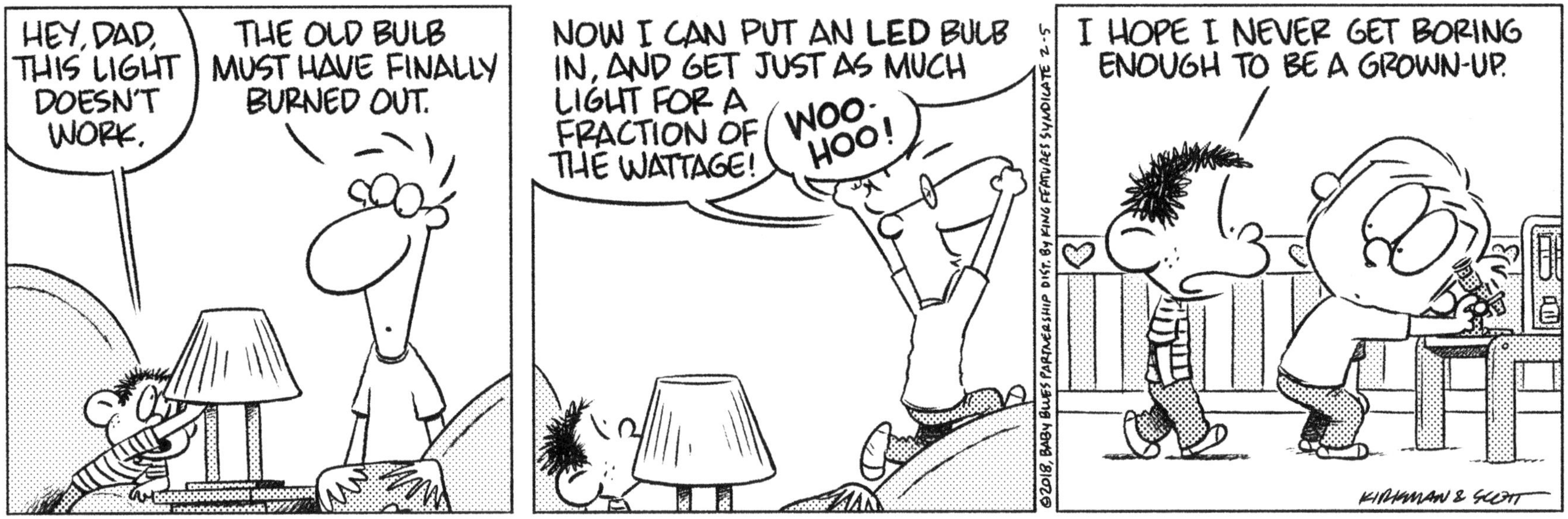
HEY, DAD, THIS LIGHT DOESN'T WORK.
THE OLD BULB MUST HAVE FINALLY BURNED OUT.
NOW I CAN PUT AN LED BULB IN, AND GET JUST AS MUCH LIGHT FOR A FRACTION OF THE WATTAGE!
WOO-HOO!
I HOPE I NEVER GET BORING ENOUGH TO BE A GROWN-UP.
©2018, BABY BLUES PARTNERSHIP DIST. BY KING FEATURES SYNDICATE 2-5
KIRKMAN & SCOTT

Rick: Now I feel like I'm not the only one.

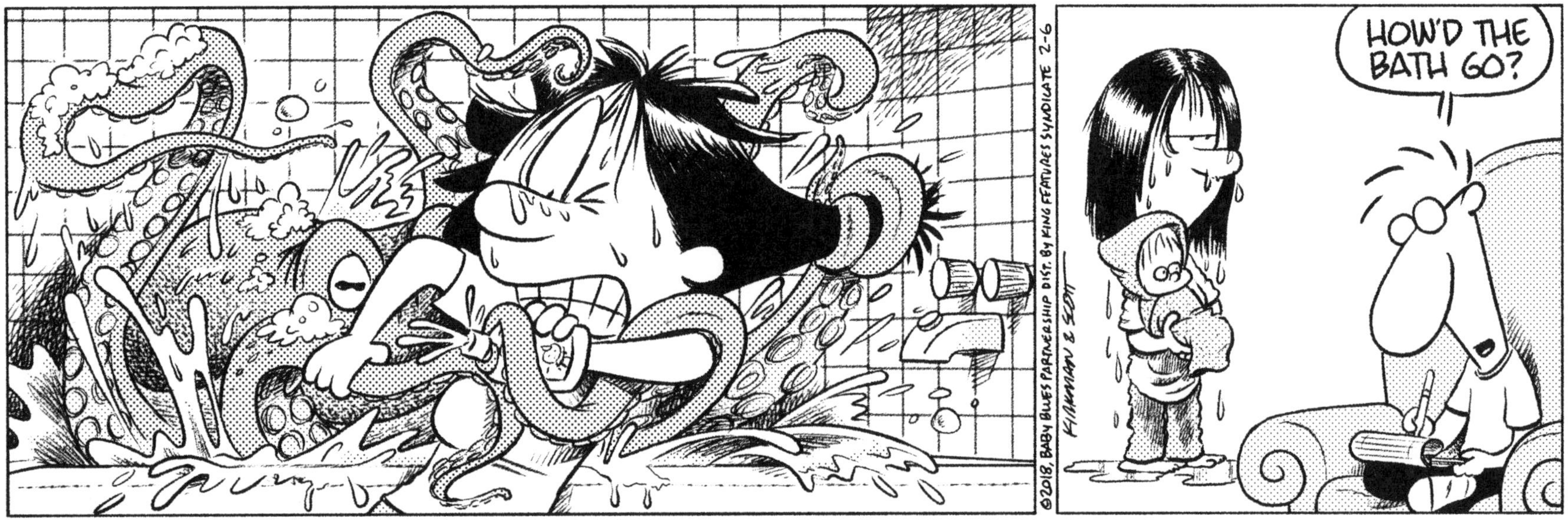
©2018, BABY BLUES PARTNERSHIP DIST. BY KING FEATURES SYNDICATE 2-6
KIRKMAN & SCOTT
HOW'D THE BATH GO?

Rick: I dread it when Jerry types just a few words that mean an extra half hour to an hour of drawing for me, but this was a blast to draw.

Jerry: Awesome octopus drawing, Rick!

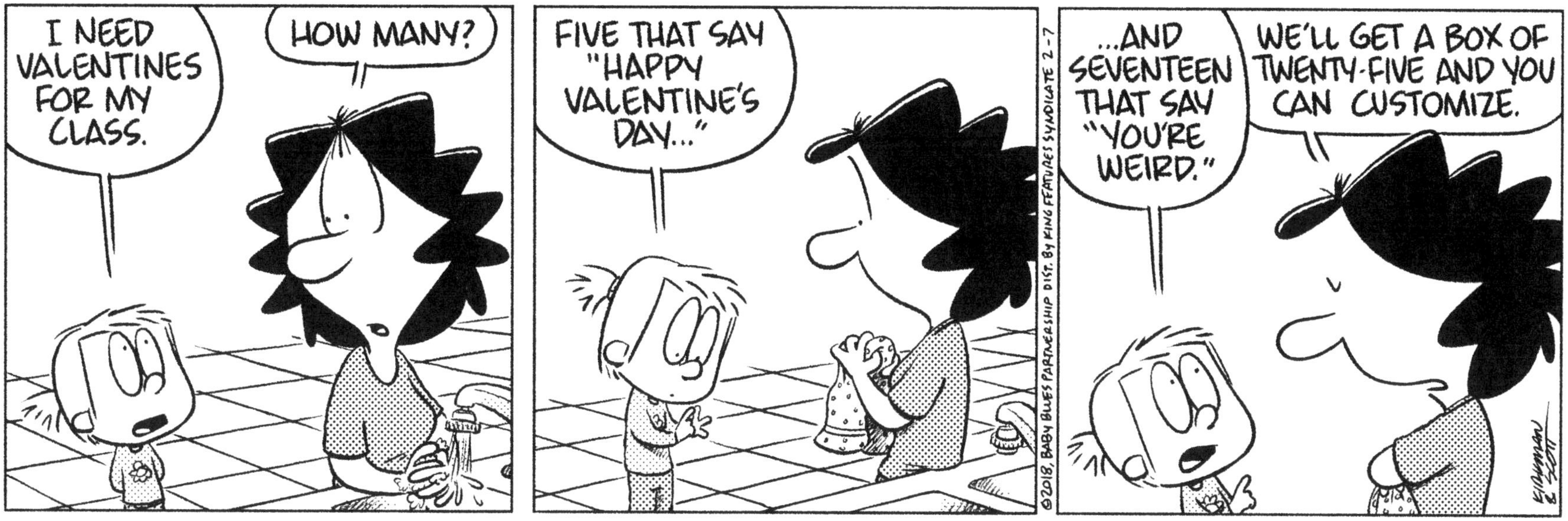
I NEED VALENTINES FOR MY CLASS.
HOW MANY?
FIVE THAT SAY "HAPPY VALENTINE'S DAY..."
©2018, BABY BLUES PARTNERSHIP DIST. BY KING FEATURES SYNDICATE 2-7
...AND SEVENTEEN THAT SAY "YOU'RE WEIRD."
WE'LL GET A BOX OF TWENTY-FIVE AND YOU CAN CUSTOMIZE.
KIRKMAN & SCOTT

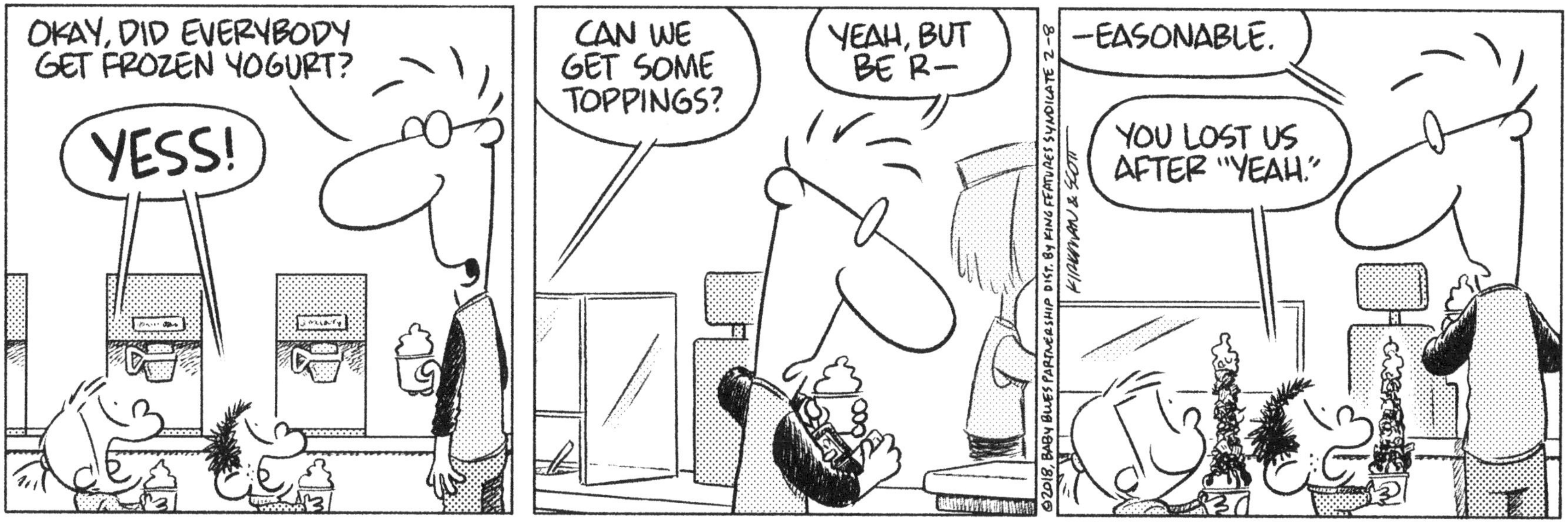
OKAY, DID EVERYBODY GET FROZEN YOGURT?
YESS!
CAN WE GET SOME TOPPINGS?
YEAH, BUT BE R—
©2018, BABY BLUES PARTNERSHIP DIST. BY KING FEATURES SYNDICATE 2-8
KIRKMAN & SCOTT
—EASONABLE.
YOU LOST US AFTER "YEAH."

Rick: I hope this frozen yogurt shop factored Zoe and Hammie into their pricing.

Jerry: When I take my kid to the frozen yogurt shop, the toppings always outweigh the yogurt.

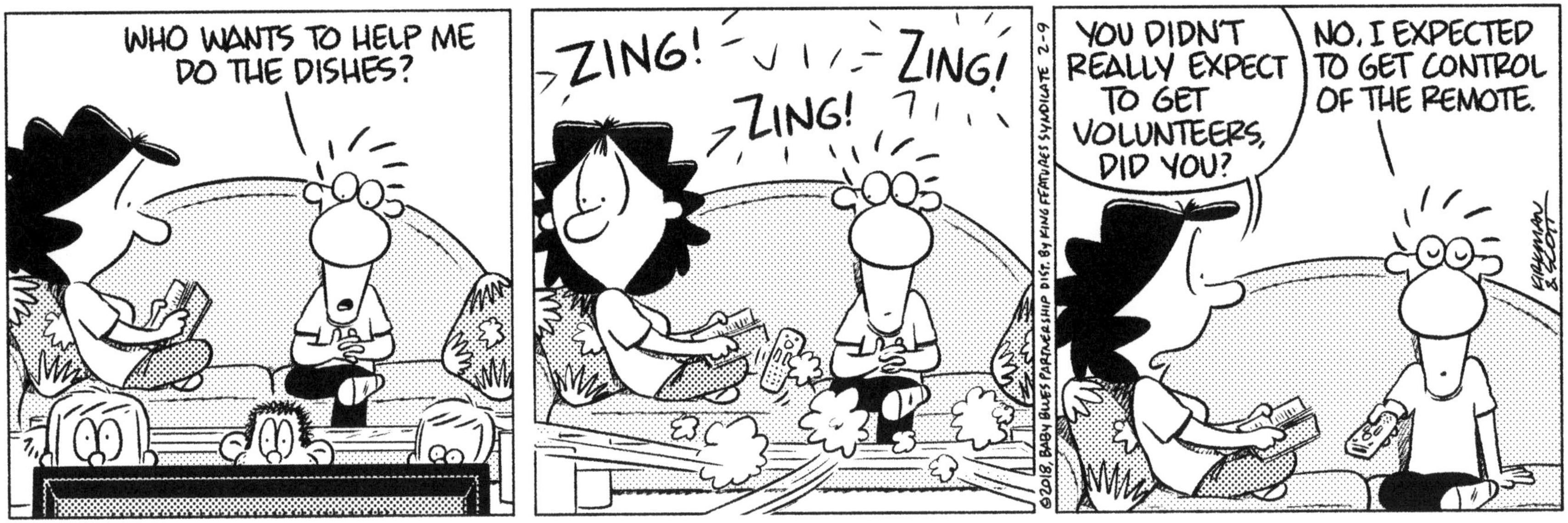
WHO WANTS TO HELP ME DO THE DISHES?
ZING!
ZING!
ZING!
©2018, BABY BLUES PARTNERSHIP DIST. BY KING FEATURES SYNDICATE 2-9
YOU DIDN'T REALLY EXPECT TO GET VOLUNTEERS, DID YOU?
NO, I EXPECTED TO GET CONTROL OF THE REMOTE.
KIRKMAN & SCOTT

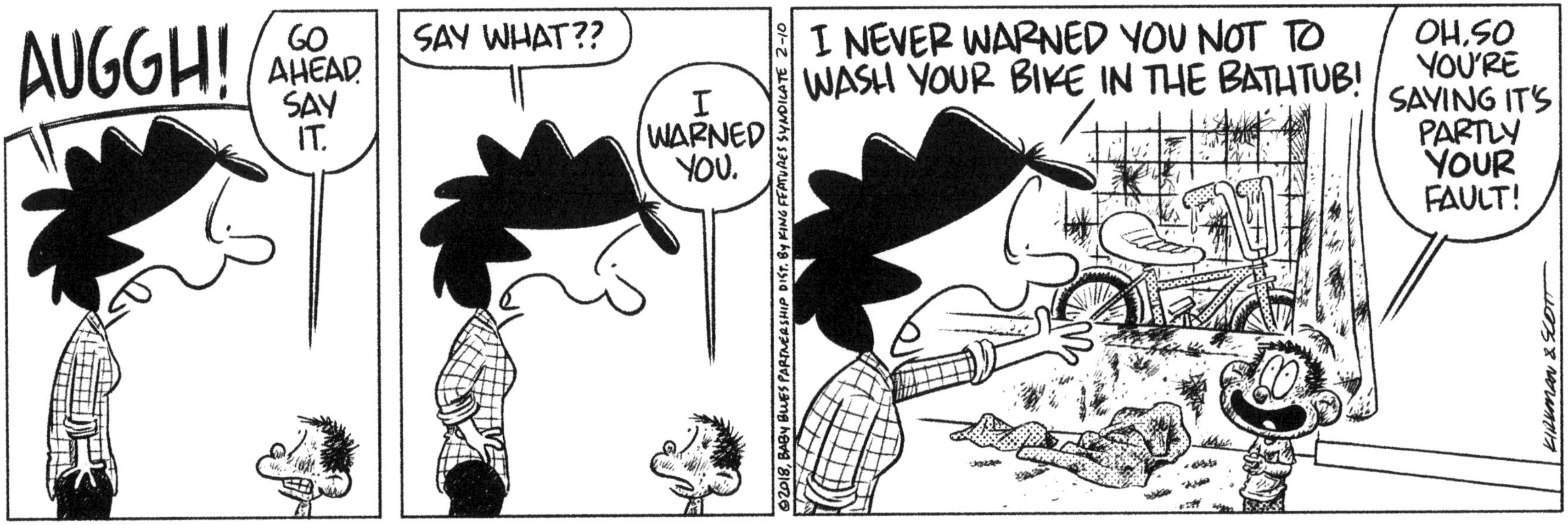
AUGGH!
GO AHEAD. SAY IT.
SAY WHAT??
I WARNED YOU.
©2018, BABY BLUES PARTNERSHIP DIST. BY KING FEATURES SYNDICATE 2-10
I NEVER WARNED YOU NOT TO WASH YOUR BIKE IN THE BATHTUB!
OH, SO YOU'RE SAYING IT'S PARTLY YOUR FAULT!
KIRKMAN & SCOTT

BAM! SMASH! SPLATT!
UH-OH.

BAM! SMASH! SPLATT!
UH-OH.
FIRST ONE TO FLINCH HAS TO GO DEAL WITH THAT.
BRING IT.
©2018, BABY BLUES PARTNERSHIP DIST. BY KING FEATURES SYNDICATE
I TOLD YOU WE SHOULDN'T HAVE GRAPE JUICE IN HERE!
YOU POURED IT!
BOY, IT'S REALLY PURPLE, ISN'T IT?
DON'T JUST STAND THERE! GO FIND SOMETHING TO WIPE IT UP WITH!
WHAT ABOUT THIS?
PERFECT!
MOM PRACTICALLY NEVER USES THIS TABLECLOTH. IT'S LIKE A HUNDRED YEARS OLD.
2-18
KIRKMAN & SCOTT
YOU FLINCHED!

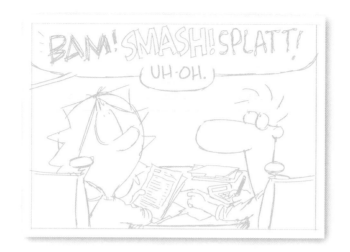

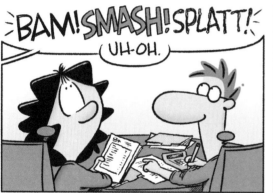

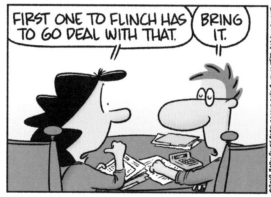

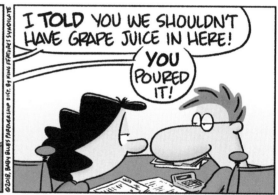

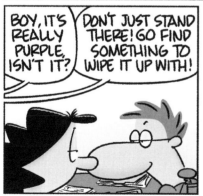

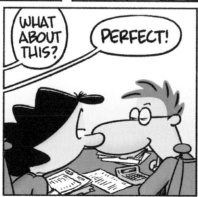

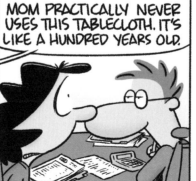

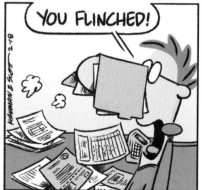

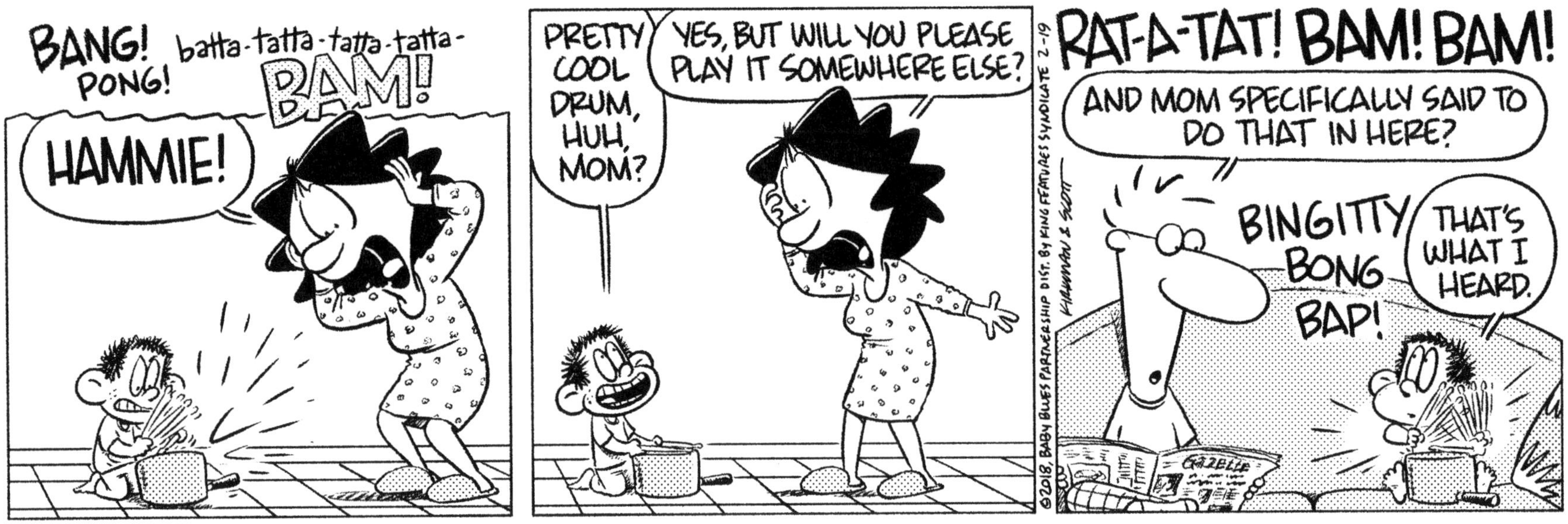
BANG! PONG! batta-tatta-tatta-tatta-BAM!
HAMMIE!
PRETTY COOL DRUM, HUH, MOM?
YES, BUT WILL YOU PLEASE PLAY IT SOMEWHERE ELSE?
©2018, BABY BLUES PARTNERSHIP DIST. BY KING FEATURES SYNDICATE 2-19
KIRKMAN & SCOTT
RAT-A-TAT! BAM! BAM!
AND MOM SPECIFICALLY SAID TO DO THAT IN HERE?
BINGITTY BONG BAP!
THAT'S WHAT I HEARD.
GAZETTE

Rick: Curse of the aspiring drummer, always being told to do that somewhere else.

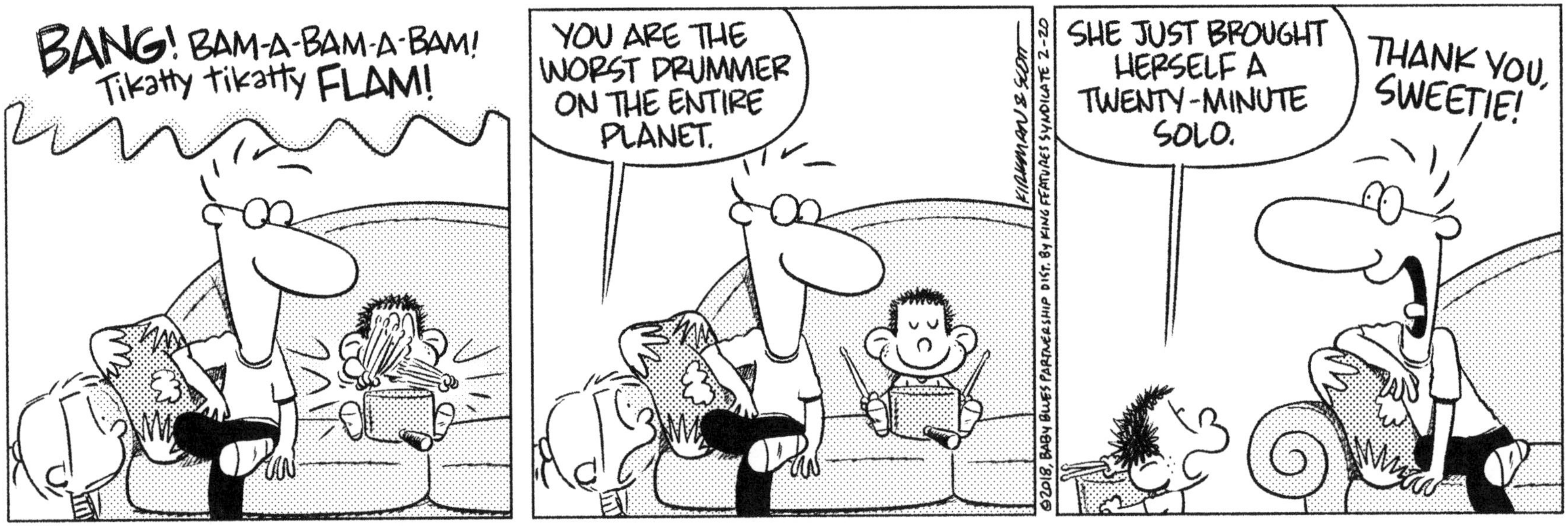
BANG! BAM-A-BAM-A-BAM! Tikatty tikatty FLAM!
YOU ARE THE WORST DRUMMER ON THE ENTIRE PLANET.
KIRKMAN & SCOTT
©2018, BABY BLUES PARTNERSHIP DIST. BY KING FEATURES SYNDICATE 2-20
SHE JUST BROUGHT HERSELF A TWENTY-MINUTE SOLO.
THANK YOU, SWEETIE!

Rick: *In-A-Gadda-Da-Vida*, Zoe. **Jerry:** Criticize the drummer at your own peril.

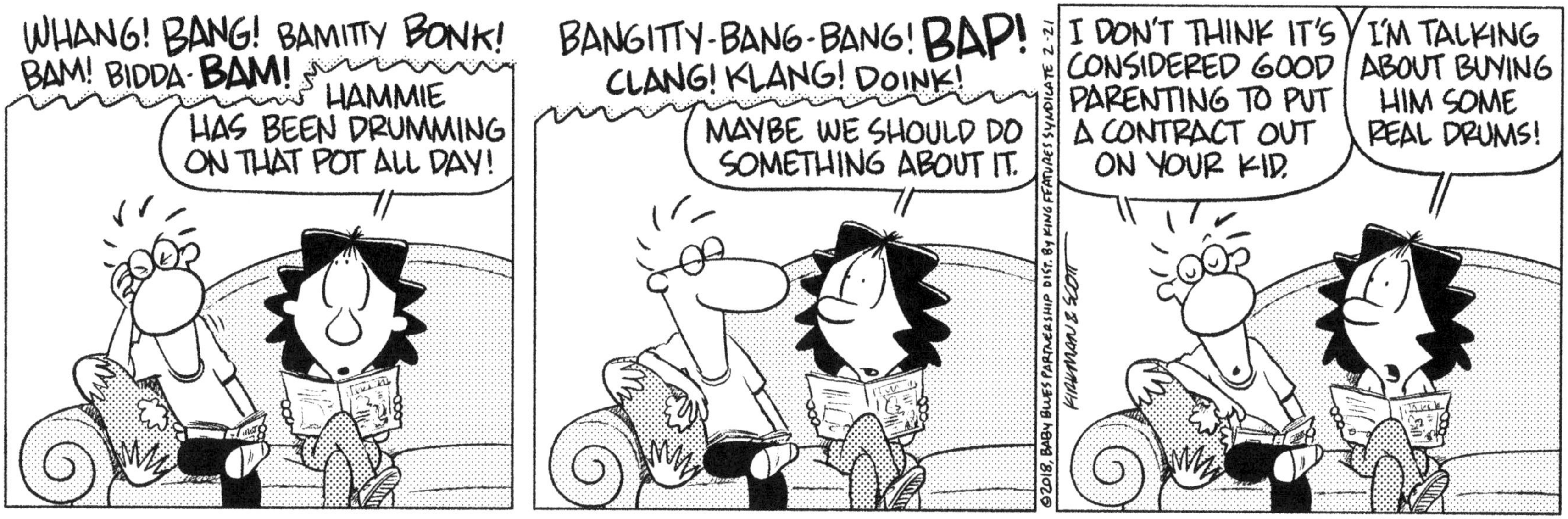
WHANG! BANG! BAMITTY BONK! BAM! BIDDA-BAM!
HAMMIE HAS BEEN DRUMMING ON THAT POT ALL DAY!
BANGITTY-BANG-BANG! BAP! CLANG! KLANG! DOINK!
MAYBE WE SHOULD DO SOMETHING ABOUT IT.
©2018, BABY BLUES PARTNERSHIP DIST. BY KING FEATURES SYNDICATE 2-21
KIRKMAN & SCOTT
I DON'T THINK IT'S CONSIDERED GOOD PARENTING TO PUT A CONTRACT OUT ON YOUR KID.
I'M TALKING ABOUT BUYING HIM SOME REAL DRUMS!

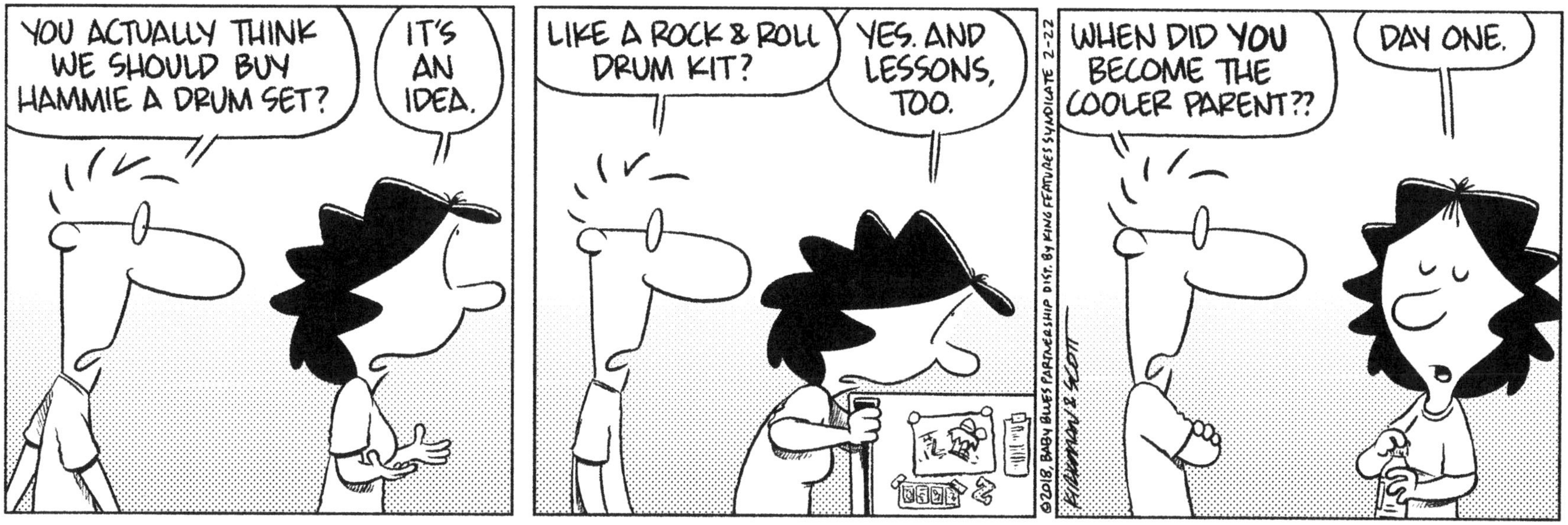
YOU ACTUALLY THINK WE SHOULD BUY HAMMIE A DRUM SET?
IT'S AN IDEA.
LIKE A ROCK & ROLL DRUM KIT?
YES. AND LESSONS, TOO.
©2018, BABY BLUES PARTNERSHIP DIST. BY KING FEATURES SYNDICATE 2-22
KIRKMAN & SCOTT
WHEN DID YOU BECOME THE COOLER PARENT??
DAY ONE.

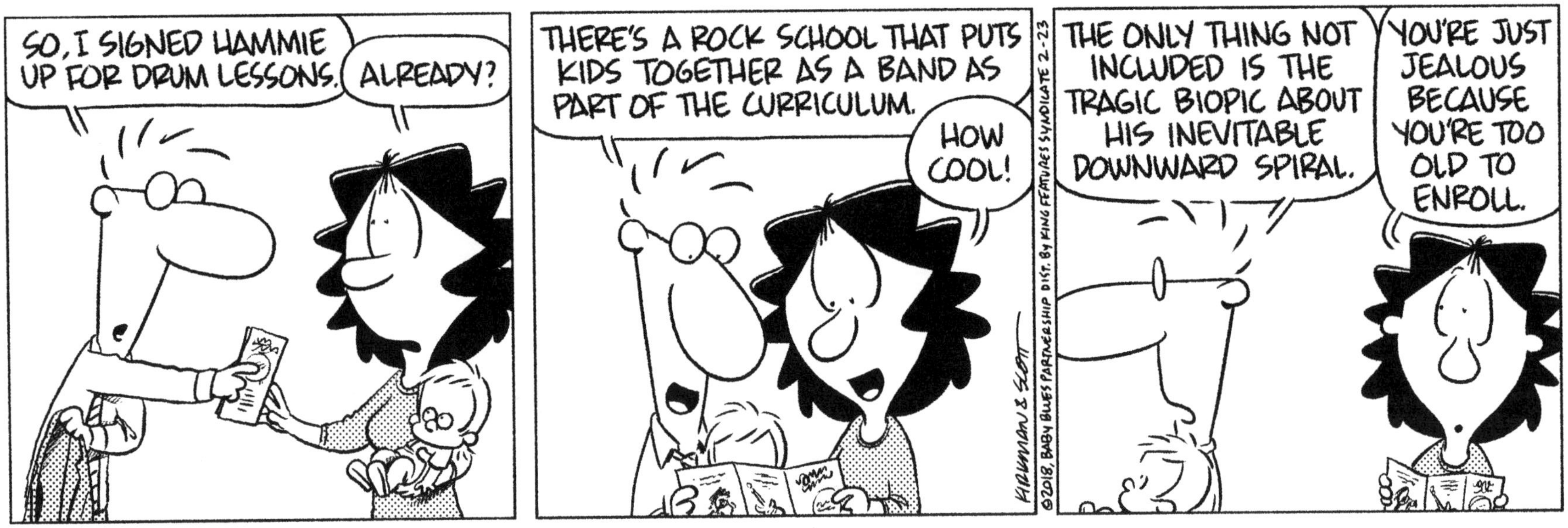
SO, I SIGNED HAMMIE UP FOR DRUM LESSONS.
ALREADY?
THERE'S A ROCK SCHOOL THAT PUTS KIDS TOGETHER AS A BAND AS PART OF THE CURRICULUM.
HOW COOL!
©2018, BABY BLUES PARTNERSHIP DIST. BY KING FEATURES SYNDICATE 2-23
KIRKMAN & SCOTT
THE ONLY THING NOT INCLUDED IS THE TRAGIC BIOPIC ABOUT HIS INEVITABLE DOWNWARD SPIRAL.
YOU'RE JUST JEALOUS BECAUSE YOU'RE TOO OLD TO ENROLL.

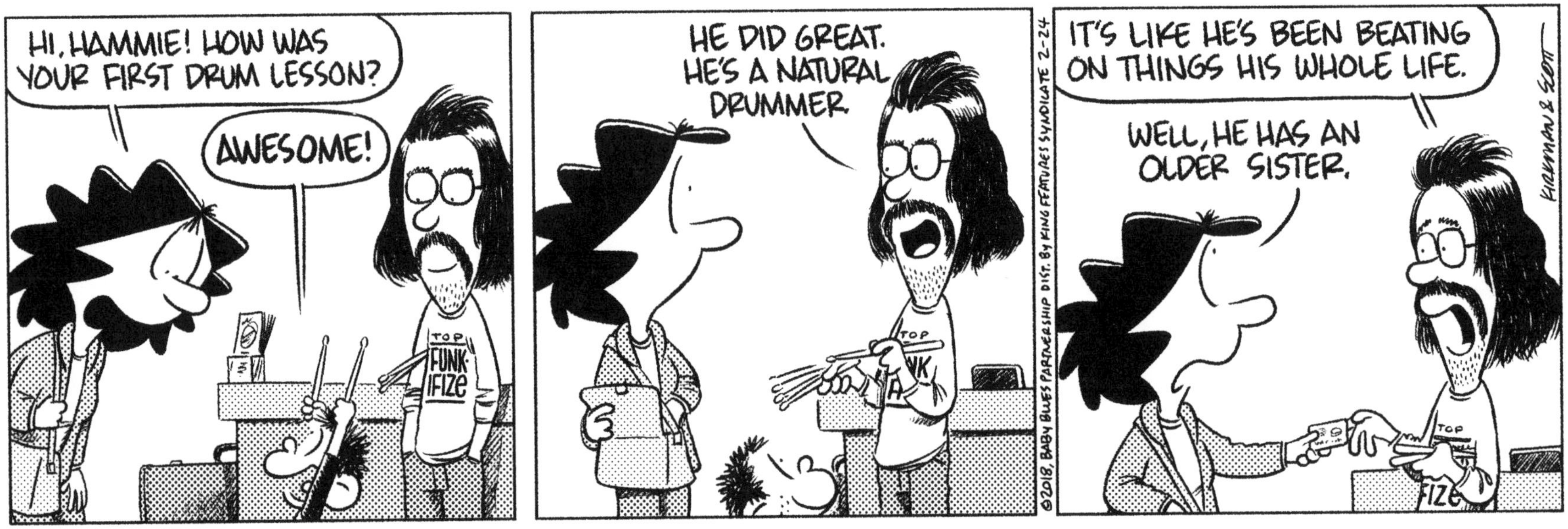
HI, HAMMIE! HOW WAS YOUR FIRST DRUM LESSON?
AWESOME!
TOP FUNK-IFIZE
HE DID GREAT. HE'S A NATURAL DRUMMER.
©2018, BABY BLUES PARTNERSHIP DIST. BY KING FEATURES SYNDICATE 2-24
IT'S LIKE HE'S BEEN BEATING ON THINGS HIS WHOLE LIFE.
WELL, HE HAS AN OLDER SISTER.
KIRKMAN & SCOTT

Rick: He looks a little like my drum teacher I had when I was fifty. I snuck in a little nod to one of my favorite bands, Tower of Power.

Jerry: Sometimes a punchline comes soooo naturally. Sorry, sis.

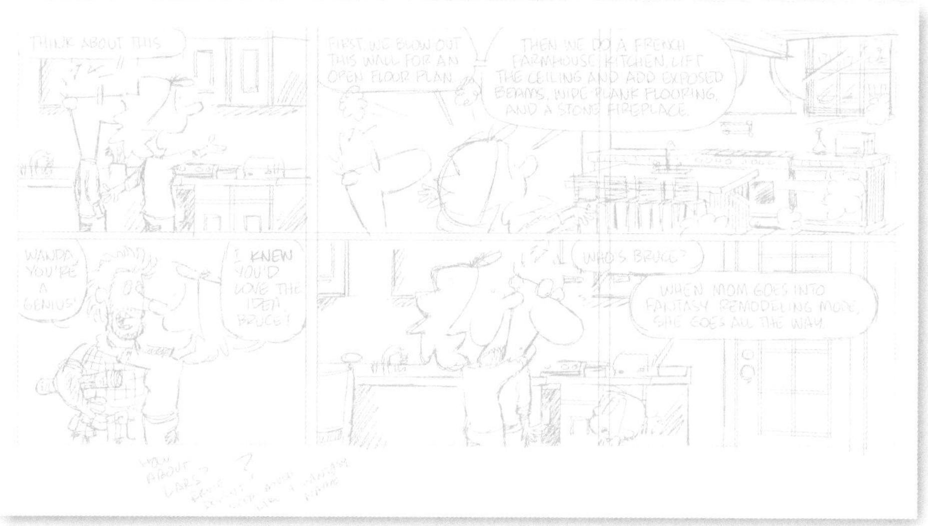

THINK ABOUT THIS
FIRST, WE BLOW OUT THIS WALL FOR AN OPEN FLOOR PLAN.
THEN WE DO A FRENCH FARMHOUSE KITCHEN, LIFT THE CEILING AND ADD EXPOSED BEAMS, WIDE PLANK FLOORING, AND A STONE FIREPLACE.
WANDA, YOU'RE A GENIUS!
I KNEW YOU'D LOVE THE IDEA BRUCE!
WHO'S BRUCE?
WHEN MOM GOES INTO FANTASY REMODELING MODE, SHE GOES ALL THE WAY.

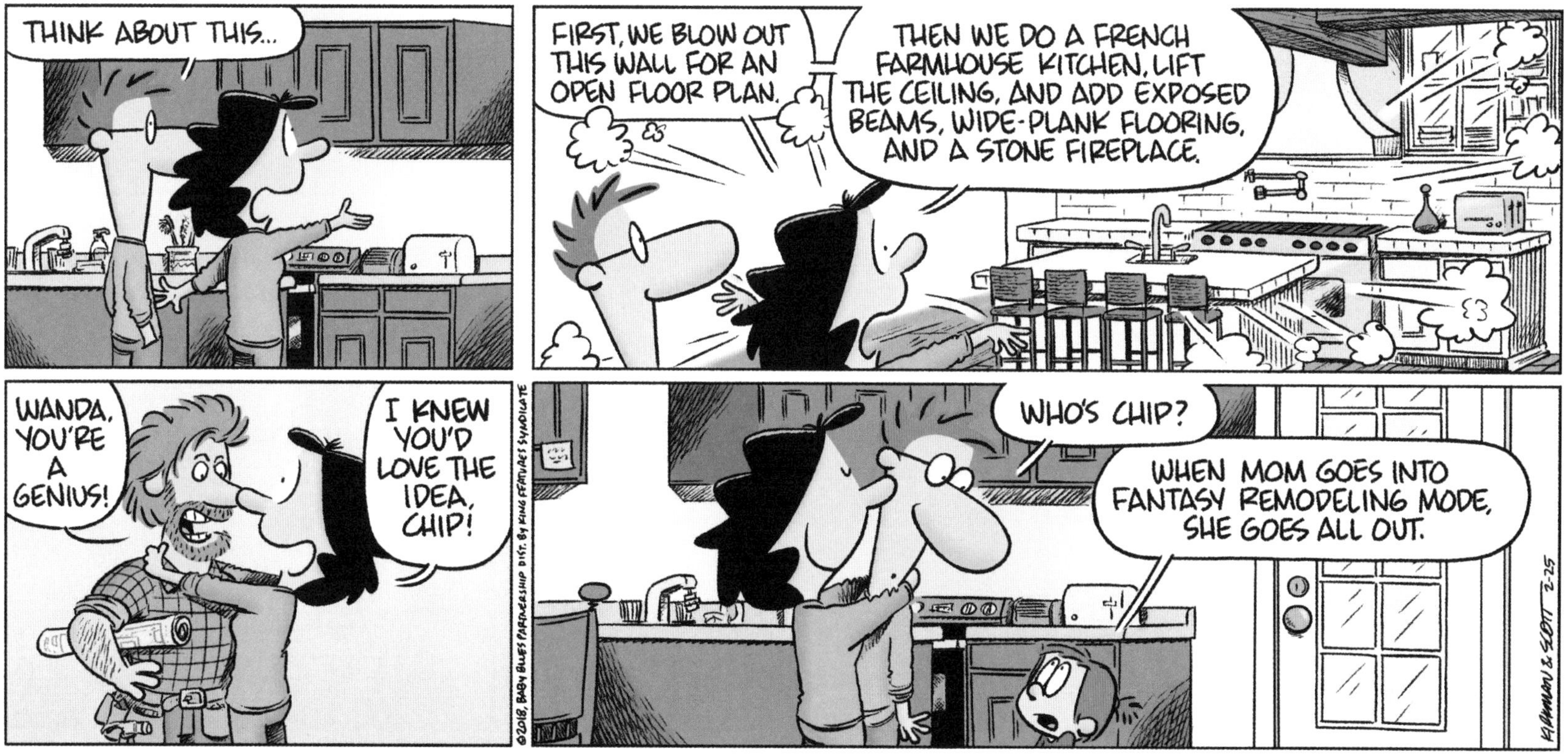

THINK ABOUT THIS...
FIRST, WE BLOW OUT THIS WALL FOR AN OPEN FLOOR PLAN.
THEN WE DO A FRENCH FARMHOUSE KITCHEN, LIFT THE CEILING, AND ADD EXPOSED BEAMS, WIDE-PLANK FLOORING, AND A STONE FIREPLACE.
WANDA, YOU'RE A GENIUS!
I KNEW YOU'D LOVE THE IDEA, CHIP!
©2018, BABY BLUES PARTNERSHIP DIST. BY KING FEATURES SYNDICATE
WHO'S CHIP?
WHEN MOM GOES INTO FANTASY REMODELING MODE, SHE GOES ALL OUT.
KIRKMAN & SCOTT 2-25

Rick: Another last-minute change, when I questioned the name Bruce. Jerry changed it to Chip. I have to admit, I didn't know there was a real Chip when I sketched this.

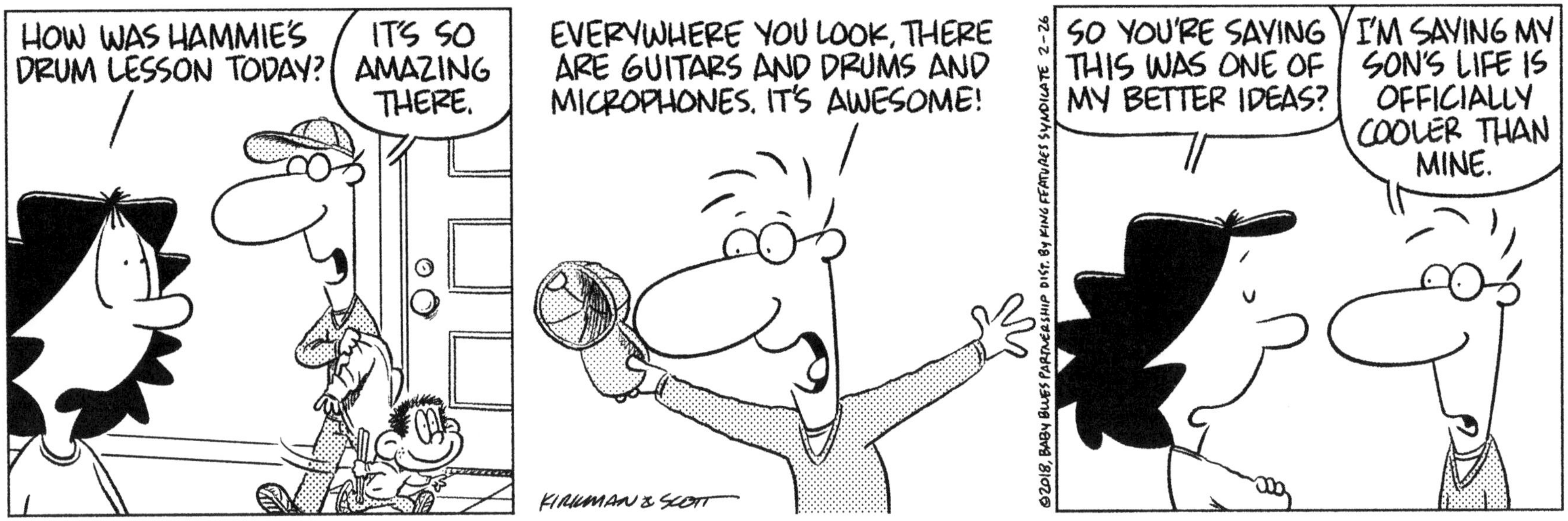
HOW WAS HAMMIE'S DRUM LESSON TODAY?
IT'S SO AMAZING THERE.
EVERYWHERE YOU LOOK, THERE ARE GUITARS AND DRUMS AND MICROPHONES. IT'S AWESOME!
KIRKMAN & SCOTT
©2018, BABY BLUES PARTNERSHIP DIST. BY KING FEATURES SYNDICATE 2-26
SO YOU'RE SAYING THIS WAS ONE OF MY BETTER IDEAS?
I'M SAYING MY SON'S LIFE IS OFFICIALLY COOLER THAN MINE.

Rick: All I can say is get used to it, Darryl.

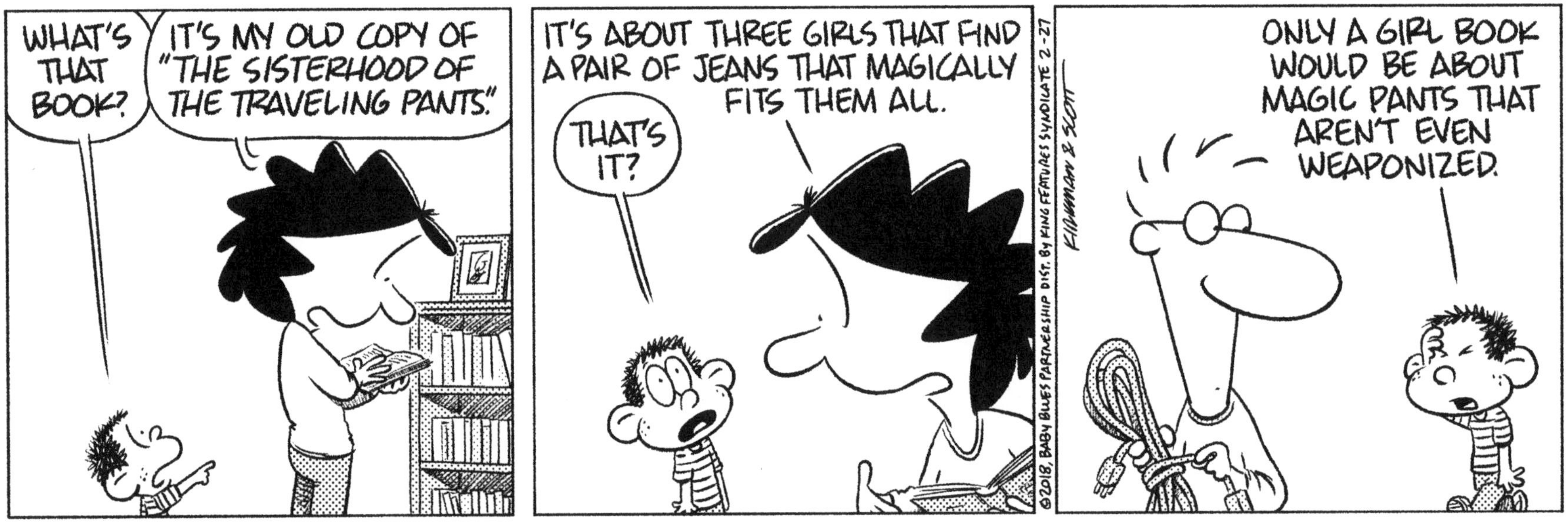
WHAT'S THAT BOOK?
IT'S MY OLD COPY OF "THE SISTERHOOD OF THE TRAVELING PANTS."
IT'S ABOUT THREE GIRLS THAT FIND A PAIR OF JEANS THAT MAGICALLY FITS THEM ALL.
THAT'S IT?
©2018, BABY BLUES PARTNERSHIP DIST. BY KING FEATURES SYNDICATE 2-27
KIRKMAN & SCOTT
ONLY A GIRL BOOK WOULD BE ABOUT MAGIC PANTS THAT AREN'T EVEN WEAPONIZED.

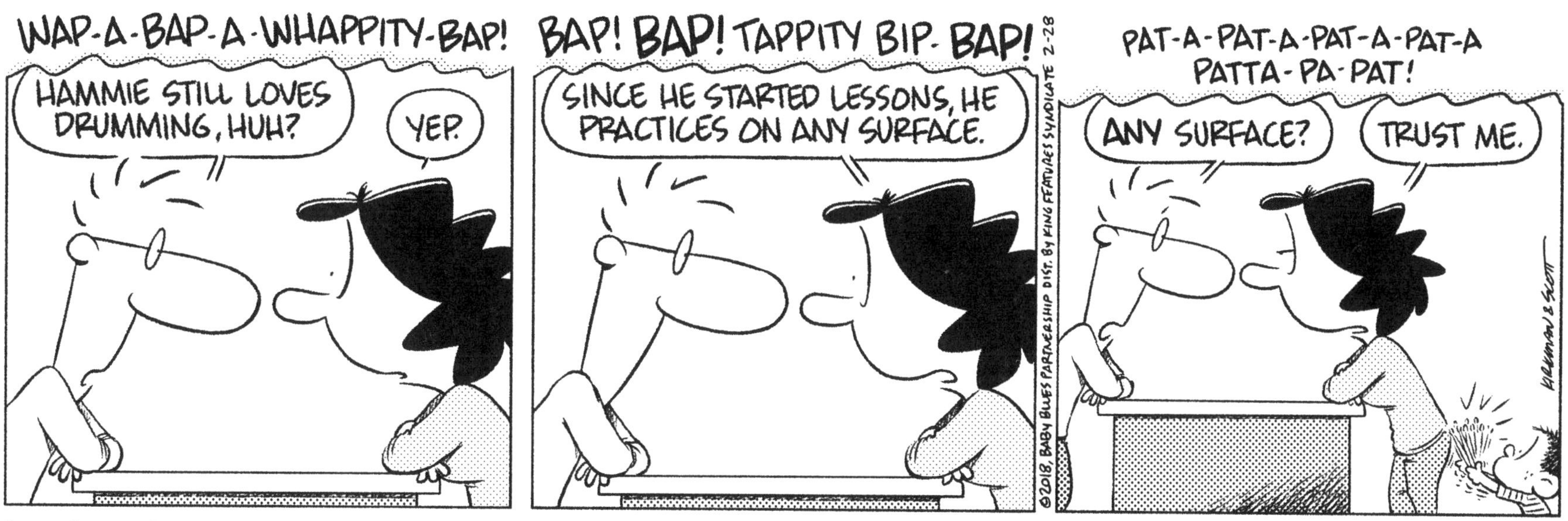
WAP-A-BAP-A-WHAPPITY-BAP!
HAMMIE STILL LOVES DRUMMING, HUH?
YEP.
BAP! BAP! TAPPITY BIP-BAP!
SINCE HE STARTED LESSONS, HE PRACTICES ON ANY SURFACE.
©2018, BABY BLUES PARTNERSHIP DIST. BY KING FEATURES SYNDICATE 2-28
PAT-A-PAT-A-PAT-A-PAT-A PATTA-PA-PAT!
ANY SURFACE?
TRUST ME.
KIRKMAN & SCOTT

Jerry: Any surface.

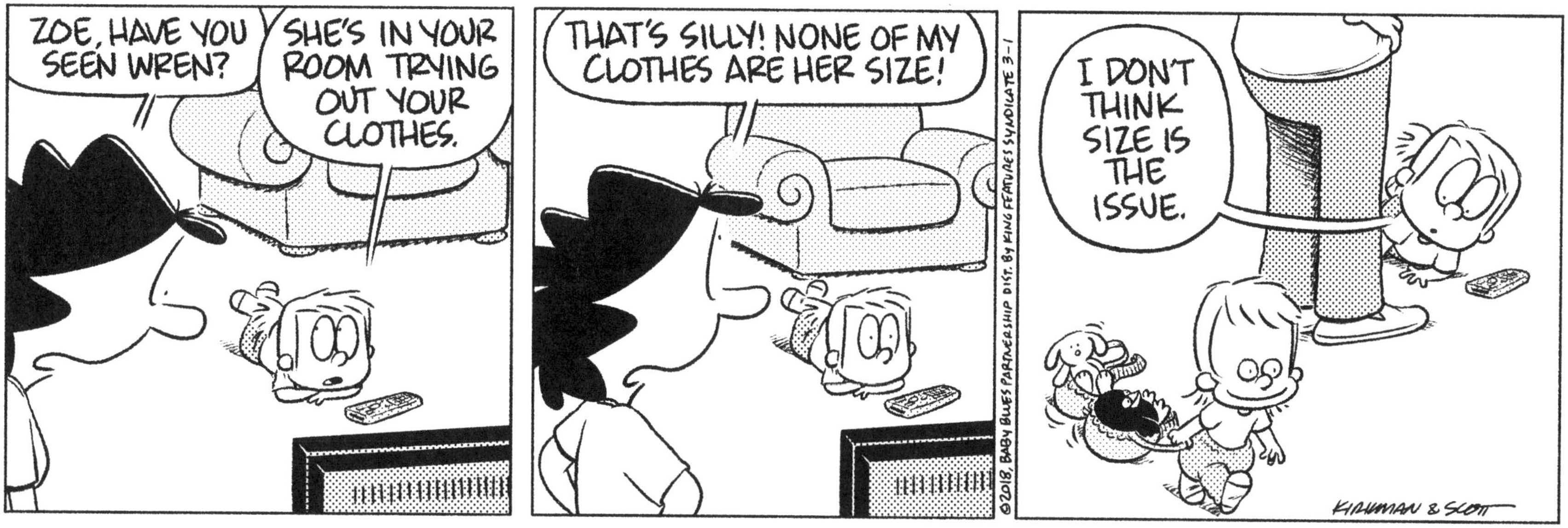
ZOE, HAVE YOU SEEN WREN?
SHE'S IN YOUR ROOM TRYING OUT YOUR CLOTHES.
THAT'S SILLY! NONE OF MY CLOTHES ARE HER SIZE!
©2018, BABY BLUES PARTNERSHIP DIST. BY KING FEATURES SYNDICATE 3-1
I DON'T THINK SIZE IS THE ISSUE.
KIRKMAN & SCOTT

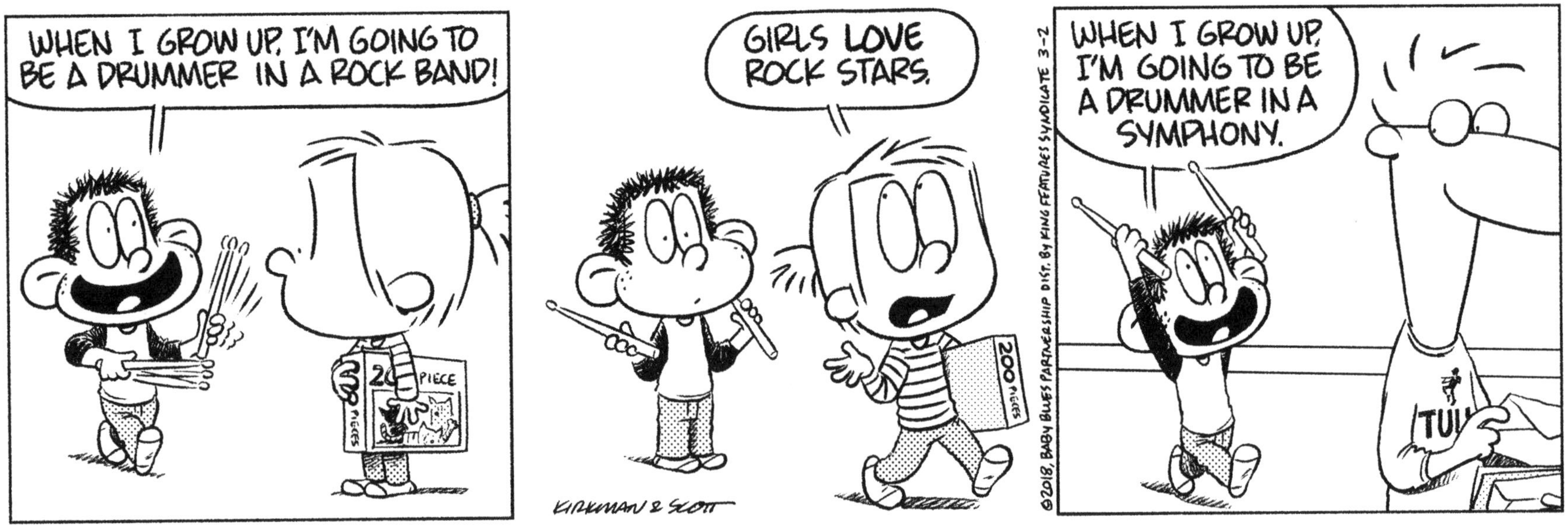
WHEN I GROW UP, I'M GOING TO BE A DRUMMER IN A ROCK BAND!
200 PIECE
GIRLS LOVE ROCK STARS.
200 PIECES
KIRKMAN & SCOTT
©2018, BABY BLUES PARTNERSHIP DIST. BY KING FEATURES SYNDICATE 3-2
WHEN I GROW UP, I'M GOING TO BE A DRUMMER IN A SYMPHONY.
TULL

Rick: Darryl is trying to show his rock cred with the (Jethro) Tull T-shirt. We won't mention the Grammy fiasco.

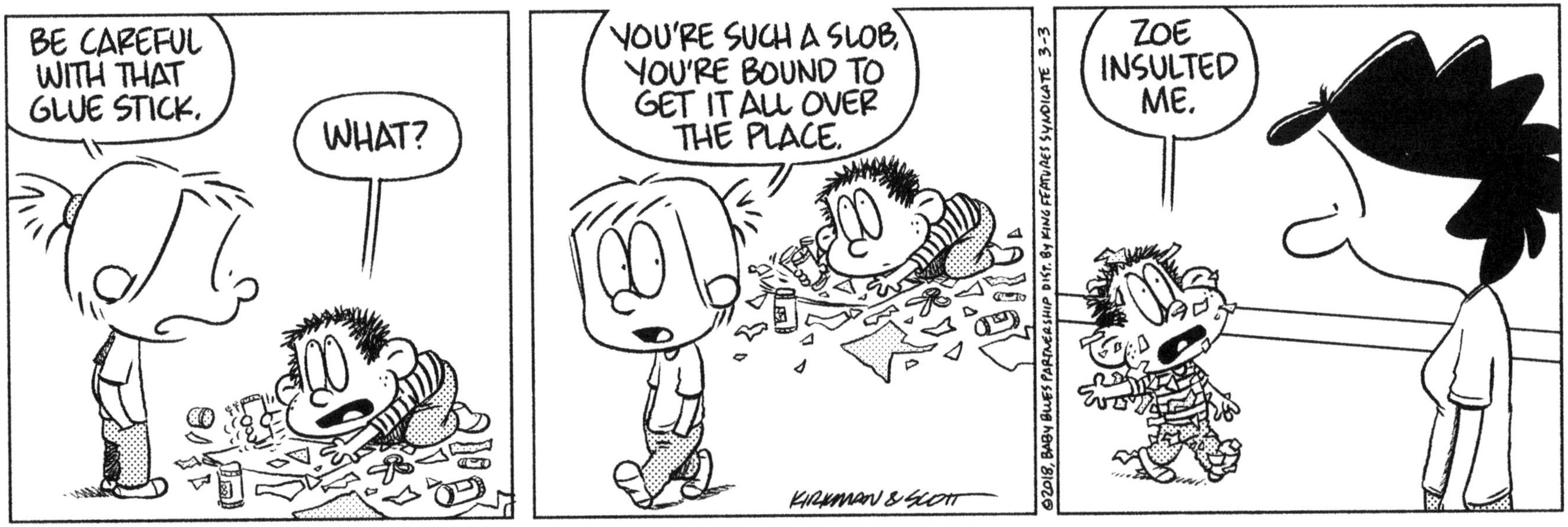
BE CAREFUL WITH THAT GLUE STICK.
WHAT?
YOU'RE SUCH A SLOB, YOU'RE BOUND TO GET IT ALL OVER THE PLACE.
KIRKMAN & SCOTT
©2018, BABY BLUES PARTNERSHIP DIST. BY KING FEATURES SYNDICATE 3-3
ZOE INSULTED ME.

BABY BLUES®
BY RICK KIRKMAN / JERRY SCOTT

NEXT IS ARUGULA. CAN YOU SAY "ARUGULA," WREN?
WOOGALOO!
OH MY GOSH, SHE'S ADORABLE!
OH, THANKS.
WOOGALOO!
WOOGALOO!
SHE'S A LUCKY LITTLE GIRL TO HAVE SUCH A GOOD DADDY.
I GUESS SO.
ALL IT TAKES IS UNCONDITIONAL LOVE, ENDLESS PATIENCE, STEADY DISCIPLINE...
-NO-NO-NO-NO-NO!
...AND ABOVE ALL, CONSTANT SUPERVISION...
UM, SHE HAS THE PRODUCE GUY CORNERED WITH A VEGETABLE SPRAYER.
AAAUUUGH!
3-4
©2018, BABY BLUES PARTNERSHIP DIST. BY KING FEATURES SYNDICATE

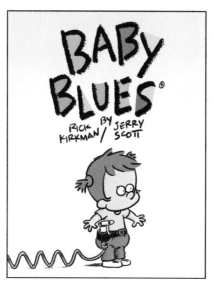

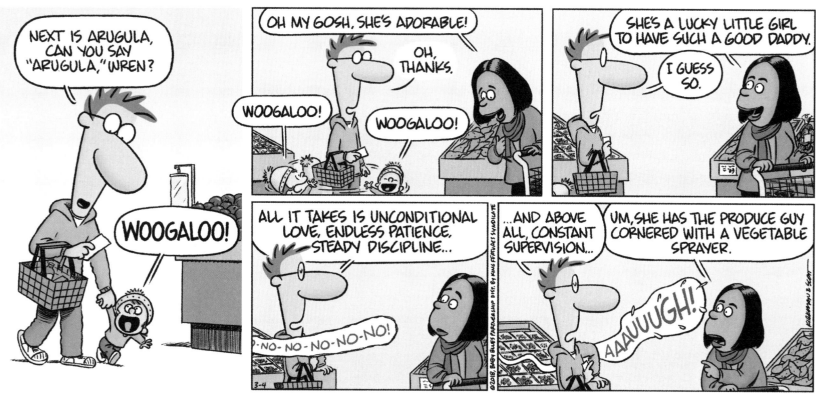

Rick: Why do men get praised for shopping with their kids? Really, that needs to end.

Jerry: "Woogaloo" is a better word for it than "arugula." Just sayin'.

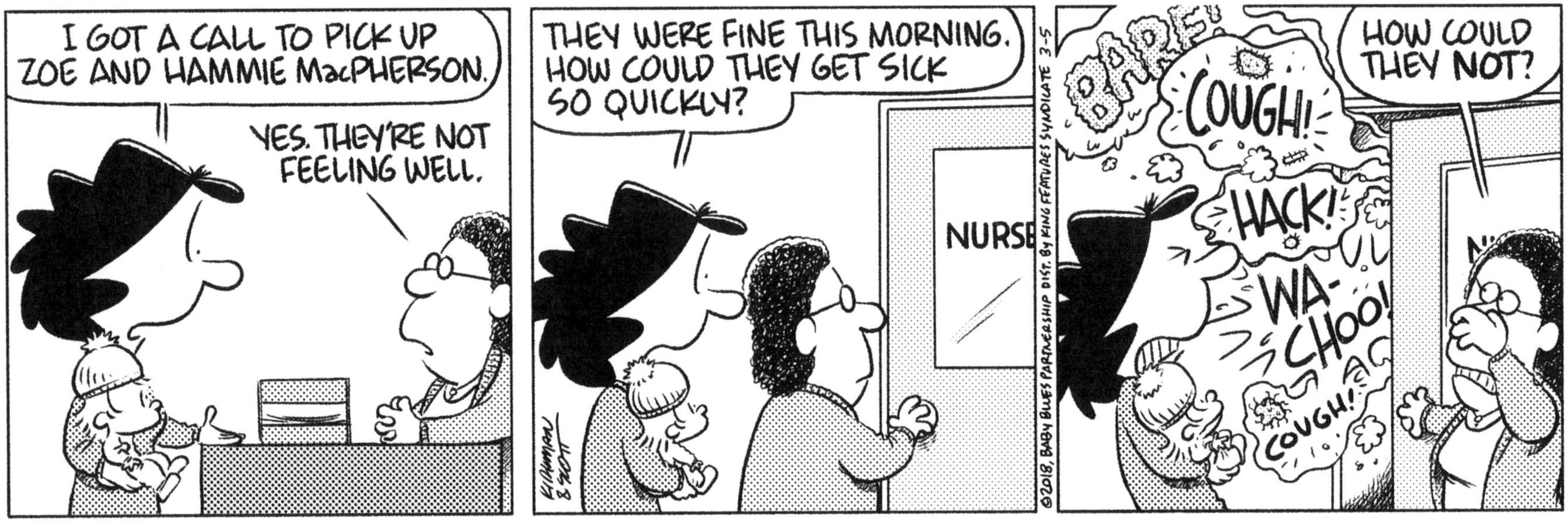
I GOT A CALL TO PICK UP ZOE AND HAMMIE MacPHERSON.
YES. THEY'RE NOT FEELING WELL.
THEY WERE FINE THIS MORNING. HOW COULD THEY GET SICK SO QUICKLY?
NURSE
©2018, BABY BLUES PARTNERSHIP DIST. BY KING FEATURES SYNDICATE 3-5
BARF!
COUGH!
HACK!
WA-CHOO!
COUGH!
HOW COULD THEY NOT?

Rick: I actually start coughing when I look at this one.

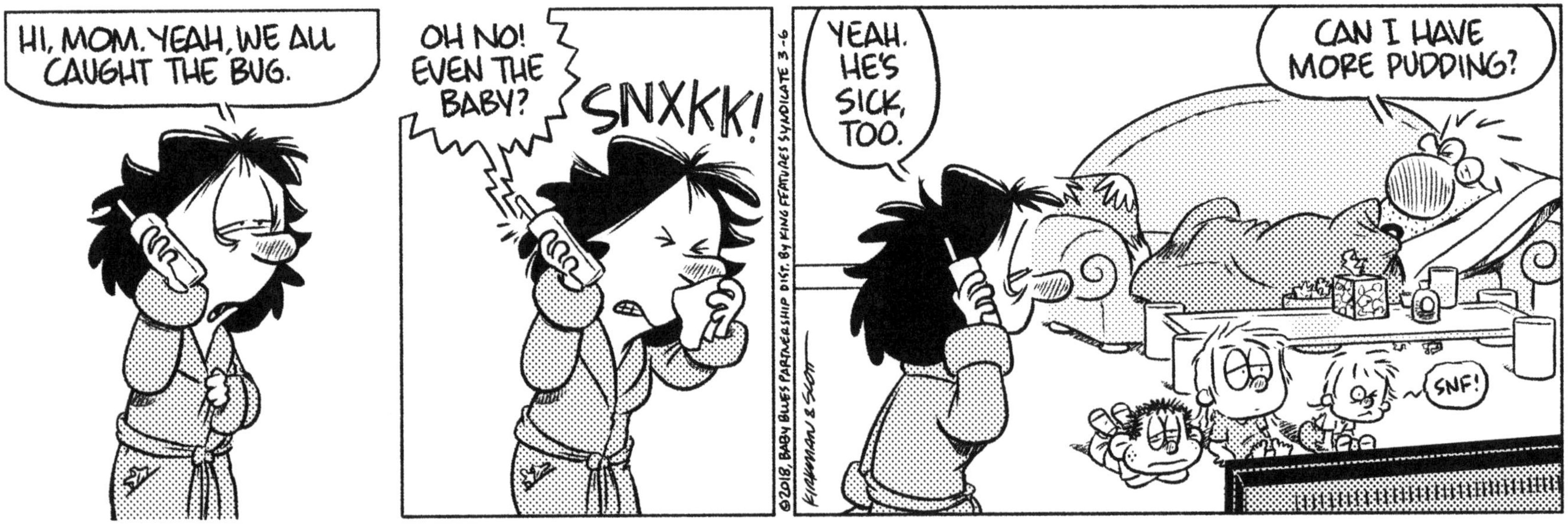
HI, MOM. YEAH, WE ALL CAUGHT THE BUG.
OH NO! EVEN THE BABY?
SNXKK!
©2018, BABY BLUES PARTNERSHIP DIST. BY KING FEATURES SYNDICATE 3-6
YEAH. HE'S SICK, TOO.
CAN I HAVE MORE PUDDING?
SNF!

Rick: My favorite part about this drawing is Wren.

Jerry: Research shows that the man-cold is much worse than a normal cold. My research, anyway.

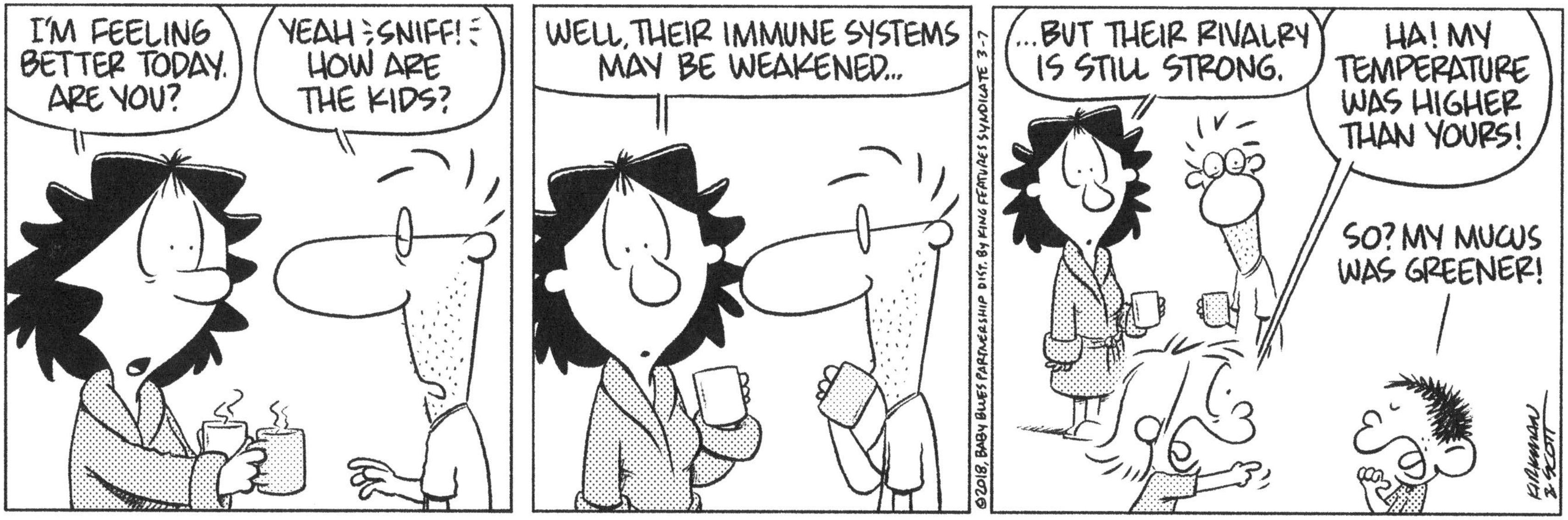
I'M FEELING BETTER TODAY. ARE YOU?
YEAH ~SNIFF!~ HOW ARE THE KIDS?
WELL, THEIR IMMUNE SYSTEMS MAY BE WEAKENED...
©2018, BABY BLUES PARTNERSHIP DIST. BY KING FEATURES SYNDICATE 3-7
...BUT THEIR RIVALRY IS STILL STRONG.
HA! MY TEMPERATURE WAS HIGHER THAN YOURS!
SO? MY MUCUS WAS GREENER!
KIRKMAN & SCOTT

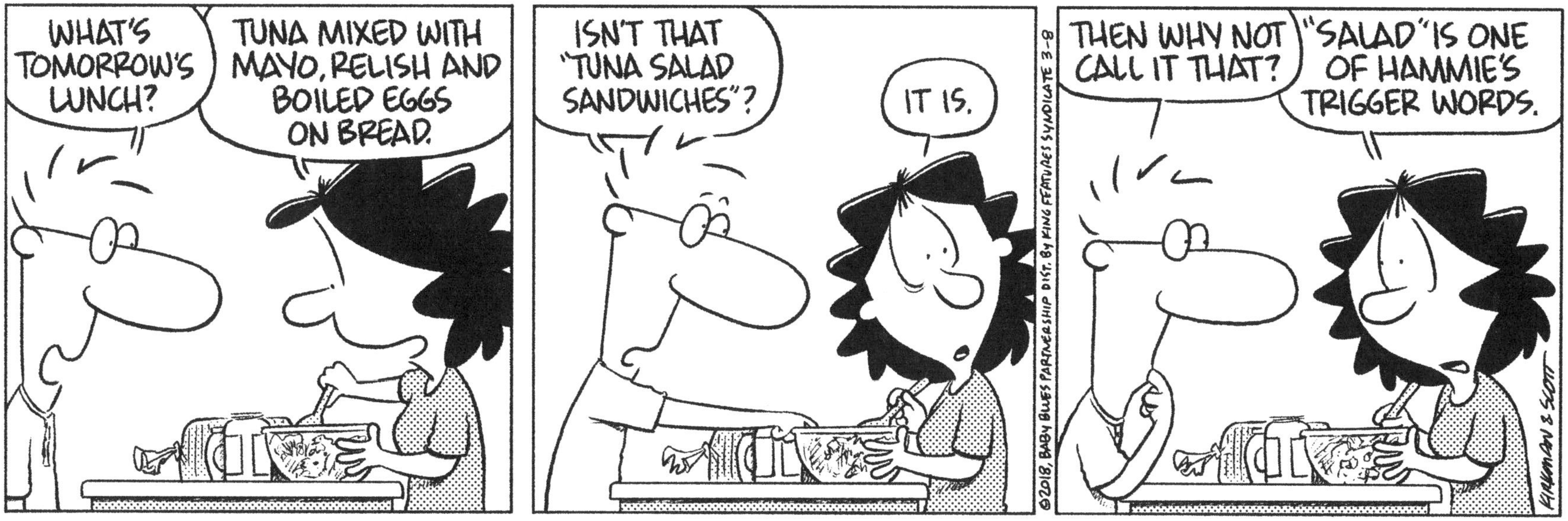
WHAT'S TOMORROW'S LUNCH?
TUNA MIXED WITH MAYO, RELISH AND BOILED EGGS ON BREAD.
ISN'T THAT "TUNA SALAD SANDWICHES"?
IT IS.
©2018, BABY BLUES PARTNERSHIP DIST. BY KING FEATURES SYNDICATE 3-8
THEN WHY NOT CALL IT THAT?
"SALAD" IS ONE OF HAMMIE'S TRIGGER WORDS.
KIRKMAN & SCOTT

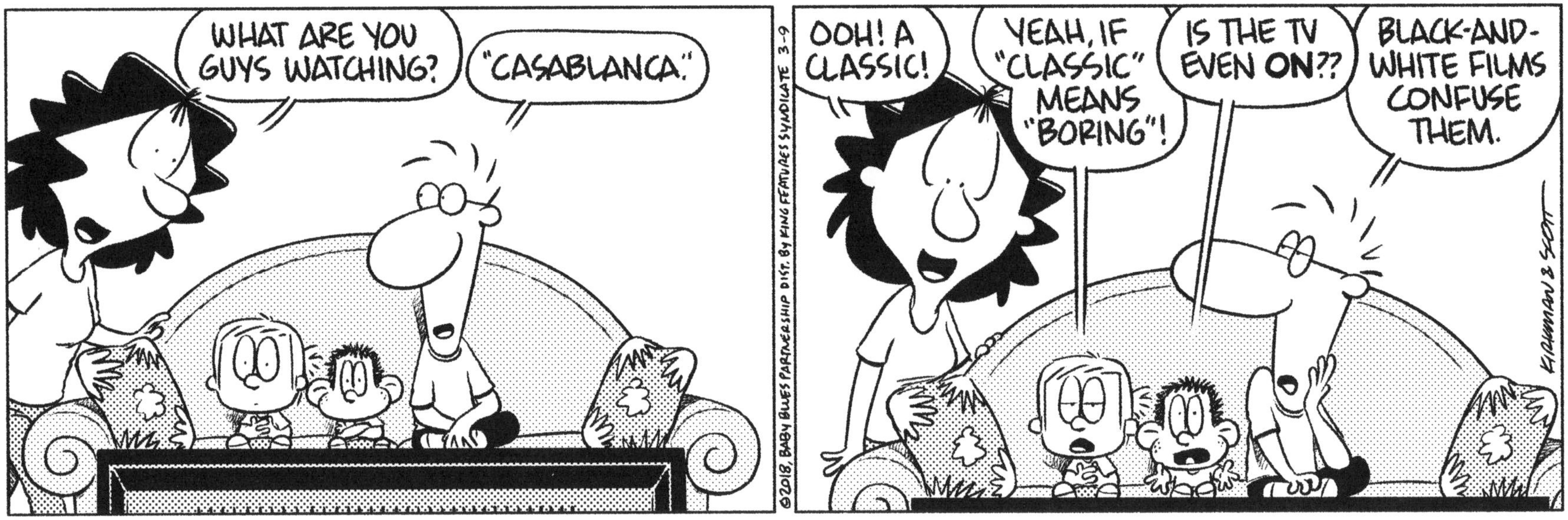
WHAT ARE YOU GUYS WATCHING?
"CASABLANCA."
©2018, BABY BLUES PARTNERSHIP DIST. BY KING FEATURES SYNDICATE 3-9
OOH! A CLASSIC!
YEAH, IF "CLASSIC" MEANS "BORING"!
IS THE TV EVEN **ON**??
BLACK-AND-WHITE FILMS CONFUSE THEM.
KIRKMAN & SCOTT

Rick: My kids actually told me Darryl's last line. They found characters hard to tell apart in black-and-white movies and TV shows. I want science to explain that one.

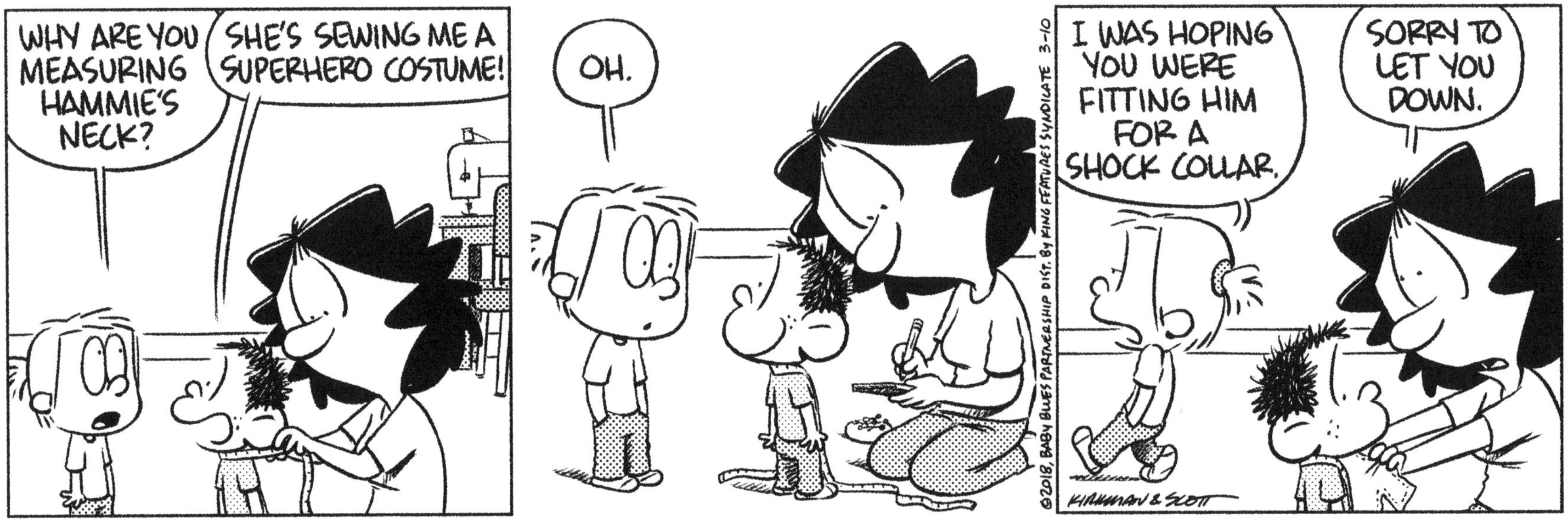
WHY ARE YOU MEASURING HAMMIE'S NECK?
SHE'S SEWING ME A SUPERHERO COSTUME!
OH.
©2018, BABY BLUES PARTNERSHIP DIST. BY KING FEATURES SYNDICATE 3-10
I WAS HOPING YOU WERE FITTING HIM FOR A SHOCK COLLAR.
SORRY TO LET YOU DOWN.
KIRKMAN & SCOTT

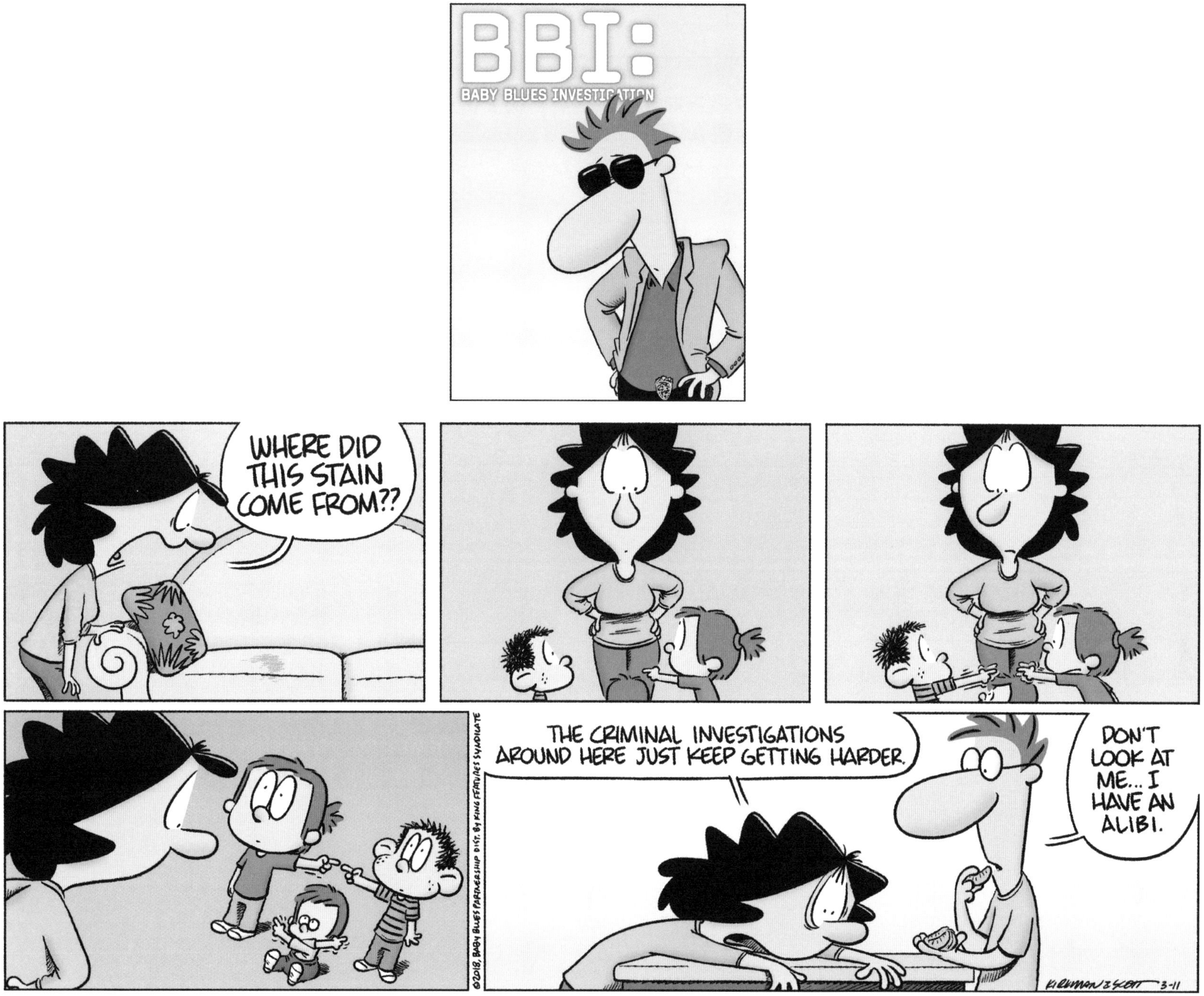
BBI:
BABY BLUES INVESTIGATION
WHERE DID THIS STAIN COME FROM??
THE CRIMINAL INVESTIGATIONS AROUND HERE JUST KEEP GETTING HARDER.
DON'T LOOK AT ME... I HAVE AN ALIBI.
©2018, BABY BLUES PARTNERSHIP DIST. BY KING FEATURES SYNDICATE
KIRKMAN & SCOTT 3-11

Rick: In case you couldn't tell, that was supposed to be Darryl as David Caruso as Horatio Caine.

Jerry: This title panel made me laugh. I saw David Caruso in a restaurant once. He looked just like himself.

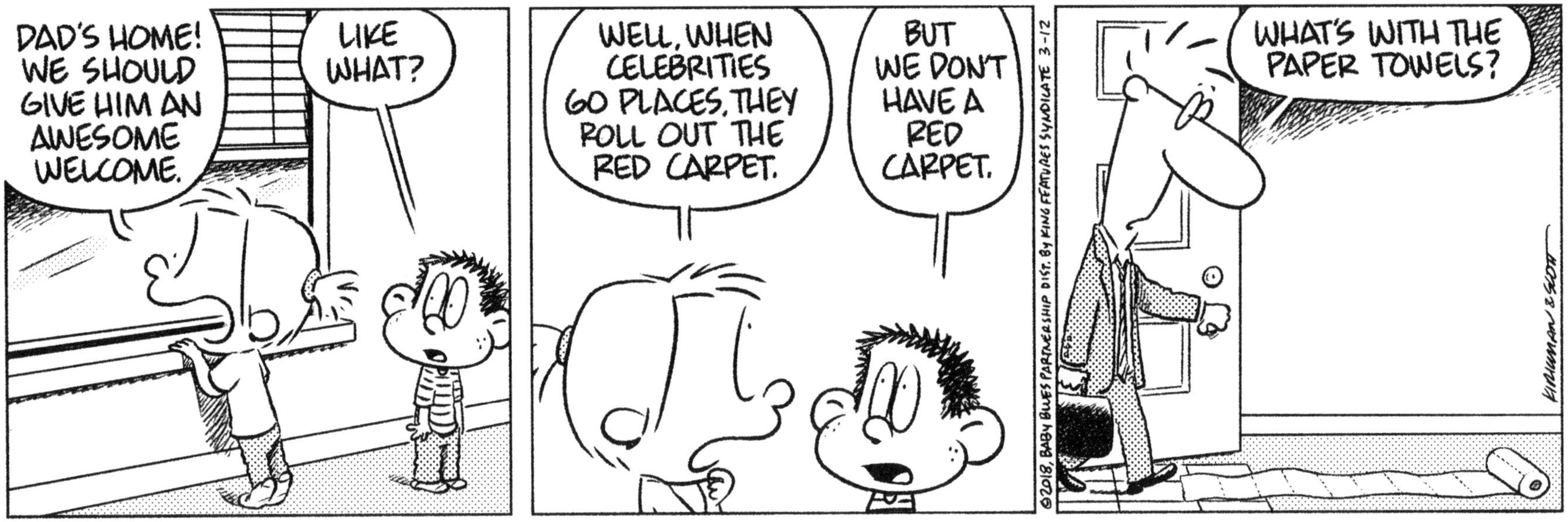
DAD'S HOME! WE SHOULD GIVE HIM AN AWESOME WELCOME.
LIKE WHAT?
WELL, WHEN CELEBRITIES GO PLACES, THEY ROLL OUT THE RED CARPET.
BUT WE DON'T HAVE A RED CARPET.
©2018, BABY BLUES PARTNERSHIP DIST. BY KING FEATURES SYNDICATE 3-12
WHAT'S WITH THE PAPER TOWELS?
KIRKMAN & SCOTT

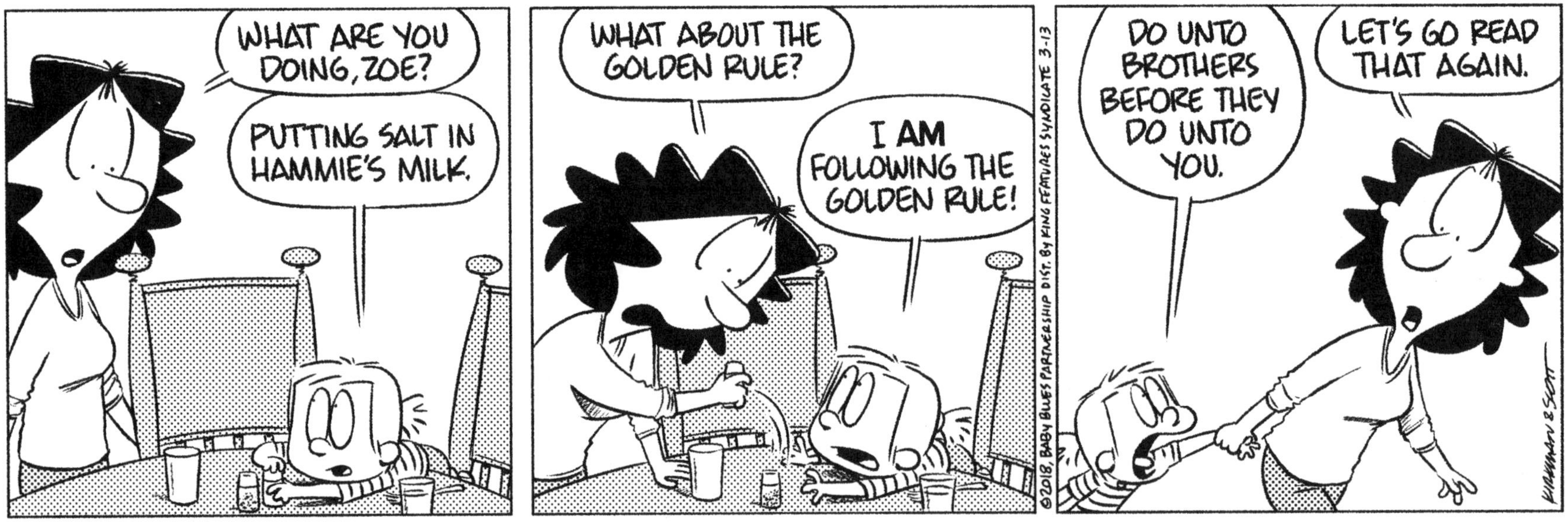
WHAT ARE YOU DOING, ZOE?
PUTTING SALT IN HAMMIE'S MILK.
WHAT ABOUT THE GOLDEN RULE?
I **AM** FOLLOWING THE GOLDEN RULE!
©2018, BABY BLUES PARTNERSHIP DIST. BY KING FEATURES SYNDICATE 3-13
DO UNTO BROTHERS BEFORE THEY DO UNTO YOU.
LET'S GO READ THAT AGAIN.
KIRKMAN & SCOTT

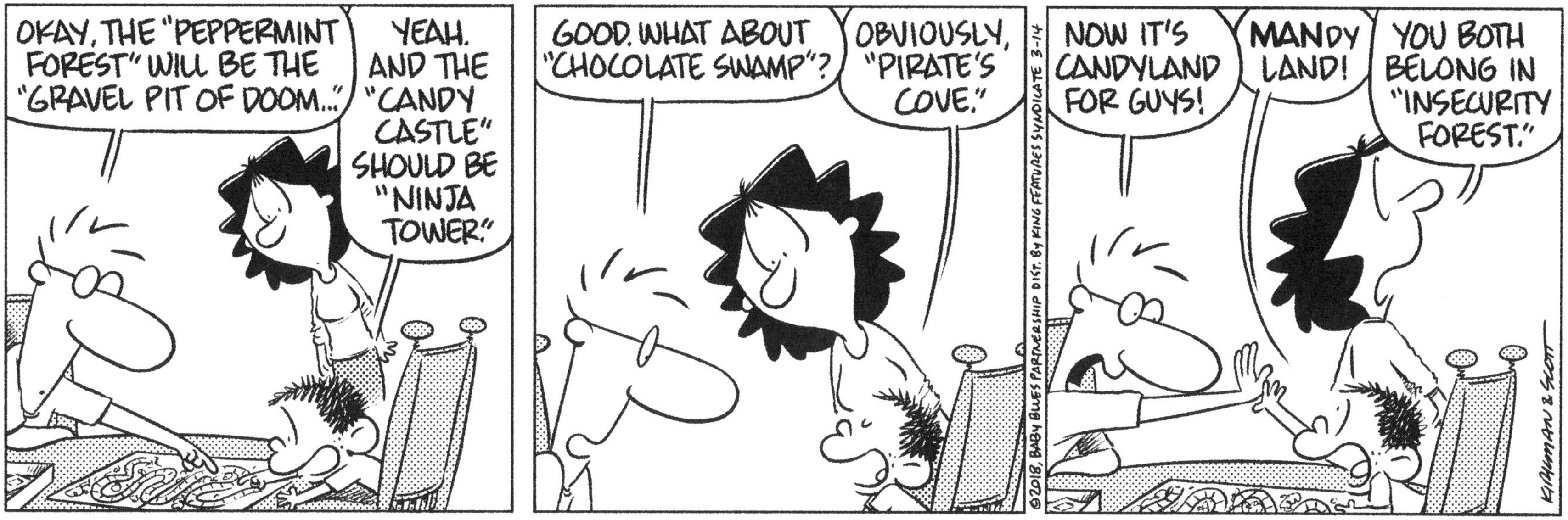
OKAY, THE "PEPPERMINT FOREST" WILL BE THE "GRAVEL PIT OF DOOM..."
YEAH. AND THE "CANDY CASTLE" SHOULD BE "NINJA TOWER."
GOOD. WHAT ABOUT "CHOCOLATE SWAMP"?
OBVIOUSLY, "PIRATE'S COVE."
©2018, BABY BLUES PARTNERSHIP DIST. BY KING FEATURES SYNDICATE 3-14
NOW IT'S CANDYLAND FOR GUYS!
MANDY LAND!
YOU BOTH BELONG IN "INSECURITY FOREST."
KIRKMAN & SCOTT

Rick: Sometimes words are too long to fit in the space available. This one took a little back and forth about the names in the game. Quite a conversation—a couple of grown men debating over "Lollipop Palace" and "Licorice Lagoon," neither of which made the cut.

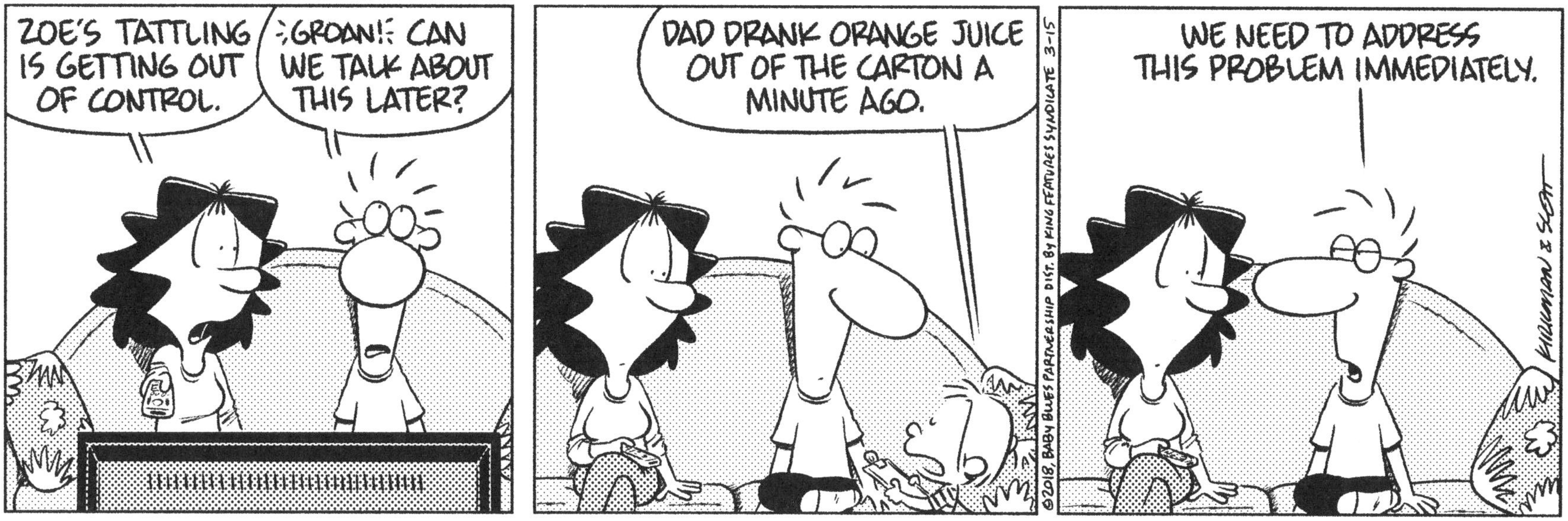
ZOE'S TATTLING IS GETTING OUT OF CONTROL.
:GROAN!: CAN WE TALK ABOUT THIS LATER?
DAD DRANK ORANGE JUICE OUT OF THE CARTON A MINUTE AGO.
©2018, BABY BLUES PARTNERSHIP DIST. BY KING FEATURES SYNDICATE 3-15
WE NEED TO ADDRESS THIS PROBLEM IMMEDIATELY.
KIRKMAN & SCOTT

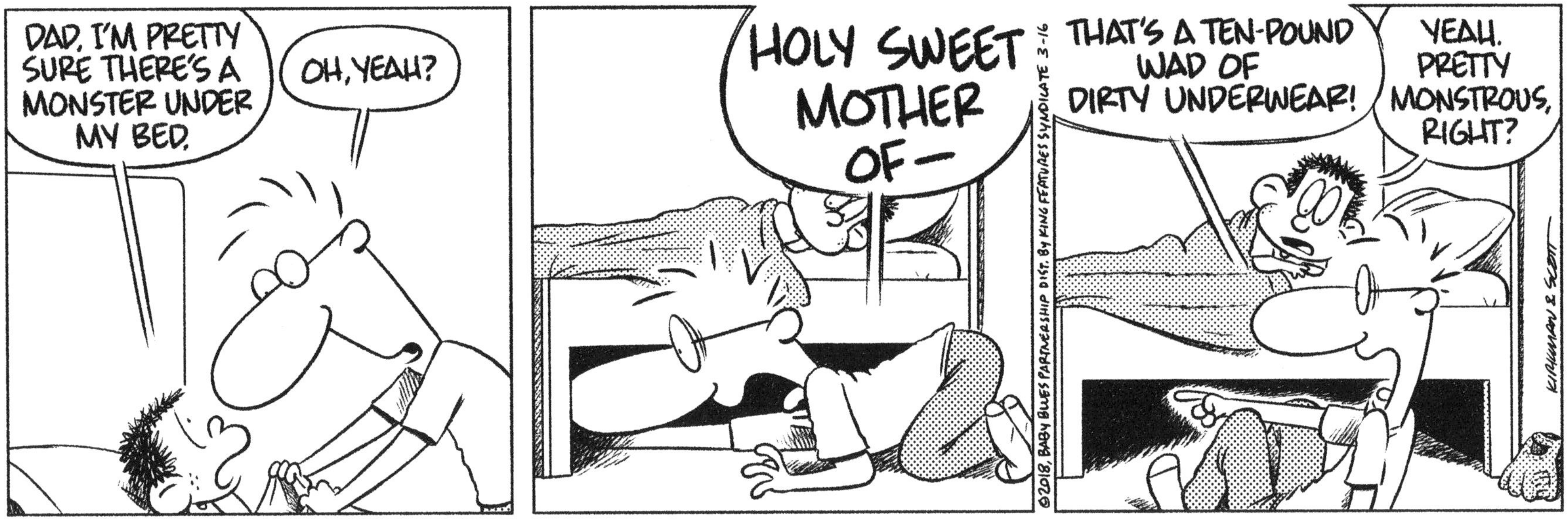
DAD, I'M PRETTY SURE THERE'S A MONSTER UNDER MY BED.
OH, YEAH?
HOLY SWEET MOTHER OF—
©2018, BABY BLUES PARTNERSHIP DIST. BY KING FEATURES SYNDICATE 3-16
THAT'S A TEN-POUND WAD OF DIRTY UNDERWEAR!
YEAH. PRETTY MONSTROUS, RIGHT?
KIRKMAN & SCOTT

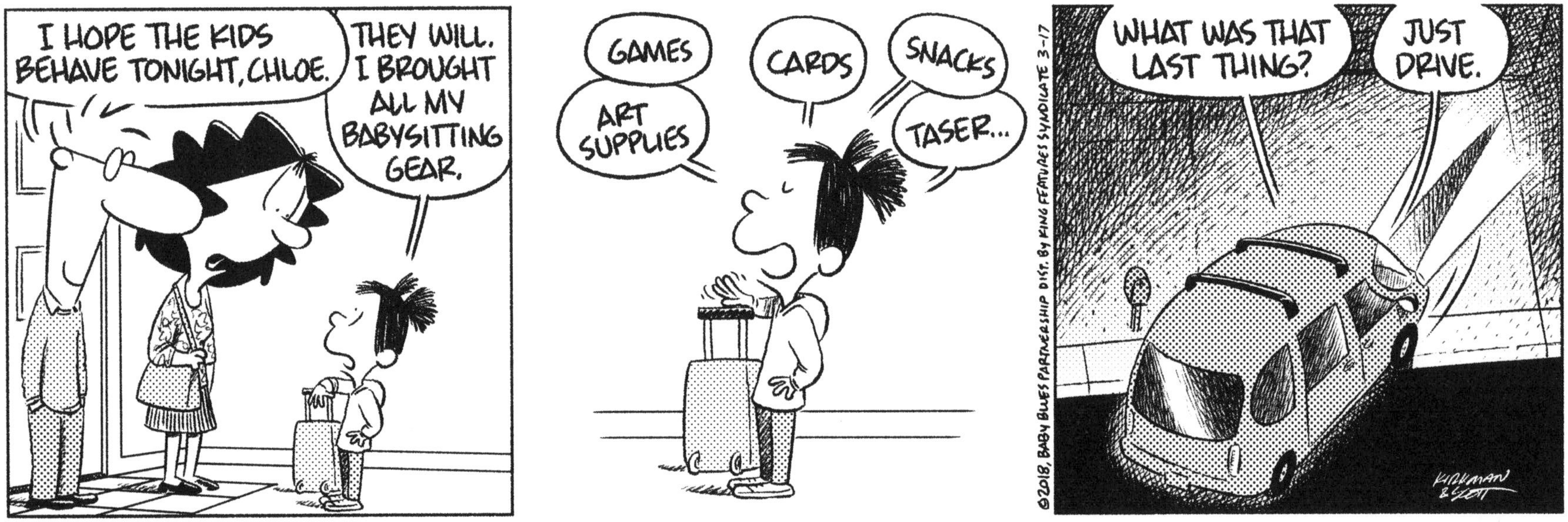
I HOPE THE KIDS BEHAVE TONIGHT, CHLOE.
THEY WILL. I BROUGHT ALL MY BABYSITTING GEAR.
GAMES
ART SUPPLIES
CARDS
SNACKS
TASER...
©2018, BABY BLUES PARTNERSHIP DIST. BY KING FEATURES SYNDICATE 3-17
WHAT WAS THAT LAST THING?
JUST DRIVE.
KIRKMAN & SCOTT

Rick: Heh-heh. **Jerry:** A good babysitter is prepared for anything. Even Hammie.

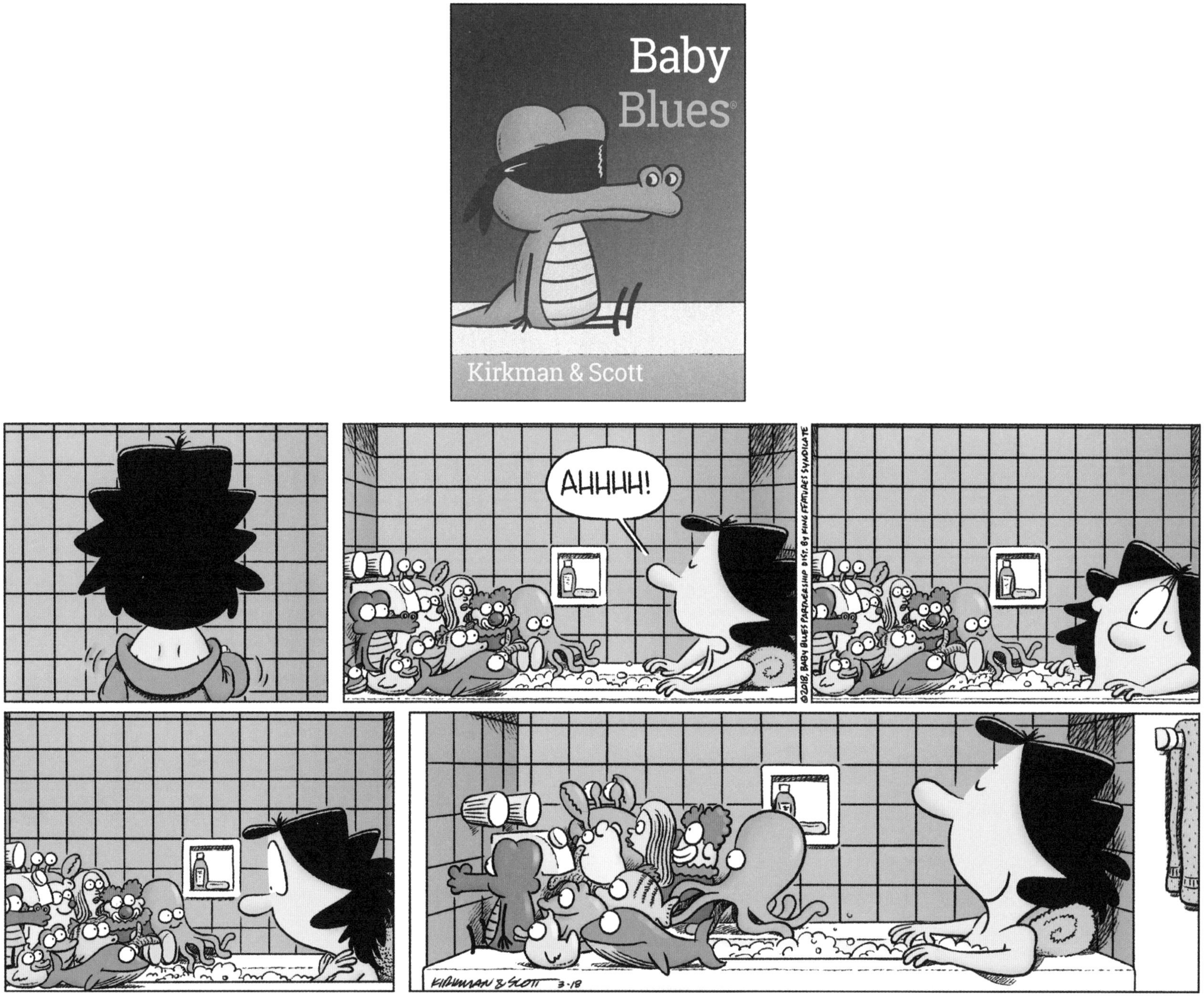
Baby
Blues®
Kirkman & Scott
AHHHH!
©2018, BABY BLUES PARTNERSHIP DIST. BY KING FEATURES SYNDICATE
KIRKMAN & SCOTT 3-18

Rick: Since there were a bunch of funny bath toys, I slipped one of the *Pearls Before Swine* crocs in there. Then took it a step further by putting him in the title panel, referencing a popular, and racy, novel series. I guess I was bored that day.

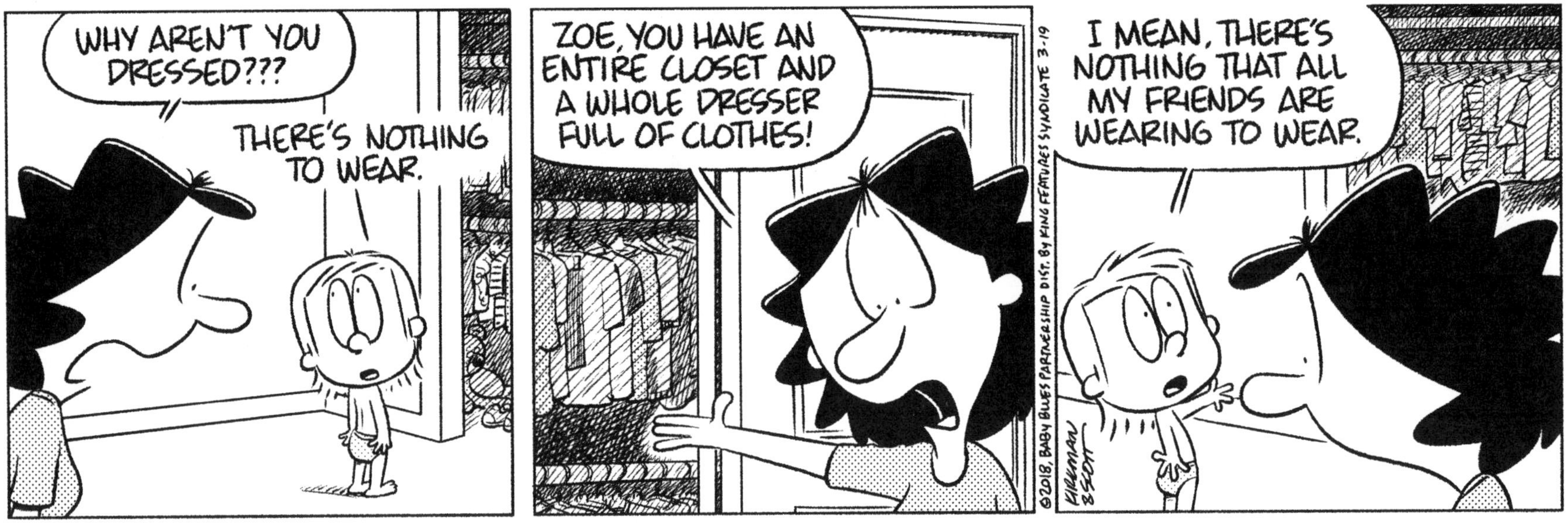
WHY AREN'T YOU DRESSED???
THERE'S NOTHING TO WEAR.
ZOE, YOU HAVE AN ENTIRE CLOSET AND A WHOLE DRESSER FULL OF CLOTHES!
©2018, BABY BLUES PARTNERSHIP DIST. BY KING FEATURES SYNDICATE 3-19
KIRKMAN & SCOTT
I MEAN, THERE'S NOTHING THAT ALL MY FRIENDS ARE WEARING TO WEAR.

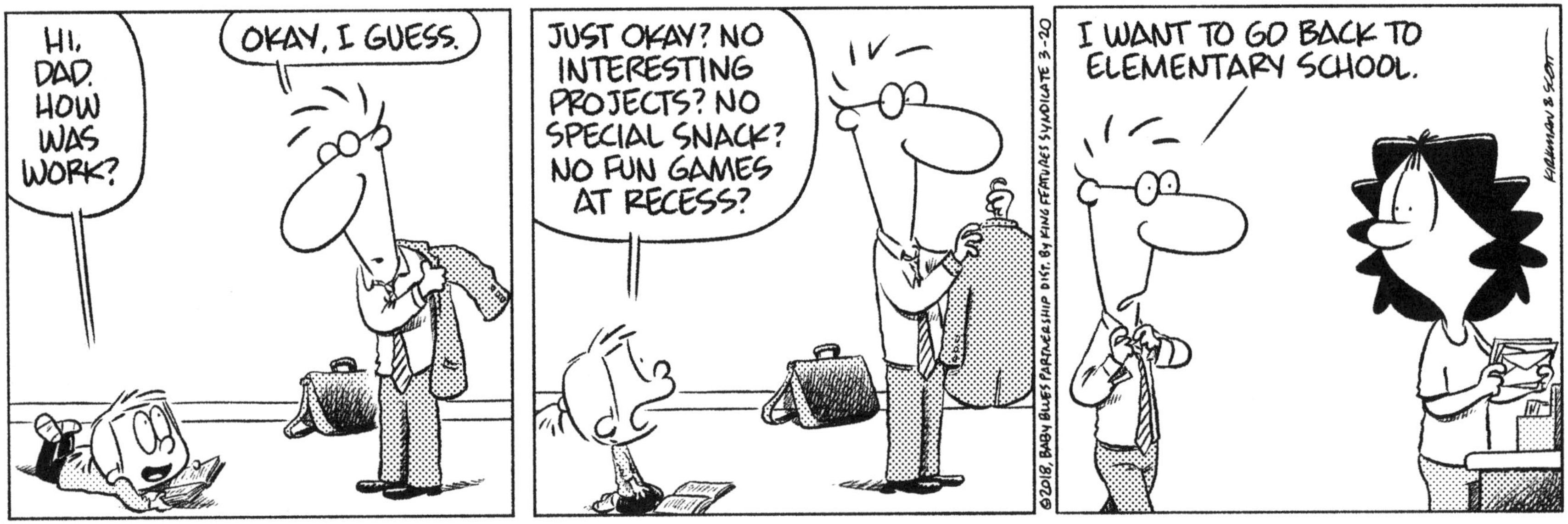
HI, DAD. HOW WAS WORK?
OKAY, I GUESS.
JUST OKAY? NO INTERESTING PROJECTS? NO SPECIAL SNACK? NO FUN GAMES AT RECESS?
©2018, BABY BLUES PARTNERSHIP DIST. BY KING FEATURES SYNDICATE 3-20
I WANT TO GO BACK TO ELEMENTARY SCHOOL.
KIRKMAN & SCOTT

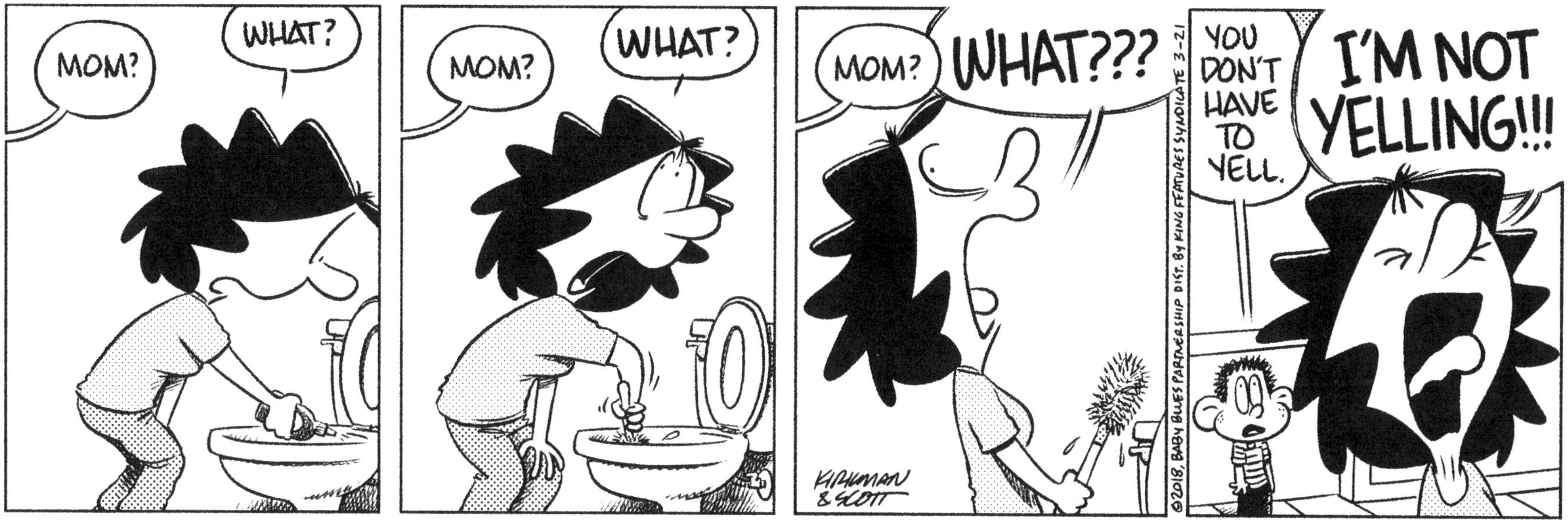
MOM?
WHAT?
MOM?
WHAT?
MOM?
WHAT???
KIRKMAN & SCOTT
©2018, BABY BLUES PARTNERSHIP DIST. BY KING FEATURES SYNDICATE 3-21
YOU DON'T HAVE TO YELL.
I'M NOT YELLING!!!

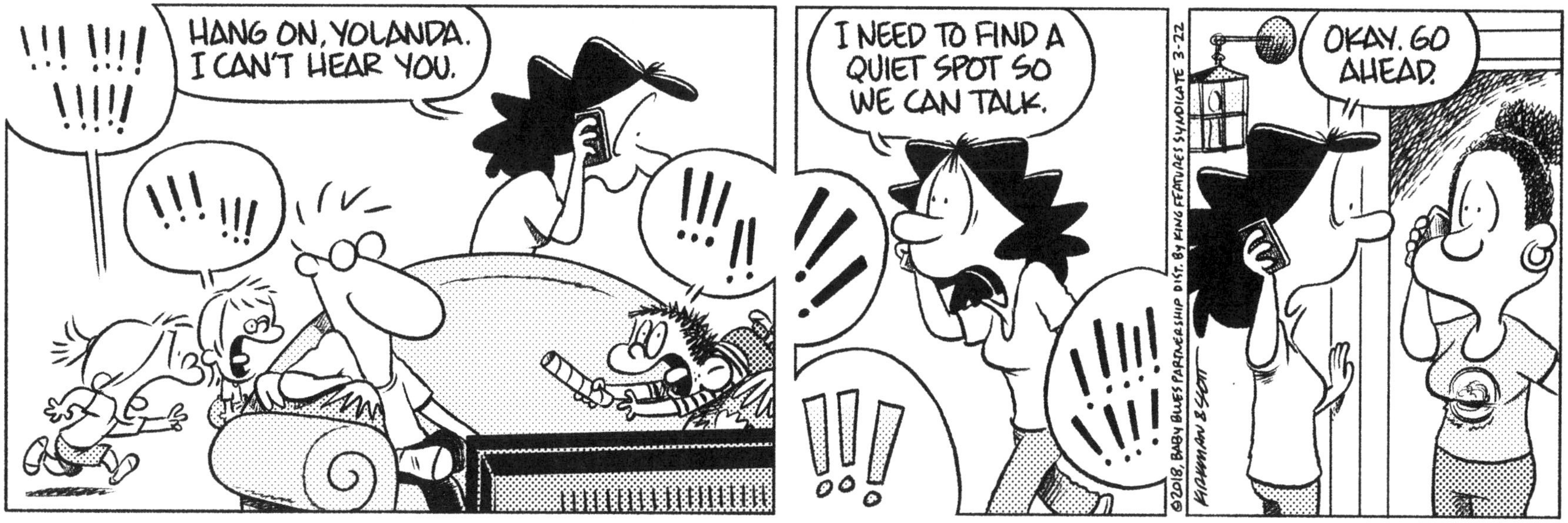
!!! !!!! !!!!!
HANG ON, YOLANDA. I CAN'T HEAR YOU.
!!! !!!
!!! !!
I NEED TO FIND A QUIET SPOT SO WE CAN TALK.
!!!
!!!
!!!! !!!!
©2018, BABY BLUES PARTNERSHIP DIST. BY KING FEATURES SYNDICATE 3-22
KIRKMAN & SCOTT
OKAY. GO AHEAD.

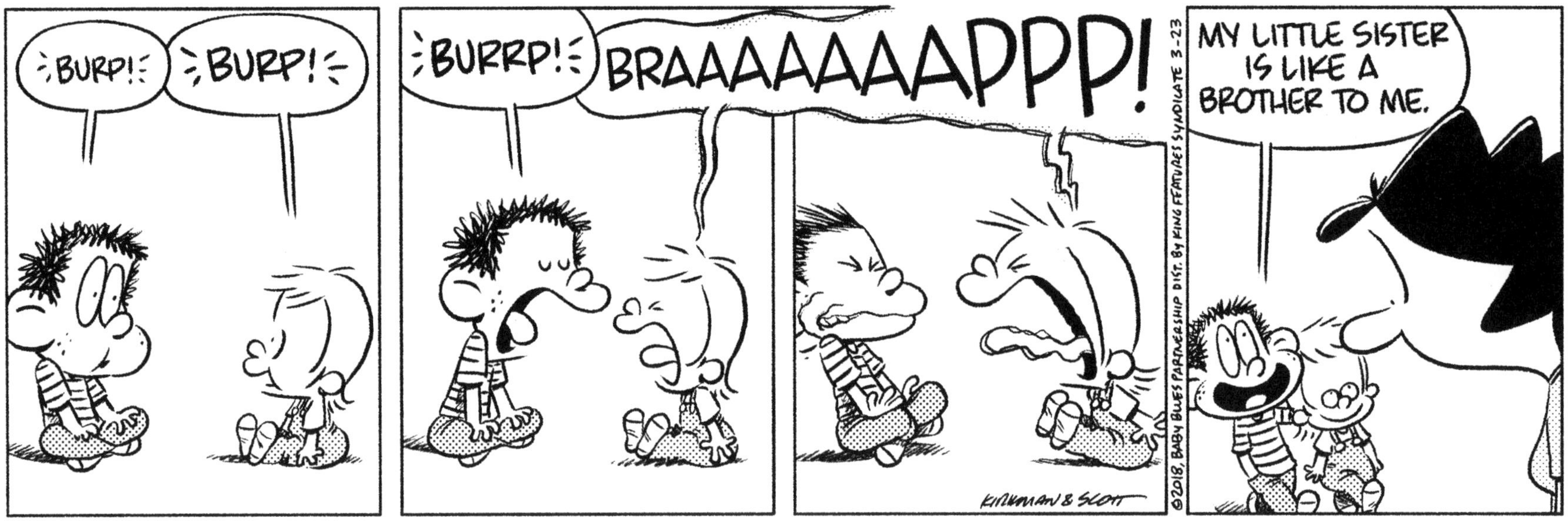
BURP!
BURP!
BURRP!
BRAAAAAAAPPP!
MY LITTLE SISTER IS LIKE A BROTHER TO ME.
KIRKMAN & SCOTT
©2018, BABY BLUES PARTNERSHIP DIST. BY KING FEATURES SYNDICATE 3-23

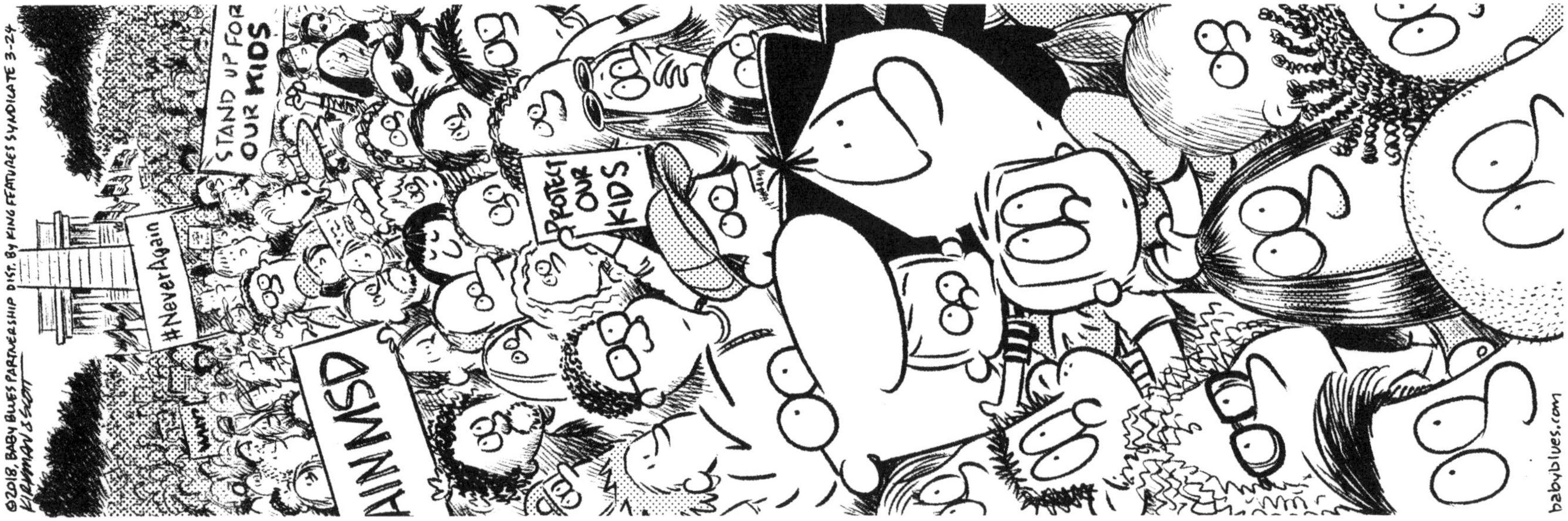
©2018, BABY BLUES PARTNERSHIP DIST. BY KING FEATURES SYNDICATE 3-24
KIRKMAN & SCOTT
STAND UP FOR OUR KIDS
PROTECT OUR KIDS
#NeverAgain
babyblues.com

Rick: A rare solemn moment for the March for Our Lives. The only time I've *not* hated drawing a crowd scene.

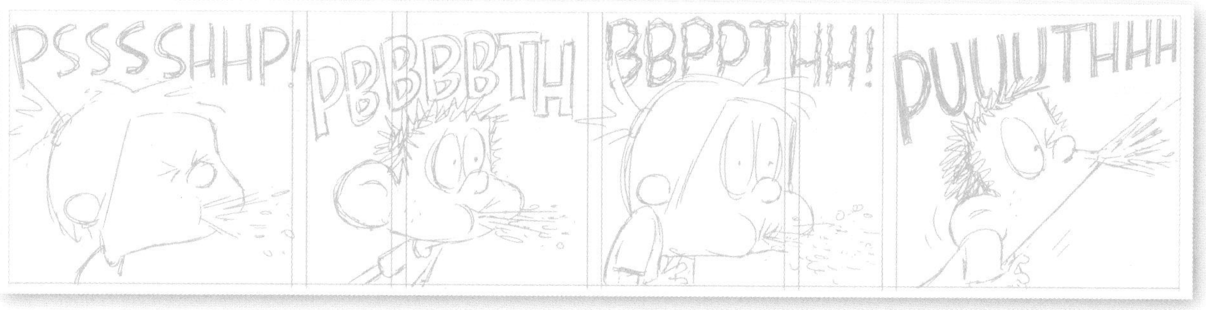
PSSSSHHP!
PBBBBTH
BBPPTHH!
PUUUTHHH

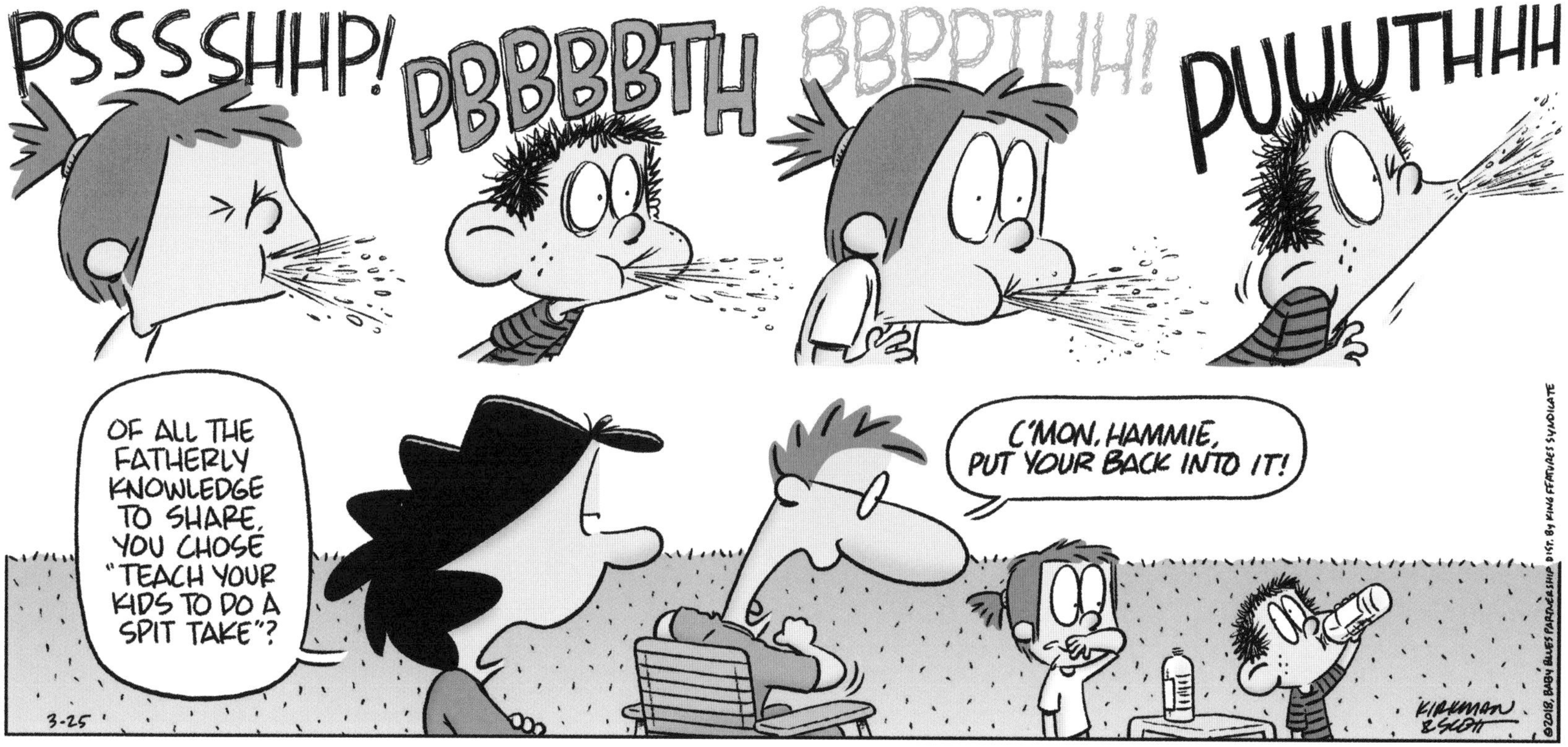
PSSSSHHP!
PBBBBTH
BBPPTHH!
PUUUTHHH
OF ALL THE FATHERLY KNOWLEDGE TO SHARE, YOU CHOSE "TEACH YOUR KIDS TO DO A SPIT TAKE"?
C'MON, HAMMIE, PUT YOUR BACK INTO IT!
3-25
KIRKMAN & SCOTT
©2018, BABY BLUES PARTNERSHIP DIST. BY KING FEATURES SYNDICATE

Rick: Parents have a responsibility to teach their kids essential life skills.

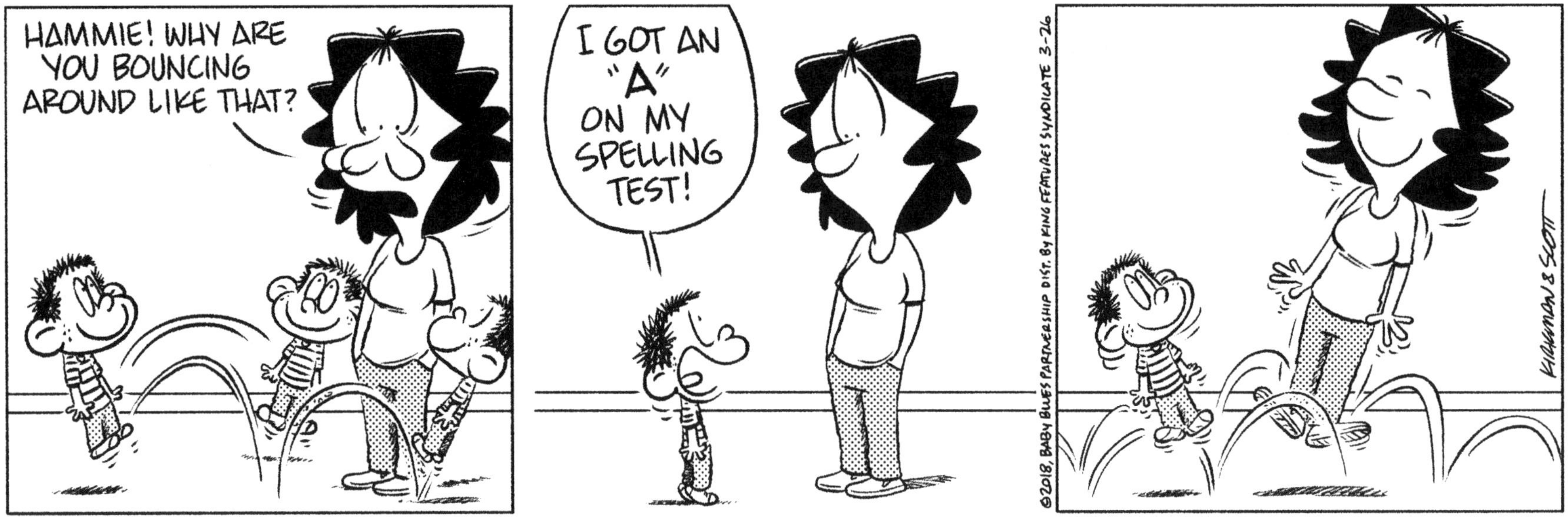
HAMMIE! WHY ARE YOU BOUNCING AROUND LIKE THAT?
I GOT AN "A" ON MY SPELLING TEST!
©2018, BABY BLUES PARTNERSHIP DIST. BY KING FEATURES SYNDICATE 3-26
KIRKMAN & SCOTT

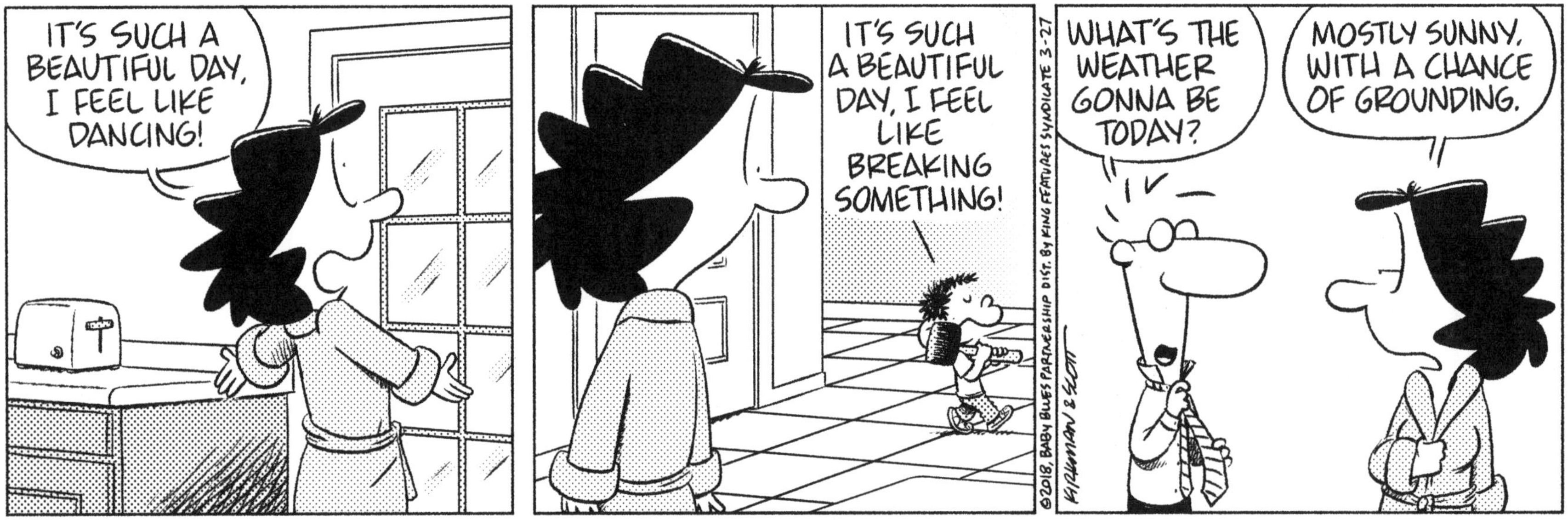
IT'S SUCH A BEAUTIFUL DAY, I FEEL LIKE DANCING!
IT'S SUCH A BEAUTIFUL DAY, I FEEL LIKE BREAKING SOMETHING!
WHAT'S THE WEATHER GONNA BE TODAY?
MOSTLY SUNNY, WITH A CHANCE OF GROUNDING.
©2018, BABY BLUES PARTNERSHIP DIST. BY KING FEATURES SYNDICATE 3-27
KIRKMAN & SCOTT

Jerry: That sounds like a familiar weather report.

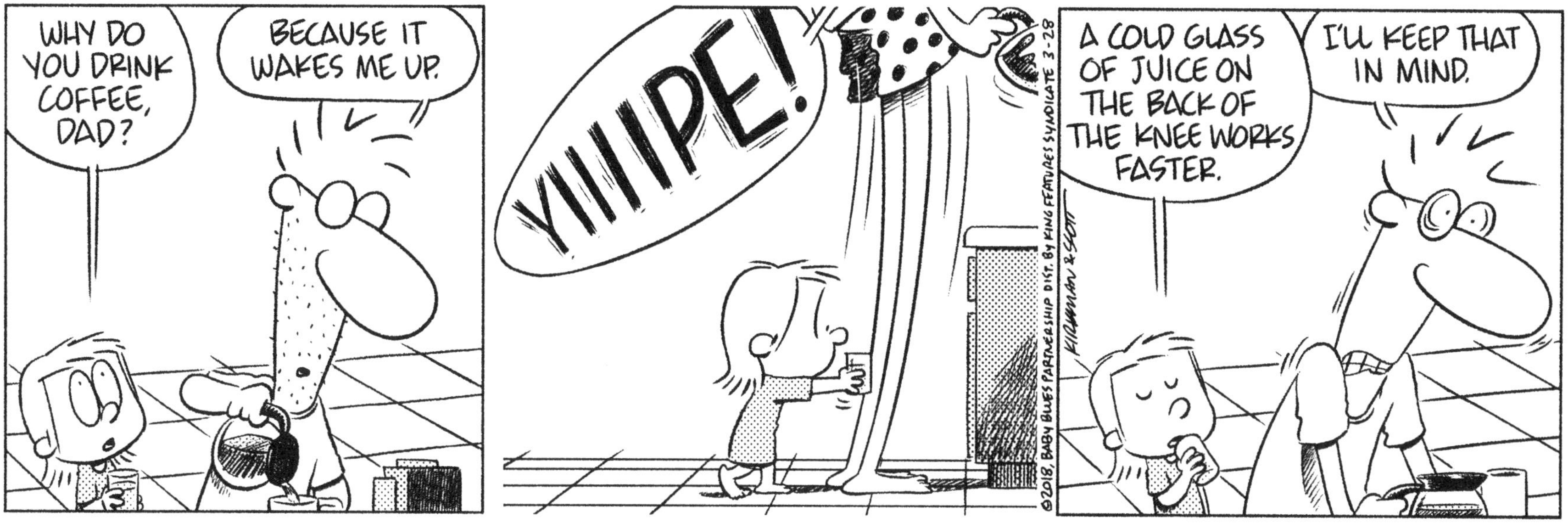
WHY DO YOU DRINK COFFEE, DAD?
BECAUSE IT WAKES ME UP.
YIIIIPE!
©2018, BABY BLUES PARTNERSHIP DIST. BY KING FEATURES SYNDICATE 3-28
KIRKMAN & SCOTT
A COLD GLASS OF JUICE ON THE BACK OF THE KNEE WORKS FASTER.
I'LL KEEP THAT IN MIND.

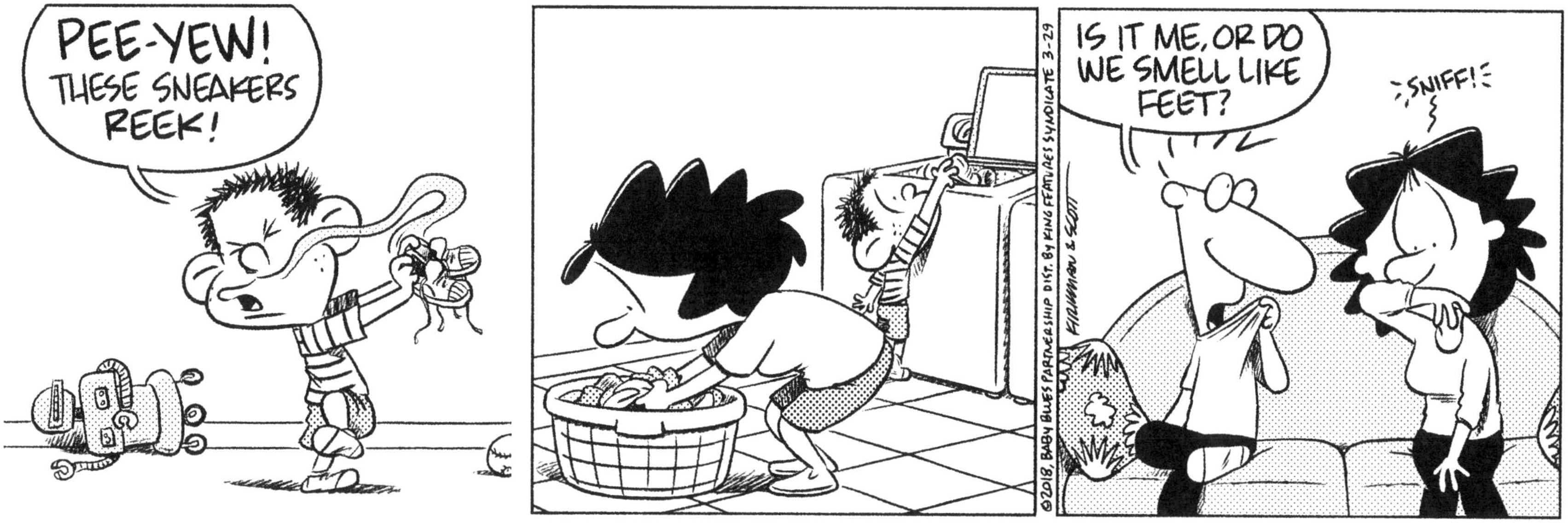
PEE-YEW! THESE SNEAKERS REEK!
©2018, BABY BLUES PARTNERSHIP DIST. BY KING FEATURES SYNDICATE 3-29
KIRKMAN & SCOTT
IS IT ME, OR DO WE SMELL LIKE FEET?
SNIFF!

Rick: That last line makes me laugh.

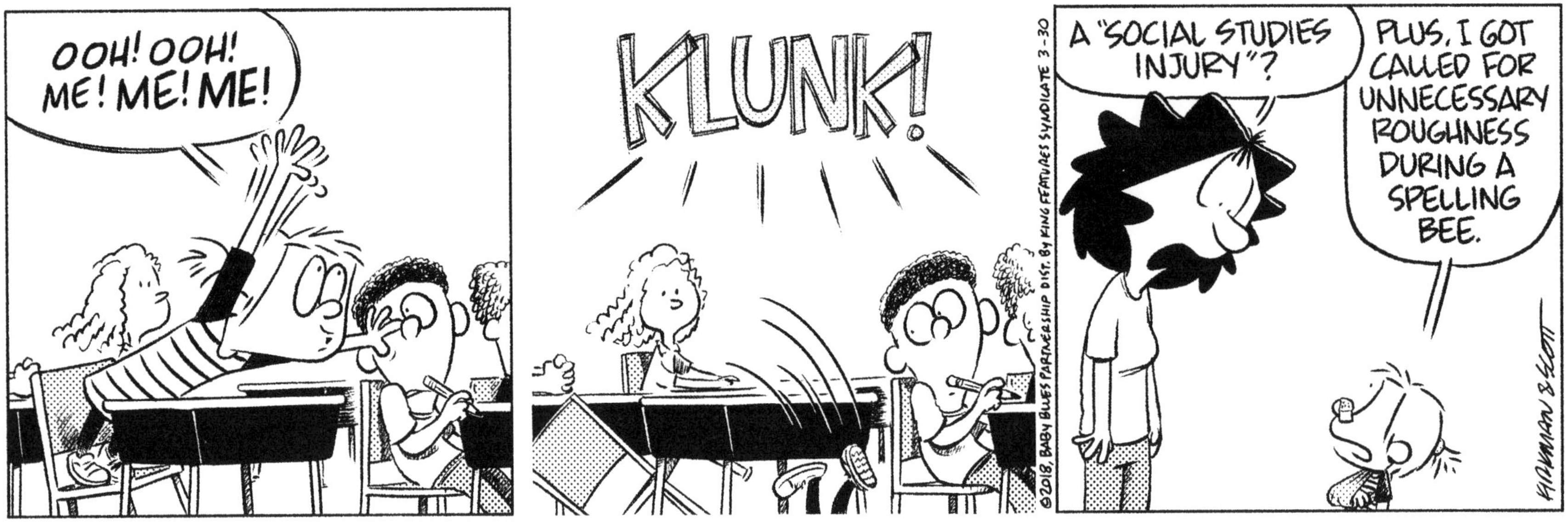
OOH! OOH! ME! ME! ME!
KLUNK!
A "SOCIAL STUDIES INJURY"?
PLUS, I GOT CALLED FOR UNNECESSARY ROUGHNESS DURING A SPELLING BEE.
©2018, BABY BLUES PARTNERSHIP DIST. BY KING FEATURES SYNDICATE 3-30
KIRKMAN & SCOTT

Jerry: The academics game ain't for sissies.

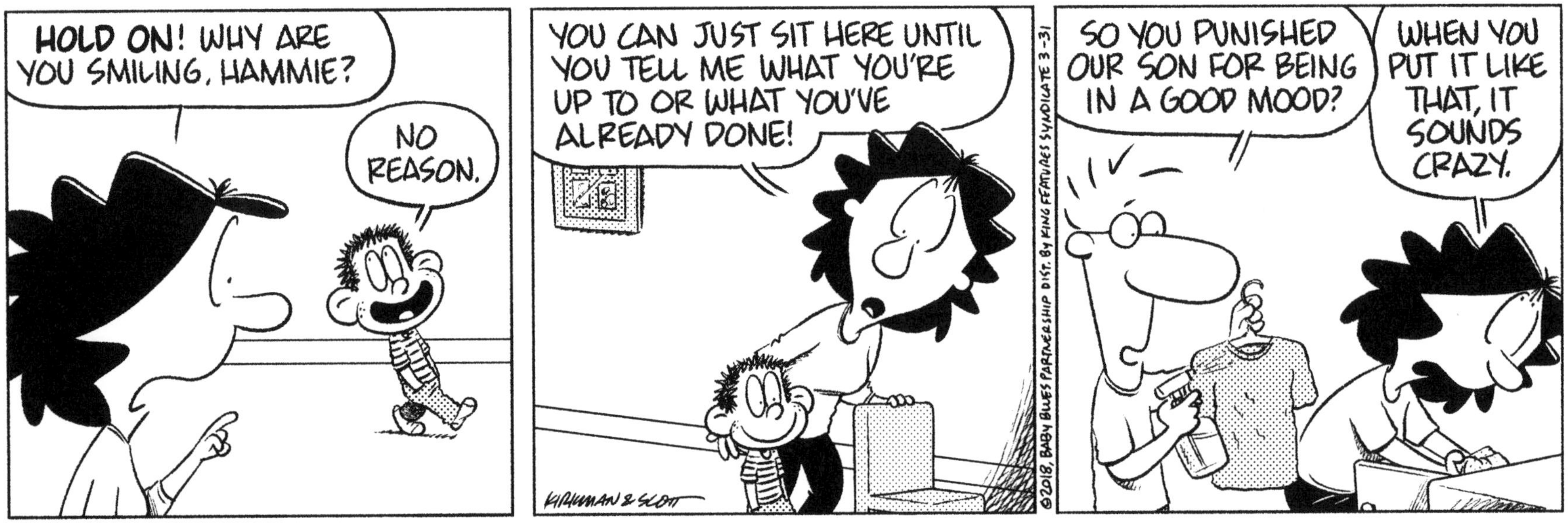
HOLD ON! WHY ARE YOU SMILING, HAMMIE?
NO REASON.
YOU CAN JUST SIT HERE UNTIL YOU TELL ME WHAT YOU'RE UP TO OR WHAT YOU'VE ALREADY DONE!
KIRKMAN & SCOTT
©2018, BABY BLUES PARTNERSHIP DIST. BY KING FEATURES SYNDICATE 3-31
SO YOU PUNISHED OUR SON FOR BEING IN A GOOD MOOD?
WHEN YOU PUT IT LIKE THAT, IT SOUNDS CRAZY.

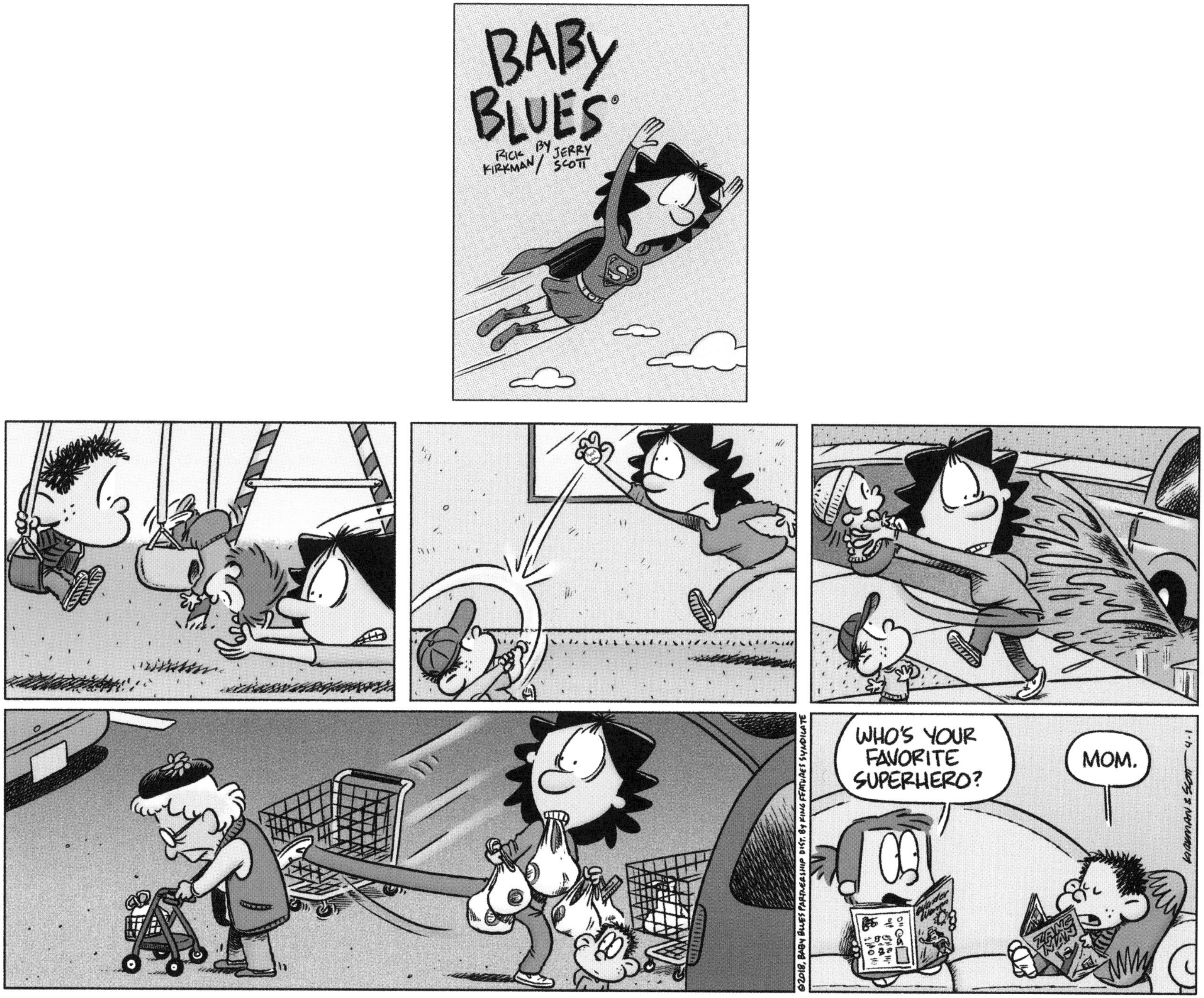
BABY BLUES®
BY RICK KIRKMAN / JERRY SCOTT
©2018, BABY BLUES PARTNERSHIP DIST. BY KING FEATURES SYNDICATE
WHO'S YOUR FAVORITE SUPERHERO?
MOM.
KIRKMAN & SCOTT
ZANG MAN

Rick: My hero. Also, I'd like to know more about this *Zang Man* on Hammie's comic.

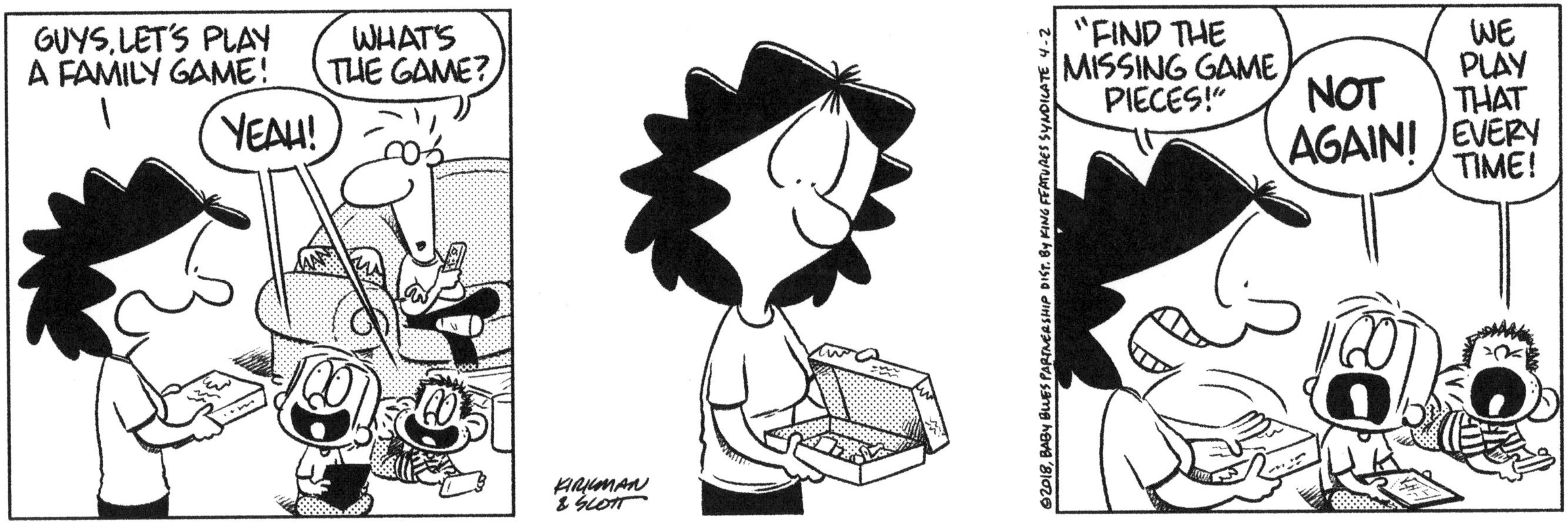
GUYS, LET'S PLAY A FAMILY GAME!
YEAH!
WHAT'S THE GAME?
KIRKMAN & SCOTT
©2018, BABY BLUES PARTNERSHIP DIST. BY KING FEATURES SYNDICATE 4-2
"FIND THE MISSING GAME PIECES!"
NOT AGAIN!
WE PLAY THAT EVERY TIME!

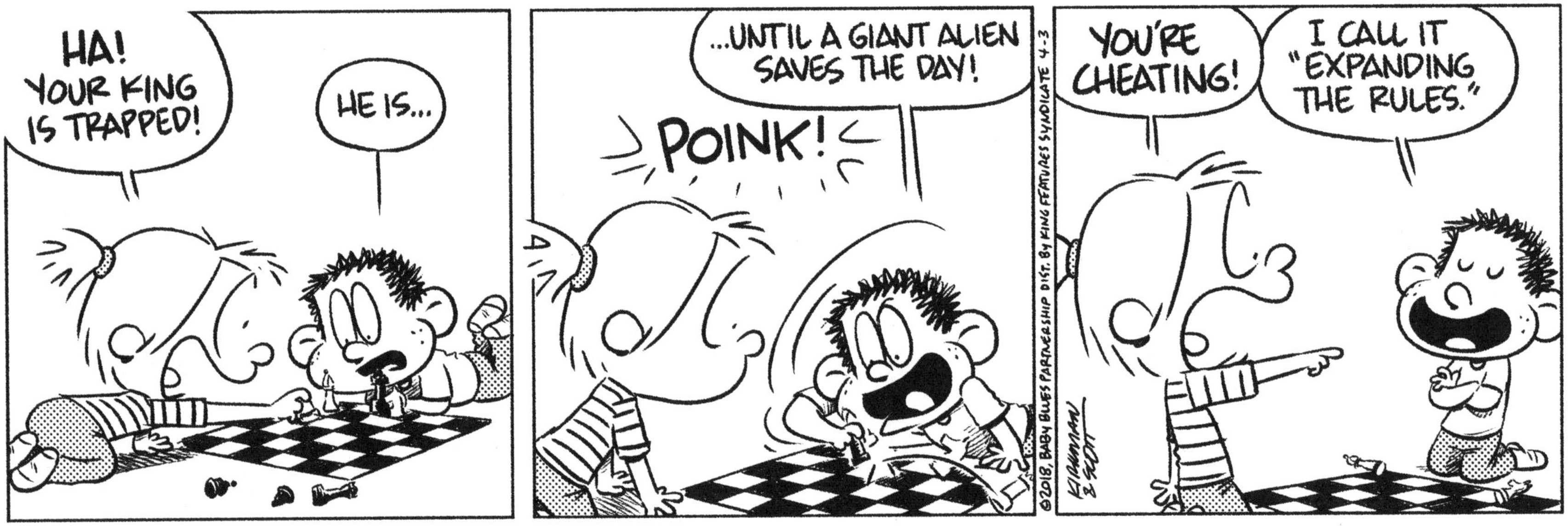
HA! YOUR KING IS TRAPPED!
HE IS...
...UNTIL A GIANT ALIEN SAVES THE DAY!
POINK!
©2018, BABY BLUES PARTNERSHIP DIST. BY KING FEATURES SYNDICATE 4-3
KIRKMAN & SCOTT
YOU'RE CHEATING!
I CALL IT "EXPANDING THE RULES."

Rick: Did I say I hate drawing checkers and chess games?

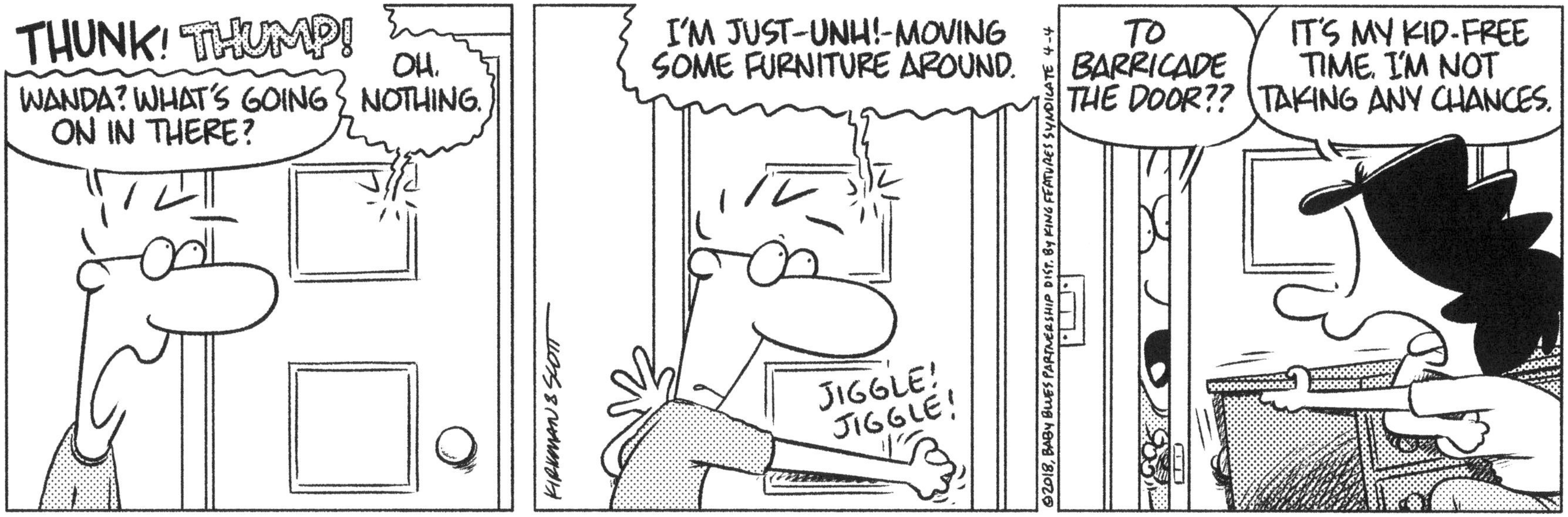
THUNK! THUMP!
WANDA? WHAT'S GOING ON IN THERE?
OH. NOTHING.
I'M JUST-UNH!-MOVING SOME FURNITURE AROUND.
JIGGLE! JIGGLE!
TO BARRICADE THE DOOR??
IT'S MY KID-FREE TIME. I'M NOT TAKING ANY CHANCES.
KIRKMAN & SCOTT
©2018, BABY BLUES PARTNERSHIP DIST. BY KING FEATURES SYNDICATE 4-4

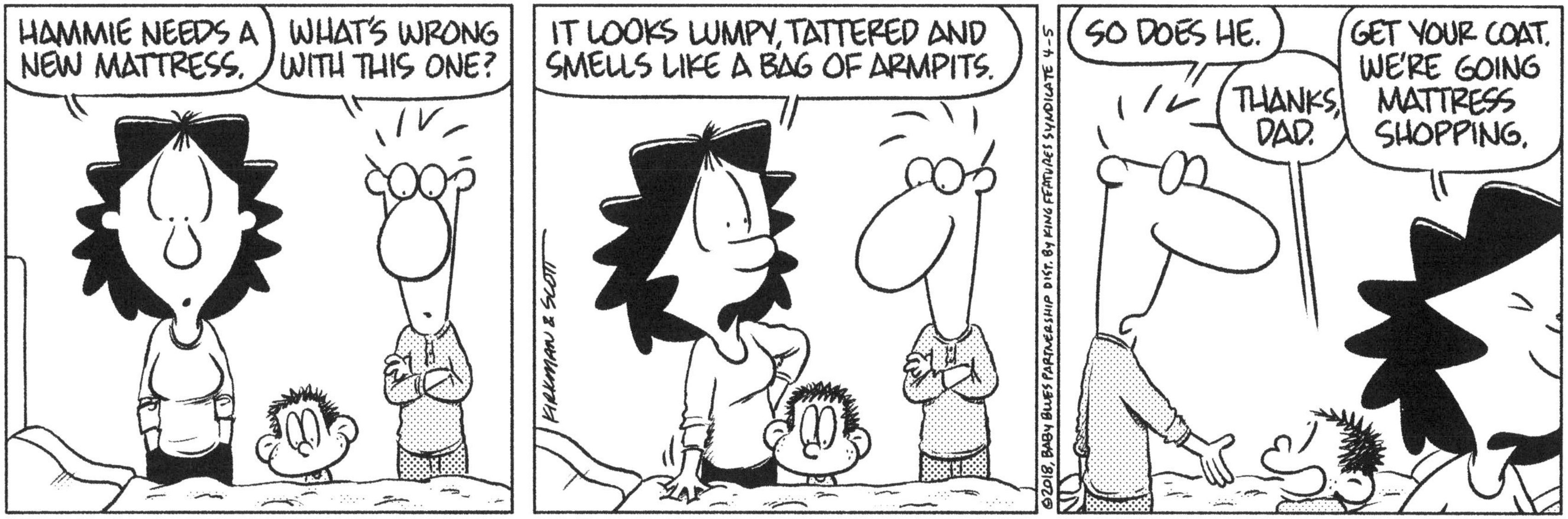
HAMMIE NEEDS A NEW MATTRESS.
WHAT'S WRONG WITH THIS ONE?
IT LOOKS LUMPY, TATTERED AND SMELLS LIKE A BAG OF ARMPITS.
SO DOES HE.
THANKS, DAD.
GET YOUR COAT. WE'RE GOING MATTRESS SHOPPING.
KIRKMAN & SCOTT
©2018, BABY BLUES PARTNERSHIP DIST. BY KING FEATURES SYNDICATE 4-5

Rick: Ha! Ha! "Bag of armpits"!

Jerry: If boys don't smell like a bag of armpits by the end of the day, they're not trying hard enough.

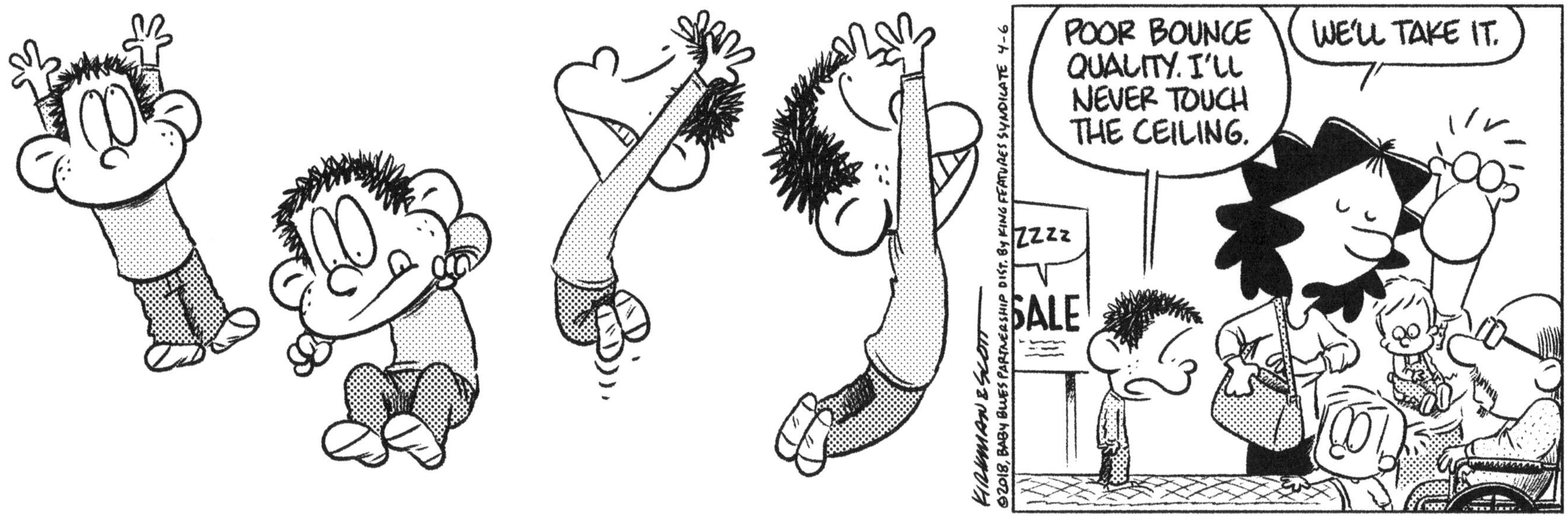
KIRKMAN & SCOTT
©2018, BABY BLUES PARTNERSHIP DIST. BY KING FEATURES SYNDICATE 4-6
POOR BOUNCE QUALITY. I'LL NEVER TOUCH THE CEILING.
WE'LL TAKE IT.
ZZZZ
SALE

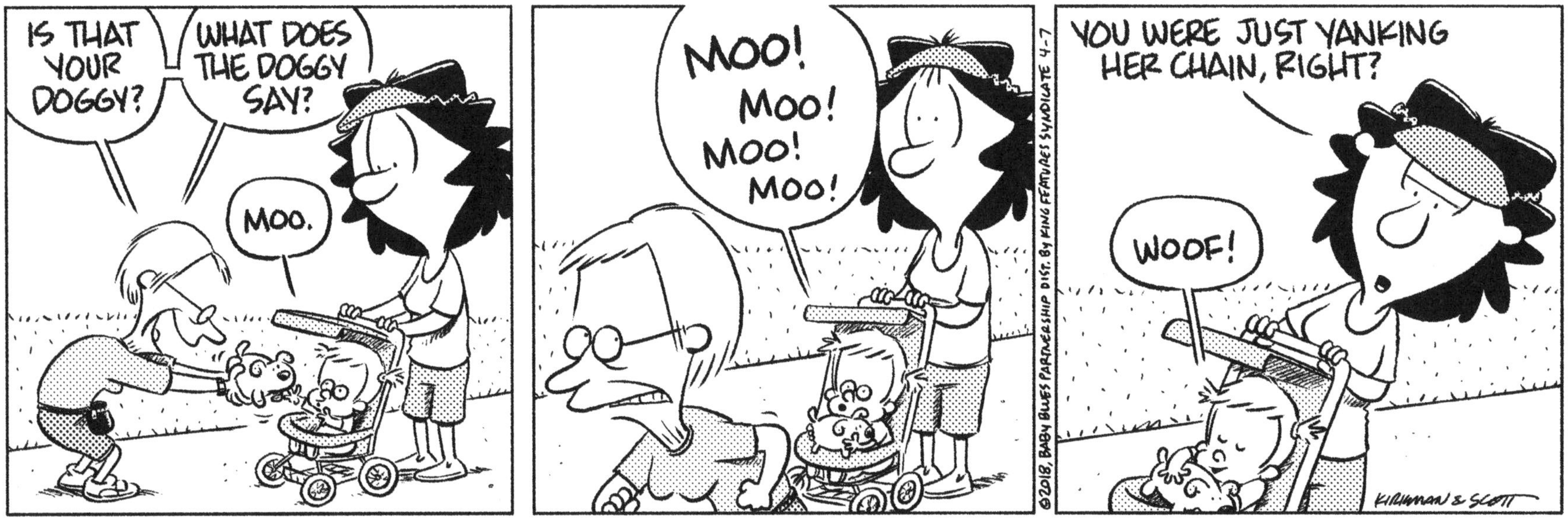
IS THAT YOUR DOGGY?
WHAT DOES THE DOGGY SAY?
MOO.
MOO! MOO! MOO! MOO!
©2018, BABY BLUES PARTNERSHIP DIST. BY KING FEATURES SYNDICATE 4-7
YOU WERE JUST YANKING HER CHAIN, RIGHT?
WOOF!
KIRKMAN & SCOTT

Baby Blues
Rick Kirkman & Jerry Scott
ZZZZZZ

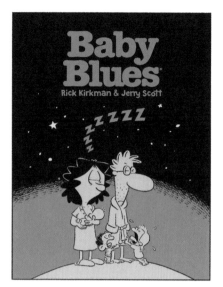

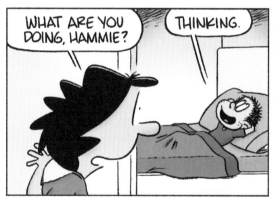

WHAT ARE YOU DOING, HAMMIE?
THINKING.
THINKING ABOUT WHAT?
TODAY.
WHAT ABOUT TODAY?
THAT IN A FEW YEARS, WE'LL ALL LOOK BACK ON IT AND LAUGH.
LOOK BACK AT WHAT? LAUGH AT **WHAT??**
REALISTICALLY, FIVE YEARS.
©2018, BABY BLUES PARTNERSHIP DIST. BY KING FEATURES SYNDICATE
TEN AT THE MOST, DEPENDING ON THE DAMAGE.
KIRKMAN & SCOTT 4-8
DARRYL?!!

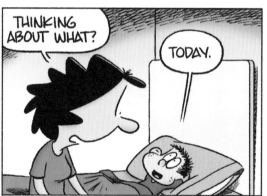

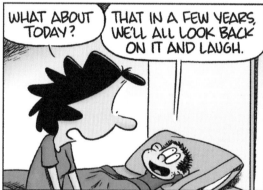

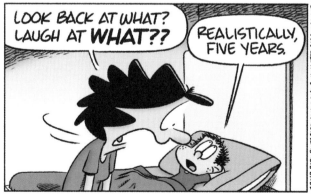

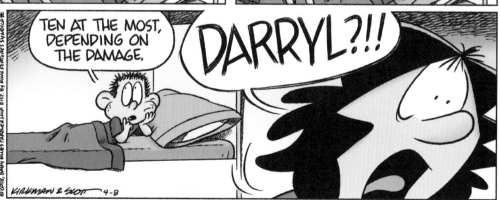

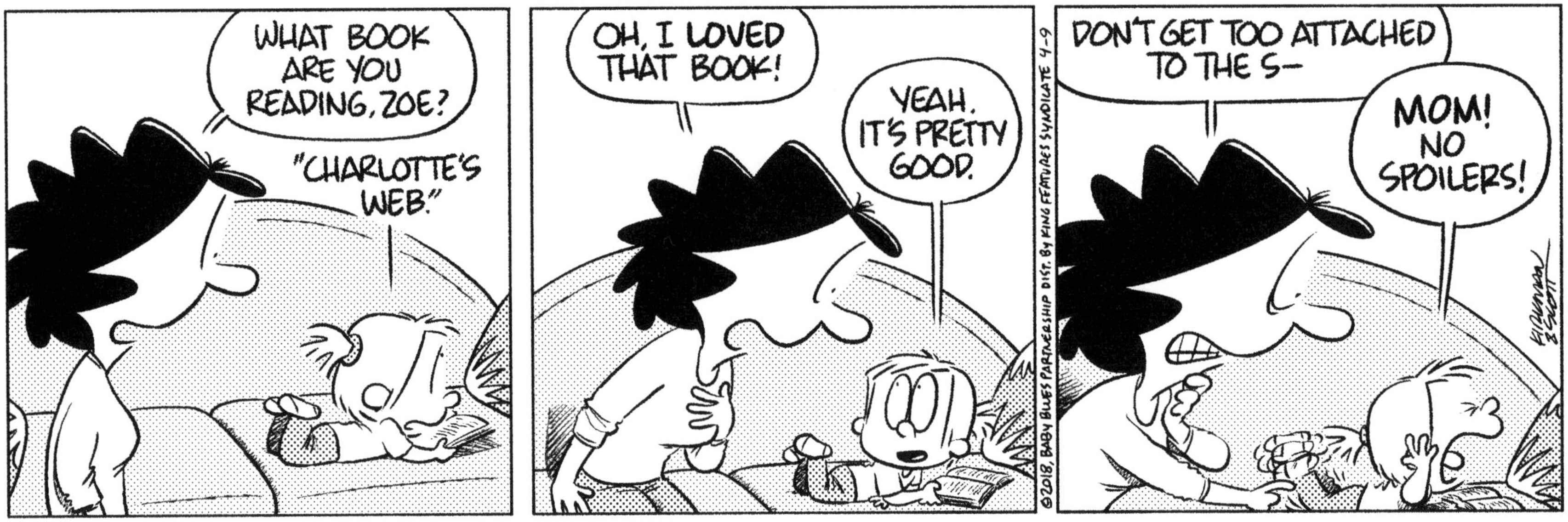
WHAT BOOK ARE YOU READING, ZOE?
"CHARLOTTE'S WEB."
OH, I LOVED THAT BOOK!
YEAH. IT'S PRETTY GOOD.
©2018, BABY BLUES PARTNERSHIP DIST. BY KING FEATURES SYNDICATE 4-9
DON'T GET TOO ATTACHED TO THE S—
MOM! NO SPOILERS!
KIRKMAN & SCOTT

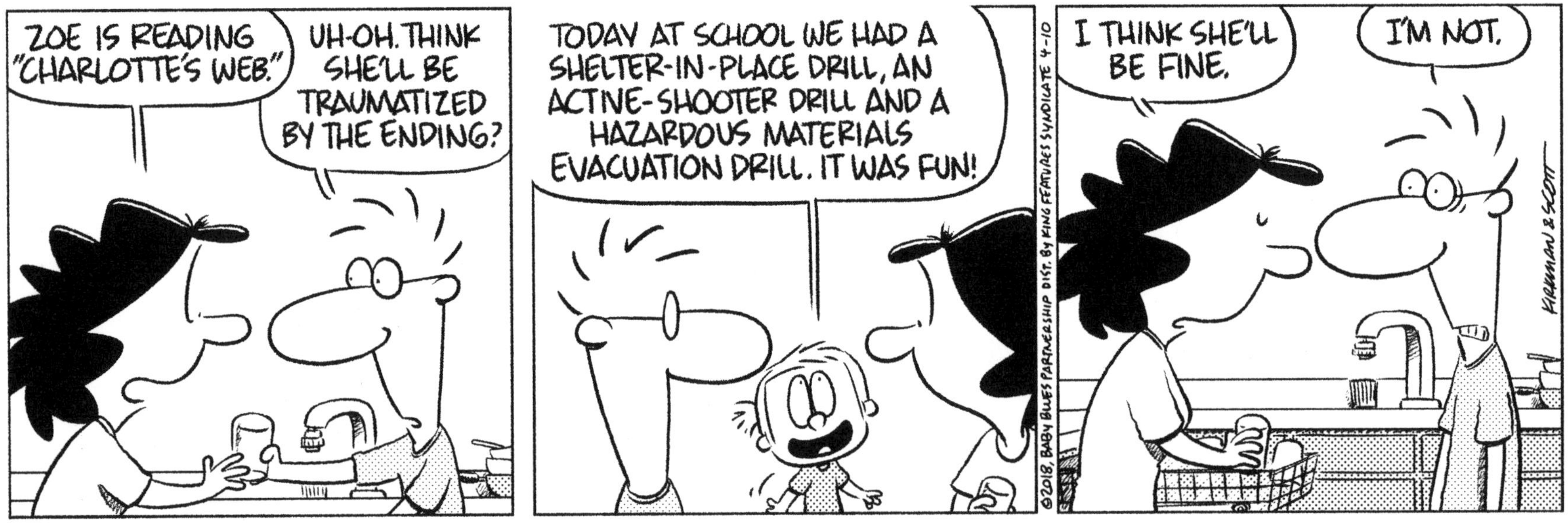
ZOE IS READING "CHARLOTTE'S WEB."
UH-OH. THINK SHE'LL BE TRAUMATIZED BY THE ENDING?
TODAY AT SCHOOL WE HAD A SHELTER-IN-PLACE DRILL, AN ACTIVE-SHOOTER DRILL AND A HAZARDOUS MATERIALS EVACUATION DRILL. IT WAS FUN!
©2018, BABY BLUES PARTNERSHIP DIST. BY KING FEATURES SYNDICATE 4-10
I THINK SHE'LL BE FINE.
I'M NOT.
KIRKMAN & SCOTT

Rick: *I'm* still shaken by Zoe's line.

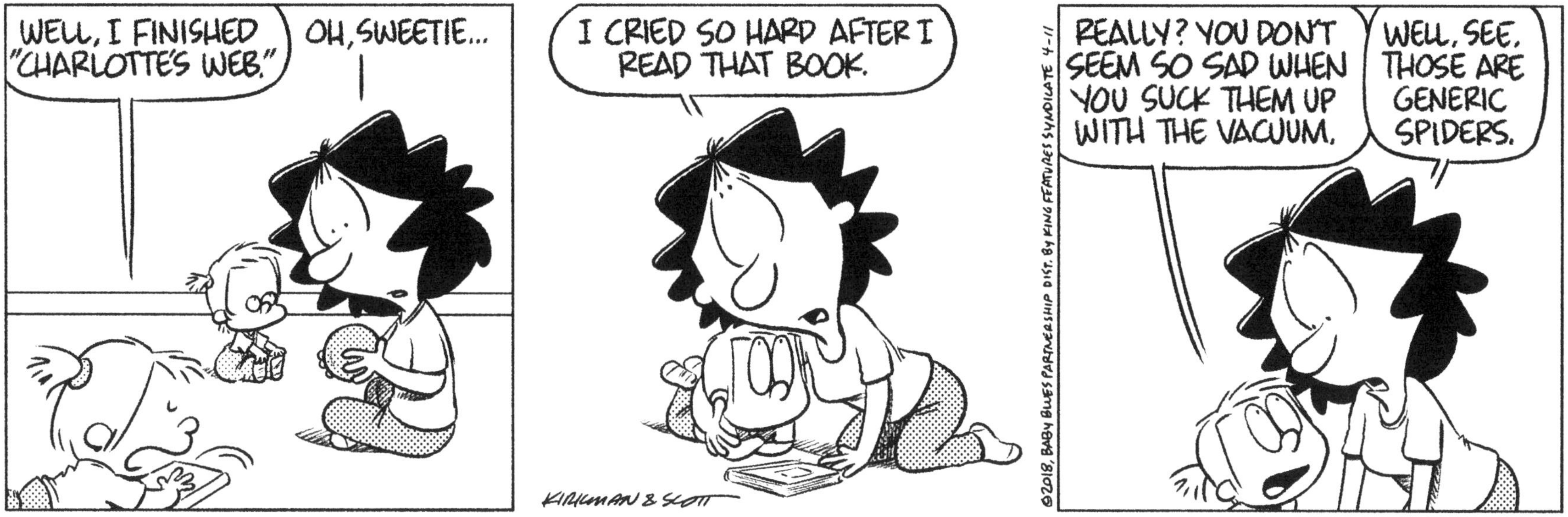
WELL, I FINISHED "CHARLOTTE'S WEB."
OH, SWEETIE...
I CRIED SO HARD AFTER I READ THAT BOOK.
KIRKMAN & SCOTT
©2018, BABY BLUES PARTNERSHIP DIST. BY KING FEATURES SYNDICATE 4-11
REALLY? YOU DON'T SEEM SO SAD WHEN YOU SUCK THEM UP WITH THE VACUUM.
WELL, SEE, THOSE ARE GENERIC SPIDERS.

Rick: Yeah, Mom, what's with that?

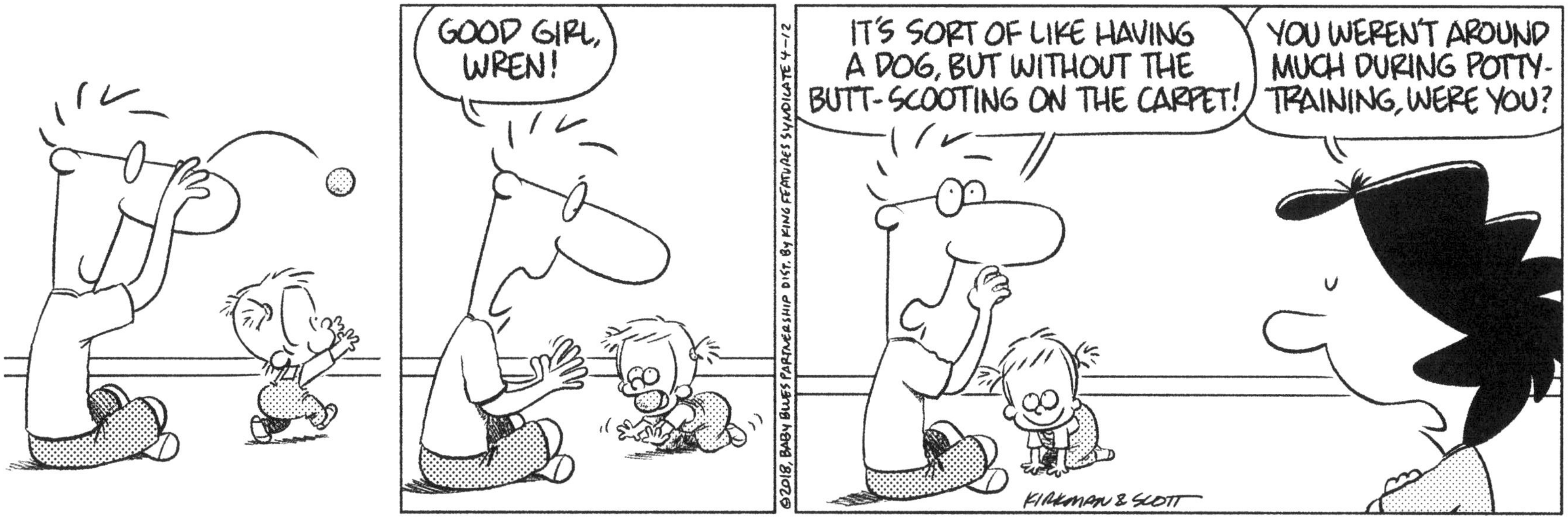
GOOD GIRL, WREN!
©2018, BABY BLUES PARTNERSHIP DIST. BY KING FEATURES SYNDICATE 4-12
IT'S SORT OF LIKE HAVING A DOG, BUT WITHOUT THE BUTT-SCOOTING ON THE CARPET!
YOU WEREN'T AROUND MUCH DURING POTTY-TRAINING, WERE YOU?
KIRKMAN & SCOTT

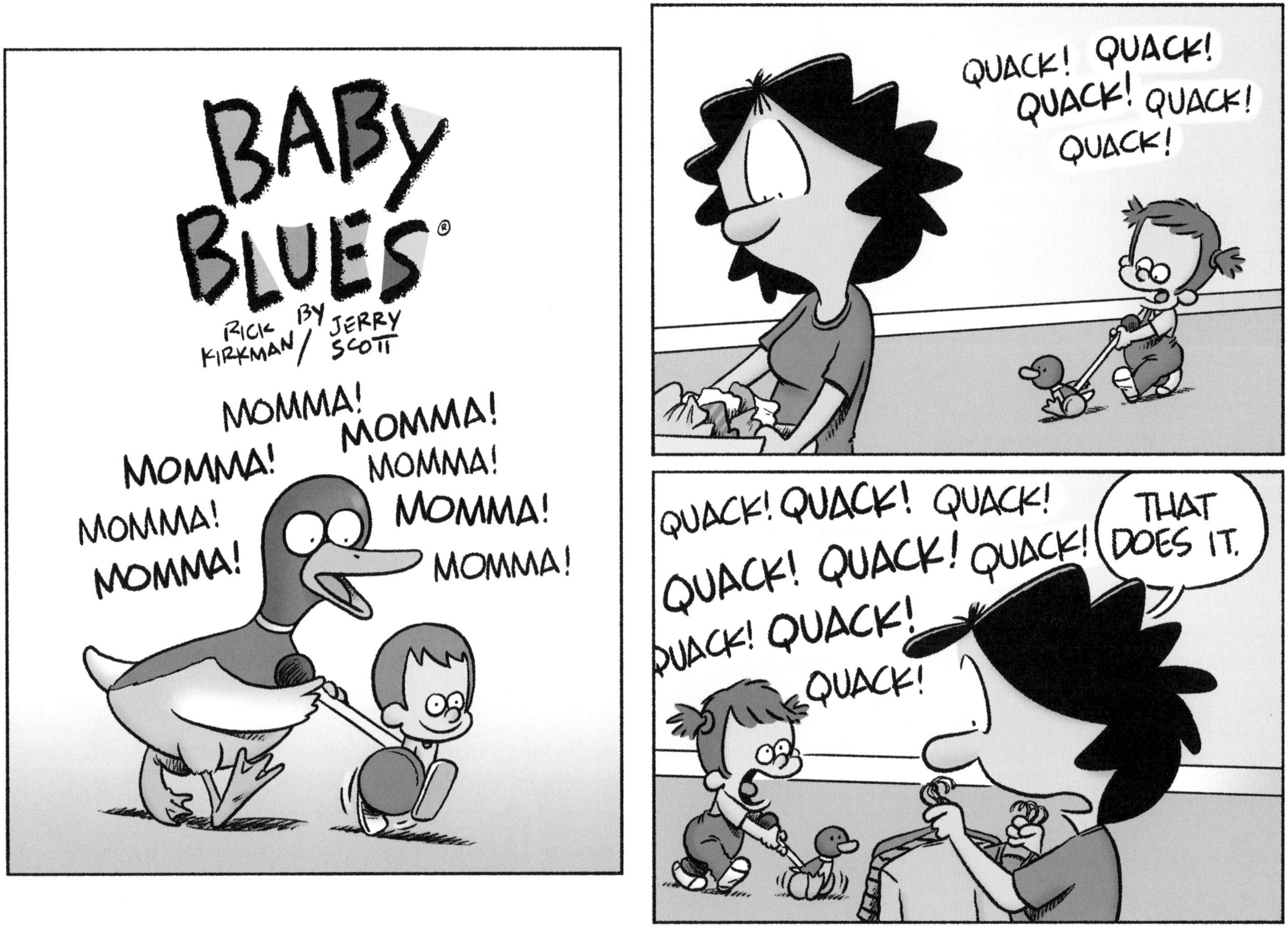
BABY BLUES®
BY RICK KIRKMAN / JERRY SCOTT
MOMMA! MOMMA! MOMMA! MOMMA! MOMMA! MOMMA! MOMMA! MOMMA!
QUACK! QUACK! QUACK! QUACK! QUACK!
QUACK! QUACK! QUACK! QUACK! QUACK! QUACK! QUACK! QUACK!
THAT DOES IT.

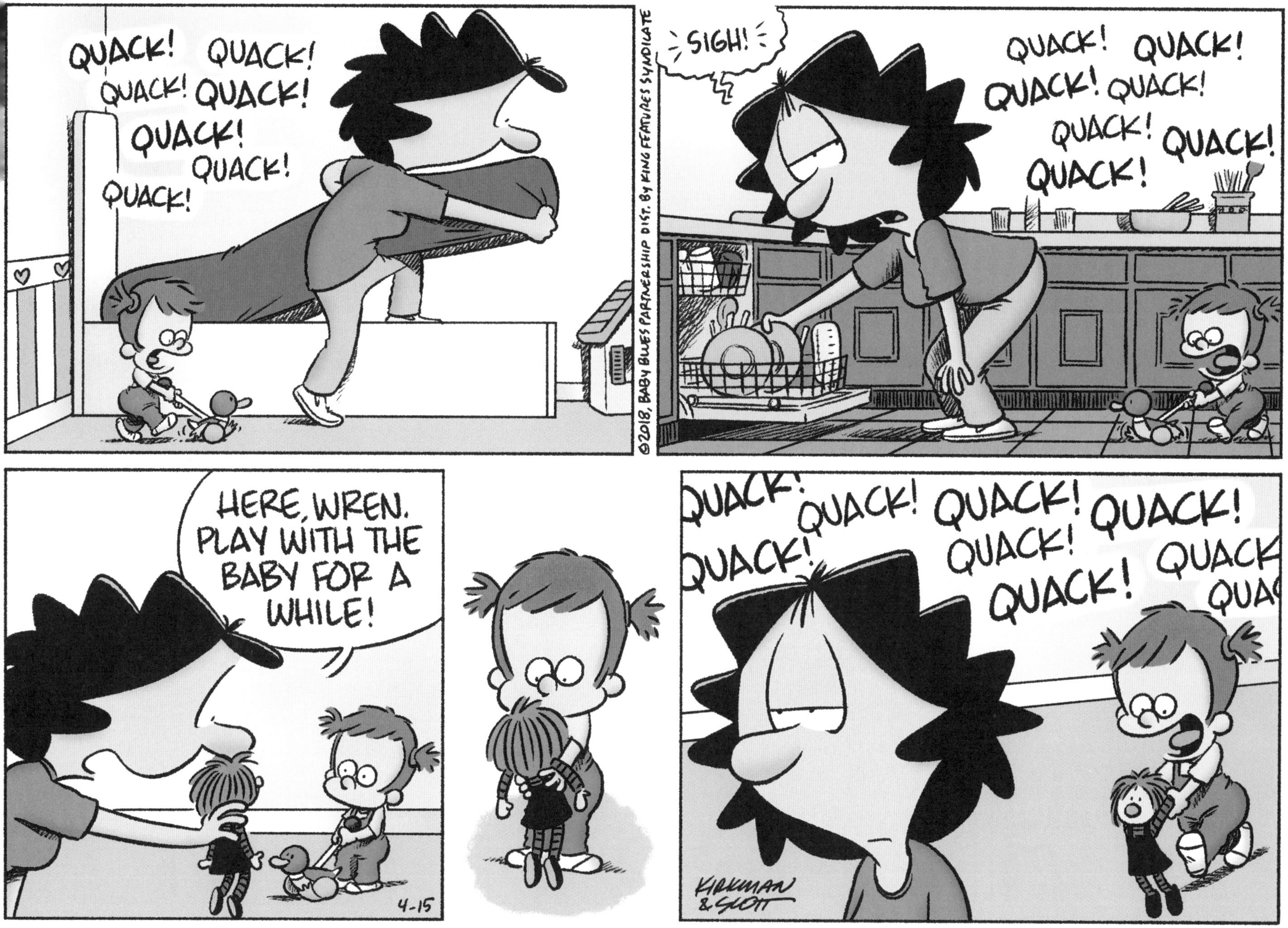
QUACK! QUACK! QUACK! QUACK! QUACK! QUACK! QUACK!
©2018, BABY BLUES PARTNERSHIP DIST. BY KING FEATURES SYNDICATE
SIGH!
QUACK! QUACK! QUACK! QUACK! QUACK! QUACK! QUACK!
HERE, WREN. PLAY WITH THE BABY FOR A WHILE!
4-15
QUACK! QUACK! QUACK! QUACK! QUACK! QUACK! QUACK
KIRKMAN & SCOTT

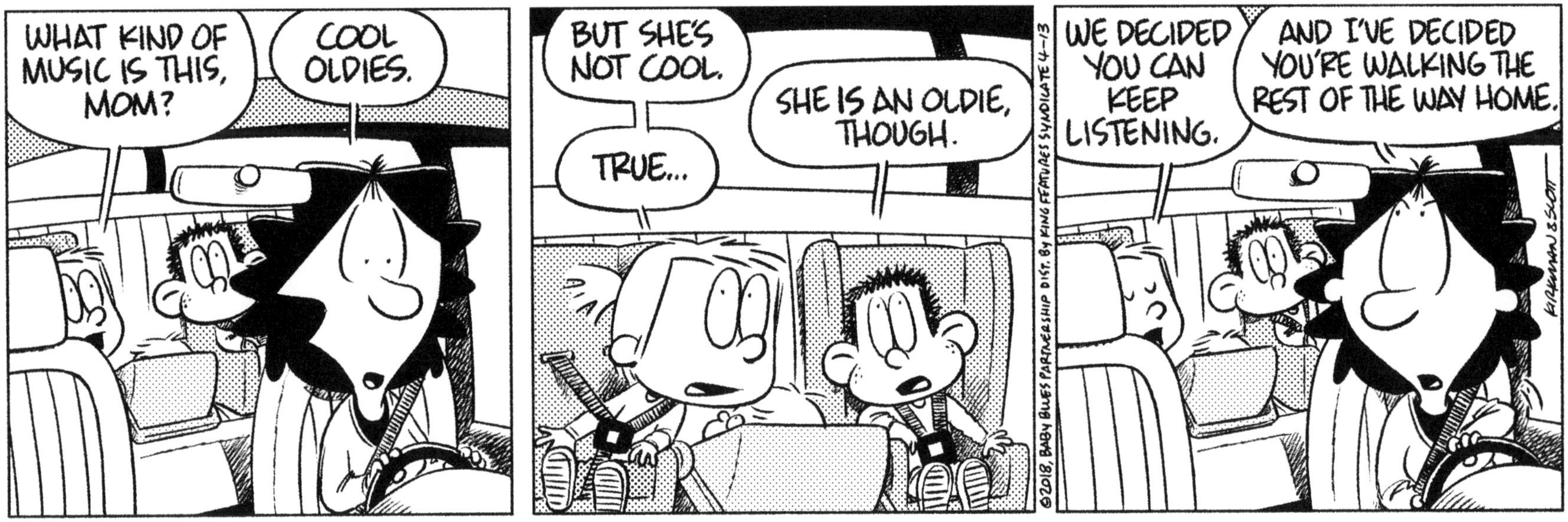
WHAT KIND OF MUSIC IS THIS, MOM?
COOL OLDIES.
BUT SHE'S NOT COOL.
TRUE...
SHE IS AN OLDIE, THOUGH.
©2018, BABY BLUES PARTNERSHIP DIST. BY KING FEATURES SYNDICATE 4-13
WE DECIDED YOU CAN KEEP LISTENING.
AND I'VE DECIDED YOU'RE WALKING THE REST OF THE WAY HOME.
KIRKMAN & SCOTT

Rick: Ouch.

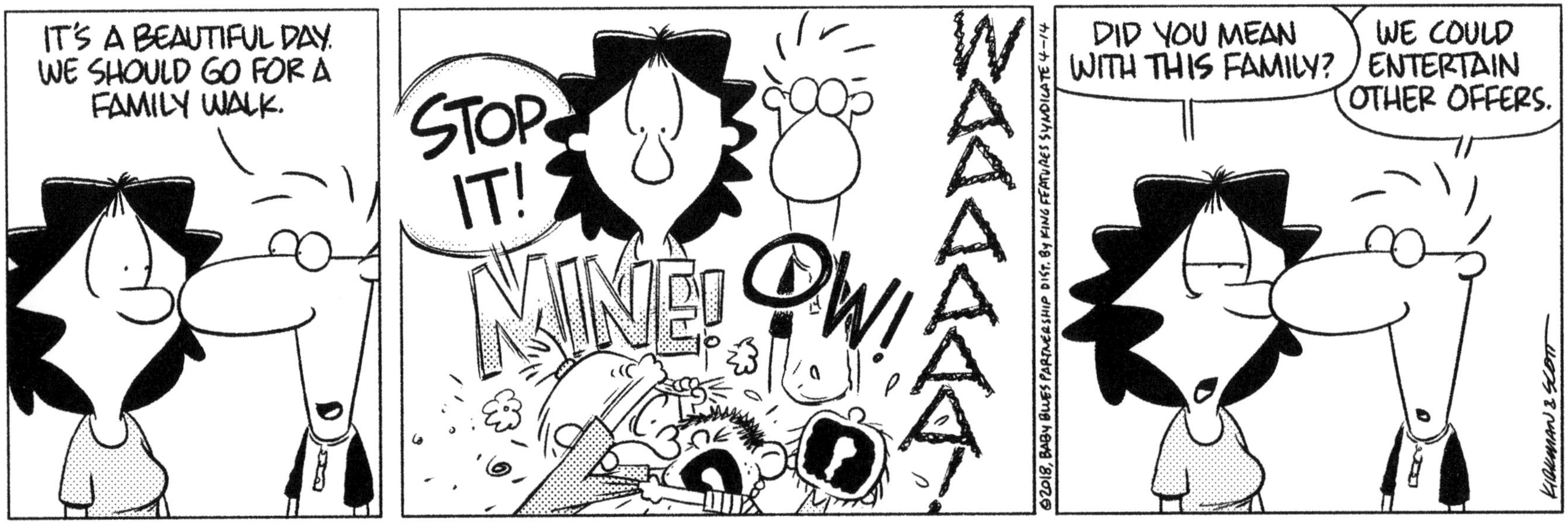
IT'S A BEAUTIFUL DAY. WE SHOULD GO FOR A FAMILY WALK.
STOP IT!
MINE!
OW!
WAAAAAA!
©2018, BABY BLUES PARTNERSHIP DIST. BY KING FEATURES SYNDICATE 4-14
DID YOU MEAN WITH THIS FAMILY?
WE COULD ENTERTAIN OTHER OFFERS.
KIRKMAN & SCOTT

Jerry: The families in toothpaste and fabric softener commercials seem especially happy to me. I'd go for a walk with them.

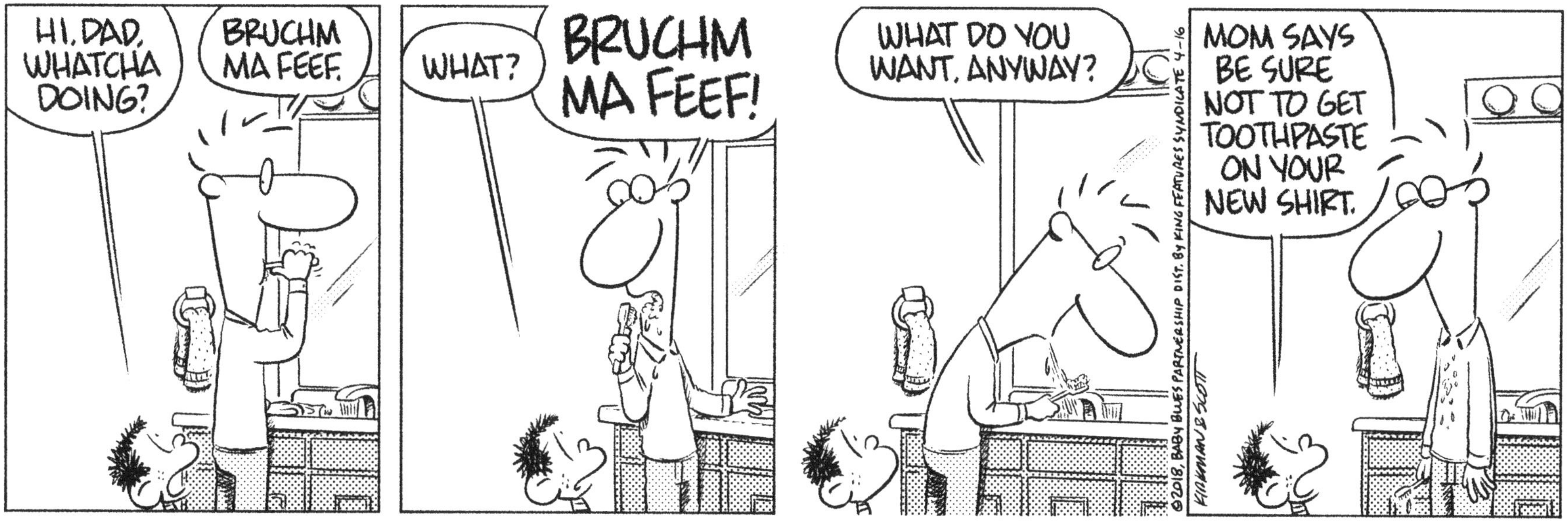
HI, DAD, WHATCHA DOING?
BRUCHM MA FEEF.
WHAT?
BRUCHM MA FEEF!
WHAT DO YOU WANT, ANYWAY?
MOM SAYS BE SURE NOT TO GET TOOTHPASTE ON YOUR NEW SHIRT.
©2018, BABY BLUES PARTNERSHIP DIST. BY KING FEATURES SYNDICATE 4-16
KIRKMAN & SCOTT

Rick: Perfect toothbrushing-speak, Jerry.

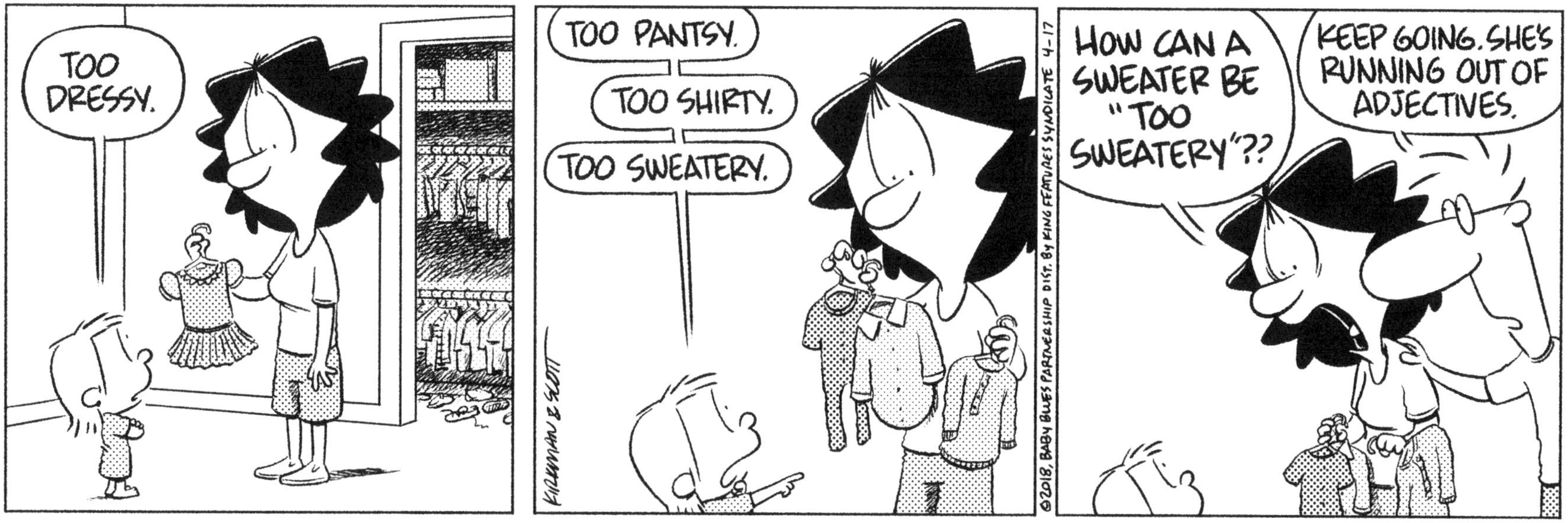
TOO DRESSY.
TOO PANTSY.
TOO SHIRTY.
TOO SWEATERY.
KIRKMAN & SCOTT
©2018, BABY BLUES PARTNERSHIP DIST. BY KING FEATURES SYNDICATE 4-17
HOW CAN A SWEATER BE "TOO SWEATERY"??
KEEP GOING. SHE'S RUNNING OUT OF ADJECTIVES.

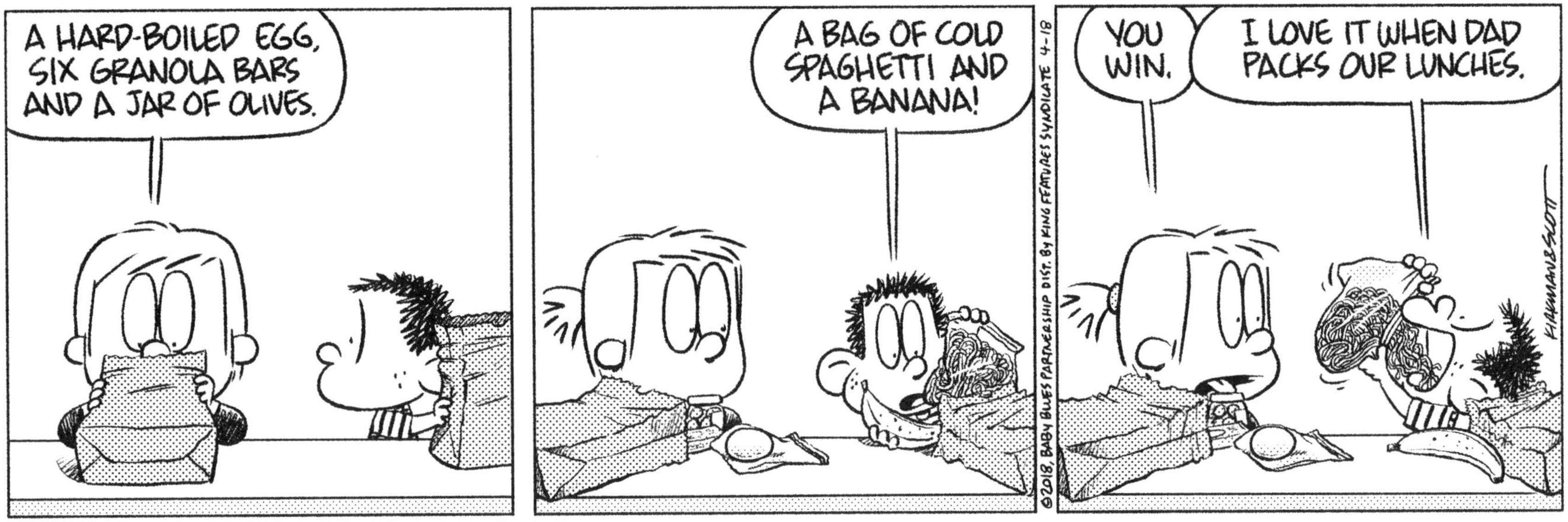
A HARD-BOILED EGG, SIX GRANOLA BARS AND A JAR OF OLIVES.
A BAG OF COLD SPAGHETTI AND A BANANA!
YOU WIN.
I LOVE IT WHEN DAD PACKS OUR LUNCHES.
©2018, BABY BLUES PARTNERSHIP DIST. BY KING FEATURES SYNDICATE 4-18
KIRKMAN & SCOTT

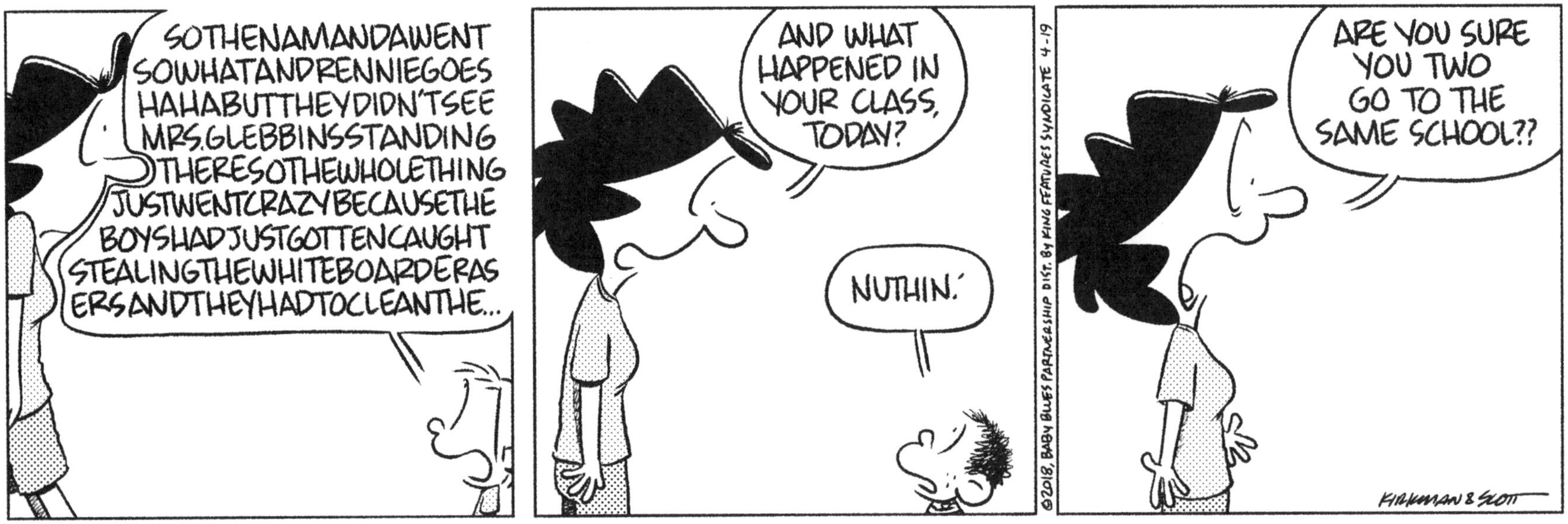
SOTHENAMANDAWENT SOWHATANDRENNIEGOES HAHABUTTHEYDIDN'TSEE MRS.GLEBBINSSTANDING THERESOTHEWHOLETHING JUSTWENTCRAZYBECAUSETHE BOYSHADJUSTGOTTENCAUGHT STEALINGTHEWHITEBOARDERAS ERSANDTHEYHADTOCLEANTHE...
AND WHAT HAPPENED IN YOUR CLASS, TODAY?
NUTHIN'.
ARE YOU SURE YOU TWO GO TO THE SAME SCHOOL??
©2018, BABY BLUES PARTNERSHIP DIST. BY KING FEATURES SYNDICATE 4-19
KIRKMAN & SCOTT

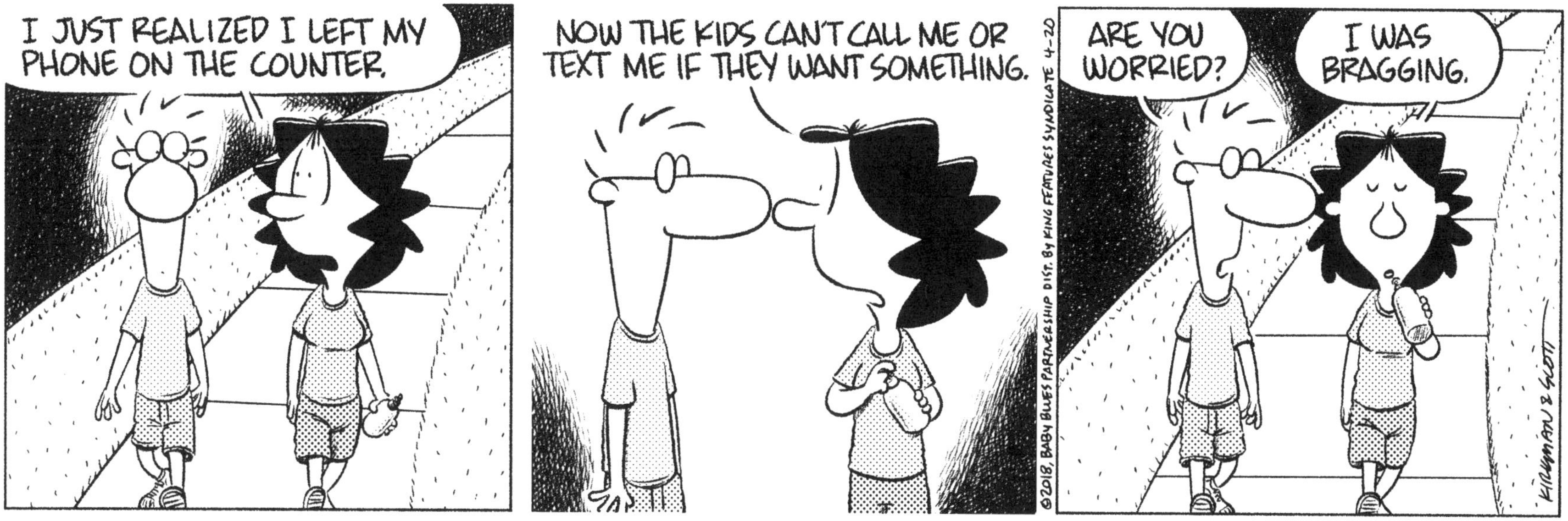
I JUST REALIZED I LEFT MY PHONE ON THE COUNTER.
NOW THE KIDS CAN'T CALL ME OR TEXT ME IF THEY WANT SOMETHING.
ARE YOU WORRIED?
I WAS BRAGGING.
KIRKMAN & SCOTT

Rick: Love this.

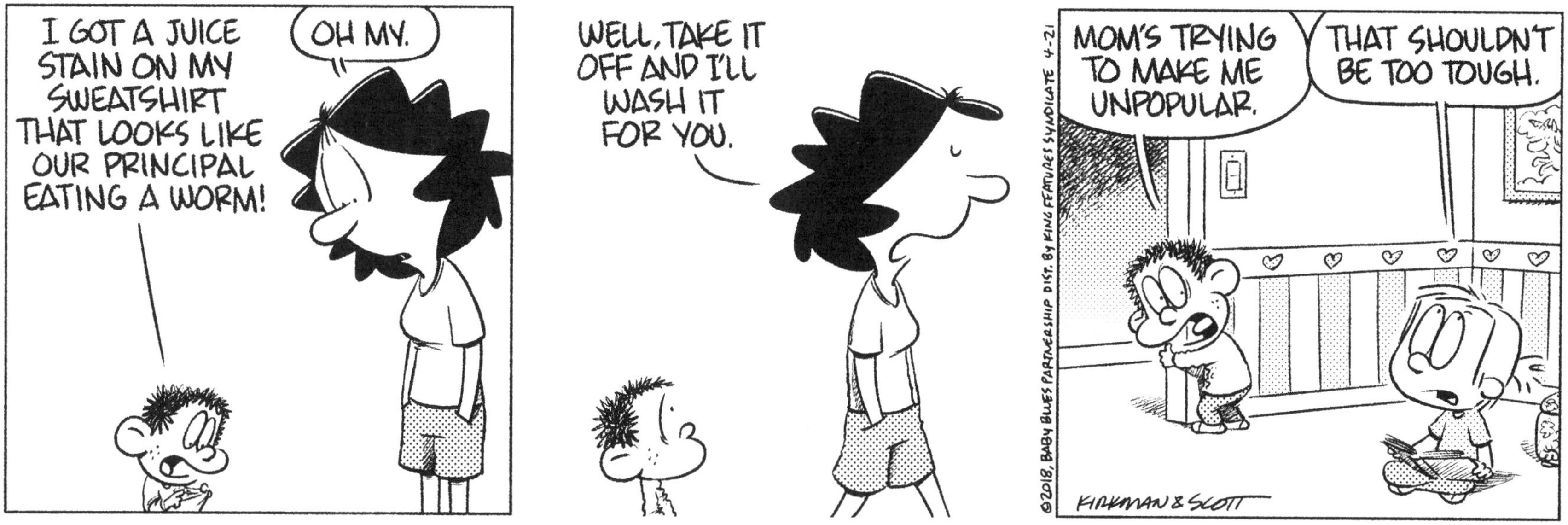
I GOT A JUICE STAIN ON MY SWEATSHIRT THAT LOOKS LIKE OUR PRINCIPAL EATING A WORM!
OH MY.
WELL, TAKE IT OFF AND I'LL WASH IT FOR YOU.
MOM'S TRYING TO MAKE ME UNPOPULAR.
THAT SHOULDN'T BE TOO TOUGH.
KIRKMAN & SCOTT

BOOO OOO!

BOOO OOO!
THIS WOULD LOOK CUTE TODAY.
PBBBBTHH!
NAPTIME, WREN.
HISSSSSSS!
LOOSERRRR!
©2018, BABY BLUES PARTNERSHIP DIST. BY KING FEATURES SYNDICATE
4-22
I AM NOT LETTING WREN SIT BY YOU AT ZOE'S SOCCER GAMES ANYMORE.
KIRKMAN & SCOTT

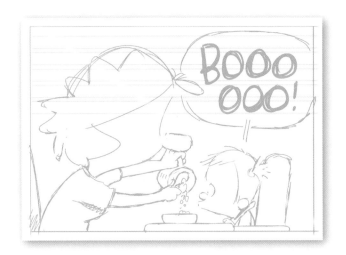

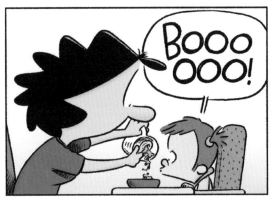

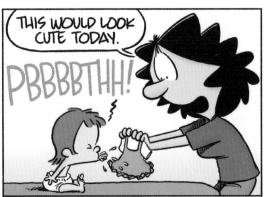

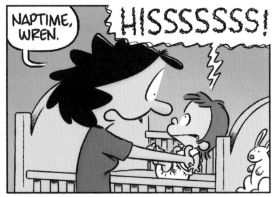

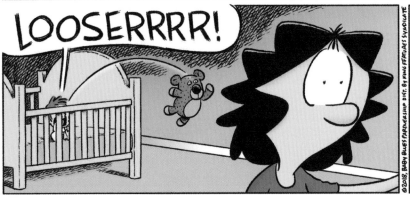

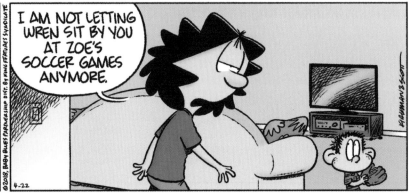

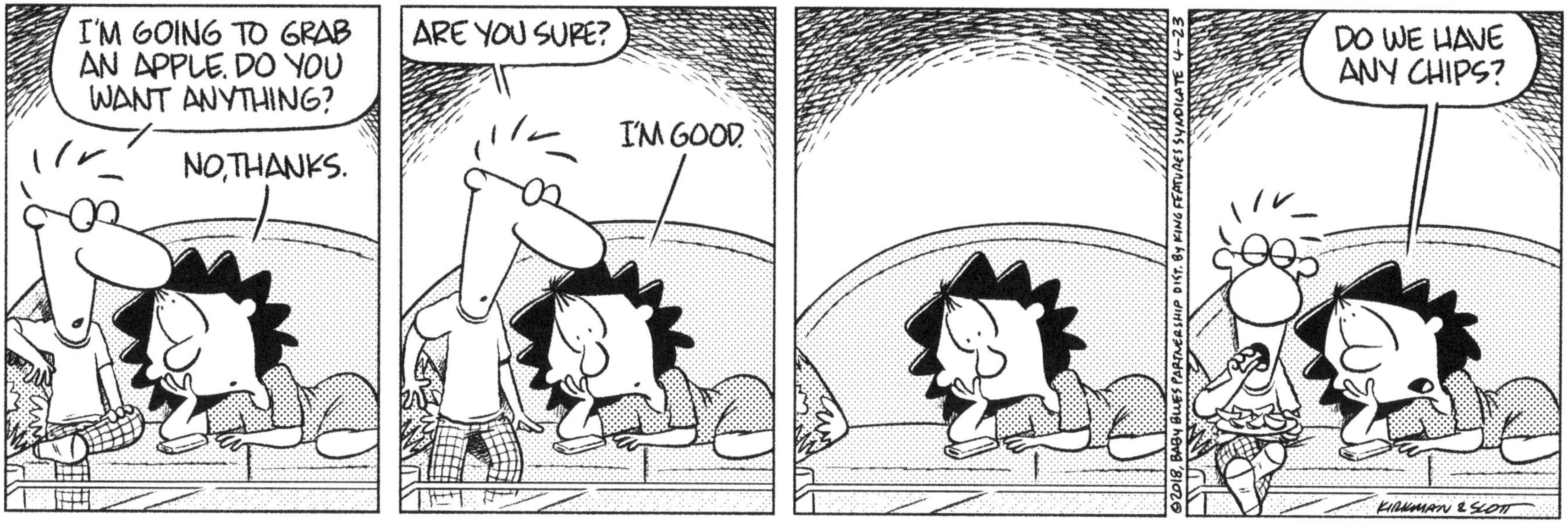
I'M GOING TO GRAB AN APPLE. DO YOU WANT ANYTHING?
NO, THANKS.
ARE YOU SURE?
I'M GOOD.
©2018, BABY BLUES PARTNERSHIP DIST. BY KING FEATURES SYNDICATE 4-23
DO WE HAVE ANY CHIPS?
KIRKMAN & SCOTT

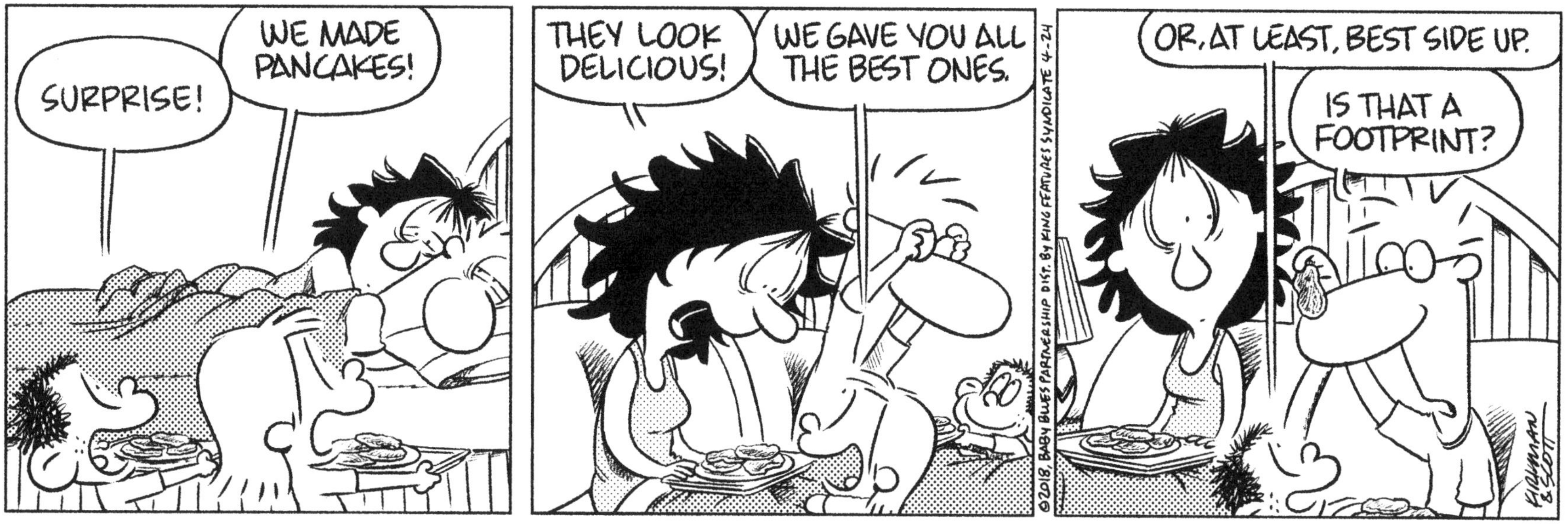
SURPRISE!
WE MADE PANCAKES!
THEY LOOK DELICIOUS!
WE GAVE YOU ALL THE BEST ONES.
©2018, BABY BLUES PARTNERSHIP DIST. BY KING FEATURES SYNDICATE 4-24
OR, AT LEAST, BEST SIDE UP.
IS THAT A FOOTPRINT?
KIRKMAN & SCOTT

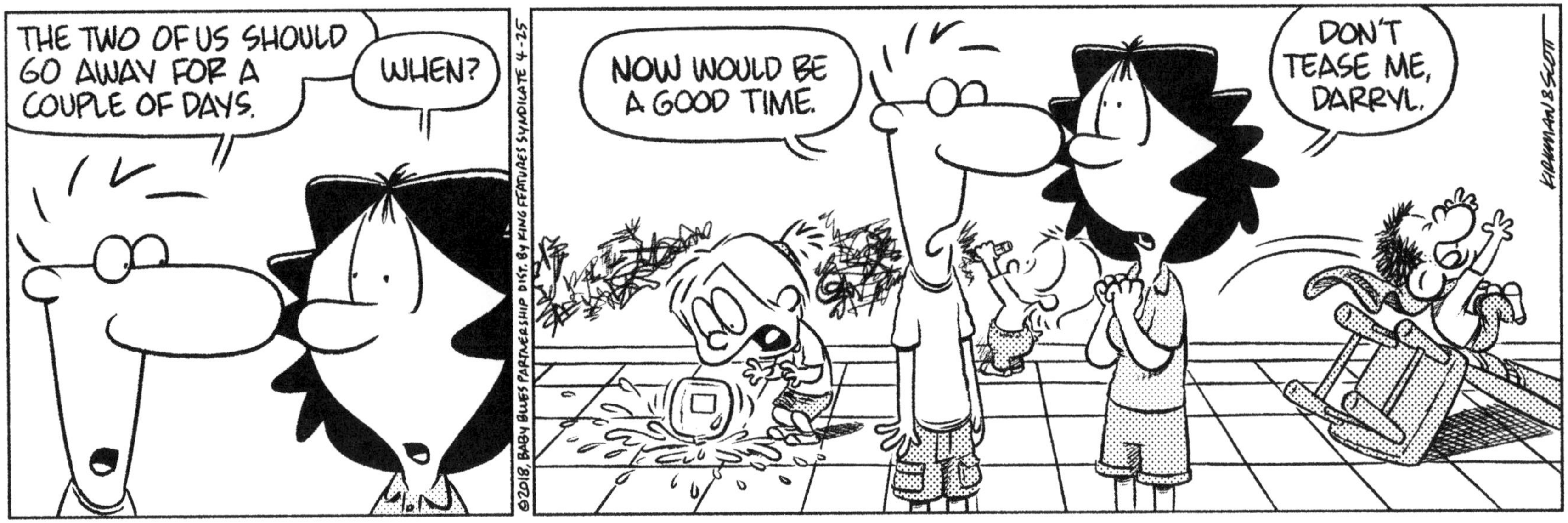
THE TWO OF US SHOULD GO AWAY FOR A COUPLE OF DAYS.
WHEN?
NOW WOULD BE A GOOD TIME.
DON'T TEASE ME, DARRYL.
©2018, BABY BLUES PARTNERSHIP DIST. BY KING FEATURES SYNDICATE 4-25
KIRKMAN & SCOTT

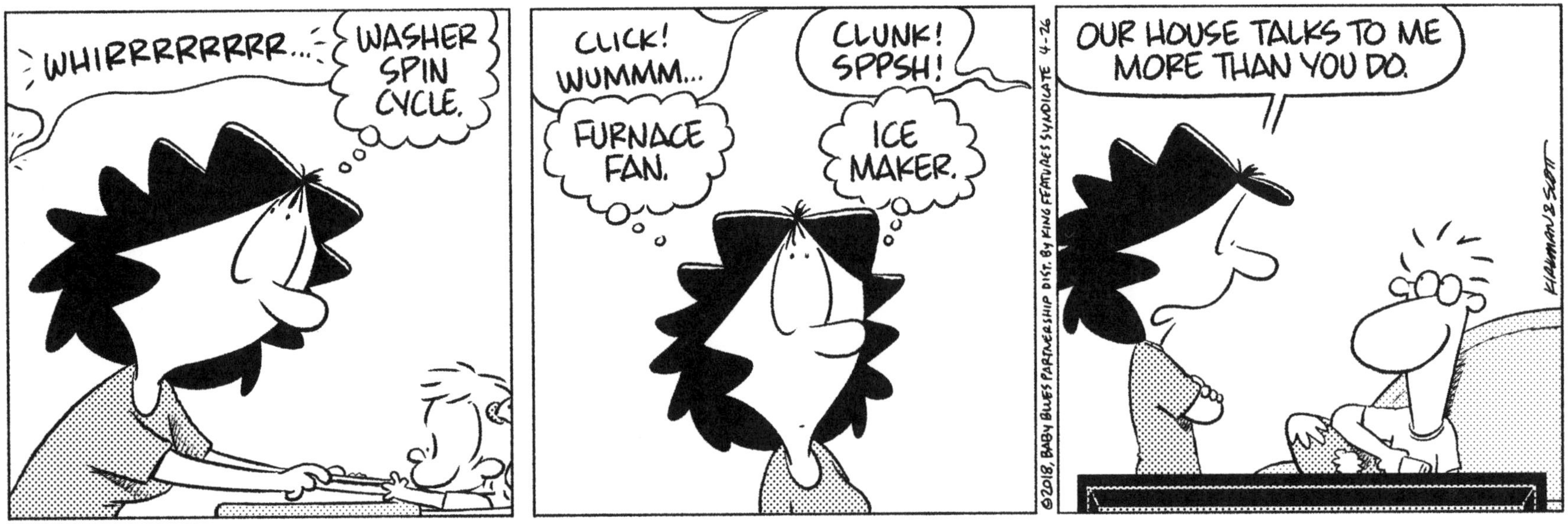
WHIRRRRRRRR...
WASHER SPIN CYCLE.
CLICK! WUMMM...
FURNACE FAN.
CLUNK! SPPSH!
ICE MAKER.
OUR HOUSE TALKS TO ME MORE THAN YOU DO.
©2018, BABY BLUES PARTNERSHIP DIST. BY KING FEATURES SYNDICATE 4-26
KIRKMAN & SCOTT

Jerry: Guys, if you see this posted on your refrigerator door, it's time to up your game.

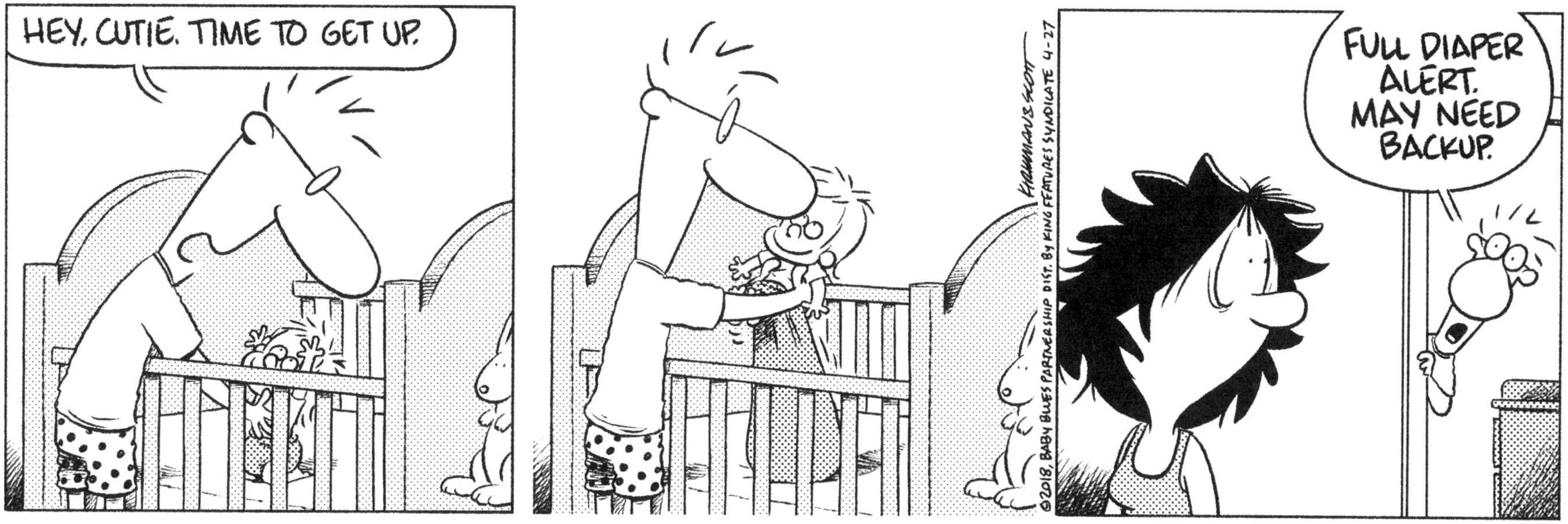
HEY, CUTIE. TIME TO GET UP.
KIRKMAN & SCOTT
©2018, BABY BLUES PARTNERSHIP DIST. BY KING FEATURES SYNDICATE 4-27
FULL DIAPER ALERT. MAY NEED BACKUP.

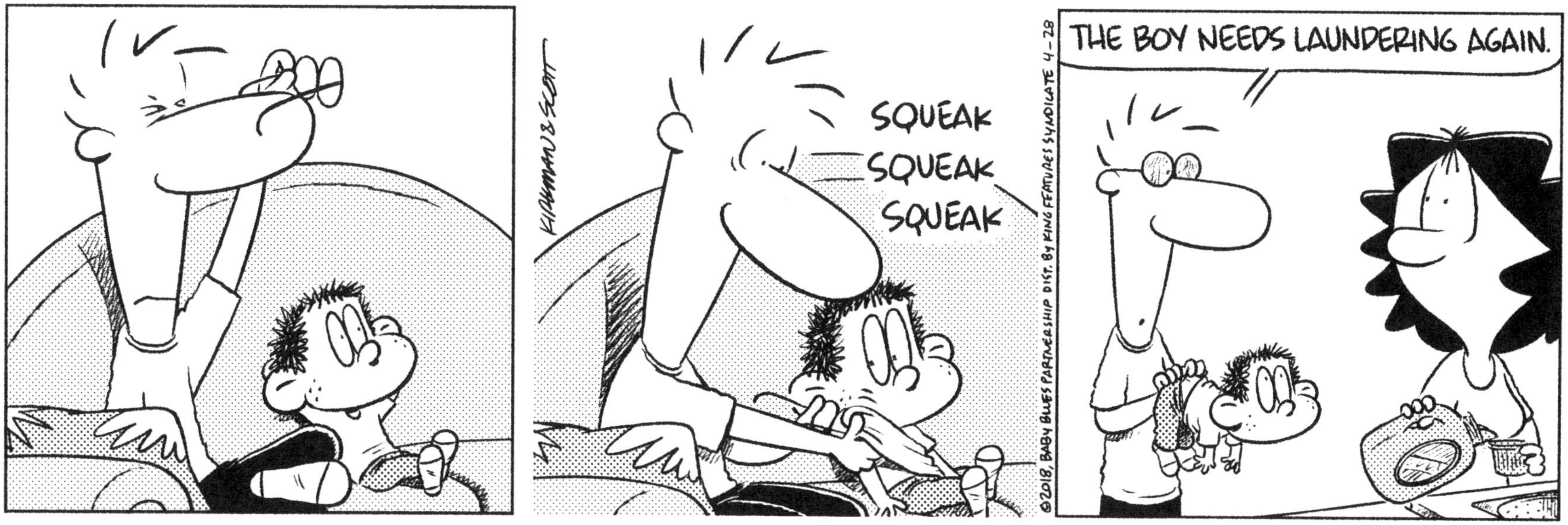
KIRKMAN & SCOTT
SQUEAK
SQUEAK
SQUEAK
©2018, BABY BLUES PARTNERSHIP DIST. BY KING FEATURES SYNDICATE 4-28
THE BOY NEEDS LAUNDERING AGAIN.

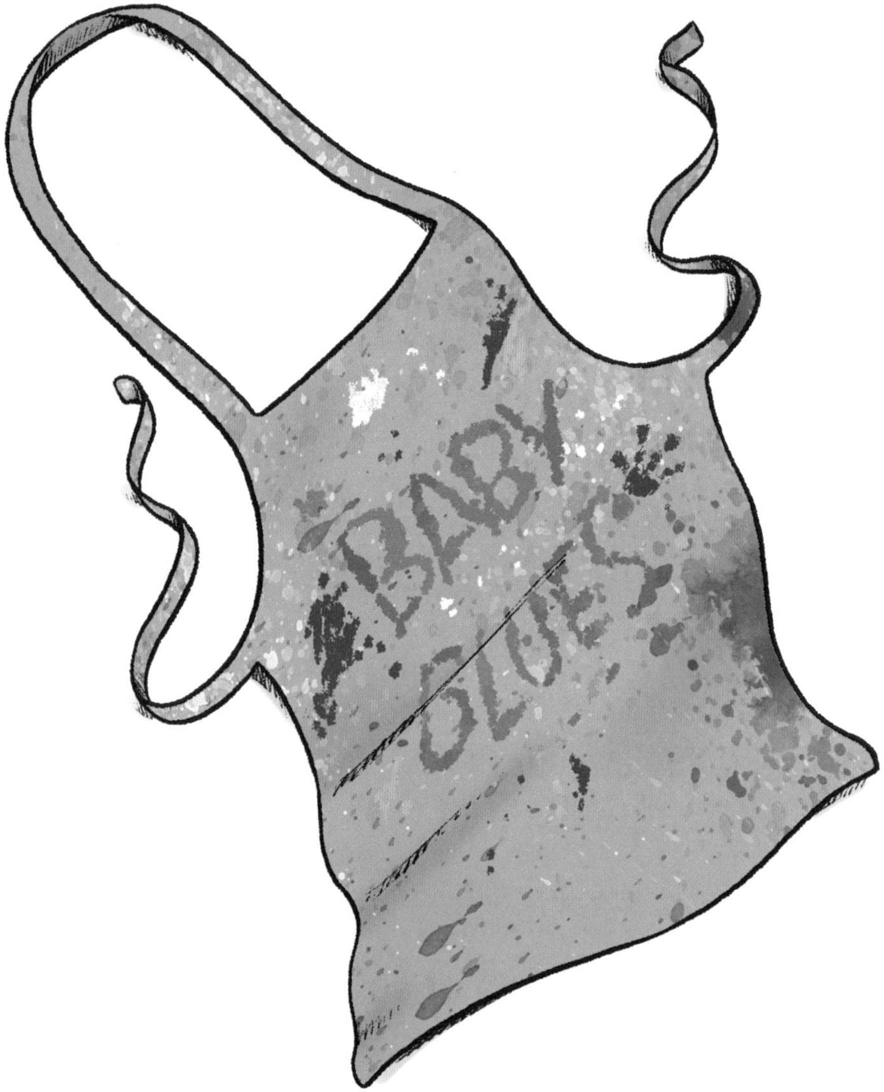
BABY BLUES!

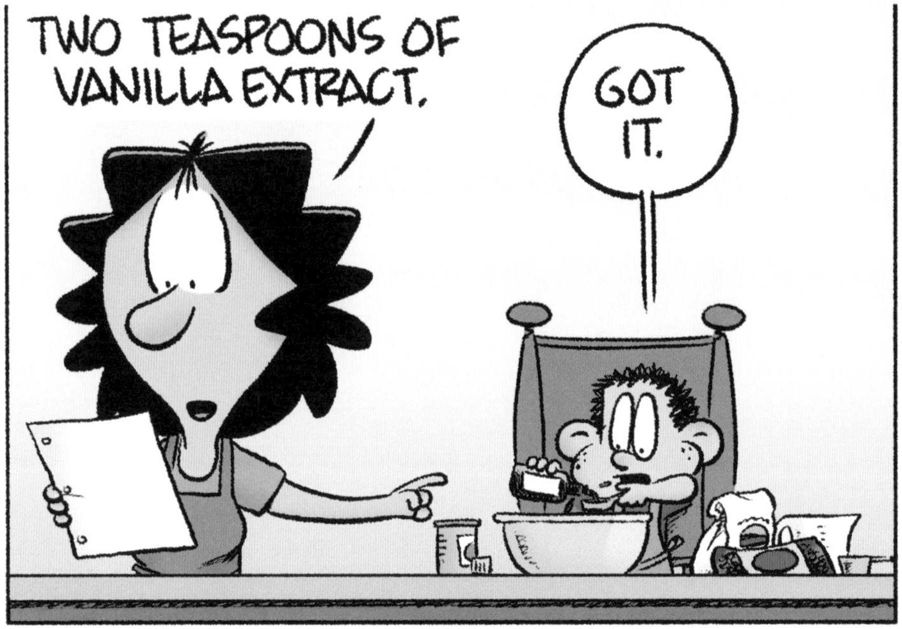
TWO TEASPOONS OF VANILLA EXTRACT.
GOT IT.

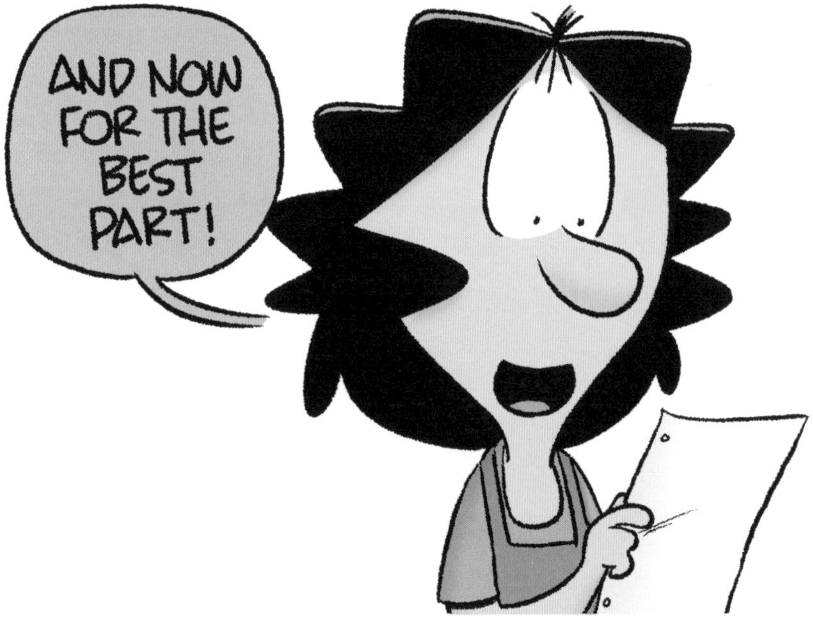
AND NOW FOR THE BEST PART!

Rick: Coloring the title panel was a fun challenge. It would've been a mess to create in real life (or IRL, as the kids say). Thank goodness for splatter brushes in Photoshop!

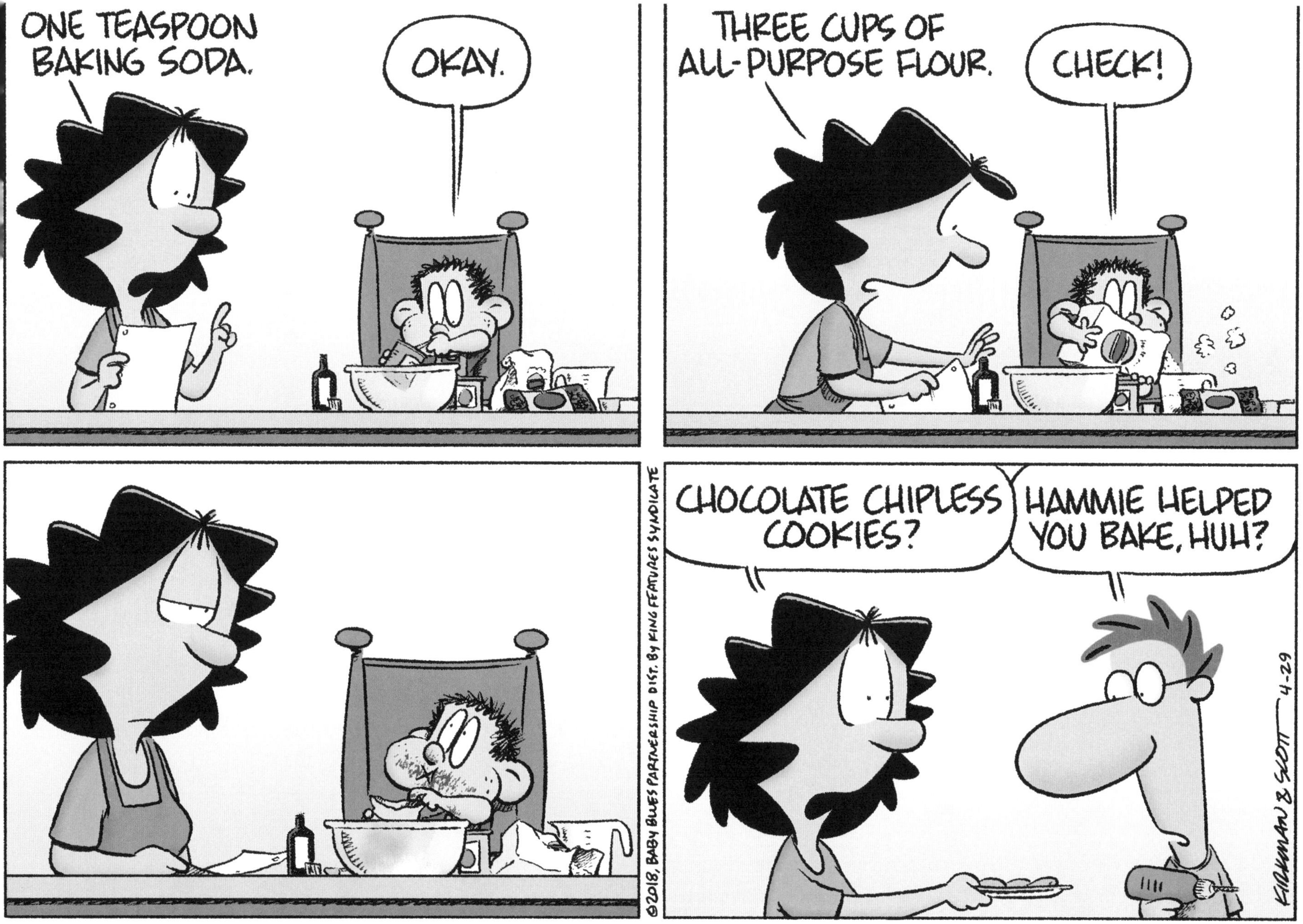
ONE TEASPOON BAKING SODA.
OKAY.
THREE CUPS OF ALL-PURPOSE FLOUR.
CHECK!
CHOCOLATE CHIPLESS COOKIES?
HAMMIE HELPED YOU BAKE, HUH?
©2018, BABY BLUES PARTNERSHIP DIST. BY KING FEATURES SYNDICATE
KIRKMAN & SCOTT 4-29

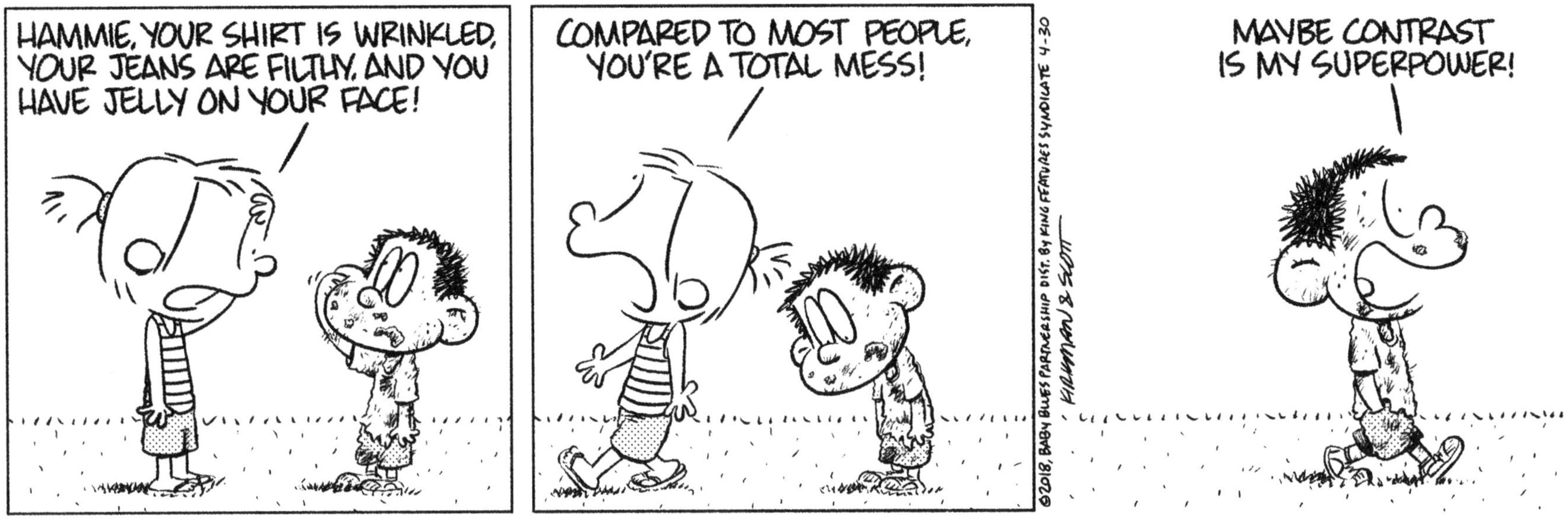
HAMMIE, YOUR SHIRT IS WRINKLED, YOUR JEANS ARE FILTHY, AND YOU HAVE JELLY ON YOUR FACE!
COMPARED TO MOST PEOPLE, YOU'RE A TOTAL MESS!
©2018, BABY BLUES PARTNERSHIP DIST. BY KING FEATURES SYNDICATE 4-30
KIRKMAN & SCOTT
MAYBE CONTRAST IS MY SUPERPOWER!

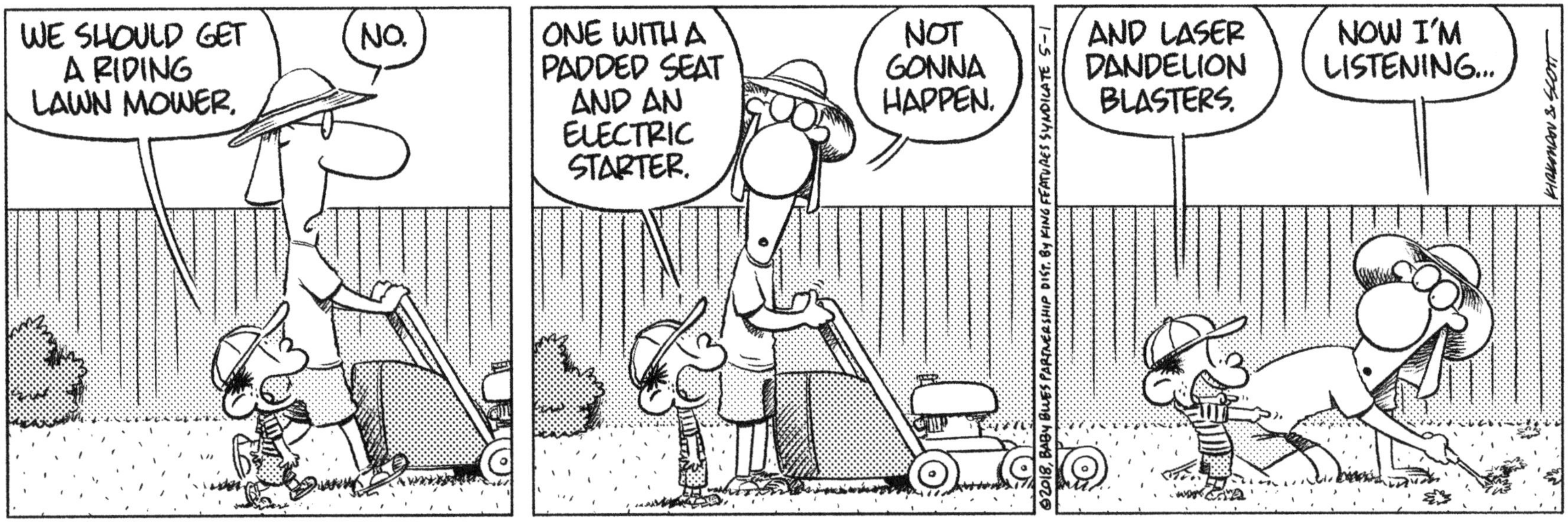
WE SHOULD GET A RIDING LAWN MOWER.
NO.
ONE WITH A PADDED SEAT AND AN ELECTRIC STARTER.
NOT GONNA HAPPEN.
©2018, BABY BLUES PARTNERSHIP DIST. BY KING FEATURES SYNDICATE 5-1
AND LASER DANDELION BLASTERS.
NOW I'M LISTENING...
KIRKMAN & SCOTT

Jerry: Patent pending.

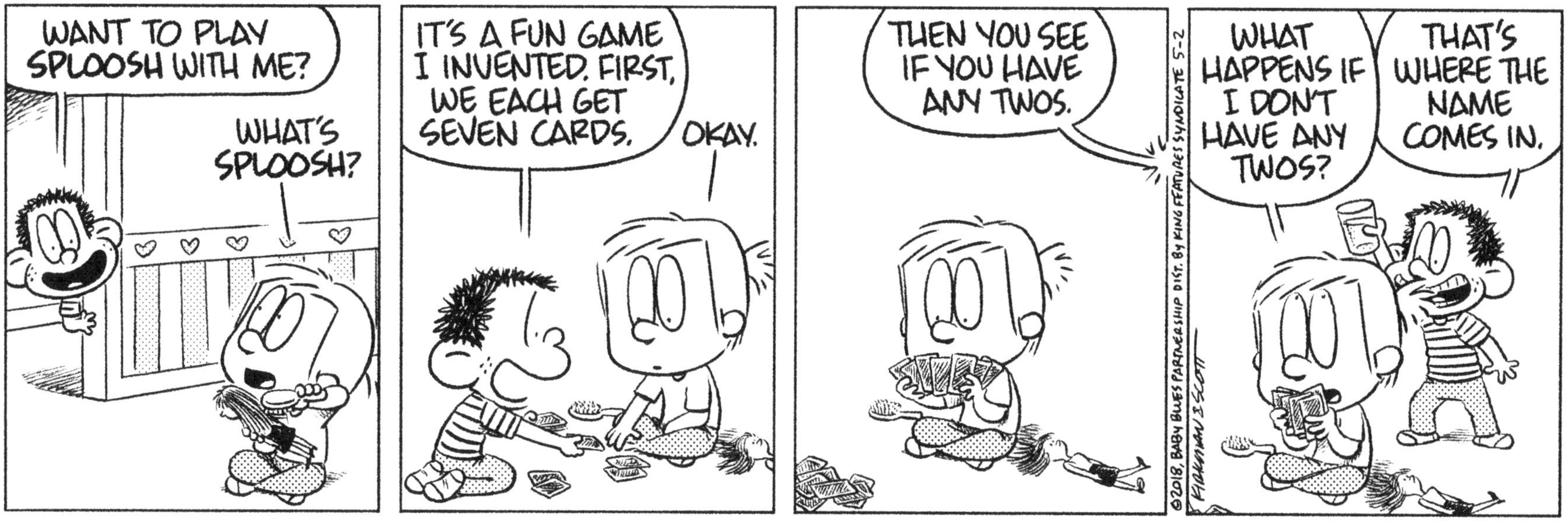
WANT TO PLAY SPLOOSH WITH ME?
WHAT'S SPLOOSH?
IT'S A FUN GAME I INVENTED. FIRST, WE EACH GET SEVEN CARDS.
OKAY.
THEN YOU SEE IF YOU HAVE ANY TWOS.
WHAT HAPPENS IF I DON'T HAVE ANY TWOS?
THAT'S WHERE THE NAME COMES IN.
©2018, BABY BLUES PARTNERSHIP DIST. BY KING FEATURES SYNDICATE 5-2
KIRKMAN & SCOTT

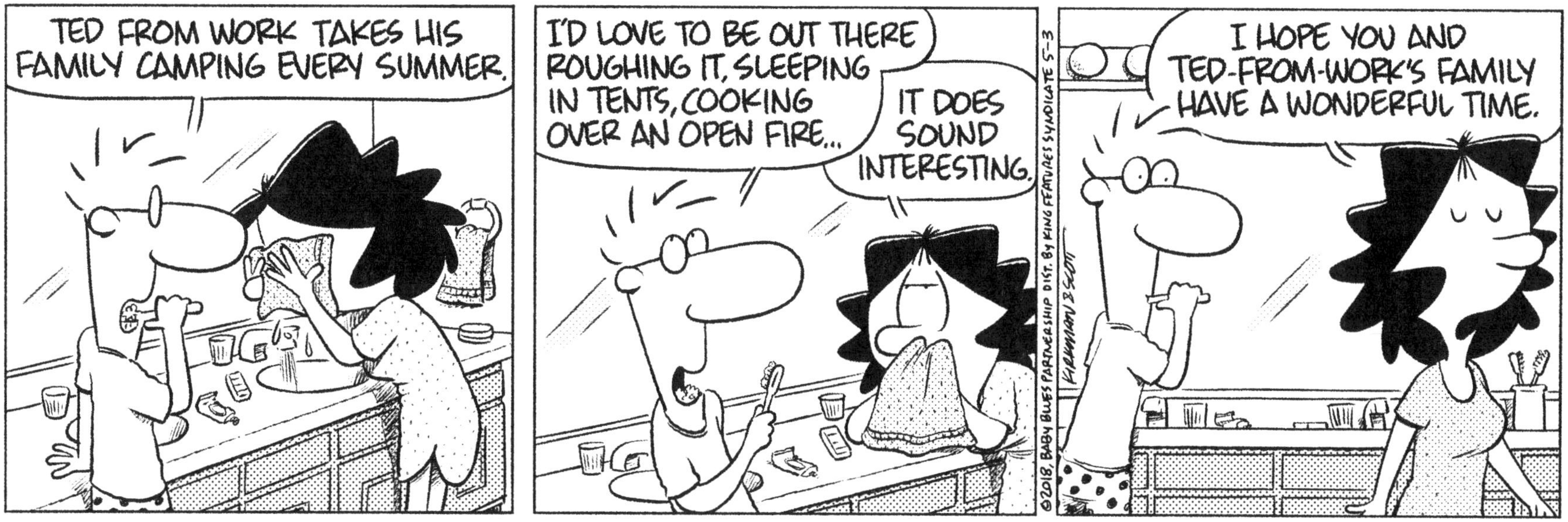
TED FROM WORK TAKES HIS FAMILY CAMPING EVERY SUMMER.
I'D LOVE TO BE OUT THERE ROUGHING IT, SLEEPING IN TENTS, COOKING OVER AN OPEN FIRE...
IT DOES SOUND INTERESTING.
I HOPE YOU AND TED-FROM-WORK'S FAMILY HAVE A WONDERFUL TIME.
©2018, BABY BLUES PARTNERSHIP DIST. BY KING FEATURES SYNDICATE 5-3
KIRKMAN & SCOTT

Rick: You look at these strips over and over while you're working on them. I don't know why I didn't notice accidentally putting a light dot tone in Wanda's nightshirt in the last panel.

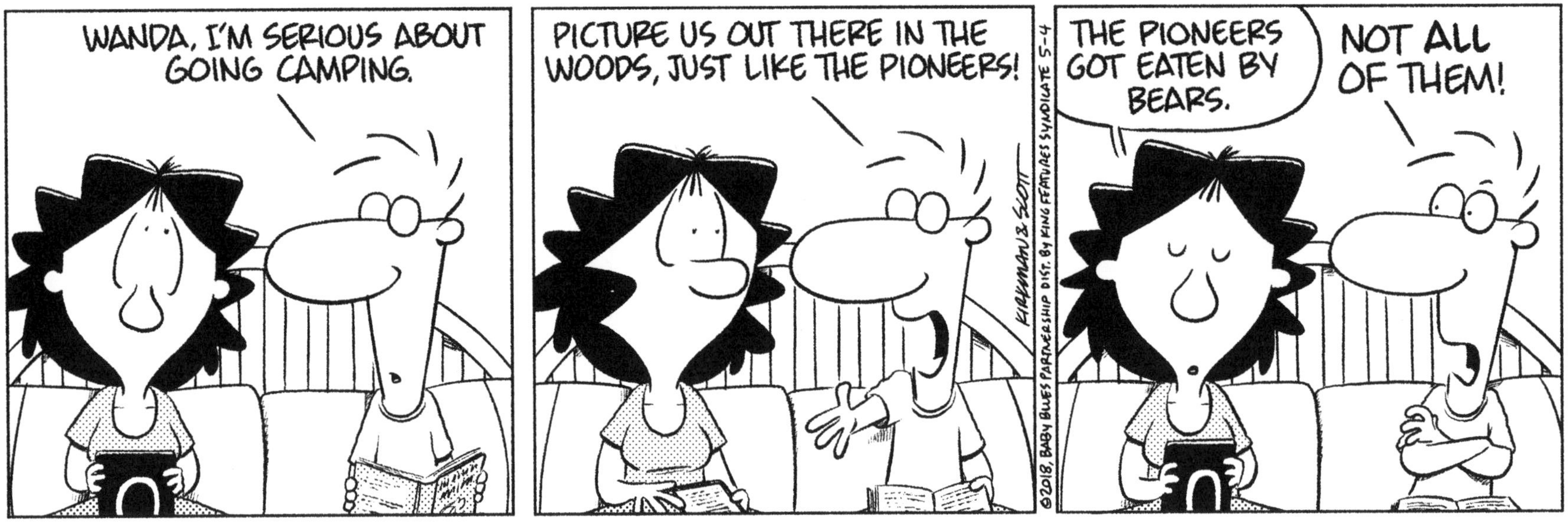
WANDA, I'M SERIOUS ABOUT GOING CAMPING.
PICTURE US OUT THERE IN THE WOODS, JUST LIKE THE PIONEERS!
KIRKMAN & SCOTT
©2018, BABY BLUES PARTNERSHIP DIST. BY KING FEATURES SYNDICATE 5-4
THE PIONEERS GOT EATEN BY BEARS.
NOT ALL OF THEM!

Jerry: Almost every camping experience I've had has ended in some level of disaster. I'm with Wanda on this one.

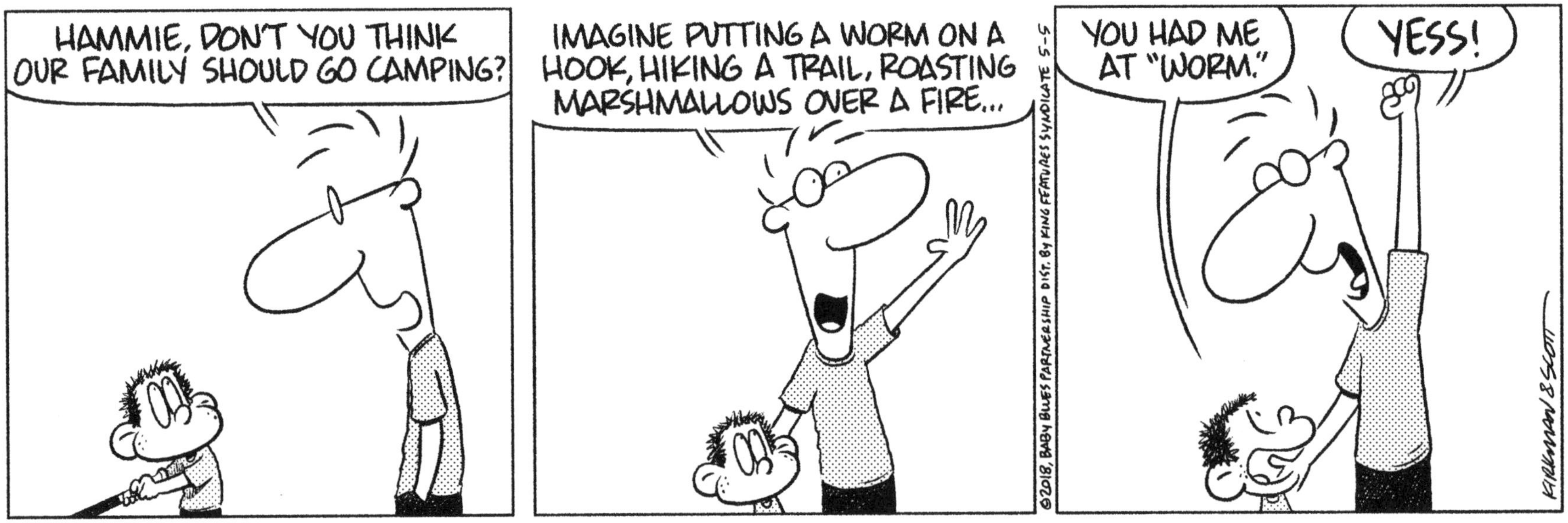
HAMMIE, DON'T YOU THINK OUR FAMILY SHOULD GO CAMPING?
IMAGINE PUTTING A WORM ON A HOOK, HIKING A TRAIL, ROASTING MARSHMALLOWS OVER A FIRE...
©2018, BABY BLUES PARTNERSHIP DIST. BY KING FEATURES SYNDICATE 5-5
YOU HAD ME AT "WORM."
YESS!
KIRKMAN & SCOTT

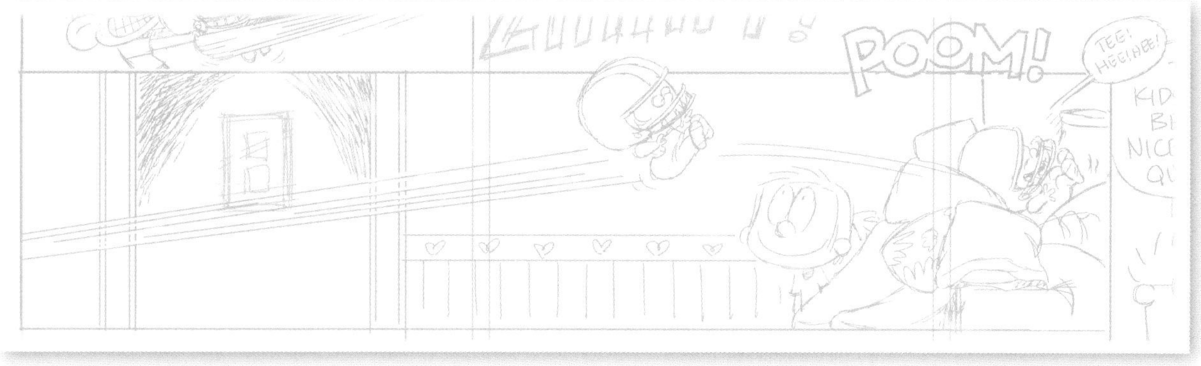
POOM!
TEE! HEE!HEE!

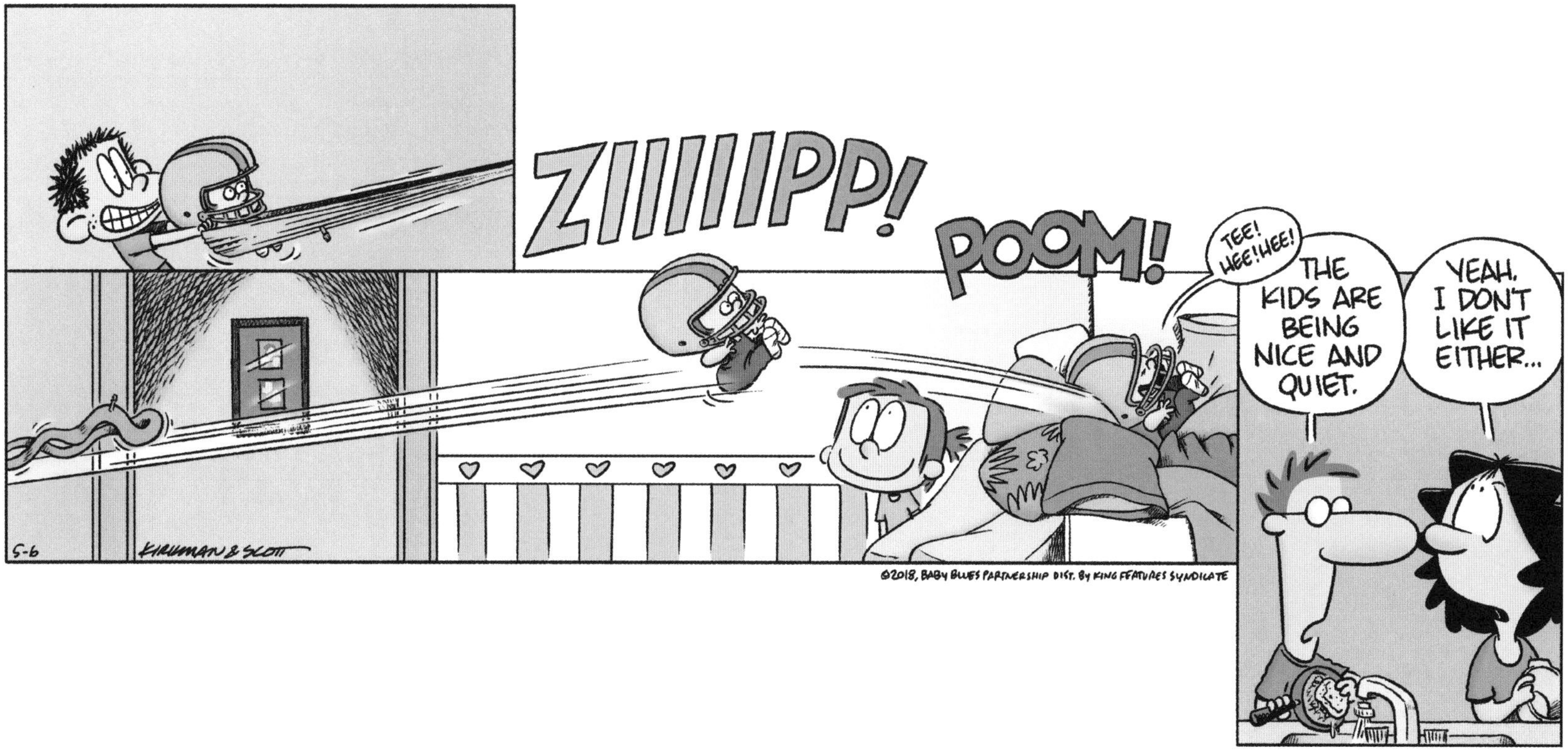
ZIIIIIPP!
POOM!
TEE! HEE!HEE!
THE KIDS ARE BEING NICE AND QUIET.
YEAH, I DON'T LIKE IT EITHER...
5-6
KIRKMAN & SCOTT
©2018, BABY BLUES PARTNERSHIP DIST. BY KING FEATURES SYNDICATE

Rick: Great opportunity to play with the layout, using the action across the strip to lead to the last panel.

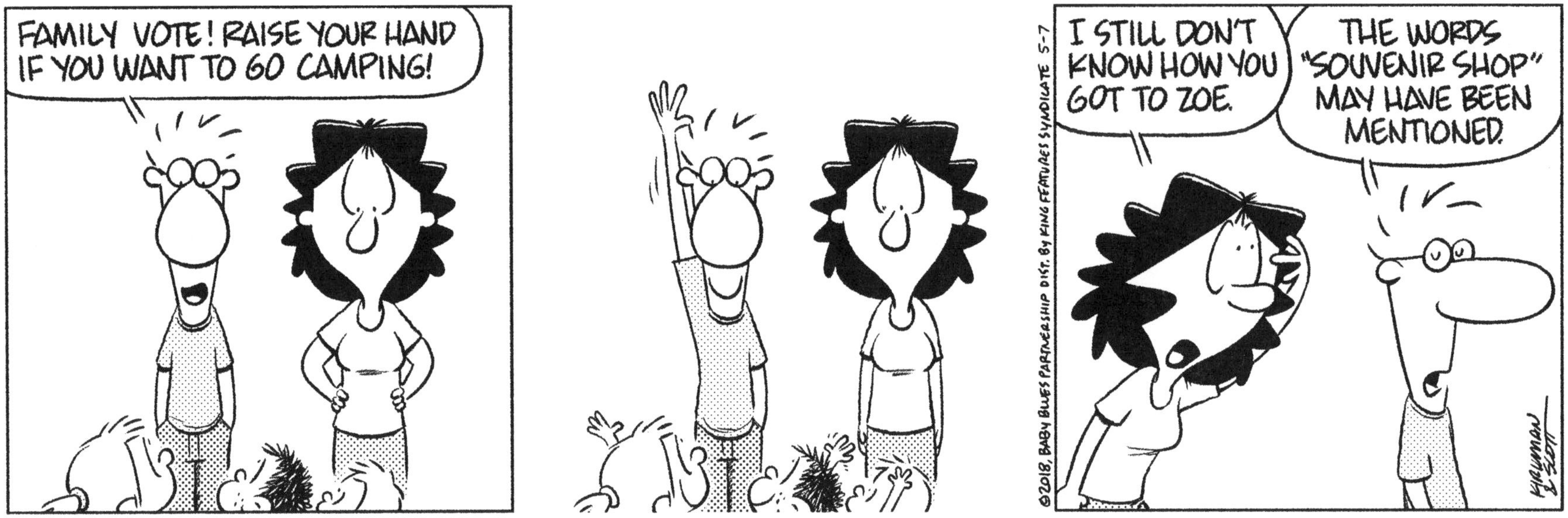
FAMILY VOTE! RAISE YOUR HAND IF YOU WANT TO GO CAMPING!
I STILL DON'T KNOW HOW YOU GOT TO ZOE.
THE WORDS "SOUVENIR SHOP" MAY HAVE BEEN MENTIONED.
©2018, BABY BLUES PARTNERSHIP DIST. BY KING FEATURES SYNDICATE 5-7
KIRKMAN & SCOTT

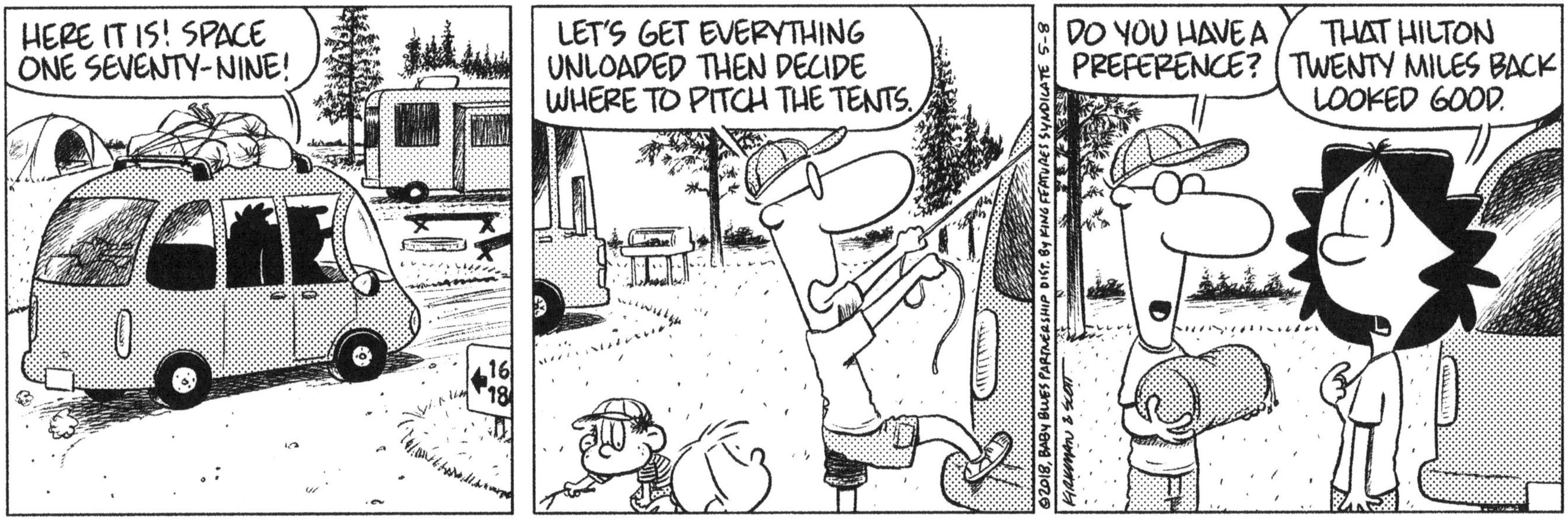
HERE IT IS! SPACE ONE SEVENTY-NINE!
LET'S GET EVERYTHING UNLOADED THEN DECIDE WHERE TO PITCH THE TENTS.
DO YOU HAVE A PREFERENCE?
THAT HILTON TWENTY MILES BACK LOOKED GOOD.
©2018, BABY BLUES PARTNERSHIP DIST. BY KING FEATURES SYNDICATE 5-8
KIRKMAN & SCOTT

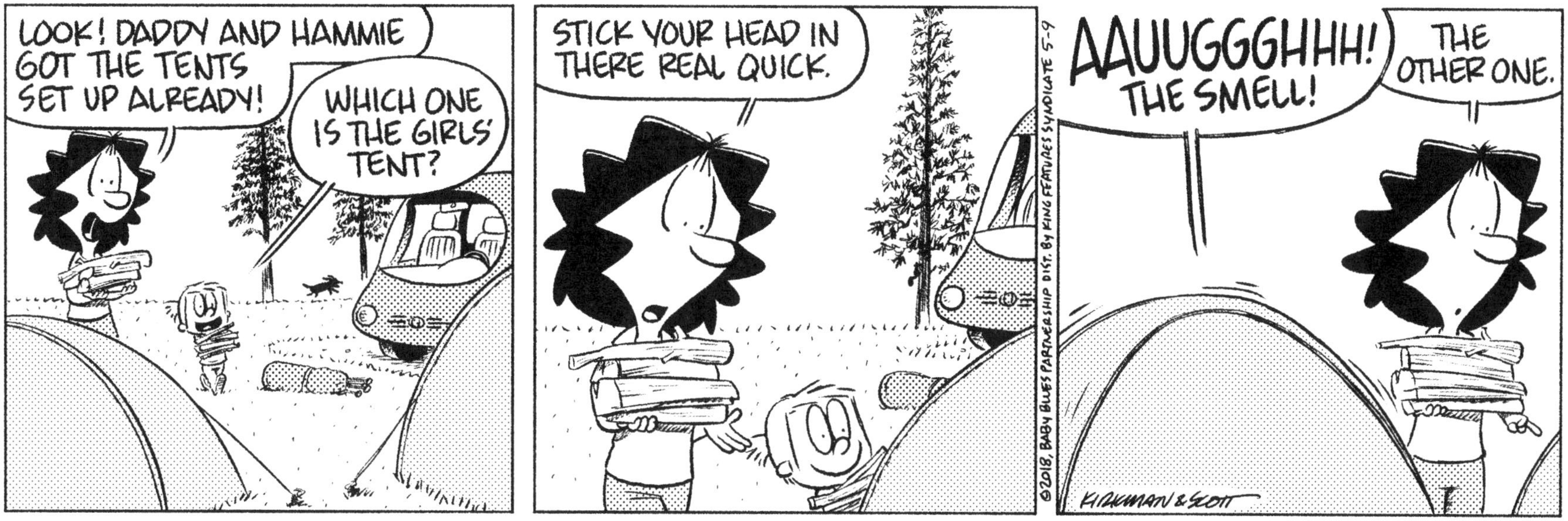
LOOK! DADDY AND HAMMIE GOT THE TENTS SET UP ALREADY!
WHICH ONE IS THE GIRLS' TENT?
STICK YOUR HEAD IN THERE REAL QUICK.
©2018, BABY BLUES PARTNERSHIP DIST. BY KING FEATURES SYNDICATE 5-9
AAUUGGGHHH! THE SMELL!
THE OTHER ONE.
KIRKMAN & SCOTT

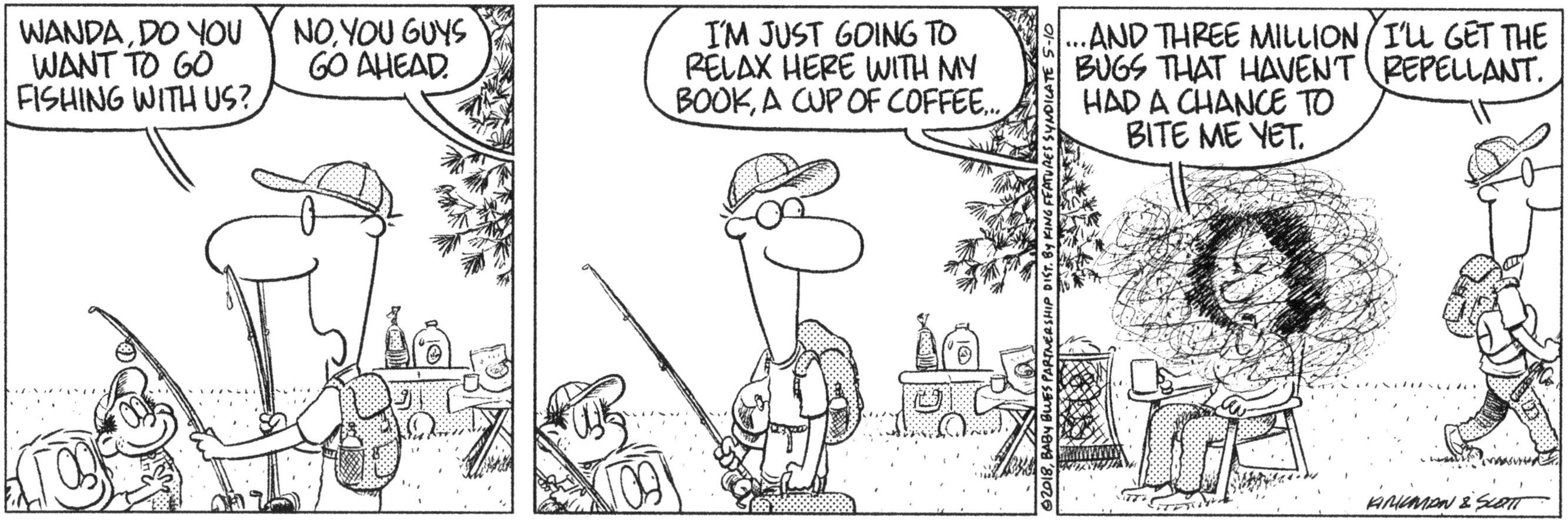
WANDA, DO YOU WANT TO GO FISHING WITH US?
NO, YOU GUYS GO AHEAD.
I'M JUST GOING TO RELAX HERE WITH MY BOOK, A CUP OF COFFEE...
©2018, BABY BLUES PARTNERSHIP DIST. BY KING FEATURES SYNDICATE 5-10
...AND THREE MILLION BUGS THAT HAVEN'T HAD A CHANCE TO BITE ME YET.
I'LL GET THE REPELLANT.
KIRKMAN & SCOTT

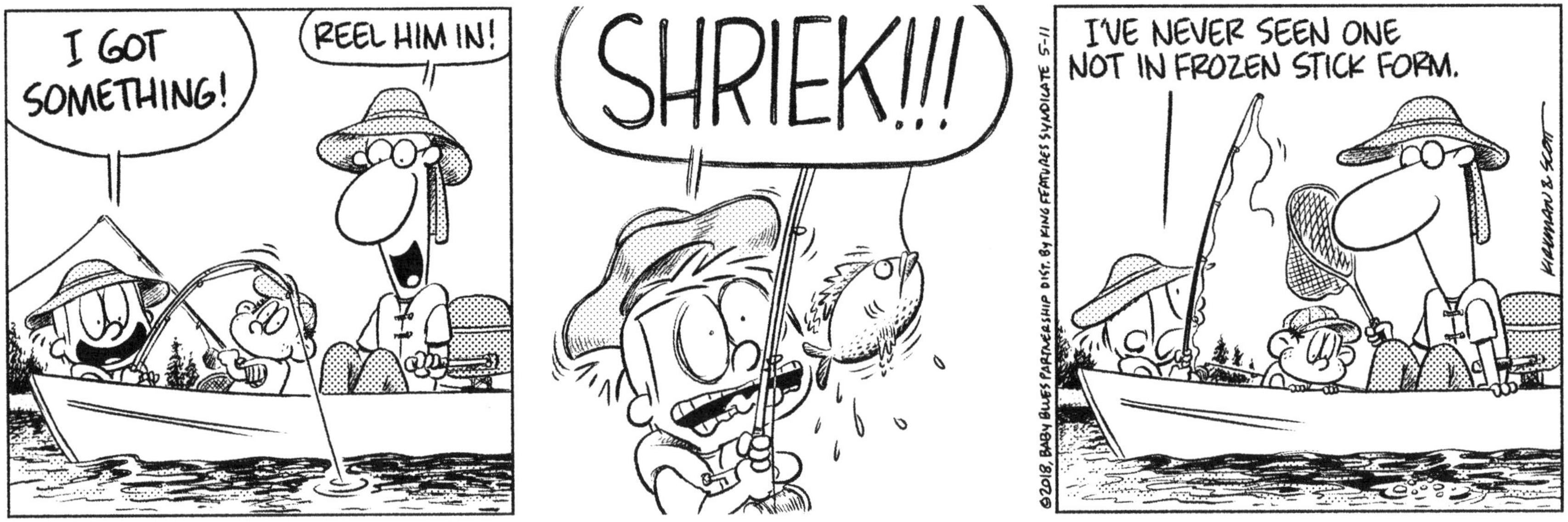
I GOT SOMETHING!
REEL HIM IN!
SHRIEK!!!
©2018, BABY BLUES PARTNERSHIP DIST. BY KING FEATURES SYNDICATE 5-11
I'VE NEVER SEEN ONE NOT IN FROZEN STICK FORM.
KIRKMAN & SCOTT

Rick: I love to draw fear and fish. I wonder what that says about me?

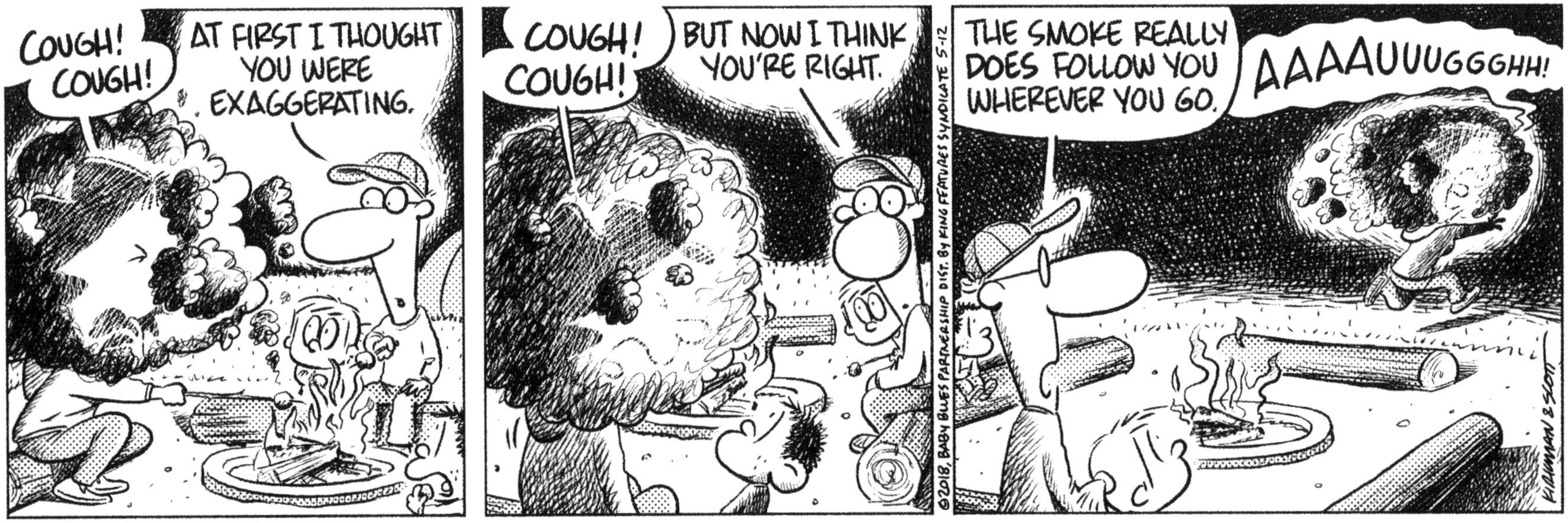
COUGH! COUGH!
AT FIRST I THOUGHT YOU WERE EXAGGERATING.
COUGH! COUGH!
BUT NOW I THINK YOU'RE RIGHT.
©2018, BABY BLUES PARTNERSHIP DIST. BY KING FEATURES SYNDICATE 5-12
THE SMOKE REALLY DOES FOLLOW YOU WHEREVER YOU GO.
AAAAUUUGGGHH!
KIRKMAN & SCOTT

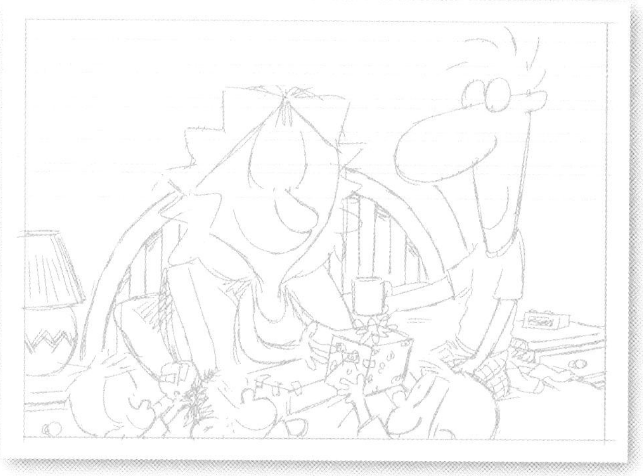

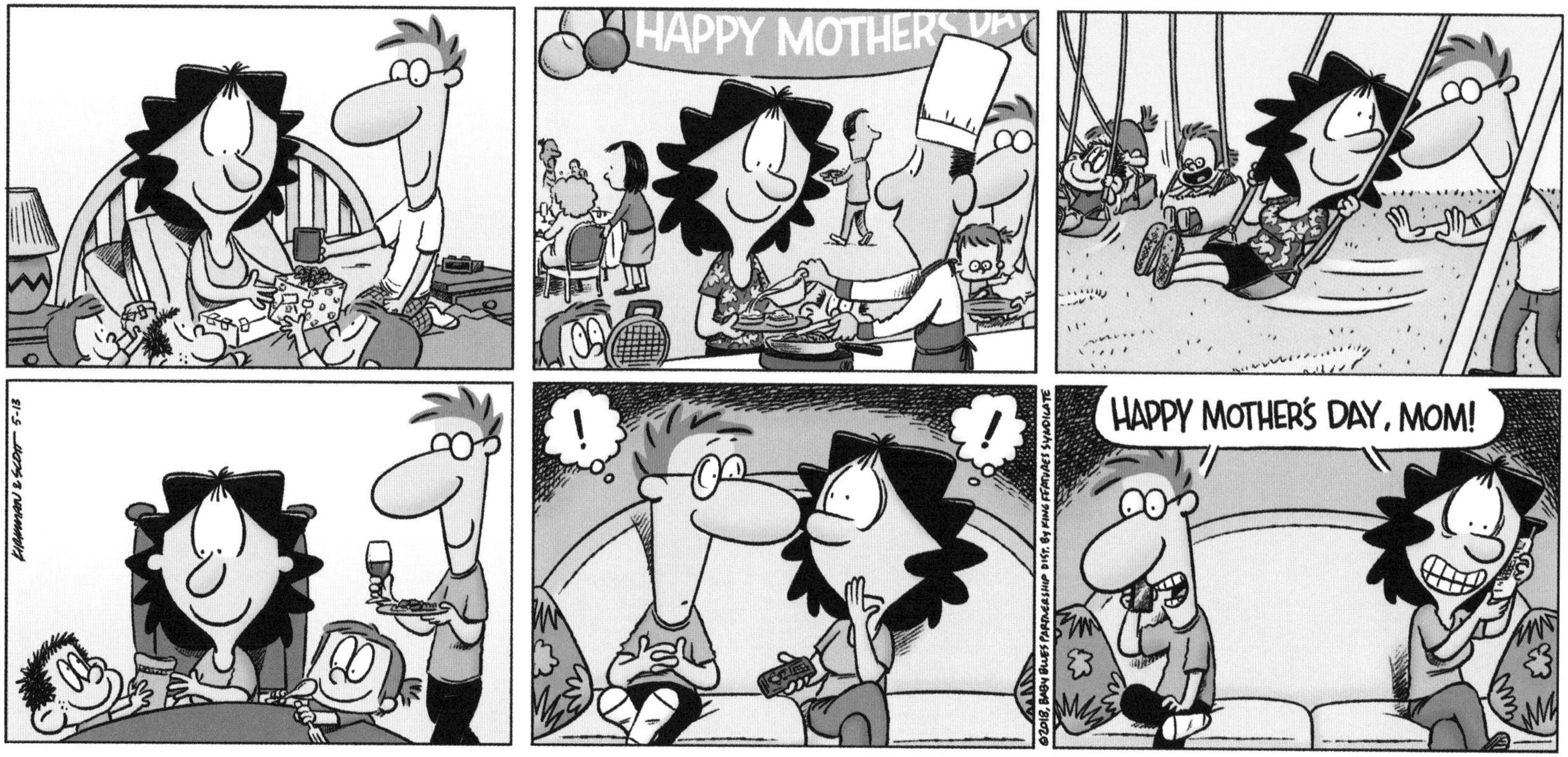
HAPPY MOTHERS
KIRKMAN & SCOTT 5-13
!
!
©2018, BABY BLUES PARTNERSHIP DIST. BY KING FEATURES SYNDICATE
HAPPY MOTHER'S DAY, MOM!

Rick: Whoops!

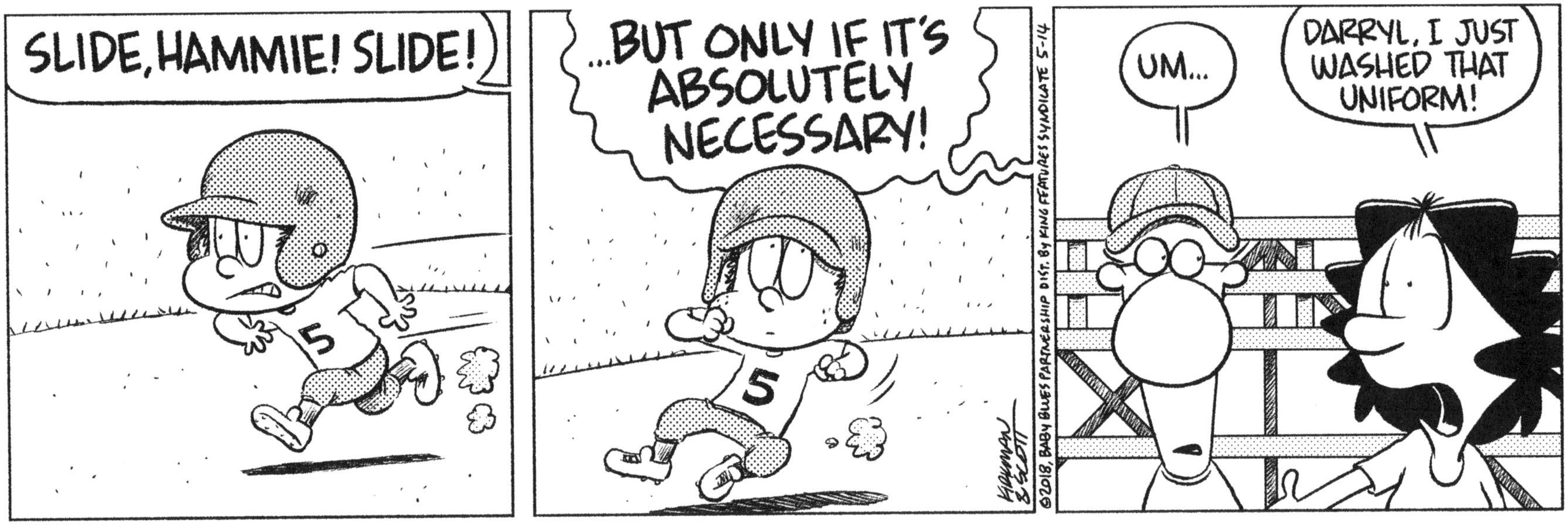
SLIDE, HAMMIE! SLIDE!
...BUT ONLY IF IT'S ABSOLUTELY NECESSARY!
©2018, BABY BLUES PARTNERSHIP DIST. BY KING FEATURES SYNDICATE 5-14
KIRKMAN & SCOTT
UM...
DARRYL, I JUST WASHED THAT UNIFORM!

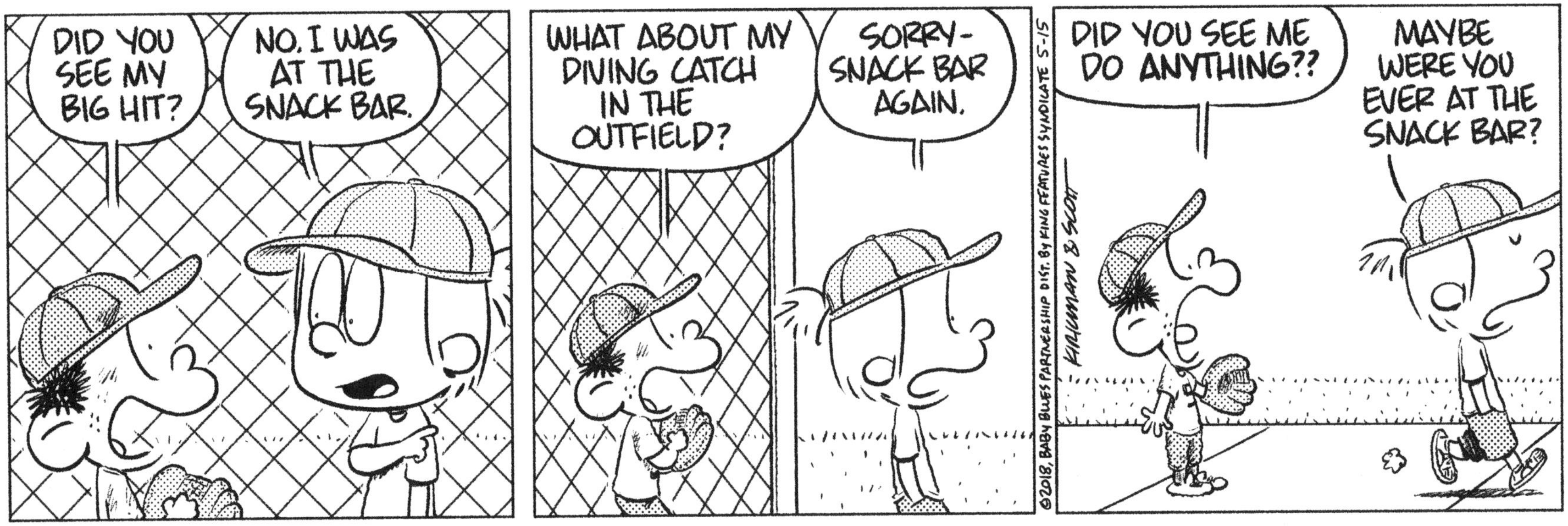
DID YOU SEE MY BIG HIT?
NO. I WAS AT THE SNACK BAR.
WHAT ABOUT MY DIVING CATCH IN THE OUTFIELD?
SORRY-SNACK BAR AGAIN.
©2018, BABY BLUES PARTNERSHIP DIST. BY KING FEATURES SYNDICATE 5-15
KIRKMAN & SCOTT
DID YOU SEE ME DO ANYTHING??
MAYBE WERE YOU EVER AT THE SNACK BAR?

Rick: Argh! I left the period off after "Maybe" in the last panel. Feel free to get a pen and put it in for me. Just don't use a Sharpie: it'll bleed through the page on the other side—possibly giving a character an extra eye or a big freckle.

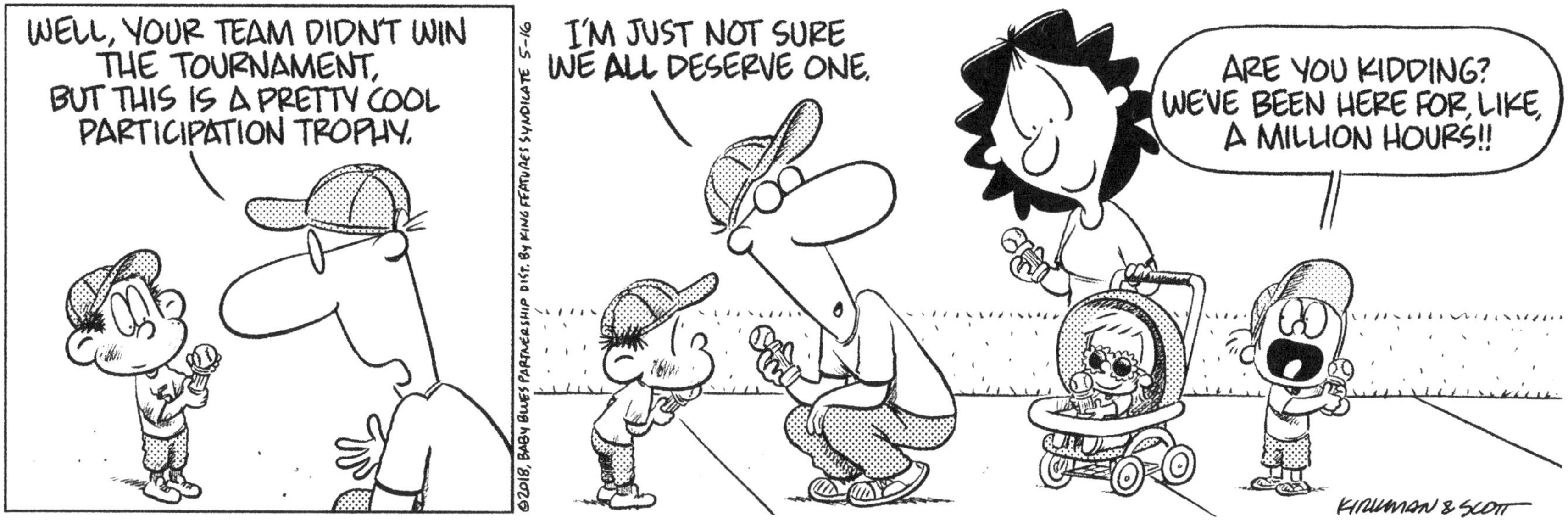
WELL, YOUR TEAM DIDN'T WIN THE TOURNAMENT, BUT THIS IS A PRETTY COOL PARTICIPATION TROPHY.
©2018, BABY BLUES PARTNERSHIP DIST. BY KING FEATURES SYNDICATE 5-16
I'M JUST NOT SURE WE ALL DESERVE ONE.
ARE YOU KIDDING? WE'VE BEEN HERE FOR, LIKE, A MILLION HOURS!!
KIRKMAN & SCOTT

Jerry: If they gave trophies for dance recital attendance, I'd need a bigger mantle.

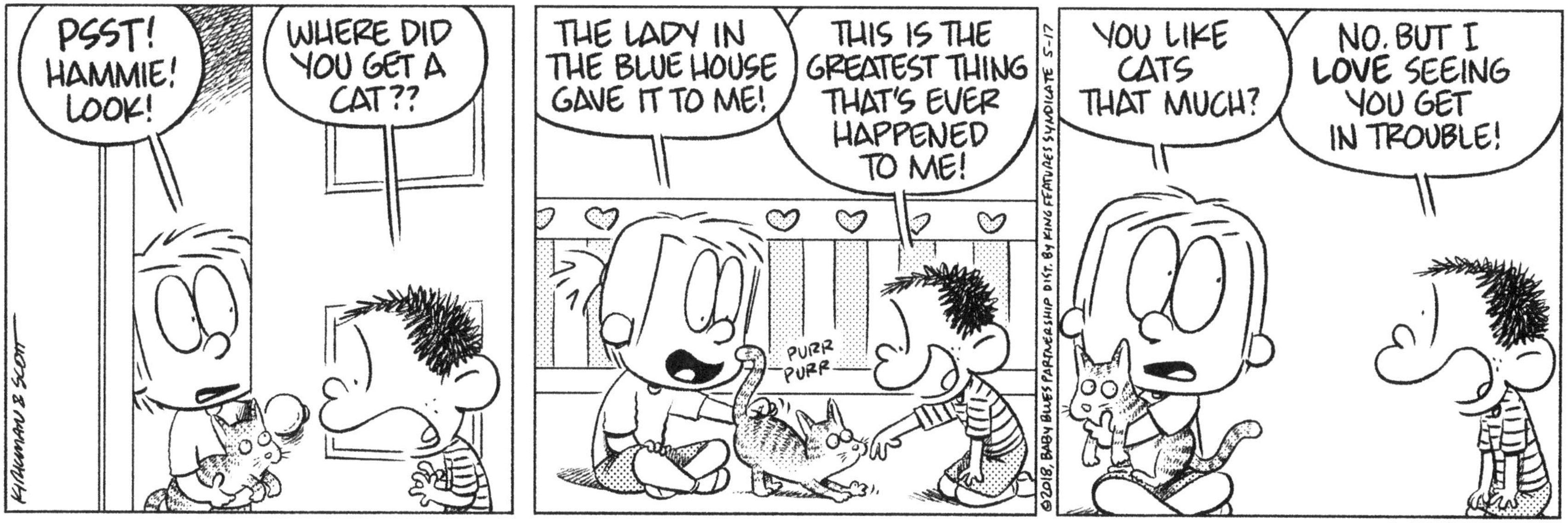
PSST! HAMMIE! LOOK!
WHERE DID YOU GET A CAT??
KIRKMAN & SCOTT
THE LADY IN THE BLUE HOUSE GAVE IT TO ME!
THIS IS THE GREATEST THING THAT'S EVER HAPPENED TO ME!
PURR PURR
©2018, BABY BLUES PARTNERSHIP DIST. BY KING FEATURES SYNDICATE 5-17
YOU LIKE CATS THAT MUCH?
NO. BUT I LOVE SEEING YOU GET IN TROUBLE!

Rick: I feel a sneeze coming on just looking at that.

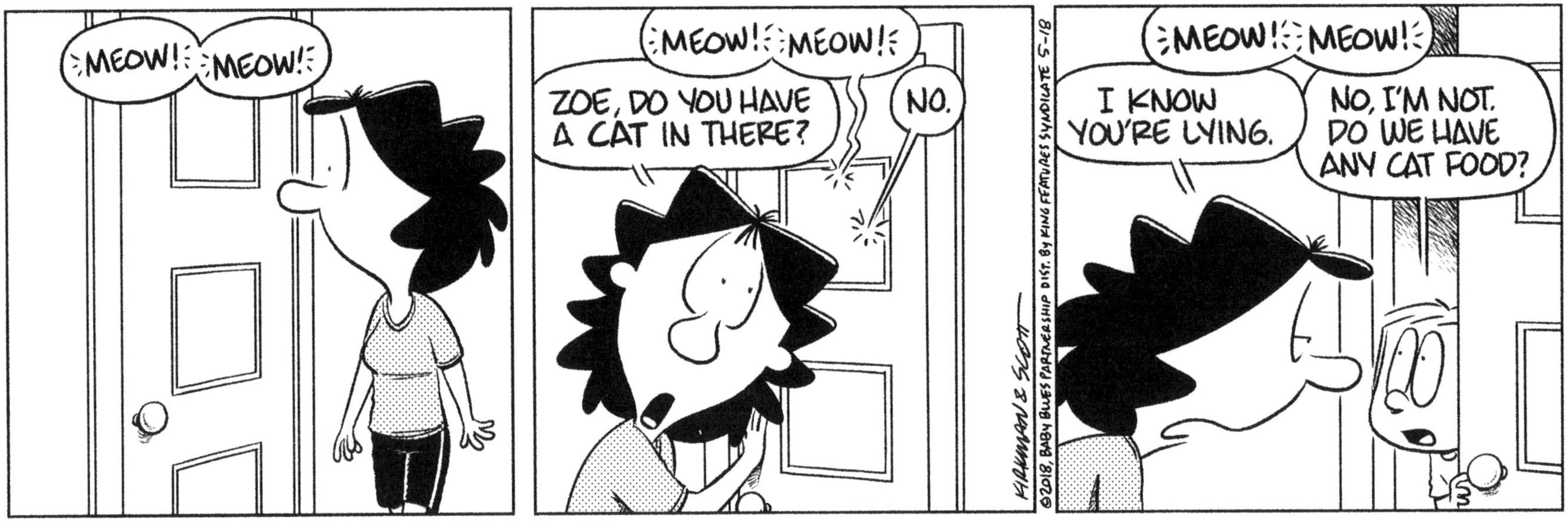
MEOW! MEOW!
MEOW! MEOW!
ZOE, DO YOU HAVE A CAT IN THERE?
NO.
KIRKMAN & SCOTT
©2018, BABY BLUES PARTNERSHIP DIST. BY KING FEATURES SYNDICATE 5-18
MEOW! MEOW!
I KNOW YOU'RE LYING.
NO, I'M NOT. DO WE HAVE ANY CAT FOOD?

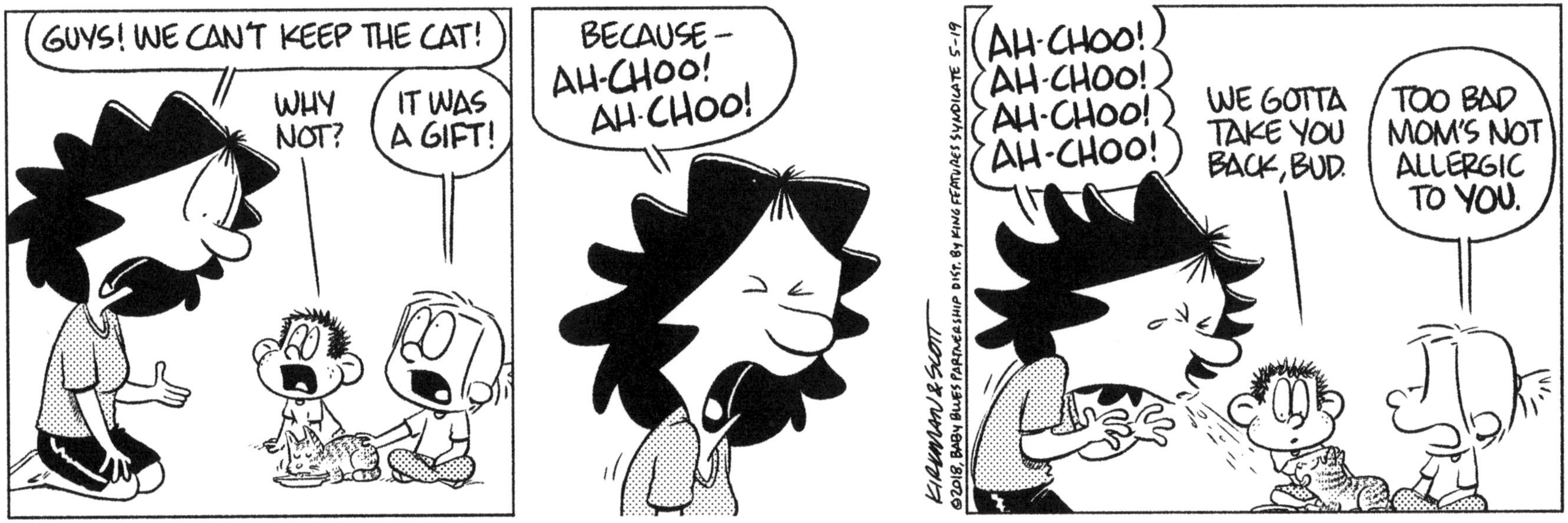
GUYS! WE CAN'T KEEP THE CAT!
WHY NOT?
IT WAS A GIFT!
BECAUSE— AH-CHOO! AH-CHOO!
©2018, BABY BLUES PARTNERSHIP DIST. BY KING FEATURES SYNDICATE 5-19
KIRKMAN & SCOTT
AH-CHOO! AH-CHOO! AH-CHOO! AH-CHOO!
WE GOTTA TAKE YOU BACK, BUD.
TOO BAD MOM'S NOT ALLERGIC TO YOU.

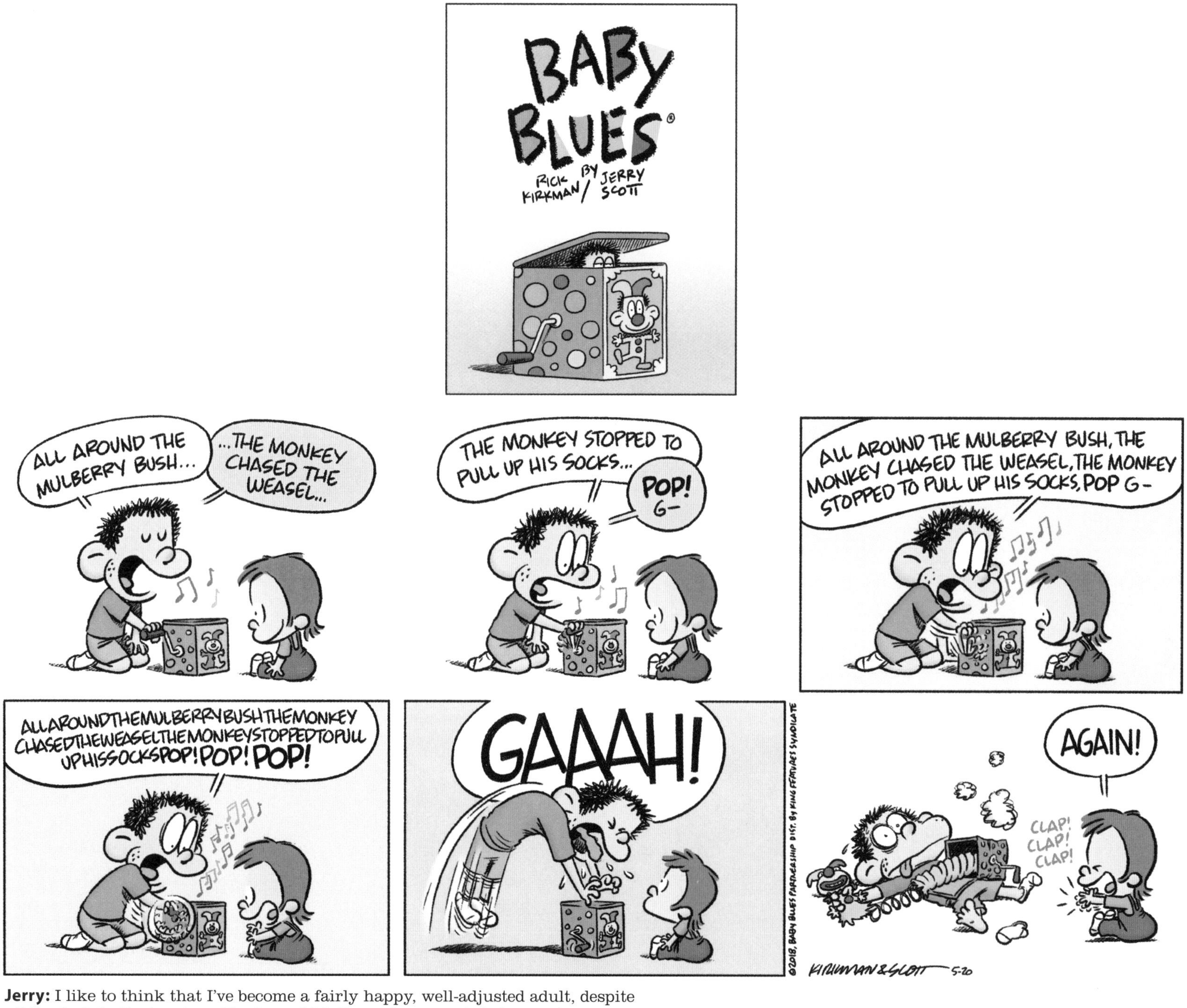
BABY BLUES®
BY RICK KIRKMAN / JERRY SCOTT
ALL AROUND THE MULBERRY BUSH...
...THE MONKEY CHASED THE WEASEL...
THE MONKEY STOPPED TO PULL UP HIS SOCKS...
POP! G–
ALL AROUND THE MULBERRY BUSH, THE MONKEY CHASED THE WEASEL, THE MONKEY STOPPED TO PULL UP HIS SOCKS, POP G–
ALLAROUNDTHEMULBERRYBUSHTHEMONKEY CHASEDTHEWEASELTHEMONKEYSTOPPEDTOPULL UPHISSOCKSPOP! POP! POP!
GAAAH!
AGAIN!
CLAP! CLAP! CLAP!
©2018, BABY BLUES PARTNERSHIP DIST. BY KING FEATURES SYNDICATE
KIRKMAN & SCOTT 5-20

Jerry: I like to think that I've become a fairly happy, well-adjusted adult, despite all the jack-in-the-box toys I had as a kid. They always weirded me out.

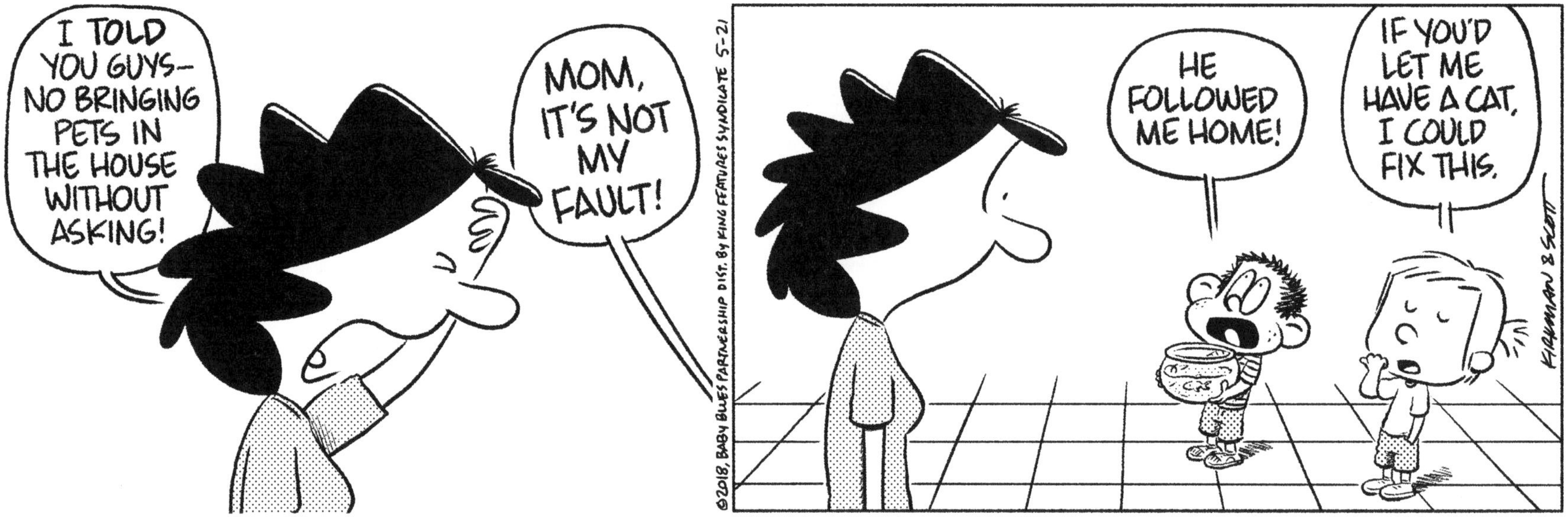
I TOLD YOU GUYS— NO BRINGING PETS IN THE HOUSE WITHOUT ASKING!
MOM, IT'S NOT MY FAULT!
HE FOLLOWED ME HOME!
IF YOU'D LET ME HAVE A CAT, I COULD FIX THIS.
©2018, BABY BLUES PARTNERSHIP DIST. BY KING FEATURES SYNDICATE 5-21
KIRKMAN & SCOTT

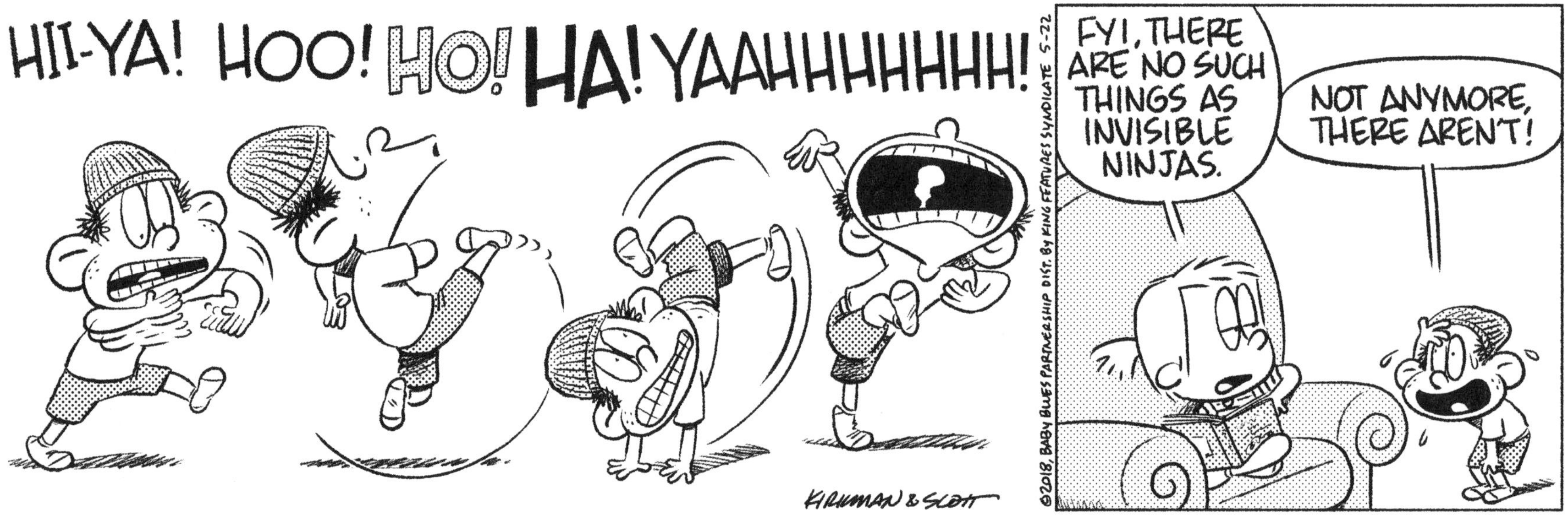
HII-YA! HOO! HO! HA! YAAHHHHHHH!
FYI, THERE ARE NO SUCH THINGS AS INVISIBLE NINJAS.
NOT ANYMORE, THERE AREN'T!
©2018, BABY BLUES PARTNERSHIP DIST. BY KING FEATURES SYNDICATE 5-22
KIRKMAN & SCOTT

Rick: I had to release my Inner Ninja to draw this. Should've seen me in front of the mirror.

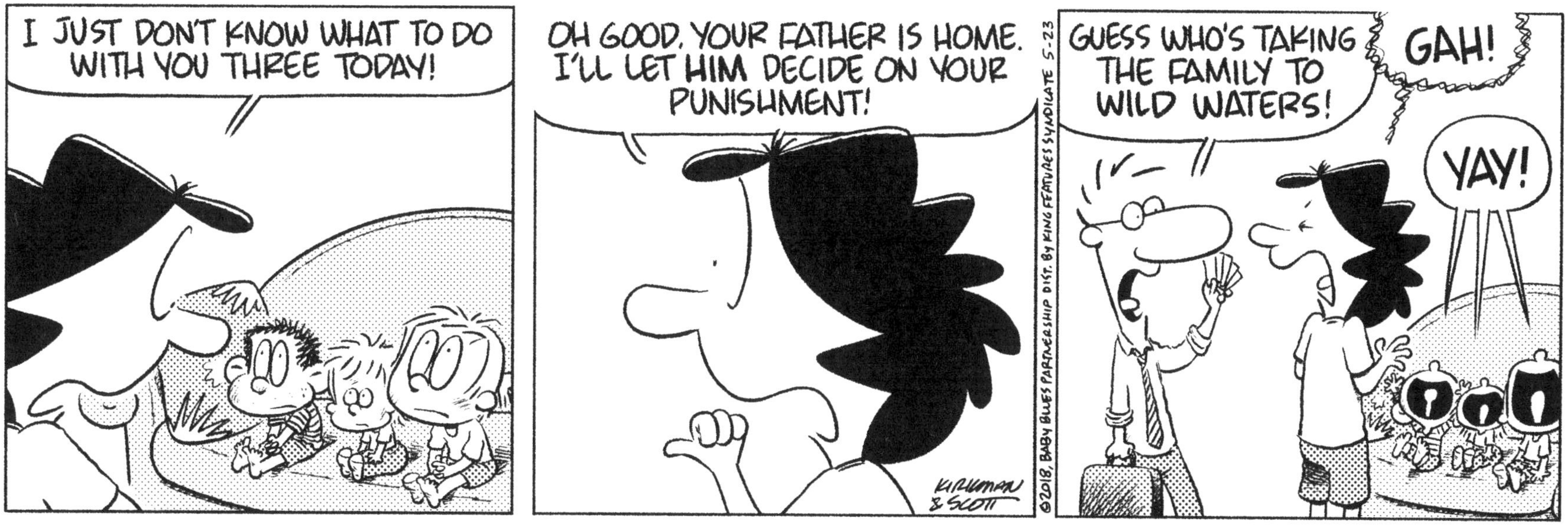
I JUST DON'T KNOW WHAT TO DO WITH YOU THREE TODAY!
OH GOOD. YOUR FATHER IS HOME. I'LL LET HIM DECIDE ON YOUR PUNISHMENT!
KIRKMAN & SCOTT
©2018, BABY BLUES PARTNERSHIP DIST. BY KING FEATURES SYNDICATE 5-23
GUESS WHO'S TAKING THE FAMILY TO WILD WATERS!
GAH!
YAY!

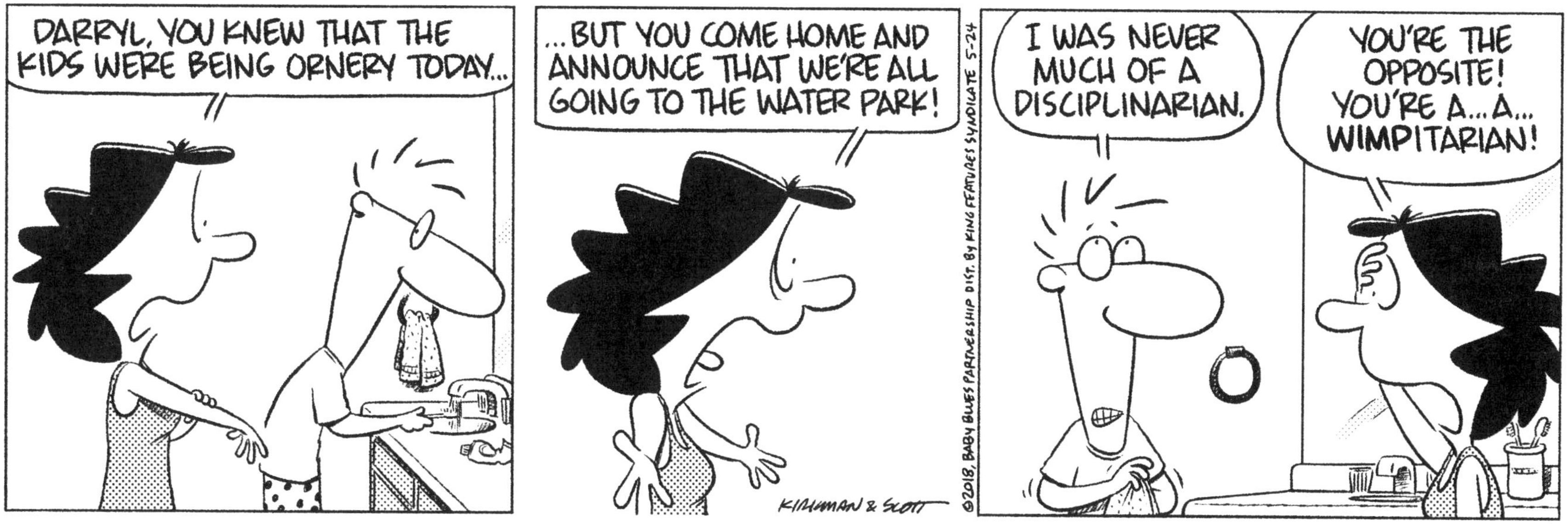
DARRYL, YOU KNEW THAT THE KIDS WERE BEING ORNERY TODAY...
...BUT YOU COME HOME AND ANNOUNCE THAT WE'RE ALL GOING TO THE WATER PARK!
KIRKMAN & SCOTT
©2018, BABY BLUES PARTNERSHIP DIST. BY KING FEATURES SYNDICATE 5-24
I WAS NEVER MUCH OF A DISCIPLINARIAN.
YOU'RE THE OPPOSITE! YOU'RE A...A... WIMPITARIAN!

Rick: Great word. Look that up in your Funk & Wagnalls. (Ask your parents. No, ask your grandparents.)

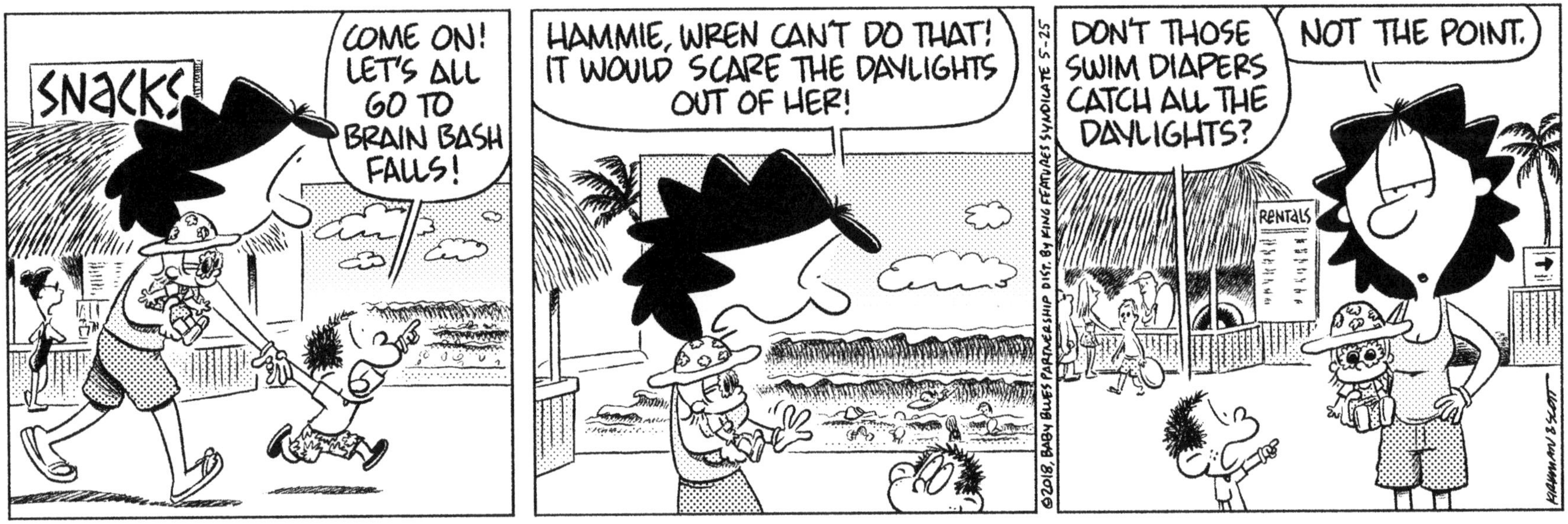
SNACKS
COME ON! LET'S ALL GO TO BRAIN BASH FALLS!
HAMMIE, WREN CAN'T DO THAT! IT WOULD SCARE THE DAYLIGHTS OUT OF HER!
©2018, BABY BLUES PARTNERSHIP DIST. BY KING FEATURES SYNDICATE 5-25
DON'T THOSE SWIM DIAPERS CATCH ALL THE DAYLIGHTS?
NOT THE POINT.
RENTALS
KIRKMAN & SCOTT

Rick: Challenge: Make it look like a water park in three tiny panels.

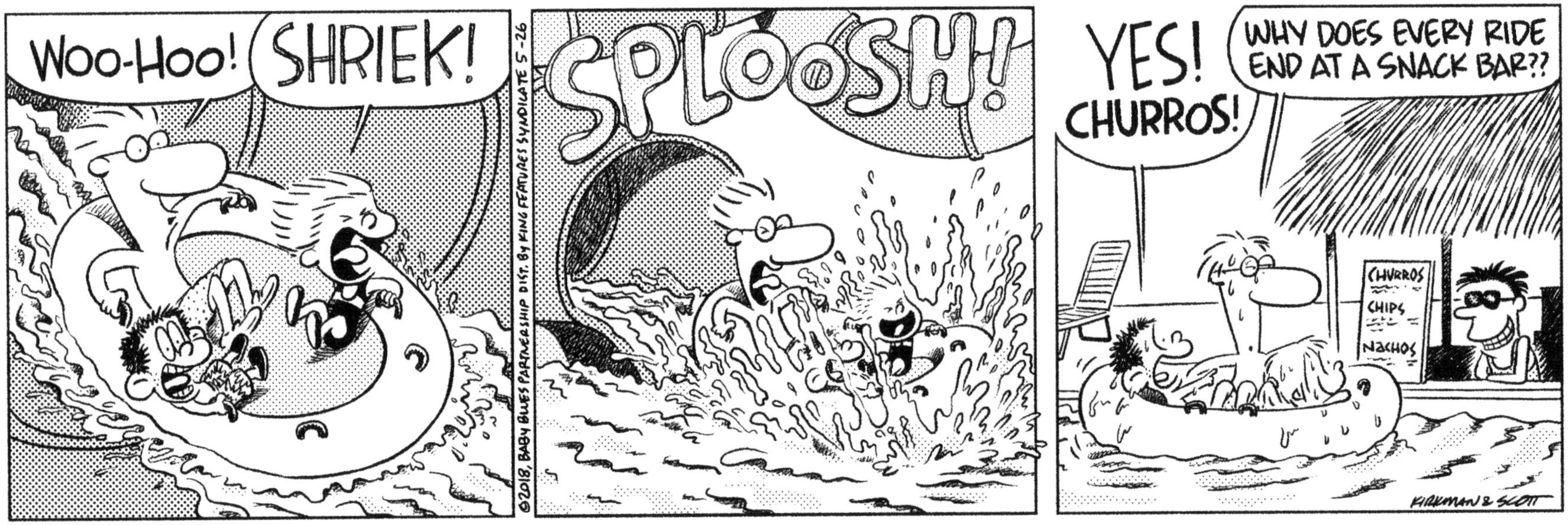
WOO-HOO!
SHRIEK!
©2018, BABY BLUES PARTNERSHIP DIST. BY KING FEATURES SYNDICATE 5-26
SPLOOSH!
YES! CHURROS!
WHY DOES EVERY RIDE END AT A SNACK BAR??
CHURROS
CHIPS
NACHOS
KIRKMAN & SCOTT

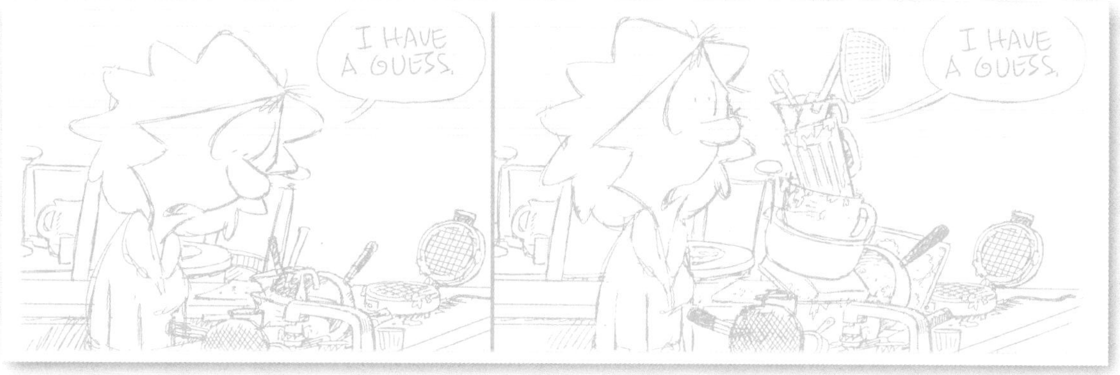
I HAVE A GUESS.
I HAVE A GUESS.

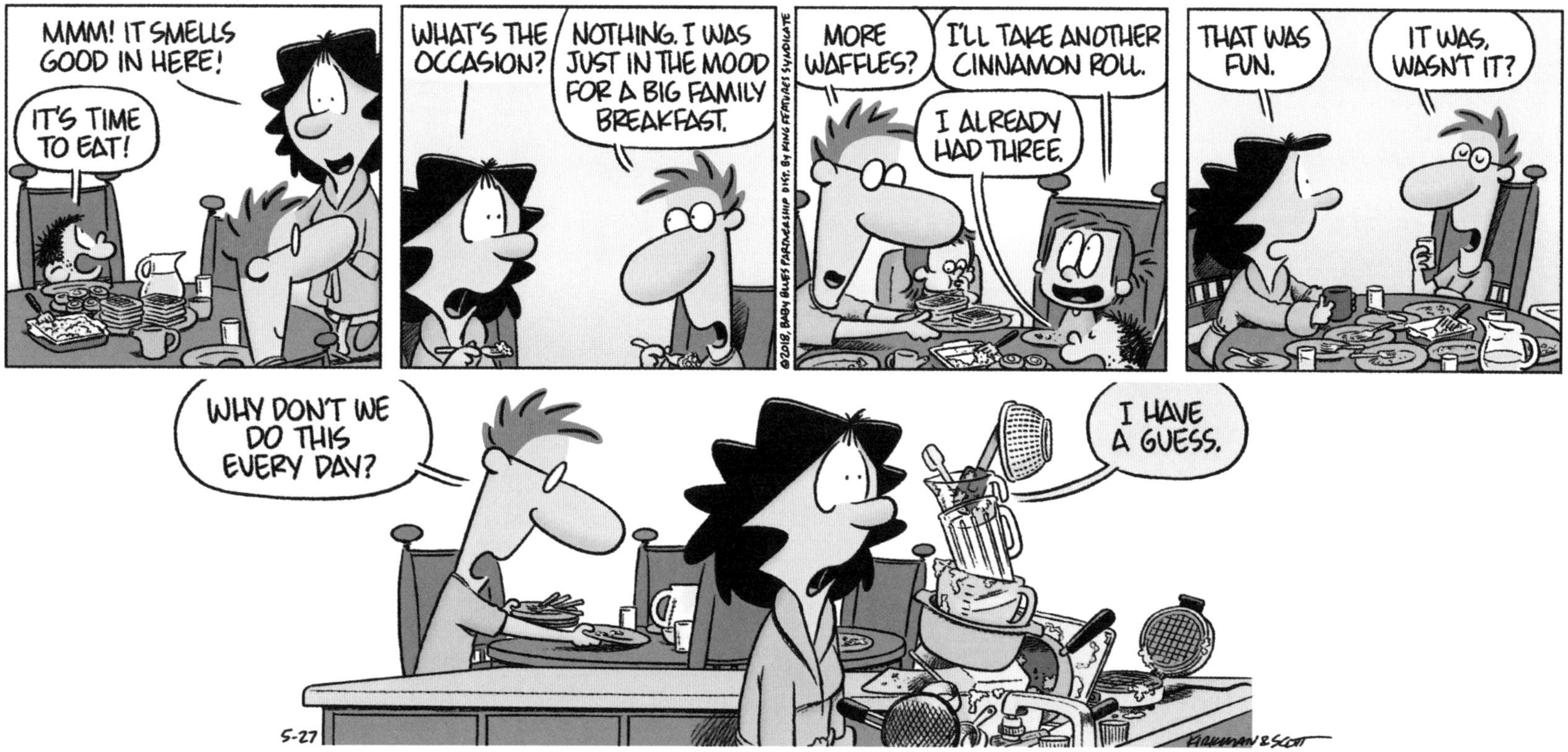
MMM! IT SMELLS GOOD IN HERE!
IT'S TIME TO EAT!
WHAT'S THE OCCASION?
NOTHING. I WAS JUST IN THE MOOD FOR A BIG FAMILY BREAKFAST.
©2018, BABY BLUES PARTNERSHIP DIST. BY KING FEATURES SYNDICATE
MORE WAFFLES?
I'LL TAKE ANOTHER CINNAMON ROLL.
I ALREADY HAD THREE.
THAT WAS FUN.
IT WAS, WASN'T IT?
WHY DON'T WE DO THIS EVERY DAY?
I HAVE A GUESS.
5-27
KIRKMAN & SCOTT

Rick: Sometimes I don't quite go far enough in a drawing. Here, Jerry wanted me to push it more. Good call.

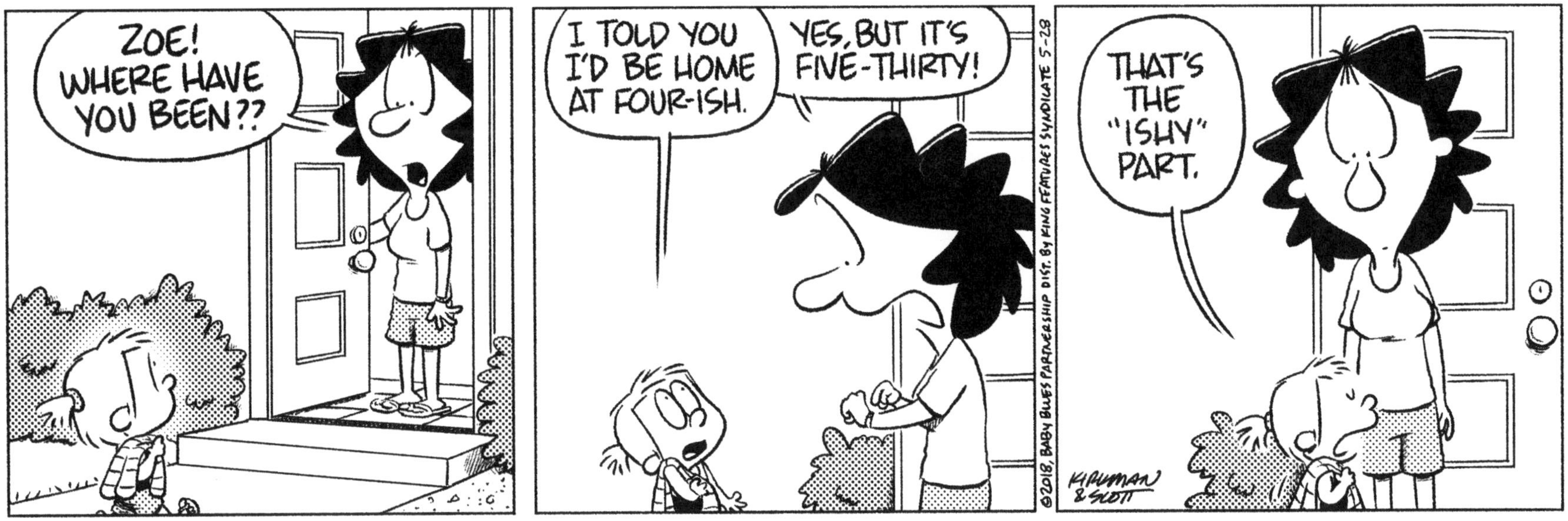
ZOE! WHERE HAVE YOU BEEN??
I TOLD YOU I'D BE HOME AT FOUR-ISH.
YES, BUT IT'S FIVE-THIRTY!
©2018, BABY BLUES PARTNERSHIP DIST. BY KING FEATURES SYNDICATE 5-28
THAT'S THE "ISHY" PART.
KIRKMAN & SCOTT

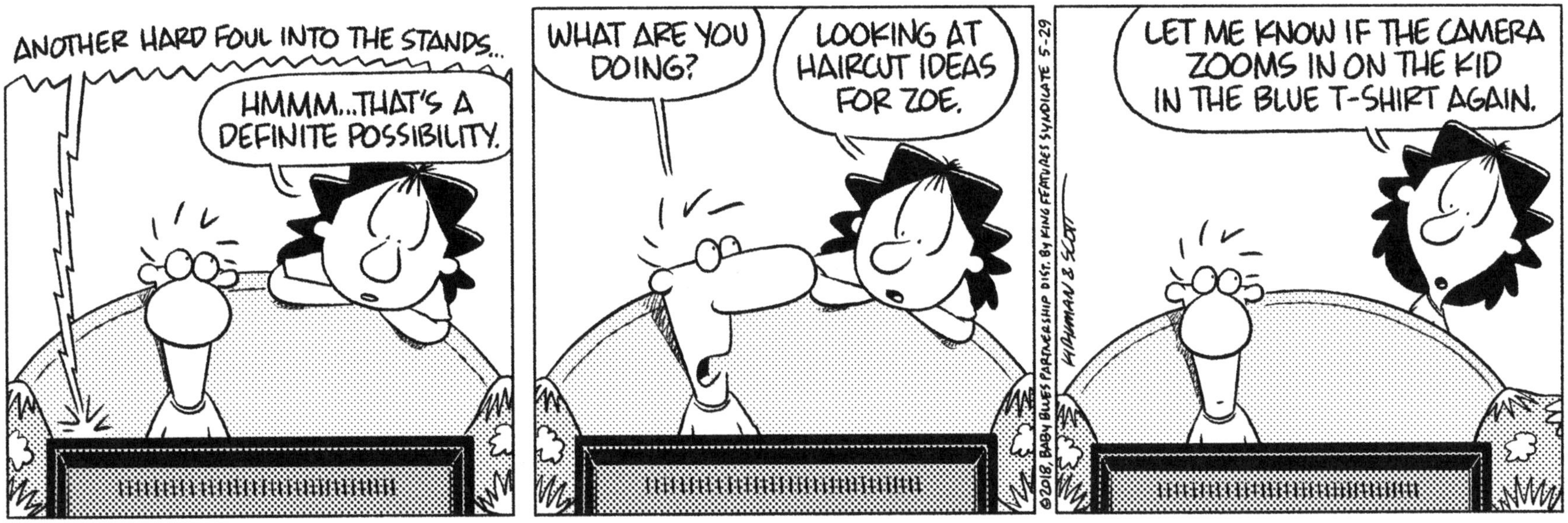
ANOTHER HARD FOUL INTO THE STANDS...
HMMM...THAT'S A DEFINITE POSSIBILITY.
WHAT ARE YOU DOING?
LOOKING AT HAIRCUT IDEAS FOR ZOE.
©2018, BABY BLUES PARTNERSHIP DIST. BY KING FEATURES SYNDICATE 5-29
KIRKMAN & SCOTT
LET ME KNOW IF THE CAMERA ZOOMS IN ON THE KID IN THE BLUE T-SHIRT AGAIN.

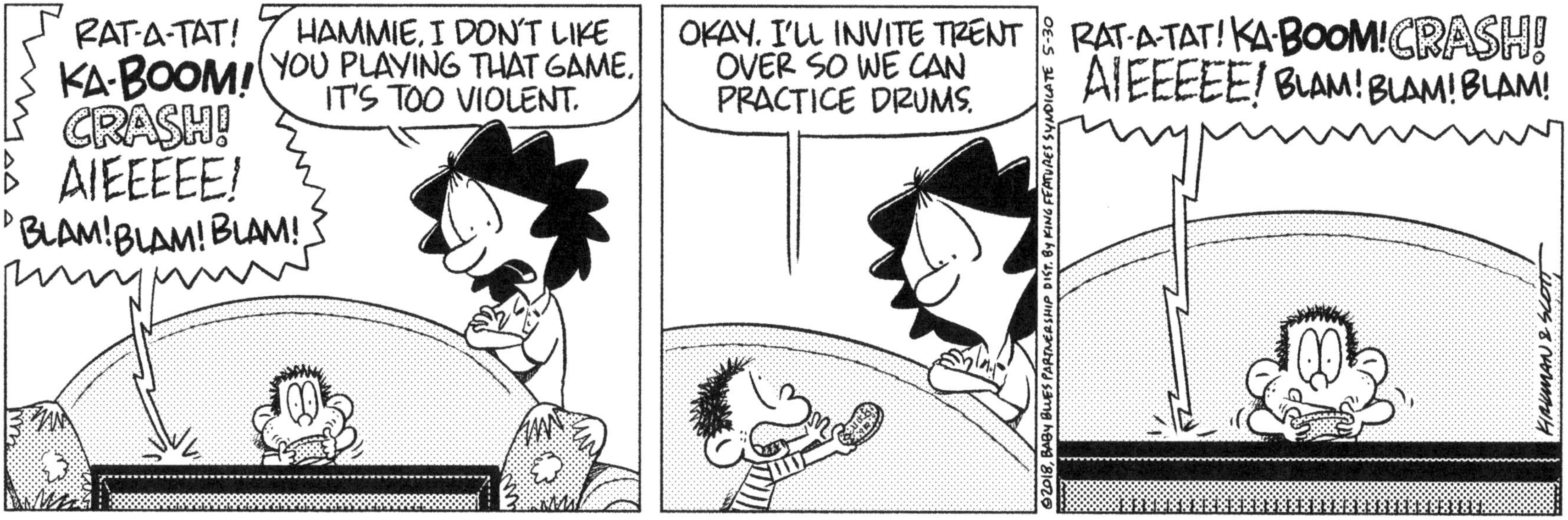
RAT-A-TAT! KA-BOOM! CRASH! AIEEEEE! BLAM! BLAM! BLAM!
HAMMIE, I DON'T LIKE YOU PLAYING THAT GAME. IT'S TOO VIOLENT.
OKAY. I'LL INVITE TRENT OVER SO WE CAN PRACTICE DRUMS.
RAT-A-TAT! KA-BOOM! CRASH! AIEEEEE! BLAM! BLAM! BLAM!
©2018, BABY BLUES PARTNERSHIP DIST. BY KING FEATURES SYNDICATE 5-30
KIRKMAN & SCOTT

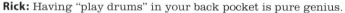

Rick: Having "play drums" in your back pocket is pure genius.

Jerry: One of the details Rick and I put a lot of effort into is the acting. A lot of information is communicated through a character's body language. I really like the way Wanda is leaning on the couch with one elbow. There's something really mom-ish about it.

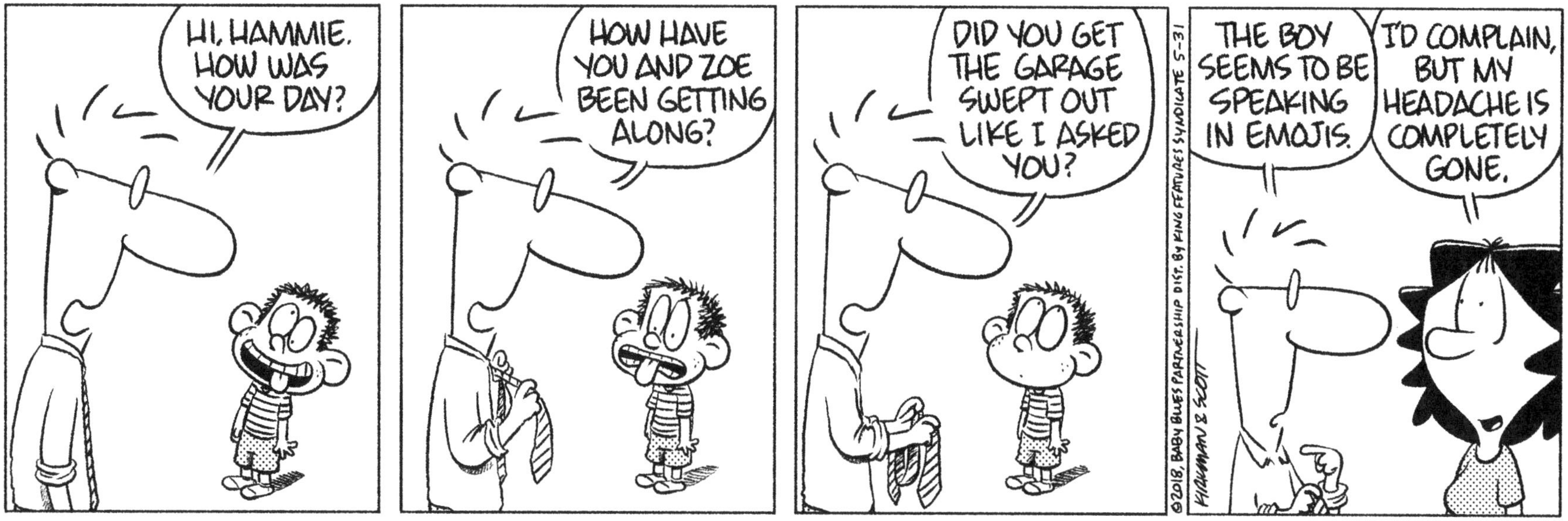
HI, HAMMIE. HOW WAS YOUR DAY?
HOW HAVE YOU AND ZOE BEEN GETTING ALONG?
DID YOU GET THE GARAGE SWEPT OUT LIKE I ASKED YOU?
©2018, BABY BLUES PARTNERSHIP DIST. BY KING FEATURES SYNDICATE 5-31
KIRKMAN & SCOTT
THE BOY SEEMS TO BE SPEAKING IN EMOJIS.
I'D COMPLAIN, BUT MY HEADACHE IS COMPLETELY GONE.

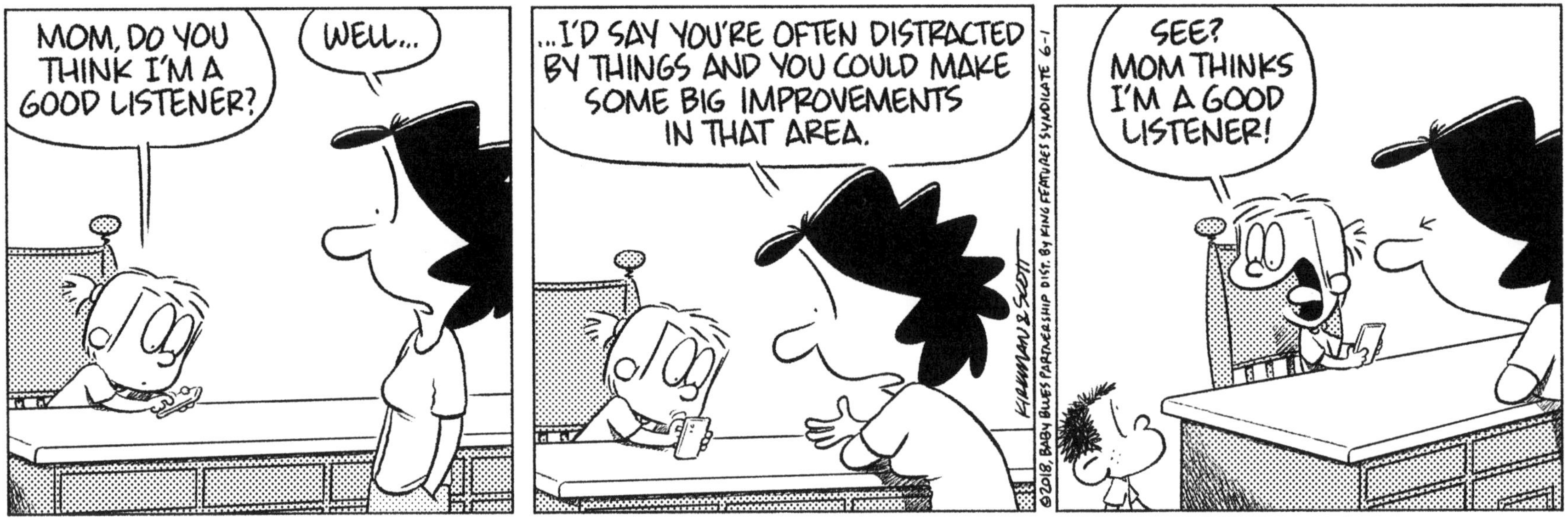
MOM, DO YOU THINK I'M A GOOD LISTENER?
WELL...
...I'D SAY YOU'RE OFTEN DISTRACTED BY THINGS AND YOU COULD MAKE SOME BIG IMPROVEMENTS IN THAT AREA.
KIRKMAN & SCOTT
©2018, BABY BLUES PARTNERSHIP DIST. BY KING FEATURES SYNDICATE 6-1
SEE? MOM THINKS I'M A GOOD LISTENER!

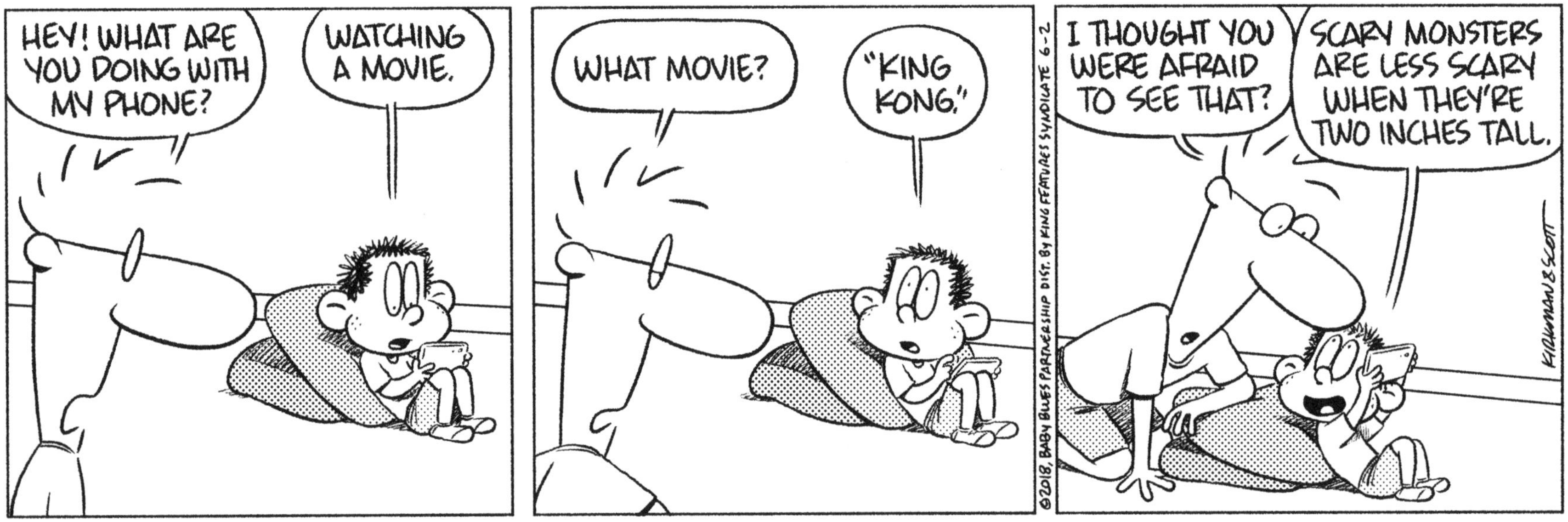
HEY! WHAT ARE YOU DOING WITH MY PHONE?
WATCHING A MOVIE.
WHAT MOVIE?
"KING KONG."
©2018, BABY BLUES PARTNERSHIP DIST. BY KING FEATURES SYNDICATE 6-2
I THOUGHT YOU WERE AFRAID TO SEE THAT?
SCARY MONSTERS ARE LESS SCARY WHEN THEY'RE TWO INCHES TALL.
KIRKMAN & SCOTT

Rick: The logic in this is indisputable.

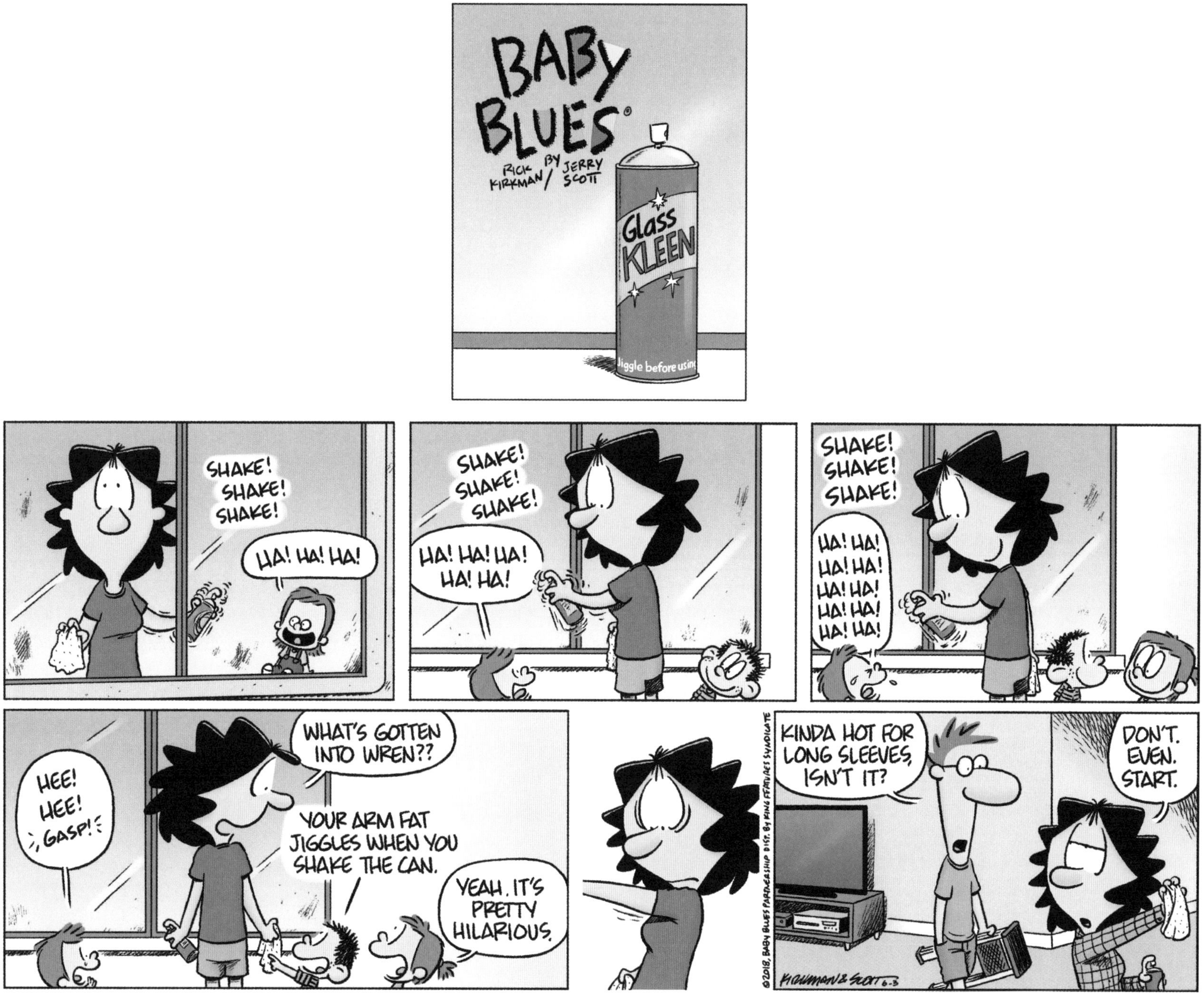
BABY BLUES®
BY RICK KIRKMAN / JERRY SCOTT
Glass KLEEN
Jiggle before using
SHAKE! SHAKE! SHAKE!
HA! HA! HA!
SHAKE! SHAKE! SHAKE!
HA! HA! HA! HA! HA!
SHAKE! SHAKE! SHAKE!
HA! HA! HA! HA! HA! HA! HA! HA! HA! HA!
HEE! HEE! GASP!
WHAT'S GOTTEN INTO WREN??
YOUR ARM FAT JIGGLES WHEN YOU SHAKE THE CAN.
YEAH, IT'S PRETTY HILARIOUS.
KINDA HOT FOR LONG SLEEVES, ISN'T IT?
DON'T. EVEN. START.
©2018, BABY BLUES PARTNERSHIP DIST. BY KING FEATURES SYNDICATE
KIRKMAN & SCOTT 6-3

Rick: I seem to recall an angry note about this one.

Jerry: My grandma had Olympic quality jiggling arm fat, but I knew better than to laugh.

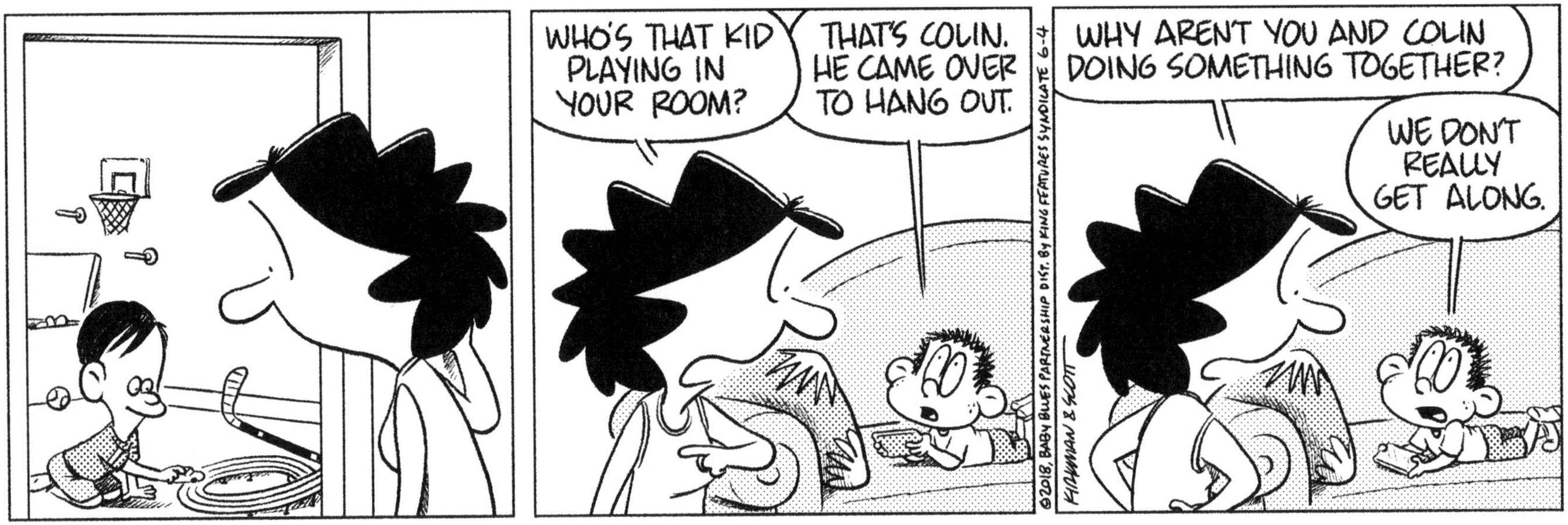
WHO'S THAT KID PLAYING IN YOUR ROOM?
THAT'S COLIN. HE CAME OVER TO HANG OUT.
©2018, BABY BLUES PARTNERSHIP DIST. BY KING FEATURES SYNDICATE 6-4
KIRKMAN & SCOTT
WHY AREN'T YOU AND COLIN DOING SOMETHING TOGETHER?
WE DON'T REALLY GET ALONG.

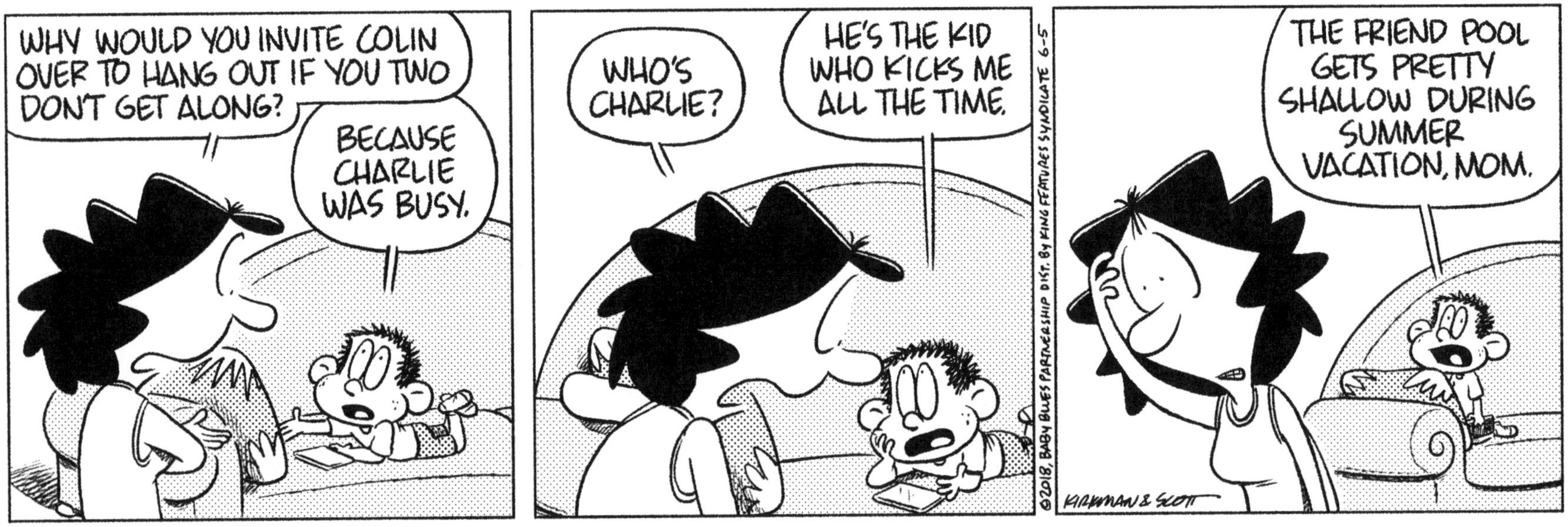
WHY WOULD YOU INVITE COLIN OVER TO HANG OUT IF YOU TWO DON'T GET ALONG?
BECAUSE CHARLIE WAS BUSY.
WHO'S CHARLIE?
HE'S THE KID WHO KICKS ME ALL THE TIME.
©2018, BABY BLUES PARTNERSHIP DIST. BY KING FEATURES SYNDICATE 6-5
KIRKMAN & SCOTT
THE FRIEND POOL GETS PRETTY SHALLOW DURING SUMMER VACATION, MOM.

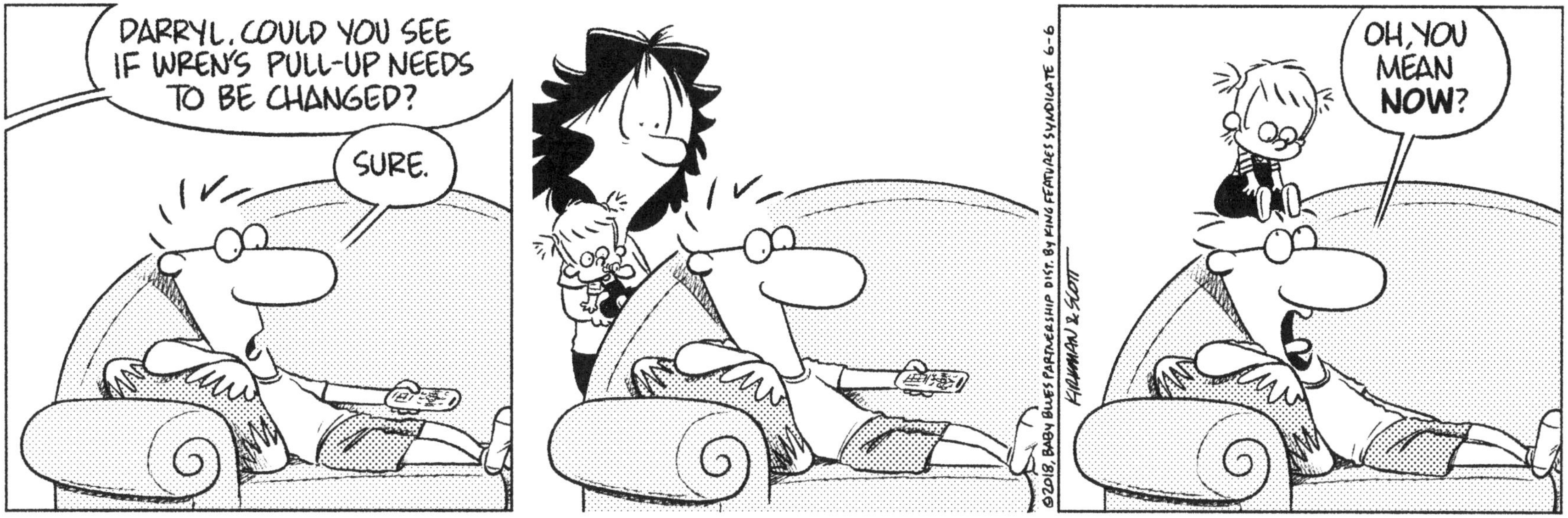
DARRYL, COULD YOU SEE IF WREN'S PULL-UP NEEDS TO BE CHANGED?
SURE.
OH, YOU MEAN **NOW**?
©2018, BABY BLUES PARTNERSHIP DIST. BY KING FEATURES SYNDICATE 6-6
KIRKMAN & SCOTT

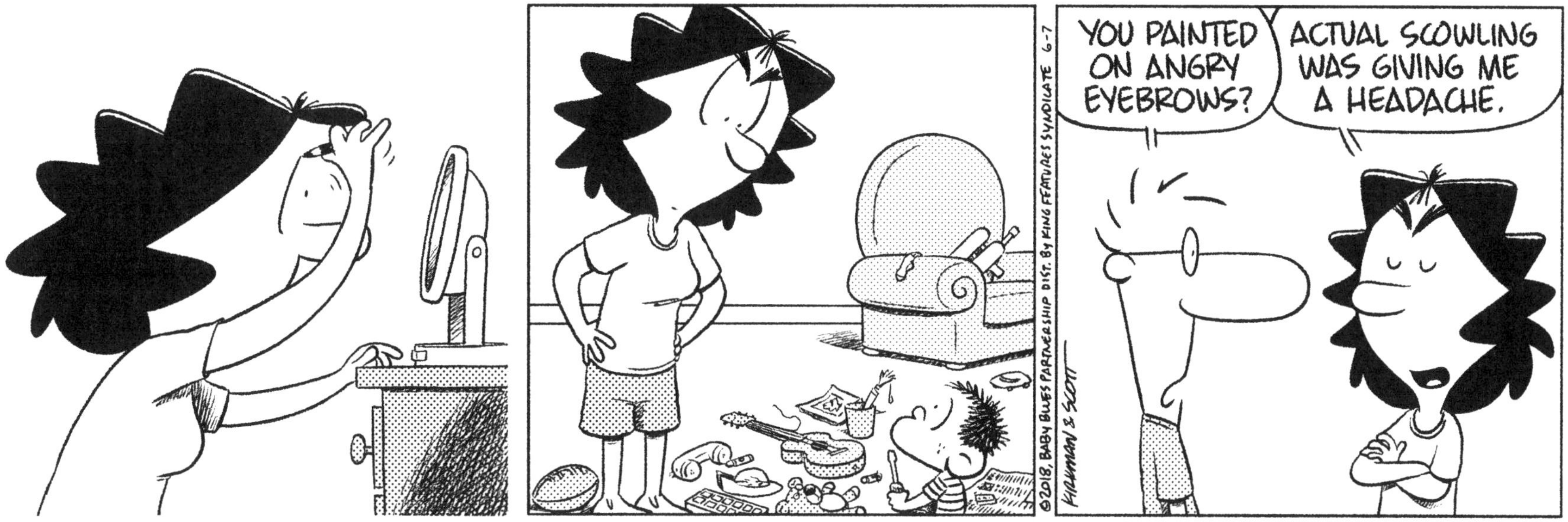
©2018, BABY BLUES PARTNERSHIP DIST. BY KING FEATURES SYNDICATE 6-7
KIRKMAN & SCOTT
YOU PAINTED ON ANGRY EYEBROWS?
ACTUAL SCOWLING WAS GIVING ME A HEADACHE.

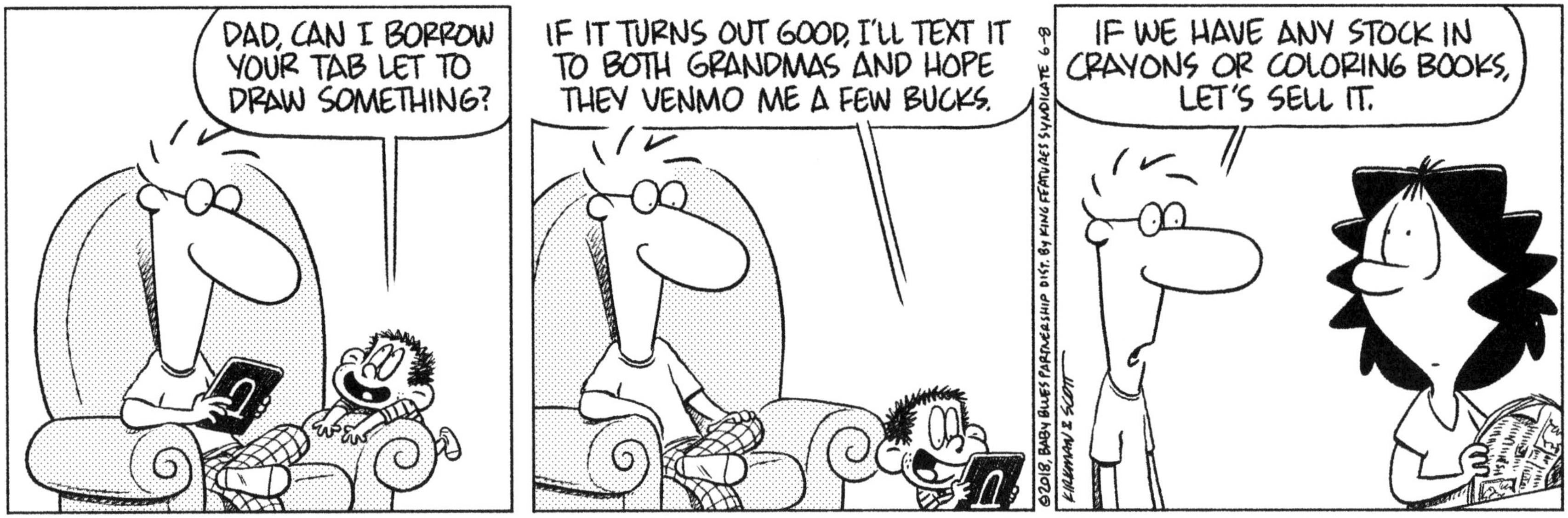
DAD, CAN I BORROW YOUR TAB LET TO DRAW SOMETHING?
IF IT TURNS OUT GOOD, I'LL TEXT IT TO BOTH GRANDMAS AND HOPE THEY VENMO ME A FEW BUCKS.
IF WE HAVE ANY STOCK IN CRAYONS OR COLORING BOOKS, LET'S SELL IT.
©2018, BABY BLUES PARTNERSHIP DIST. BY KING FEATURES SYNDICATE 6-8
KIRKMAN & SCOTT

Rick: New game: Find the mistake in the first panel. I'll wait. My internal spell-check must've been on the fritz.

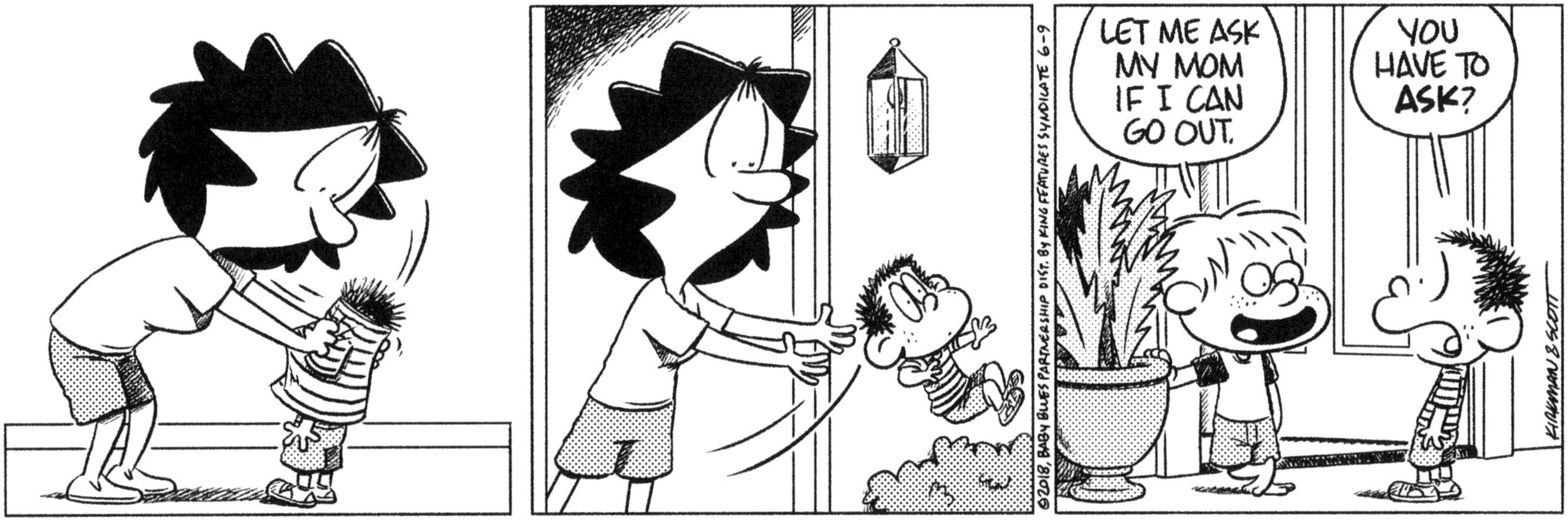
©2018, BABY BLUES PARTNERSHIP DIST. BY KING FEATURES SYNDICATE 6-9
LET ME ASK MY MOM IF I CAN GO OUT.
YOU HAVE TO **ASK**?
KIRKMAN & SCOTT

Jerry: This is pretty much how it was during my summer vacations.

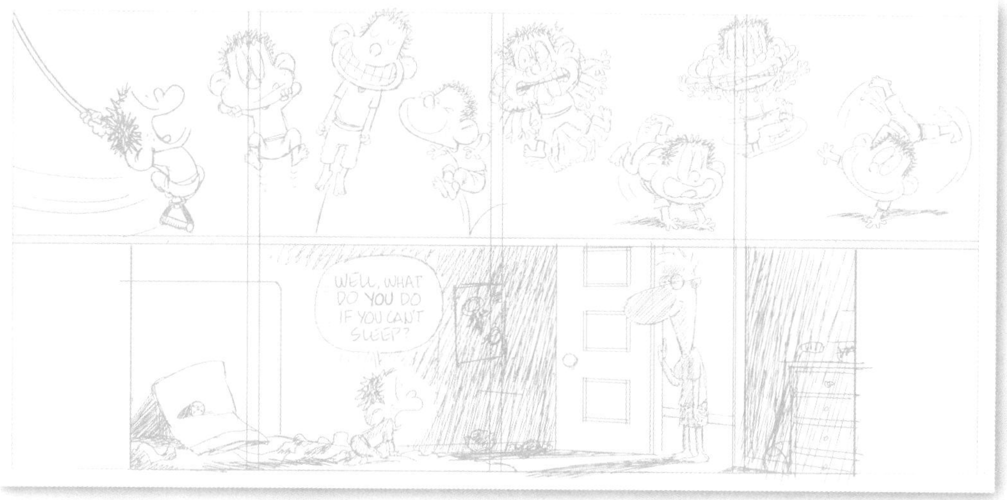
WELL, WHAT DO YOU DO IF YOU CAN'T SLEEP?

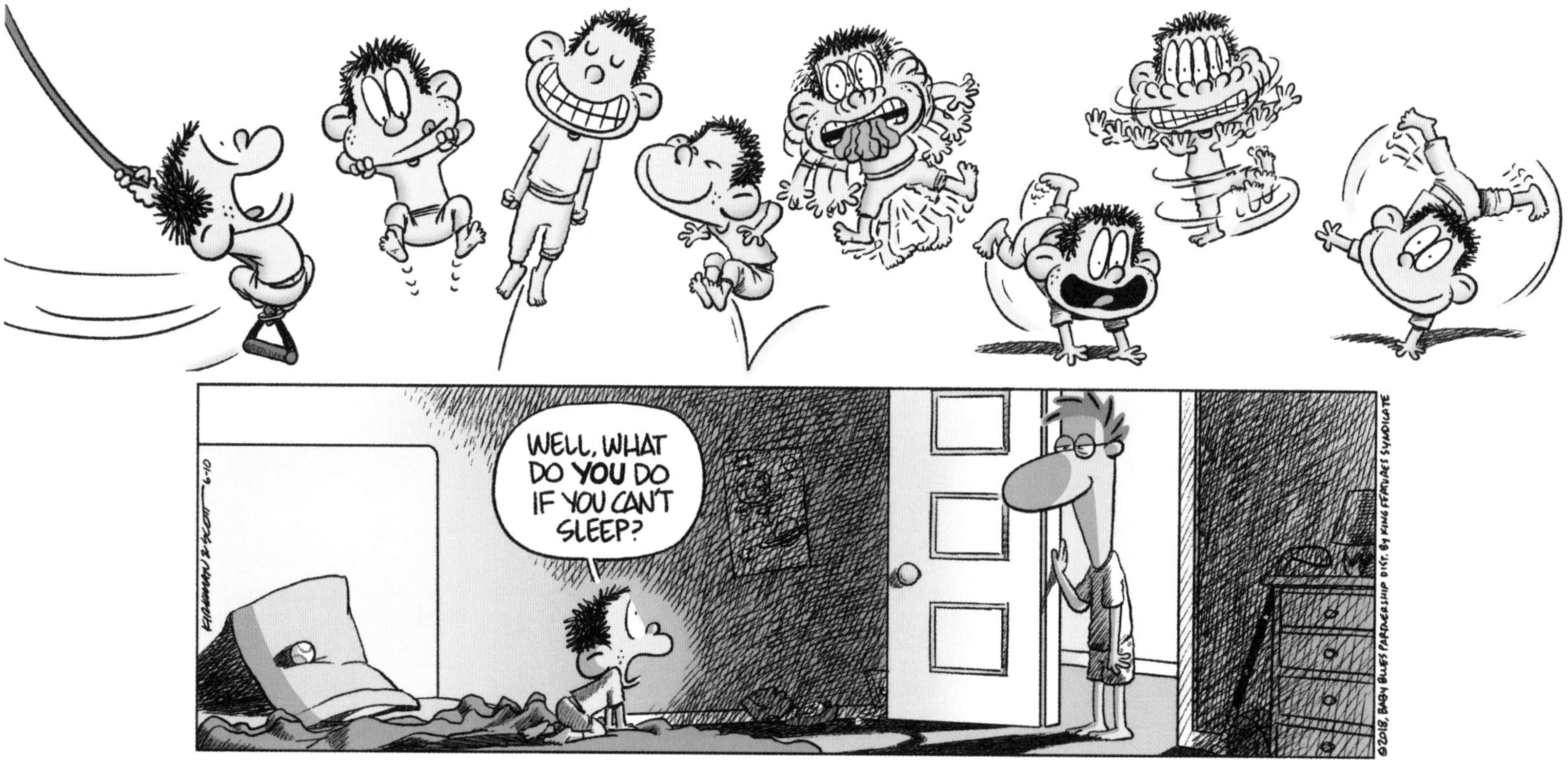
WELL, WHAT DO **YOU** DO IF YOU CAN'T SLEEP?
©2018, BABY BLUES PARTNERSHIP DIST. BY KING FEATURES SYNDICATE

Rick: One of my favorite things to draw: kid action. Back to Hammie's question: Not that. Even on my best day, I'd end up in the ER.

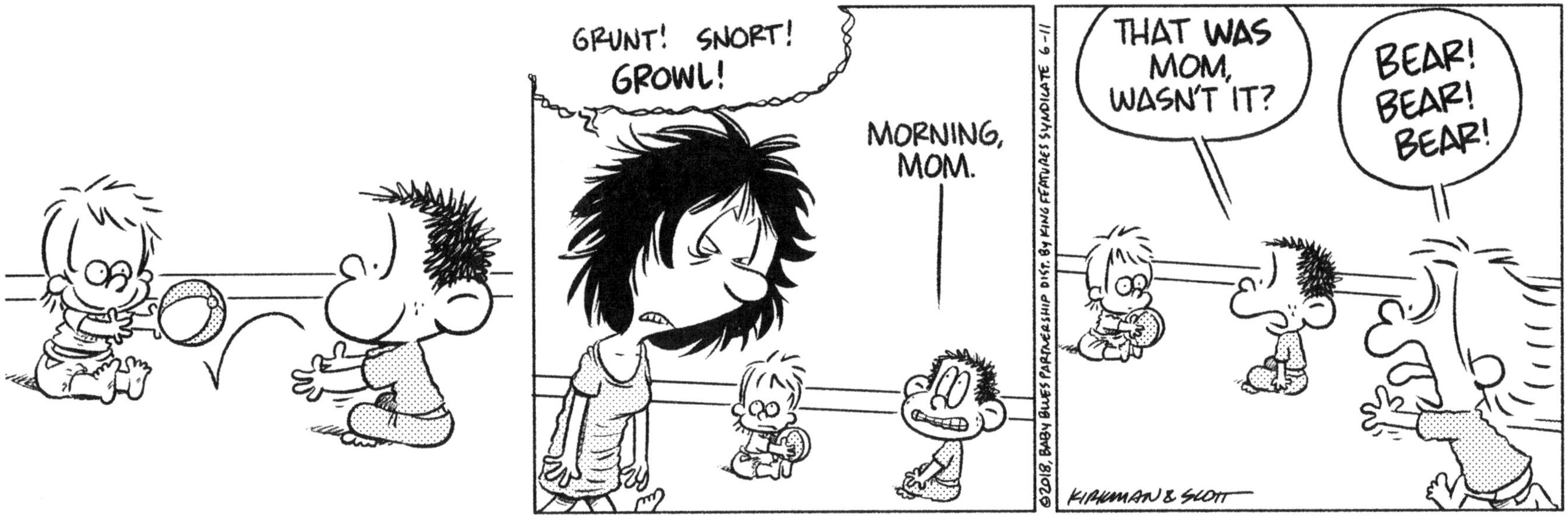
GRUNT! SNORT! GROWL!
MORNING, MOM.
©2018, BABY BLUES PARTNERSHIP DIST. BY KING FEATURES SYNDICATE 6-11
THAT WAS MOM, WASN'T IT?
BEAR! BEAR! BEAR!
KIRKMAN & SCOTT

Rick: I love Grizzled Wanda.

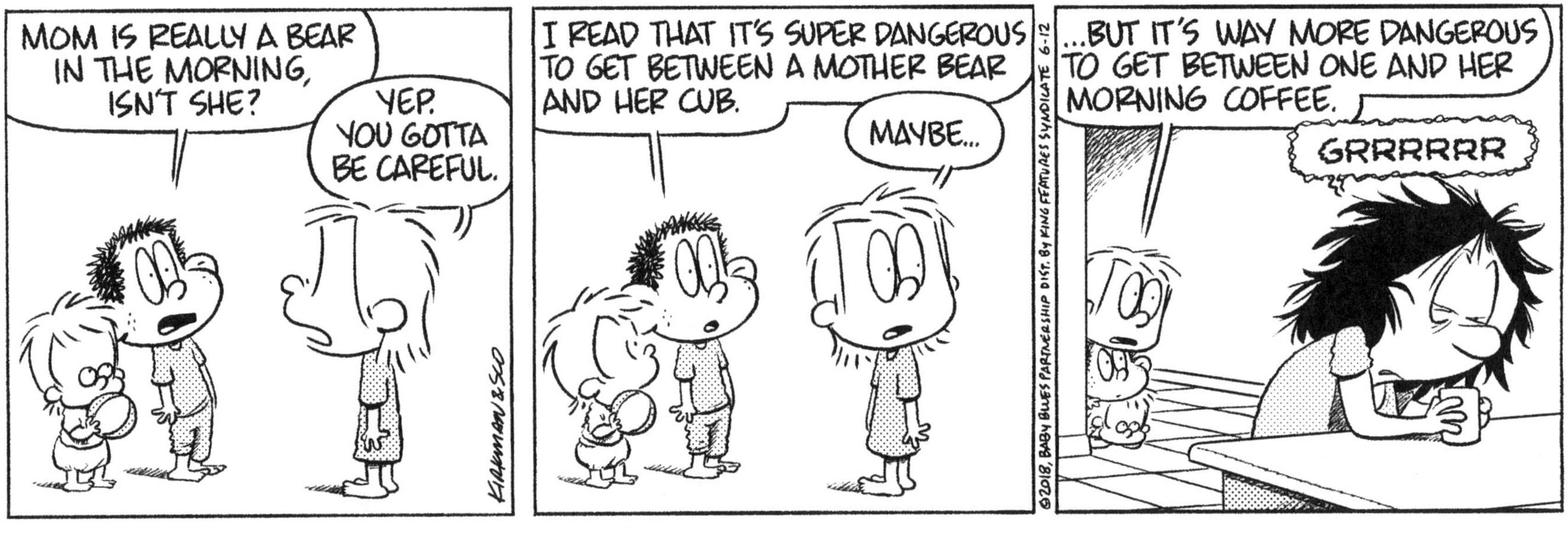
MOM IS REALLY A BEAR IN THE MORNING, ISN'T SHE?
YEP. YOU GOTTA BE CAREFUL.
KIRKMAN & SCO
I READ THAT IT'S SUPER DANGEROUS TO GET BETWEEN A MOTHER BEAR AND HER CUB.
MAYBE...
©2018, BABY BLUES PARTNERSHIP DIST. BY KING FEATURES SYNDICATE 6-12
...BUT IT'S WAY MORE DANGEROUS TO GET BETWEEN ONE AND HER MORNING COFFEE.
GRRRRRR

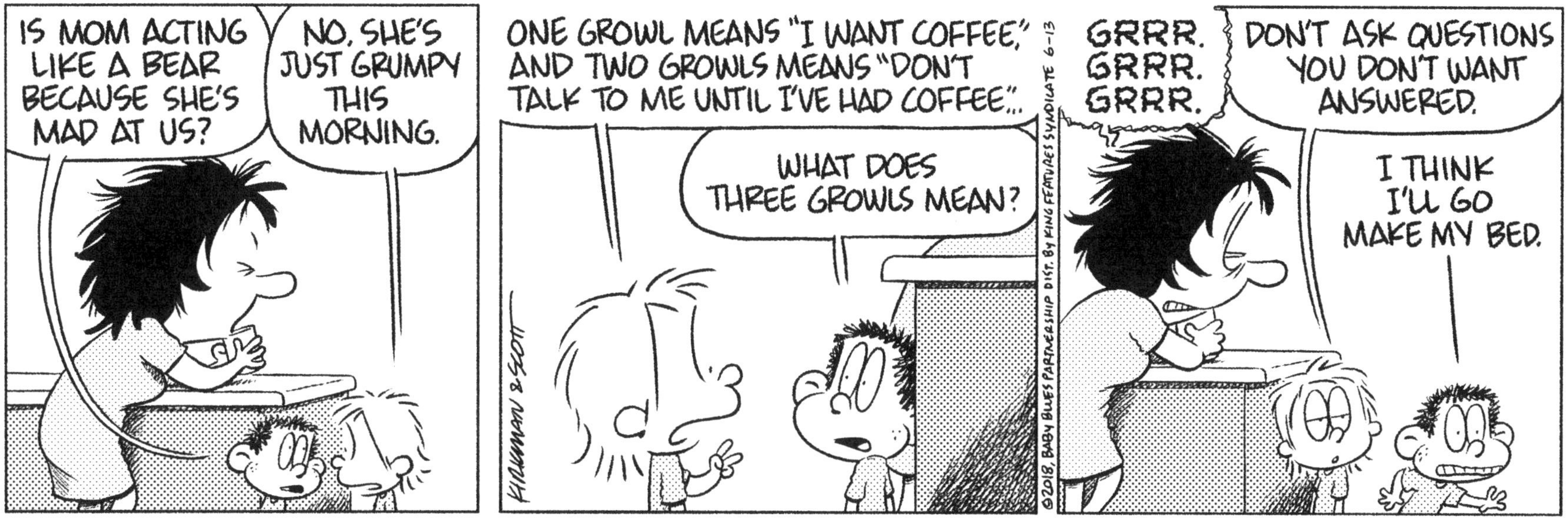
IS MOM ACTING LIKE A BEAR BECAUSE SHE'S MAD AT US?
NO, SHE'S JUST GRUMPY THIS MORNING.
ONE GROWL MEANS "I WANT COFFEE," AND TWO GROWLS MEANS "DON'T TALK TO ME UNTIL I'VE HAD COFFEE."...
WHAT DOES THREE GROWLS MEAN?
KIRKMAN & SCOTT
©2018, BABY BLUES PARTNERSHIP DIST. BY KING FEATURES SYNDICATE 6-13
GRRR. GRRR. GRRR.
DON'T ASK QUESTIONS YOU DON'T WANT ANSWERED.
I THINK I'LL GO MAKE MY BED.

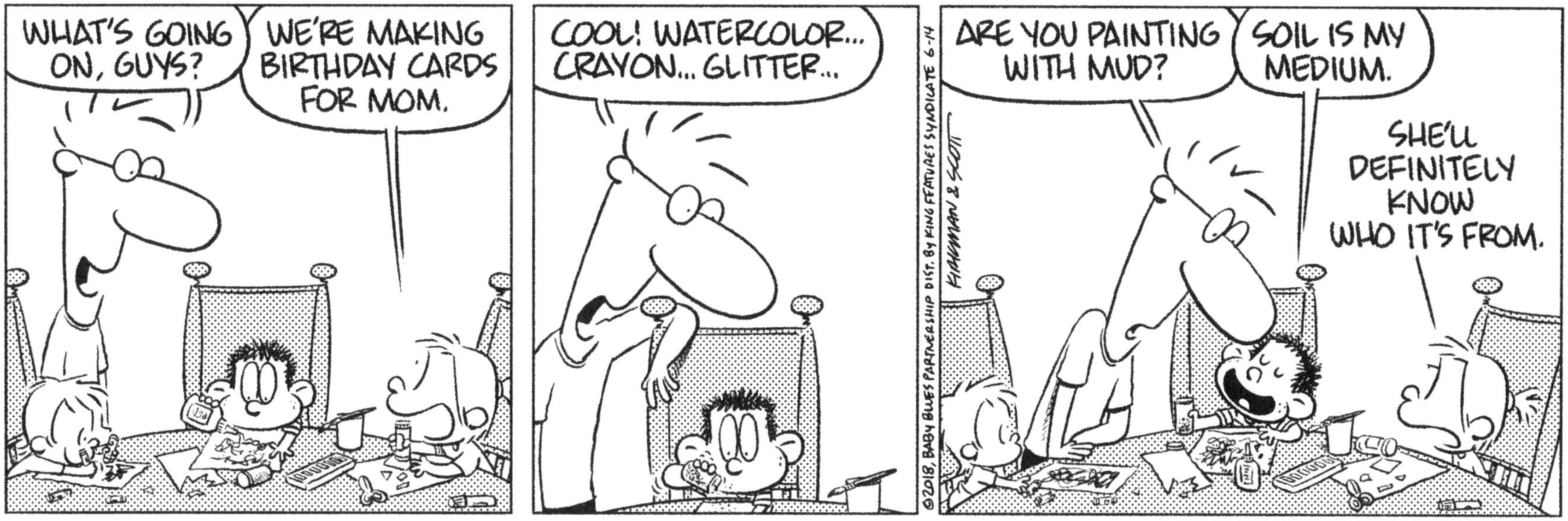
WHAT'S GOING ON, GUYS?
WE'RE MAKING BIRTHDAY CARDS FOR MOM.
COOL! WATERCOLOR... CRAYON... GLITTER...
©2018, BABY BLUES PARTNERSHIP DIST. BY KING FEATURES SYNDICATE 6-14
KIRKMAN & SCOTT
ARE YOU PAINTING WITH MUD?
SOIL IS MY MEDIUM.
SHE'LL DEFINITELY KNOW WHO IT'S FROM.

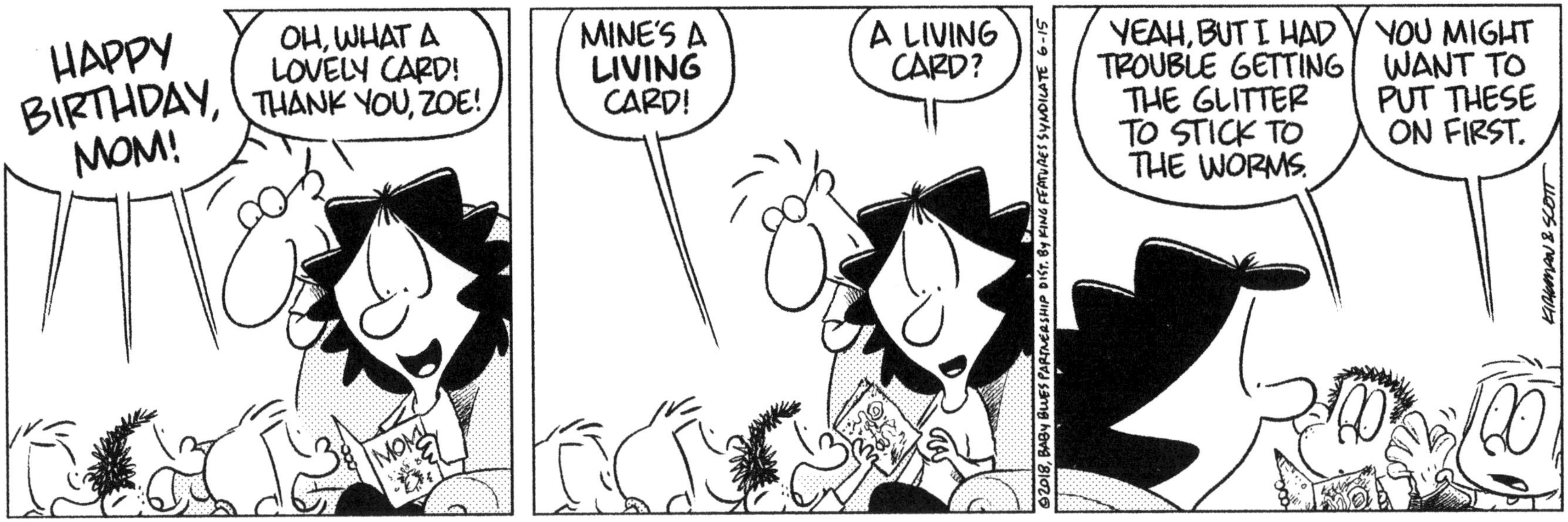
HAPPY BIRTHDAY, MOM!
OH, WHAT A LOVELY CARD! THANK YOU, ZOE!
MOM
MINE'S A **LIVING** CARD!
A LIVING CARD?
©2018, BABY BLUES PARTNERSHIP DIST. BY KING FEATURES SYNDICATE 6-15
YEAH, BUT I HAD TROUBLE GETTING THE GLITTER TO STICK TO THE WORMS.
YOU MIGHT WANT TO PUT THESE ON FIRST.
KIRKMAN & SCOTT

Jerry: You won't find a card like that at Hallmark.

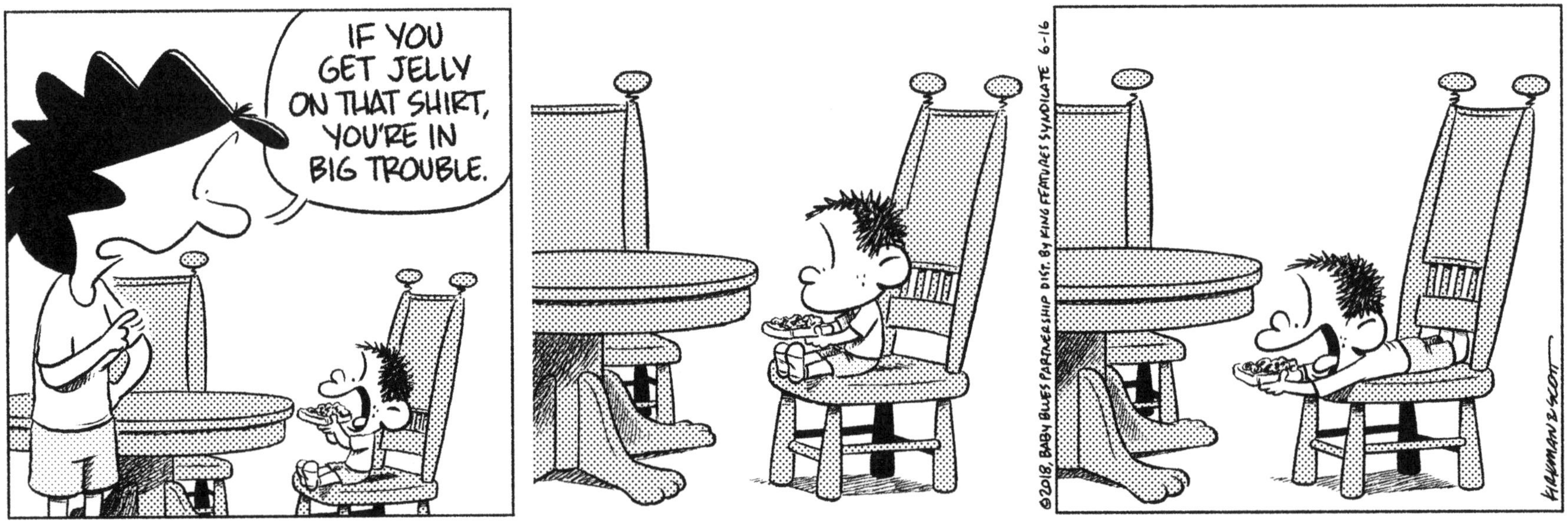
IF YOU GET JELLY ON THAT SHIRT, YOU'RE IN BIG TROUBLE.
©2018, BABY BLUES PARTNERSHIP DIST. BY KING FEATURES SYNDICATE 6-16
KIRKMAN & SCOTT

BABY BLUES®

by Rick Kirkman / Jerry Scott

WOW! NEW SWIM TRUNKS!
LET'S ALL GO TO THE LAKE SO DADDY CAN TRY THEM OUT!
YAY!
ICE
©2018, BABY BLUES PARTNERSHIP DIST. BY KING FEATURES SYNDICATE
WAS THERE A GROUPON DEAL ON THESE SWIM TRUNKS?
WHAT MAKES YOU THINK THAT?
KIRKMAN & SCOTT 6-17

Rick: Gags sometimes seem better when they're typed than when they're drawn. Seven emails later, the last-panel dialogue was ratified. And I had to apologize to my coloring assistant for that pattern.

Jerry: This is a peek into my wardrobe: Generic Dadwear On Sale.

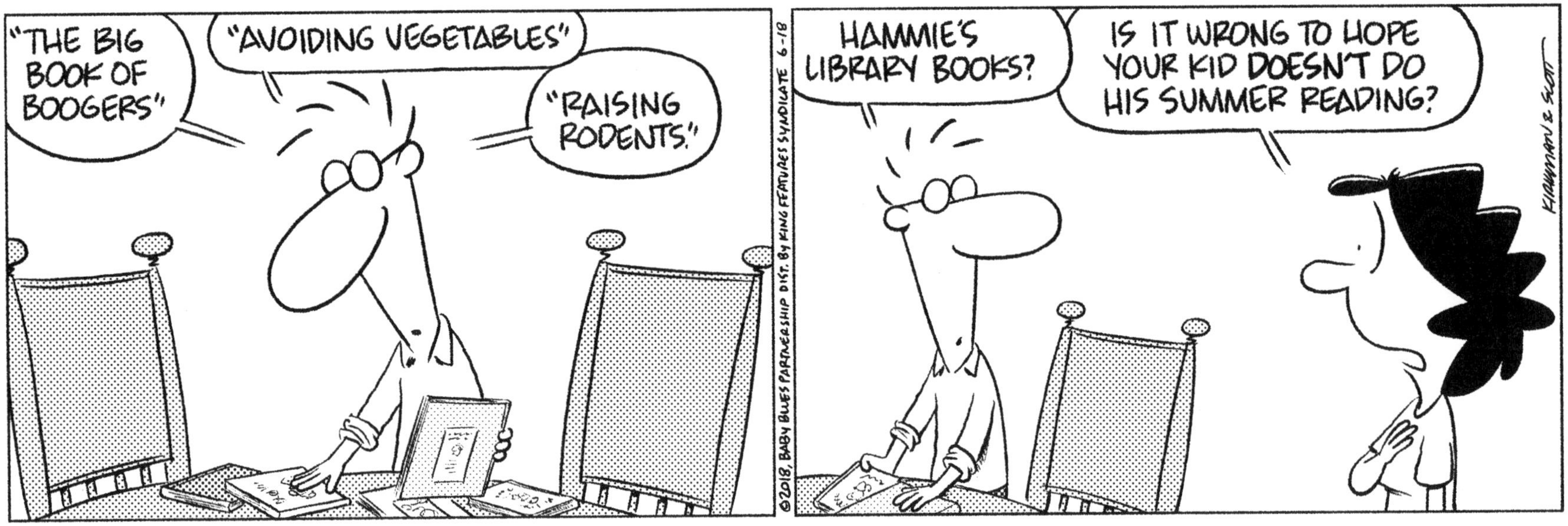
"THE BIG BOOK OF BOOGERS"
"AVOIDING VEGETABLES"
"RAISING RODENTS."
©2018, BABY BLUES PARTNERSHIP DIST. BY KING FEATURES SYNDICATE 6-18
HAMMIE'S LIBRARY BOOKS?
IS IT WRONG TO HOPE YOUR KID DOESN'T DO HIS SUMMER READING?
KIRKMAN & SCOTT

Rick: I'm sure that first book would be a big hit.

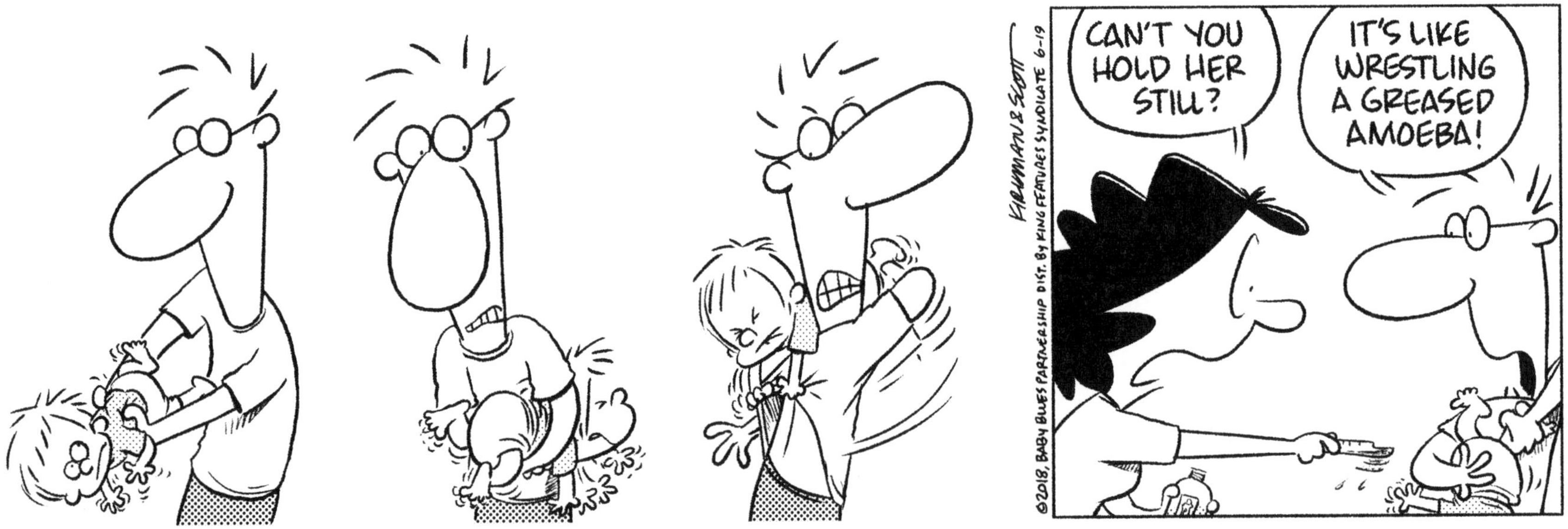
KIRKMAN & SCOTT
©2018, BABY BLUES PARTNERSHIP DIST. BY KING FEATURES SYNDICATE 6-19
CAN'T YOU HOLD HER STILL?
IT'S LIKE WRESTLING A GREASED AMOEBA!

Rick: Wow. This one takes me back.

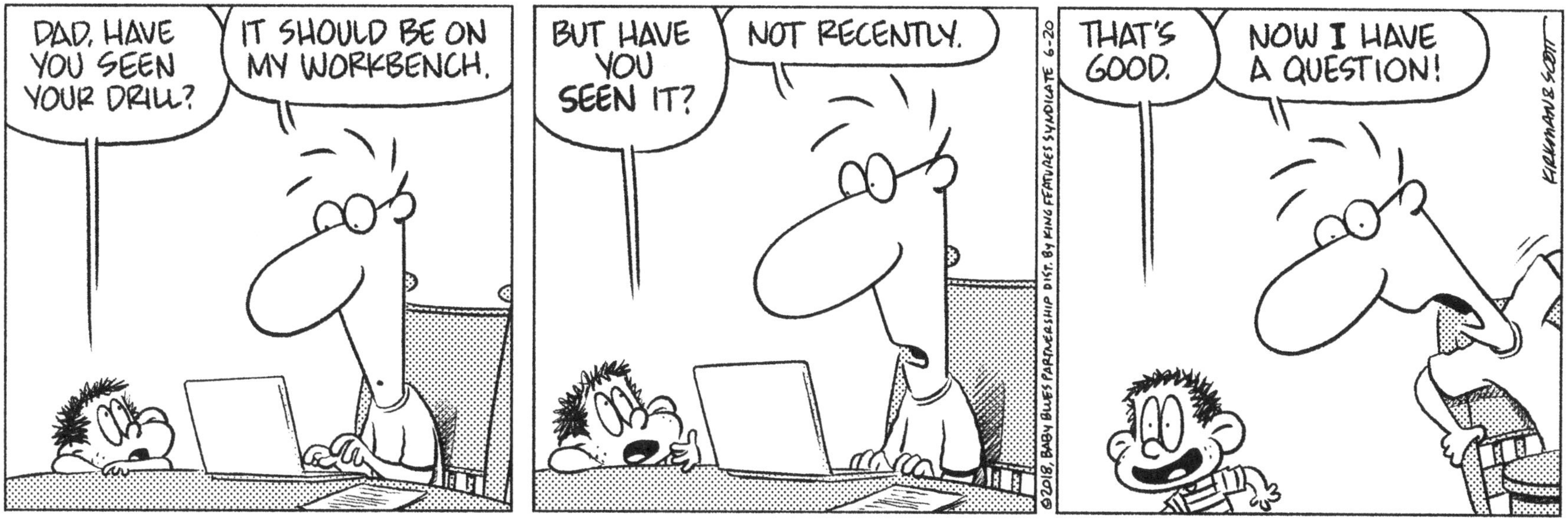
DAD, HAVE YOU SEEN YOUR DRILL?
IT SHOULD BE ON MY WORKBENCH.
BUT HAVE YOU SEEN IT?
NOT RECENTLY.
©2018, BABY BLUES PARTNERSHIP DIST. BY KING FEATURES SYNDICATE 6-20
THAT'S GOOD.
NOW I HAVE A QUESTION!
KIRKMAN & SCOTT

Rick: There should be a name for this kind of question: one where you only want a literal answer to avoid self-incrimination.

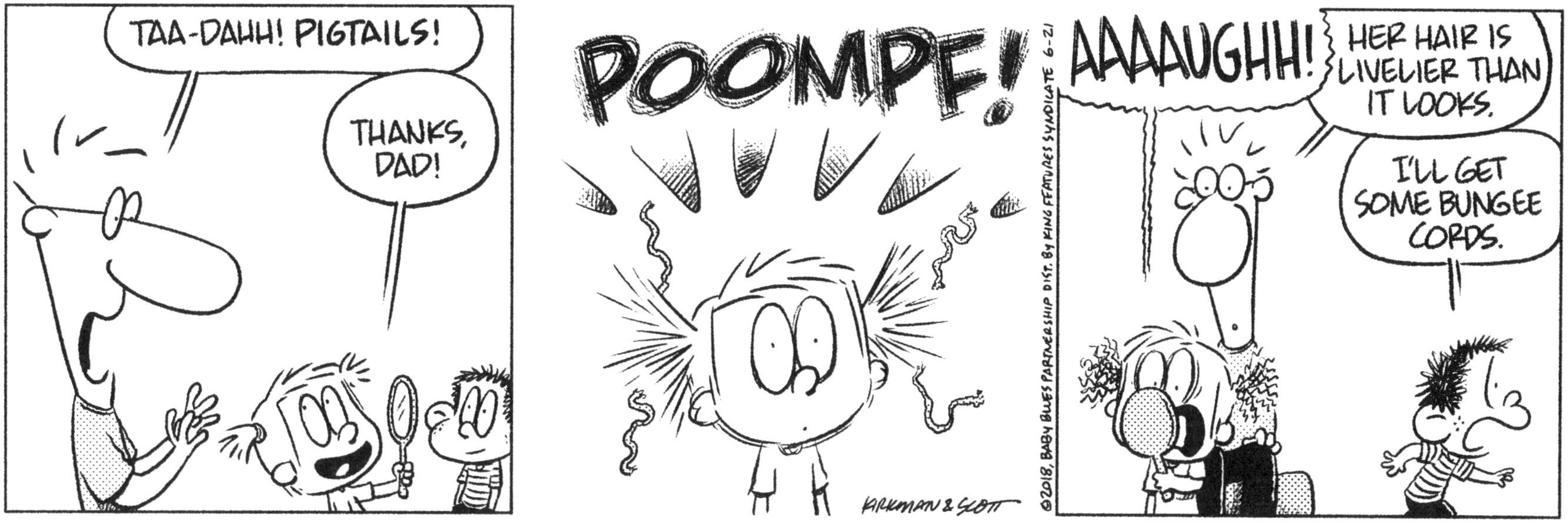
TAA-DAHH! PIGTAILS!
THANKS, DAD!
POOMPF!
KIRKMAN & SCOTT
©2018, BABY BLUES PARTNERSHIP DIST. BY KING FEATURES SYNDICATE 6-21
AAAAUGHH!
HER HAIR IS LIVELIER THAN IT LOOKS.
I'LL GET SOME BUNGEE CORDS.

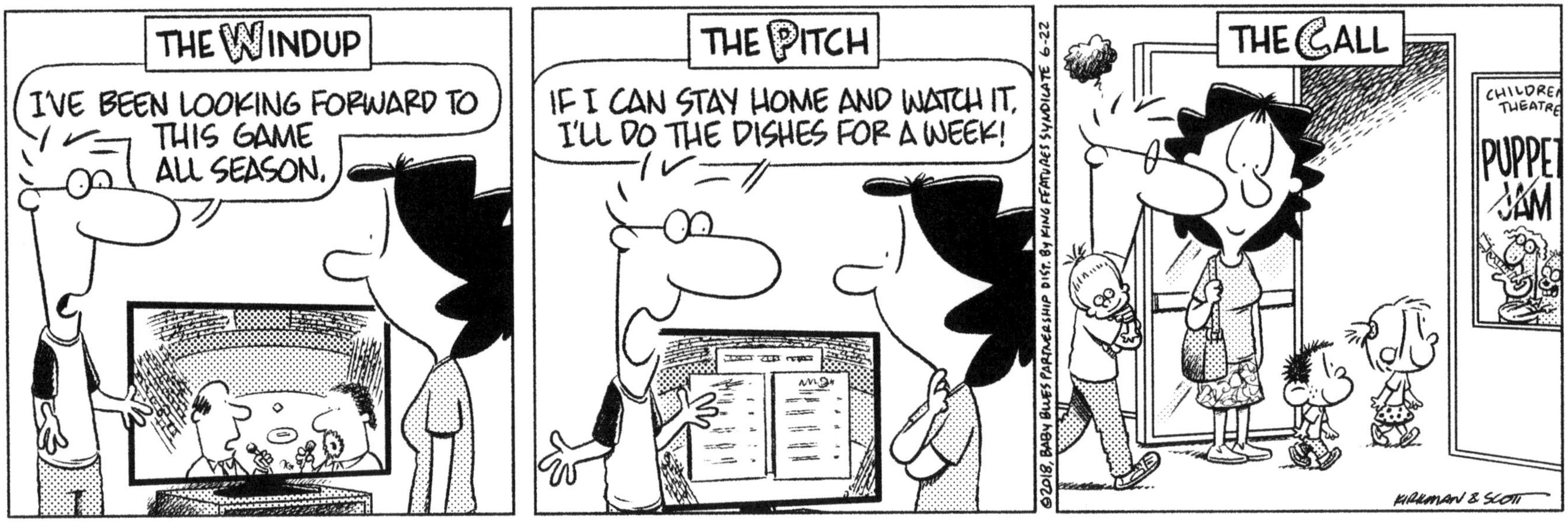
THE WINDUP
I'VE BEEN LOOKING FORWARD TO THIS GAME ALL SEASON.
THE PITCH
IF I CAN STAY HOME AND WATCH IT, I'LL DO THE DISHES FOR A WEEK!
THE CALL
CHILDREN THEATRE
PUPPET JAM
©2018, BABY BLUES PARTNERSHIP DIST. BY KING FEATURES SYNDICATE 6-22
KIRKMAN & SCOTT

Rick: It's not just baseball where you can't argue balls and strikes.

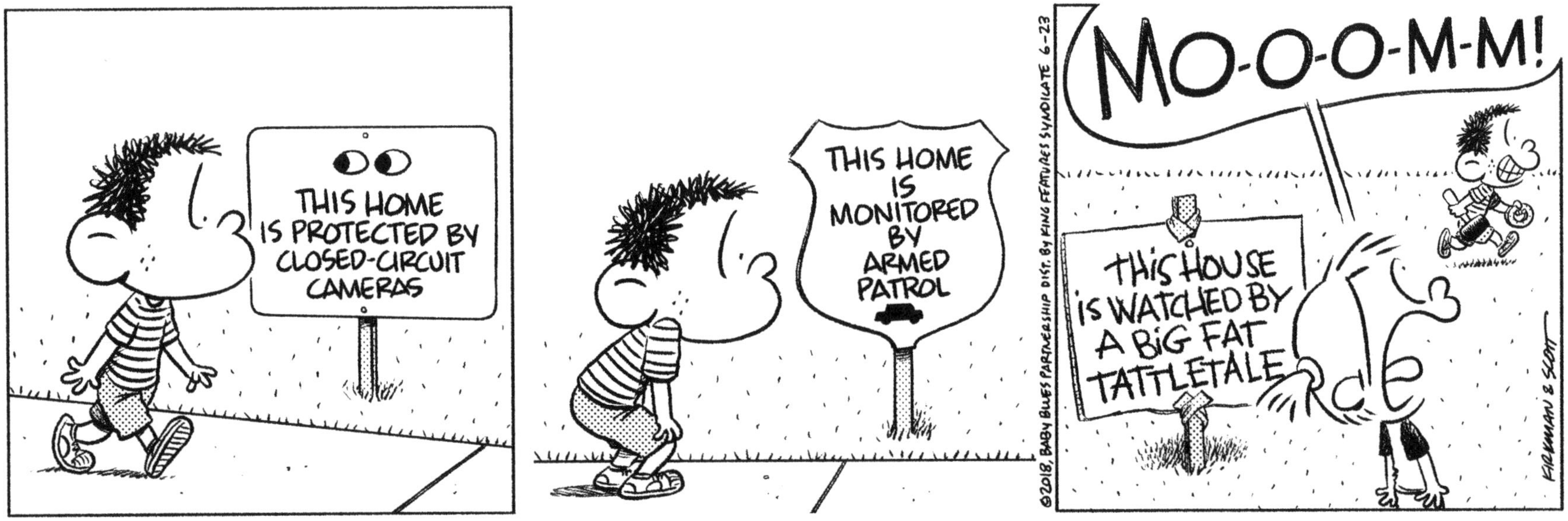
THIS HOME IS PROTECTED BY CLOSED-CIRCUIT CAMERAS
THIS HOME IS MONITORED BY ARMED PATROL
MO-O-O-M-M!
THIS HOUSE IS WATCHED BY A BIG FAT TATTLETALE
©2018, BABY BLUES PARTNERSHIP DIST. BY KING FEATURES SYNDICATE 6-23
KIRKMAN & SCOTT

BIP!
BOOP!
BEP!

BIP!
BOOP!
BEP!
GROAN! HI, DAR-RYL.
HEY, SWEETIE. WHAT'S NEW?
©2018, BABY BLUES PARTNERSHIP DIST. BY KING FEATURES SYNDICATE
NOT TOO MUCH. BUT MY ABS ARE KILLING ME.
DID YOU GO TO THE GYM?
OOF! NO.
NEW WORKOUT VIDEO?
UNH! NO.
CRUNCHES?
OW. SOME-THING LIKE THAT.
SQUISHY!
KIRKMAN & SCOTT 6-24

Rick: P90-OWW!

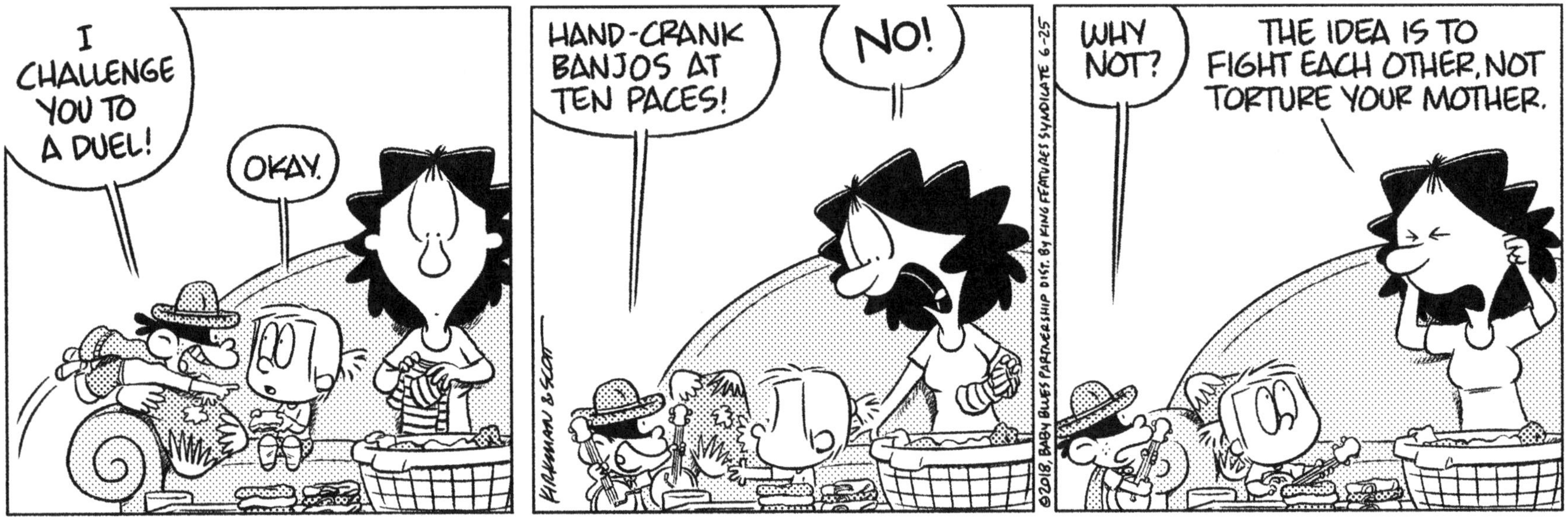
I CHALLENGE YOU TO A DUEL!
OKAY.
HAND-CRANK BANJOS AT TEN PACES!
NO!
WHY NOT?
THE IDEA IS TO FIGHT EACH OTHER, NOT TORTURE YOUR MOTHER.
KIRKMAN & SCOTT
©2018, BABY BLUES PARTNERSHIP DIST. BY KING FEATURES SYNDICATE 6-25

Rick: Now that's dueling banjos.

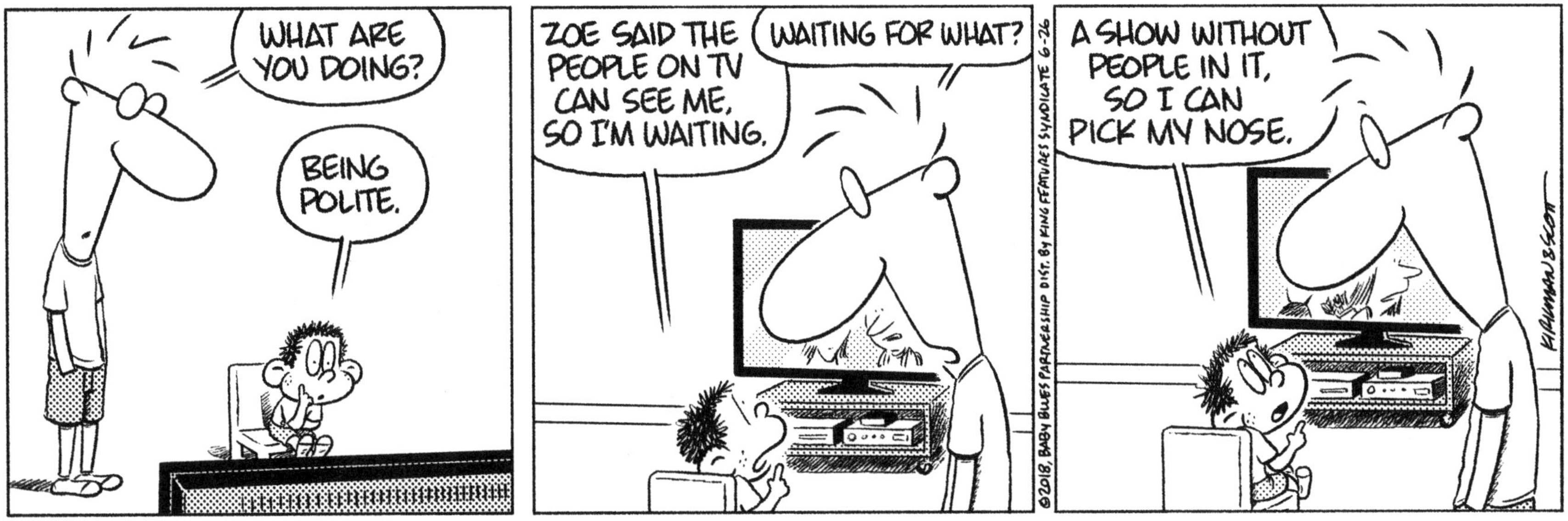
WHAT ARE YOU DOING?
BEING POLITE.
ZOE SAID THE PEOPLE ON TV CAN SEE ME, SO I'M WAITING.
WAITING FOR WHAT?
A SHOW WITHOUT PEOPLE IN IT, SO I CAN PICK MY NOSE.
KIRKMAN & SCOTT
©2018, BABY BLUES PARTNERSHIP DIST. BY KING FEATURES SYNDICATE 6-26

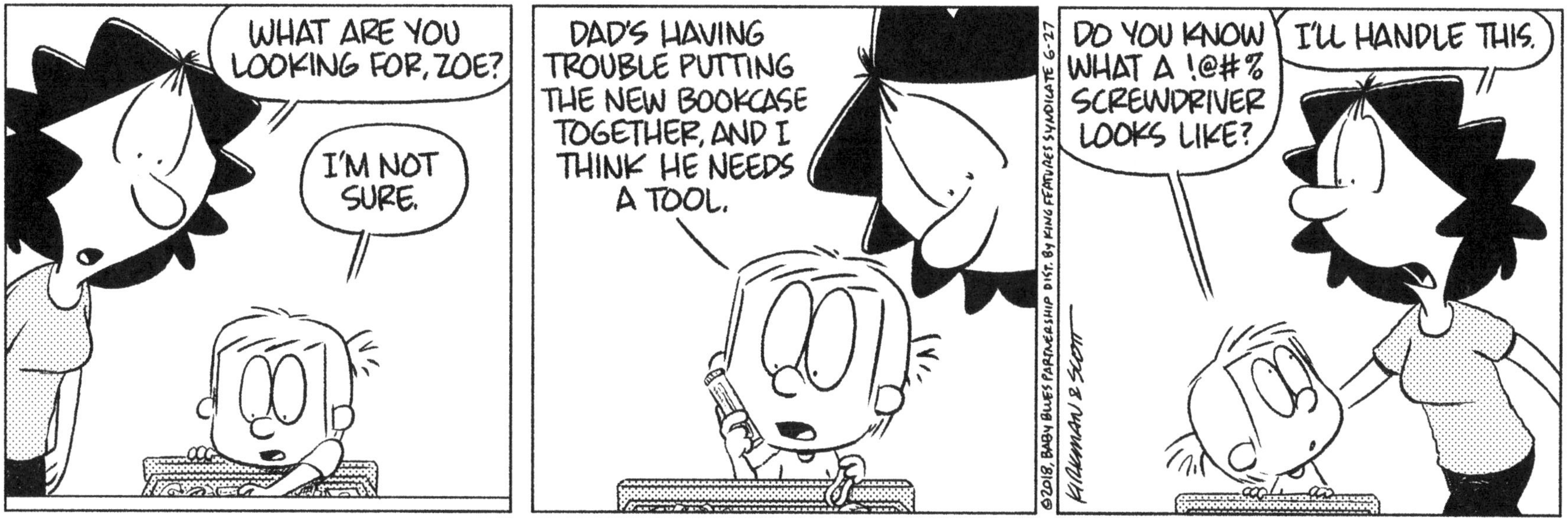
WHAT ARE YOU LOOKING FOR, ZOE?
I'M NOT SURE.
DAD'S HAVING TROUBLE PUTTING THE NEW BOOKCASE TOGETHER, AND I THINK HE NEEDS A TOOL.
©2018, BABY BLUES PARTNERSHIP DIST. BY KING FEATURES SYNDICATE 6-27
KIRKMAN & SCOTT
DO YOU KNOW WHAT A !@#% SCREWDRIVER LOOKS LIKE?
I'LL HANDLE THIS.

Jerry: The !@#% screwdriver is one of my most useful tools.

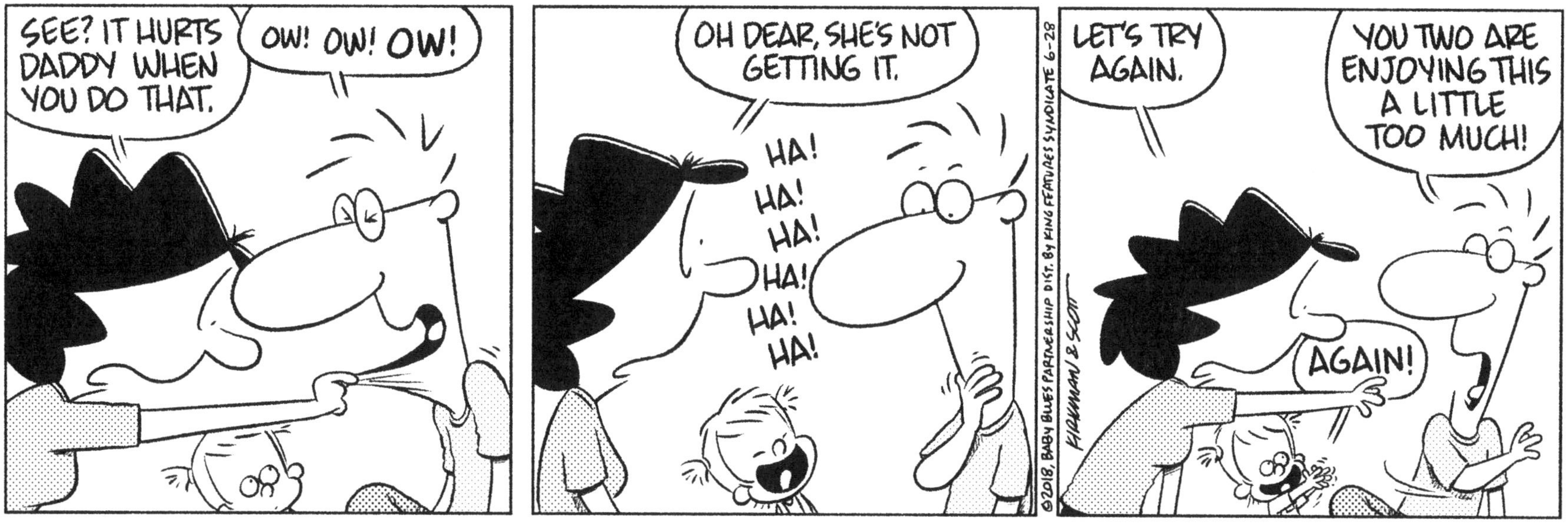
SEE? IT HURTS DADDY WHEN YOU DO THAT.
OW! OW! OW!
OH DEAR, SHE'S NOT GETTING IT.
HA! HA! HA! HA! HA! HA!
©2018, BABY BLUES PARTNERSHIP DIST. BY KING FEATURES SYNDICATE 6-28
KIRKMAN & SCOTT
LET'S TRY AGAIN.
YOU TWO ARE ENJOYING THIS A LITTLE TOO MUCH!
AGAIN!

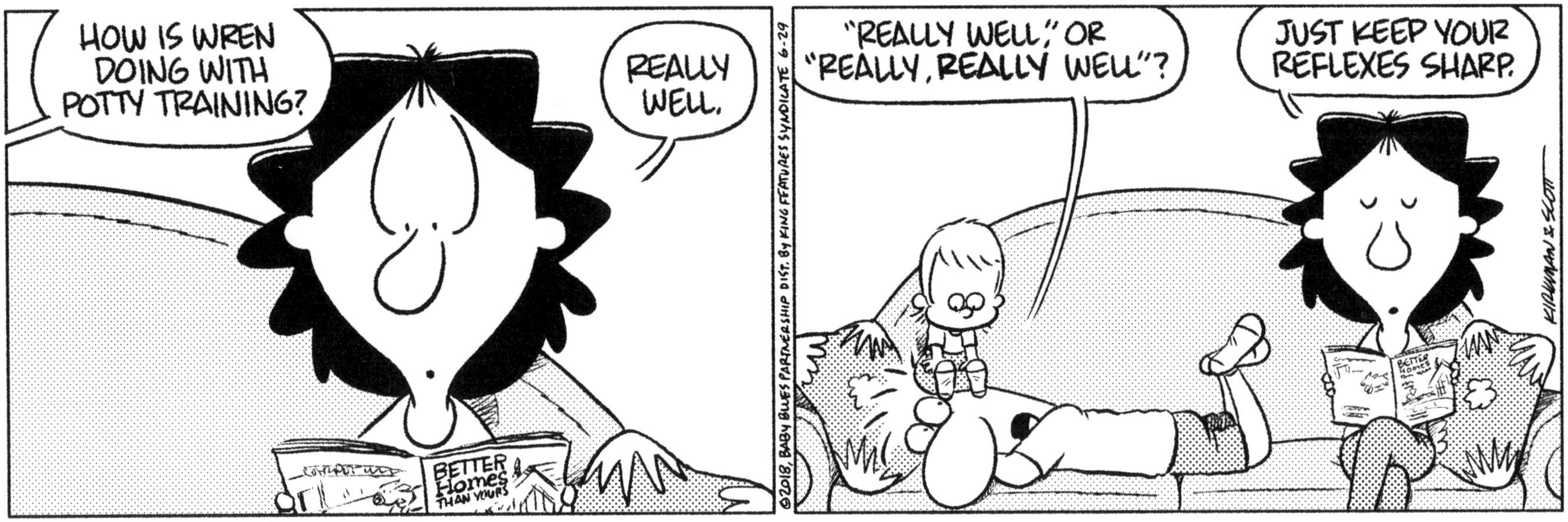
HOW IS WREN DOING WITH POTTY TRAINING?
REALLY WELL.
©2018, BABY BLUES PARTNERSHIP DIST. BY KING FEATURES SYNDICATE 6-29
"REALLY WELL," OR "REALLY, REALLY WELL"?
JUST KEEP YOUR REFLEXES SHARP.
BETTER Homes THAN YOURS
KIRKMAN & SCOTT

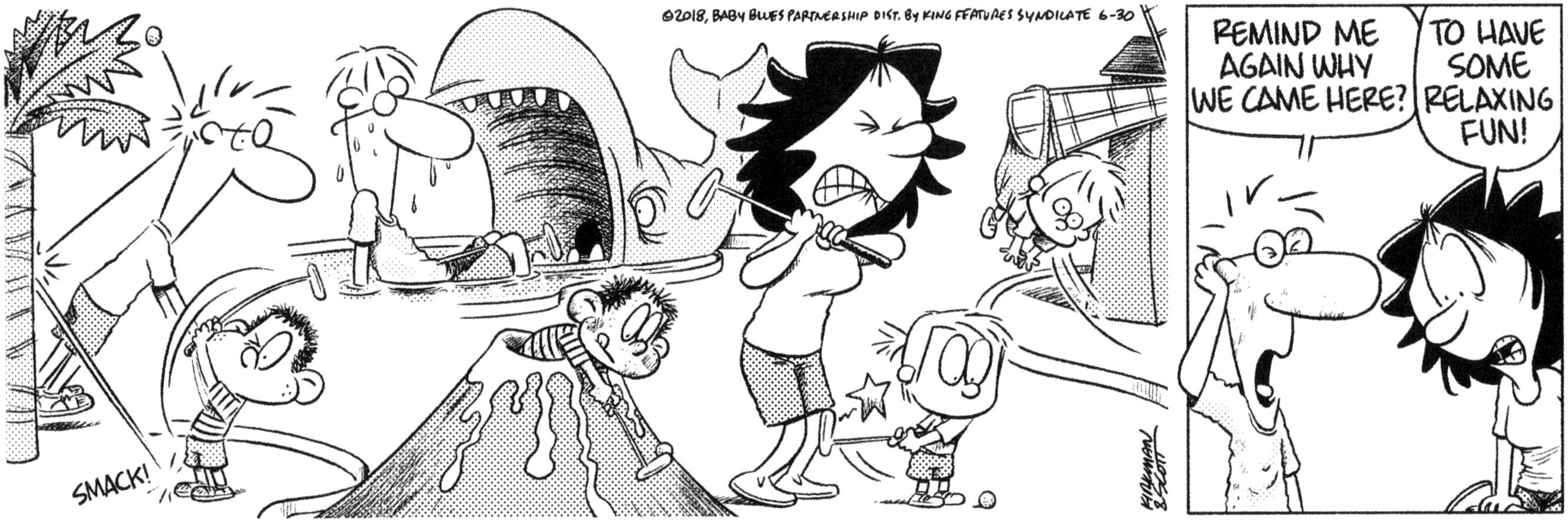
©2018, BABY BLUES PARTNERSHIP DIST. BY KING FEATURES SYNDICATE 6-30
SMACK!
KIRKMAN & SCOTT
REMIND ME AGAIN WHY WE CAME HERE?
TO HAVE SOME RELAXING FUN!

Rick: This goofy golf strip was a lot of fun to draw, to get in all the action and locations and imply the serpentine course with very little room.

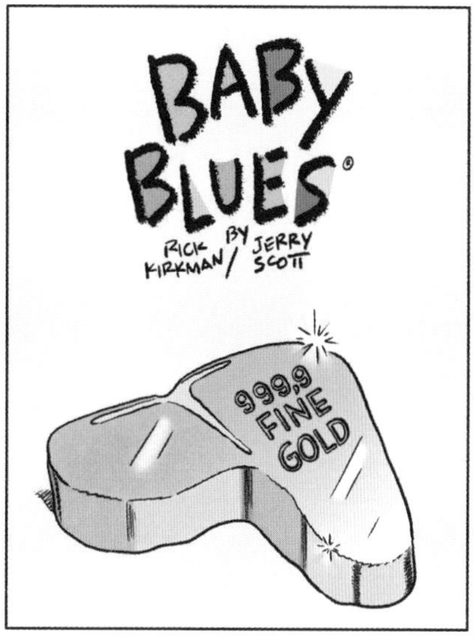
BABY BLUES®
BY RICK KIRKMAN / JERRY SCOTT
999.9 FINE GOLD

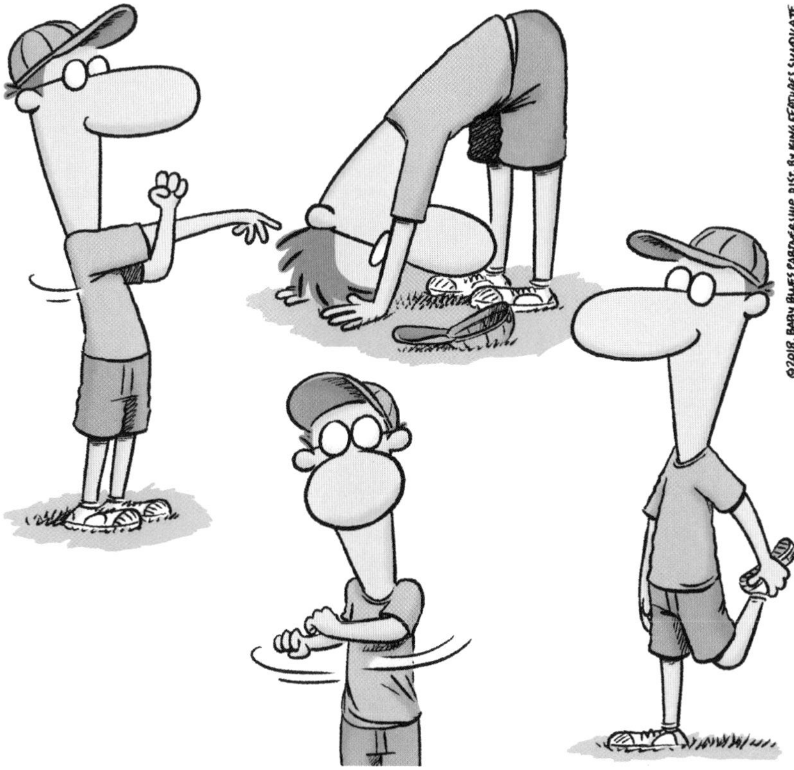

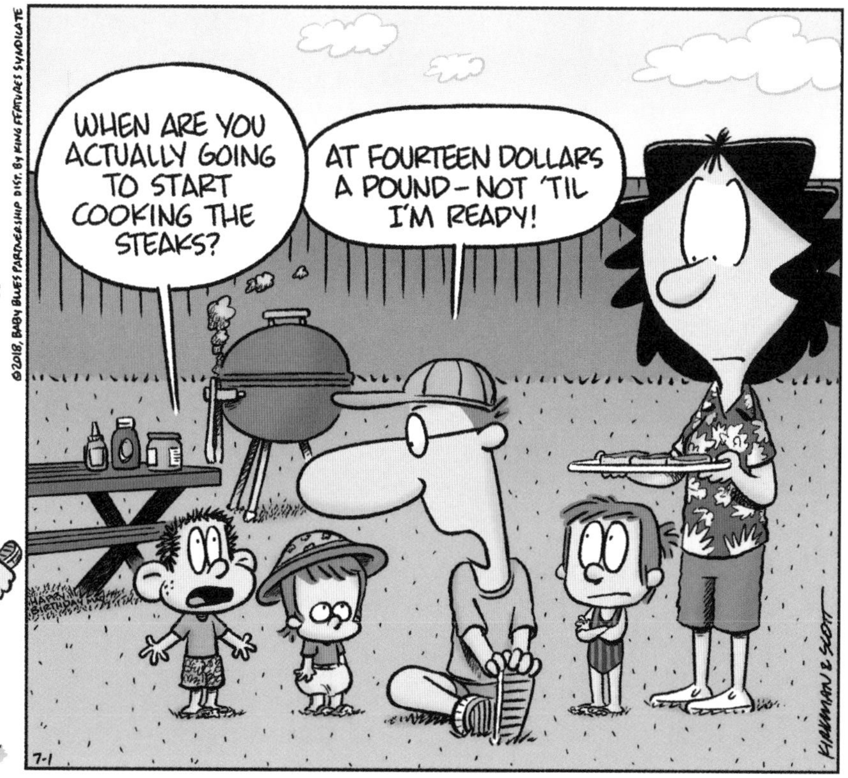
©2018, BABY BLUES PARTNERSHIP DIST. BY KING FEATURES SYNDICATE
WHEN ARE YOU ACTUALLY GOING TO START COOKING THE STEAKS?
AT FOURTEEN DOLLARS A POUND–NOT 'TIL I'M READY!
7-1
KIRKMAN & SCOTT

Rick: Now that I see it in print, I think I'll be changing my stretching routine.

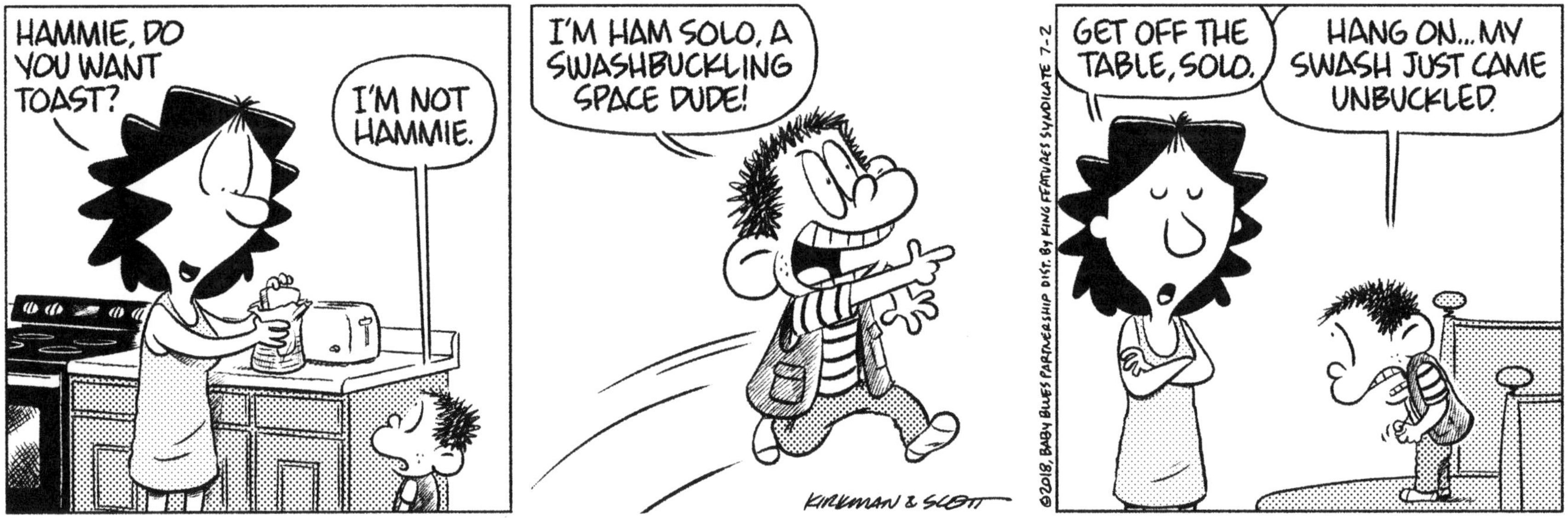
HAMMIE, DO YOU WANT TOAST?
I'M NOT HAMMIE.
I'M HAM SOLO, A SWASHBUCKLING SPACE DUDE!
KIRKMAN & SCOTT
©2018, BABY BLUES PARTNERSHIP DIST. BY KING FEATURES SYNDICATE 7-2
GET OFF THE TABLE, SOLO.
HANG ON... MY SWASH JUST CAME UNBUCKLED.

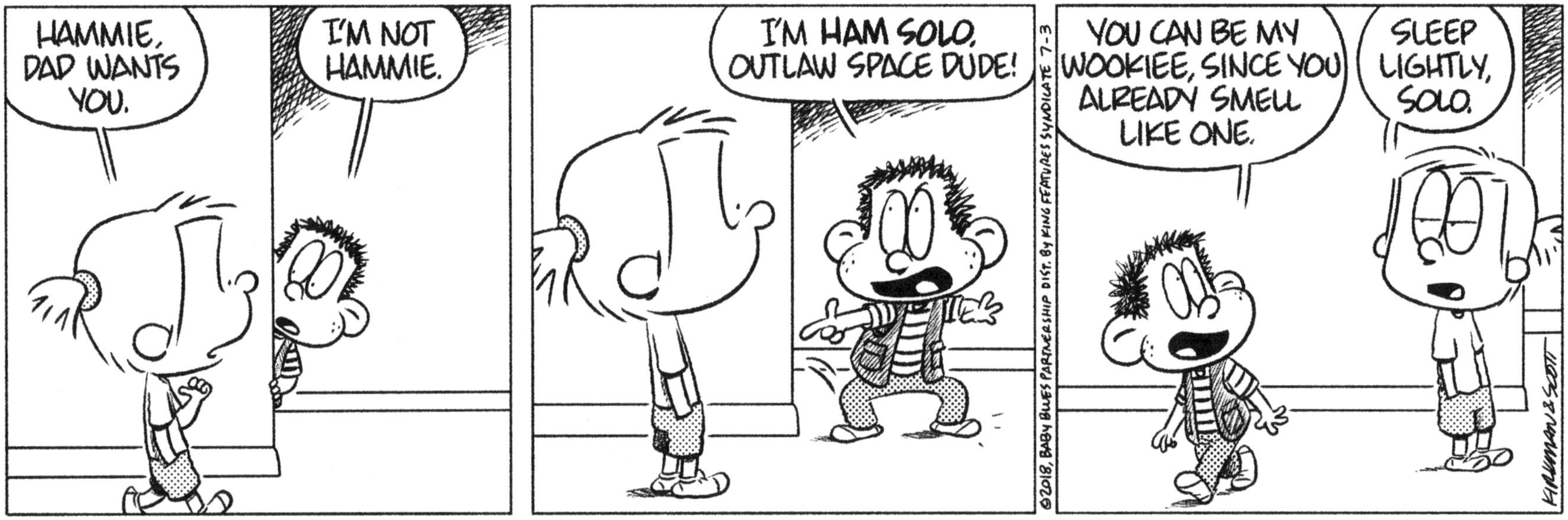
HAMMIE, DAD WANTS YOU.
I'M NOT HAMMIE.
I'M HAM SOLO, OUTLAW SPACE DUDE!
©2018, BABY BLUES PARTNERSHIP DIST. BY KING FEATURES SYNDICATE 7-3
YOU CAN BE MY WOOKIEE, SINCE YOU ALREADY SMELL LIKE ONE.
SLEEP LIGHTLY, SOLO.
KIRKMAN & SCOTT

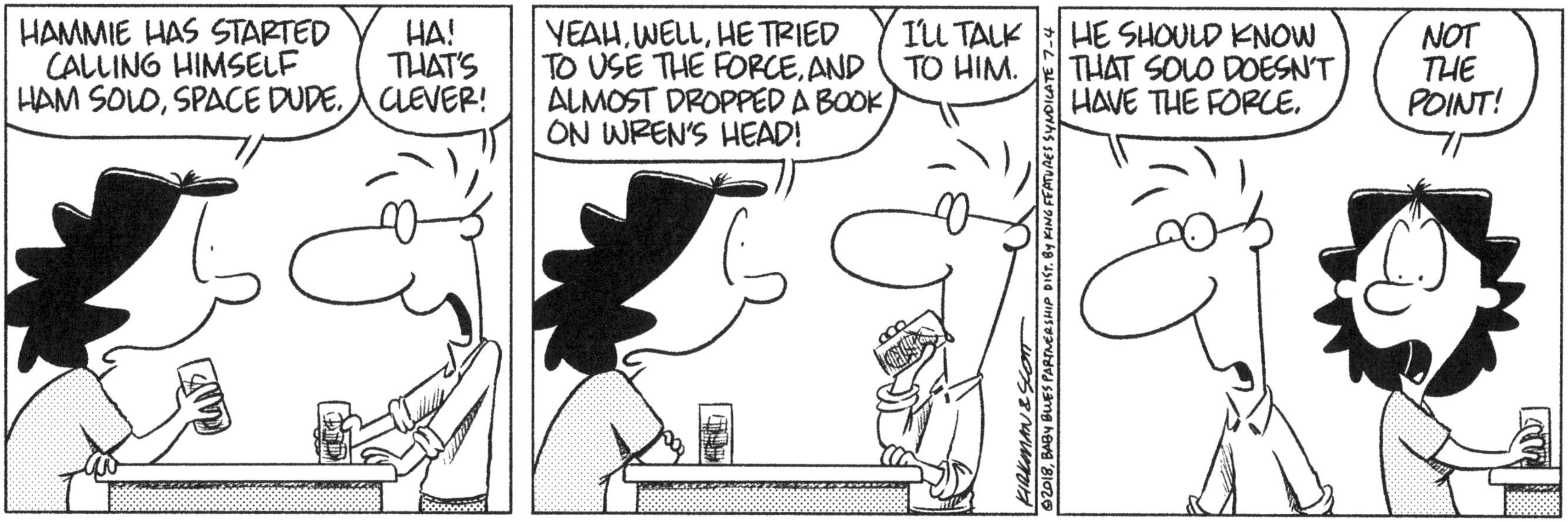
HAMMIE HAS STARTED CALLING HIMSELF HAM SOLO, SPACE DUDE.
HA! THAT'S CLEVER!
YEAH, WELL, HE TRIED TO USE THE FORCE, AND ALMOST DROPPED A BOOK ON WREN'S HEAD!
I'LL TALK TO HIM.
KIRKMAN & SCOTT
©2018, BABY BLUES PARTNERSHIP DIST. BY KING FEATURES SYNDICATE 7-4
HE SHOULD KNOW THAT SOLO DOESN'T HAVE THE FORCE.
NOT THE POINT!

Rick: Hard to get a nerd to focus on anything else when *Star Wars* is mentioned.

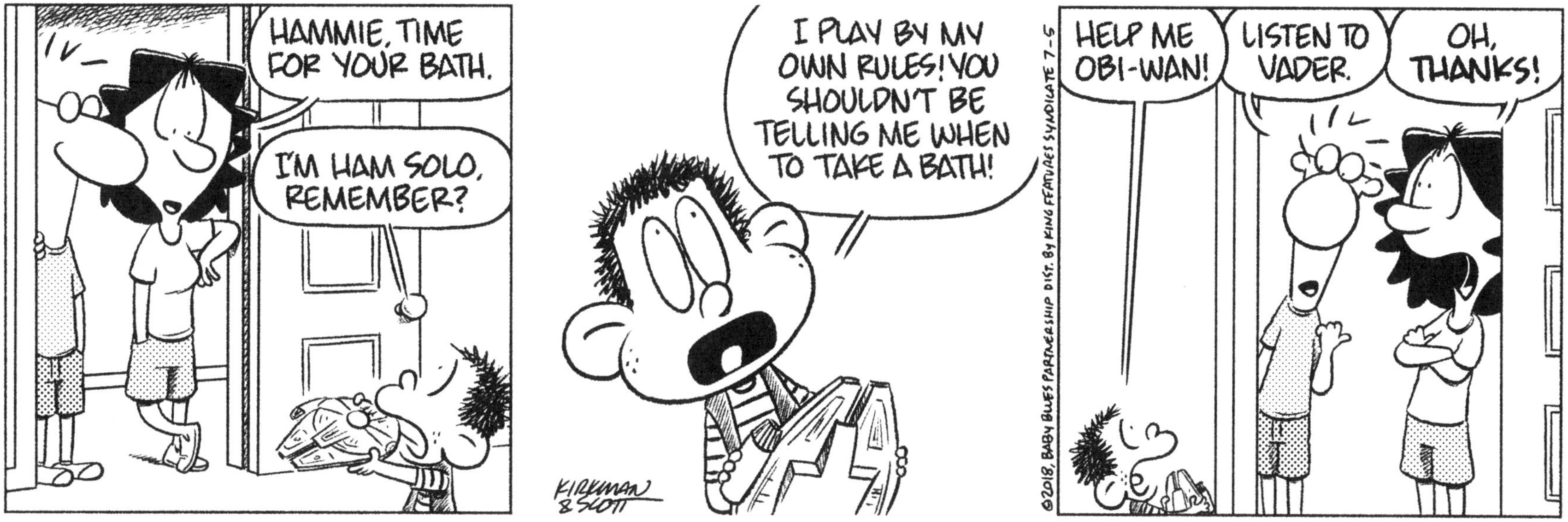
HAMMIE, TIME FOR YOUR BATH.
I'M HAM SOLO, REMEMBER?
I PLAY BY MY OWN RULES! YOU SHOULDN'T BE TELLING ME WHEN TO TAKE A BATH!
KIRKMAN & SCOTT
©2018, BABY BLUES PARTNERSHIP DIST. BY KING FEATURES SYNDICATE 7-5
HELP ME OBI-WAN!
LISTEN TO VADER.
OH, THANKS!

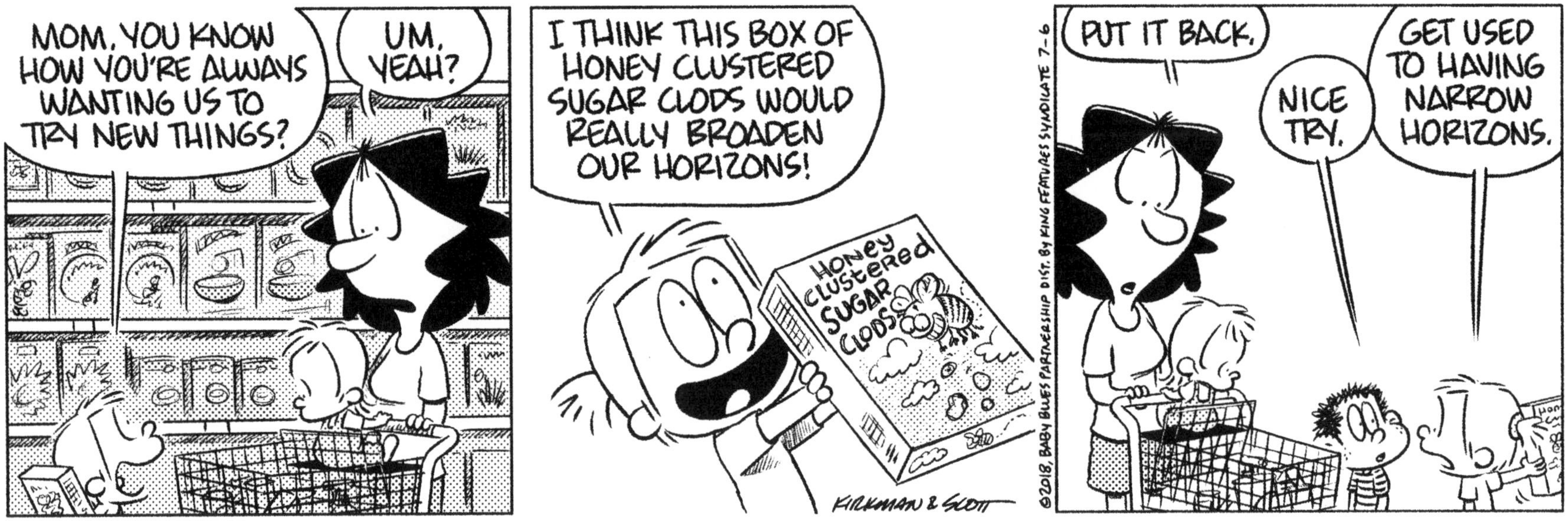
MOM, YOU KNOW HOW YOU'RE ALWAYS WANTING US TO TRY NEW THINGS?
UM, YEAH?
I THINK THIS BOX OF HONEY CLUSTERED SUGAR CLODS WOULD REALLY BROADEN OUR HORIZONS!
Honey Clustered SUGAR CLODS
KIRKMAN & SCOTT
©2018, BABY BLUES PARTNERSHIP DIST. BY KING FEATURES SYNDICATE 7-6
PUT IT BACK.
NICE TRY.
GET USED TO HAVING NARROW HORIZONS.

Rick: Great cereal name, Jer.

Jerry: Honey Clustered Sugar Clods would be good with chocolate milk, I bet.

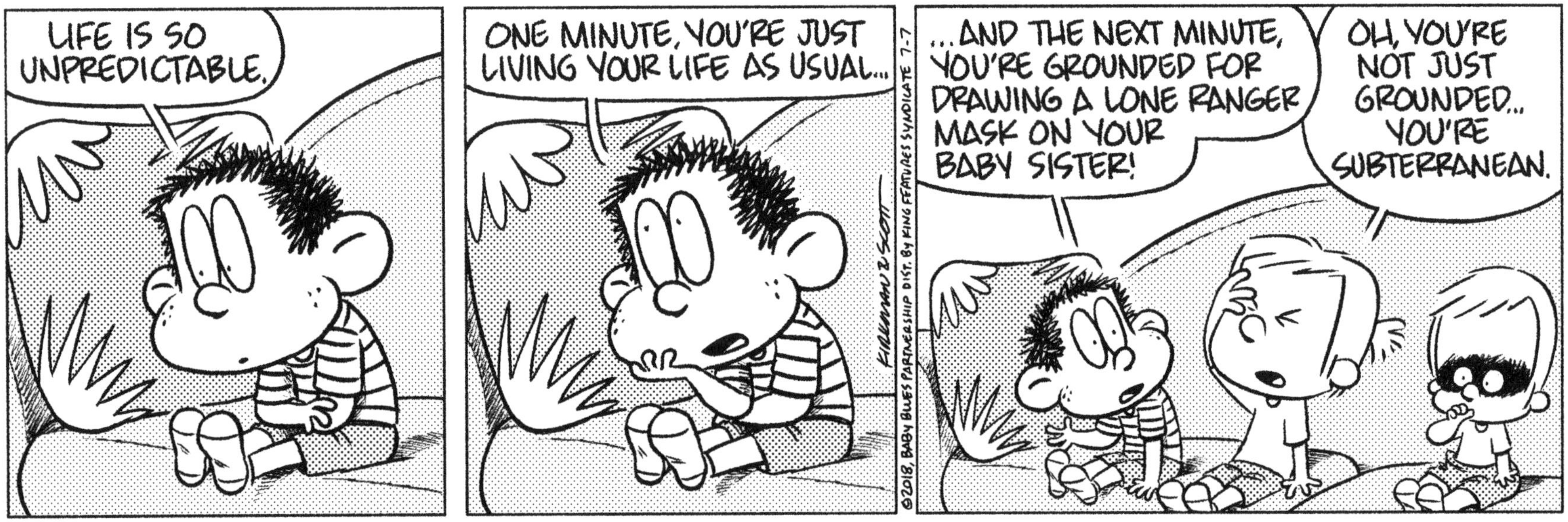
LIFE IS SO UNPREDICTABLE.
ONE MINUTE, YOU'RE JUST LIVING YOUR LIFE AS USUAL...
KIRKMAN & SCOTT
©2018, BABY BLUES PARTNERSHIP DIST. BY KING FEATURES SYNDICATE 7-7
...AND THE NEXT MINUTE, YOU'RE GROUNDED FOR DRAWING A LONE RANGER MASK ON YOUR BABY SISTER!
OH, YOU'RE NOT JUST GROUNDED... YOU'RE SUBTERRANEAN.

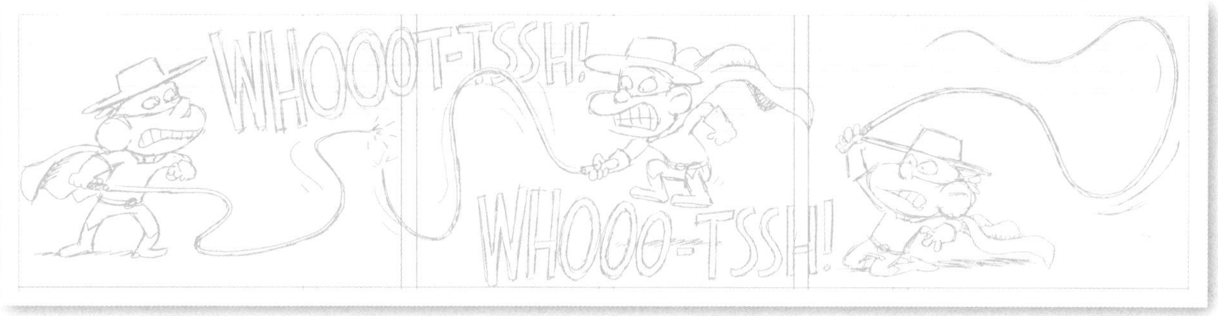
WHOOOT-TSSH!
WHOOO-TSSH!

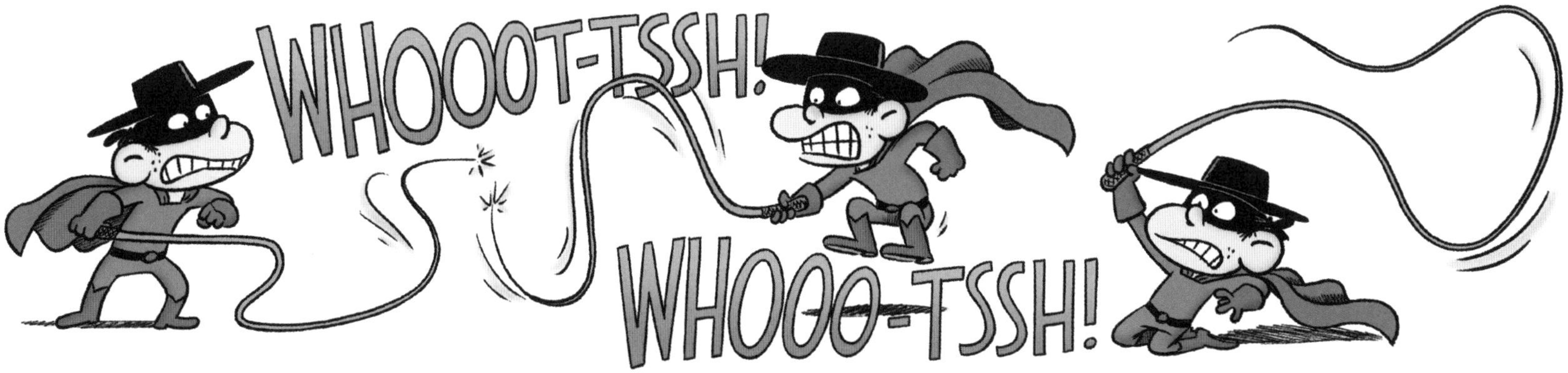
WHOOOT-TSSH!
WHOOO-TSSH!

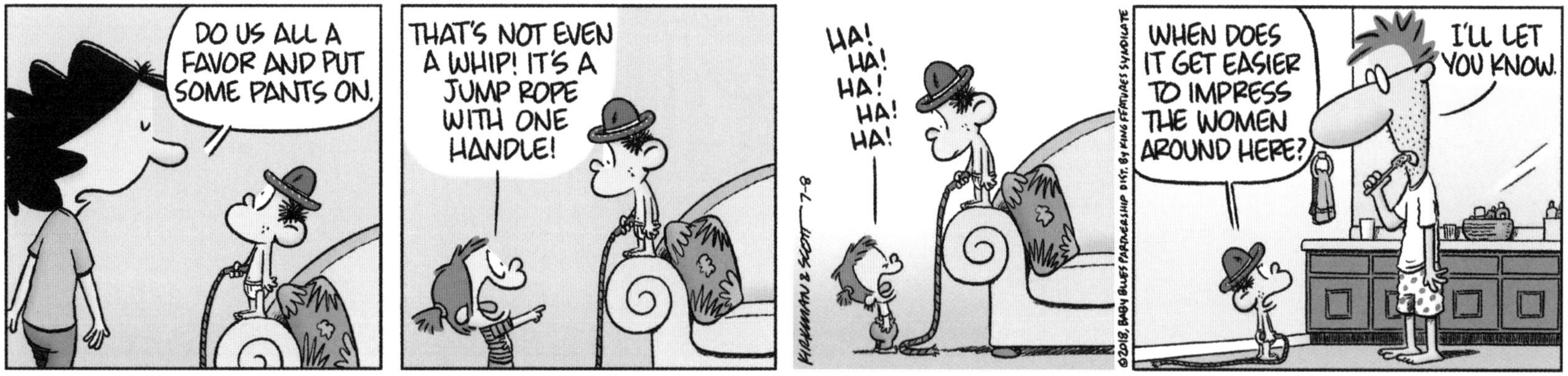
DO US ALL A FAVOR AND PUT SOME PANTS ON.
THAT'S NOT EVEN A WHIP! IT'S A JUMP ROPE WITH ONE HANDLE!
KIRKMAN & SCOTT 7-8
HA! HA! HA! HA! HA!
©2018, BABY BLUES PARTNERSHIP DIST. BY KING FEATURES SYNDICATE
WHEN DOES IT GET EASIER TO IMPRESS THE WOMEN AROUND HERE?
I'LL LET YOU KNOW.

Rick: In a family of all other women, I never figured that out, either. As fun as Hammie's Zorro-like alter ego is, I really like his real-life look.

Jerry: Hammie's reality costume in this strip cracks me up every time.

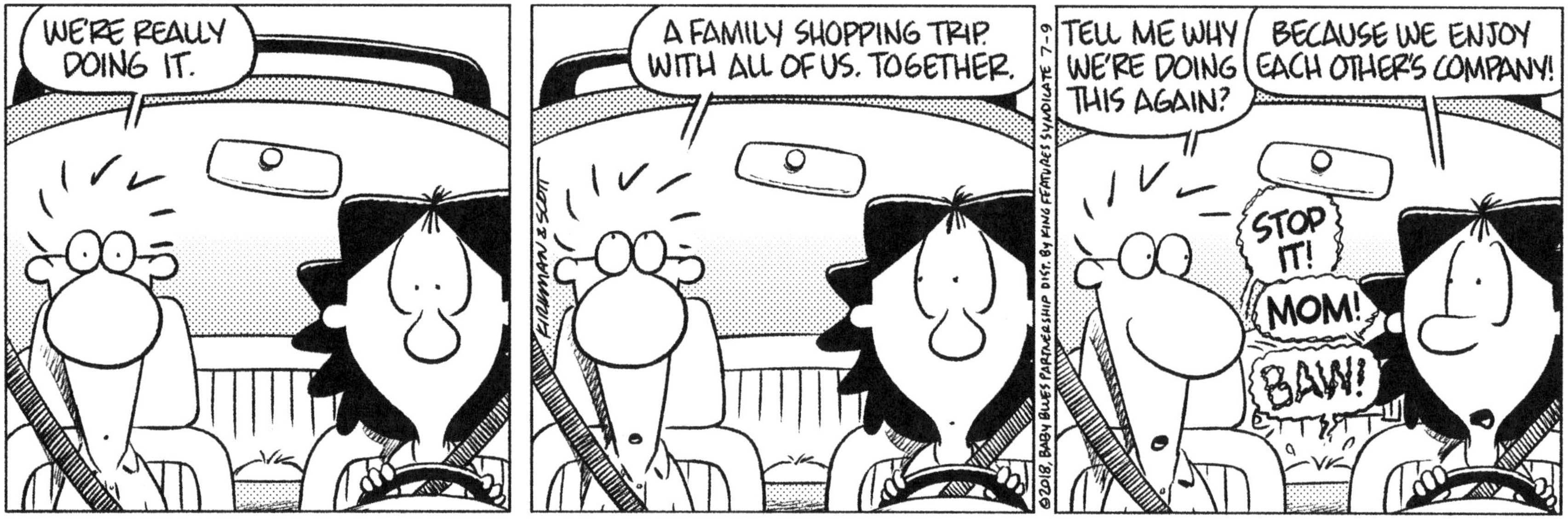
WE'RE REALLY DOING IT.
A FAMILY SHOPPING TRIP. WITH ALL OF US. TOGETHER.
KIRKMAN & SCOTT
©2018, BABY BLUES PARTNERSHIP DIST. BY KING FEATURES SYNDICATE 7-9
TELL ME WHY WE'RE DOING THIS AGAIN?
BECAUSE WE ENJOY EACH OTHER'S COMPANY!
STOP IT!
MOM!
BAW!

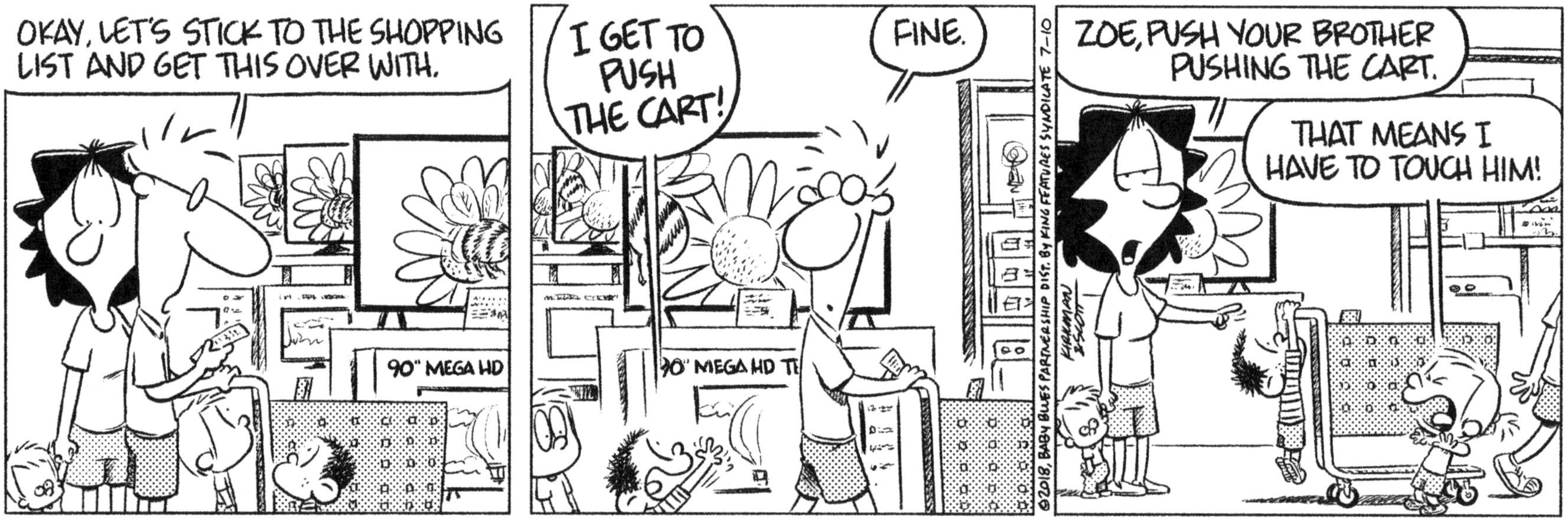
OKAY, LET'S STICK TO THE SHOPPING LIST AND GET THIS OVER WITH.
90" MEGA HD
I GET TO PUSH THE CART!
FINE.
©2018, BABY BLUES PARTNERSHIP DIST. BY KING FEATURES SYNDICATE 7-10
ZOE, PUSH YOUR BROTHER PUSHING THE CART.
THAT MEANS I HAVE TO TOUCH HIM!
KIRKMAN & SCOTT

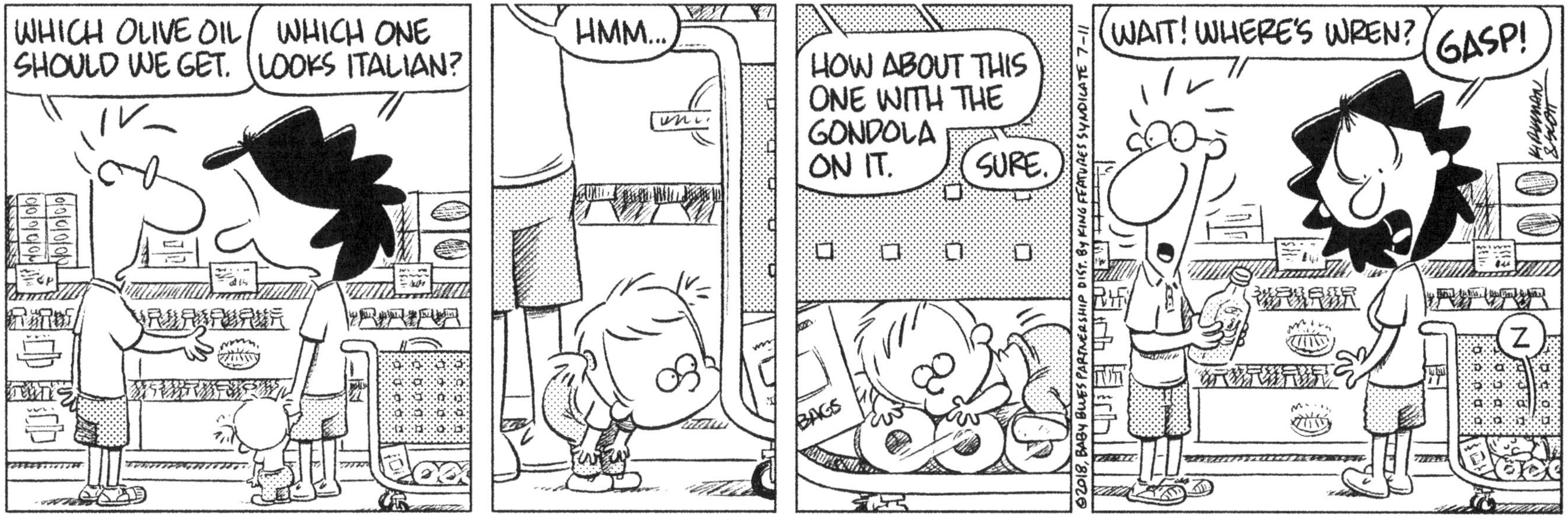
WHICH OLIVE OIL SHOULD WE GET.
WHICH ONE LOOKS ITALIAN?
HMM...
HOW ABOUT THIS ONE WITH THE GONDOLA ON IT.
SURE.
BAGS
©2018, BABY BLUES PARTNERSHIP DIST. BY KING FEATURES SYNDICATE 7-11
WAIT! WHERE'S WREN?
GASP!
Z
KIRKMAN & SCOTT

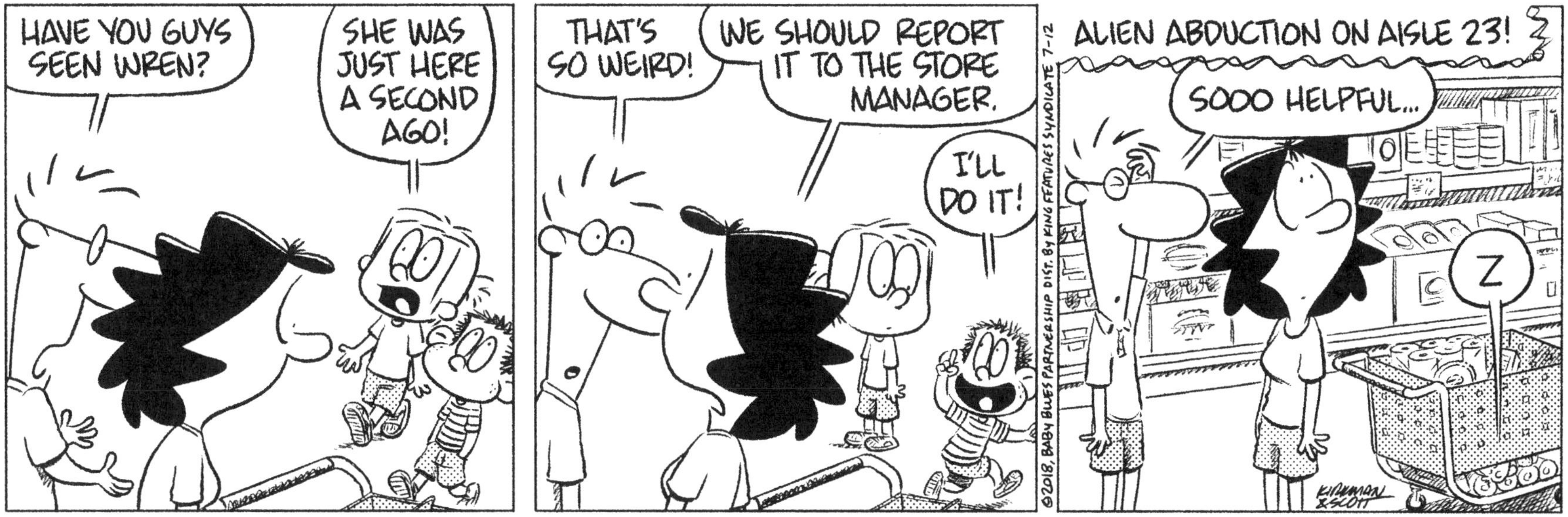
HAVE YOU GUYS SEEN WREN?
SHE WAS JUST HERE A SECOND AGO!
THAT'S SO WEIRD!
WE SHOULD REPORT IT TO THE STORE MANAGER.
I'LL DO IT!
©2018, BABY BLUES PARTNERSHIP DIST. BY KING FEATURES SYNDICATE 7-12
ALIEN ABDUCTION ON AISLE 23!
SOOO HELPFUL...
Z
KIRKMAN & SCOTT

GUYS, WE NEED YOUR HELP FINDING WREN.

OKAY.

NO PROBLEM.

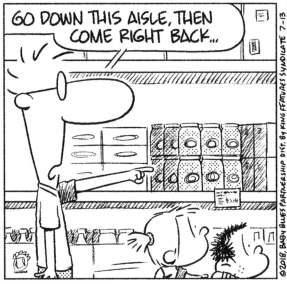

GO DOWN THIS AISLE, THEN COME RIGHT BACK...

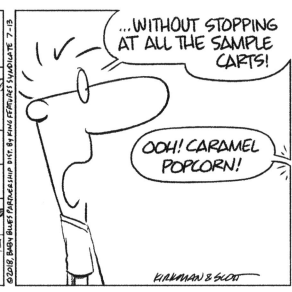

...WITHOUT STOPPING AT ALL THE SAMPLE CARTS!

OOH! CARAMEL POPCORN!

KIRKMAN & SCOTT

©2018, BABY BLUES PARTNERSHIP DIST. BY KING FEATURES SYNDICATE 7-13

I FOUND HER!

WHERE WAS SHE??

SHE FELL ASLEEP ON THE PACKAGE OF TOILET PAPER.

YOU'RE KIDDING.

WREN!

KIRKMAN & SCOTT

©2018, BABY BLUES PARTNERSHIP DIST. BY KING FEATURES SYNDICATE 7-14

WOW! IT'S SUPER-COMFY DOWN HERE.

FOR SAFETY'S SAKE, MAYBE WE SHOULD SWITCH TO SINGLE-PLY.

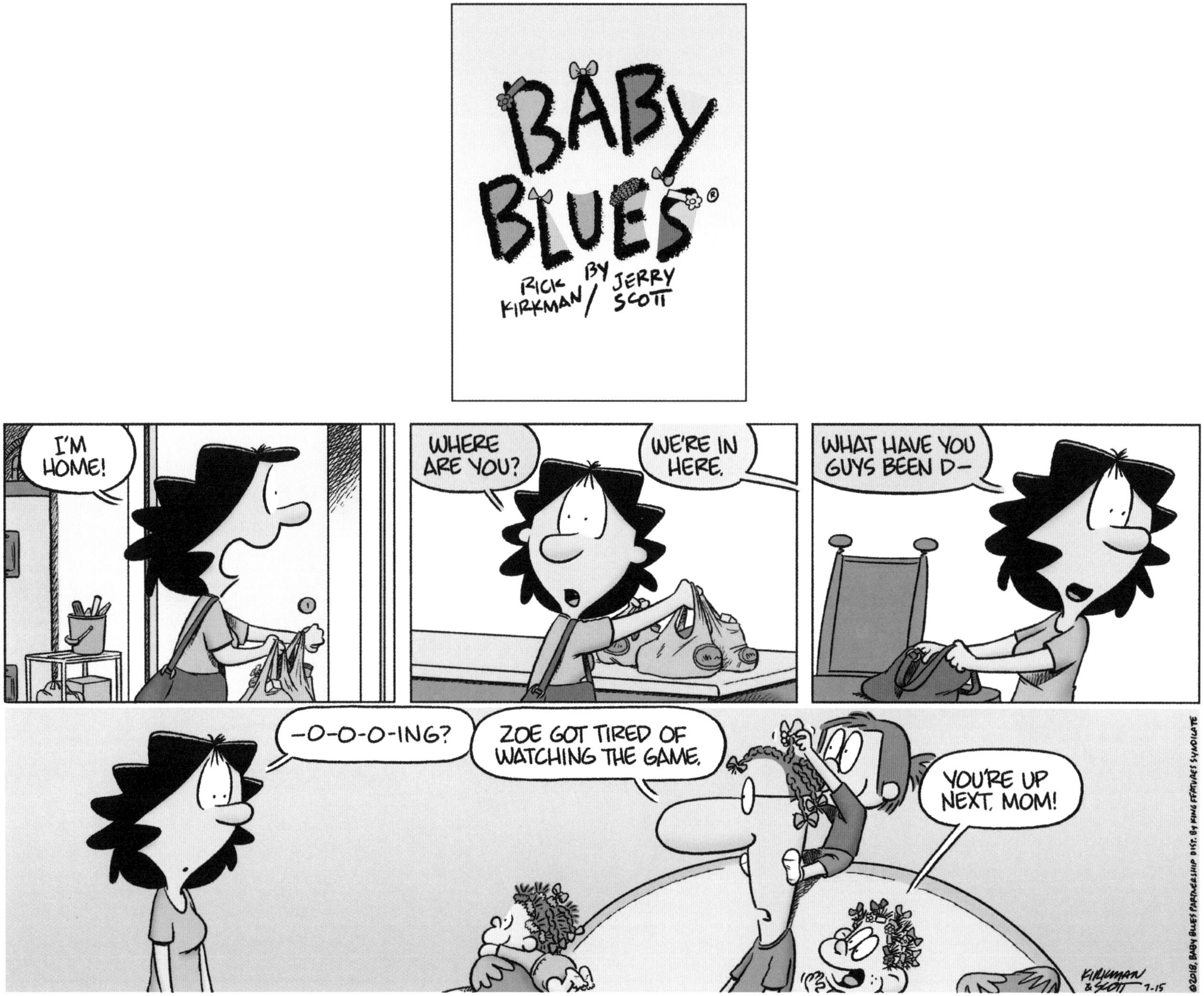
BABY BLUES®
BY RICK KIRKMAN / JERRY SCOTT
I'M HOME!
WHERE ARE YOU?
WE'RE IN HERE.
WHAT HAVE YOU GUYS BEEN D–
–O-O-O-ING?
ZOE GOT TIRED OF WATCHING THE GAME.
YOU'RE UP NEXT, MOM!
KIRKMAN & SCOTT 7-15
©2018, BABY BLUES PARTNERSHIP DIST. BY KING FEATURES SYNDICATE

Rick: One key to successful parenting is to lose all vanity. At least, that's what I told myself.

Jerry: I don't know how Zoe got multiple braids out of Darryl's five or six hairs. And yeah, I'm a little envious.

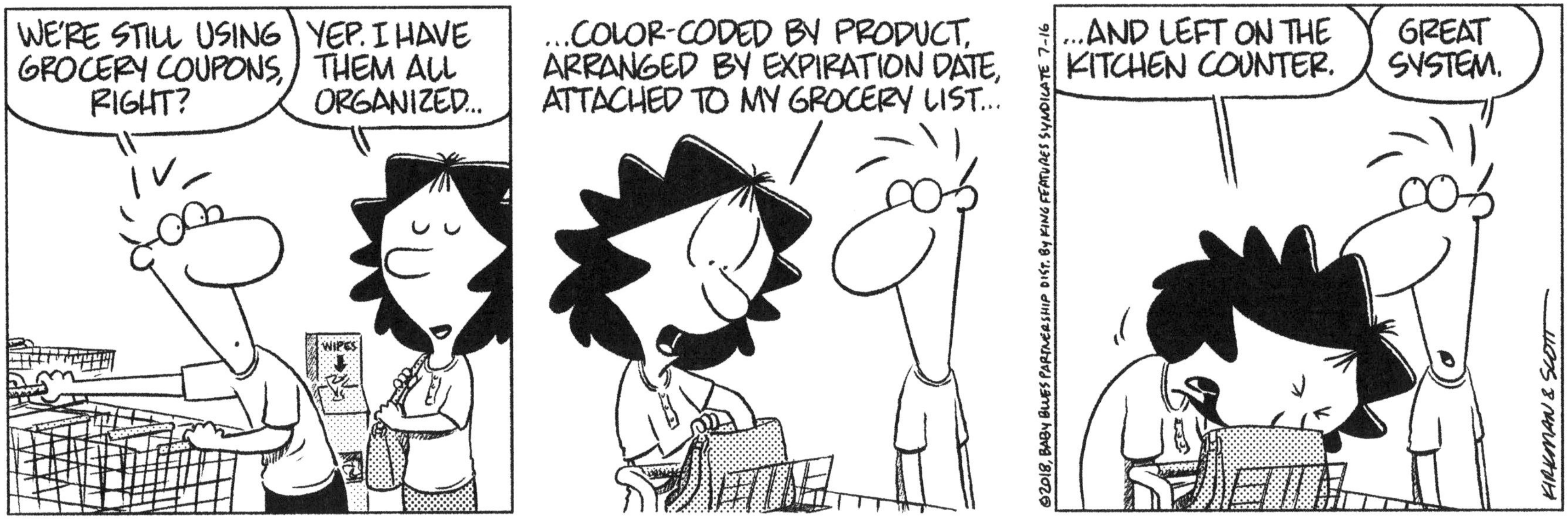
WE'RE STILL USING GROCERY COUPONS, RIGHT?
YEP. I HAVE THEM ALL ORGANIZED...
WIPES
...COLOR-CODED BY PRODUCT, ARRANGED BY EXPIRATION DATE, ATTACHED TO MY GROCERY LIST...
...AND LEFT ON THE KITCHEN COUNTER.
GREAT SYSTEM.
©2018, BABY BLUES PARTNERSHIP DIST. BY KING FEATURES SYNDICATE 7-16
KIRKMAN & SCOTT

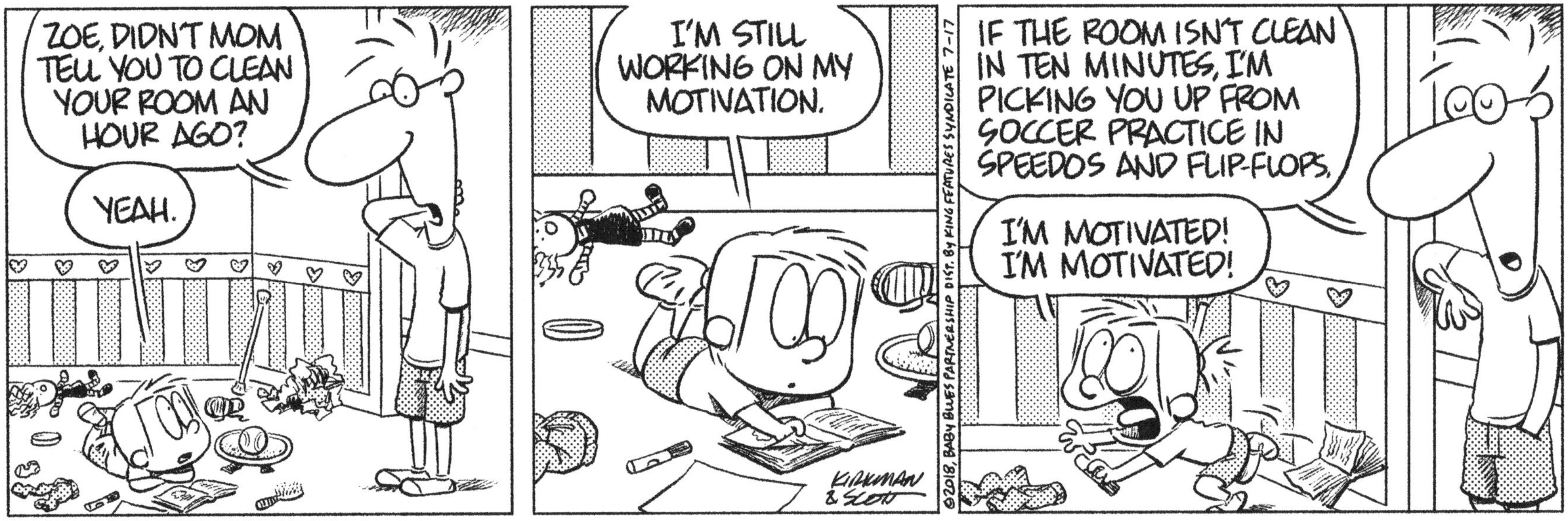
ZOE, DIDN'T MOM TELL YOU TO CLEAN YOUR ROOM AN HOUR AGO?
YEAH.
I'M STILL WORKING ON MY MOTIVATION.
KIRKMAN & SCOTT
©2018, BABY BLUES PARTNERSHIP DIST. BY KING FEATURES SYNDICATE 7-17
IF THE ROOM ISN'T CLEAN IN TEN MINUTES, I'M PICKING YOU UP FROM SOCCER PRACTICE IN SPEEDOS AND FLIP-FLOPS.
I'M MOTIVATED! I'M MOTIVATED!

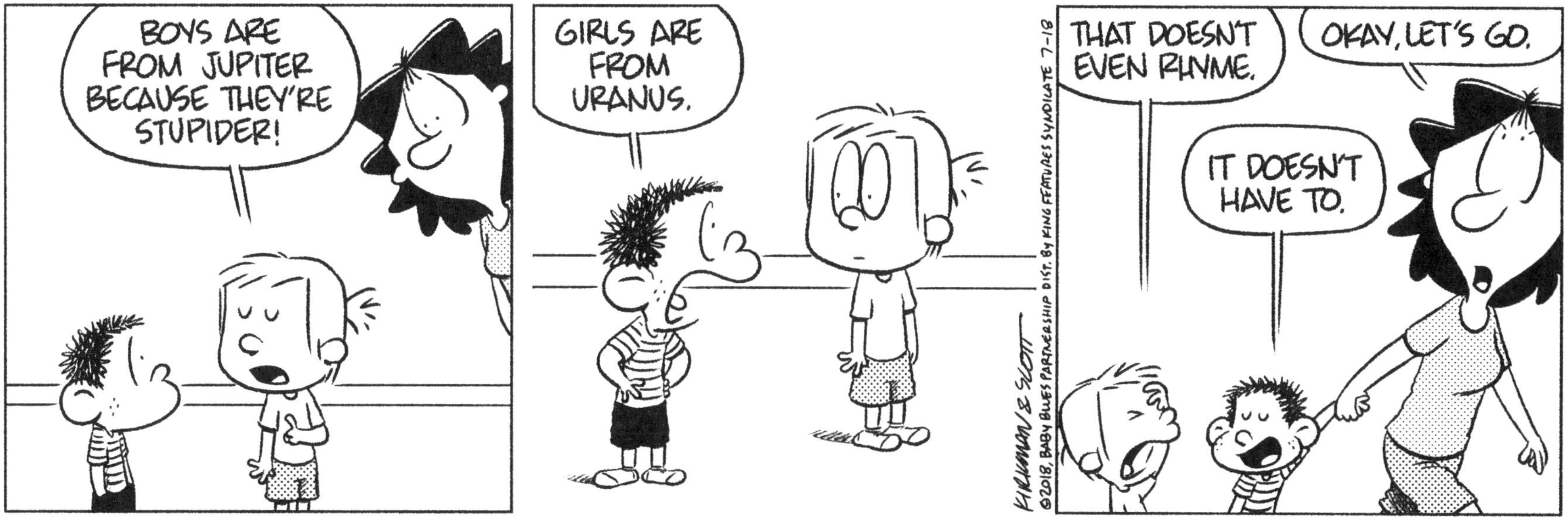
BOYS ARE FROM JUPITER BECAUSE THEY'RE STUPIDER!
GIRLS ARE FROM URANUS.
THAT DOESN'T EVEN RHYME.
IT DOESN'T HAVE TO.
OKAY, LET'S GO.
KIRKMAN & SCOTT
©2018, BABY BLUES PARTNERSHIP DIST. BY KING FEATURES SYNDICATE 7-18

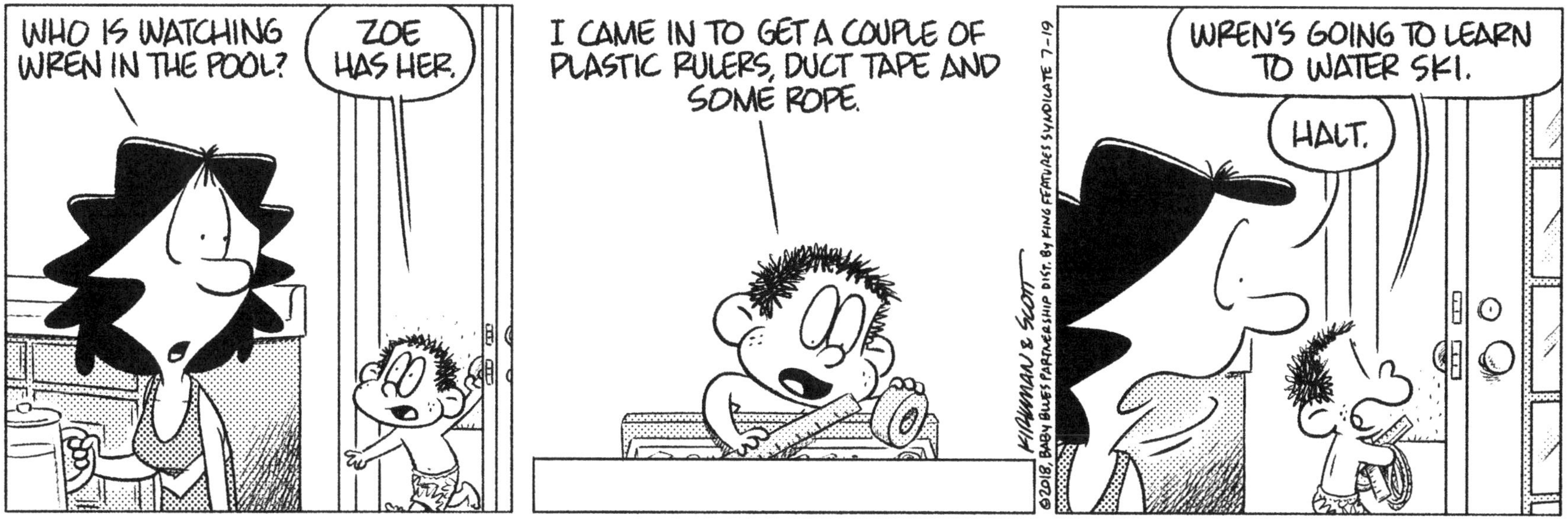
WHO IS WATCHING WREN IN THE POOL?
ZOE HAS HER.
I CAME IN TO GET A COUPLE OF PLASTIC RULERS, DUCT TAPE AND SOME ROPE.
WREN'S GOING TO LEARN TO WATER SKI.
HALT.
KIRKMAN & SCOTT
©2018, BABY BLUES PARTNERSHIP DIST. BY KING FEATURES SYNDICATE 7-19

Rick: A reader called us out on this one for having Hammie watch Wren in the pool. It's not a real pool with real water, just like Hammie doesn't really have a way to teach Wren to water ski. Or does he?

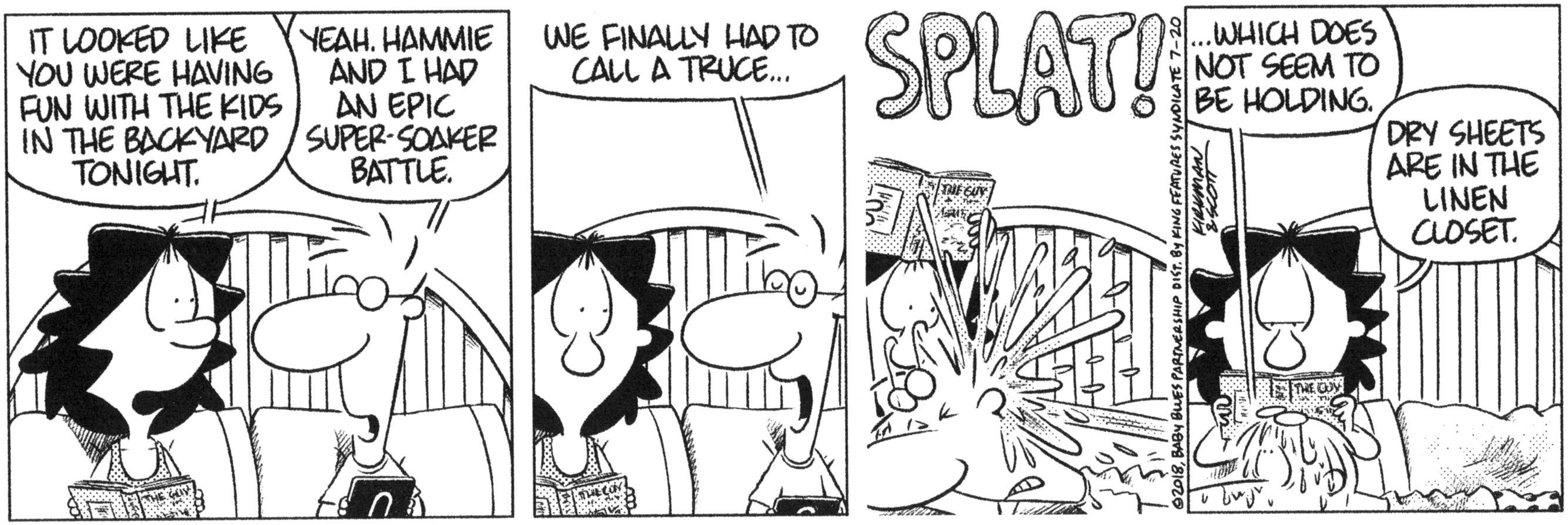
IT LOOKED LIKE YOU WERE HAVING FUN WITH THE KIDS IN THE BACKYARD TONIGHT.
YEAH. HAMMIE AND I HAD AN EPIC SUPER-SOAKER BATTLE.
WE FINALLY HAD TO CALL A TRUCE...
SPLAT!
©2018, BABY BLUES PARTNERSHIP DIST. BY KING FEATURES SYNDICATE 7-20
...WHICH DOES NOT SEEM TO BE HOLDING.
DRY SHEETS ARE IN THE LINEN CLOSET.

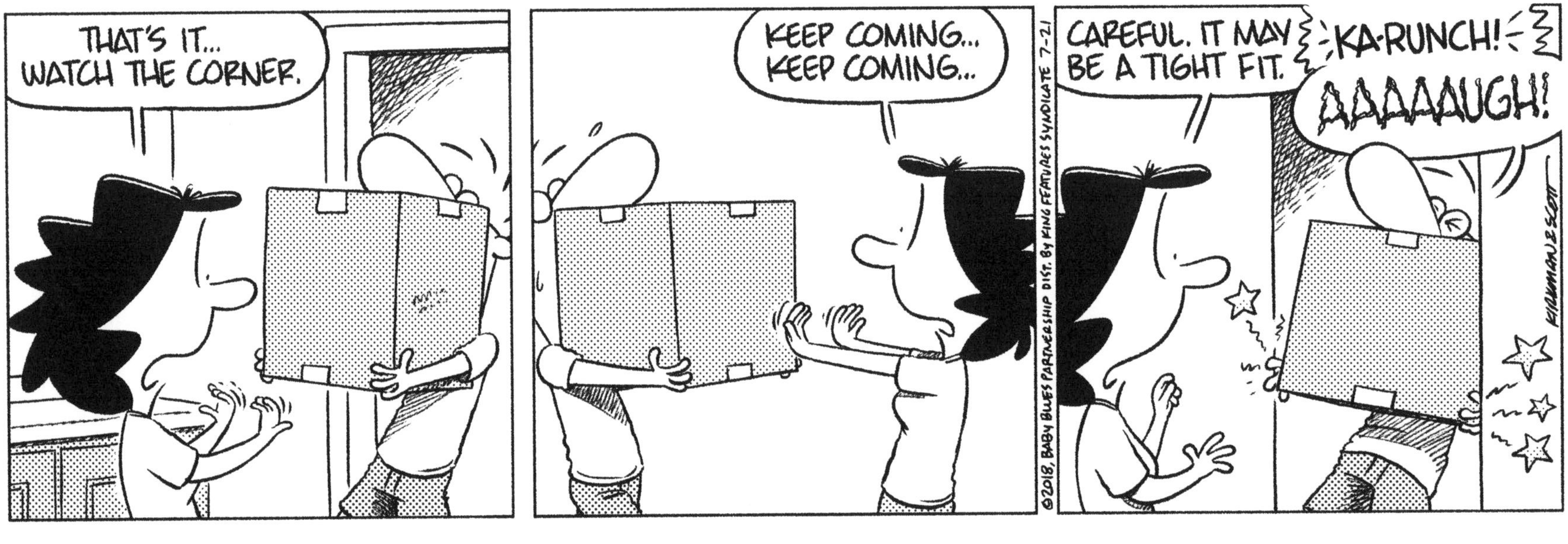
THAT'S IT... WATCH THE CORNER.
KEEP COMING... KEEP COMING...
©2018, BABY BLUES PARTNERSHIP DIST. BY KING FEATURES SYNDICATE 7-21
CAREFUL. IT MAY BE A TIGHT FIT.
KA-RUNCH!
AAAAAUGH!

BABY BLUES
Rick Kirkman & Jerry Scott
ZZZZZZ

WOW! THIS LOOKS LIKE QUITE AN ART PROJECT GOING ON OVER THERE!
I'M JUST MAKING A POSTER FOR MY ROOM.
IT'S ABOUT A BOY IN MY CLASS I SORTA LIKE.
A BOY?
YEAH. HIS NAME IS T.J. HE WEARS LEATHER BOOTS AND HAS THE LONGEST EYE-LASHES EVER!
LEATHER BOOTS?
©2018, BABY BLUES PARTNERSHIP DIST. BY KING FEATURES SYNDICATE 7-29
WHAT DO YOU THINK?
Loves me!
HoT Stuff
Loves Me Not
hunk
TJ + ZM
Loves me
Stud muffin
Loves Me Not
Loves me
I NEED A BACKGROUND CHECK ON A T.J.
ALREADY DONE. HE'S CLEAN.
Wunky Duck
KIRKMAN & SCOTT

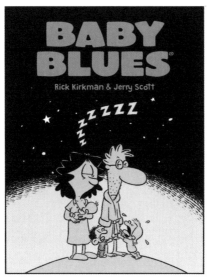

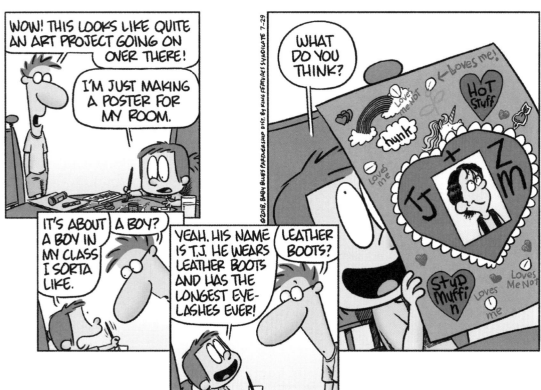

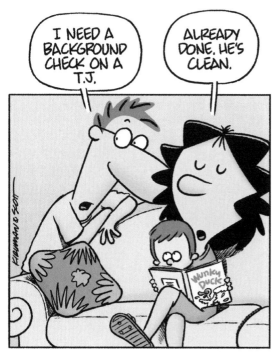

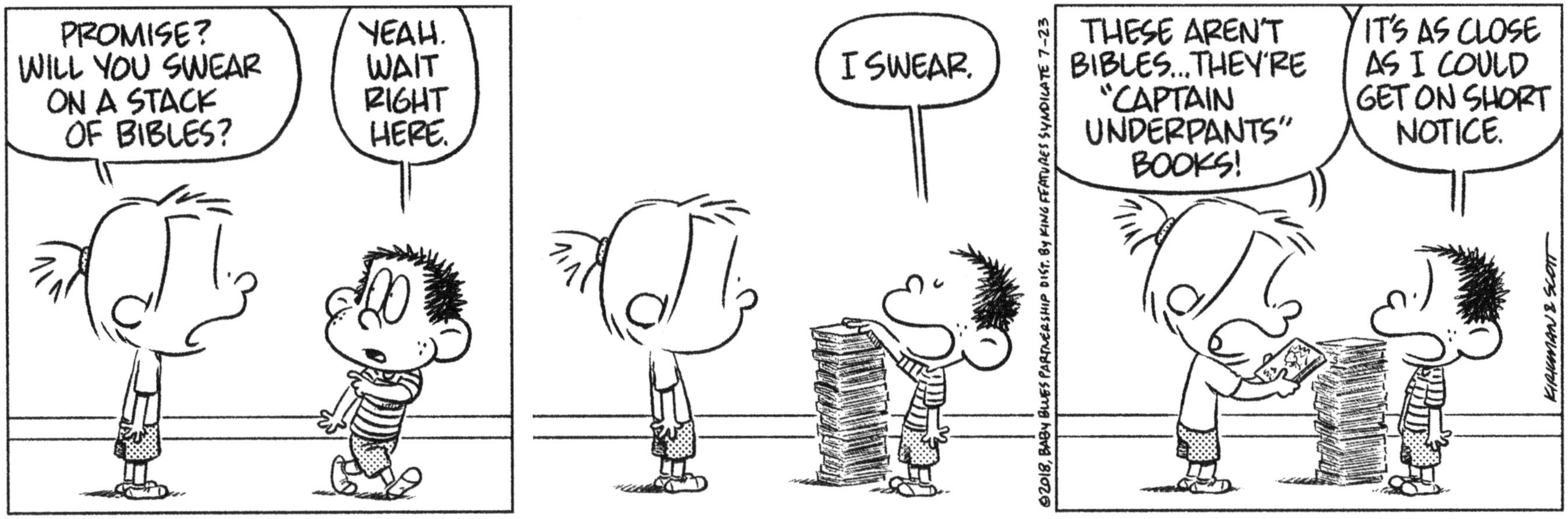
PROMISE? WILL YOU SWEAR ON A STACK OF BIBLES?
YEAH. WAIT RIGHT HERE.
I SWEAR.
©2018, BABY BLUES PARTNERSHIP DIST. BY KING FEATURES SYNDICATE 7-23
THESE AREN'T BIBLES...THEY'RE "CAPTAIN UNDERPANTS" BOOKS!
IT'S AS CLOSE AS I COULD GET ON SHORT NOTICE.
KIRKMAN & SCOTT

Jerry: The gospel according to Dav Pilkey.

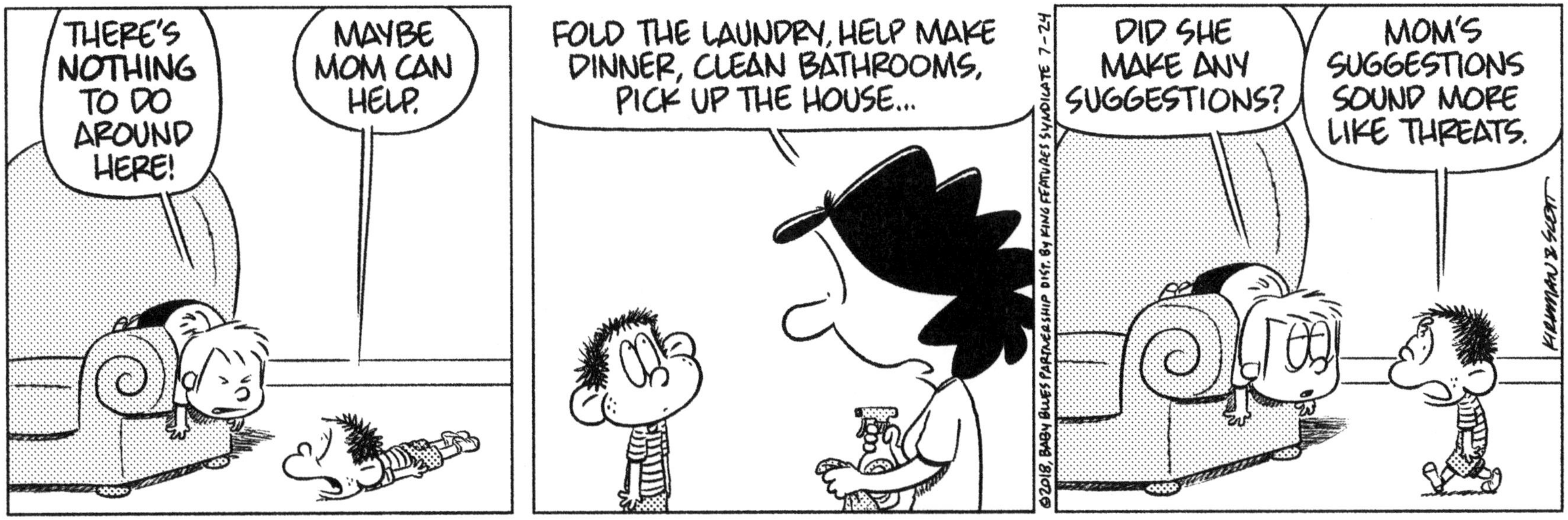
THERE'S NOTHING TO DO AROUND HERE!
MAYBE MOM CAN HELP.
FOLD THE LAUNDRY, HELP MAKE DINNER, CLEAN BATHROOMS, PICK UP THE HOUSE...
©2018, BABY BLUES PARTNERSHIP DIST. BY KING FEATURES SYNDICATE 7-24
DID SHE MAKE ANY SUGGESTIONS?
MOM'S SUGGESTIONS SOUND MORE LIKE THREATS.
KIRKMAN & SCOTT

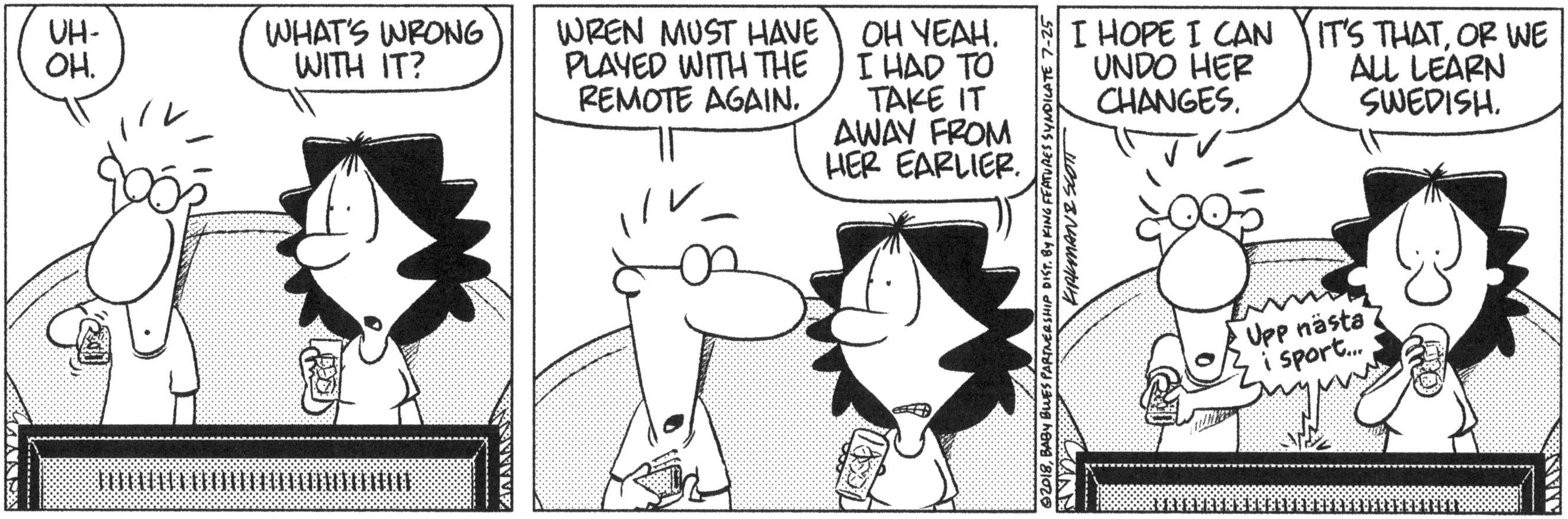

UH-OH.
WHAT'S WRONG WITH IT?
WREN MUST HAVE PLAYED WITH THE REMOTE AGAIN.
OH YEAH. I HAD TO TAKE IT AWAY FROM HER EARLIER.
I HOPE I CAN UNDO HER CHANGES.
IT'S THAT, OR WE ALL LEARN SWEDISH.
Upp nästa i sport...
©2018, BABY BLUES PARTNERSHIP DIST. BY KING FEATURES SYNDICATE 7-25
KIRKMAN & SCOTT

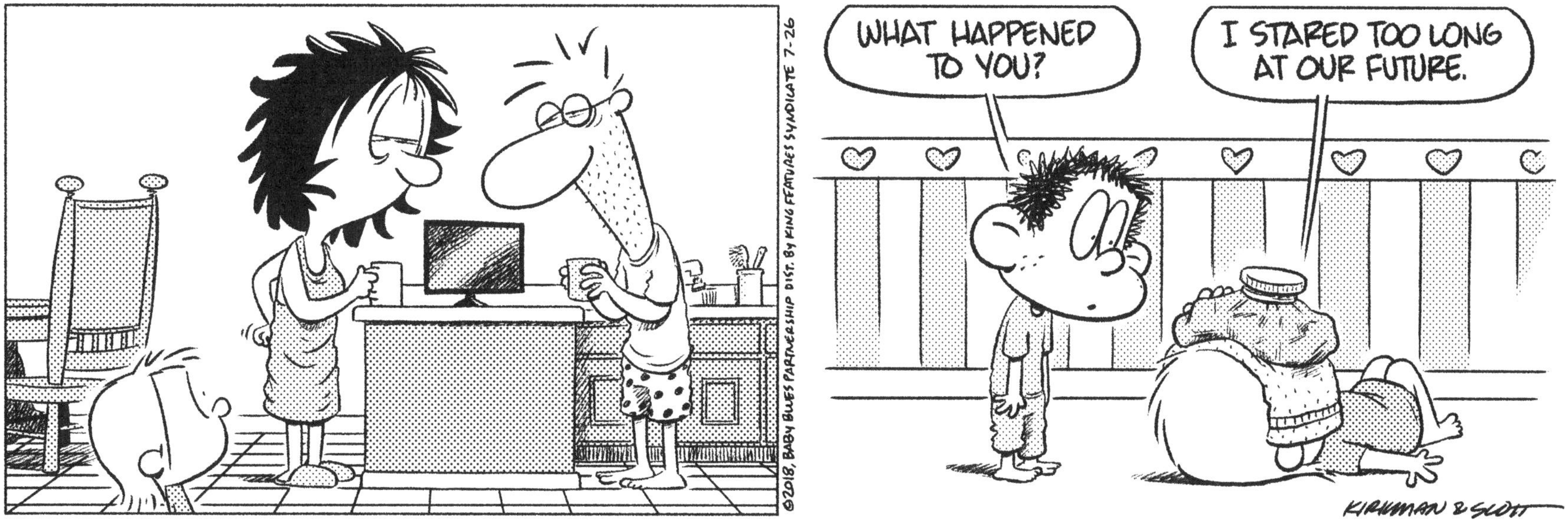

©2018, BABY BLUES PARTNERSHIP DIST. BY KING FEATURES SYNDICATE 7-26
WHAT HAPPENED TO YOU?
I STARED TOO LONG AT OUR FUTURE.
KIRKMAN & SCOTT

Rick: The horror!

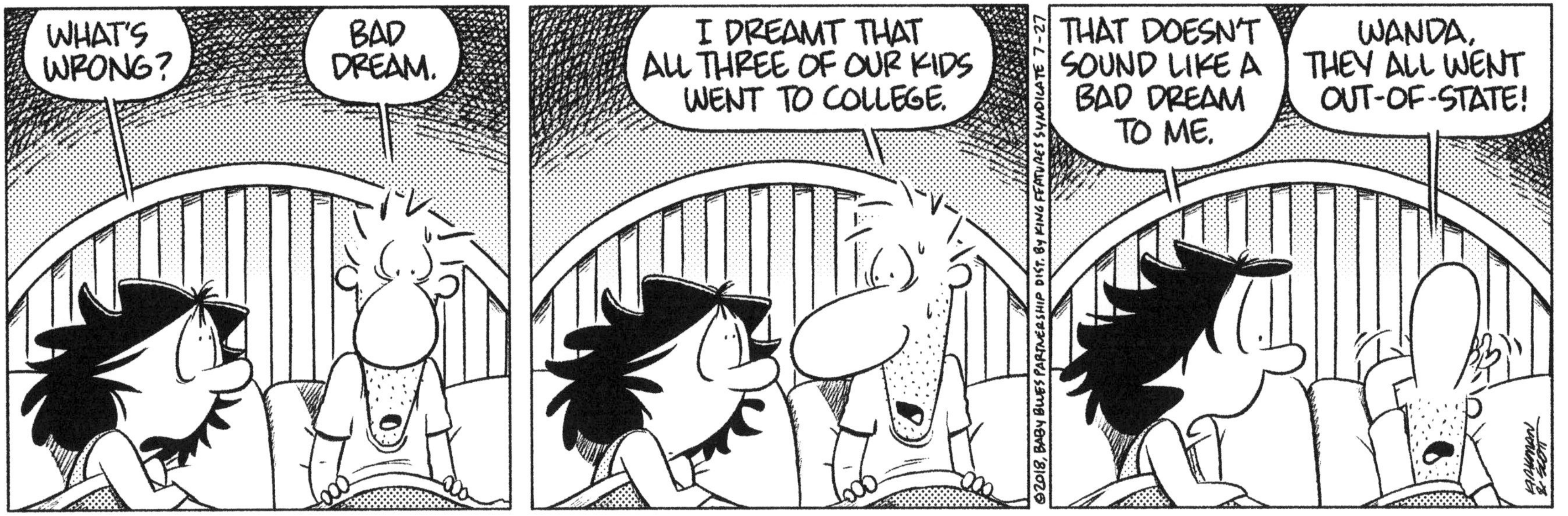
WHAT'S WRONG?
BAD DREAM.
I DREAMT THAT ALL THREE OF OUR KIDS WENT TO COLLEGE.
©2018, BABY BLUES PARTNERSHIP DIST. BY KING FEATURES SYNDICATE 7-27
THAT DOESN'T SOUND LIKE A BAD DREAM TO ME.
WANDA, THEY ALL WENT OUT-OF-STATE!
KIRKMAN & SCOTT

Rick: The horror! Part 2. **Jerry:** Been there. Paid that.

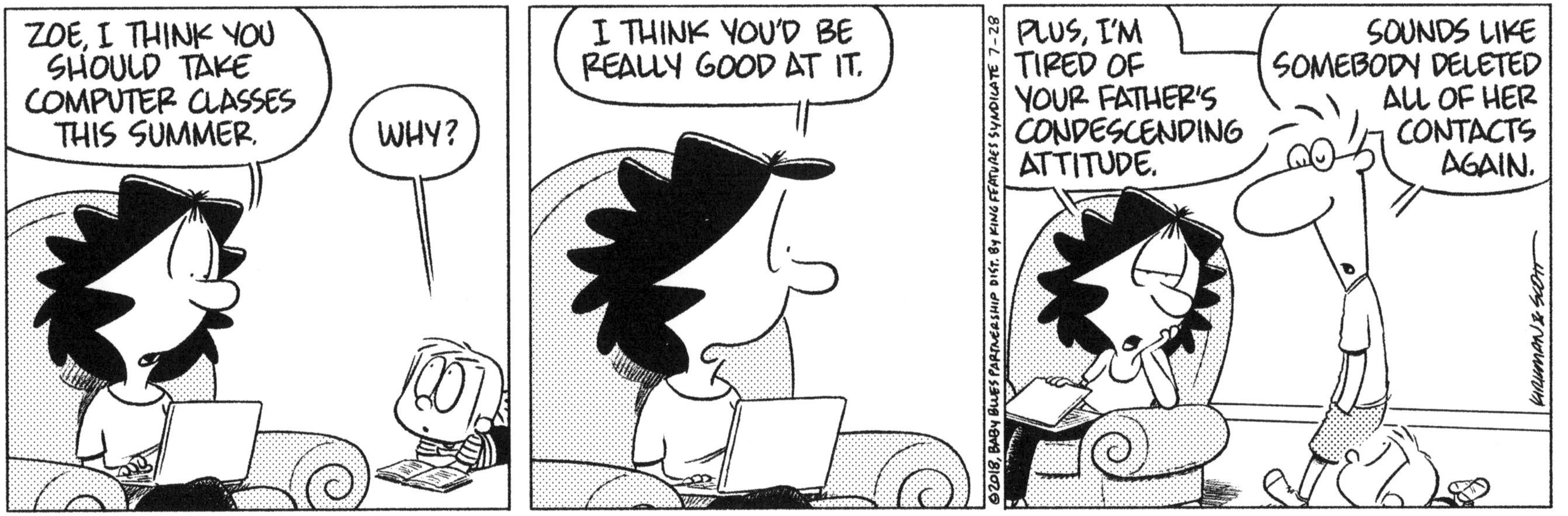
ZOE, I THINK YOU SHOULD TAKE COMPUTER CLASSES THIS SUMMER.
WHY?
I THINK YOU'D BE REALLY GOOD AT IT.
©2018, BABY BLUES PARTNERSHIP DIST. BY KING FEATURES SYNDICATE 7-28
PLUS, I'M TIRED OF YOUR FATHER'S CONDESCENDING ATTITUDE.
SOUNDS LIKE SOMEBODY DELETED ALL OF HER CONTACTS AGAIN.
KIRKMAN & SCOTT

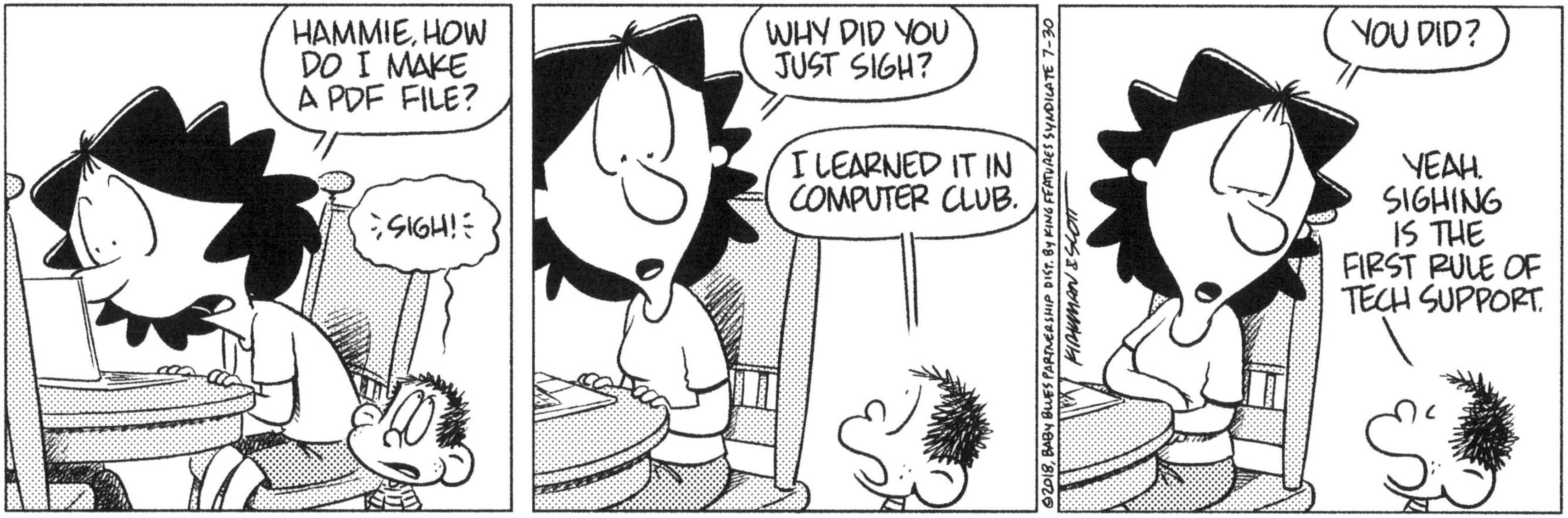
HAMMIE, HOW DO I MAKE A PDF FILE?
SIGH!
WHY DID YOU JUST SIGH?
I LEARNED IT IN COMPUTER CLUB.
YOU DID?
YEAH. SIGHING IS THE FIRST RULE OF TECH SUPPORT.
©2018, BABY BLUES PARTNERSHIP DIST. BY KING FEATURES SYNDICATE 7-30
KIRKMAN & SCOTT

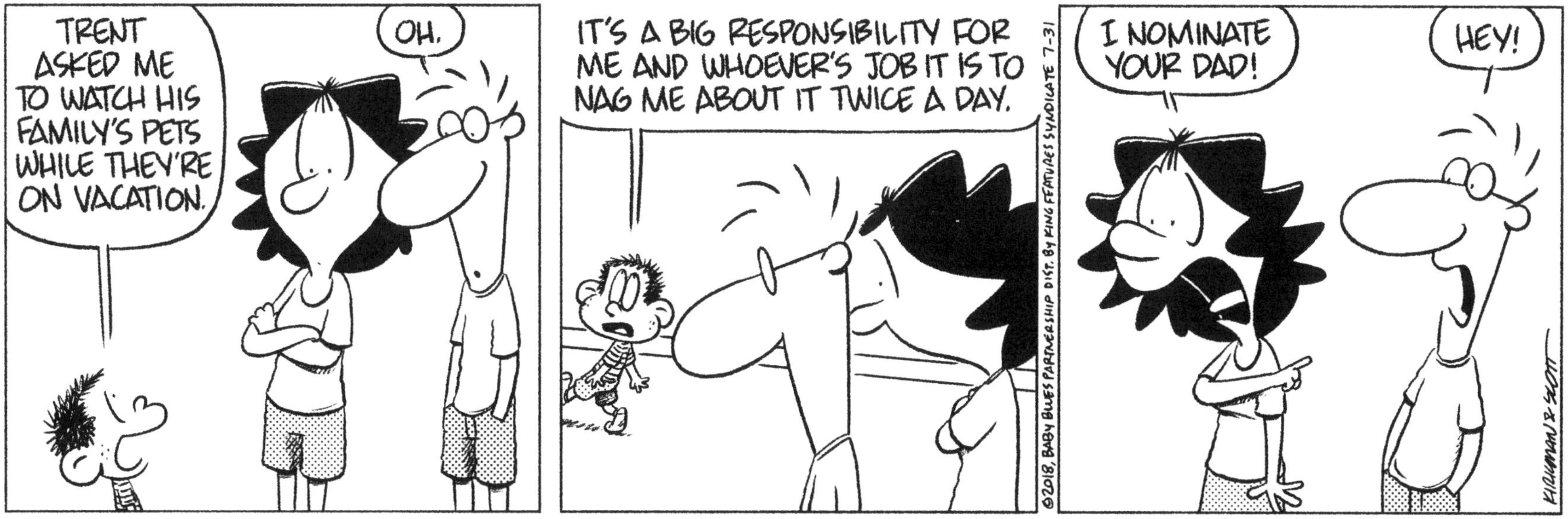
TRENT ASKED ME TO WATCH HIS FAMILY'S PETS WHILE THEY'RE ON VACATION.
OH.
IT'S A BIG RESPONSIBILITY FOR ME AND WHOEVER'S JOB IT IS TO NAG ME ABOUT IT TWICE A DAY.
I NOMINATE YOUR DAD!
HEY!
©2018, BABY BLUES PARTNERSHIP DIST. BY KING FEATURES SYNDICATE 7-31
KIRKMAN & SCOTT

Rick: Think fast, Darryl!

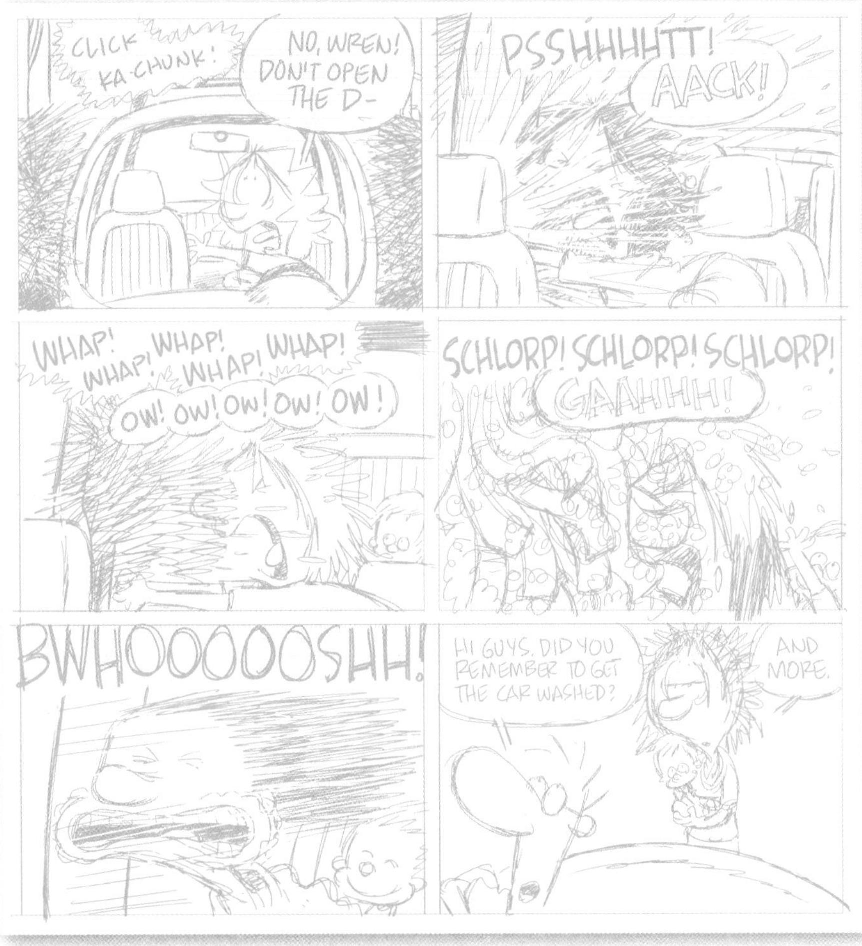
CLICK KA-CHUNK!
NO, WREN! DON'T OPEN THE D-
PSSHHHHTT!
AACK!
WHAP! WHAP! WHAP! WHAP! WHAP!
OW! OW! OW! OW! OW!
SCHLORP! SCHLORP! SCHLORP!
GAAHHH!
BWHOOOOOOSHH!
HI GUYS. DID YOU REMEMBER TO GET THE CAR WASHED?
AND MORE.

Rick: Definitely one of the most fun drawing challenges Jerry has thrown at me. The trick was to maintain the energy of the rough in the final drawing.

Jerry: This happened to one of my sister's friends. Not sure if they opted for the undercarriage rinse.

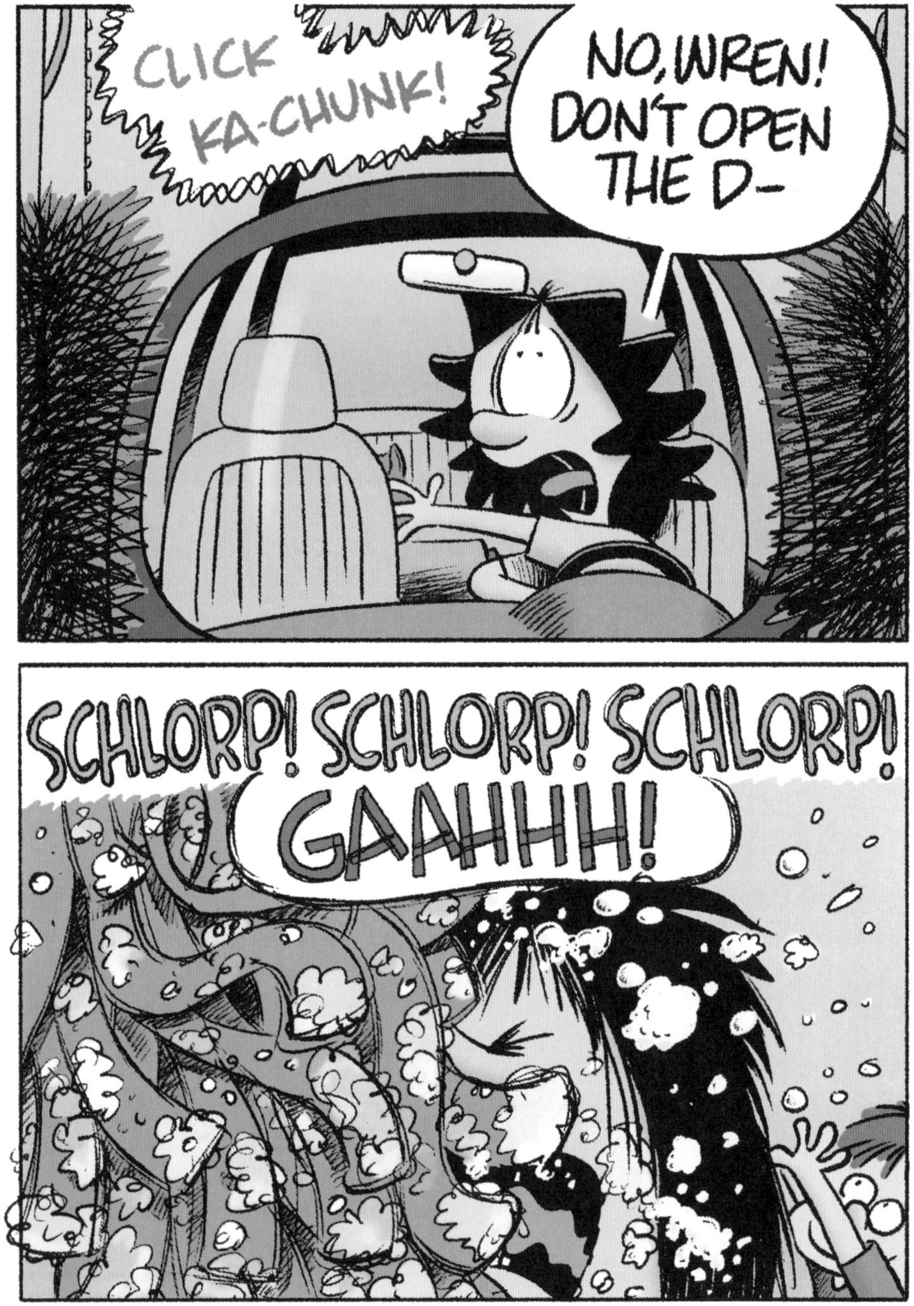
CLICK KA-CHUNK!
NO, WREN! DON'T OPEN THE D-
SCHLORP! SCHLORP! SCHLORP!
GAHHH!

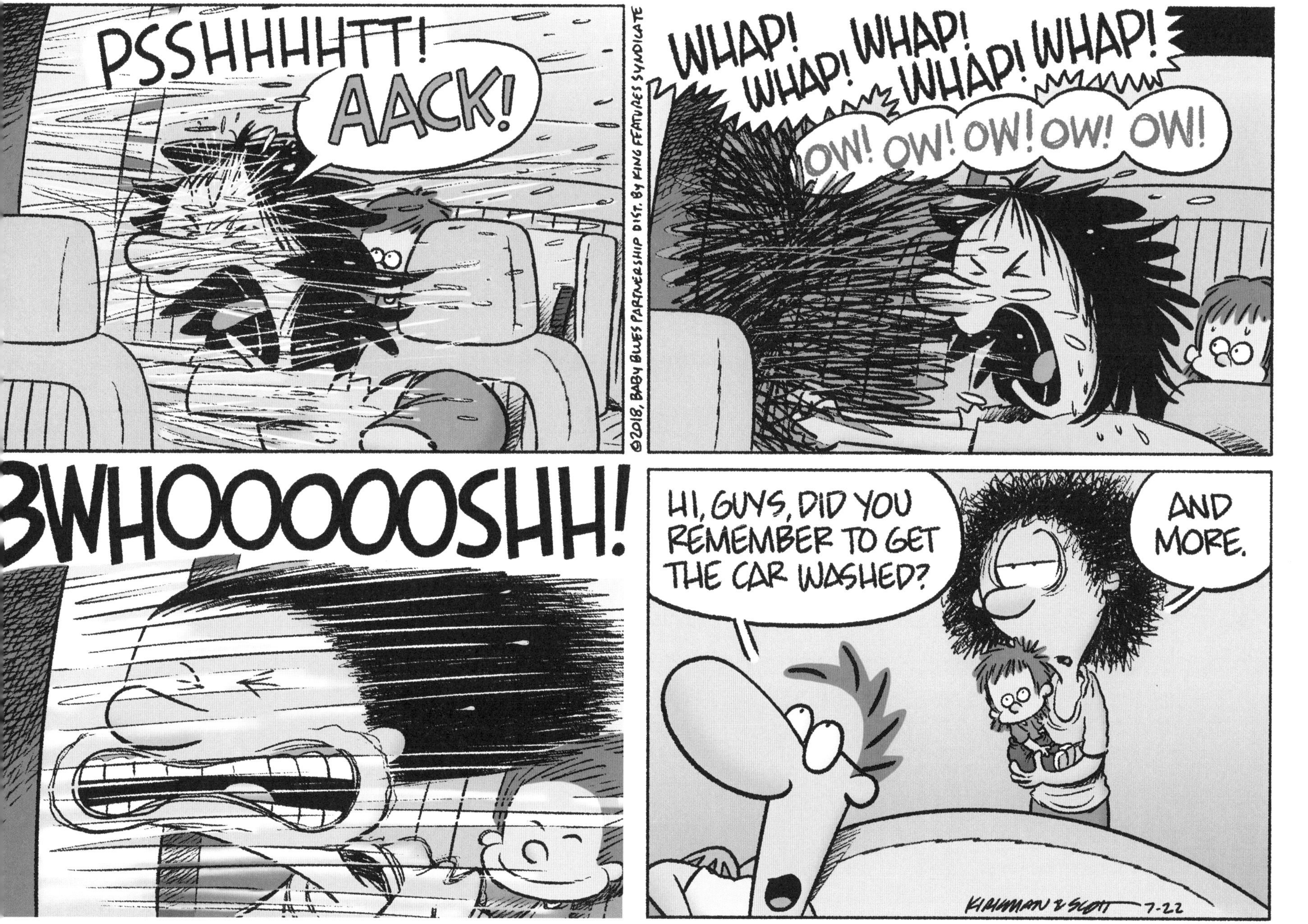
PSSHHHHTT!
AACK!
©2018, BABY BLUES PARTNERSHIP DIST. BY KING FEATURES SYNDICATE
WHAP! WHAP! WHAP! WHAP! WHAP!
OW! OW! OW! OW! OW!
BWHOOOOOOSHH!
HI, GUYS, DID YOU REMEMBER TO GET THE CAR WASHED?
AND MORE.
KIRKMAN & SCOTT 7-22

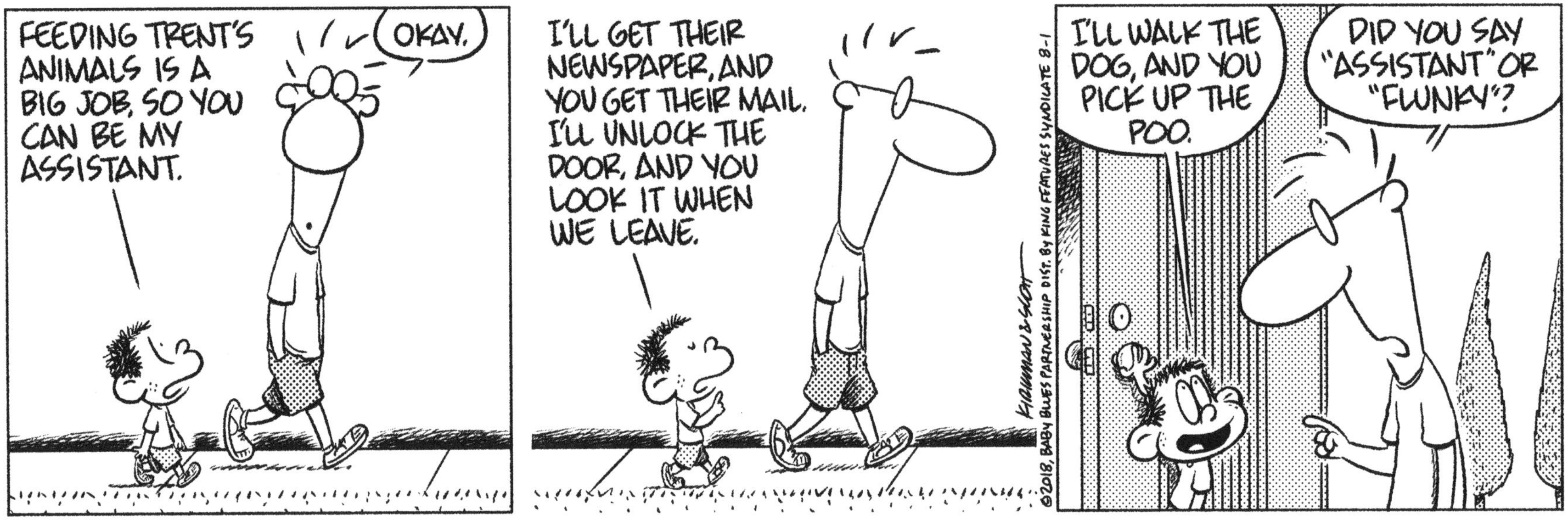
FEEDING TRENT'S ANIMALS IS A BIG JOB, SO YOU CAN BE MY ASSISTANT.
OKAY.
I'LL GET THEIR NEWSPAPER, AND YOU GET THEIR MAIL. I'LL UNLOCK THE DOOR, AND YOU LOOK IT WHEN WE LEAVE.
©2018, BABY BLUES PARTNERSHIP DIST. BY KING FEATURES SYNDICATE 8-1
I'LL WALK THE DOG, AND YOU PICK UP THE POO.
DID YOU SAY "ASSISTANT" OR "FLUNKY"?

Rick: Yikes! What do you call a "typo" when you're hand-lettering? The "typo" is in panel two. Another one I'll have to fix.

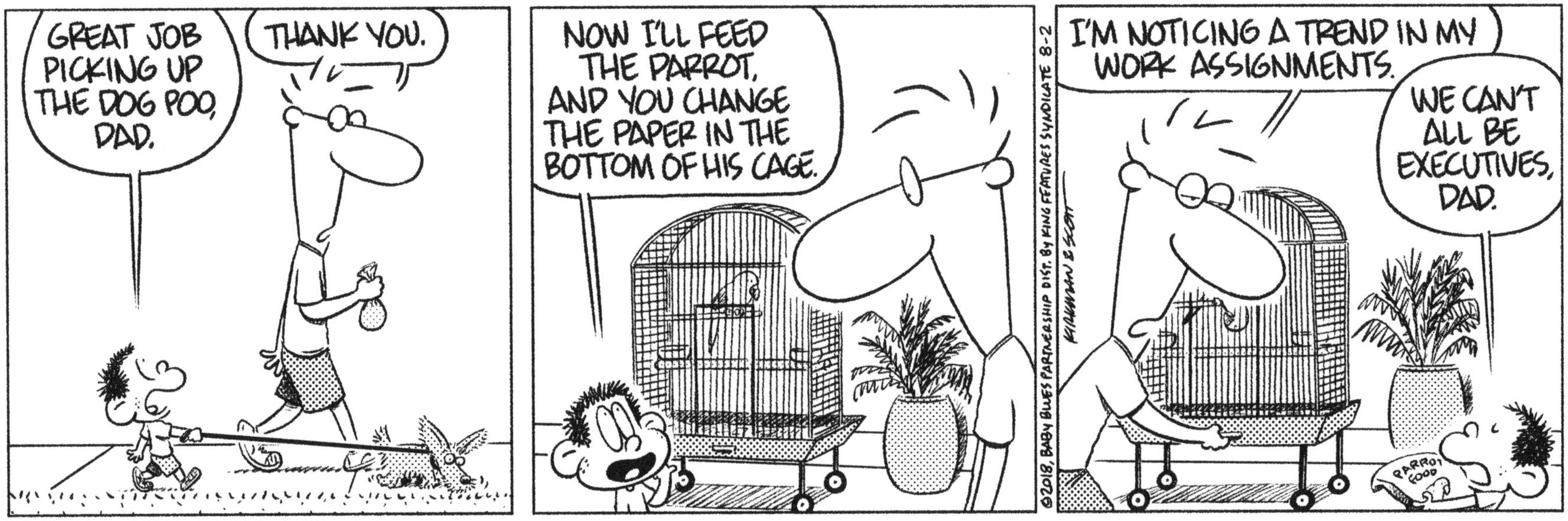
GREAT JOB PICKING UP THE DOG POO, DAD.
THANK YOU.
NOW I'LL FEED THE PARROT, AND YOU CHANGE THE PAPER IN THE BOTTOM OF HIS CAGE.
©2018, BABY BLUES PARTNERSHIP DIST. BY KING FEATURES SYNDICATE 8-2
I'M NOTICING A TREND IN MY WORK ASSIGNMENTS.
WE CAN'T ALL BE EXECUTIVES, DAD.
PARROT FOOD

Rick: I really like this dog. I'll have to try to remember to use her again sometime.

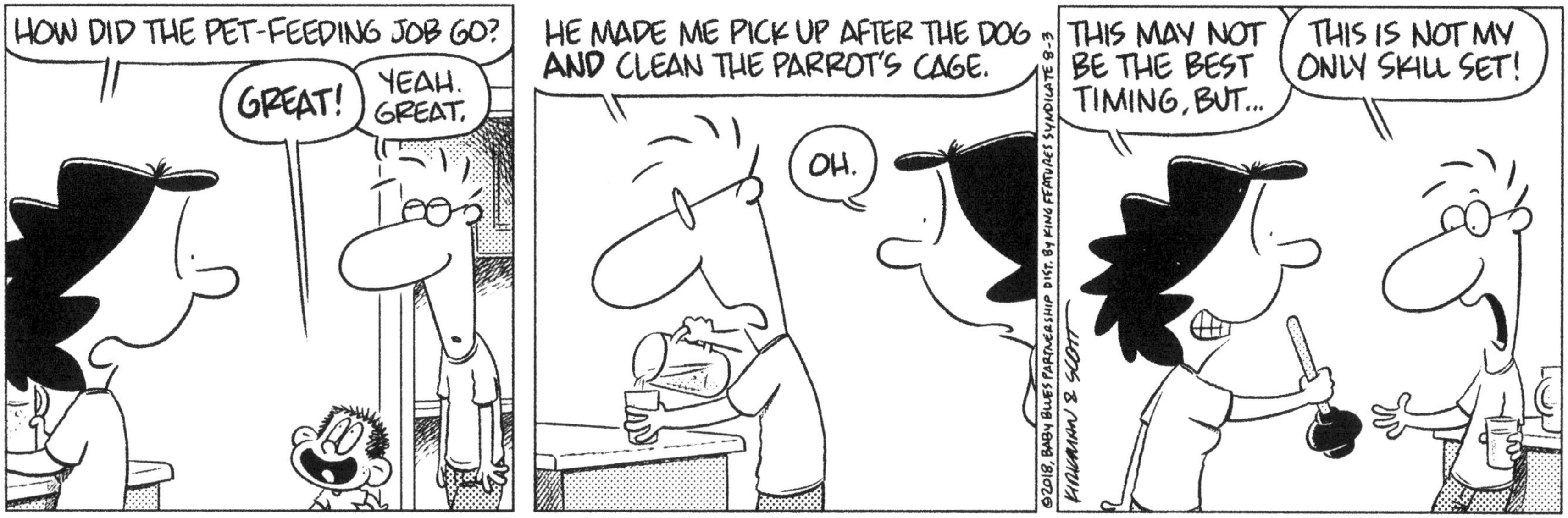
HOW DID THE PET-FEEDING JOB GO?
GREAT!
YEAH. GREAT.
HE MADE ME PICK UP AFTER THE DOG AND CLEAN THE PARROT'S CAGE.
OH.
©2018, BABY BLUES PARTNERSHIP DIST. BY KING FEATURES SYNDICATE 8-3
KIRKMAN & SCOTT
THIS MAY NOT BE THE BEST TIMING, BUT...
THIS IS NOT MY ONLY SKILL SET!

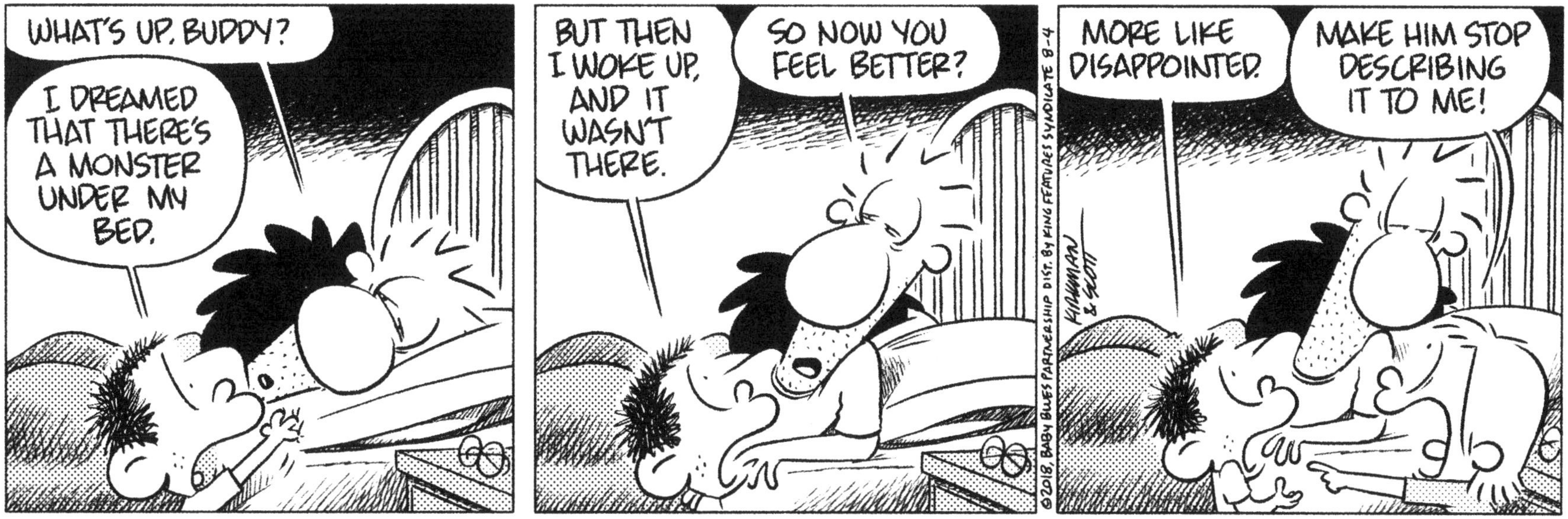
WHAT'S UP, BUDDY?
I DREAMED THAT THERE'S A MONSTER UNDER MY BED.
BUT THEN I WOKE UP, AND IT WASN'T THERE.
SO NOW YOU FEEL BETTER?
©2018, BABY BLUES PARTNERSHIP DIST. BY KING FEATURES SYNDICATE 8-4
KIRKMAN & SCOTT
MORE LIKE DISAPPOINTED.
MAKE HIM STOP DESCRIBING IT TO ME!

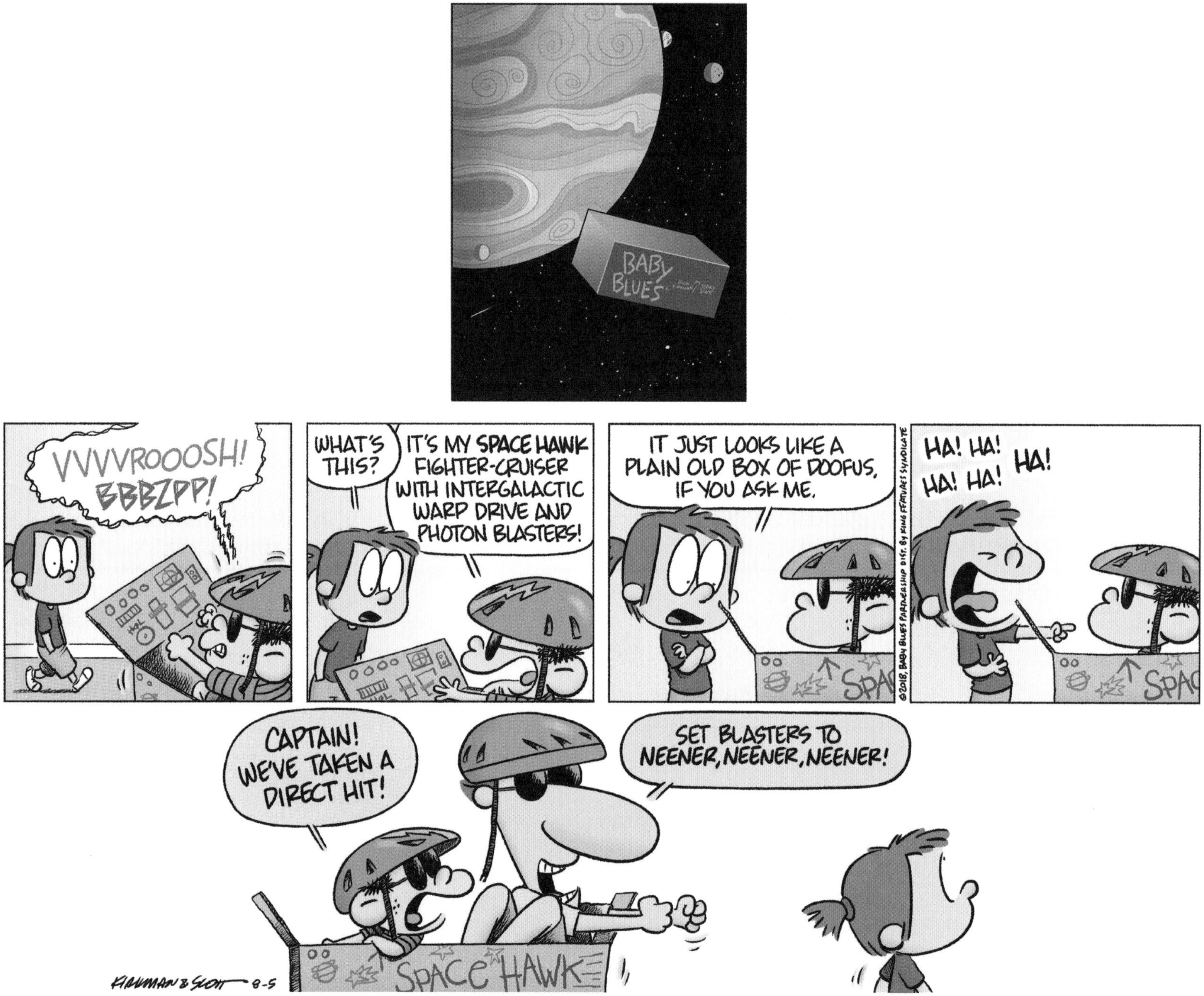
BABY BLUES
VVVVROOOSH! BBBZPP!
WHAT'S THIS?
IT'S MY SPACE HAWK FIGHTER-CRUISER WITH INTERGALACTIC WARP DRIVE AND PHOTON BLASTERS!
IT JUST LOOKS LIKE A PLAIN OLD BOX OF DOOFUS, IF YOU ASK ME.
SPAC
©2018, BABY BLUES PARTNERSHIP DIST. BY KING FEATURES SYNDICATE
HA! HA! HA! HA! HA!
SPAC
CAPTAIN! WE'VE TAKEN A DIRECT HIT!
SET BLASTERS TO NEENER, NEENER, NEENER!
KIRKMAN & SCOTT 8-5
SPACE HAWK

Rick: The title panel is my homage to the amazing *2001: A Space Odyssey*. Side note: I wanted to call this book *Neener, Neener, Neener*, but I was outvoted.

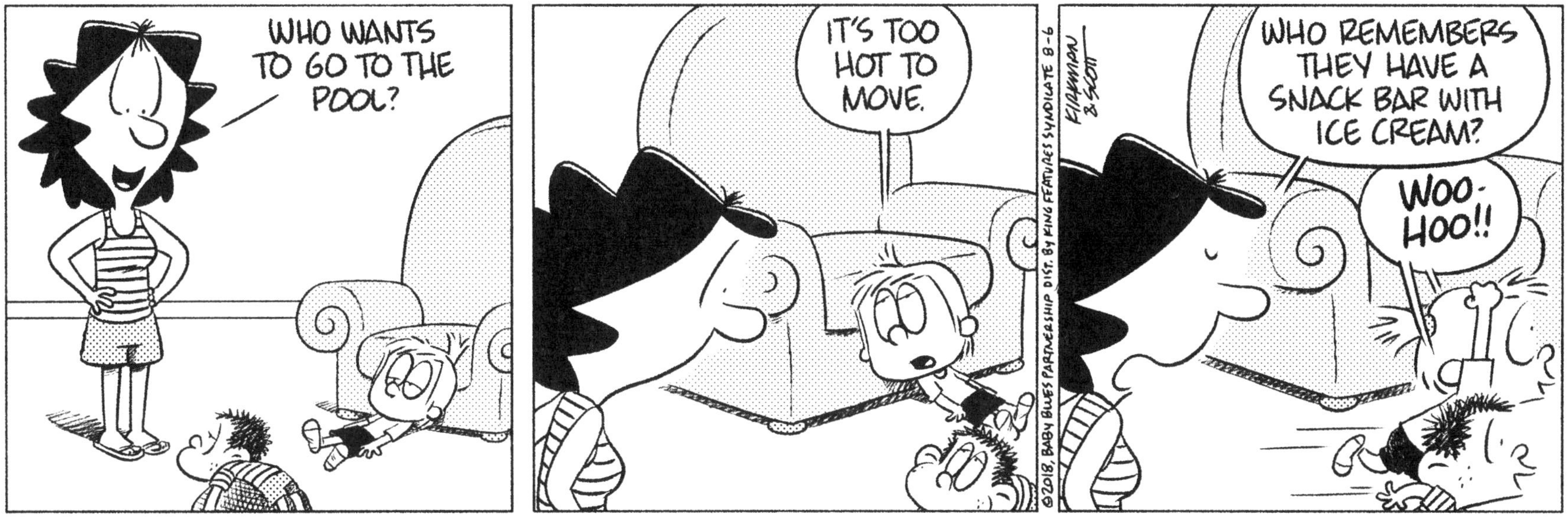
WHO WANTS TO GO TO THE POOL?
IT'S TOO HOT TO MOVE.
©2018, BABY BLUES PARTNERSHIP DIST. BY KING FEATURES SYNDICATE 8-6
KIRKMAN & SCOTT
WHO REMEMBERS THEY HAVE A SNACK BAR WITH ICE CREAM?
WOO-HOO!!

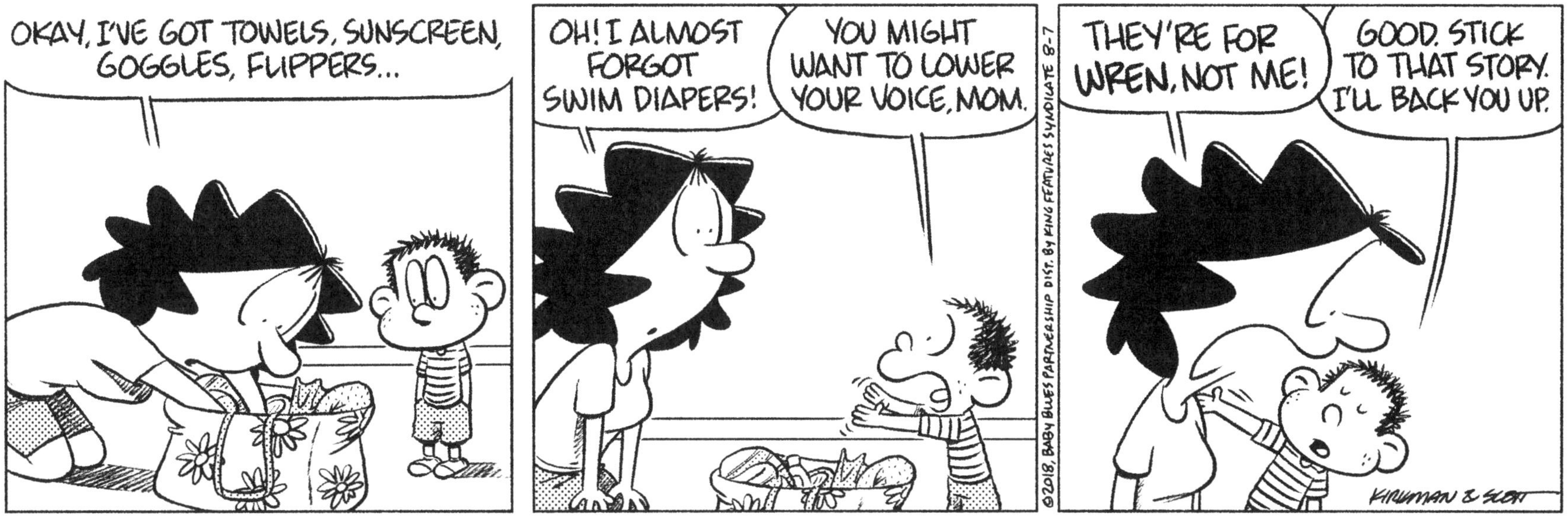
OKAY, I'VE GOT TOWELS, SUNSCREEN, GOGGLES, FLIPPERS...
OH! I ALMOST FORGOT SWIM DIAPERS!
YOU MIGHT WANT TO LOWER YOUR VOICE, MOM.
©2018, BABY BLUES PARTNERSHIP DIST. BY KING FEATURES SYNDICATE 8-7
THEY'RE FOR WREN, NOT ME!
GOOD. STICK TO THAT STORY. I'LL BACK YOU UP.
KIRKMAN & SCOTT

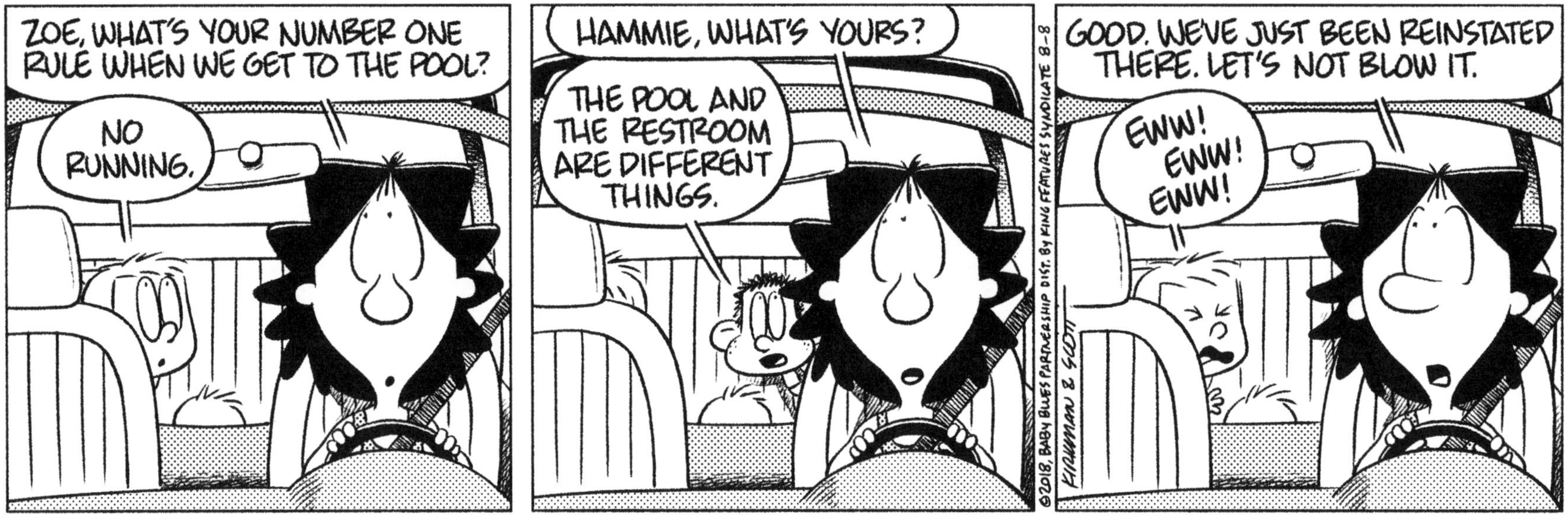
ZOE, WHAT'S YOUR NUMBER ONE RULE WHEN WE GET TO THE POOL?
NO RUNNING.
HAMMIE, WHAT'S YOURS?
THE POOL AND THE RESTROOM ARE DIFFERENT THINGS.
©2018, BABY BLUES PARTNERSHIP DIST. BY KING FEATURES SYNDICATE 8-8
KIRKMAN & SCOTT
GOOD. WE'VE JUST BEEN REINSTATED THERE. LET'S NOT BLOW IT.
EWW! EWW! EWW!

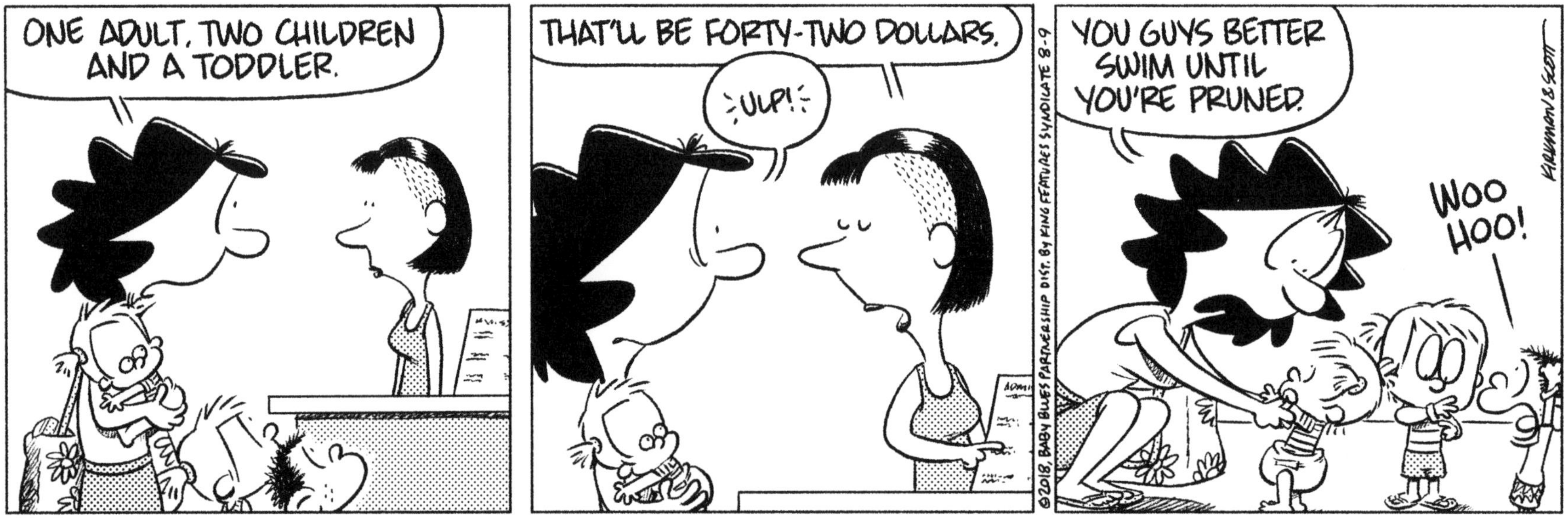
ONE ADULT, TWO CHILDREN AND A TODDLER.
THAT'LL BE FORTY-TWO DOLLARS.
ULP!
©2018, BABY BLUES PARTNERSHIP DIST. BY KING FEATURES SYNDICATE 8-9
YOU GUYS BETTER SWIM UNTIL YOU'RE PRUNED.
WOO HOO!
KIRKMAN & SCOTT

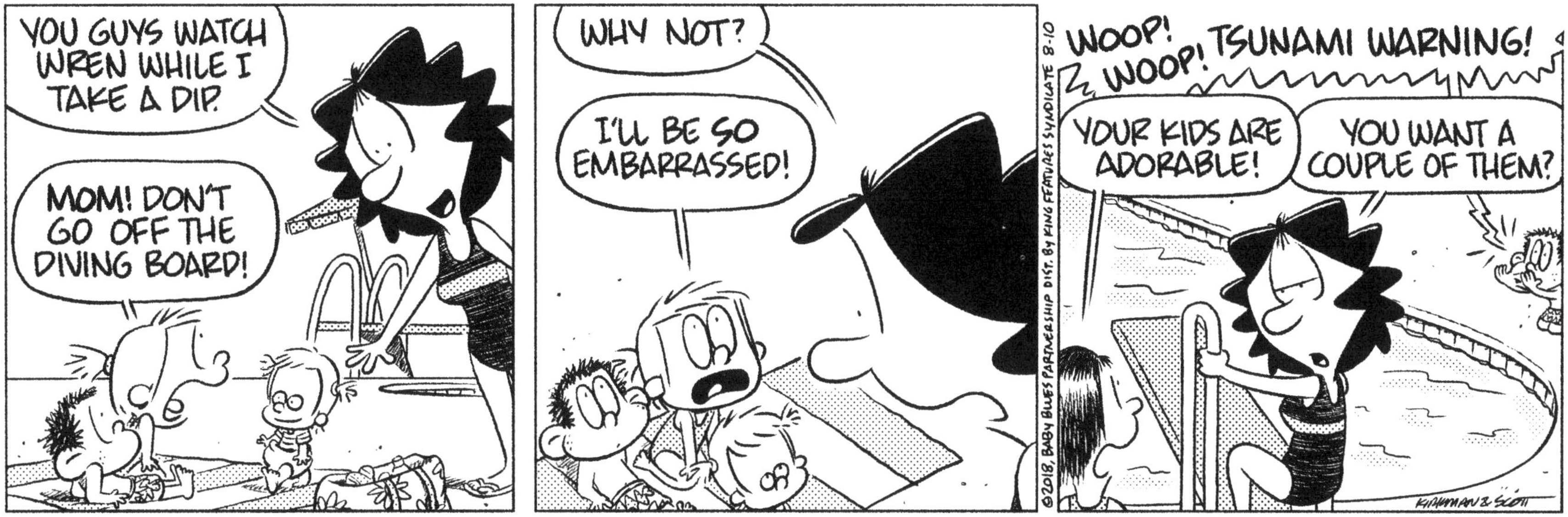
YOU GUYS WATCH WREN WHILE I TAKE A DIP.
MOM! DON'T GO OFF THE DIVING BOARD!
WHY NOT?
I'LL BE SO EMBARRASSED!
©2018, BABY BLUES PARTNERSHIP DIST. BY KING FEATURES SYNDICATE 8-10
WOOP! WOOP! TSUNAMI WARNING!
YOUR KIDS ARE ADORABLE!
YOU WANT A COUPLE OF THEM?
KIRKMAN & SCOTT

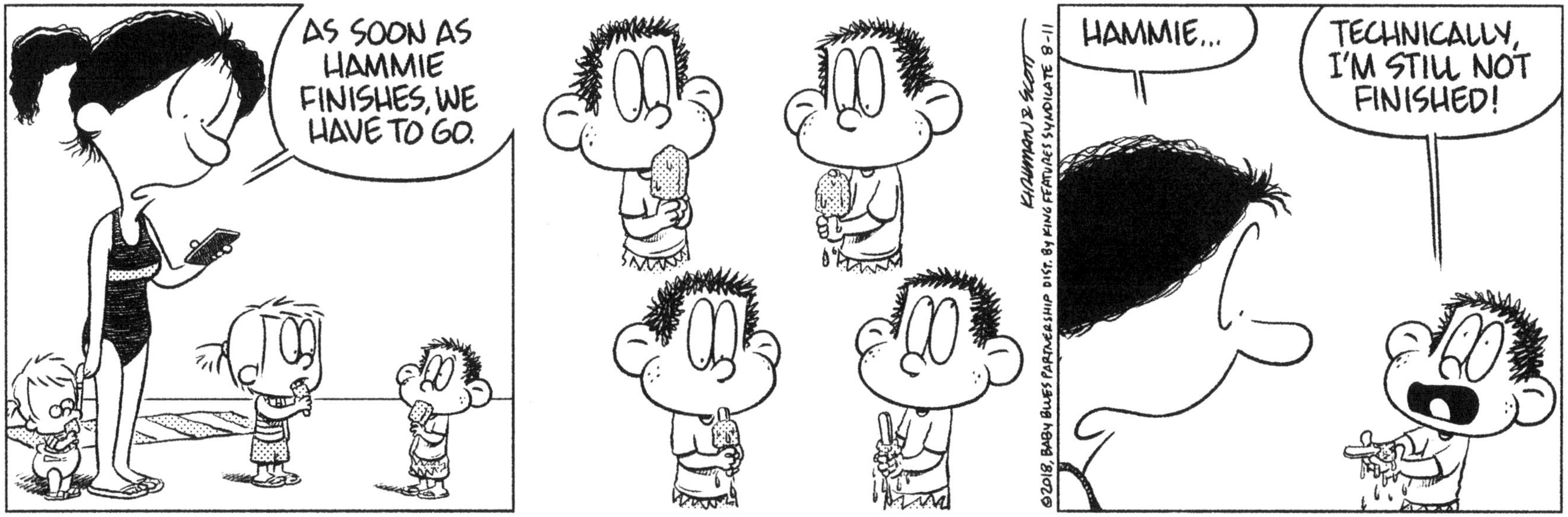
AS SOON AS HAMMIE FINISHES, WE HAVE TO GO.
KIRKMAN & SCOTT
©2018, BABY BLUES PARTNERSHIP DIST. BY KING FEATURES SYNDICATE 8-11
HAMMIE...
TECHNICALLY, I'M STILL NOT FINISHED!

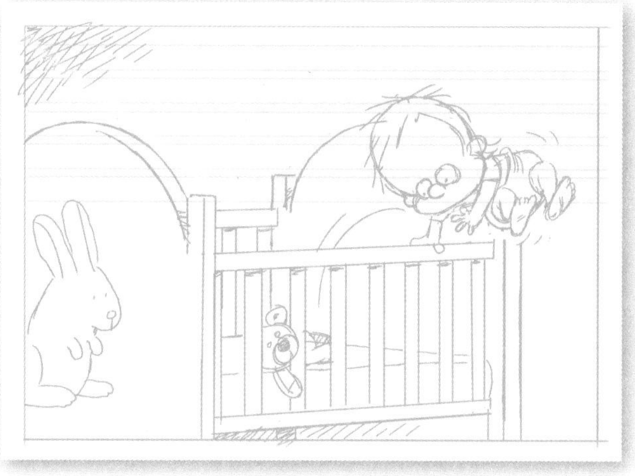

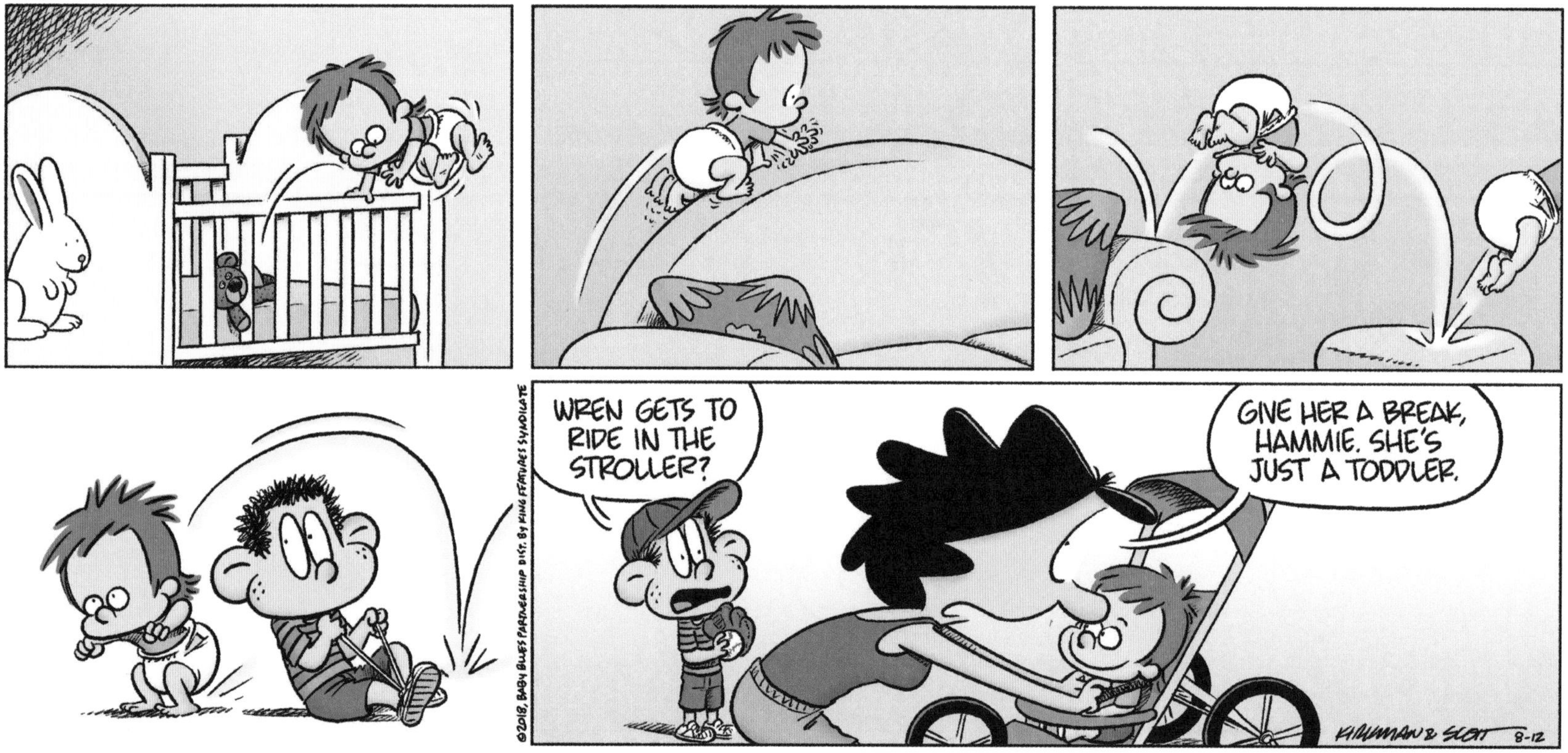
WREN GETS TO RIDE IN THE STROLLER?
GIVE HER A BREAK, HAMMIE. SHE'S JUST A TODDLER.
©2018, BABY BLUES PARTNERSHIP DIST. BY KING FEATURES SYNDICATE
KIRKMAN & SCOTT 8-12

Rick: Wren, parkour prodigy.

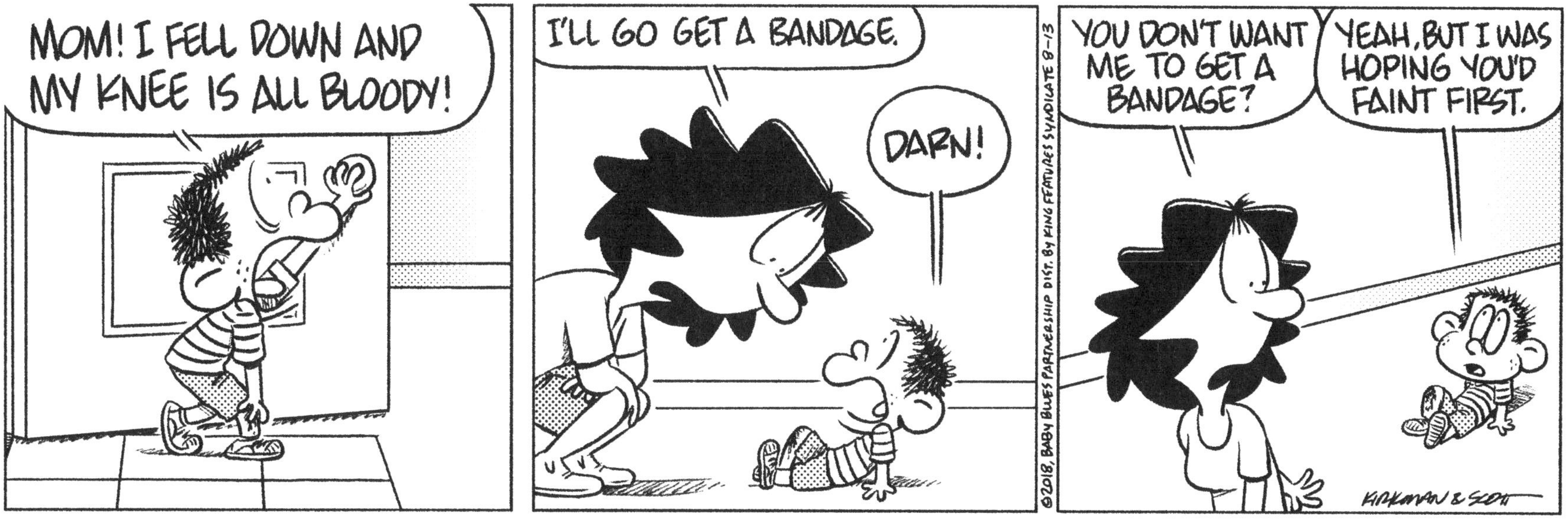
MOM! I FELL DOWN AND MY KNEE IS ALL BLOODY!
I'LL GO GET A BANDAGE.
DARN!
©2018, BABY BLUES PARTNERSHIP DIST. BY KING FEATURES SYNDICATE 8-13
YOU DON'T WANT ME TO GET A BANDAGE?
YEAH, BUT I WAS HOPING YOU'D FAINT FIRST.
KIRKMAN & SCOTT

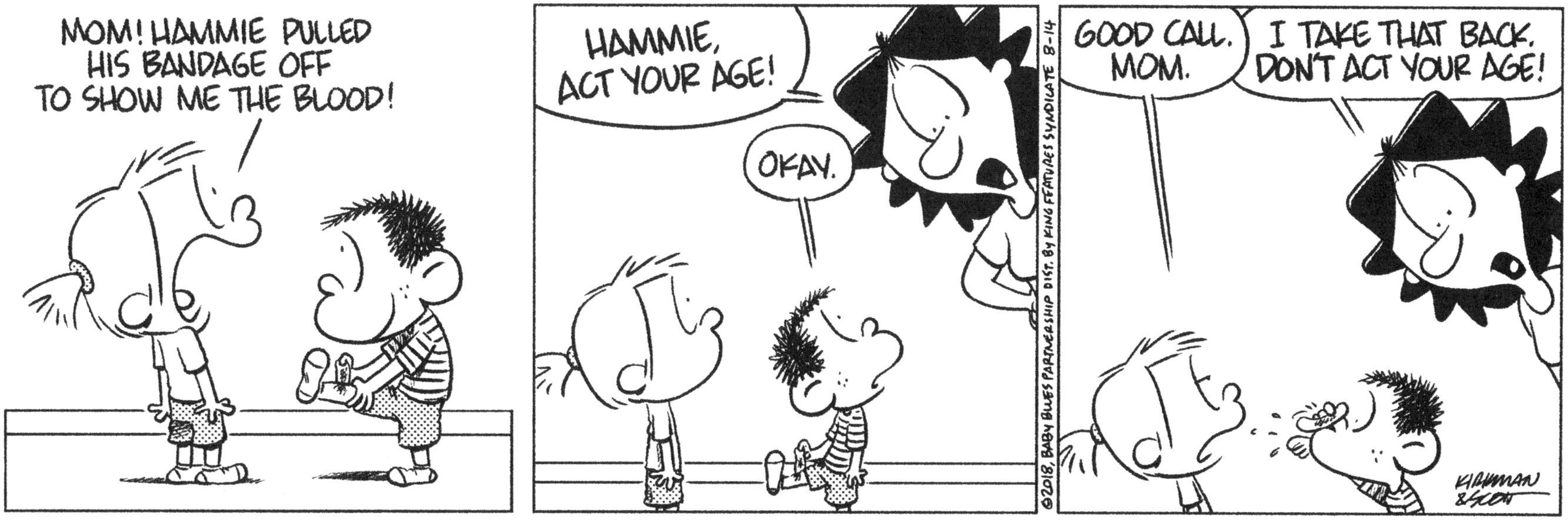
MOM! HAMMIE PULLED HIS BANDAGE OFF TO SHOW ME THE BLOOD!
HAMMIE, ACT YOUR AGE!
OKAY.
©2018, BABY BLUES PARTNERSHIP DIST. BY KING FEATURES SYNDICATE 8-14
GOOD CALL, MOM.
I TAKE THAT BACK. DON'T ACT YOUR AGE!
KIRKMAN & SCOTT

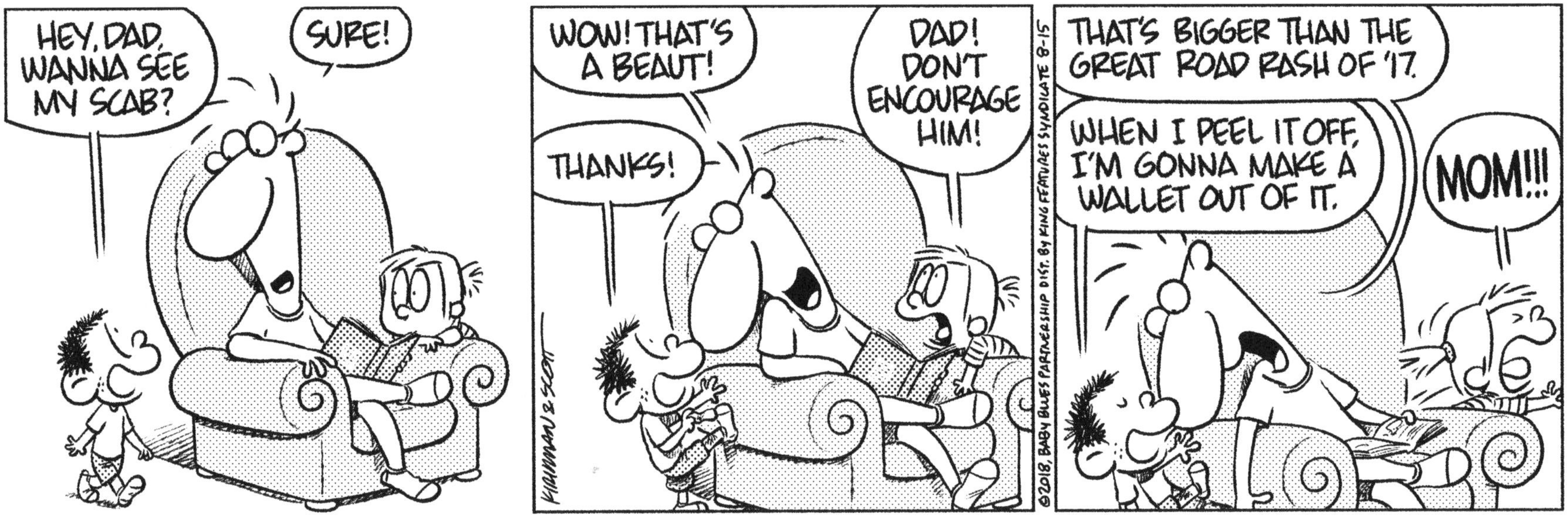

HEY, DAD, WANNA SEE MY SCAB?
SURE!
KIRKMAN & SCOTT
WOW! THAT'S A BEAUT!
THANKS!
DAD! DON'T ENCOURAGE HIM!
©2018, BABY BLUES PARTNERSHIP DIST. BY KING FEATURES SYNDICATE 8-15
THAT'S BIGGER THAN THE GREAT ROAD RASH OF '17.
WHEN I PEEL IT OFF, I'M GONNA MAKE A WALLET OUT OF IT.
MOM!!!

Jerry: Did you hear about the scab I got from a motorcycle accident once? I'll tell you sometime when you're not eating.

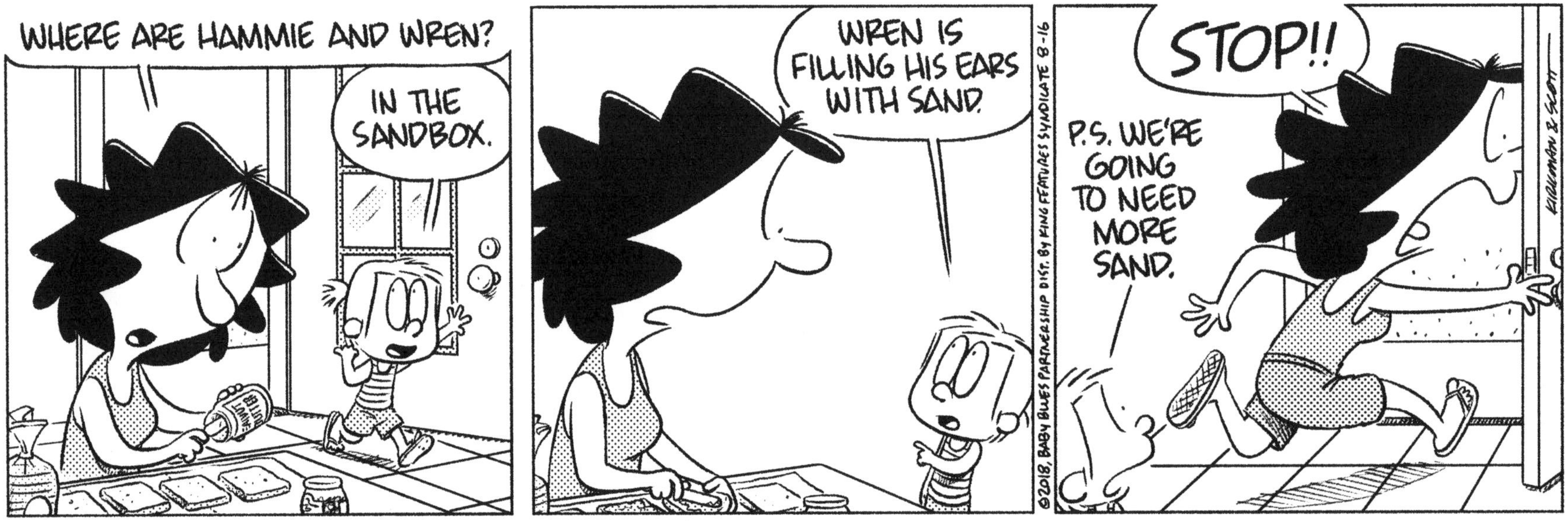

WHERE ARE HAMMIE AND WREN?
IN THE SANDBOX.
WREN IS FILLING HIS EARS WITH SAND.
©2018, BABY BLUES PARTNERSHIP DIST. BY KING FEATURES SYNDICATE 8-16
STOP!!
P.S. WE'RE GOING TO NEED MORE SAND.
KIRKMAN & SCOTT

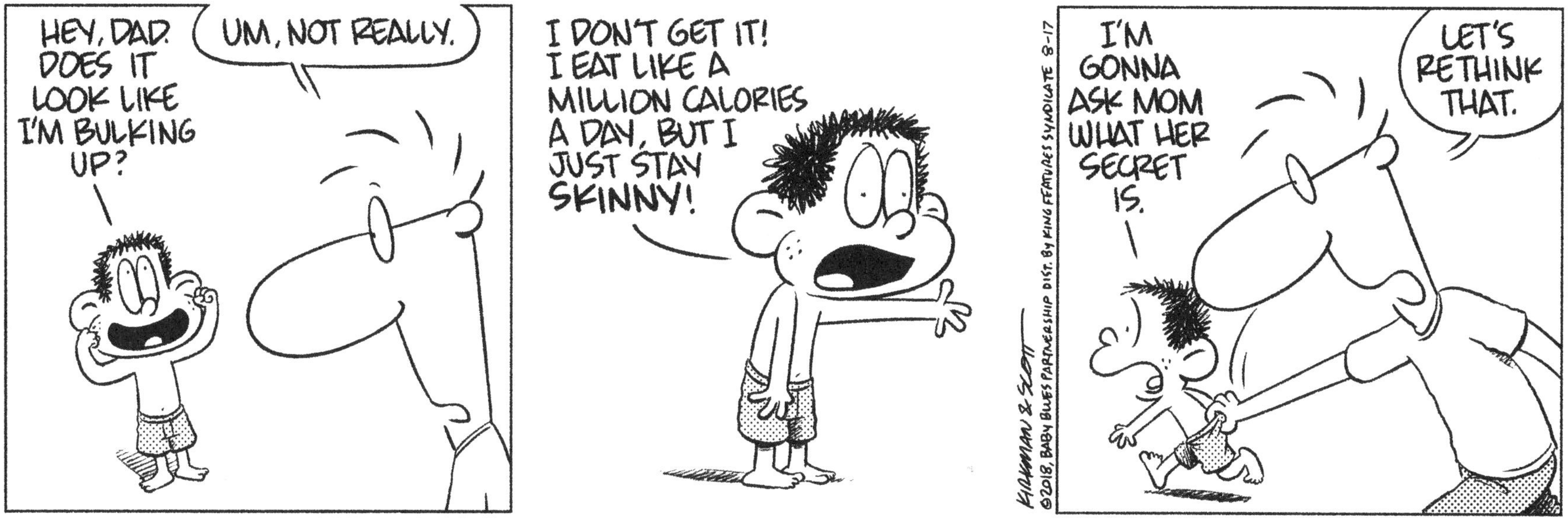
HEY, DAD. DOES IT LOOK LIKE I'M BULKING UP?
UM, NOT REALLY.
I DON'T GET IT! I EAT LIKE A MILLION CALORIES A DAY, BUT I JUST STAY SKINNY!
I'M GONNA ASK MOM WHAT HER SECRET IS.
LET'S RETHINK THAT.
KIRKMAN & SCOTT
©2018, BABY BLUES PARTNERSHIP DIST. BY KING FEATURES SYNDICATE 8-17

Rick: Better to learn these lessons young.

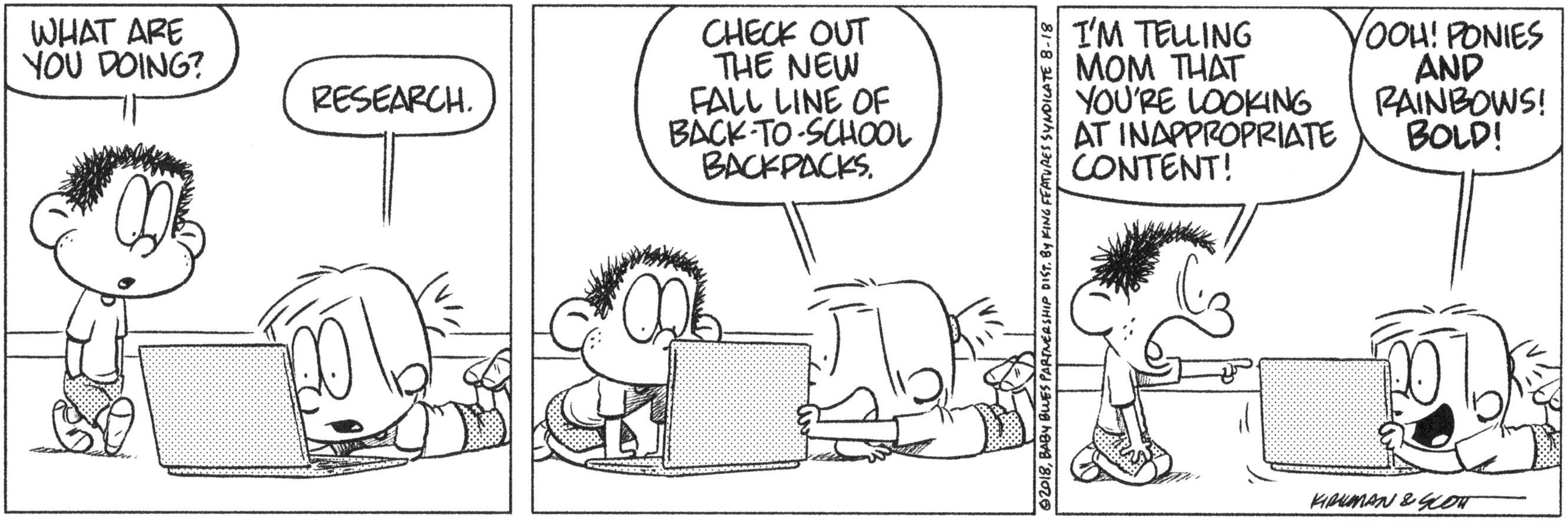
WHAT ARE YOU DOING?
RESEARCH.
CHECK OUT THE NEW FALL LINE OF BACK-TO-SCHOOL BACKPACKS.
©2018, BABY BLUES PARTNERSHIP DIST. BY KING FEATURES SYNDICATE 8-18
I'M TELLING MOM THAT YOU'RE LOOKING AT INAPPROPRIATE CONTENT!
OOH! PONIES AND RAINBOWS! BOLD!
KIRKMAN & SCOTT

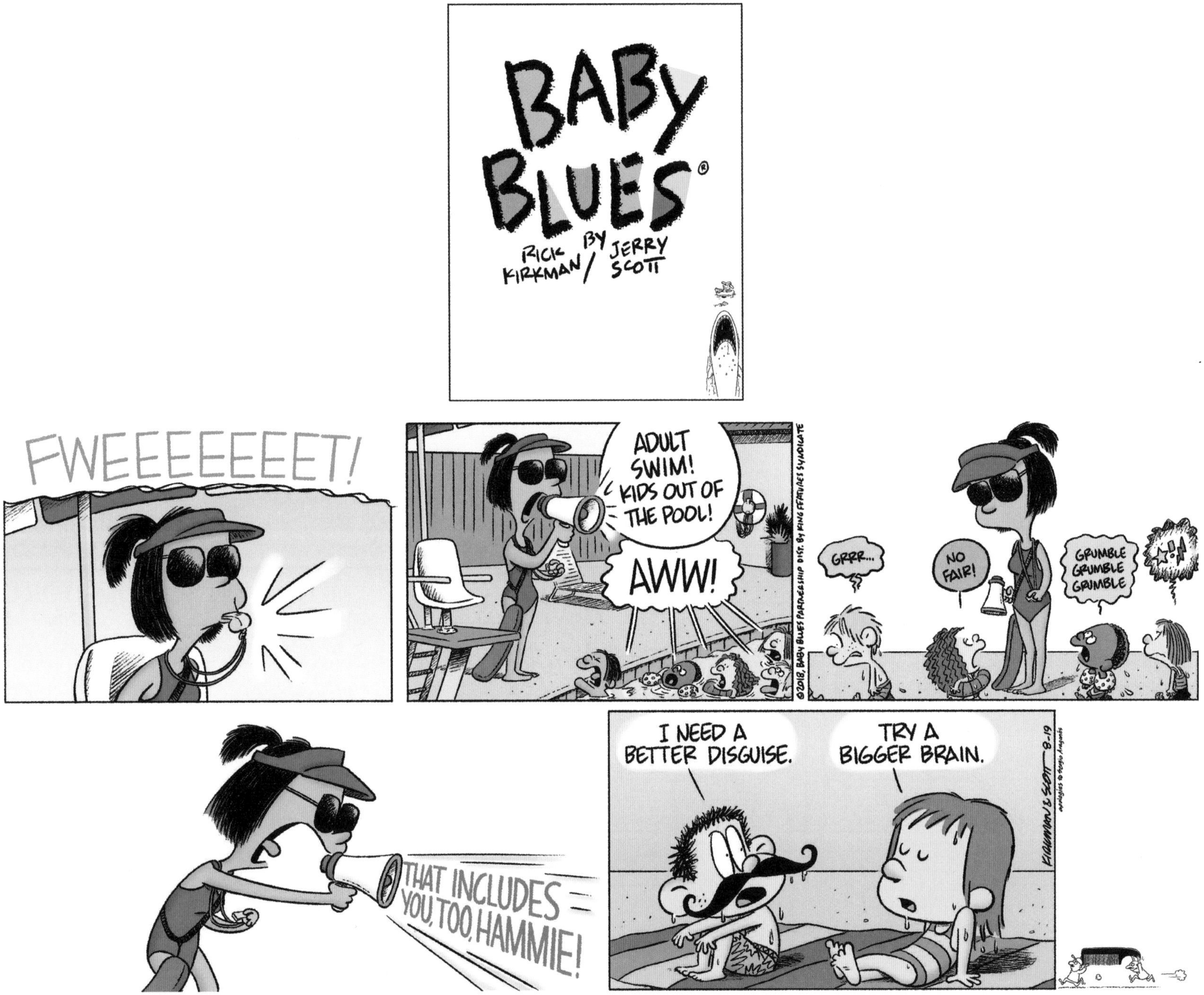
BABY BLUES®
BY RICK KIRKMAN / JERRY SCOTT
FWEEEEEEEET!
ADULT SWIM! KIDS OUT OF THE POOL!
AWW!
©2018, BABY BLUES PARTNERSHIP DIST. BY KING FEATURES SYNDICATE
GRRR...
NO FAIR!
GRUMBLE GRUMBLE GRUMBLE
THAT INCLUDES YOU, TOO, HAMMIE!
I NEED A BETTER DISGUISE.
TRY A BIGGER BRAIN.
KIRKMAN & SCOTT 8-19

Rick: Hammie's mustache reminded me of the incomparable Sergio Aragonés of *MAD* magazine fame. So I tried a couple of marginal drawings in his honor.

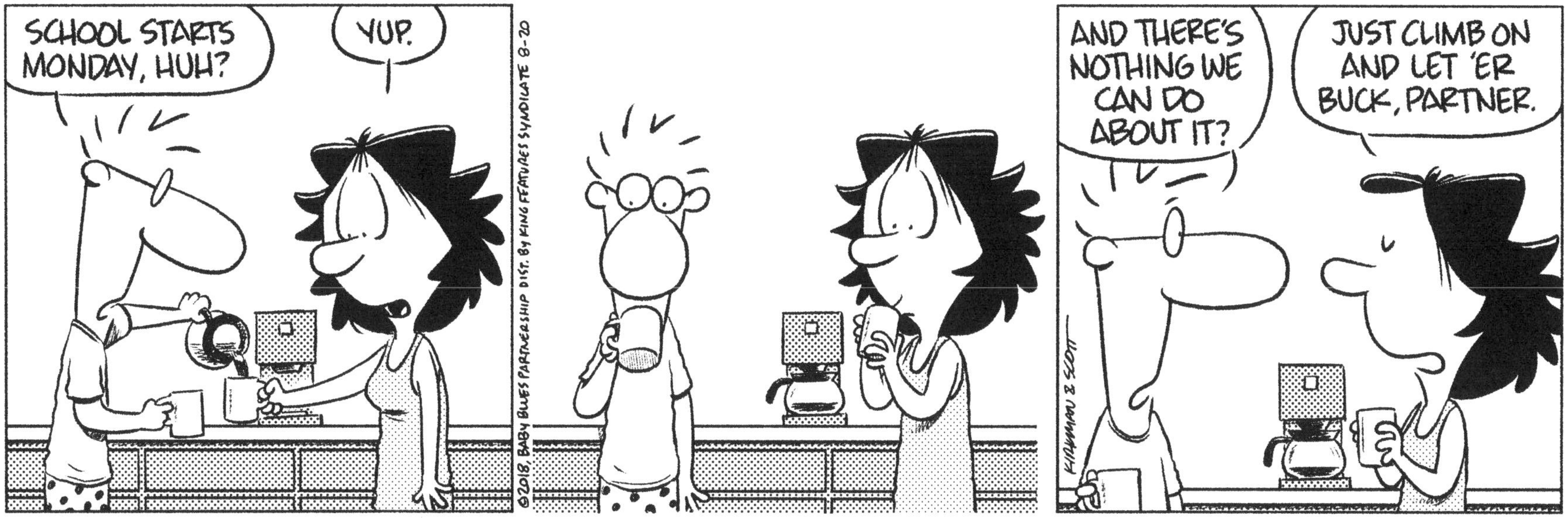
SCHOOL STARTS MONDAY, HUH?
YUP.
©2018, BABY BLUES PARTNERSHIP DIST. BY KING FEATURES SYNDICATE 8-20
AND THERE'S NOTHING WE CAN DO ABOUT IT?
JUST CLIMB ON AND LET 'ER BUCK, PARTNER.
KIRKMAN & SCOTT

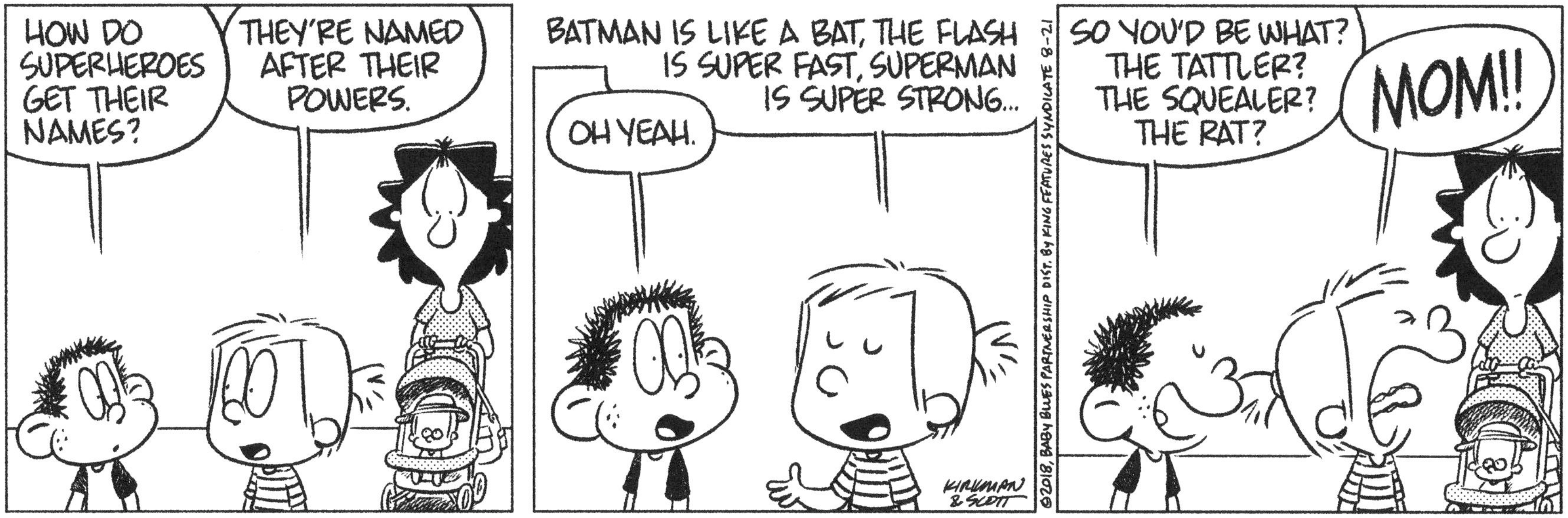
HOW DO SUPERHEROES GET THEIR NAMES?
THEY'RE NAMED AFTER THEIR POWERS.
BATMAN IS LIKE A BAT, THE FLASH IS SUPER FAST, SUPERMAN IS SUPER STRONG...
OH YEAH.
©2018, BABY BLUES PARTNERSHIP DIST. BY KING FEATURES SYNDICATE 8-21
KIRKMAN & SCOTT
SO YOU'D BE WHAT? THE TATTLER? THE SQUEALER? THE RAT?
MOM!!

Jerry: My superhero name would be Deadline Meeter. The costume is just a T-shirt and jeans.

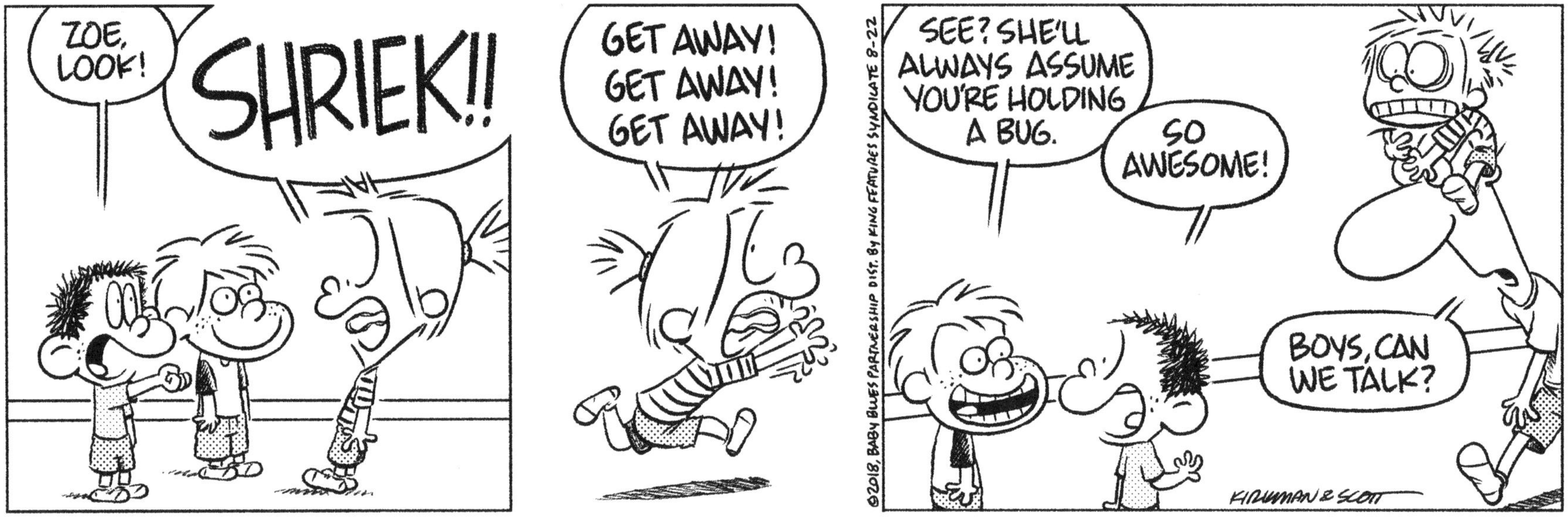

ZOE, LOOK!
SHRIEK!!
GET AWAY! GET AWAY! GET AWAY!
©2018, BABY BLUES PARTNERSHIP DIST. BY KING FEATURES SYNDICATE 8-22
SEE? SHE'LL ALWAYS ASSUME YOU'RE HOLDING A BUG.
SO AWESOME!
BOYS, CAN WE TALK?
KIRKMAN & SCOTT

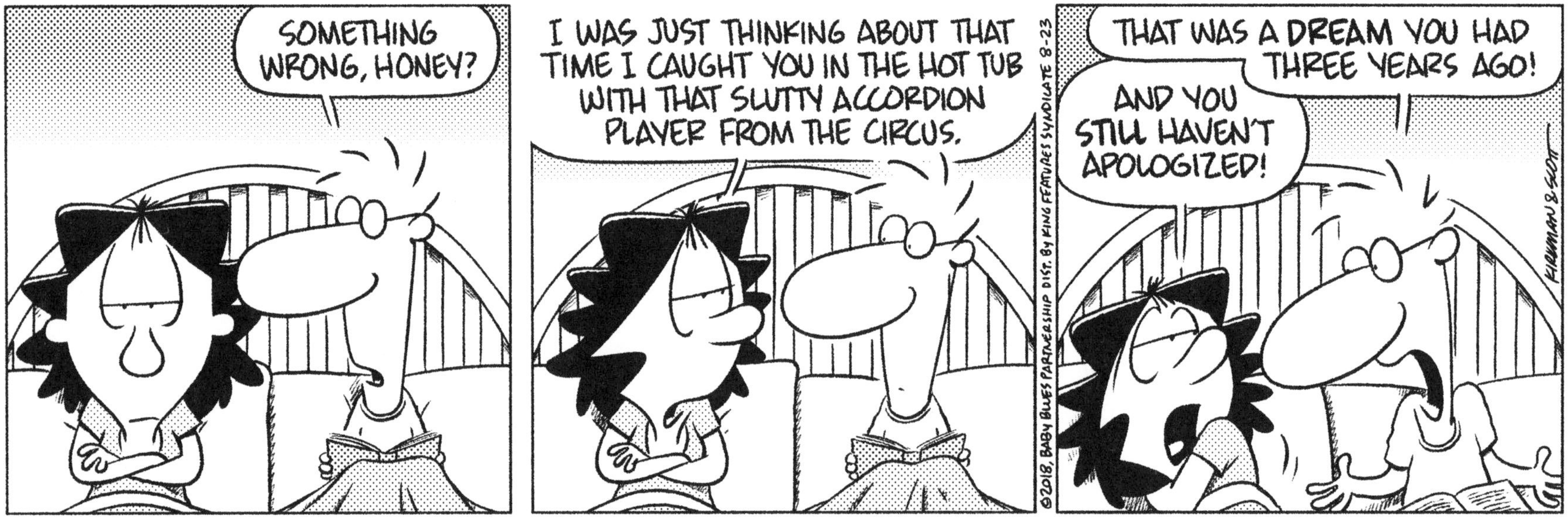

SOMETHING WRONG, HONEY?
I WAS JUST THINKING ABOUT THAT TIME I CAUGHT YOU IN THE HOT TUB WITH THAT SLUTTY ACCORDION PLAYER FROM THE CIRCUS.
©2018, BABY BLUES PARTNERSHIP DIST. BY KING FEATURES SYNDICATE 8-23
THAT WAS A DREAM YOU HAD THREE YEARS AGO!
AND YOU STILL HAVEN'T APOLOGIZED!
KIRKMAN & SCOTT

Rick: We were called to task by a reader over slut-shaming in this strip. A made-up character said it. About a dream. Dreamed by a made-up character. Who doesn't exist.

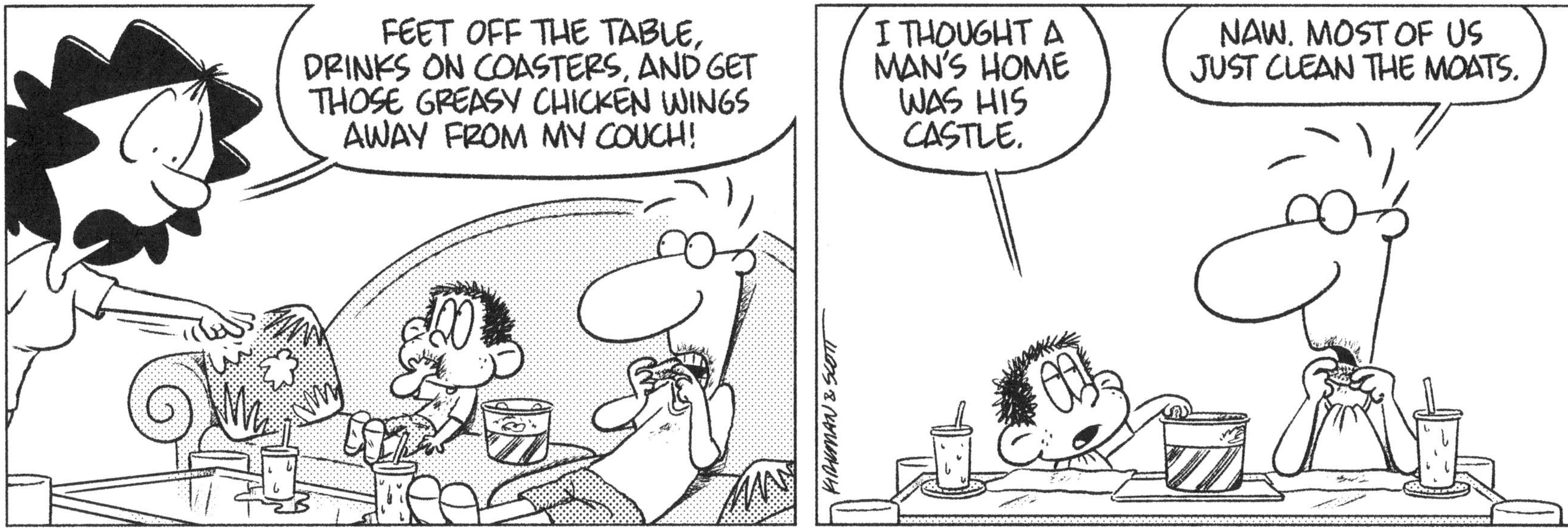
FEET OFF THE TABLE, DRINKS ON COASTERS, AND GET THOSE GREASY CHICKEN WINGS AWAY FROM MY COUCH!
KIRKMAN & SCOTT
I THOUGHT A MAN'S HOME WAS HIS CASTLE.
NAW. MOST OF US JUST CLEAN THE MOATS.
©2018, BABY BLUES PARTNERSHIP DIST. BY KING FEATURES SYNDICATE 8-24

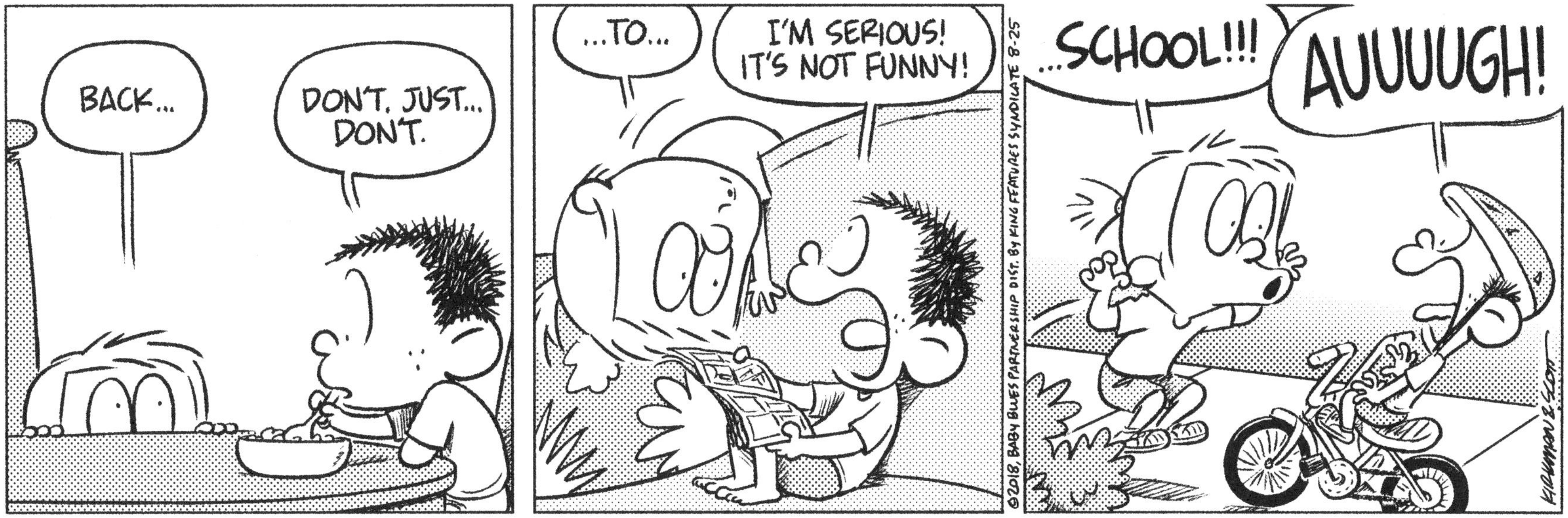
BACK...
DON'T. JUST... DON'T.
...TO...
I'M SERIOUS! IT'S NOT FUNNY!
©2018, BABY BLUES PARTNERSHIP DIST. BY KING FEATURES SYNDICATE 8-25
...SCHOOL!!!
AUUUUGH!
KIRKMAN & SCOTT

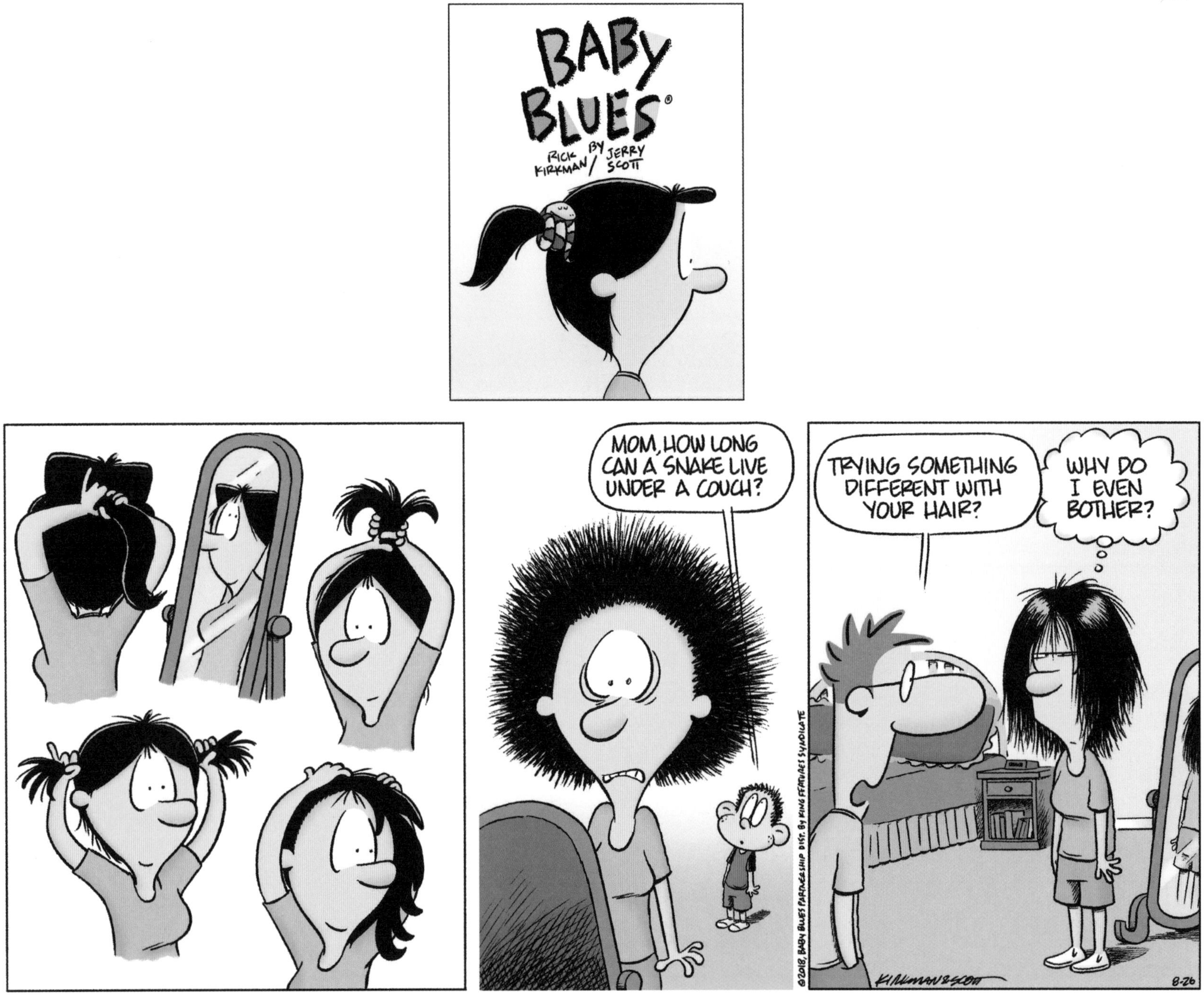
BABY BLUES®
BY RICK KIRKMAN / JERRY SCOTT
MOM, HOW LONG CAN A SNAKE LIVE UNDER A COUCH?
©2018, BABY BLUES PARTNERSHIP DIST. BY KING FEATURES SYNDICATE
TRYING SOMETHING DIFFERENT WITH YOUR HAIR?
WHY DO I EVEN BOTHER?
KIRKMAN & SCOTT
8-26

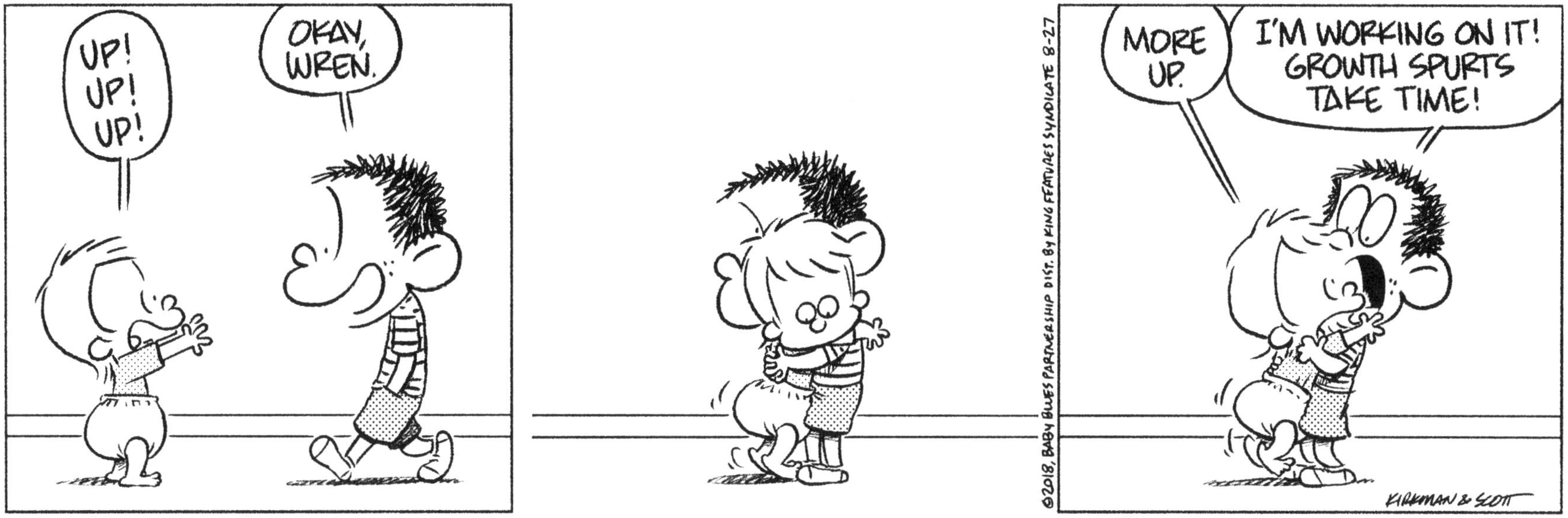
UP! UP! UP!
OKAY, WREN.
MORE UP.
I'M WORKING ON IT! GROWTH SPURTS TAKE TIME!
©2018, BABY BLUES PARTNERSHIP DIST. BY KING FEATURES SYNDICATE 8-27
KIRKMAN & SCOTT

Rick: Very subtle.

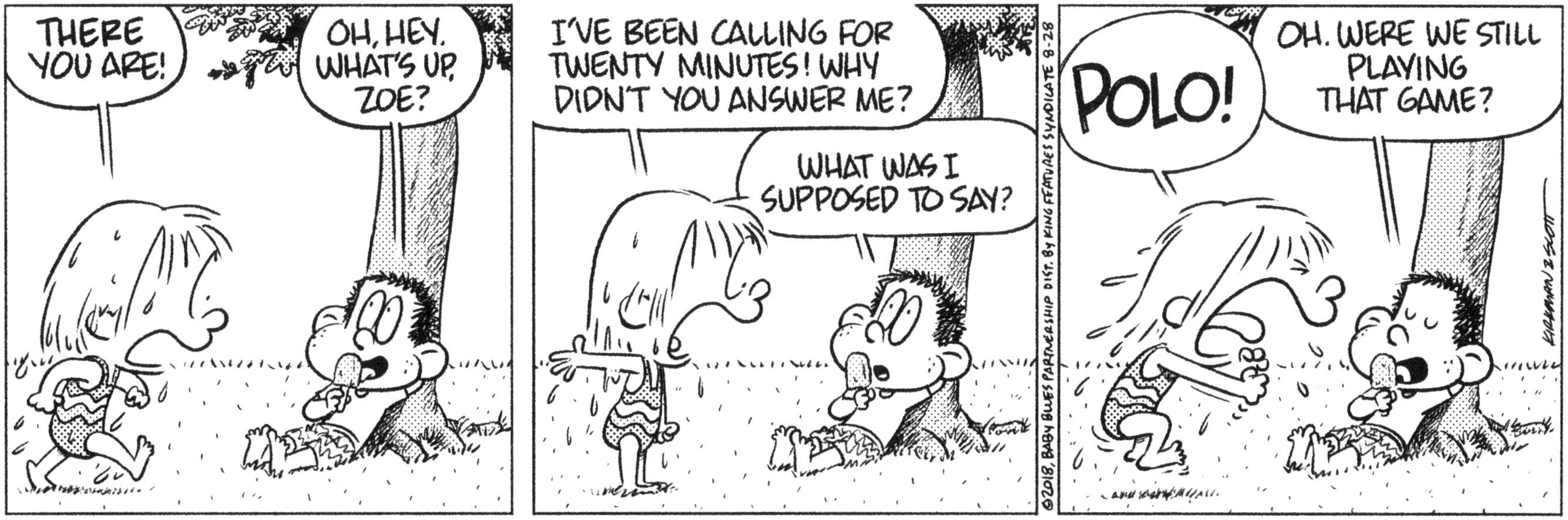
THERE YOU ARE!
OH, HEY. WHAT'S UP, ZOE?
I'VE BEEN CALLING FOR TWENTY MINUTES! WHY DIDN'T YOU ANSWER ME?
WHAT WAS I SUPPOSED TO SAY?
POLO!
OH. WERE WE STILL PLAYING THAT GAME?
©2018, BABY BLUES PARTNERSHIP DIST. BY KING FEATURES SYNDICATE 8-28
KIRKMAN & SCOTT

Rick: I love Jerry's timing in this gag. And the fact the reader needs to fill in the blank.

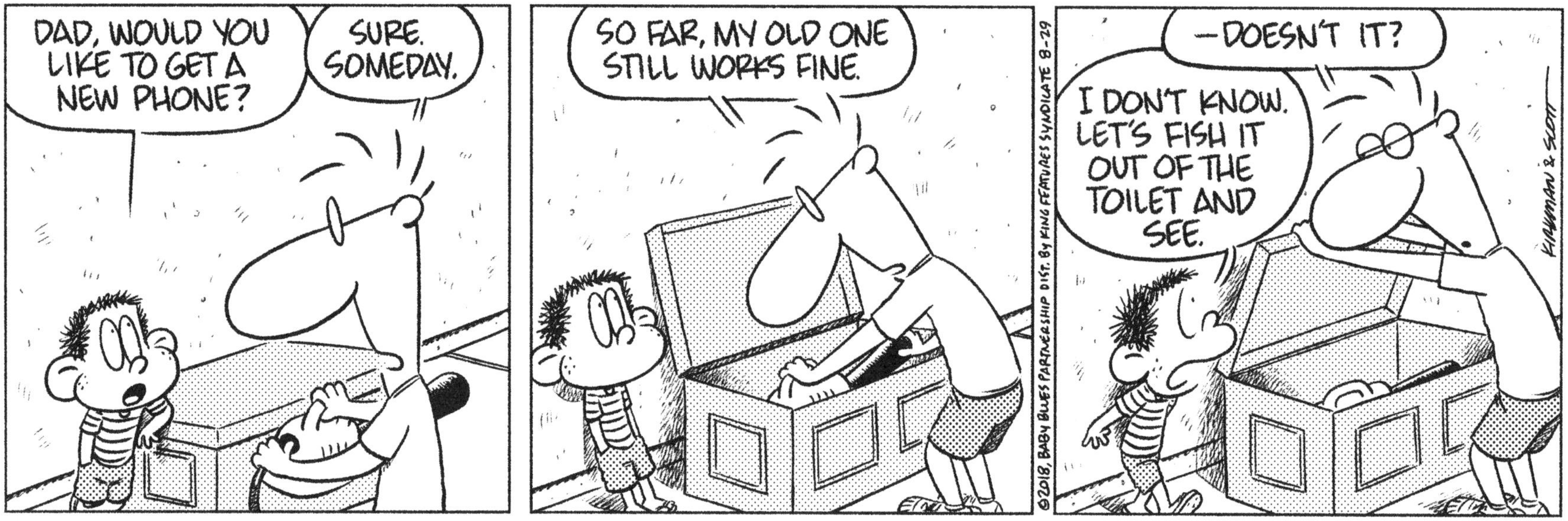
DAD, WOULD YOU LIKE TO GET A NEW PHONE?
SURE. SOMEDAY.
SO FAR, MY OLD ONE STILL WORKS FINE.
©2018, BABY BLUES PARTNERSHIP DIST. BY KING FEATURES SYNDICATE 8-29
—DOESN'T IT?
I DON'T KNOW. LET'S FISH IT OUT OF THE TOILET AND SEE.
KIRKMAN & SCOTT

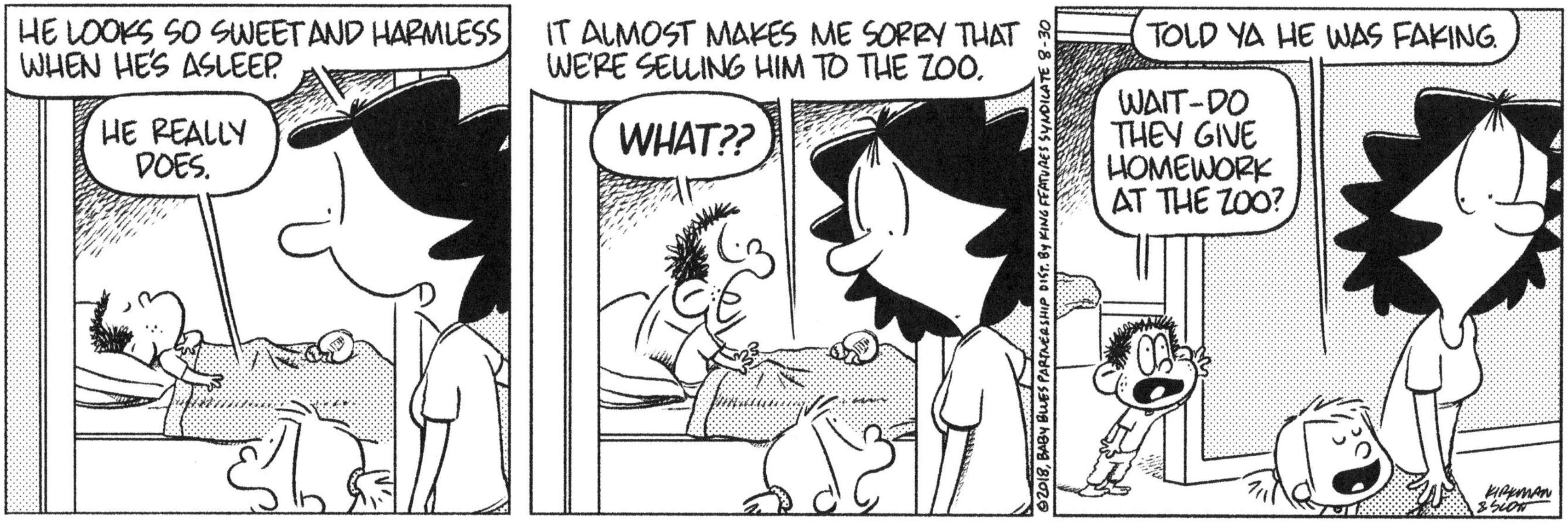
HE LOOKS SO SWEET AND HARMLESS WHEN HE'S ASLEEP.
HE REALLY DOES.
IT ALMOST MAKES ME SORRY THAT WE'RE SELLING HIM TO THE ZOO.
WHAT??
©2018, BABY BLUES PARTNERSHIP DIST. BY KING FEATURES SYNDICATE 8-30
TOLD YA HE WAS FAKING.
WAIT–DO THEY GIVE HOMEWORK AT THE ZOO?
KIRKMAN & SCOTT

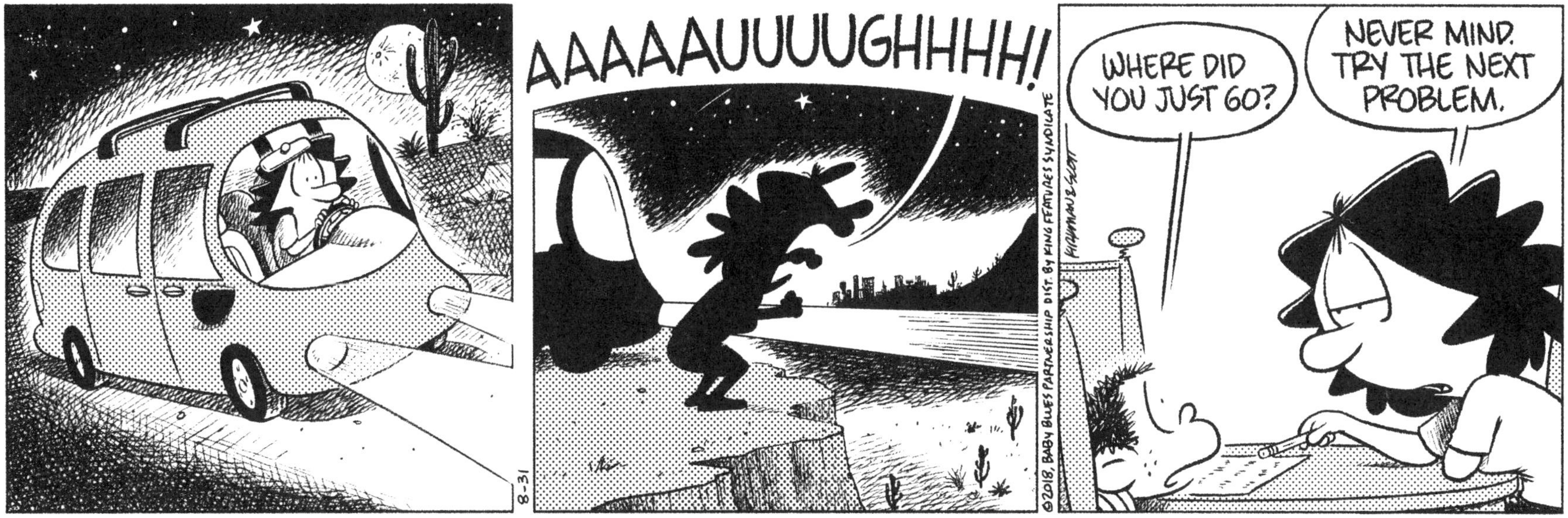
AAAAAUUUUGHHHH!
©2018, BABY BLUES PARTNERSHIP DIST. BY KING FEATURES SYNDICATE
KIRKMAN & SCOTT
WHERE DID YOU JUST GO?
NEVER MIND. TRY THE NEXT PROBLEM.

Rick: Maybe my favorite gag of the year. **Jerry:** This is an actual scene from my childhood. Let's just say I wasn't a math-y kid.

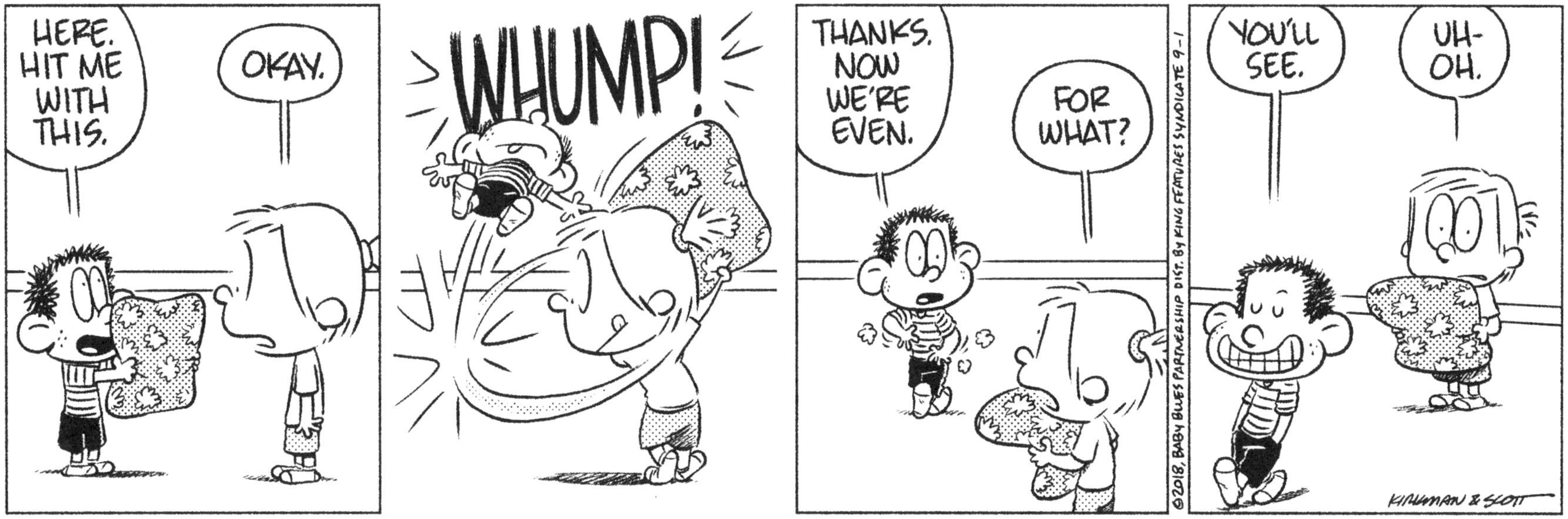
HERE. HIT ME WITH THIS.
OKAY.
WHUMP!
THANKS. NOW WE'RE EVEN.
FOR WHAT?
©2018, BABY BLUES PARTNERSHIP DIST. BY KING FEATURES SYNDICATE 9-1
YOU'LL SEE.
UH-OH.
KIRKMAN & SCOTT

Rick: I think I felt a little nudge from Sparky Schulz when I drew that second panel.

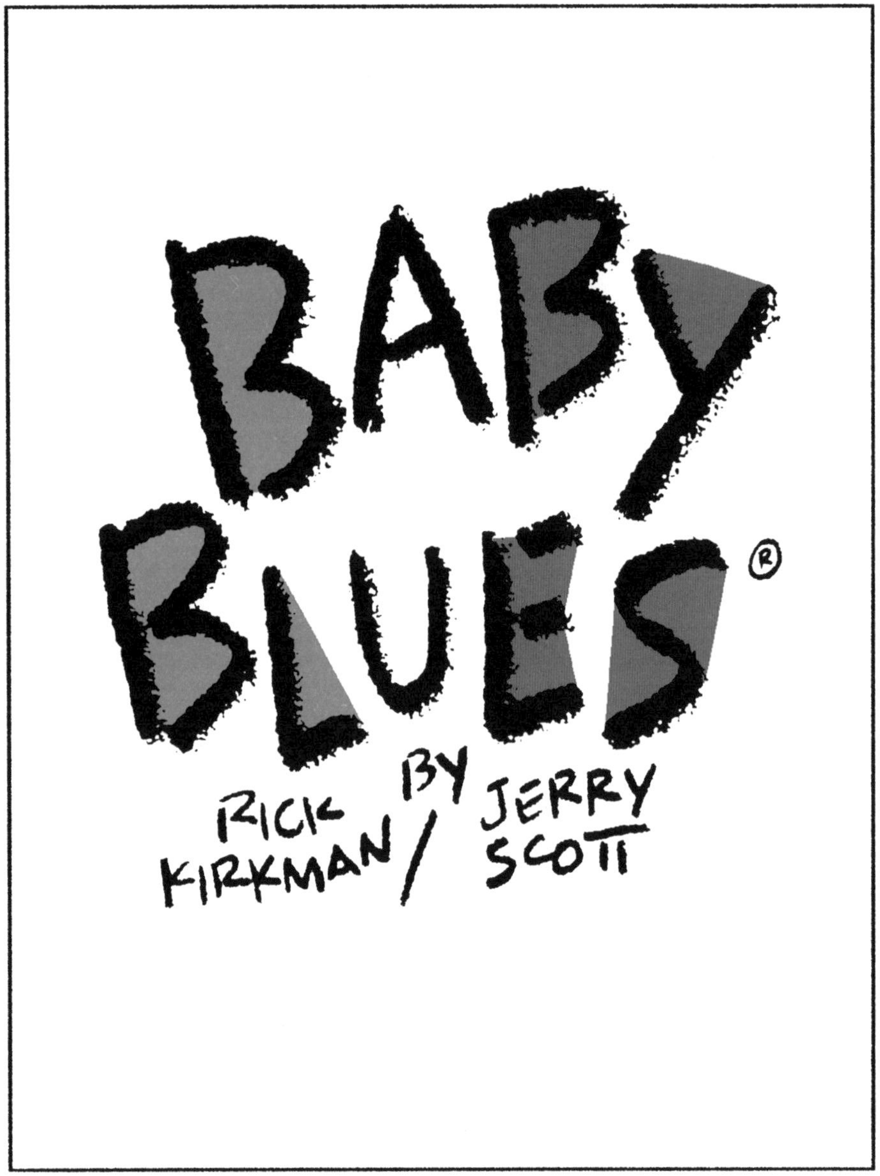
BABY BLUES®
RICK KIRKMAN / BY / JERRY SCOTT

Rick: This is such an incredibly clever concept from Jerry.

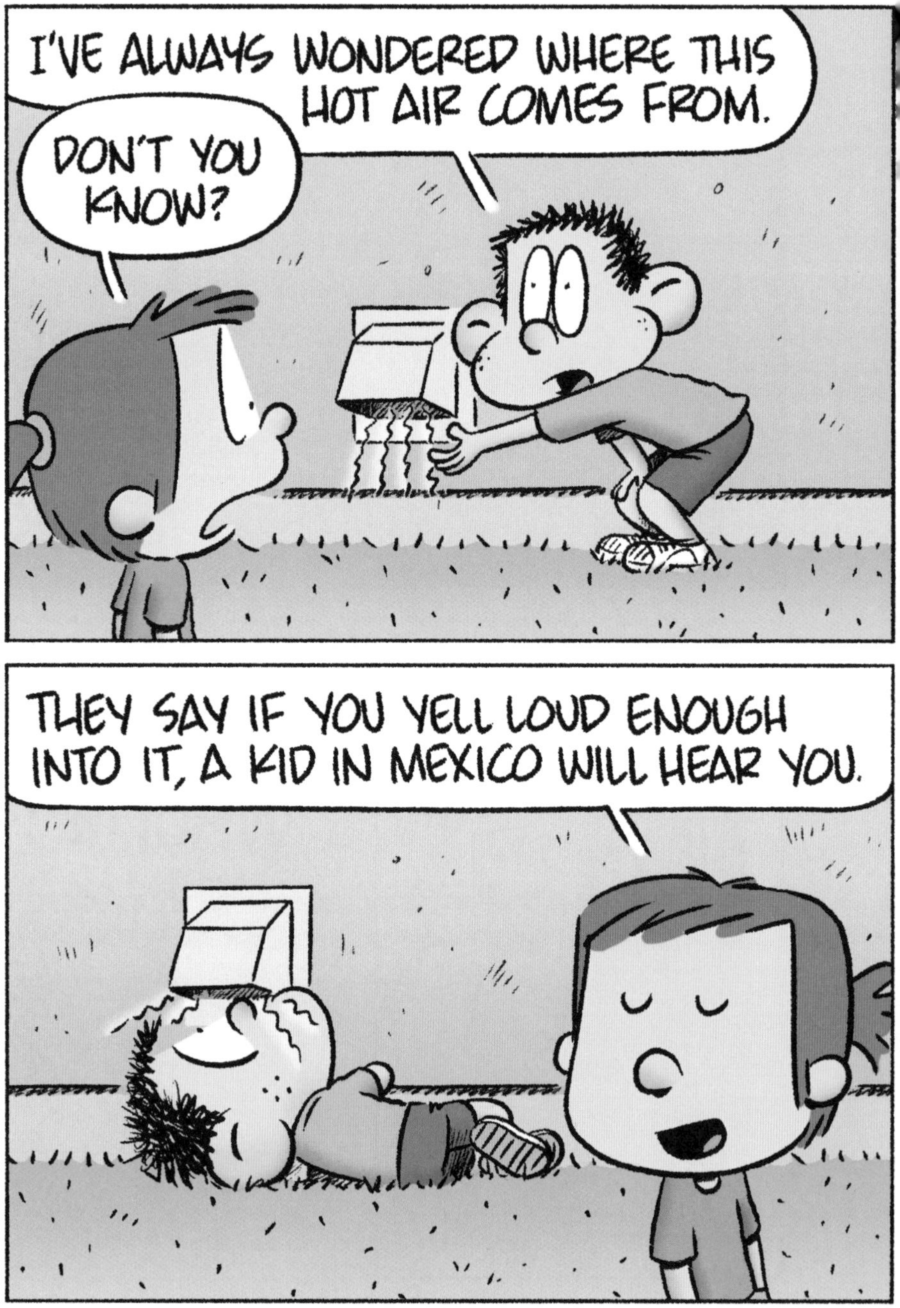
I'VE ALWAYS WONDERED WHERE THIS HOT AIR COMES FROM.
DON'T YOU KNOW?
THEY SAY IF YOU YELL LOUD ENOUGH INTO IT, A KID IN MEXICO WILL HEAR YOU.

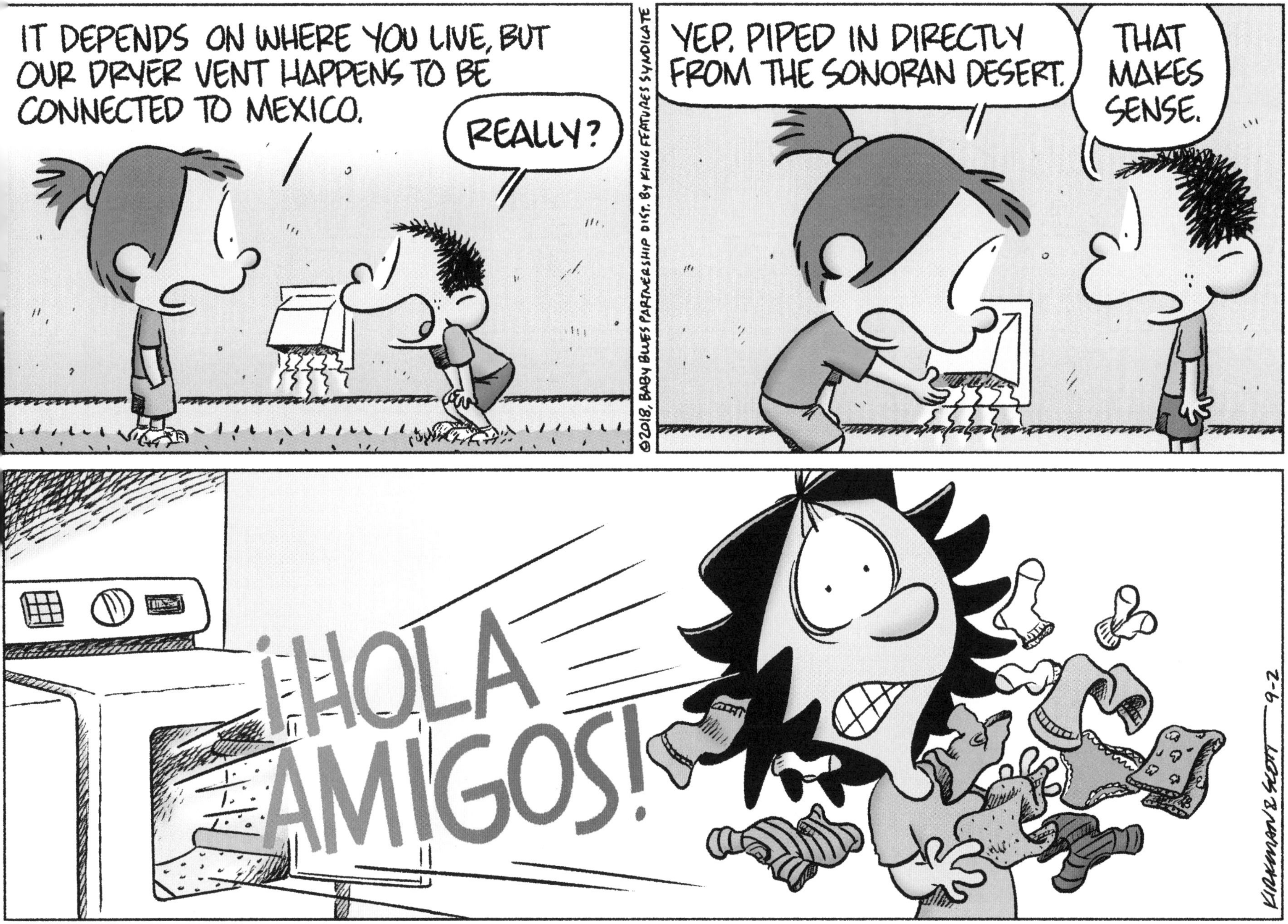

IT DEPENDS ON WHERE YOU LIVE, BUT OUR DRYER VENT HAPPENS TO BE CONNECTED TO MEXICO.
REALLY?
©2018, BABY BLUES PARTNERSHIP DIST. BY KING FEATURES SYNDICATE
YEP, PIPED IN DIRECTLY FROM THE SONORAN DESERT.
THAT MAKES SENSE.
¡HOLA AMIGOS!
KIRKMAN & SCOTT
9-2

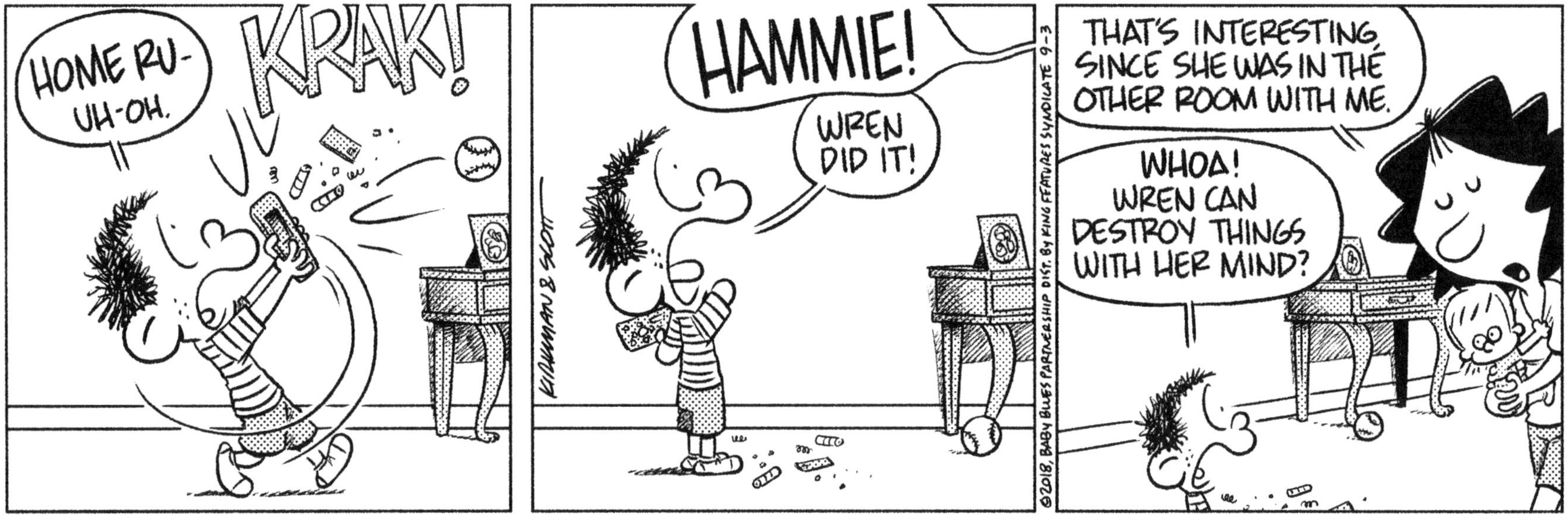
HOME RU- UH-OH.
KRAK!
HAMMIE!
WREN DID IT!
KIRKMAN & SCOTT
©2018, BABY BLUES PARTNERSHIP DIST. BY KING FEATURES SYNDICATE 9-3
THAT'S INTERESTING, SINCE SHE WAS IN THE OTHER ROOM WITH ME.
WHOA! WREN CAN DESTROY THINGS WITH HER MIND?

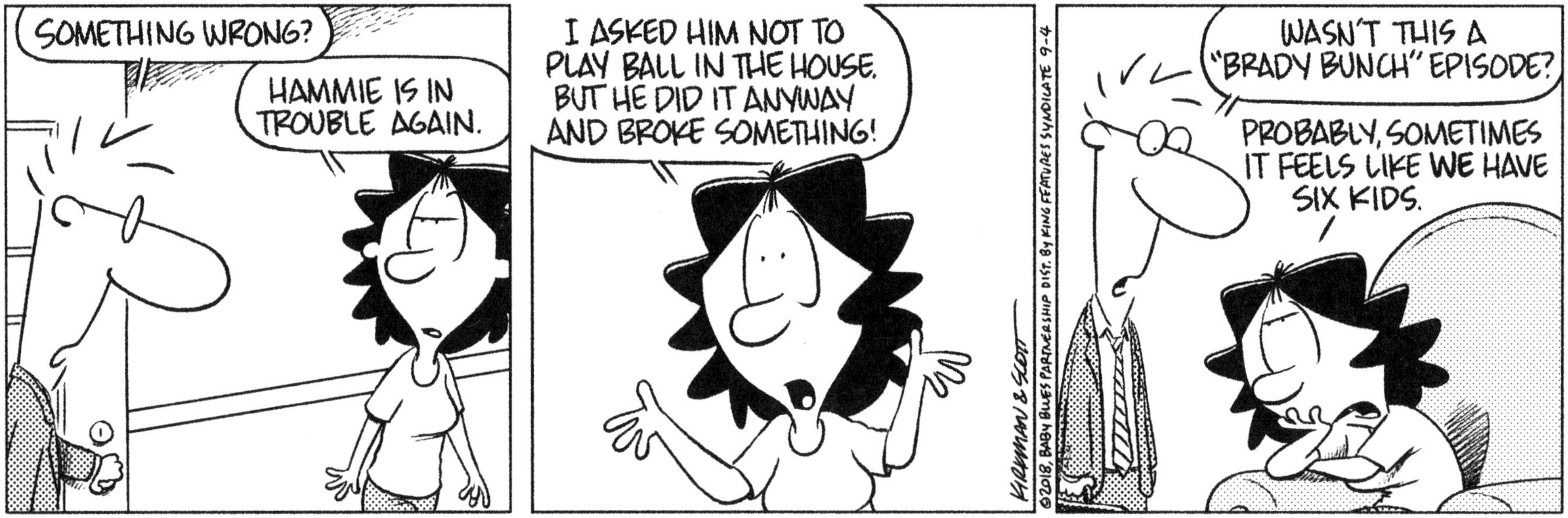
SOMETHING WRONG?
HAMMIE IS IN TROUBLE AGAIN.
I ASKED HIM NOT TO PLAY BALL IN THE HOUSE. BUT HE DID IT ANYWAY AND BROKE SOMETHING!
KIRKMAN & SCOTT
©2018, BABY BLUES PARTNERSHIP DIST. BY KING FEATURES SYNDICATE 9-4
WASN'T THIS A "BRADY BUNCH" EPISODE?
PROBABLY, SOMETIMES IT FEELS LIKE WE HAVE SIX KIDS.

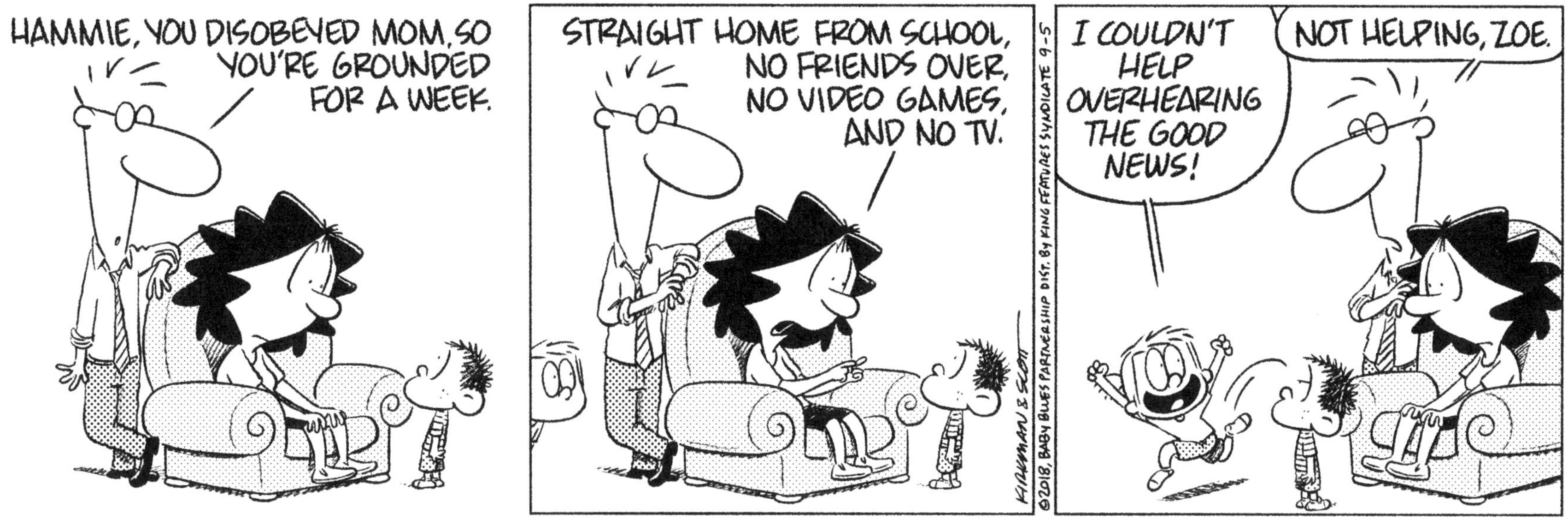
HAMMIE, YOU DISOBEYED MOM, SO YOU'RE GROUNDED FOR A WEEK.
STRAIGHT HOME FROM SCHOOL, NO FRIENDS OVER, NO VIDEO GAMES, AND NO TV.
KIRKMAN & SCOTT
©2018, BABY BLUES PARTNERSHIP DIST. BY KING FEATURES SYNDICATE 9-5
I COULDN'T HELP OVERHEARING THE GOOD NEWS!
NOT HELPING, ZOE.

Jerry: The schadenfreude is strong in this one.

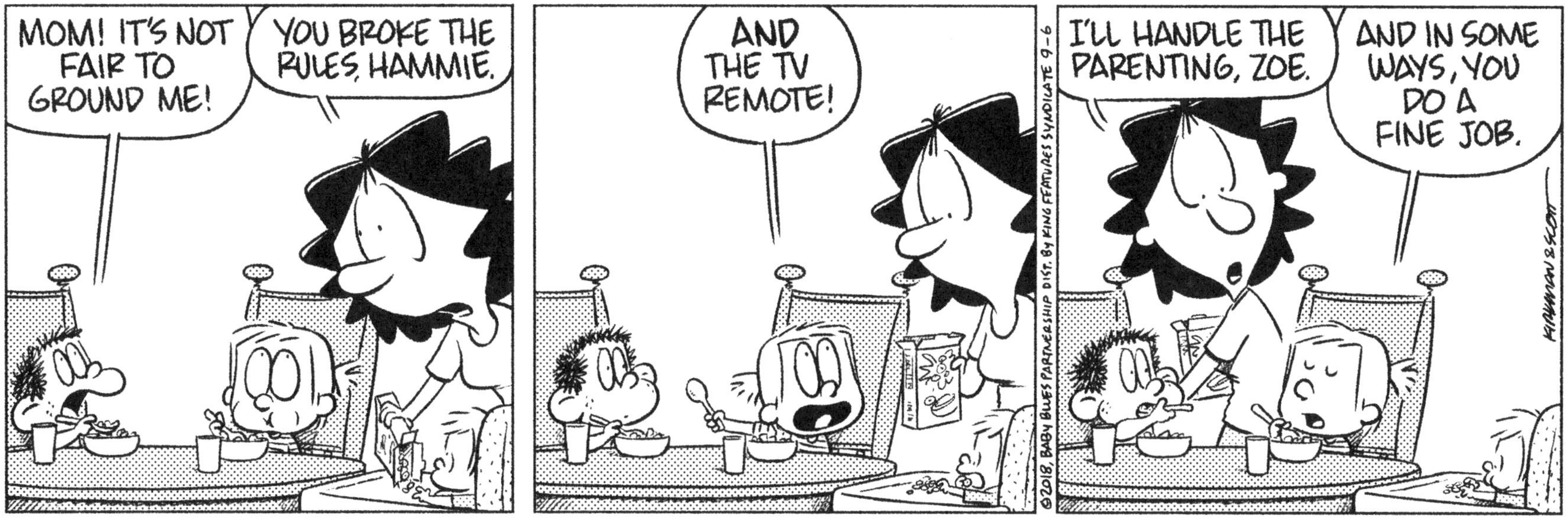
MOM! IT'S NOT FAIR TO GROUND ME!
YOU BROKE THE RULES, HAMMIE.
AND THE TV REMOTE!
©2018, BABY BLUES PARTNERSHIP DIST. BY KING FEATURES SYNDICATE 9-6
I'LL HANDLE THE PARENTING, ZOE.
AND IN SOME WAYS, YOU DO A FINE JOB.
KIRKMAN & SCOTT

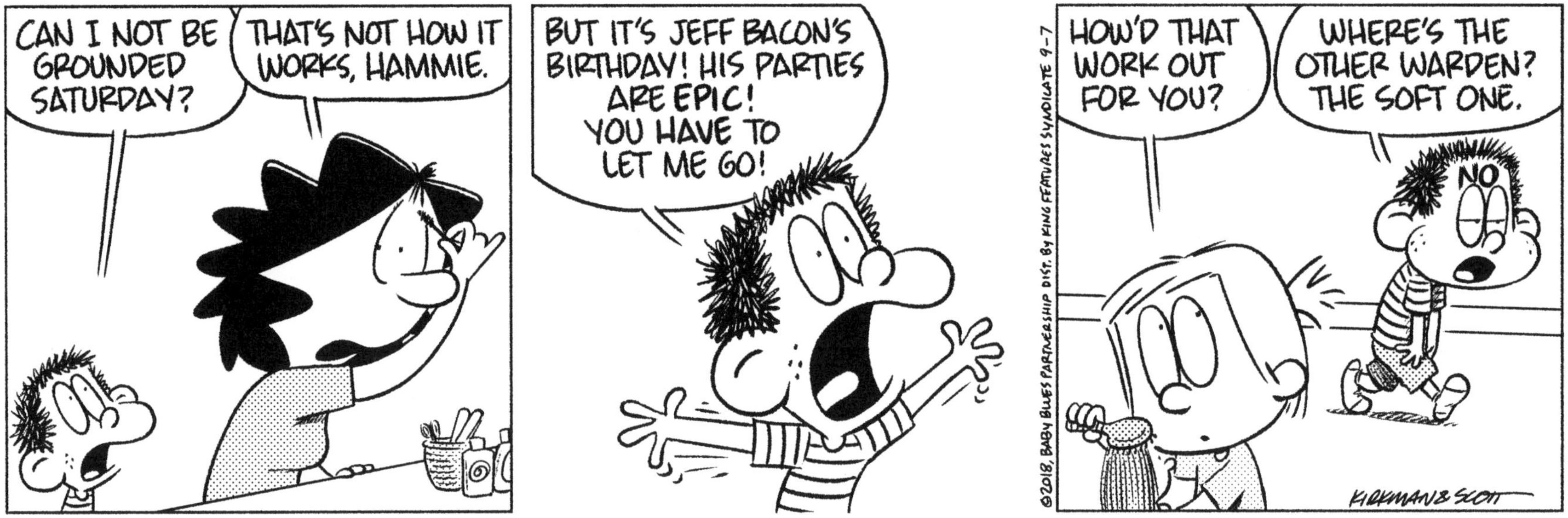
CAN I NOT BE GROUNDED SATURDAY?
THAT'S NOT HOW IT WORKS, HAMMIE.
BUT IT'S JEFF BACON'S BIRTHDAY! HIS PARTIES ARE EPIC! YOU HAVE TO LET ME GO!
HOW'D THAT WORK OUT FOR YOU?
WHERE'S THE OTHER WARDEN? THE SOFT ONE.
NO
©2018, BABY BLUES PARTNERSHIP DIST. BY KING FEATURES SYNDICATE 9-7
KIRKMAN & SCOTT

Rick: Jeff Bacon was plugged in here—he's a cartoonist buddy who led us to do USO tours for the troops. Not his birthday, though, unless you want it to be from now on.

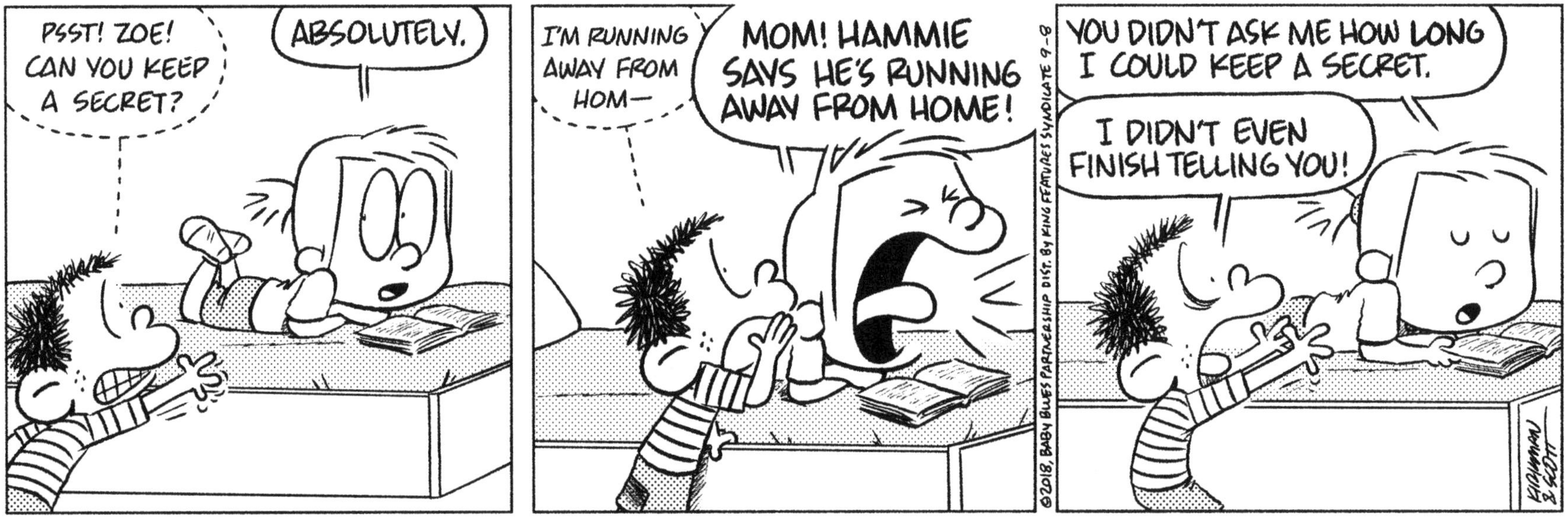
PSST! ZOE! CAN YOU KEEP A SECRET?
ABSOLUTELY.
I'M RUNNING AWAY FROM HOM—
MOM! HAMMIE SAYS HE'S RUNNING AWAY FROM HOME!
YOU DIDN'T ASK ME HOW LONG I COULD KEEP A SECRET.
I DIDN'T EVEN FINISH TELLING YOU!
©2018, BABY BLUES PARTNERSHIP DIST. BY KING FEATURES SYNDICATE 9-8
KIRKMAN & SCOTT

Jerry: With sisters you have to read the fine print.

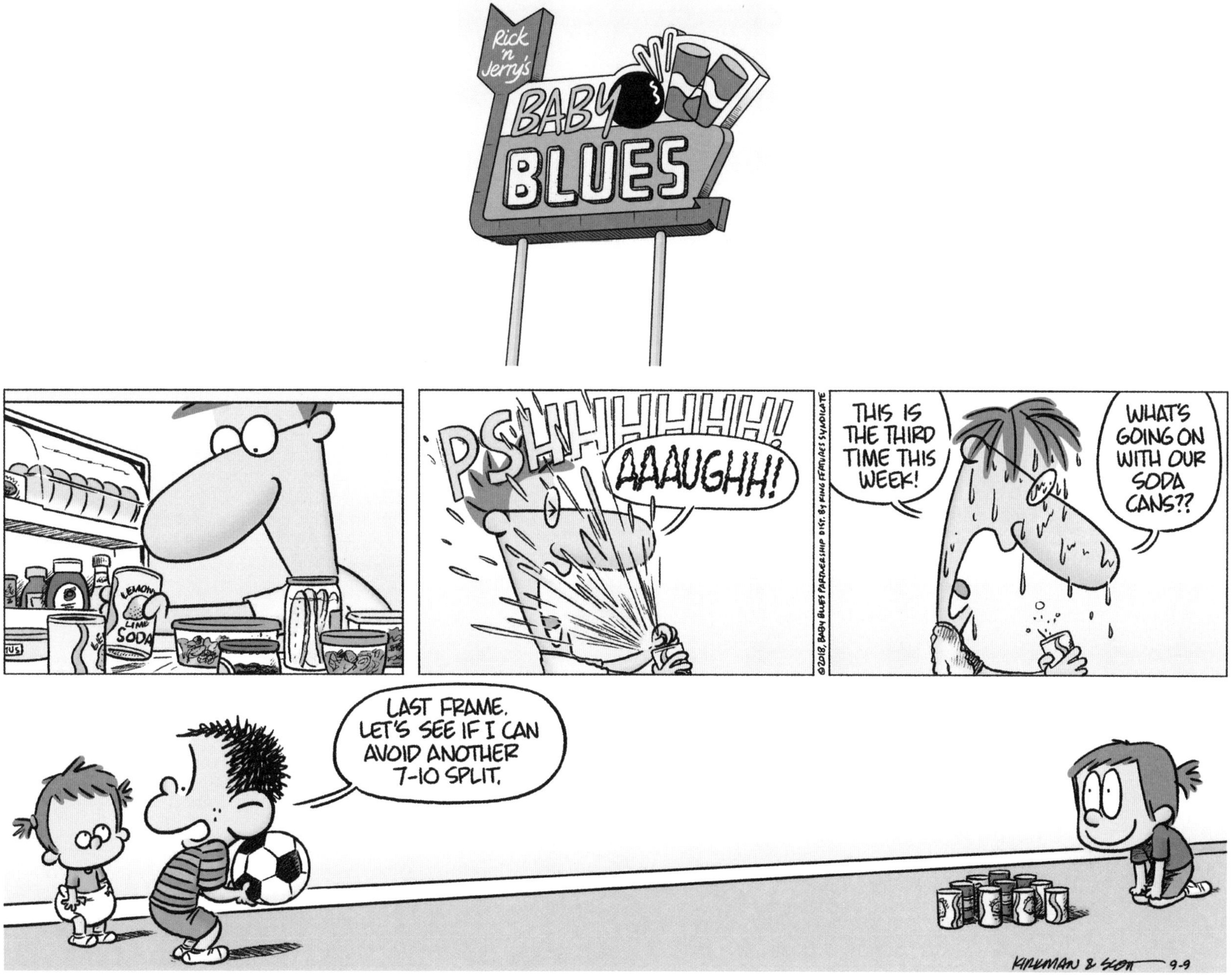
Rick 'n Jerry's
BABY BLUES
LEMON LIME SODA
PSHHHHHHH!
AAAUGHH!
©2018, BABY BLUES PARTNERSHIP DIST. BY KING FEATURES SYNDICATE
THIS IS THE THIRD TIME THIS WEEK!
WHAT'S GOING ON WITH OUR SODA CANS??
LAST FRAME. LET'S SEE IF I CAN AVOID ANOTHER 7-10 SPLIT.
KIRKMAN & SCOTT 9-9

Rick: In the old days, I would've had to drive to see an actual bowling alley sign. Yay, internet! Again, great timing, showing the moment before the event.

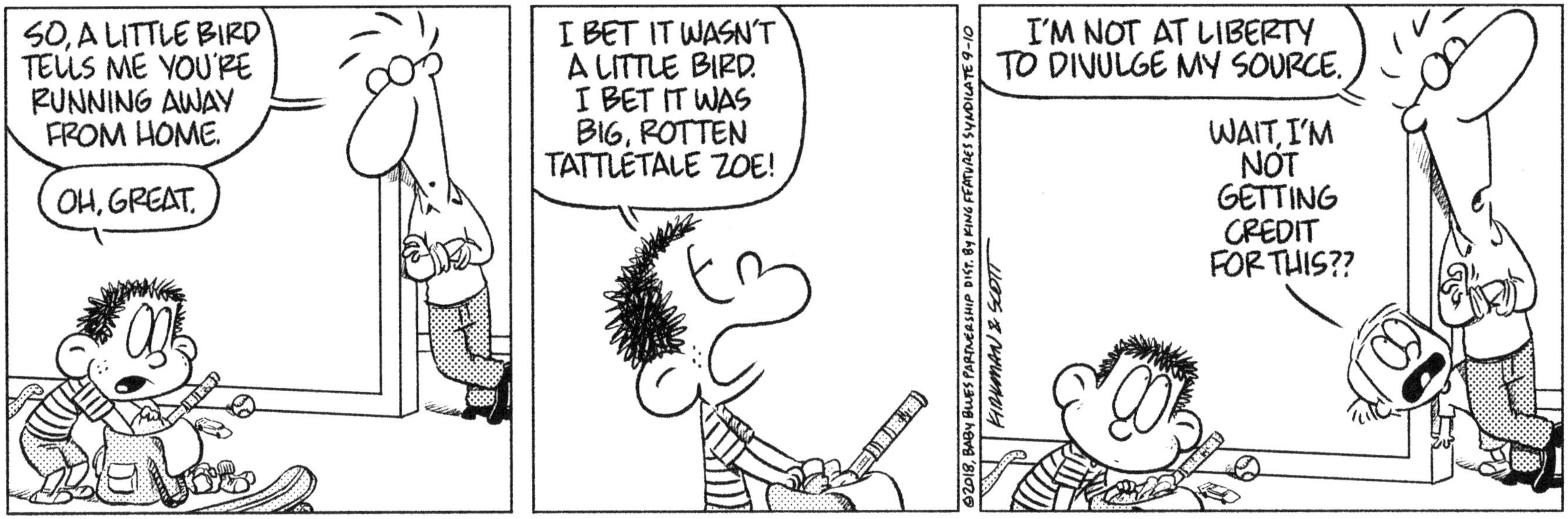
SO, A LITTLE BIRD TELLS ME YOU'RE RUNNING AWAY FROM HOME.
OH, GREAT.
I BET IT WASN'T A LITTLE BIRD. I BET IT WAS BIG, ROTTEN TATTLETALE ZOE!
©2018, BABY BLUES PARTNERSHIP DIST. BY KING FEATURES SYNDICATE 9-10
KIRKMAN & SCOTT
I'M NOT AT LIBERTY TO DIVULGE MY SOURCE.
WAIT, I'M NOT GETTING CREDIT FOR THIS??

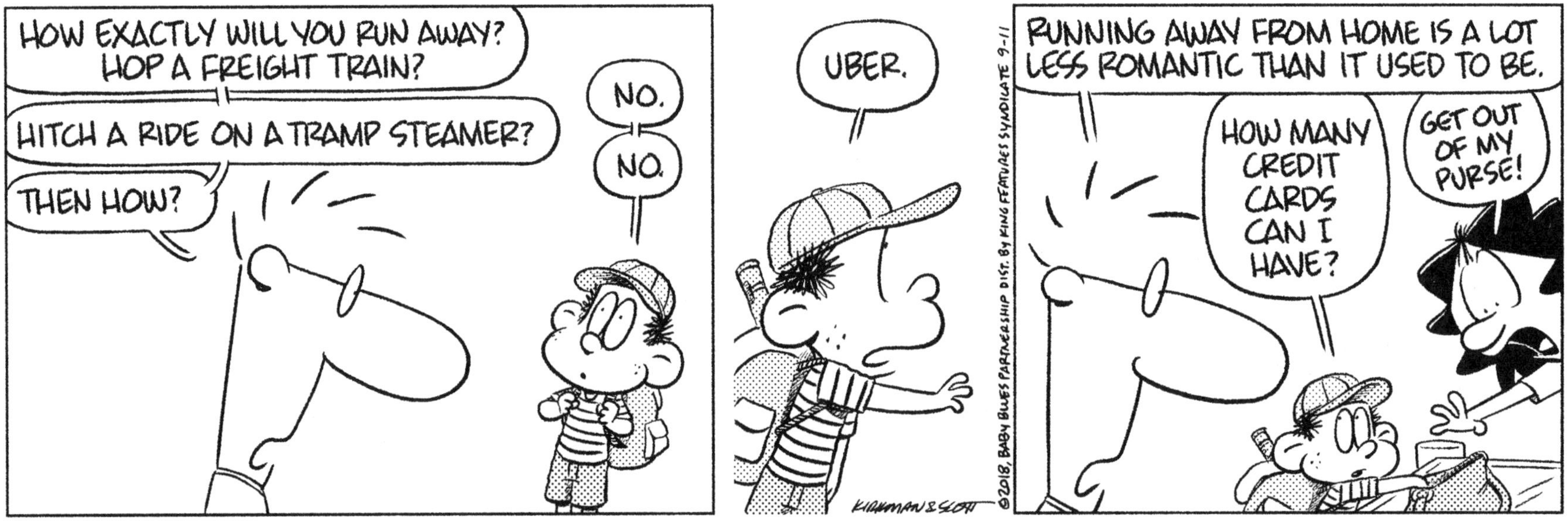
HOW EXACTLY WILL YOU RUN AWAY? HOP A FREIGHT TRAIN?
NO.
HITCH A RIDE ON A TRAMP STEAMER?
NO.
THEN HOW?
UBER.
KIRKMAN & SCOTT
©2018, BABY BLUES PARTNERSHIP DIST. BY KING FEATURES SYNDICATE 9-11
RUNNING AWAY FROM HOME IS A LOT LESS ROMANTIC THAN IT USED TO BE.
HOW MANY CREDIT CARDS CAN I HAVE?
GET OUT OF MY PURSE!

Rick: Hammie is definitely not five-star passenger material.

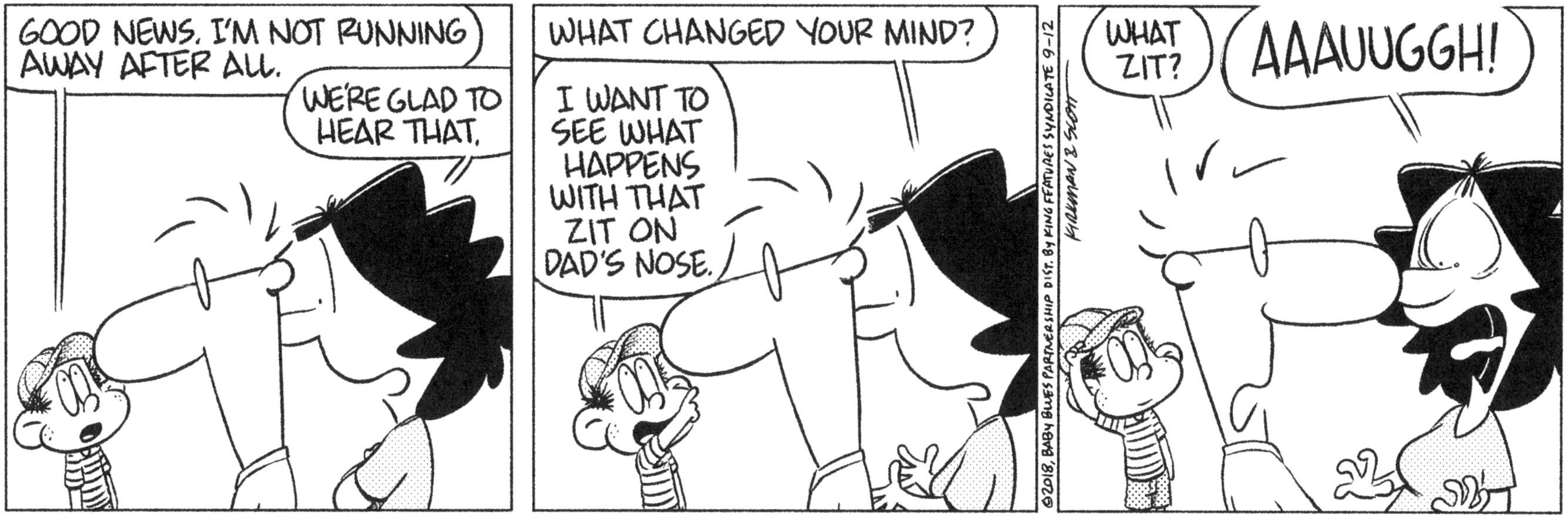
GOOD NEWS. I'M NOT RUNNING AWAY AFTER ALL.
WE'RE GLAD TO HEAR THAT.
WHAT CHANGED YOUR MIND?
I WANT TO SEE WHAT HAPPENS WITH THAT ZIT ON DAD'S NOSE.
©2018, BABY BLUES PARTNERSHIP DIST. BY KING FEATURES SYNDICATE 9-12
KIRKMAN & SCOTT
WHAT ZIT?
AAAUUGGH!

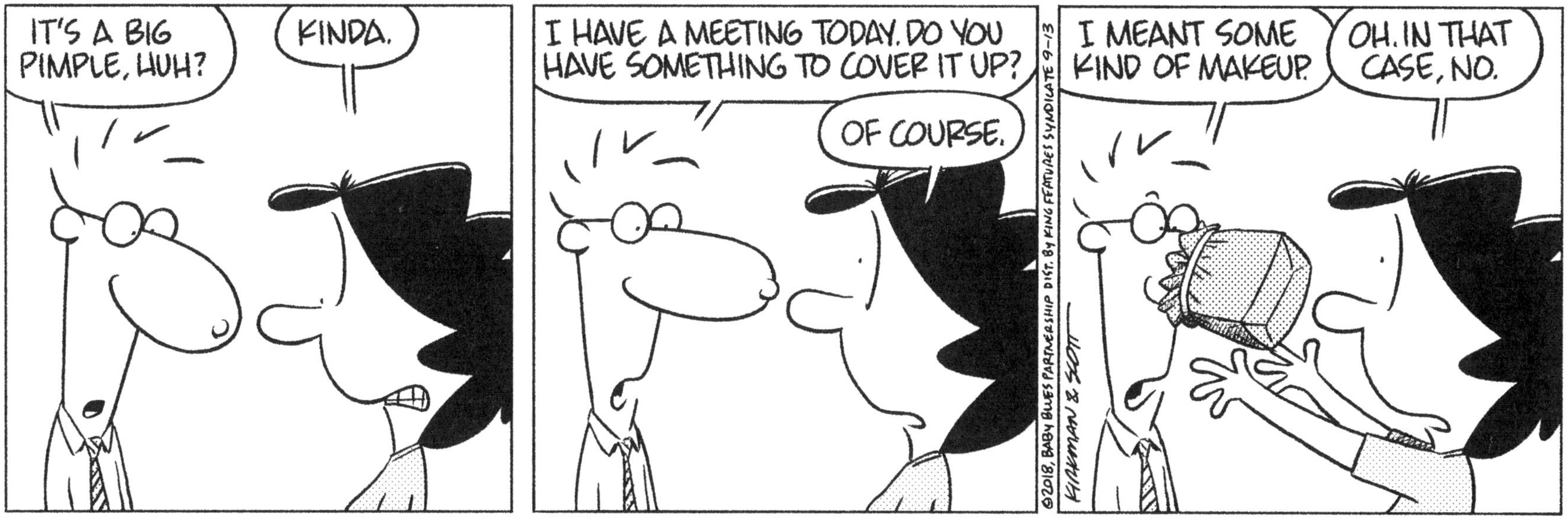
IT'S A BIG PIMPLE, HUH?
KINDA.
I HAVE A MEETING TODAY. DO YOU HAVE SOMETHING TO COVER IT UP?
OF COURSE.
©2018, BABY BLUES PARTNERSHIP DIST. BY KING FEATURES SYNDICATE 9-13
KIRKMAN & SCOTT
I MEANT SOME KIND OF MAKEUP.
OH. IN THAT CASE, NO.

Rick: Aaannnd, we get back to making fun of Darryl's nose.

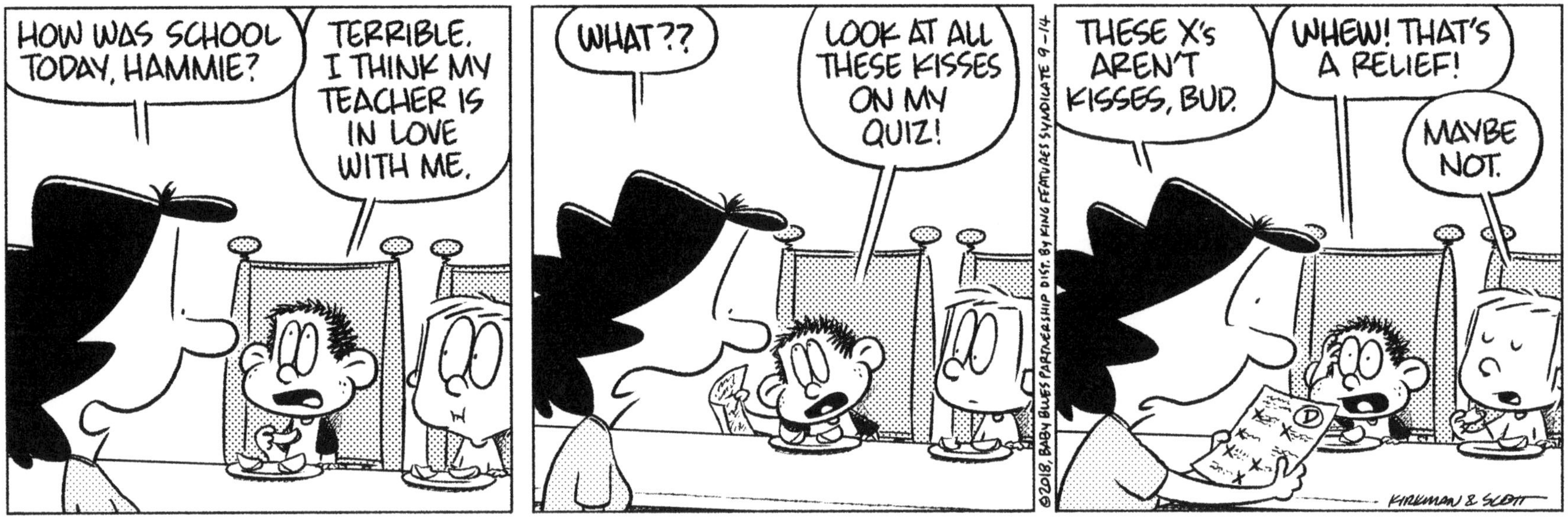
HOW WAS SCHOOL TODAY, HAMMIE?
TERRIBLE. I THINK MY TEACHER IS IN LOVE WITH ME.
WHAT??
LOOK AT ALL THESE KISSES ON MY QUIZ!
©2018, BABY BLUES PARTNERSHIP DIST. BY KING FEATURES SYNDICATE 9-14
THESE X's AREN'T KISSES, BUD.
WHEW! THAT'S A RELIEF!
MAYBE NOT.
KIRKMAN & SCOTT

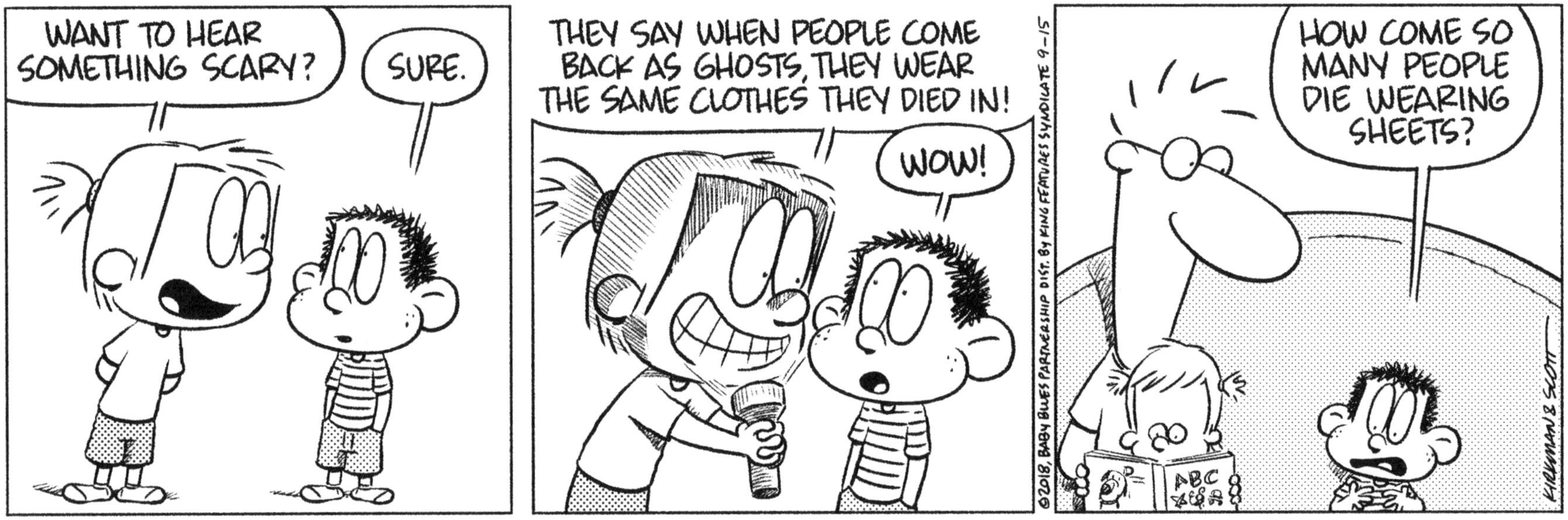
WANT TO HEAR SOMETHING SCARY?
SURE.
THEY SAY WHEN PEOPLE COME BACK AS GHOSTS, THEY WEAR THE SAME CLOTHES THEY DIED IN!
WOW!
©2018, BABY BLUES PARTNERSHIP DIST. BY KING FEATURES SYNDICATE 9-15
HOW COME SO MANY PEOPLE DIE WEARING SHEETS?
ABC
KIRKMAN & SCOTT

MAMA.
MAMA.

MAMA.
MAMA.
GOOD GIRL.
©2018, BABY BLUES PARTNERSHIP DIST. BY KING FEATURES SYNDICATE
MAMA. MAMA. MAMA.
MAMA. MAMA. MAMA.
NICE.
KIRKMAN & SCOTT 9-16
MAMA! MAMA! MAMA! MAMA! MAMA!
MAMA! MAMA! MAMA! MAMA! MAMA!
MAMA! MAMA! MAMA! MAMA! MAMA!
WHY DOESN'T SHE EVER CALL FOR YOU?
IT MUST BE NATURE'S WAY.

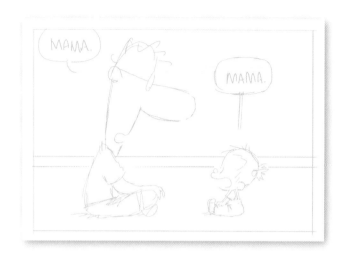

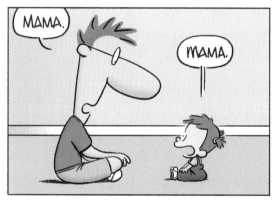

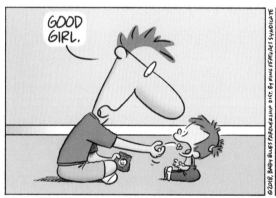

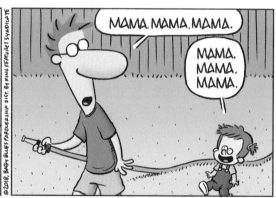

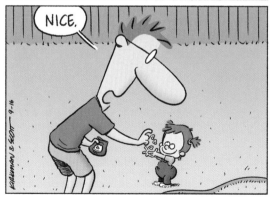

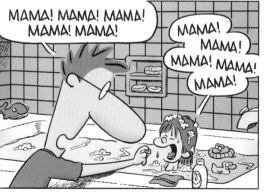

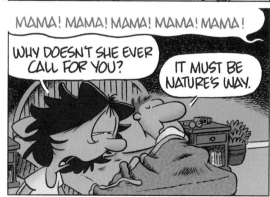

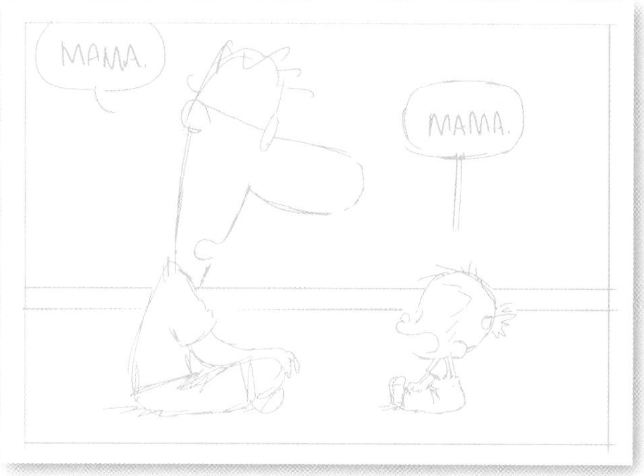

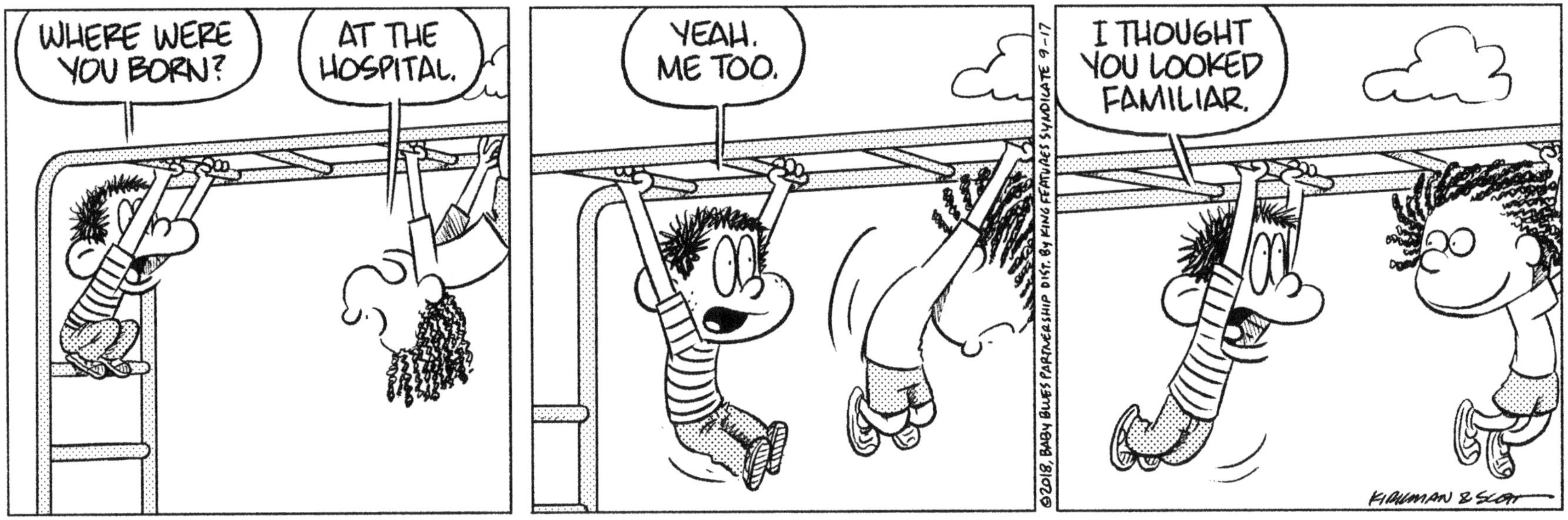
WHERE WERE YOU BORN?
AT THE HOSPITAL.
YEAH. ME TOO.
I THOUGHT YOU LOOKED FAMILIAR.

Rick: I got a kick out of drawing these. Reminds me of the days when I could do that without ripping my joints out.

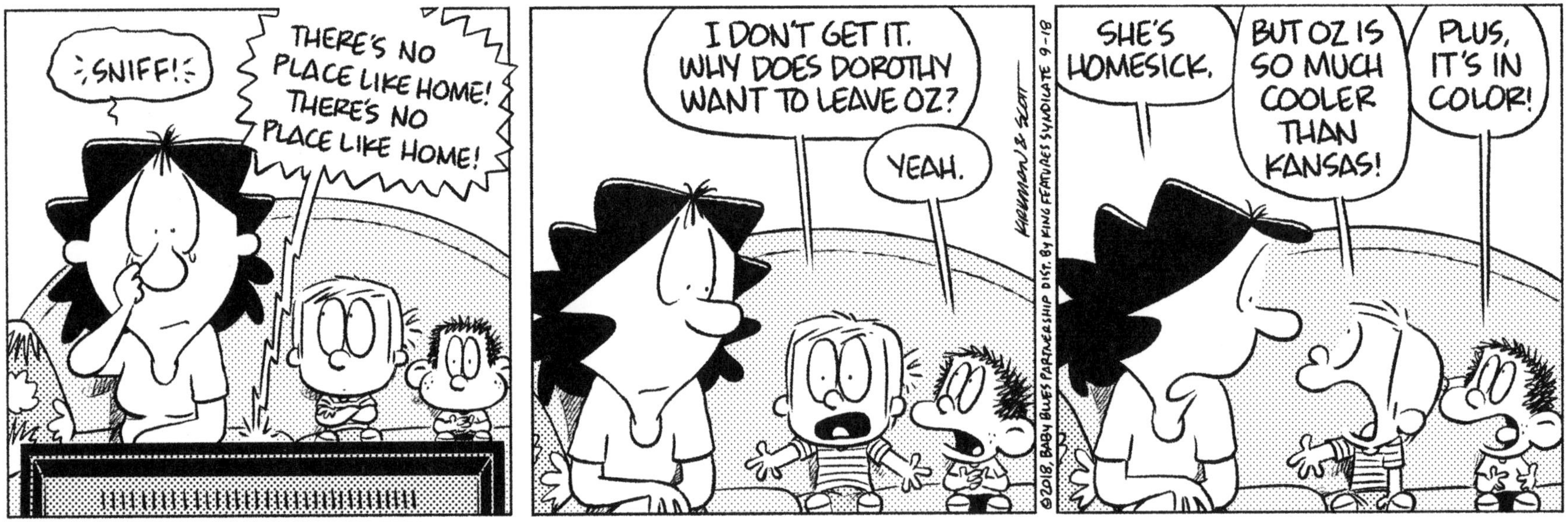
SNIFF!
THERE'S NO PLACE LIKE HOME! THERE'S NO PLACE LIKE HOME!
I DON'T GET IT. WHY DOES DOROTHY WANT TO LEAVE OZ?
YEAH.
SHE'S HOMESICK.
BUT OZ IS SO MUCH COOLER THAN KANSAS!
PLUS, IT'S IN COLOR!

Rick: They make very good points.

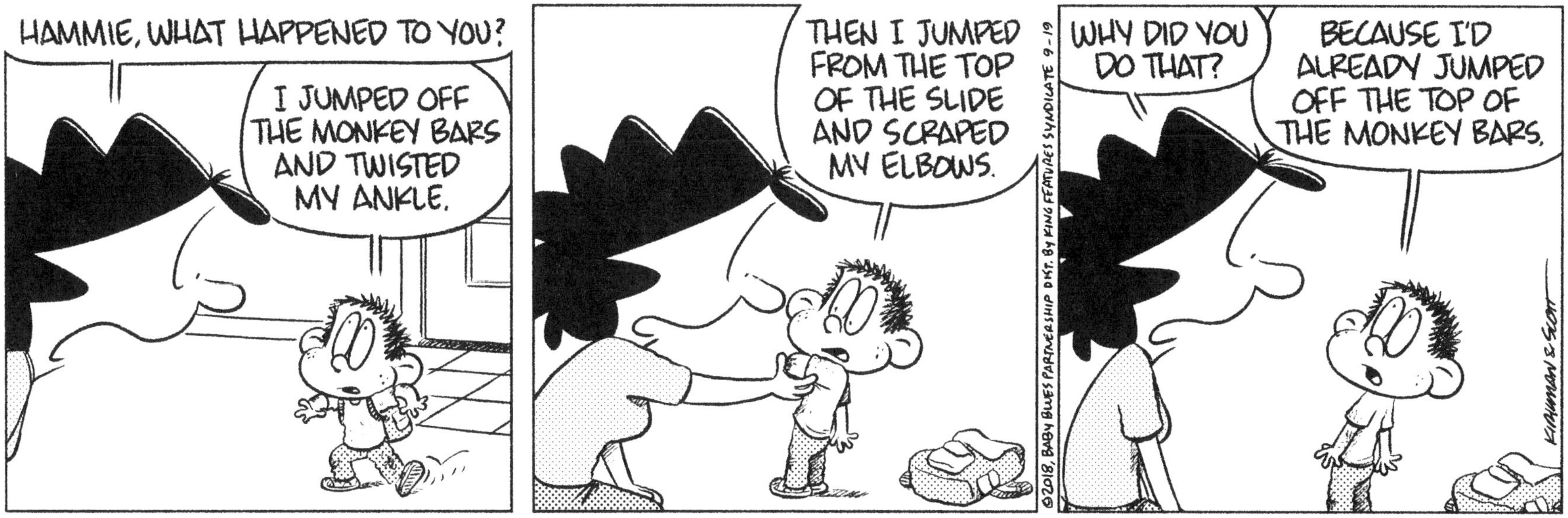
HAMMIE, WHAT HAPPENED TO YOU?
I JUMPED OFF THE MONKEY BARS AND TWISTED MY ANKLE.
THEN I JUMPED FROM THE TOP OF THE SLIDE AND SCRAPED MY ELBOWS.
©2018, BABY BLUES PARTNERSHIP DIST. BY KING FEATURES SYNDICATE 9-19
WHY DID YOU DO THAT?
BECAUSE I'D ALREADY JUMPED OFF THE TOP OF THE MONKEY BARS.
KIRKMAN & SCOTT

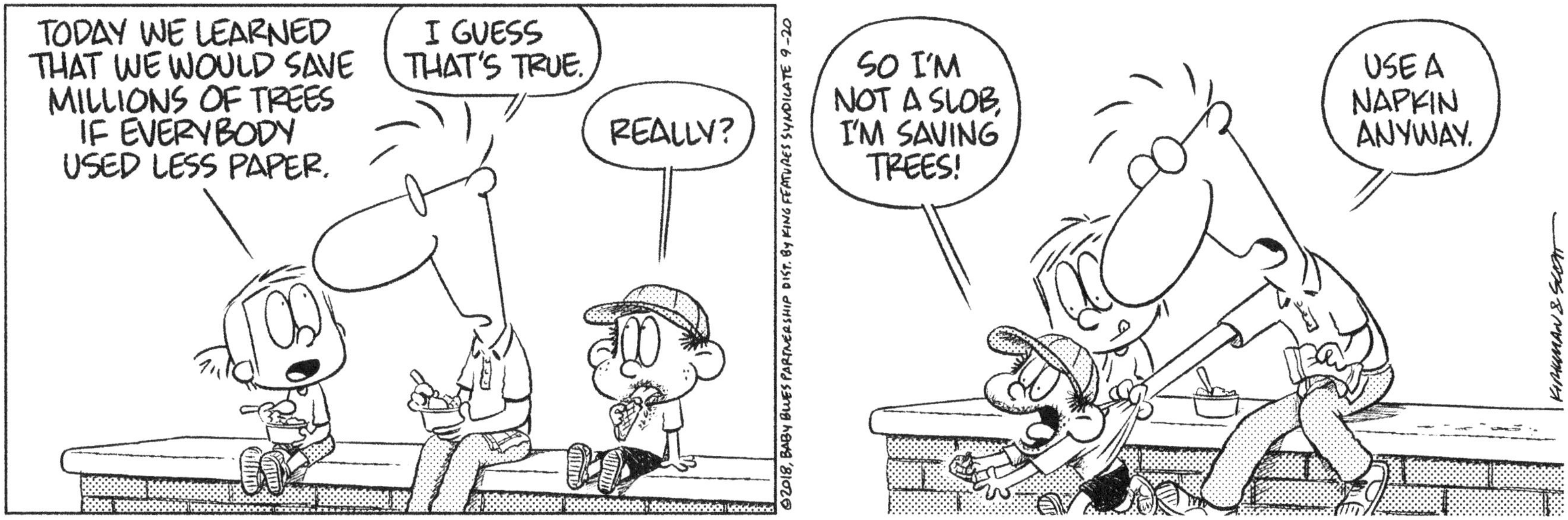
TODAY WE LEARNED THAT WE WOULD SAVE MILLIONS OF TREES IF EVERYBODY USED LESS PAPER.
I GUESS THAT'S TRUE.
REALLY?
©2018, BABY BLUES PARTNERSHIP DIST. BY KING FEATURES SYNDICATE 9-20
SO I'M NOT A SLOB, I'M SAVING TREES!
USE A NAPKIN ANYWAY.
KIRKMAN & SCOTT

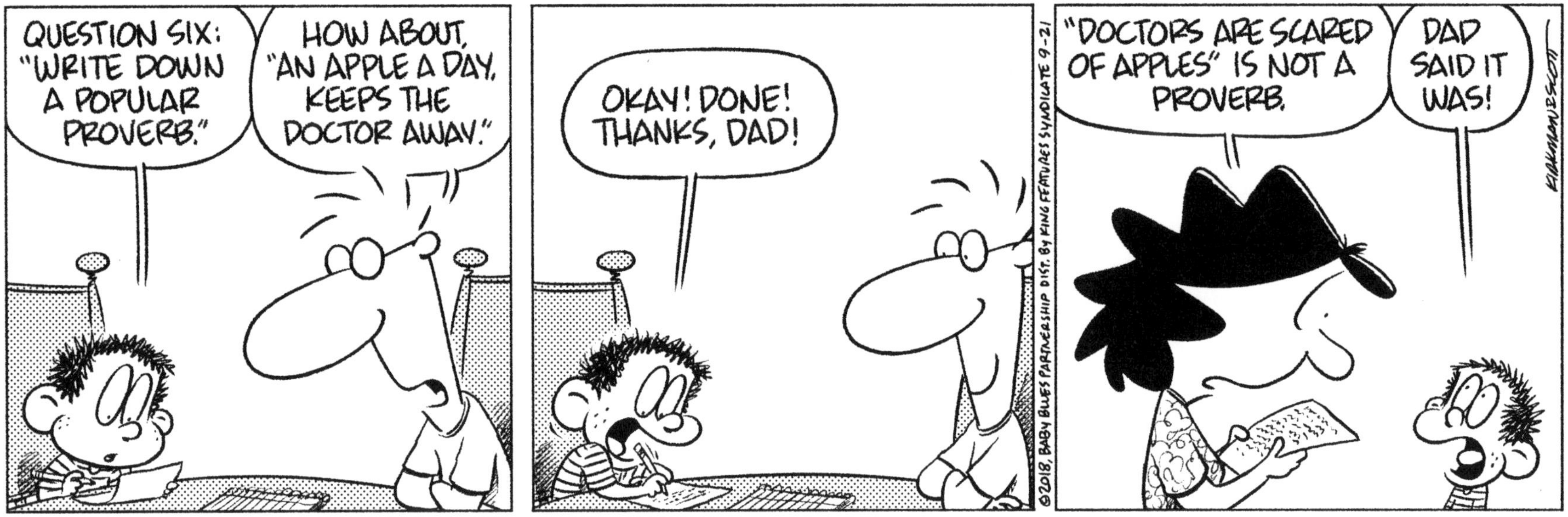
QUESTION SIX: "WRITE DOWN A POPULAR PROVERB."
HOW ABOUT, "AN APPLE A DAY, KEEPS THE DOCTOR AWAY."
OKAY! DONE! THANKS, DAD!
"DOCTORS ARE SCARED OF APPLES" IS NOT A PROVERB.
DAD SAID IT WAS!
©2018, BABY BLUES PARTNERSHIP DIST. BY KING FEATURES SYNDICATE 9-21
KIRKMAN & SCOTT

Rick: Lost in translation.

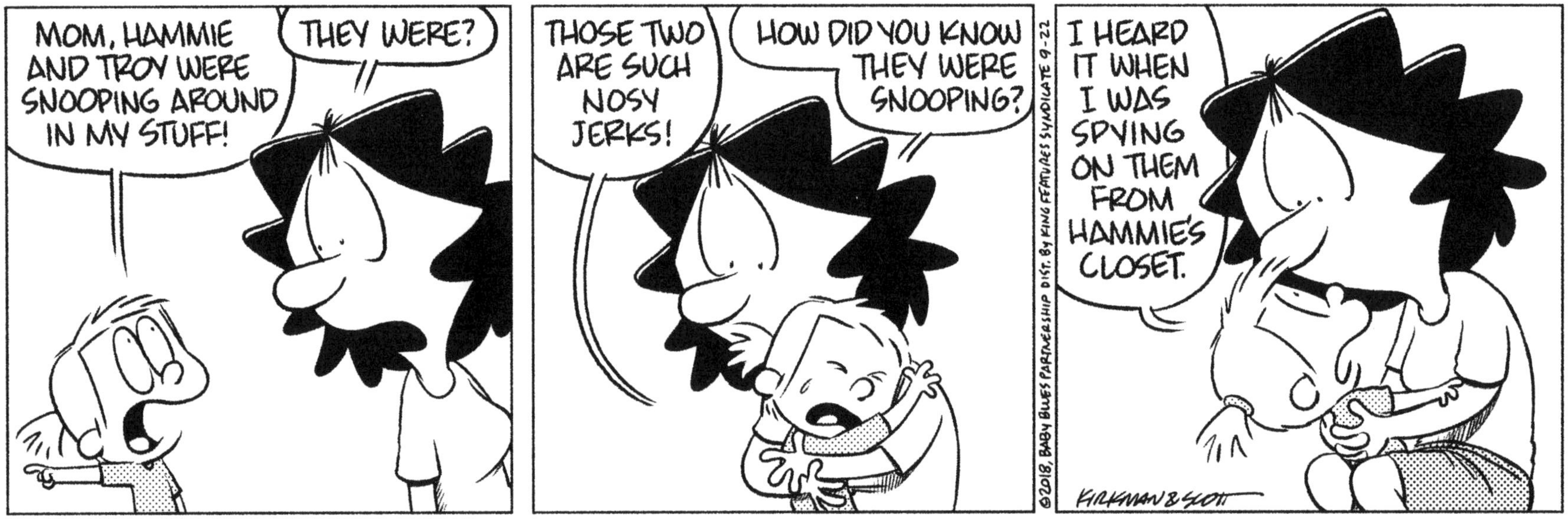
MOM, HAMMIE AND TROY WERE SNOOPING AROUND IN MY STUFF!
THEY WERE?
THOSE TWO ARE SUCH NOSY JERKS!
HOW DID YOU KNOW THEY WERE SNOOPING?
I HEARD IT WHEN I WAS SPYING ON THEM FROM HAMMIE'S CLOSET.
©2018, BABY BLUES PARTNERSHIP DIST. BY KING FEATURES SYNDICATE 9-22
KIRKMAN & SCOTT

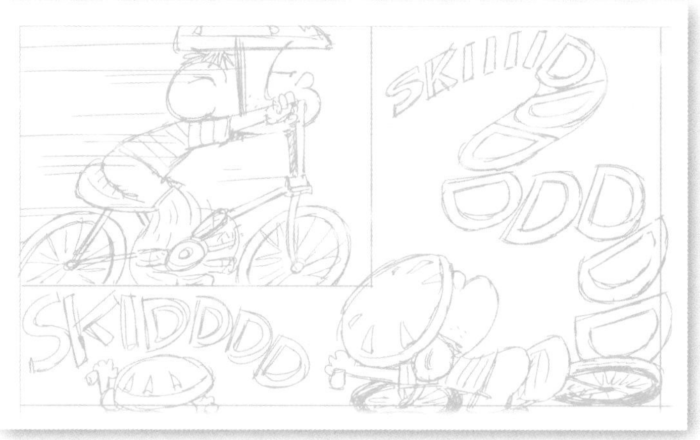

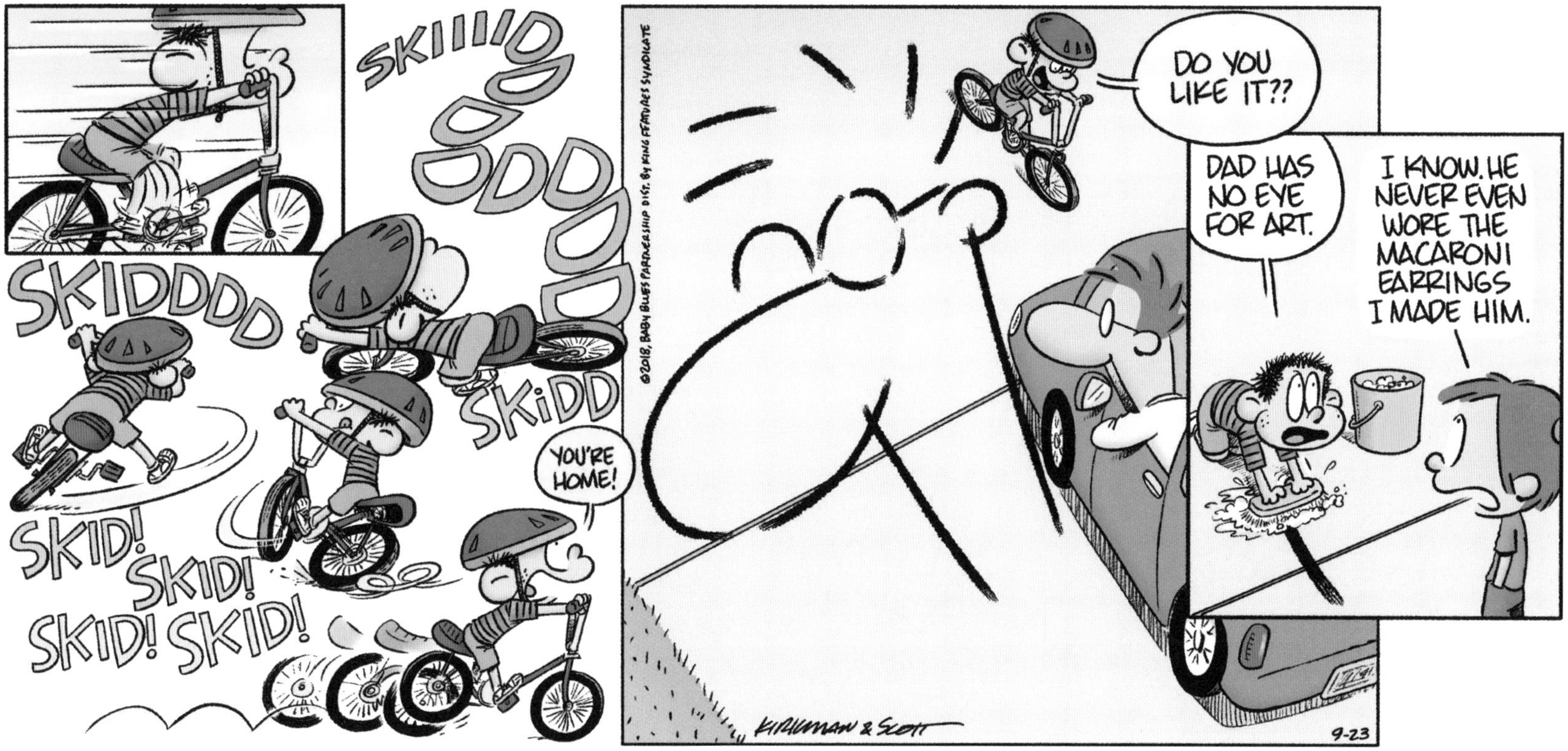
SKIIIID
SKIDDDDD
SKiDD
SKID! SKID! SKID! SKID!
YOU'RE HOME!
©2018, BABY BLUES PARTNERSHIP DIST. BY KING FEATURES SYNDICATE
DO YOU LIKE IT??
DAD HAS NO EYE FOR ART.
I KNOW. HE NEVER EVEN WORE THE MACARONI EARRINGS I MADE HIM.
KIRKMAN & SCOTT
9-23

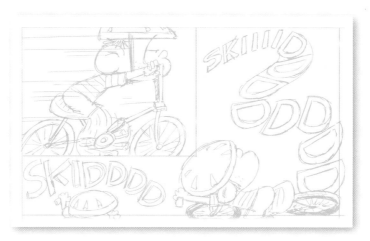

Rick: As much as I hate drawing bicycles, this was a fun challenge.

Jerry: For a guy who hates to draw bicycles, Rick sure raised the bar with this strip!

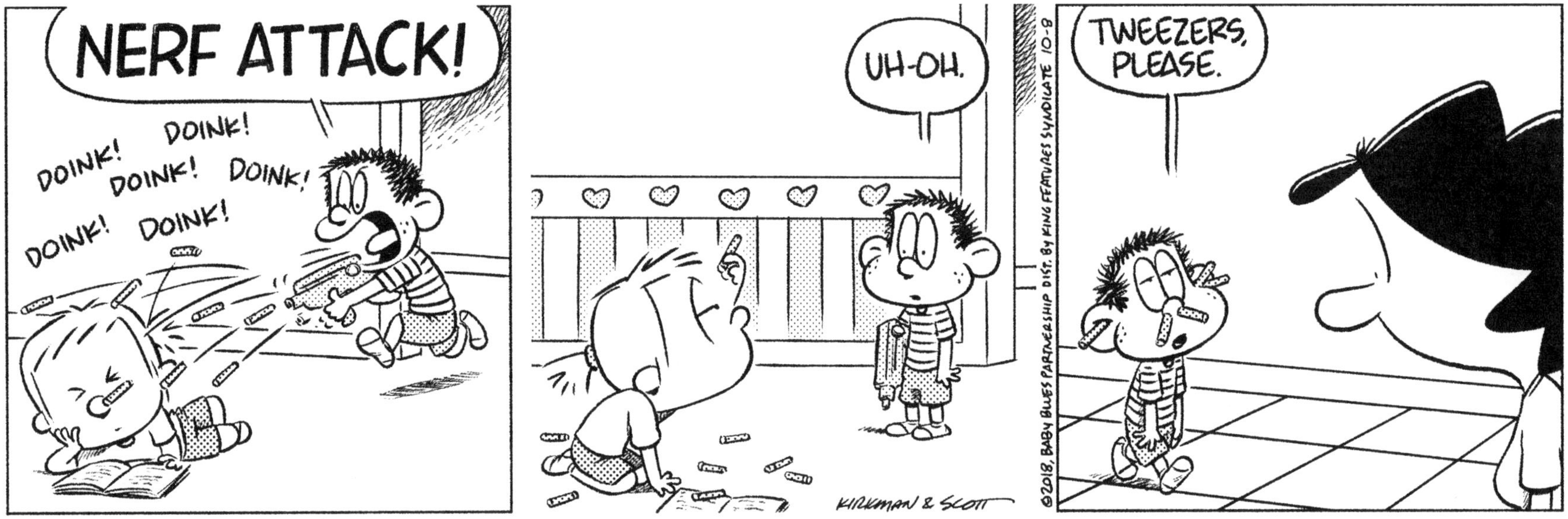
NERF ATTACK!
DOINK! DOINK! DOINK! DOINK! DOINK! DOINK!
UH-OH.
KIRKMAN & SCOTT
©2018, BABY BLUES PARTNERSHIP DIST. BY KING FEATURES SYNDICATE 10-8
TWEEZERS, PLEASE.

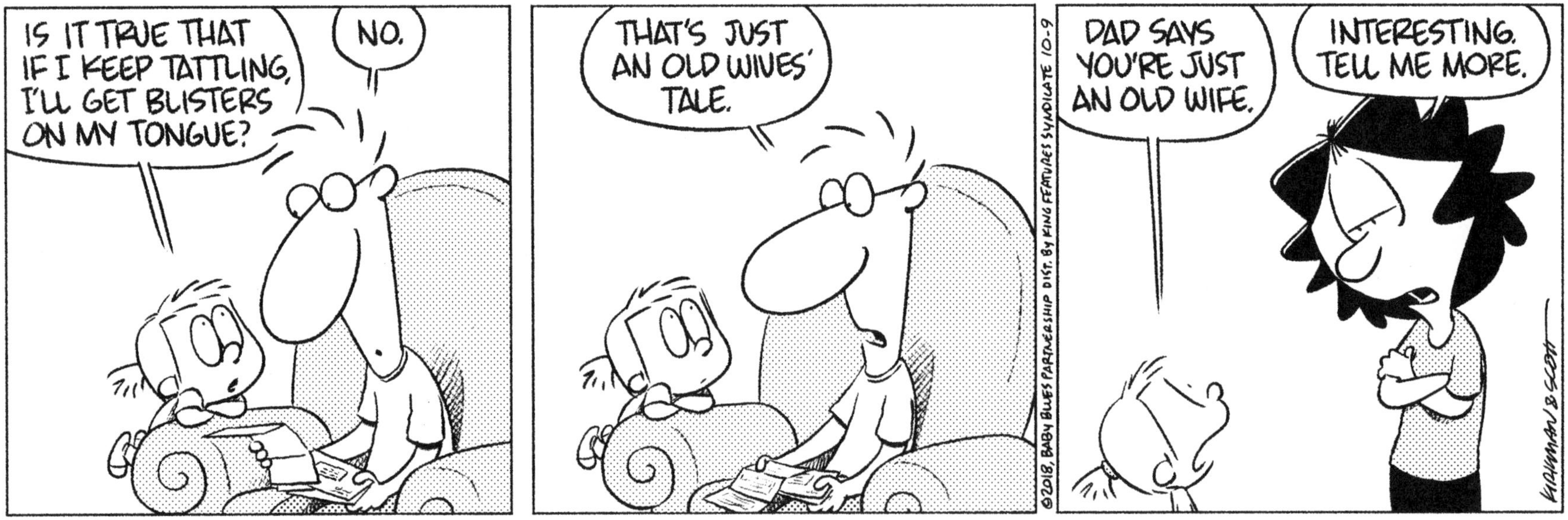
IS IT TRUE THAT IF I KEEP TATTLING, I'LL GET BLISTERS ON MY TONGUE?
NO.
THAT'S JUST AN OLD WIVES' TALE.
©2018, BABY BLUES PARTNERSHIP DIST. BY KING FEATURES SYNDICATE 10-9
DAD SAYS YOU'RE JUST AN OLD WIFE.
INTERESTING. TELL ME MORE.
KIRKMAN & SCOTT

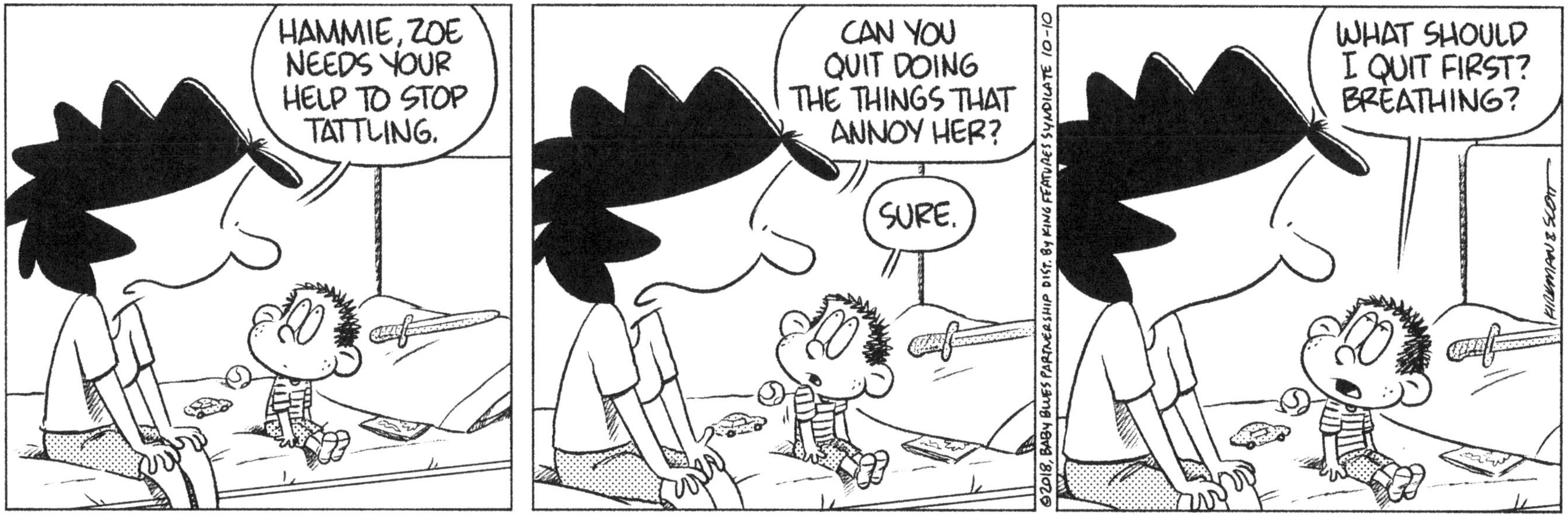
HAMMIE, ZOE NEEDS YOUR HELP TO STOP TATTLING.
CAN YOU QUIT DOING THE THINGS THAT ANNOY HER?
SURE.
WHAT SHOULD I QUIT FIRST? BREATHING?
©2018, BABY BLUES PARTNERSHIP DIST. BY KING FEATURES SYNDICATE 10-10
KIRKMAN & SCOTT

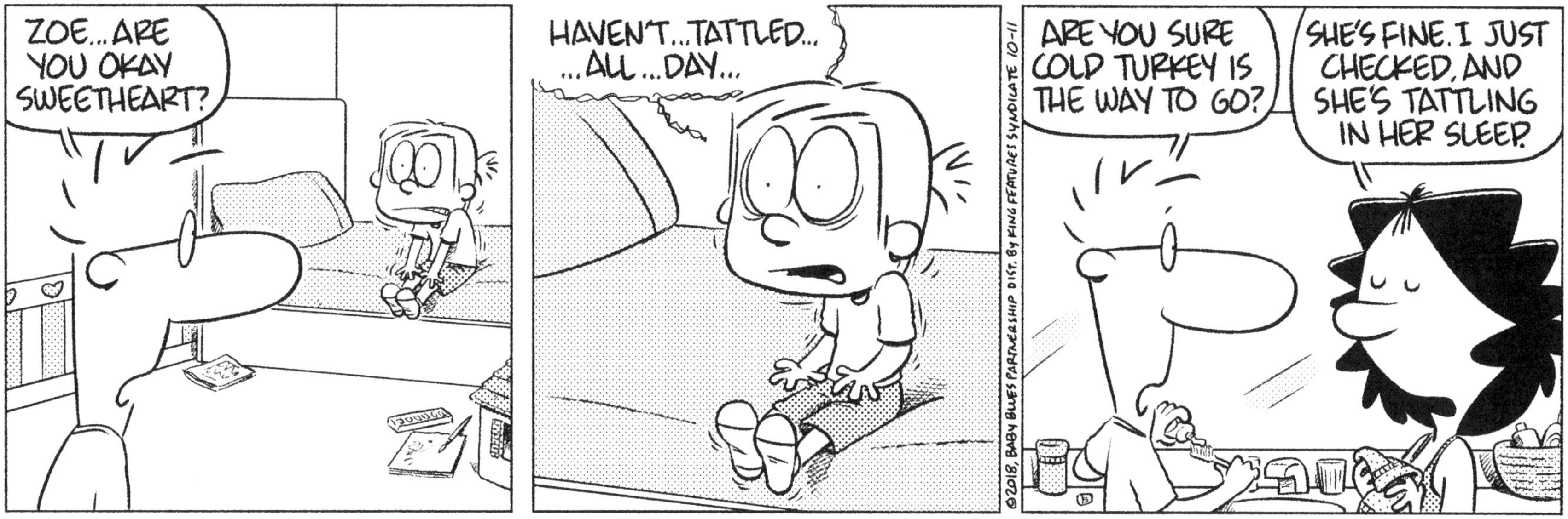
ZOE...ARE YOU OKAY SWEETHEART?
HAVEN'T...TATTLED... ...ALL...DAY...
©2018, BABY BLUES PARTNERSHIP DIST. BY KING FEATURES SYNDICATE 10-11
ARE YOU SURE COLD TURKEY IS THE WAY TO GO?
SHE'S FINE. I JUST CHECKED, AND SHE'S TATTLING IN HER SLEEP.

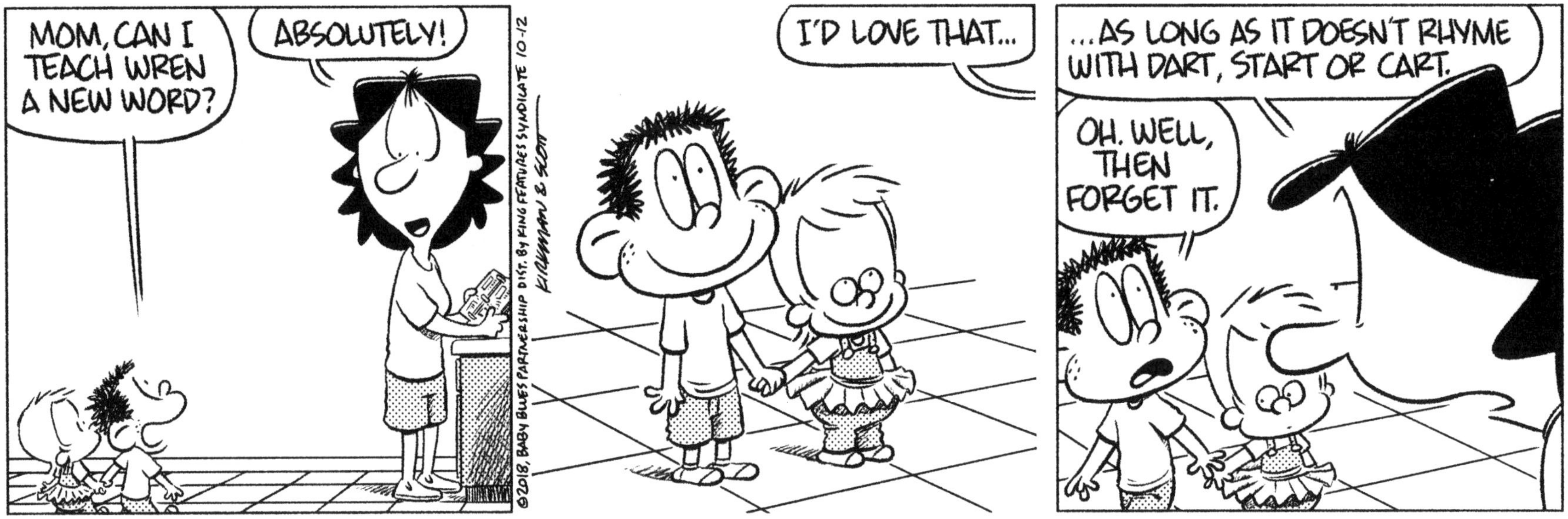
MOM, CAN I TEACH WREN A NEW WORD?
ABSOLUTELY!
I'D LOVE THAT...
...AS LONG AS IT DOESN'T RHYME WITH DART, START OR CART.
OH. WELL, THEN FORGET IT.
©2018, BABY BLUES PARTNERSHIP DIST. BY KING FEATURES SYNDICATE 10-12
KIRKMAN & SCOTT

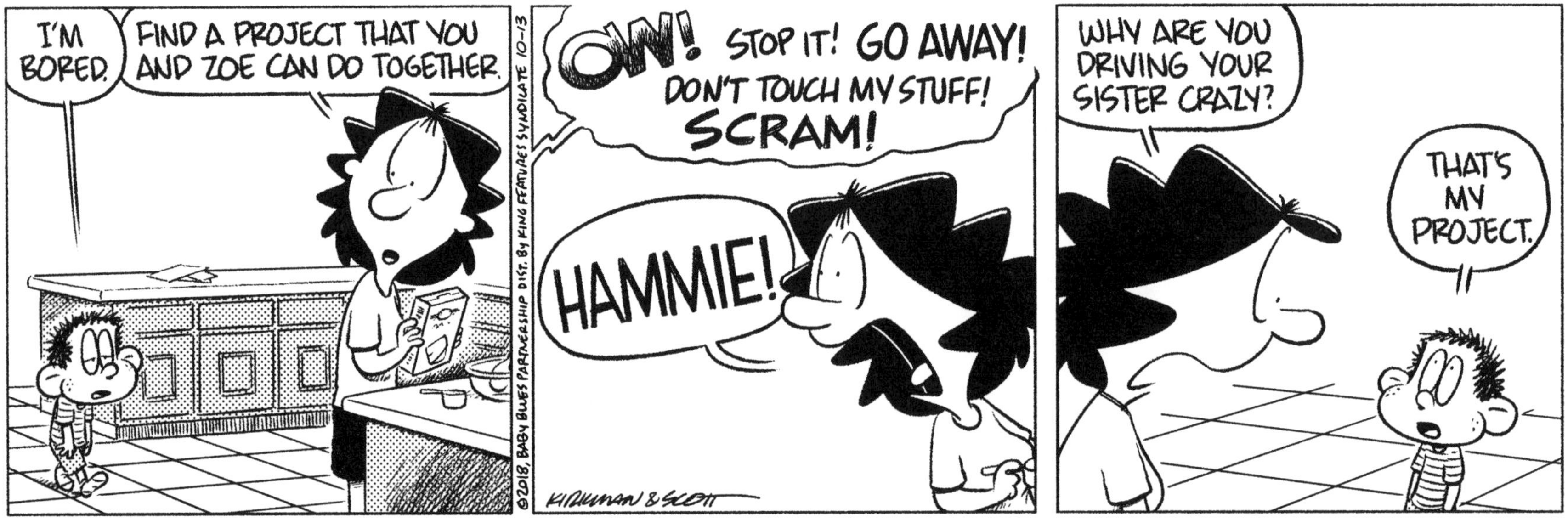
I'M BORED.
FIND A PROJECT THAT YOU AND ZOE CAN DO TOGETHER.
©2018, BABY BLUES PARTNERSHIP DIST. BY KING FEATURES SYNDICATE 10-13
OW! STOP IT! GO AWAY! DON'T TOUCH MY STUFF! SCRAM!
HAMMIE!
KIRKMAN & SCOTT
WHY ARE YOU DRIVING YOUR SISTER CRAZY?
THAT'S MY PROJECT.

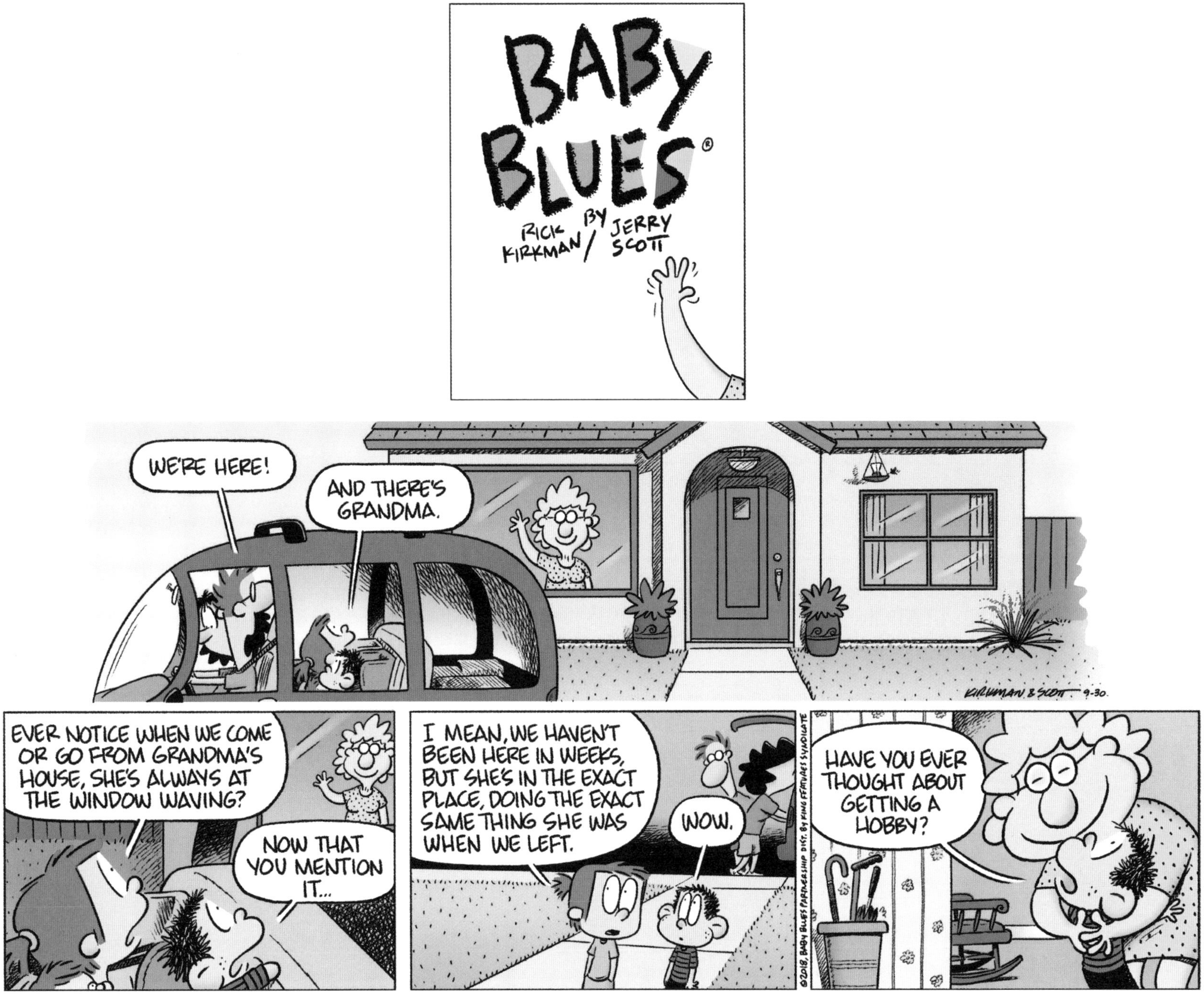
BABY BLUES®
BY RICK KIRKMAN / JERRY SCOTT
WE'RE HERE!
AND THERE'S GRANDMA.
KIRKMAN & SCOTT 9-30.
EVER NOTICE WHEN WE COME OR GO FROM GRANDMA'S HOUSE, SHE'S ALWAYS AT THE WINDOW WAVING?
NOW THAT YOU MENTION IT...
I MEAN, WE HAVEN'T BEEN HERE IN WEEKS, BUT SHE'S IN THE EXACT PLACE, DOING THE EXACT SAME THING SHE WAS WHEN WE LEFT.
WOW.
©2018, BABY BLUES PARTNERSHIP DIST. BY KING FEATURES SYNDICATE
HAVE YOU EVER THOUGHT ABOUT GETTING A HOBBY?

Rick: That's such a funny concept to me. Could be a *Twilight Zone* episode. Or maybe *The Stepford Grammas.*

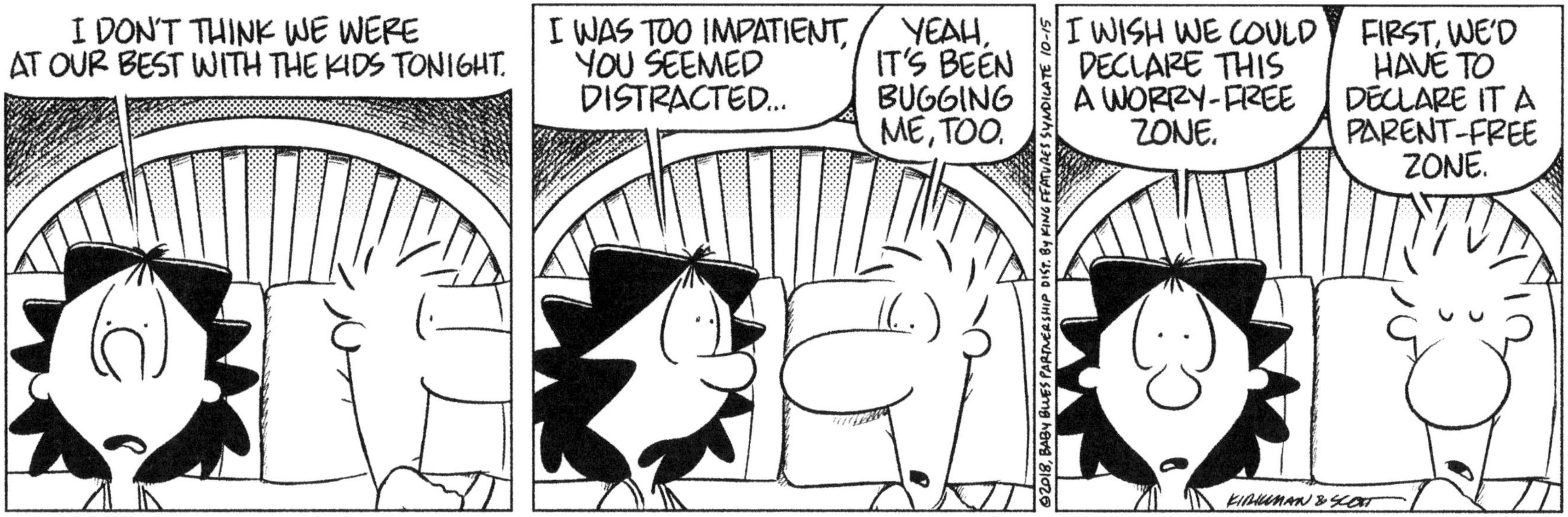
I DON'T THINK WE WERE AT OUR BEST WITH THE KIDS TONIGHT.
I WAS TOO IMPATIENT, YOU SEEMED DISTRACTED...
YEAH, IT'S BEEN BUGGING ME, TOO.
©2018, BABY BLUES PARTNERSHIP DIST. BY KING FEATURES SYNDICATE 10-15
I WISH WE COULD DECLARE THIS A WORRY-FREE ZONE.
FIRST, WE'D HAVE TO DECLARE IT A PARENT-FREE ZONE.
KIRKMAN & SCOTT

Rick: Pretty profound, if you ask me.

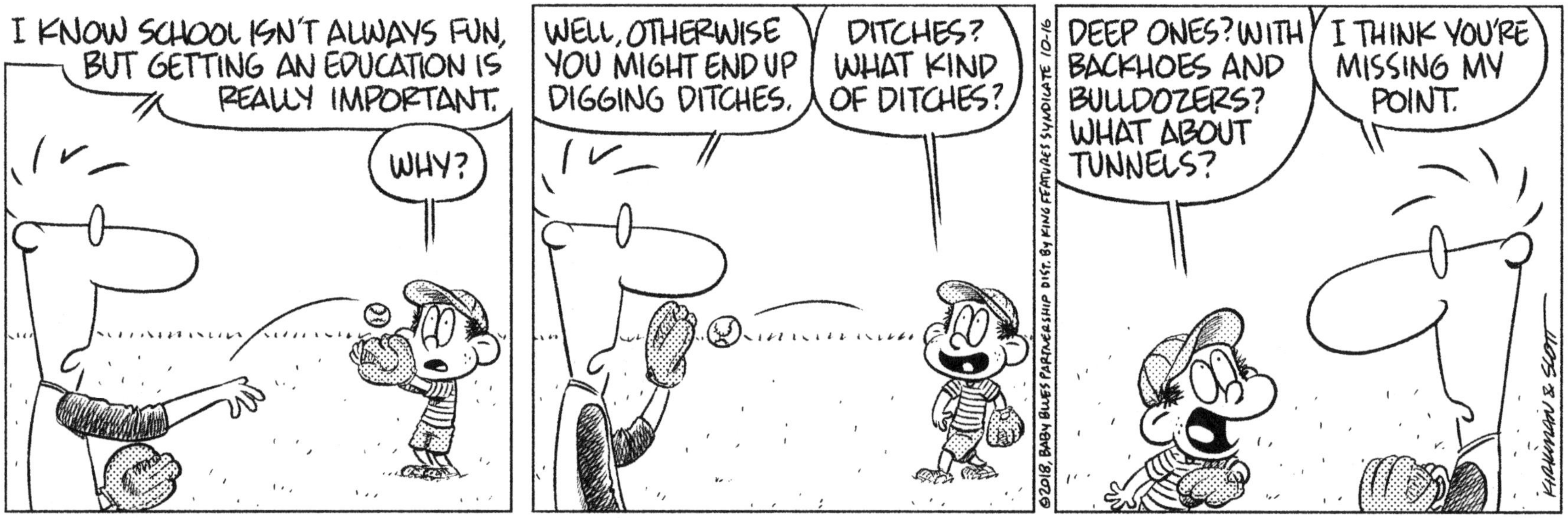
I KNOW SCHOOL ISN'T ALWAYS FUN, BUT GETTING AN EDUCATION IS REALLY IMPORTANT.
WHY?
WELL, OTHERWISE YOU MIGHT END UP DIGGING DITCHES.
DITCHES? WHAT KIND OF DITCHES?
©2018, BABY BLUES PARTNERSHIP DIST. BY KING FEATURES SYNDICATE 10-16
DEEP ONES? WITH BACKHOES AND BULLDOZERS? WHAT ABOUT TUNNELS?
I THINK YOU'RE MISSING MY POINT.
KIRKMAN & SCOTT

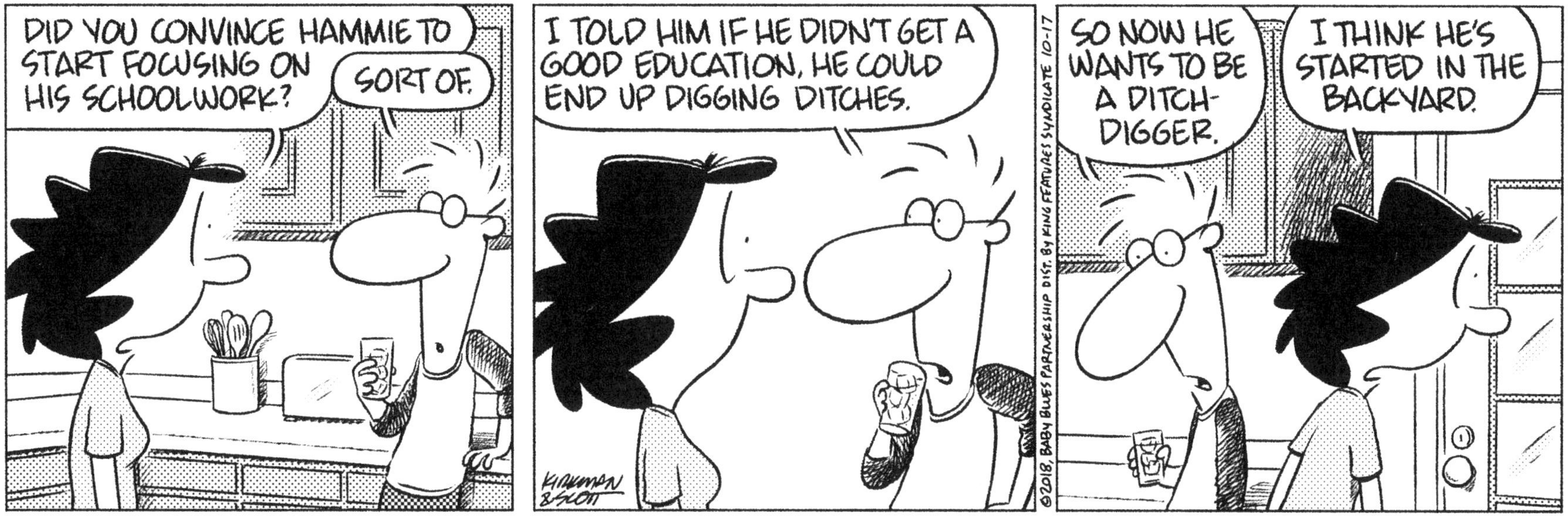
DID YOU CONVINCE HAMMIE TO START FOCUSING ON HIS SCHOOLWORK?
SORT OF.
I TOLD HIM IF HE DIDN'T GET A GOOD EDUCATION, HE COULD END UP DIGGING DITCHES.
KIRKMAN & SCOTT
©2018, BABY BLUES PARTNERSHIP DIST. BY KING FEATURES SYNDICATE 10-17
SO NOW HE WANTS TO BE A DITCH-DIGGER.
I THINK HE'S STARTED IN THE BACKYARD.

Rick: Got raked over the coals for this one, too. We were not trying to demean ditchdiggers. It's an honest living. Would "TV pundit" work better?

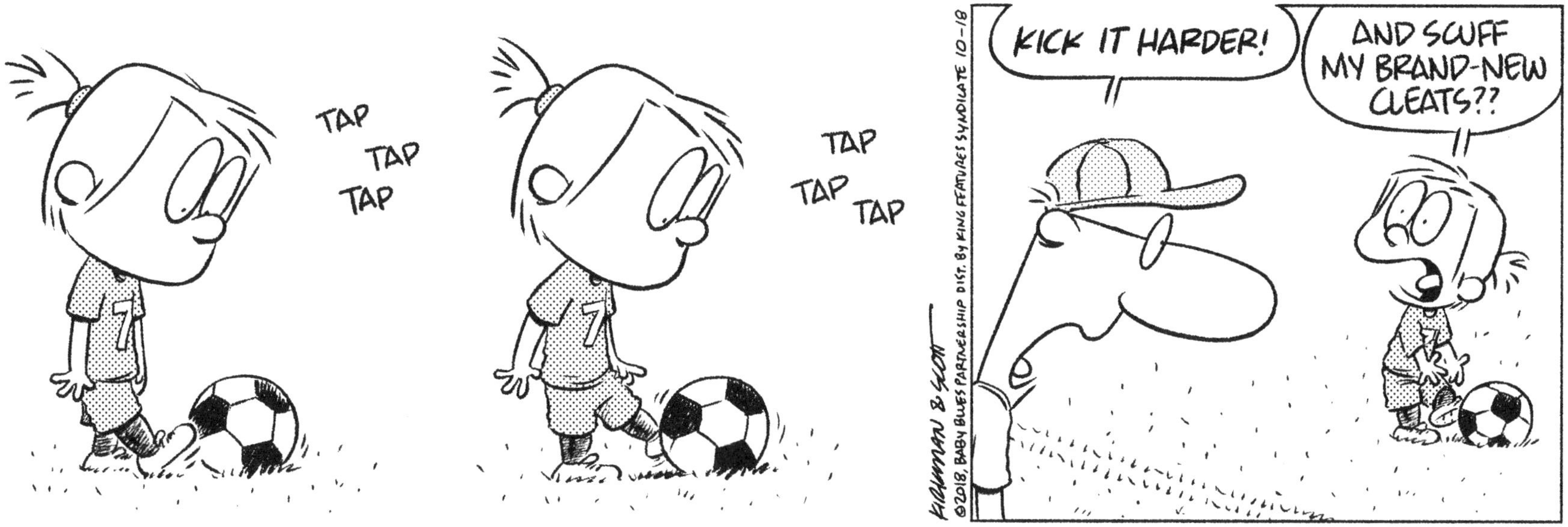
TAP
TAP
TAP
TAP
TAP
TAP
KIRKMAN & SCOTT
©2018, BABY BLUES PARTNERSHIP DIST. BY KING FEATURES SYNDICATE 10-18
KICK IT HARDER!
AND SCUFF MY BRAND-NEW CLEATS??

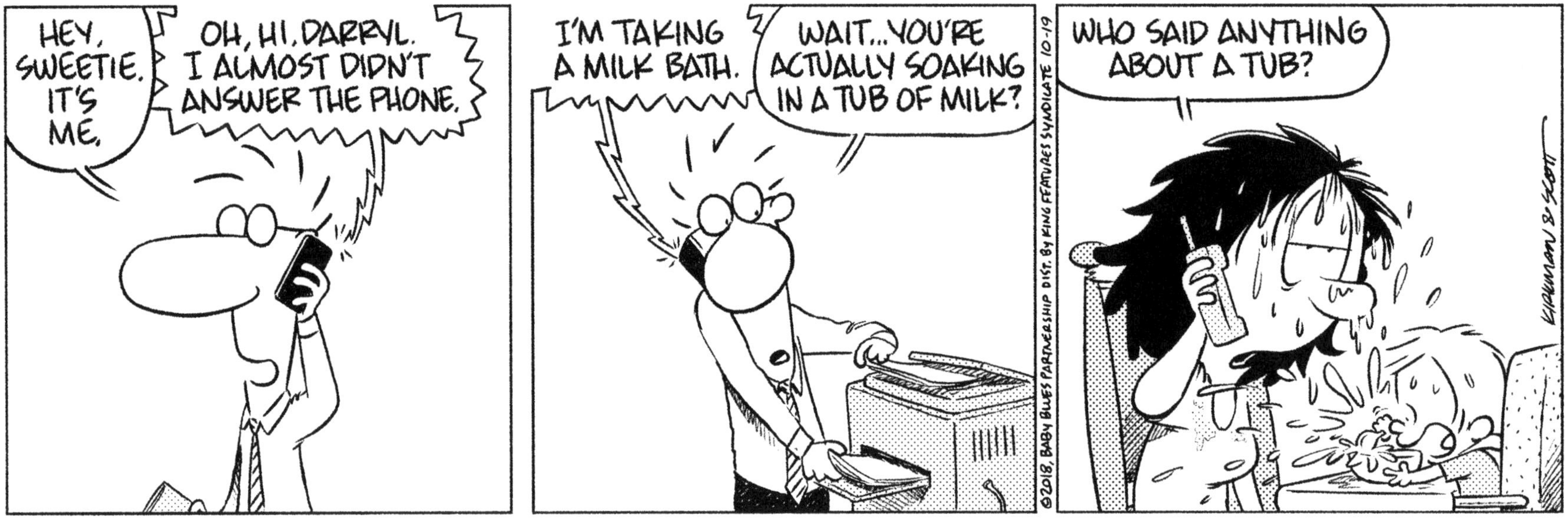
HEY, SWEETIE. IT'S ME.
OH, HI, DARRYL. I ALMOST DIDN'T ANSWER THE PHONE.
I'M TAKING A MILK BATH.
WAIT... YOU'RE ACTUALLY SOAKING IN A TUB OF MILK?
©2018, BABY BLUES PARTNERSHIP DIST. BY KING FEATURES SYNDICATE 10-19
WHO SAID ANYTHING ABOUT A TUB?
KIRKMAN & SCOTT

Rick: Rimshot, please.

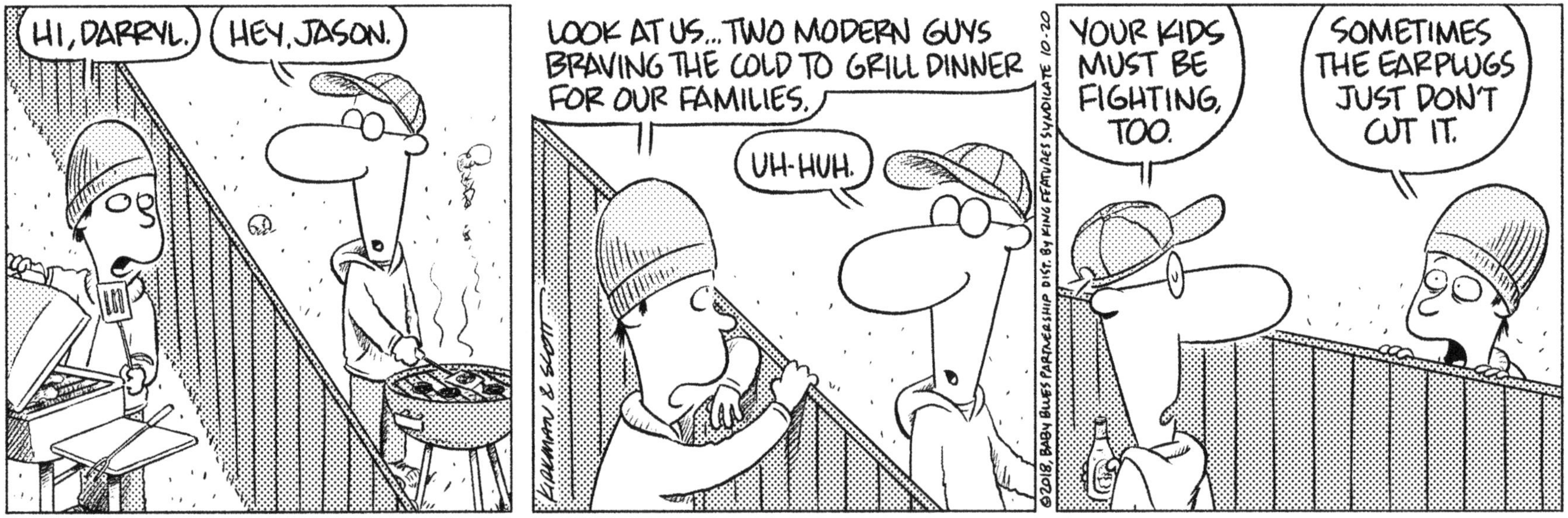
HI, DARRYL.
HEY, JASON.
KIRKMAN & SCOTT
LOOK AT US... TWO MODERN GUYS BRAVING THE COLD TO GRILL DINNER FOR OUR FAMILIES.
UH-HUH.
©2018, BABY BLUES PARTNERSHIP DIST. BY KING FEATURES SYNDICATE 10-20
YOUR KIDS MUST BE FIGHTING, TOO.
SOMETIMES THE EARPLUGS JUST DON'T CUT IT.

Rick: Then you need my new product: kid-canceling headphones.

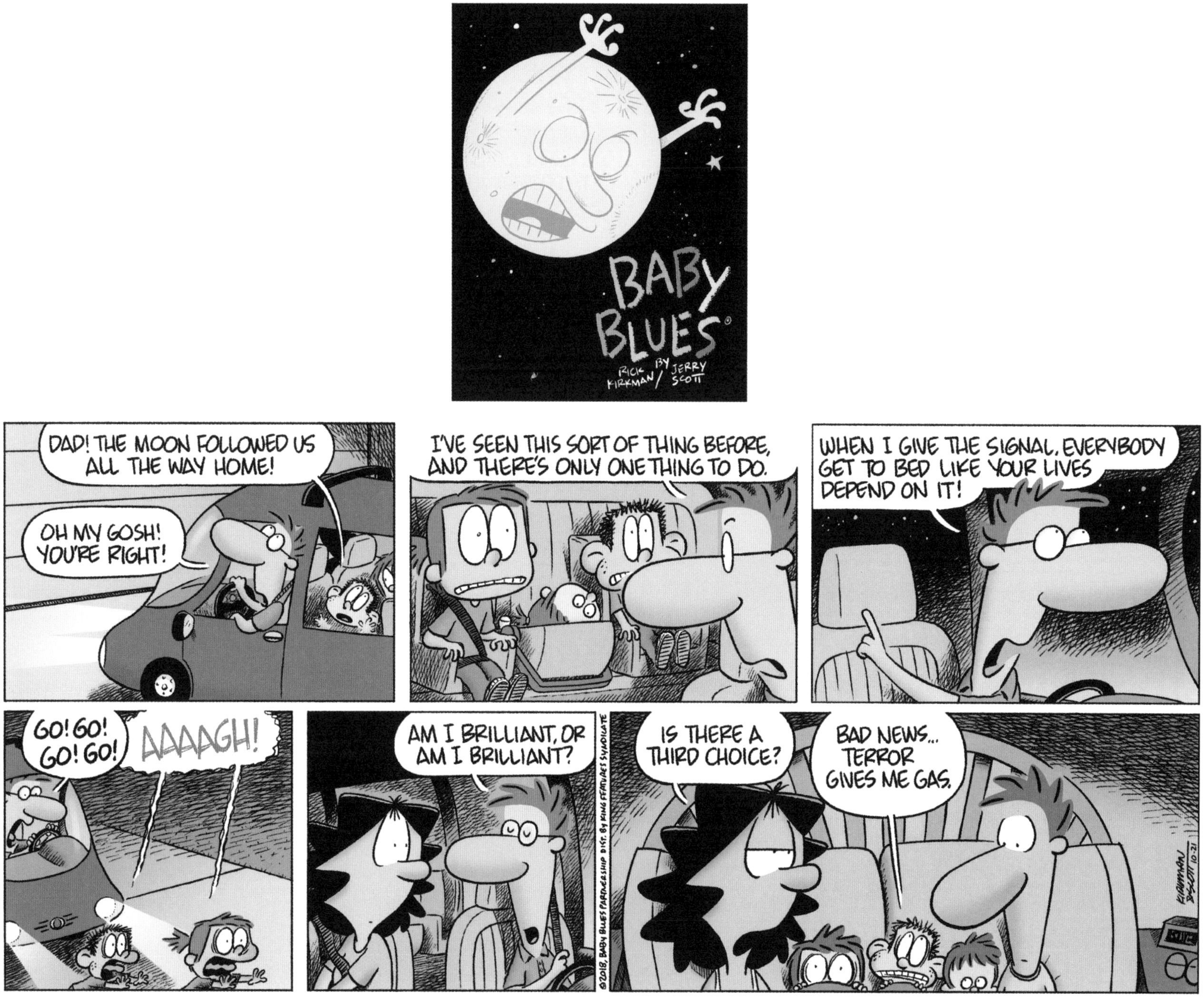
BABY BLUES
BY RICK KIRKMAN / JERRY SCOTT
DAD! THE MOON FOLLOWED US ALL THE WAY HOME!
OH MY GOSH! YOU'RE RIGHT!
I'VE SEEN THIS SORT OF THING BEFORE, AND THERE'S ONLY ONE THING TO DO.
WHEN I GIVE THE SIGNAL, EVERYBODY GET TO BED LIKE YOUR LIVES DEPEND ON IT!
GO! GO! GO! GO!
AAAAGH!
AM I BRILLIANT, OR AM I BRILLIANT?
©2018, BABY BLUES PARTNERSHIP DIST. BY KING FEATURES SYNDICATE
IS THERE A THIRD CHOICE?
BAD NEWS... TERROR GIVES ME GAS.

Rick: I thought he was brilliant, too, until the last panel.

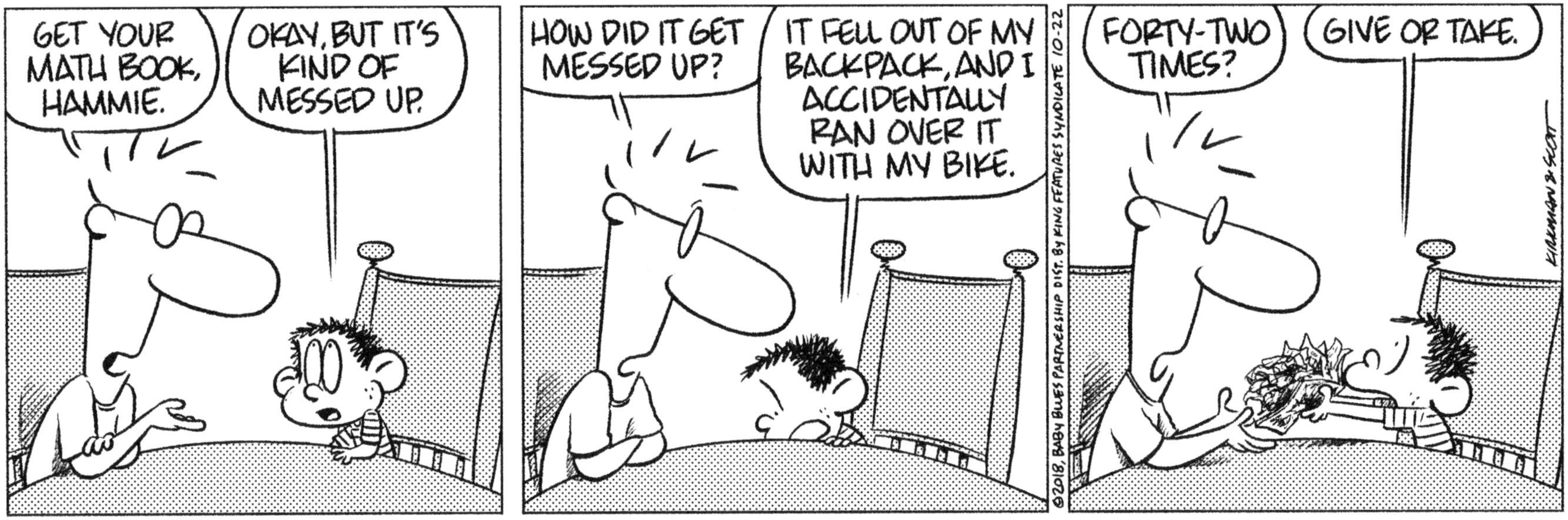
GET YOUR MATH BOOK, HAMMIE.
OKAY, BUT IT'S KIND OF MESSED UP.
HOW DID IT GET MESSED UP?
IT FELL OUT OF MY BACKPACK, AND I ACCIDENTALLY RAN OVER IT WITH MY BIKE.
©2018, BABY BLUES PARTNERSHIP DIST. BY KING FEATURES SYNDICATE 10-22
FORTY-TWO TIMES?
GIVE OR TAKE.
KIRKMAN & SCOTT

Jerry: Accidents will happen. And happen. And happen . . .

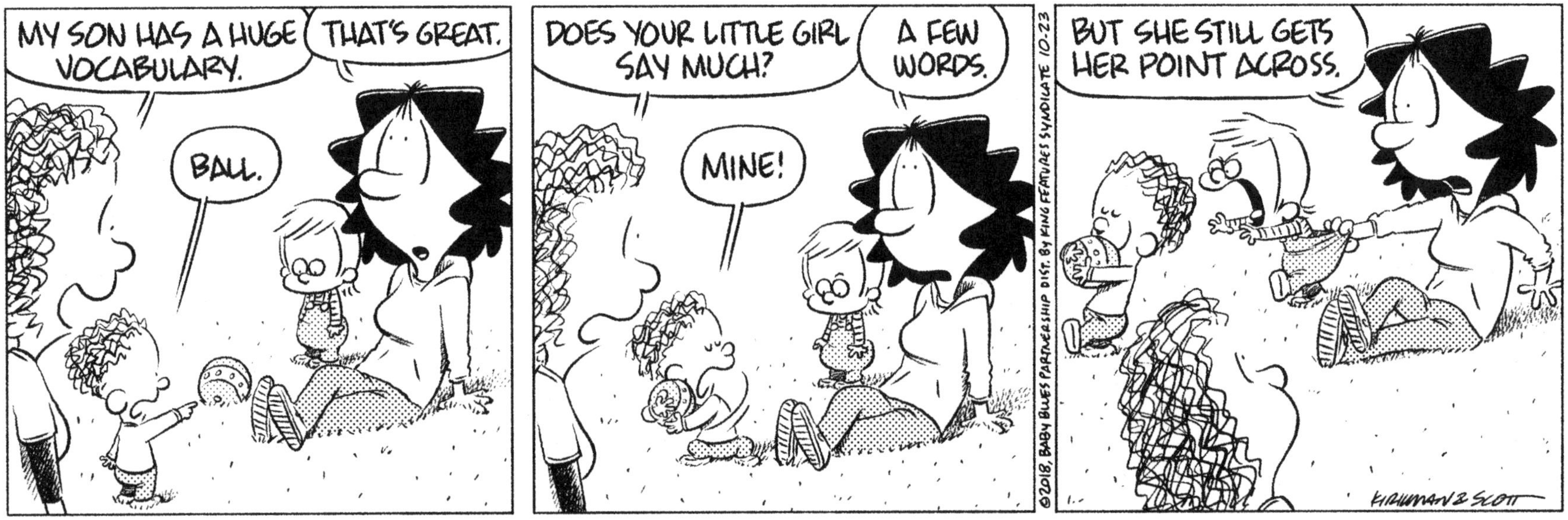
MY SON HAS A HUGE VOCABULARY.
THAT'S GREAT.
BALL.
DOES YOUR LITTLE GIRL SAY MUCH?
A FEW WORDS.
MINE!
©2018, BABY BLUES PARTNERSHIP DIST. BY KING FEATURES SYNDICATE 10-23
BUT SHE STILL GETS HER POINT ACROSS.
KIRKMAN & SCOTT

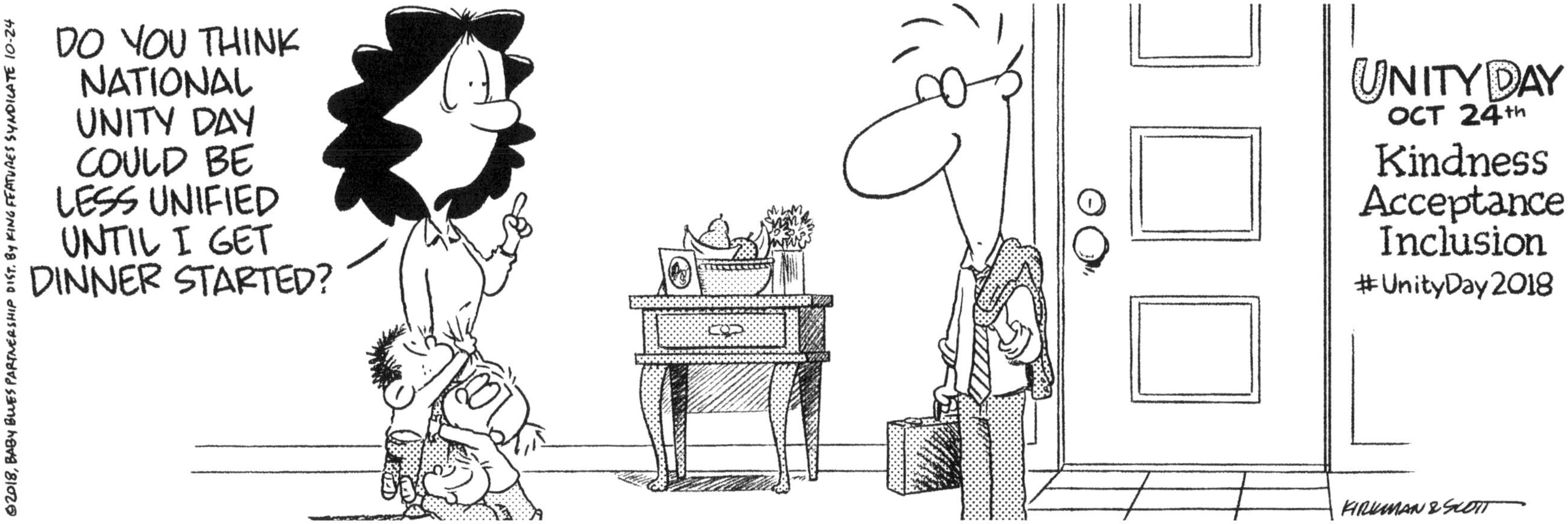
©2018, BABY BLUES PARTNERSHIP DIST. BY KING FEATURES SYNDICATE 10-24
DO YOU THINK NATIONAL UNITY DAY COULD BE LESS UNIFIED UNTIL I GET DINNER STARTED?
UNITY DAY
OCT 24th
Kindness
Acceptance
Inclusion
#UnityDay2018
KIRKMAN & SCOTT

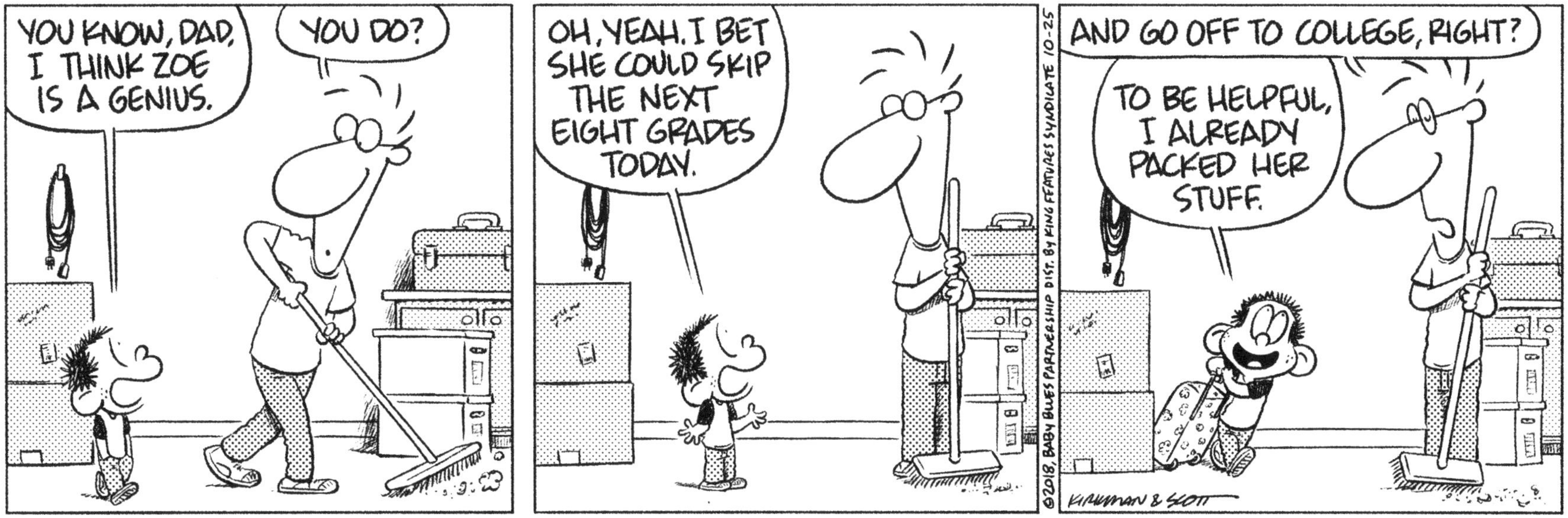
YOU KNOW, DAD, I THINK ZOE IS A GENIUS.
YOU DO?
OH, YEAH. I BET SHE COULD SKIP THE NEXT EIGHT GRADES TODAY.
©2018, BABY BLUES PARTNERSHIP DIST. BY KING FEATURES SYNDICATE 10-25
AND GO OFF TO COLLEGE, RIGHT?
TO BE HELPFUL, I ALREADY PACKED HER STUFF.
KIRKMAN & SCOTT

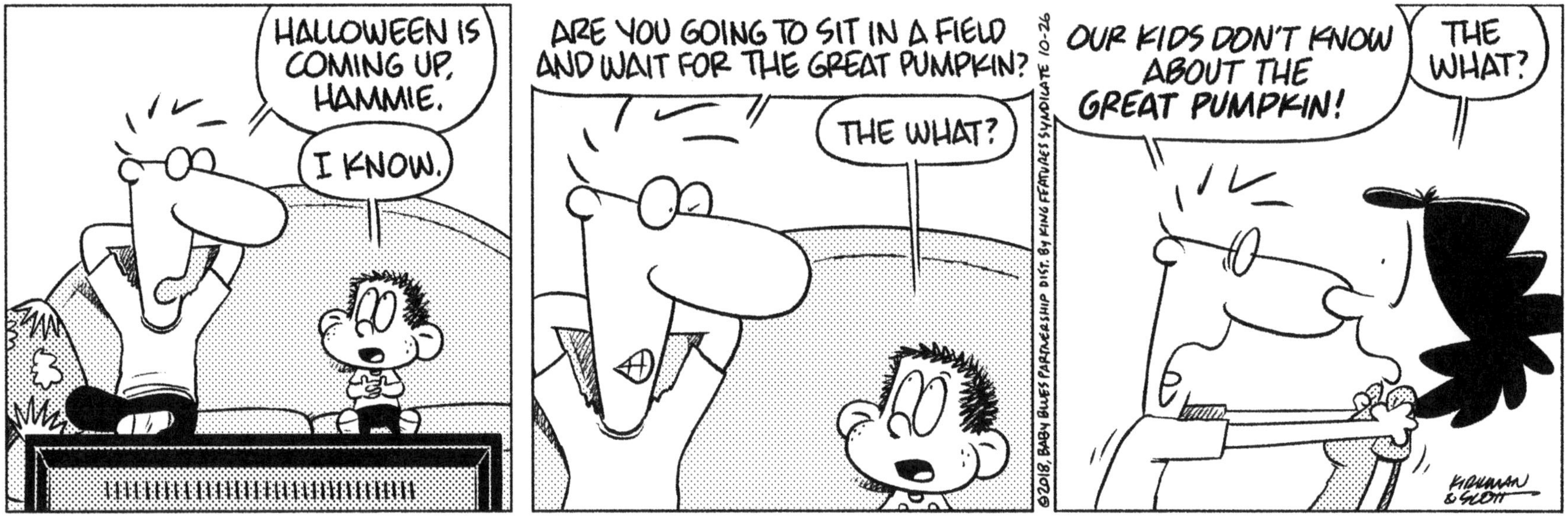
HALLOWEEN IS COMING UP, HAMMIE.
I KNOW.
ARE YOU GOING TO SIT IN A FIELD AND WAIT FOR THE GREAT PUMPKIN?
THE WHAT?
©2018, BABY BLUES PARTNERSHIP DIST. BY KING FEATURES SYNDICATE 10-26
OUR KIDS DON'T KNOW ABOUT THE GREAT PUMPKIN!
THE WHAT?
KIRKMAN & SCOTT

Rick: What's the world coming to?

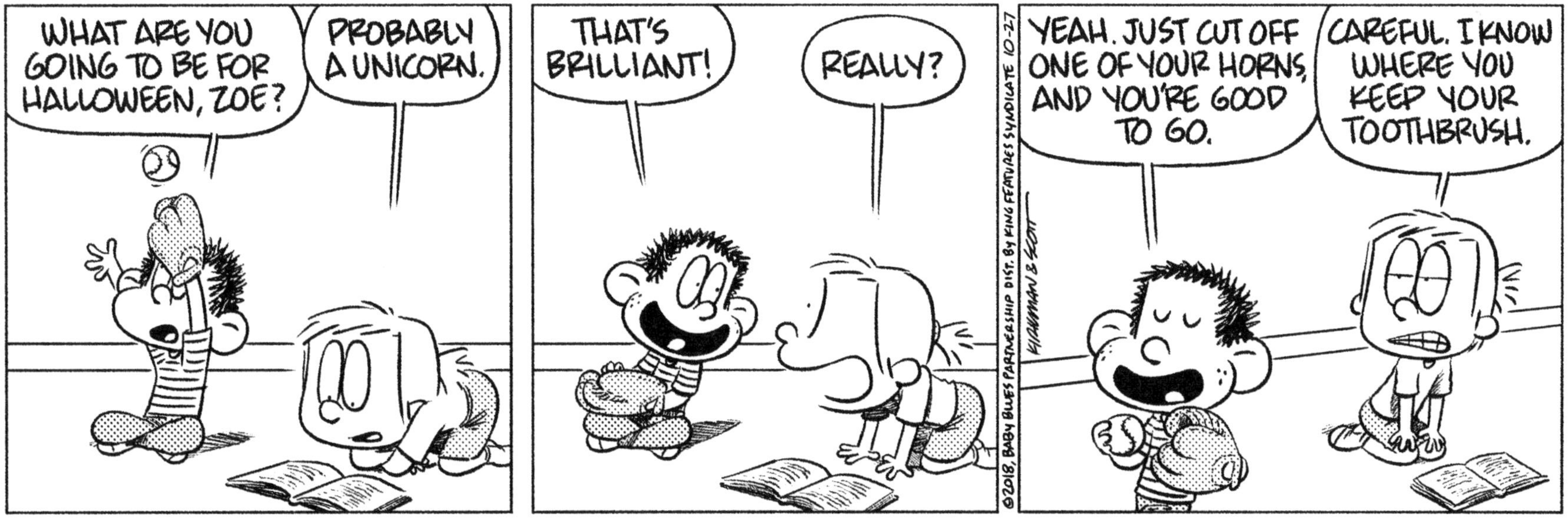
WHAT ARE YOU GOING TO BE FOR HALLOWEEN, ZOE?
PROBABLY A UNICORN.
THAT'S BRILLIANT!
REALLY?
©2018, BABY BLUES PARTNERSHIP DIST. BY KING FEATURES SYNDICATE 10-27
KIRKMAN & SCOTT
YEAH. JUST CUT OFF ONE OF YOUR HORNS, AND YOU'RE GOOD TO GO.
CAREFUL. I KNOW WHERE YOU KEEP YOUR TOOTHBRUSH.

Jerry: As a kid with two sisters, I hid my real toothbrush and left a decoy in the cup.

BABY BLUES®
Rick Kirkman & Jerry Scott
ZZZZZZ

...AND HERE'S YOUR CEREAL, HAMMIE.
ARE YOU HIDING SOMETHING BEHIND YOUR BACK?
ME? NO.
YES, YOU ARE.
WHY ARE THE MARSHMALLOW CHIPS SO SMALL?
GASP! THIS IS GENERIC CEREAL!
MOM! HOW COULD YOU?
OKAY, OKAY...
CEREAL
I DIDN'T THINK YOU COULD TELL THE CHEAP STUFF FROM THE BRAND-NAME STUFF.
HA! WHAT KIND OF DOOFUS COULDN'T TELL?
MARSH MALLO BLAST
©2018, BABY BLUES PARTNERSHIP DIST. BY KING FEATURES SYNDICATE
KIRKMAN & SCOTT 10-28
MM...GOOD CEREAL.

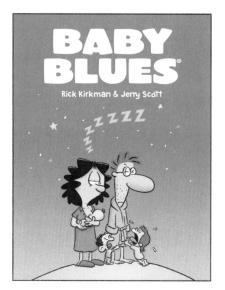

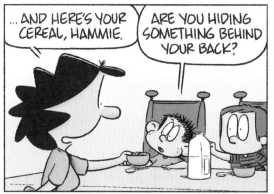

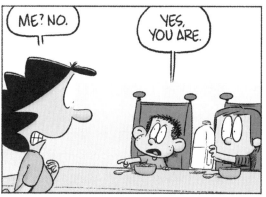

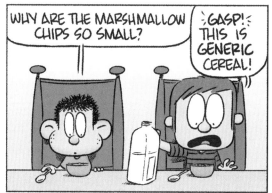

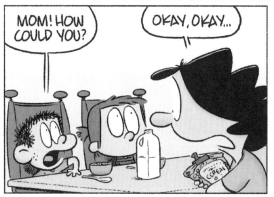

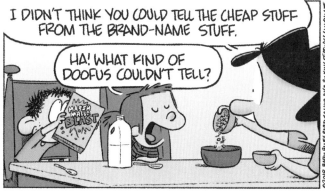

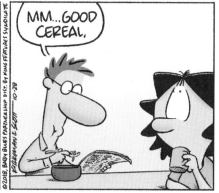

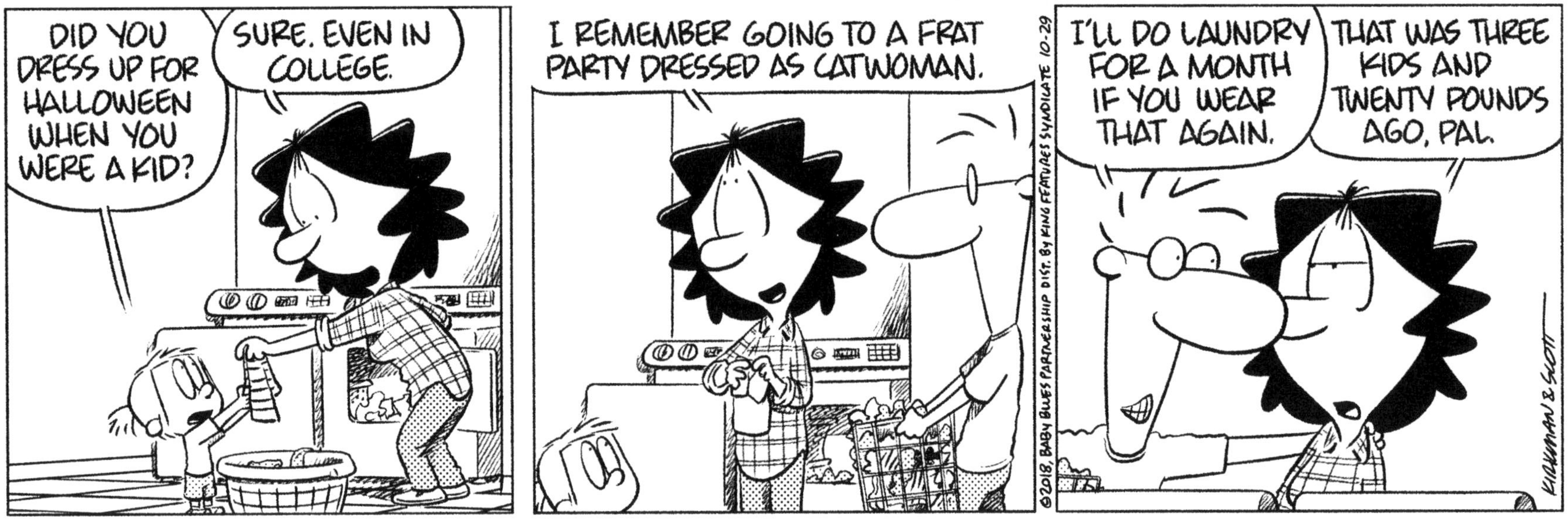
DID YOU DRESS UP FOR HALLOWEEN WHEN YOU WERE A KID?
SURE. EVEN IN COLLEGE.
I REMEMBER GOING TO A FRAT PARTY DRESSED AS CATWOMAN.
I'LL DO LAUNDRY FOR A MONTH IF YOU WEAR THAT AGAIN.
THAT WAS THREE KIDS AND TWENTY POUNDS AGO, PAL.
©2018, BABY BLUES PARTNERSHIP DIST. BY KING FEATURES SYNDICATE 10-29
KIRKMAN & SCOTT

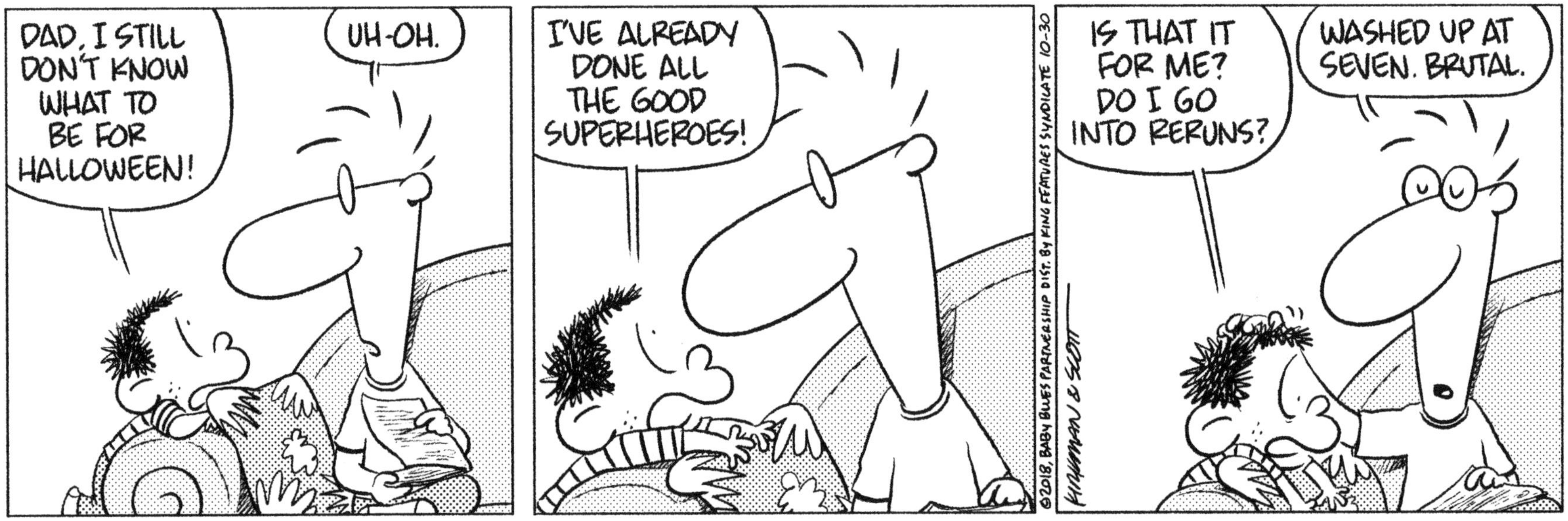
DAD, I STILL DON'T KNOW WHAT TO BE FOR HALLOWEEN!
UH-OH.
I'VE ALREADY DONE ALL THE GOOD SUPERHEROES!
IS THAT IT FOR ME? DO I GO INTO RERUNS?
WASHED UP AT SEVEN. BRUTAL.
©2018, BABY BLUES PARTNERSHIP DIST. BY KING FEATURES SYNDICATE 10-30
KIRKMAN & SCOTT

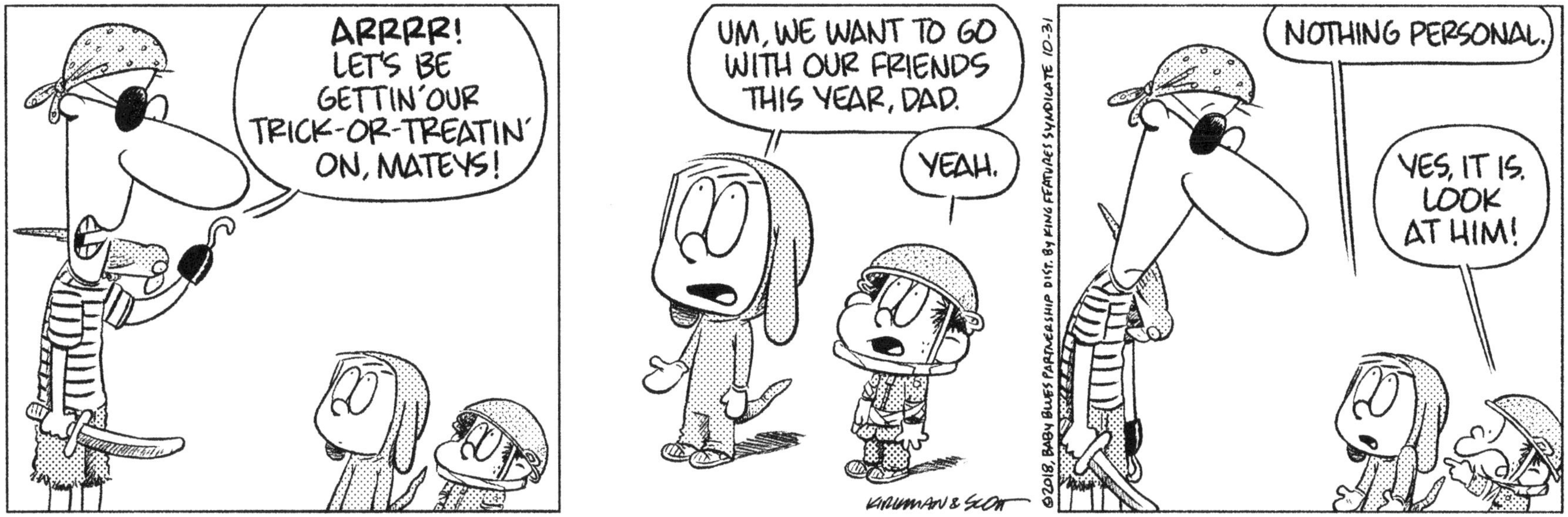

ARRRR! LET'S BE GETTIN' OUR TRICK-OR-TREATIN' ON, MATEYS!
UM, WE WANT TO GO WITH OUR FRIENDS THIS YEAR, DAD.
YEAH.
KIRKMAN & SCOTT
©2018, BABY BLUES PARTNERSHIP DIST. BY KING FEATURES SYNDICATE 10-31
NOTHING PERSONAL.
YES, IT IS. LOOK AT HIM!

Rick: And so it begins . . .

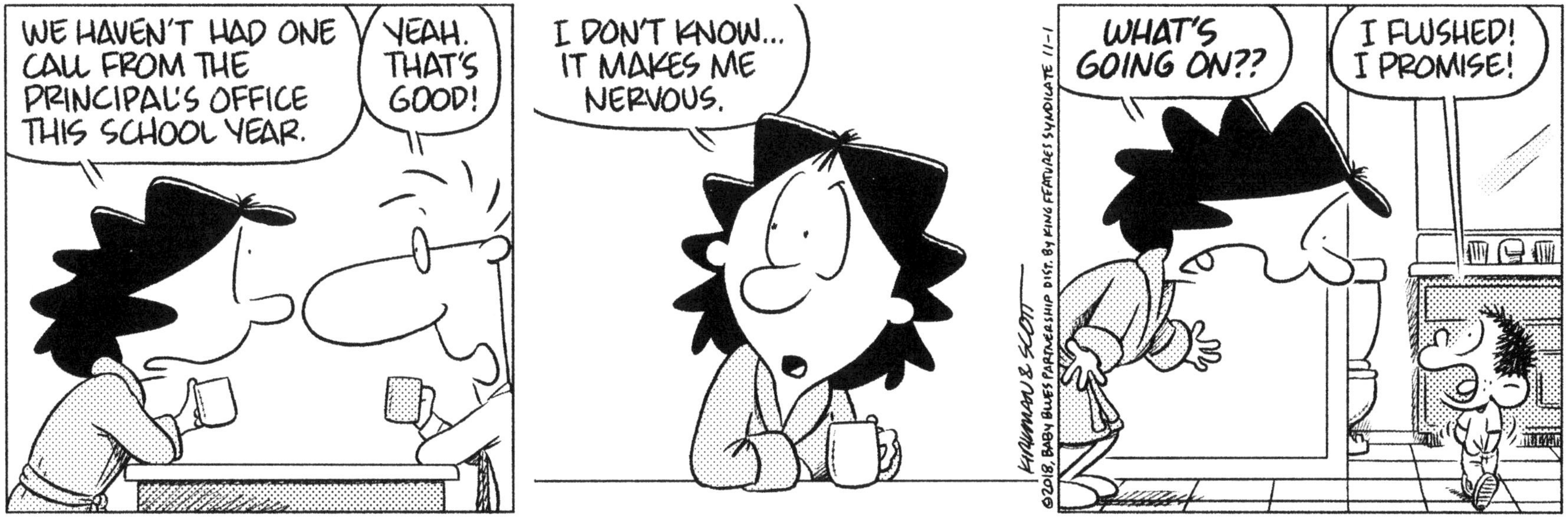

WE HAVEN'T HAD ONE CALL FROM THE PRINCIPAL'S OFFICE THIS SCHOOL YEAR.
YEAH. THAT'S GOOD!
I DON'T KNOW... IT MAKES ME NERVOUS.
KIRKMAN & SCOTT
©2018, BABY BLUES PARTNERSHIP DIST. BY KING FEATURES SYNDICATE 11-1
WHAT'S GOING ON??
I FLUSHED! I PROMISE!

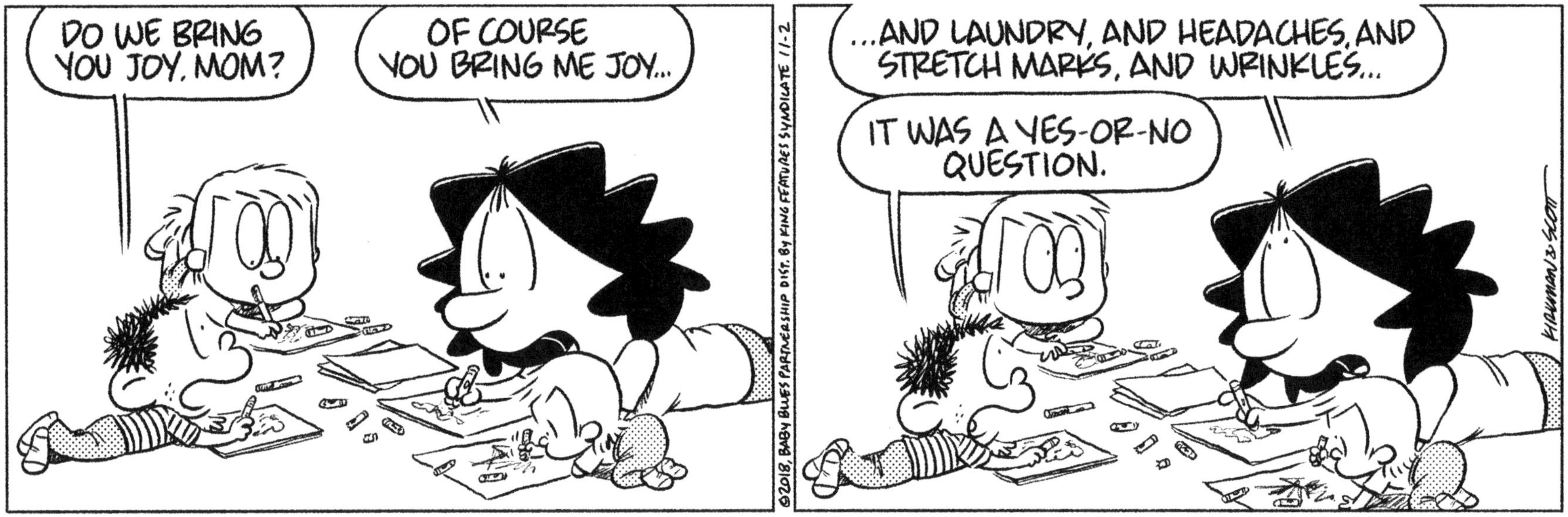
DO WE BRING YOU JOY, MOM?
OF COURSE YOU BRING ME JOY...
©2018, BABY BLUES PARTNERSHIP DIST. BY KING FEATURES SYNDICATE 11-2
...AND LAUNDRY, AND HEADACHES, AND STRETCH MARKS, AND WRINKLES...
IT WAS A YES-OR-NO QUESTION.
KIRKMAN & SCOTT

Rick: Whew! For a second, I thought that was leading to some tidying up.

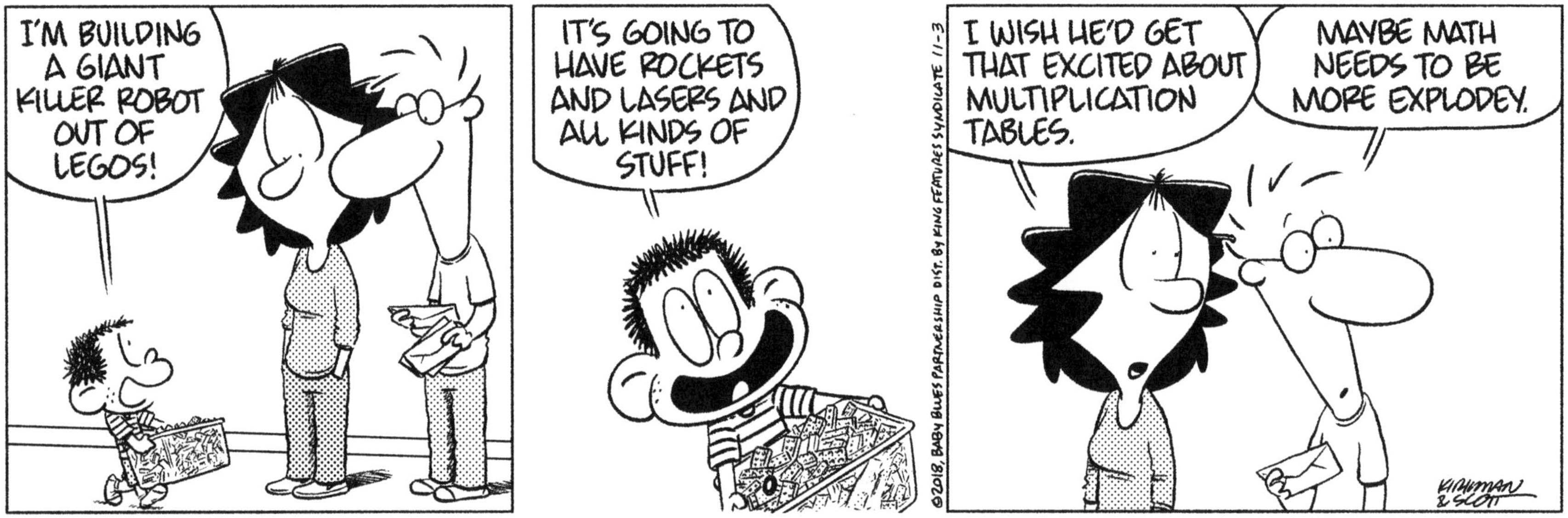
I'M BUILDING A GIANT KILLER ROBOT OUT OF LEGOS!
IT'S GOING TO HAVE ROCKETS AND LASERS AND ALL KINDS OF STUFF!
©2018, BABY BLUES PARTNERSHIP DIST. BY KING FEATURES SYNDICATE 11-3
I WISH HE'D GET THAT EXCITED ABOUT MULTIPLICATION TABLES.
MAYBE MATH NEEDS TO BE MORE EXPLODEY.
KIRKMAN & SCOTT

Rick: My vote for Word of the Year: Explodey

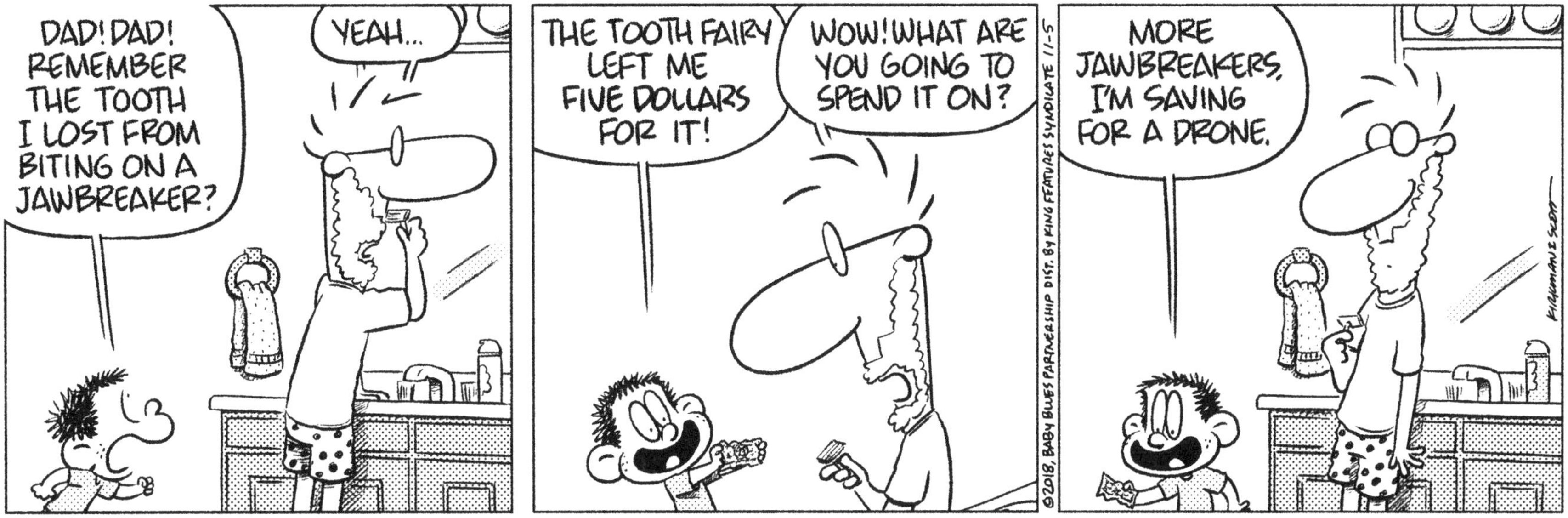
DAD! DAD! REMEMBER THE TOOTH I LOST FROM BITING ON A JAWBREAKER?
YEAH...
THE TOOTH FAIRY LEFT ME FIVE DOLLARS FOR IT!
WOW! WHAT ARE YOU GOING TO SPEND IT ON?
©2018, BABY BLUES PARTNERSHIP DIST. BY KING FEATURES SYNDICATE 11-5
MORE JAWBREAKERS, I'M SAVING FOR A DRONE.
KIRKMAN & SCOTT

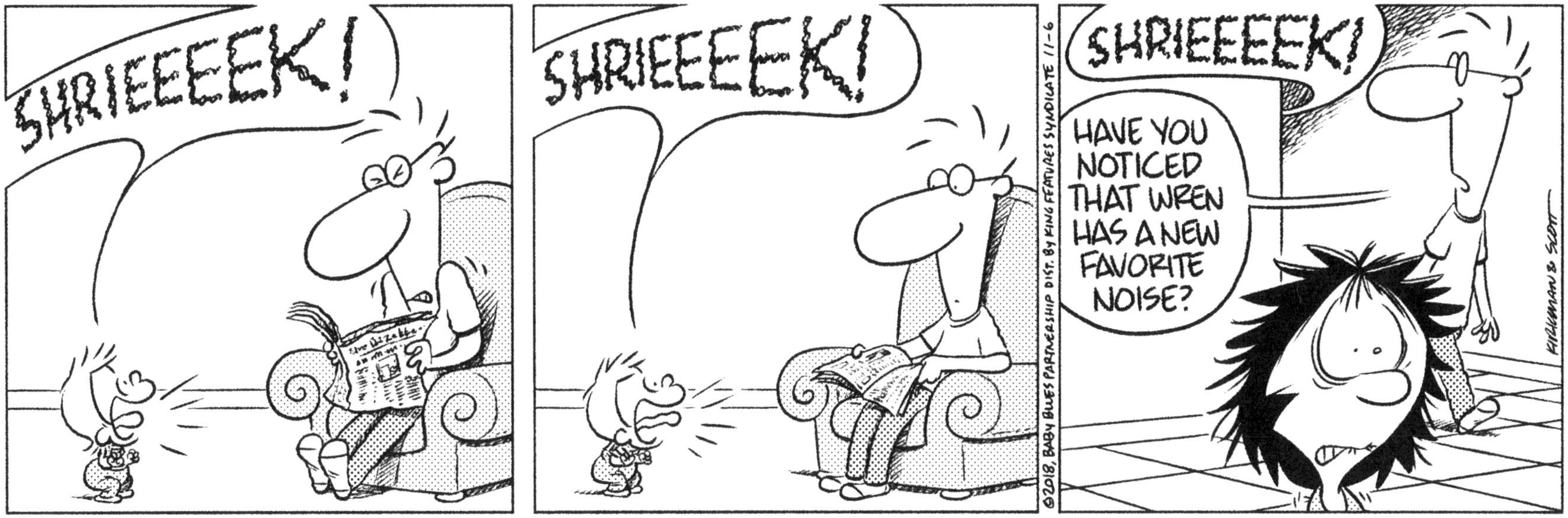
SHRIEEEEK!
SHRIEEEEK!
©2018, BABY BLUES PARTNERSHIP DIST. BY KING FEATURES SYNDICATE 11-6
SHRIEEEEK!
HAVE YOU NOTICED THAT WREN HAS A NEW FAVORITE NOISE?
KIRKMAN & SCOTT

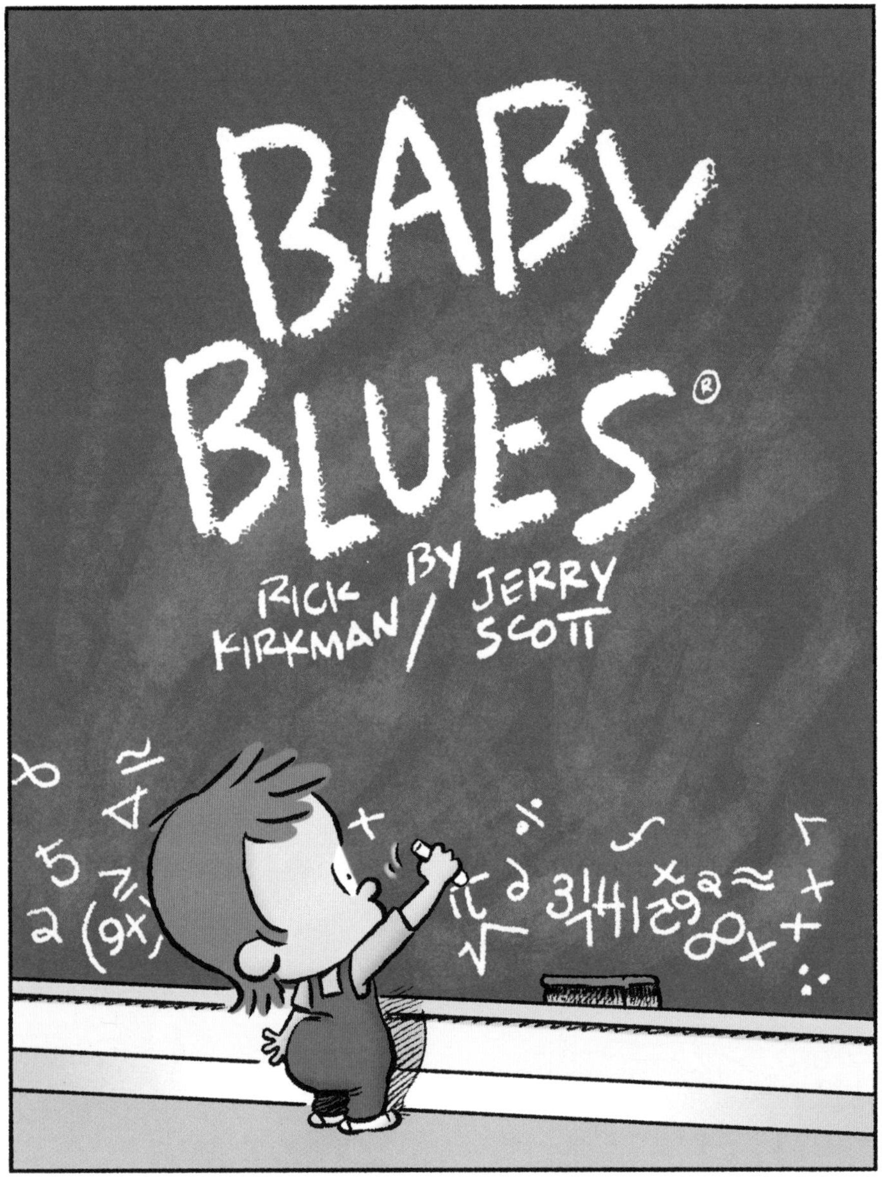
BABY BLUES®
BY
RICK KIRKMAN / JERRY SCOTT

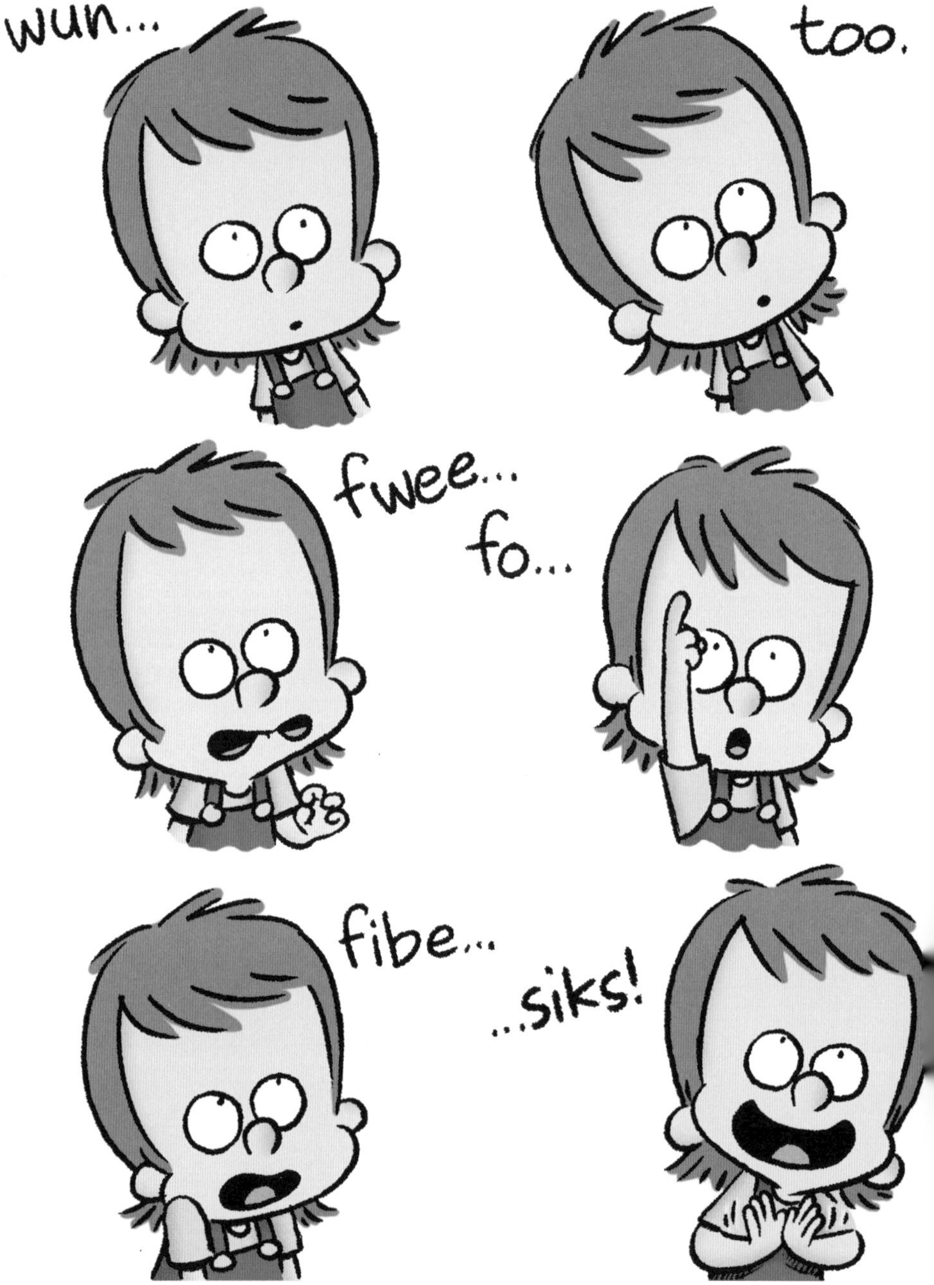
wun...
too.
fwee...
fo...
fibe...
...siks!

Rick: Wren is becoming more engaged. A mixed blessing.

Jerry: At some point while drawing this strip, Rick would have had to decide how big the nostrils should be on a nose the size of Darryl's. Think about that the next time your job seems ridiculous.

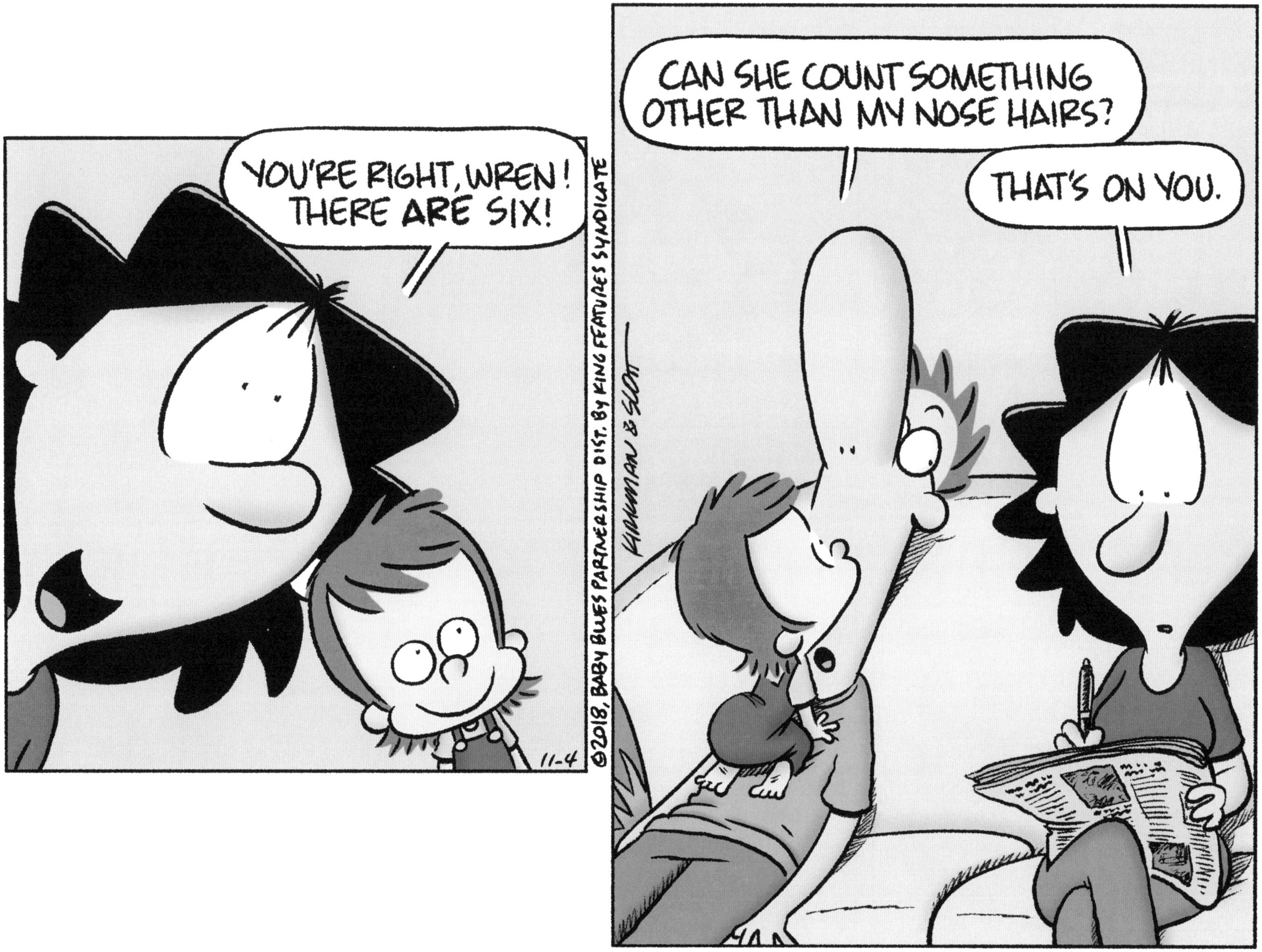
YOU'RE RIGHT, WREN! THERE ARE SIX!
11-4
©2018, BABY BLUES PARTNERSHIP DIST. BY KING FEATURES SYNDICATE
KIRKMAN & SCOTT
CAN SHE COUNT SOMETHING OTHER THAN MY NOSE HAIRS?
THAT'S ON YOU.

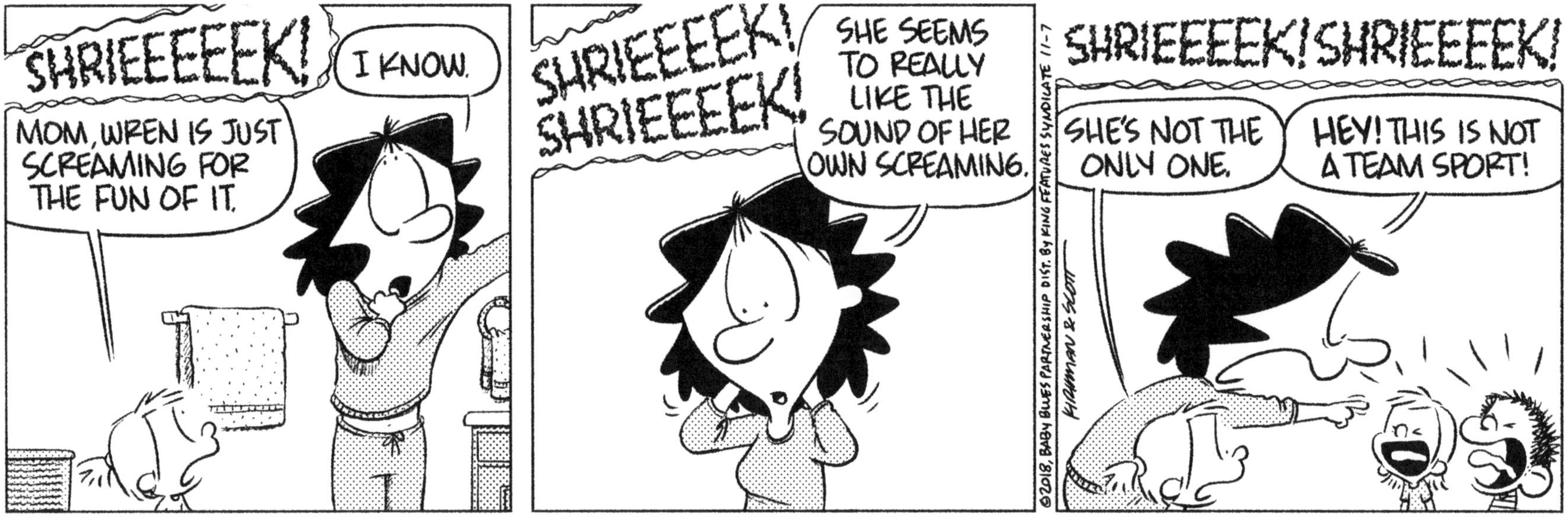
SHRIEEEEEK!
MOM, WREN IS JUST SCREAMING FOR THE FUN OF IT.
I KNOW.
SHRIEEEEEK! SHRIEEEEEK!
SHE SEEMS TO REALLY LIKE THE SOUND OF HER OWN SCREAMING.
©2018, BABY BLUES PARTNERSHIP DIST. BY KING FEATURES SYNDICATE 11-7
KIRKMAN & SCOTT
SHRIEEEEEK! SHRIEEEEEK!
SHE'S NOT THE ONLY ONE.
HEY! THIS IS NOT A TEAM SPORT!

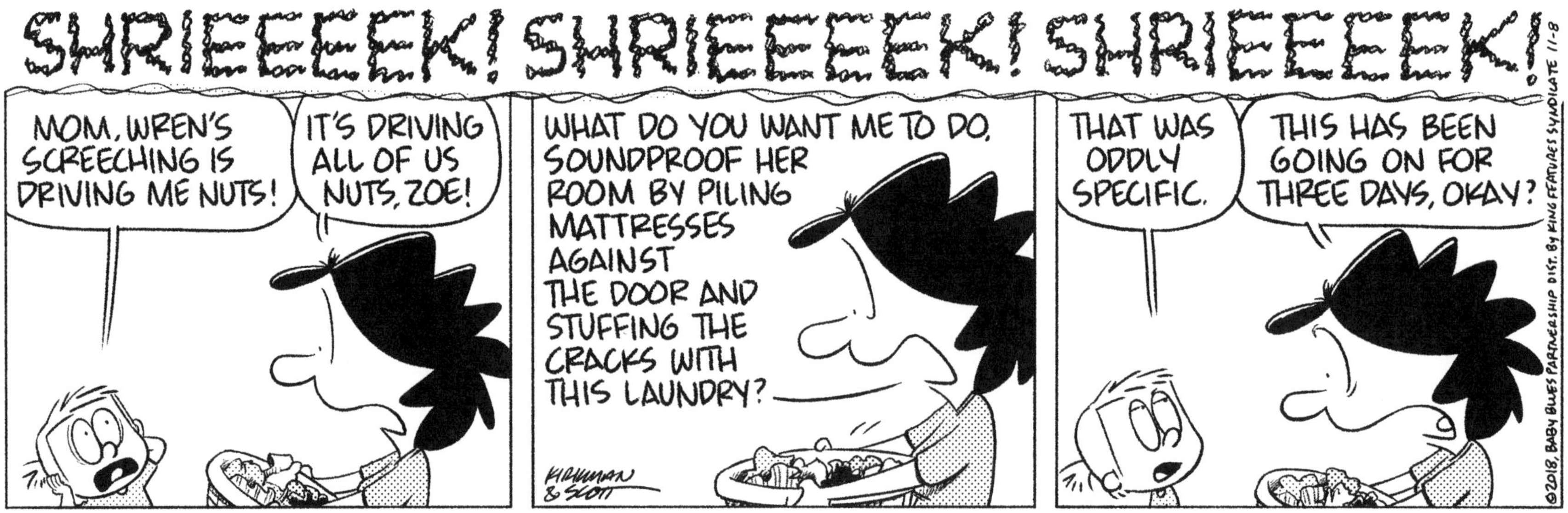
SHRIEEEEEK! SHRIEEEEEK! SHRIEEEEEK!
MOM, WREN'S SCREECHING IS DRIVING ME NUTS!
IT'S DRIVING ALL OF US NUTS, ZOE!
WHAT DO YOU WANT ME TO DO, SOUNDPROOF HER ROOM BY PILING MATTRESSES AGAINST THE DOOR AND STUFFING THE CRACKS WITH THIS LAUNDRY?
KIRKMAN & SCOTT
THAT WAS ODDLY SPECIFIC.
THIS HAS BEEN GOING ON FOR THREE DAYS, OKAY?
©2018, BABY BLUES PARTNERSHIP DIST. BY KING FEATURES SYNDICATE 11-8

Rick: I got a headache just drawing the shrieks.

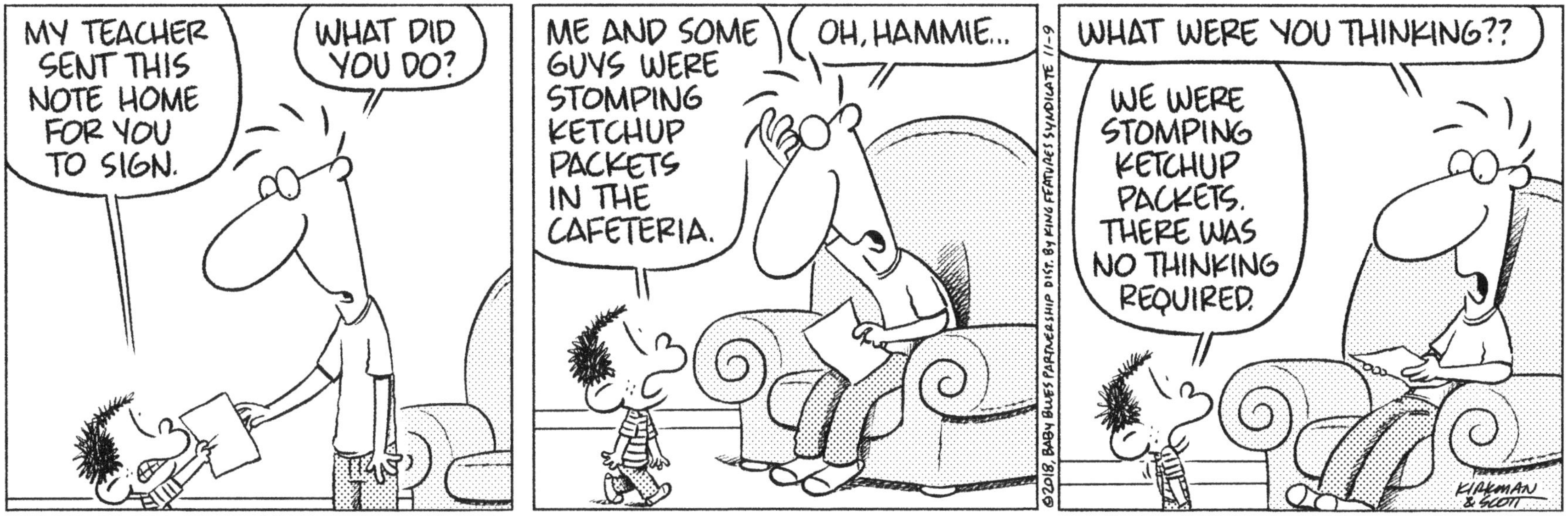
MY TEACHER SENT THIS NOTE HOME FOR YOU TO SIGN.
WHAT DID YOU DO?
ME AND SOME GUYS WERE STOMPING KETCHUP PACKETS IN THE CAFETERIA.
OH, HAMMIE...
©2018, BABY BLUES PARTNERSHIP DIST. BY KING FEATURES SYNDICATE 11-9
WHAT WERE YOU THINKING??
WE WERE STOMPING KETCHUP PACKETS. THERE WAS NO THINKING REQUIRED.
KIRKMAN & SCOTT

Rick: Makes perfect sense to me.

Jerry: Why do we always ask kids what they were thinking after their most brainless stunts? What are WE thinking?

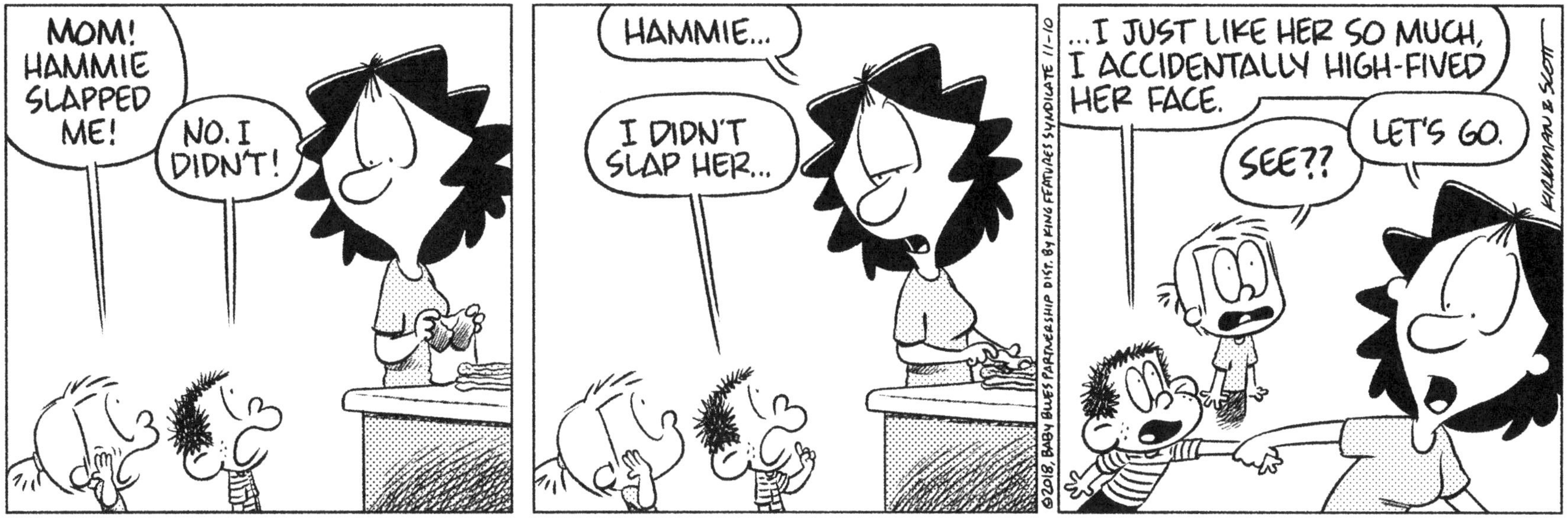
MOM! HAMMIE SLAPPED ME!
NO. I DIDN'T!
HAMMIE...
I DIDN'T SLAP HER...
©2018, BABY BLUES PARTNERSHIP DIST. BY KING FEATURES SYNDICATE 11-10
...I JUST LIKE HER SO MUCH, I ACCIDENTALLY HIGH-FIVED HER FACE.
SEE??
LET'S GO.
KIRKMAN & SCOTT

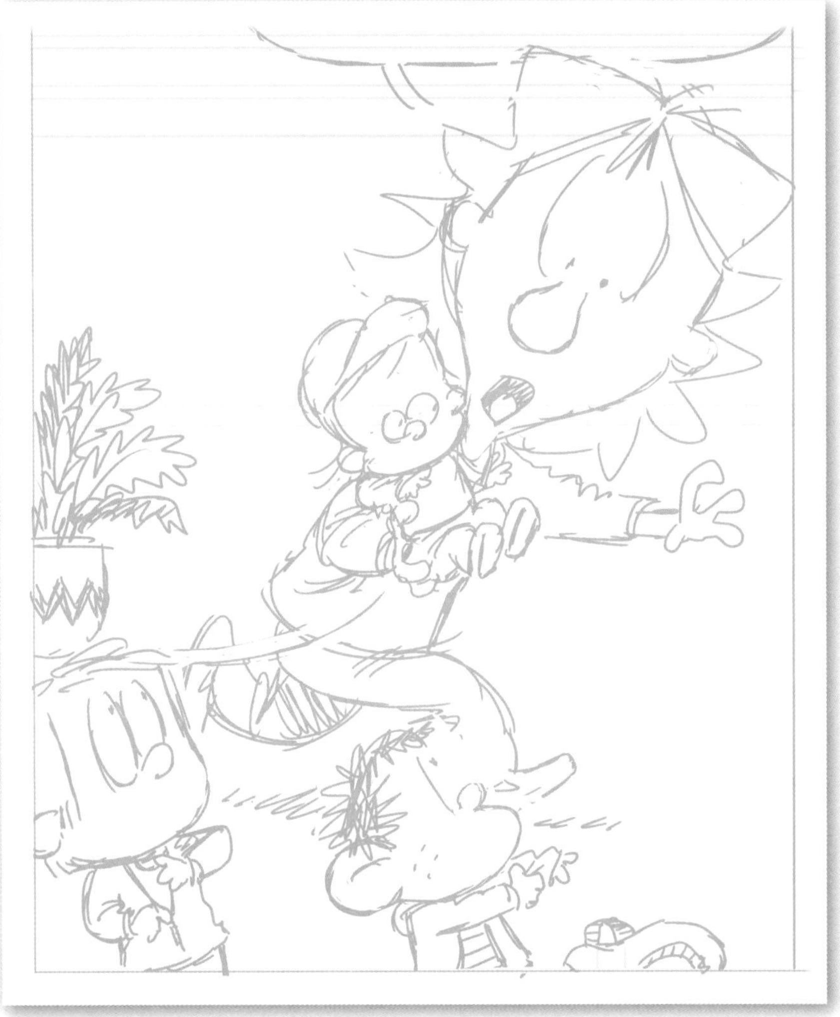

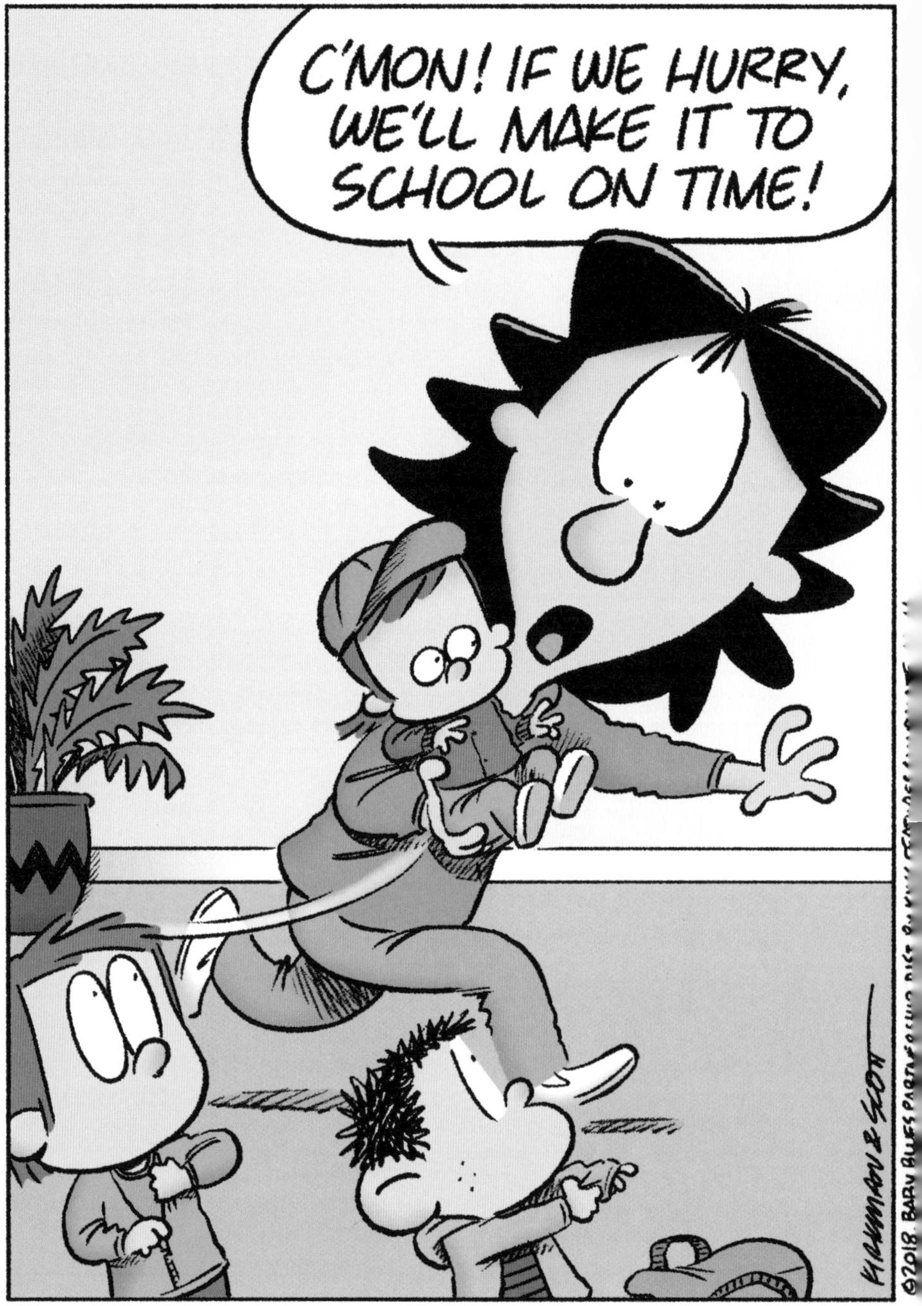
C'MON! IF WE HURRY, WE'LL MAKE IT TO SCHOOL ON TIME!
KIRKMAN & SCOTT
©2018 BABY BLUES PARTNERSHIP

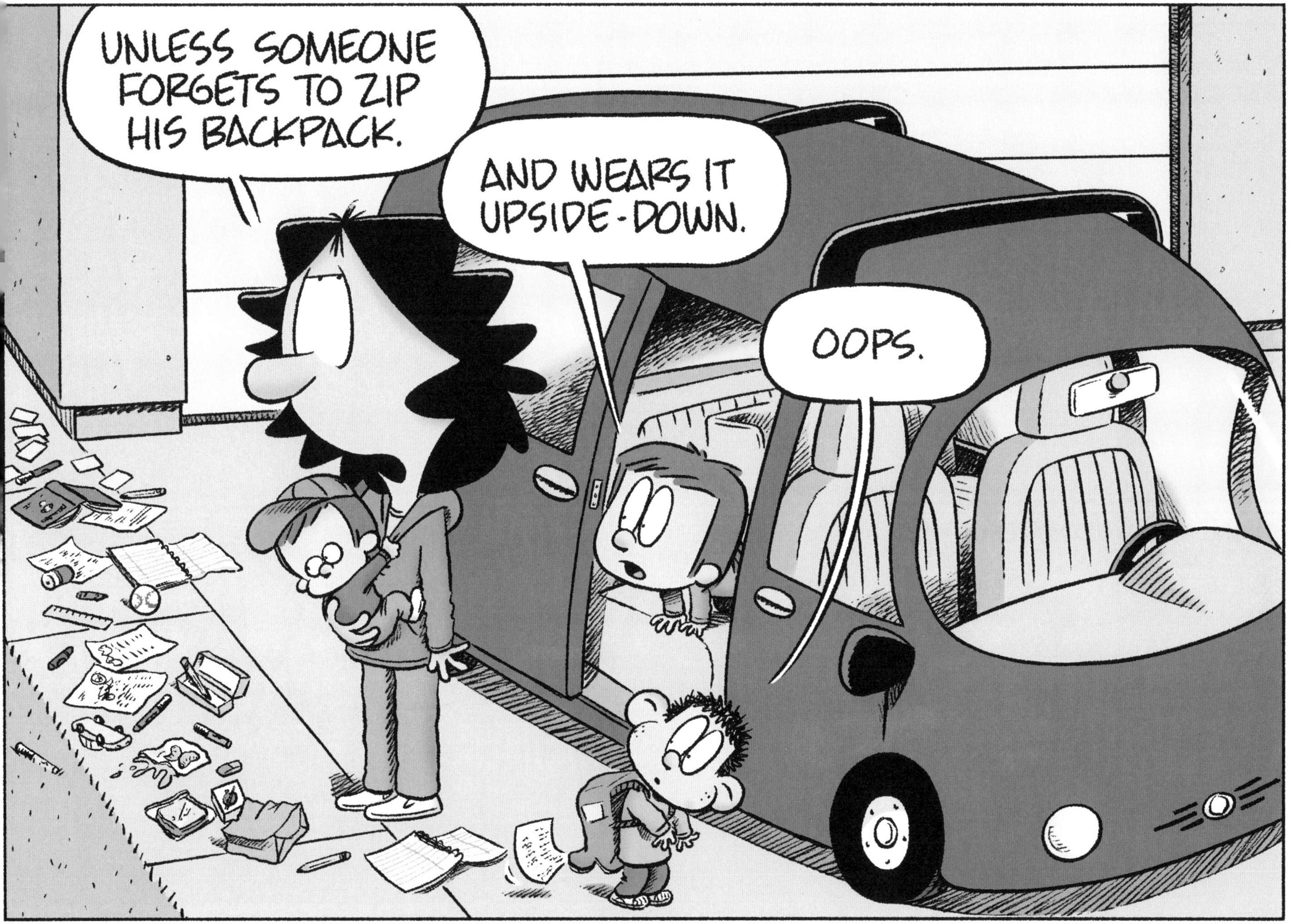
UNLESS SOMEONE FORGETS TO ZIP HIS BACKPACK.
AND WEARS IT UPSIDE-DOWN.
OOPS.

Rick: I spy with my little eye . . .

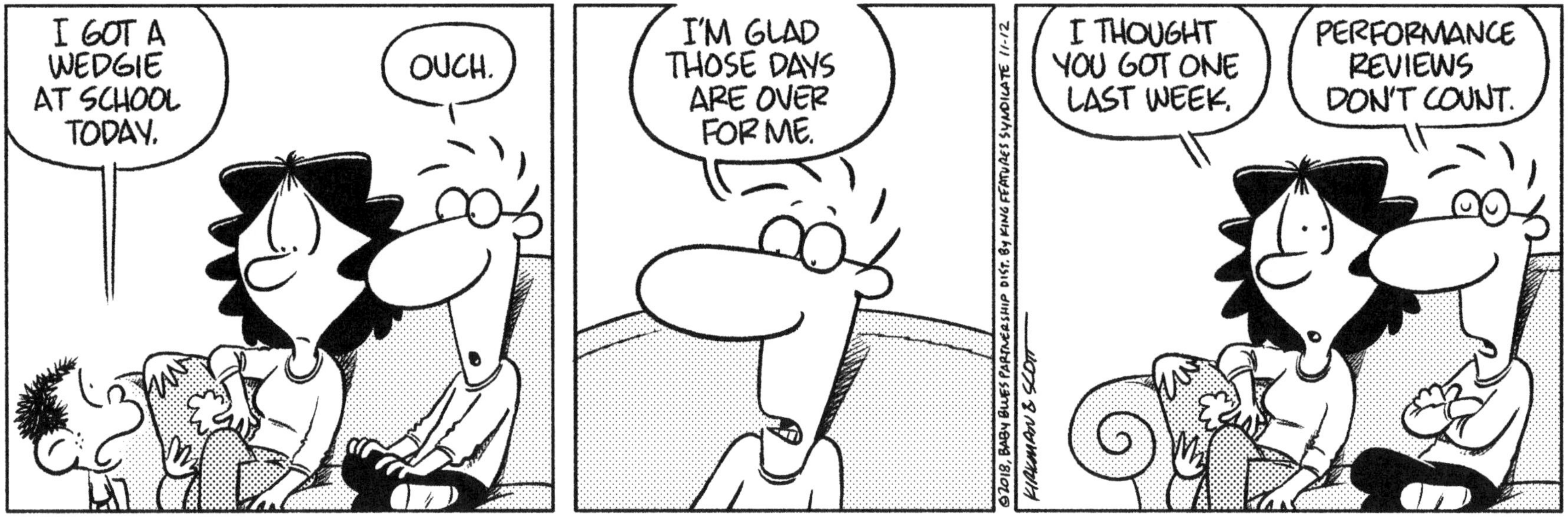
I GOT A WEDGIE AT SCHOOL TODAY.
OUCH.
I'M GLAD THOSE DAYS ARE OVER FOR ME.
©2018, BABY BLUES PARTNERSHIP DIST. BY KING FEATURES SYNDICATE 11-12
KIRKMAN & SCOTT
I THOUGHT YOU GOT ONE LAST WEEK.
PERFORMANCE REVIEWS DON'T COUNT.

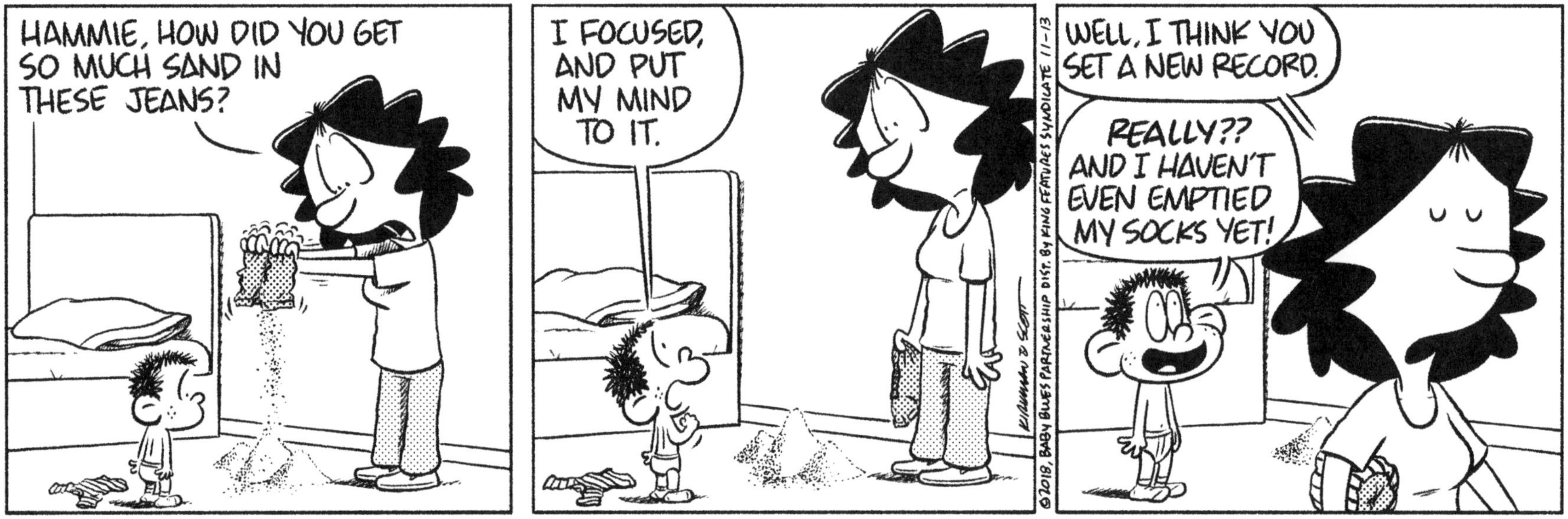
HAMMIE, HOW DID YOU GET SO MUCH SAND IN THESE JEANS?
I FOCUSED, AND PUT MY MIND TO IT.
©2018, BABY BLUES PARTNERSHIP DIST. BY KING FEATURES SYNDICATE 11-13
KIRKMAN & SCOTT
WELL, I THINK YOU SET A NEW RECORD.
REALLY?? AND I HAVEN'T EVEN EMPTIED MY SOCKS YET!

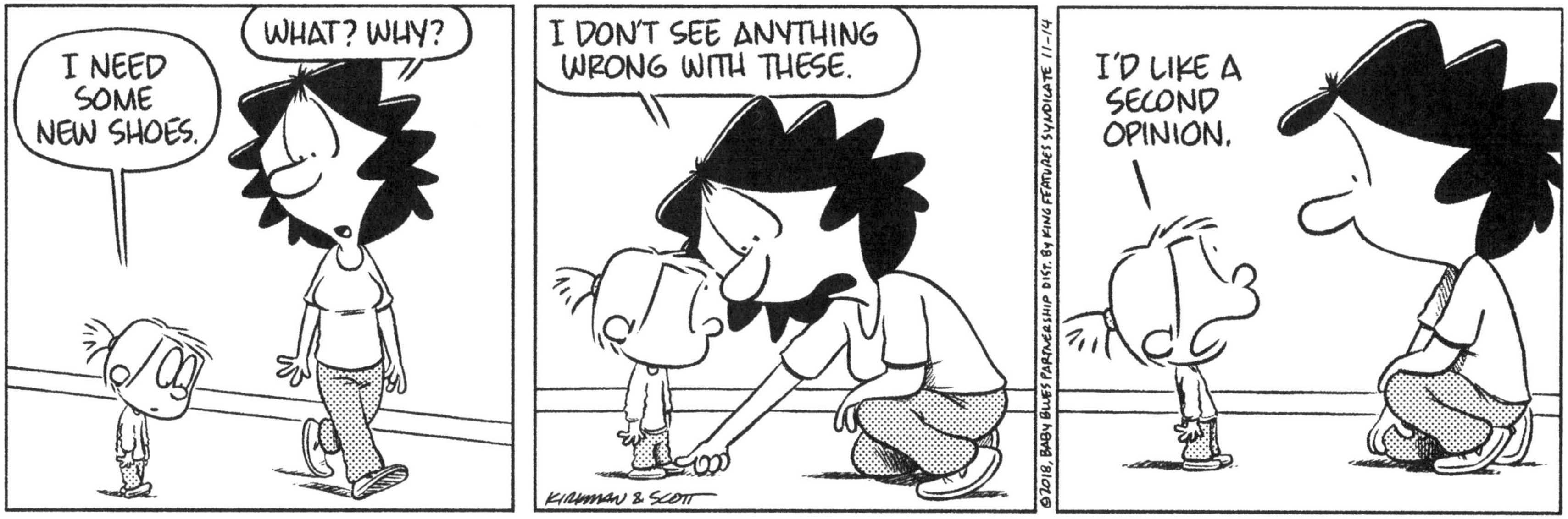
I NEED SOME NEW SHOES.
WHAT? WHY?
I DON'T SEE ANYTHING WRONG WITH THESE.
KIRKMAN & SCOTT
©2018, BABY BLUES PARTNERSHIP DIST. BY KING FEATURES SYNDICATE 11-14
I'D LIKE A SECOND OPINION.

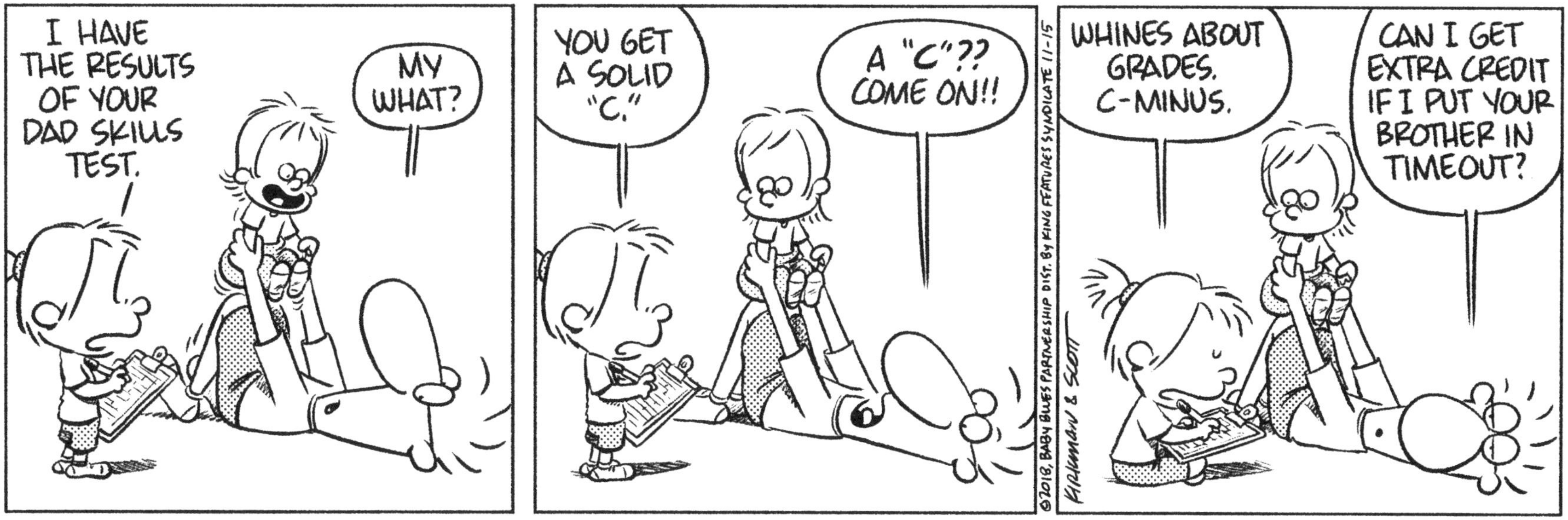
I HAVE THE RESULTS OF YOUR DAD SKILLS TEST.
MY WHAT?
YOU GET A SOLID "C."
A "C"?? COME ON!!
©2018, BABY BLUES PARTNERSHIP DIST. BY KING FEATURES SYNDICATE 11-15
KIRKMAN & SCOTT
WHINES ABOUT GRADES. C-MINUS.
CAN I GET EXTRA CREDIT IF I PUT YOUR BROTHER IN TIMEOUT?

Rick: The pressure on parents these days!

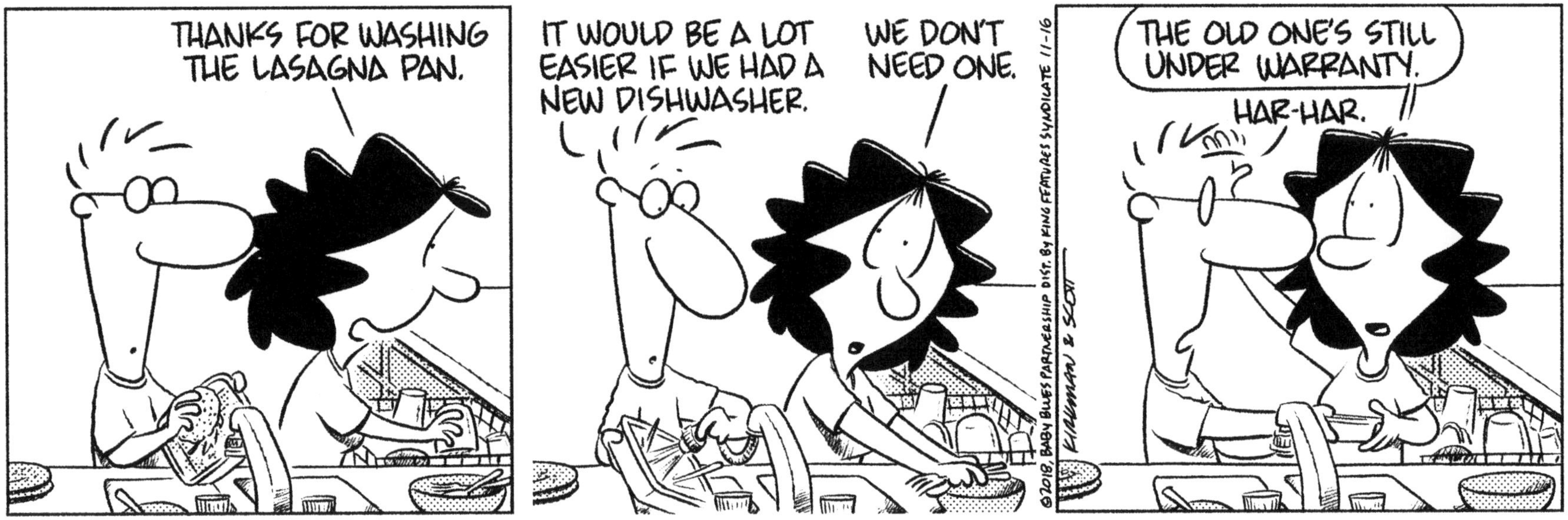
THANKS FOR WASHING THE LASAGNA PAN.
IT WOULD BE A LOT EASIER IF WE HAD A NEW DISHWASHER.
WE DON'T NEED ONE.
©2018, BABY BLUES PARTNERSHIP DIST. BY KING FEATURES SYNDICATE 11-16
KIRKMAN & SCOTT
THE OLD ONE'S STILL UNDER WARRANTY.
HAR-HAR.

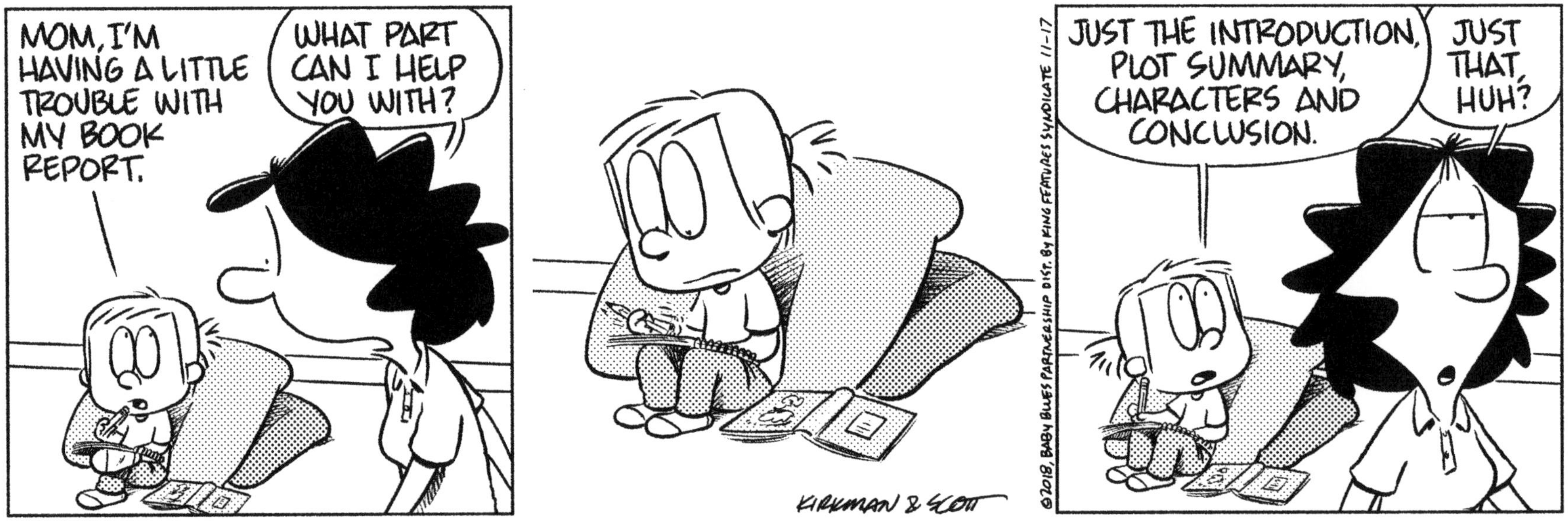
MOM, I'M HAVING A LITTLE TROUBLE WITH MY BOOK REPORT.
WHAT PART CAN I HELP YOU WITH?
KIRKMAN & SCOTT
©2018, BABY BLUES PARTNERSHIP DIST. BY KING FEATURES SYNDICATE 11-17
JUST THE INTRODUCTION, PLOT SUMMARY, CHARACTERS AND CONCLUSION.
JUST THAT, HUH?

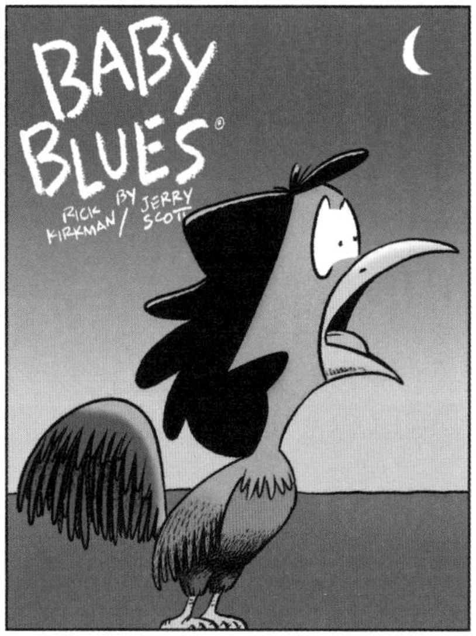
BABY BLUES®
RICK KIRKMAN / BY JERRY SCOTT

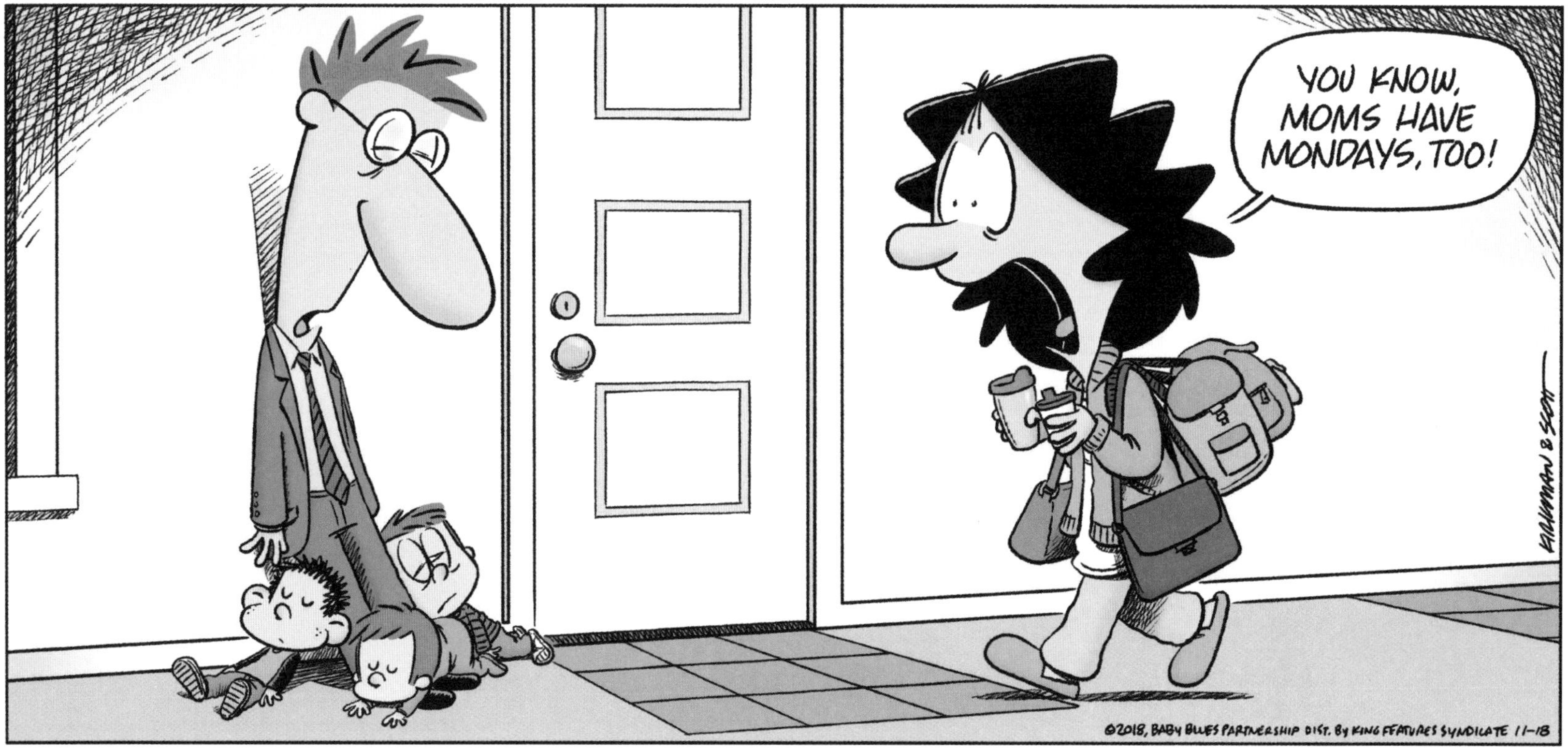
YOU KNOW, MOMS HAVE MONDAYS, TOO!
KIRKMAN & SCOTT
©2018, BABY BLUES PARTNERSHIP DIST. BY KING FEATURES SYNDICATE 11-18

Rick: This was almost the cover of this book.

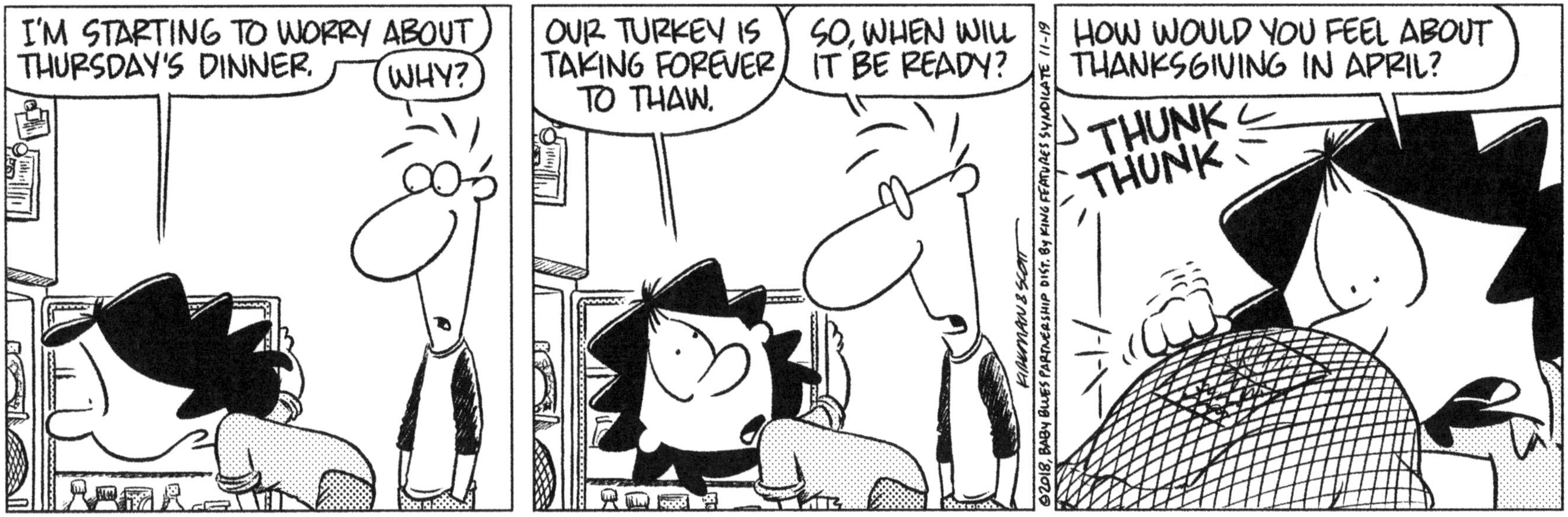
I'M STARTING TO WORRY ABOUT THURSDAY'S DINNER.
WHY?
OUR TURKEY IS TAKING FOREVER TO THAW.
SO, WHEN WILL IT BE READY?
HOW WOULD YOU FEEL ABOUT THANKSGIVING IN APRIL?
THUNK THUNK
KIRKMAN & SCOTT
©2018, BABY BLUES PARTNERSHIP DIST. BY KING FEATURES SYNDICATE 11-19

Rick: I can totally relate to this week's strips.

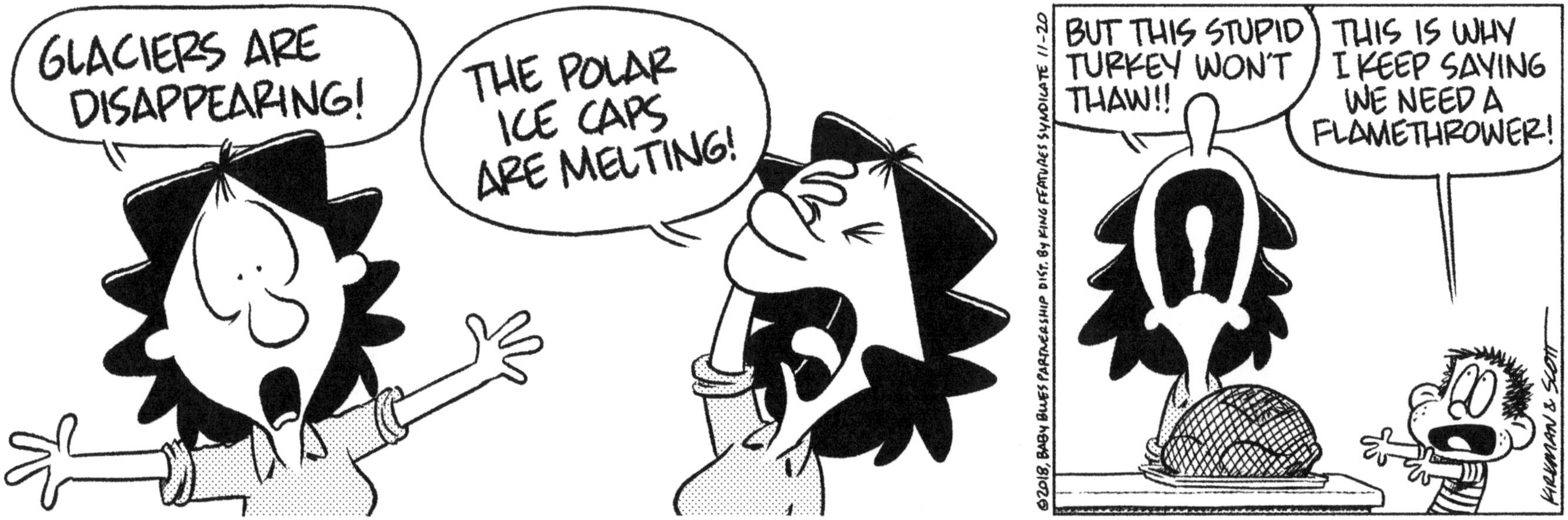
GLACIERS ARE DISAPPEARING!
THE POLAR ICE CAPS ARE MELTING!
BUT THIS STUPID TURKEY WON'T THAW!!
THIS IS WHY I KEEP SAYING WE NEED A FLAMETHROWER!
KIRKMAN & SCOTT
©2018, BABY BLUES PARTNERSHIP DIST. BY KING FEATURES SYNDICATE 11-20

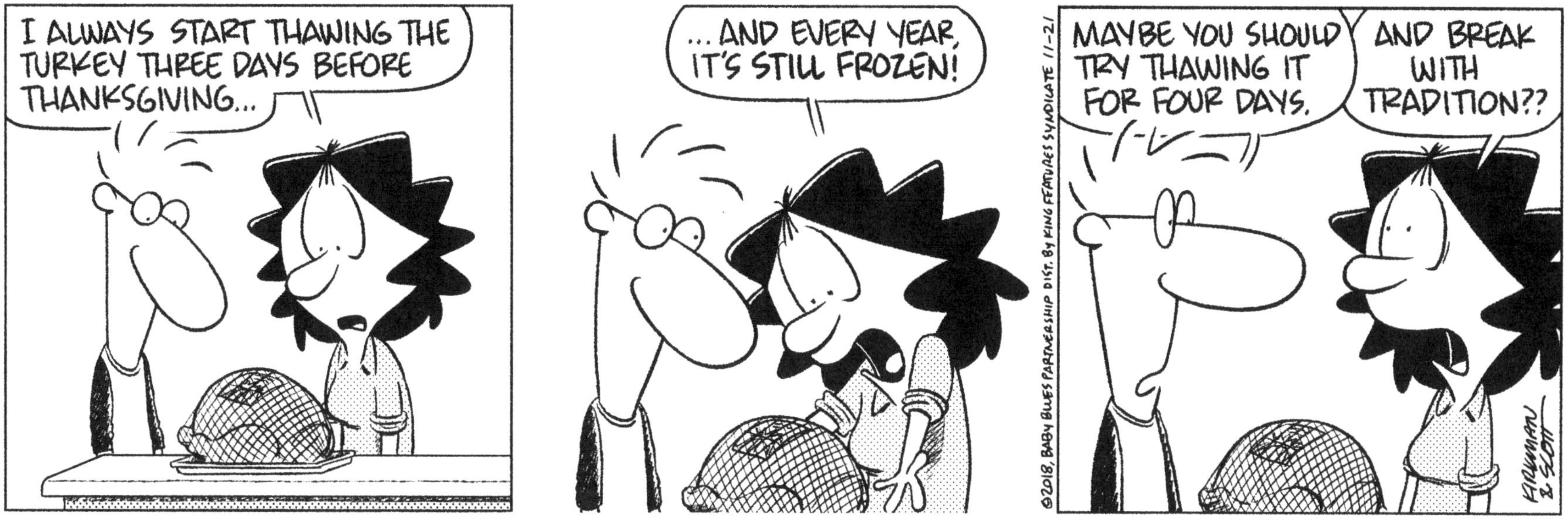
I ALWAYS START THAWING THE TURKEY THREE DAYS BEFORE THANKSGIVING...
...AND EVERY YEAR, IT'S STILL FROZEN!
©2018, BABY BLUES PARTNERSHIP DIST. BY KING FEATURES SYNDICATE 11-21
MAYBE YOU SHOULD TRY THAWING IT FOR FOUR DAYS.
AND BREAK WITH TRADITION??
KIRKMAN & SCOTT

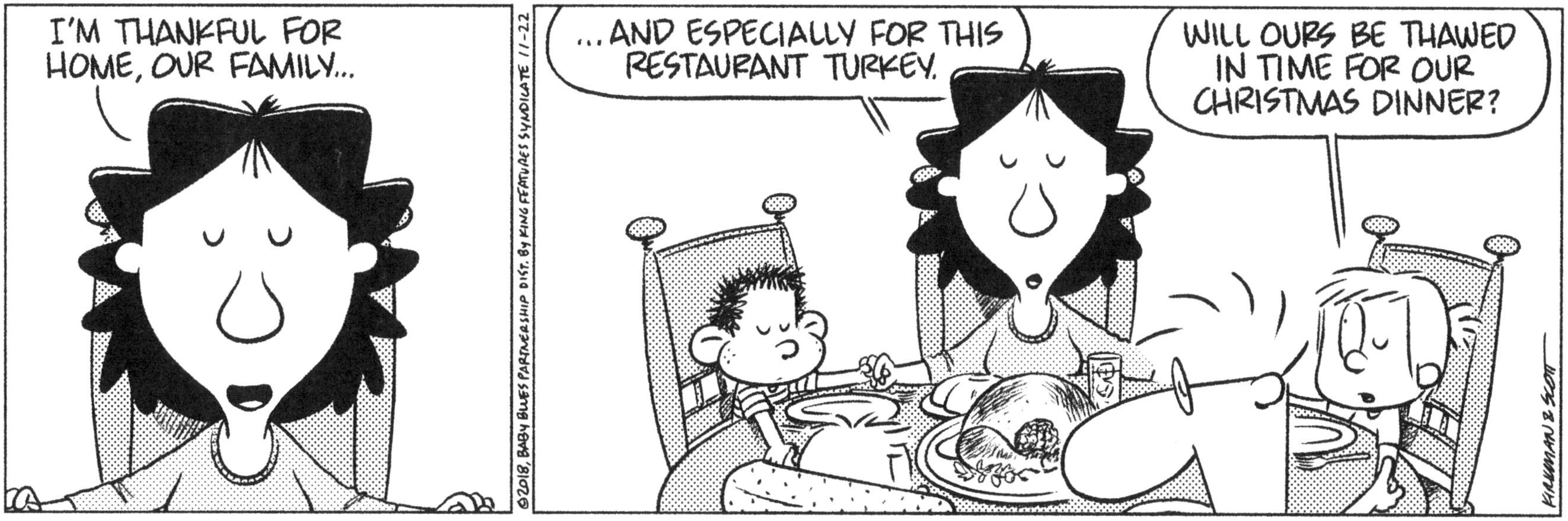
I'M THANKFUL FOR HOME, OUR FAMILY...
©2018, BABY BLUES PARTNERSHIP DIST. BY KING FEATURES SYNDICATE 11-22
...AND ESPECIALLY FOR THIS RESTAURANT TURKEY.
WILL OURS BE THAWED IN TIME FOR OUR CHRISTMAS DINNER?
KIRKMAN & SCOTT

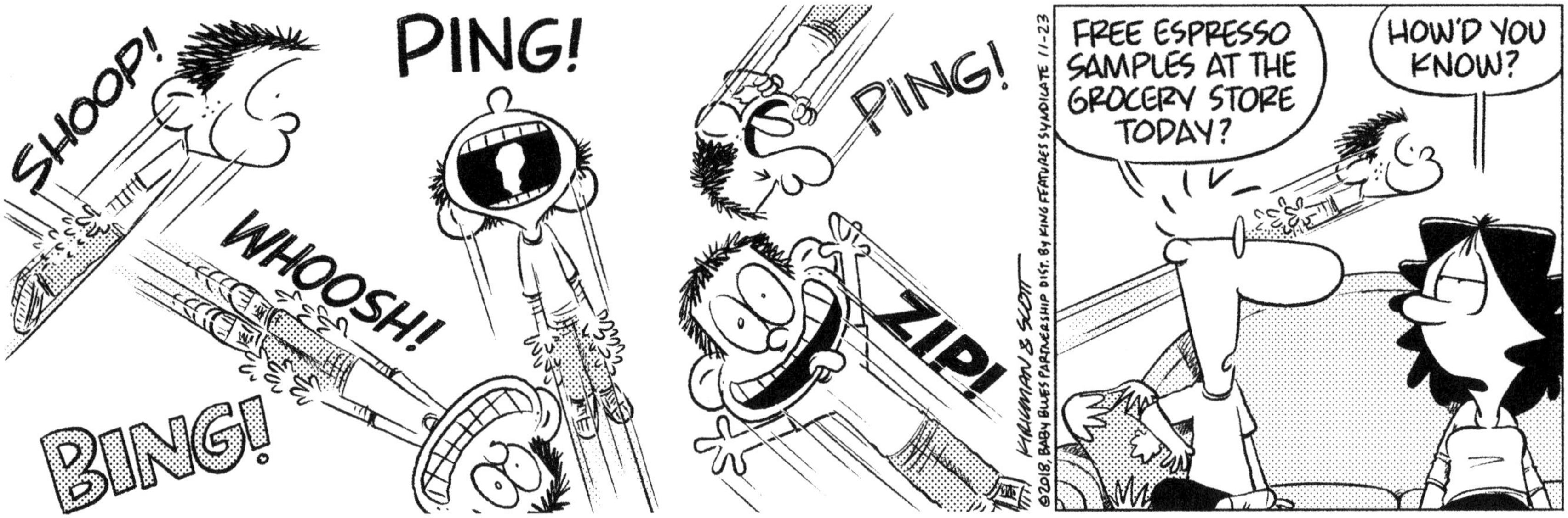
SHOOP!
PING!
WHOOSH!
BING!
PING!
ZIP!
FREE ESPRESSO SAMPLES AT THE GROCERY STORE TODAY?
HOW'D YOU KNOW?
KIRKMAN & SCOTT
©2018, BABY BLUES PARTNERSHIP DIST. BY KING FEATURES SYNDICATE 11-23

Rick: Man, what a blast to draw that first panel! Expressions, action, and lettering, oh my!

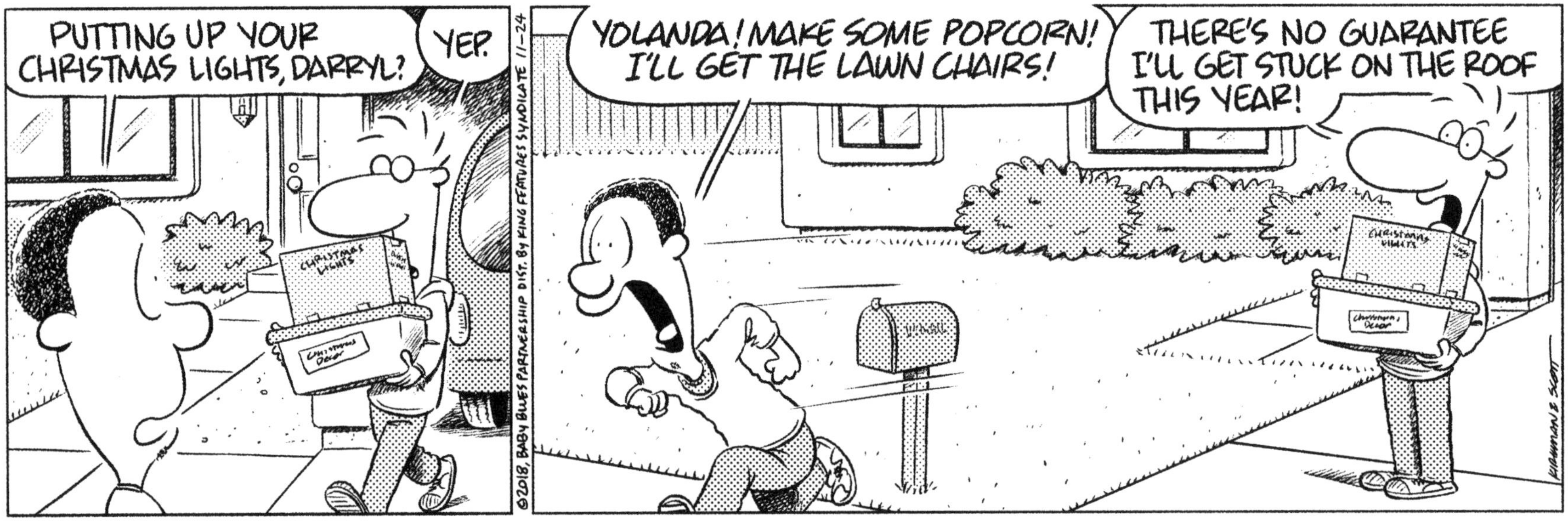
PUTTING UP YOUR CHRISTMAS LIGHTS, DARRYL?
YEP.
©2018, BABY BLUES PARTNERSHIP DIST. BY KING FEATURES SYNDICATE 11-24
YOLANDA! MAKE SOME POPCORN! I'LL GET THE LAWN CHAIRS!
THERE'S NO GUARANTEE I'LL GET STUCK ON THE ROOF THIS YEAR!
KIRKMAN & SCOTT

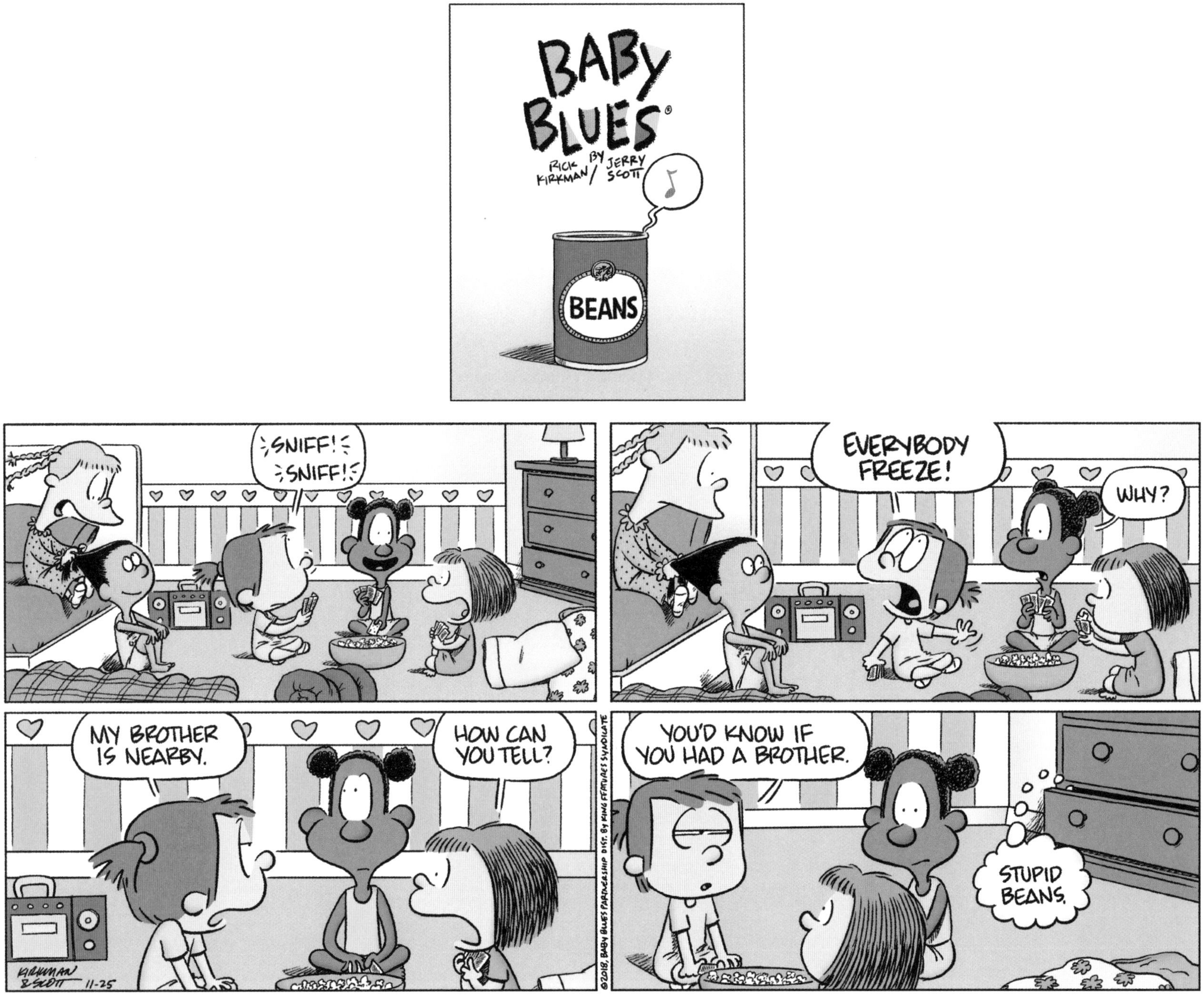
BABY BLUES®
BY RICK KIRKMAN / JERRY SCOTT
BEANS
SNIFF! SNIFF!
EVERYBODY FREEZE!
WHY?
MY BROTHER IS NEARBY.
HOW CAN YOU TELL?
KIRKMAN & SCOTT 11-25
©2018, BABY BLUES PARTNERSHIP DIST. BY KING FEATURES SYNDICATE
YOU'D KNOW IF YOU HAD A BROTHER.
STUPID BEANS.

Rick: The opposite end of the bean-joke spectrum from *Blazing Saddles*.

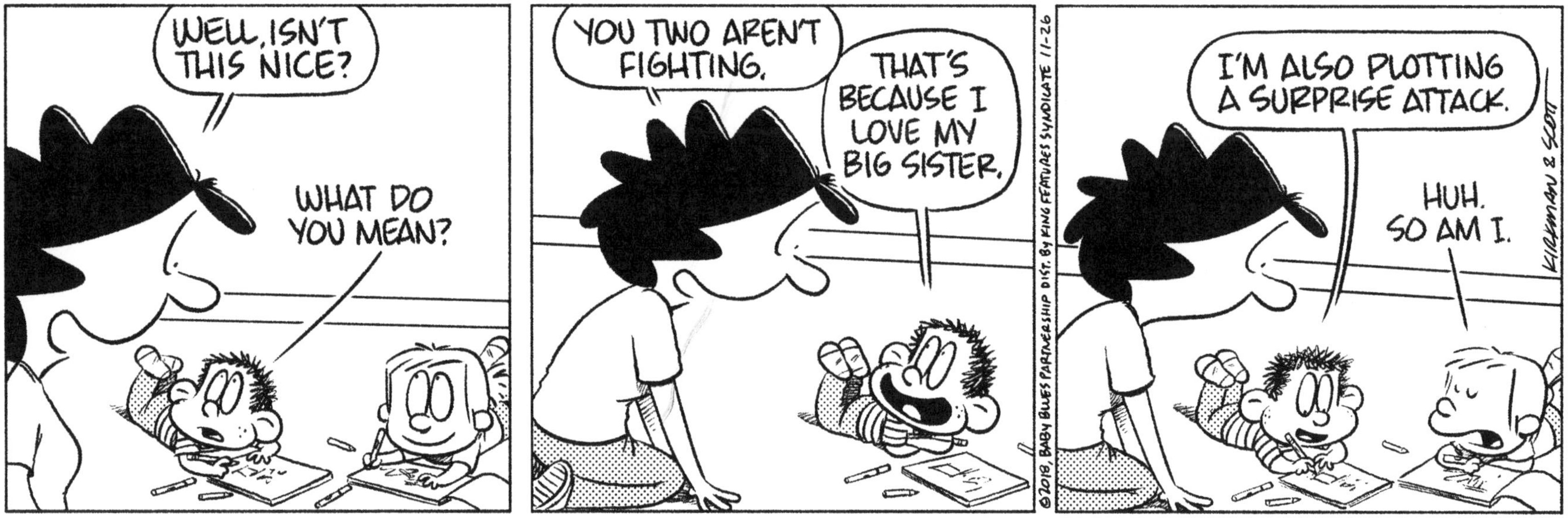
WELL, ISN'T THIS NICE?
WHAT DO YOU MEAN?
YOU TWO AREN'T FIGHTING.
THAT'S BECAUSE I LOVE MY BIG SISTER.
©2018, BABY BLUES PARTNERSHIP DIST. BY KING FEATURES SYNDICATE 11-26
I'M ALSO PLOTTING A SURPRISE ATTACK.
HUH. SO AM I.
KIRKMAN & SCOTT

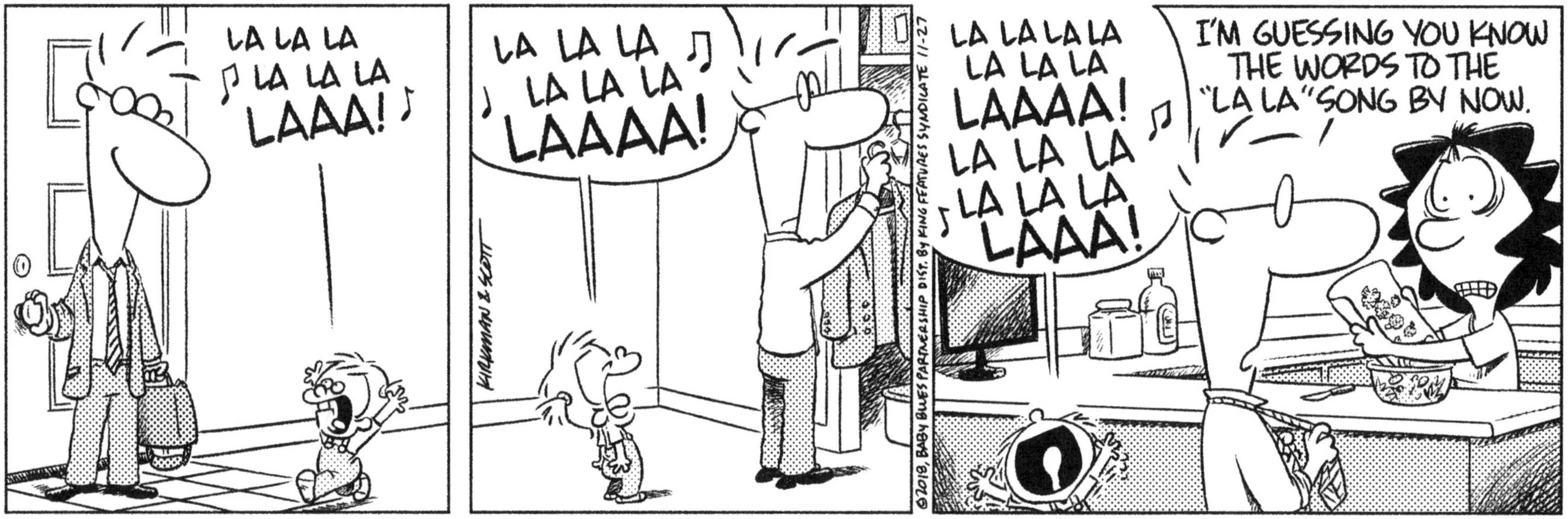
LA LA LA LA LA LA LAAA!
LA LA LA LA LA LA LAAAA!
KIRKMAN & SCOTT
©2018, BABY BLUES PARTNERSHIP DIST. BY KING FEATURES SYNDICATE 11-27
LA LA LA LA LA LA LA LAAAA! LA LA LA LA LA LA LAAA!
I'M GUESSING YOU KNOW THE WORDS TO THE "LA LA" SONG BY NOW.

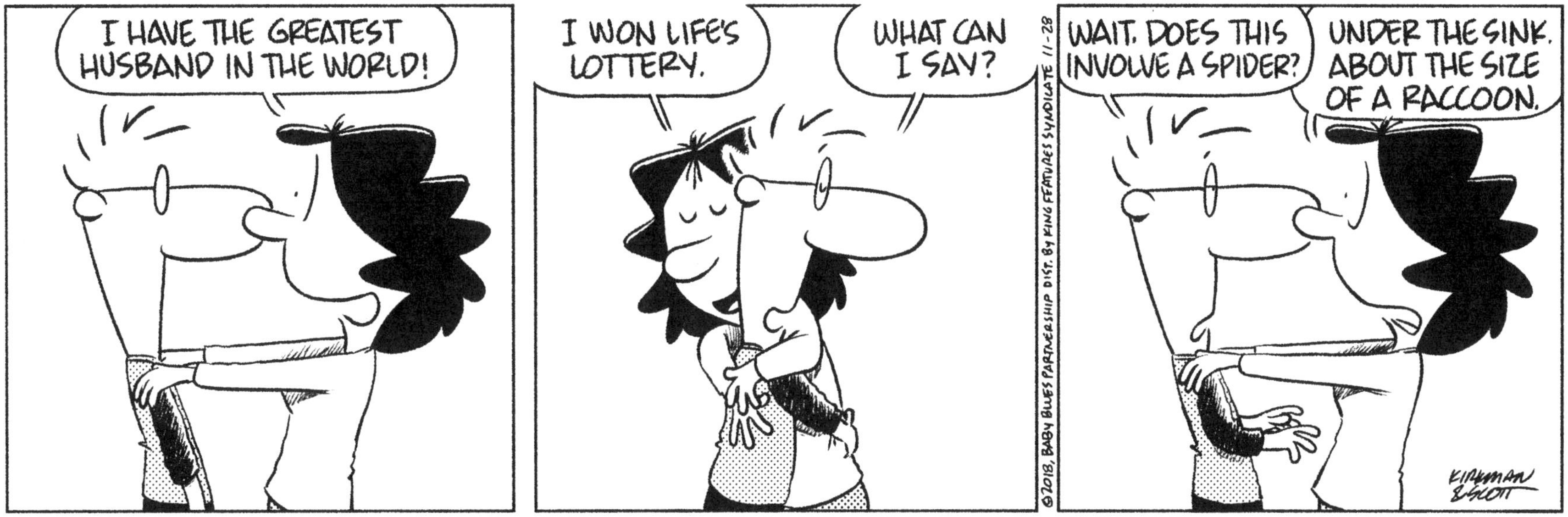
I HAVE THE GREATEST HUSBAND IN THE WORLD!
I WON LIFE'S LOTTERY.
WHAT CAN I SAY?
©2018, BABY BLUES PARTNERSHIP DIST. BY KING FEATURES SYNDICATE 11-28
WAIT. DOES THIS INVOLVE A SPIDER?
UNDER THE SINK. ABOUT THE SIZE OF A RACCOON.
KIRKMAN & SCOTT

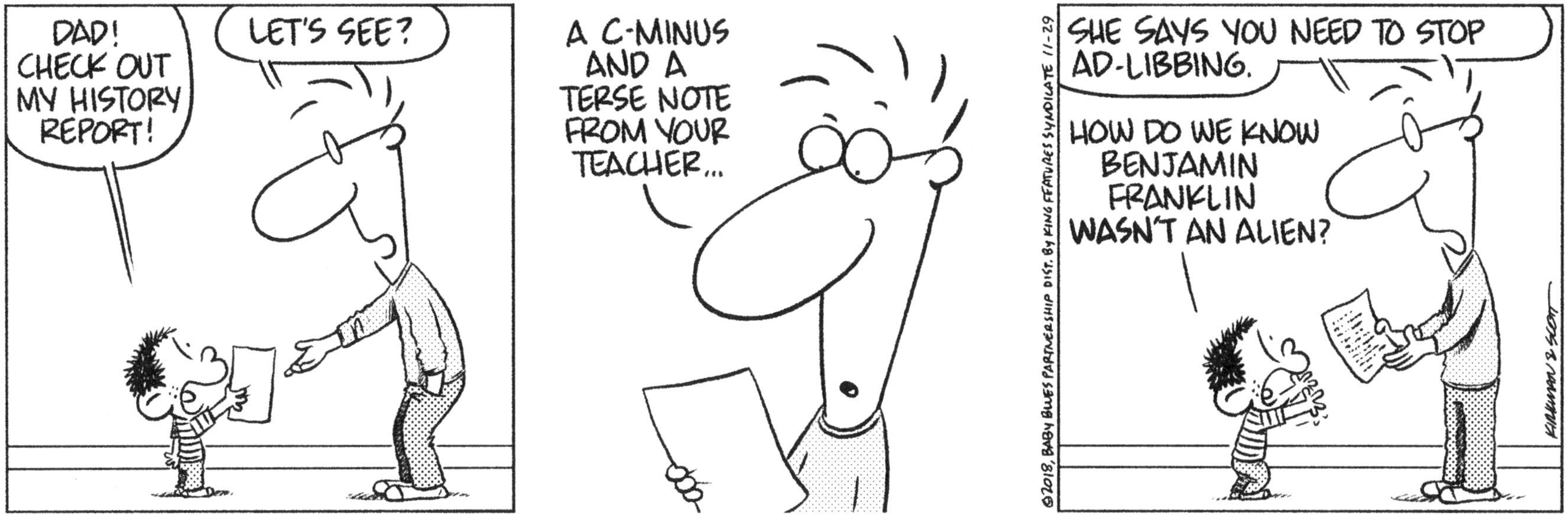
DAD! CHECK OUT MY HISTORY REPORT!
LET'S SEE?
A C-MINUS AND A TERSE NOTE FROM YOUR TEACHER...
©2018, BABY BLUES PARTNERSHIP DIST. BY KING FEATURES SYNDICATE 11-29
SHE SAYS YOU NEED TO STOP AD-LIBBING.
HOW DO WE KNOW BENJAMIN FRANKLIN WASN'T AN ALIEN?

Rick: Really, I mean, look at that hair.

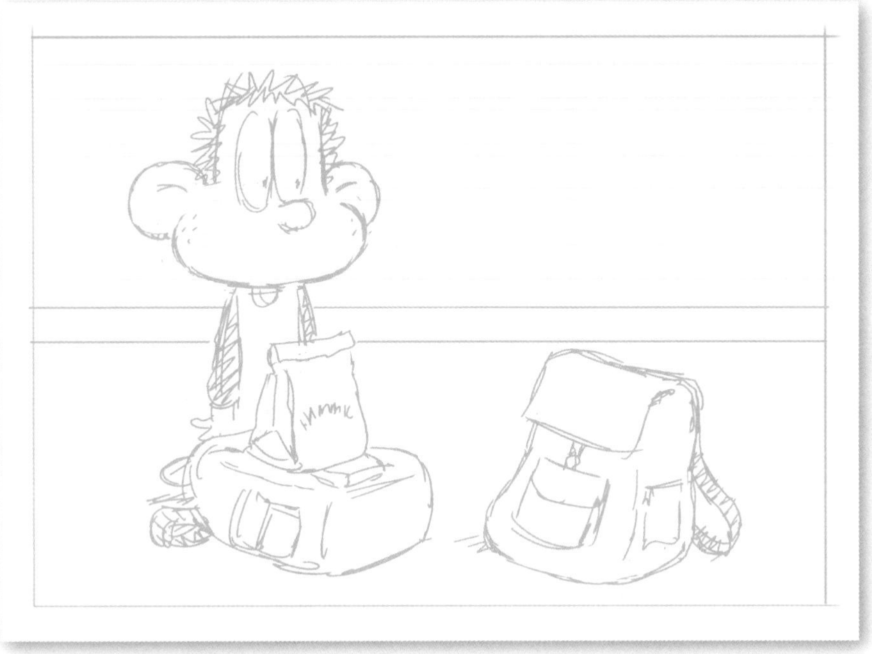

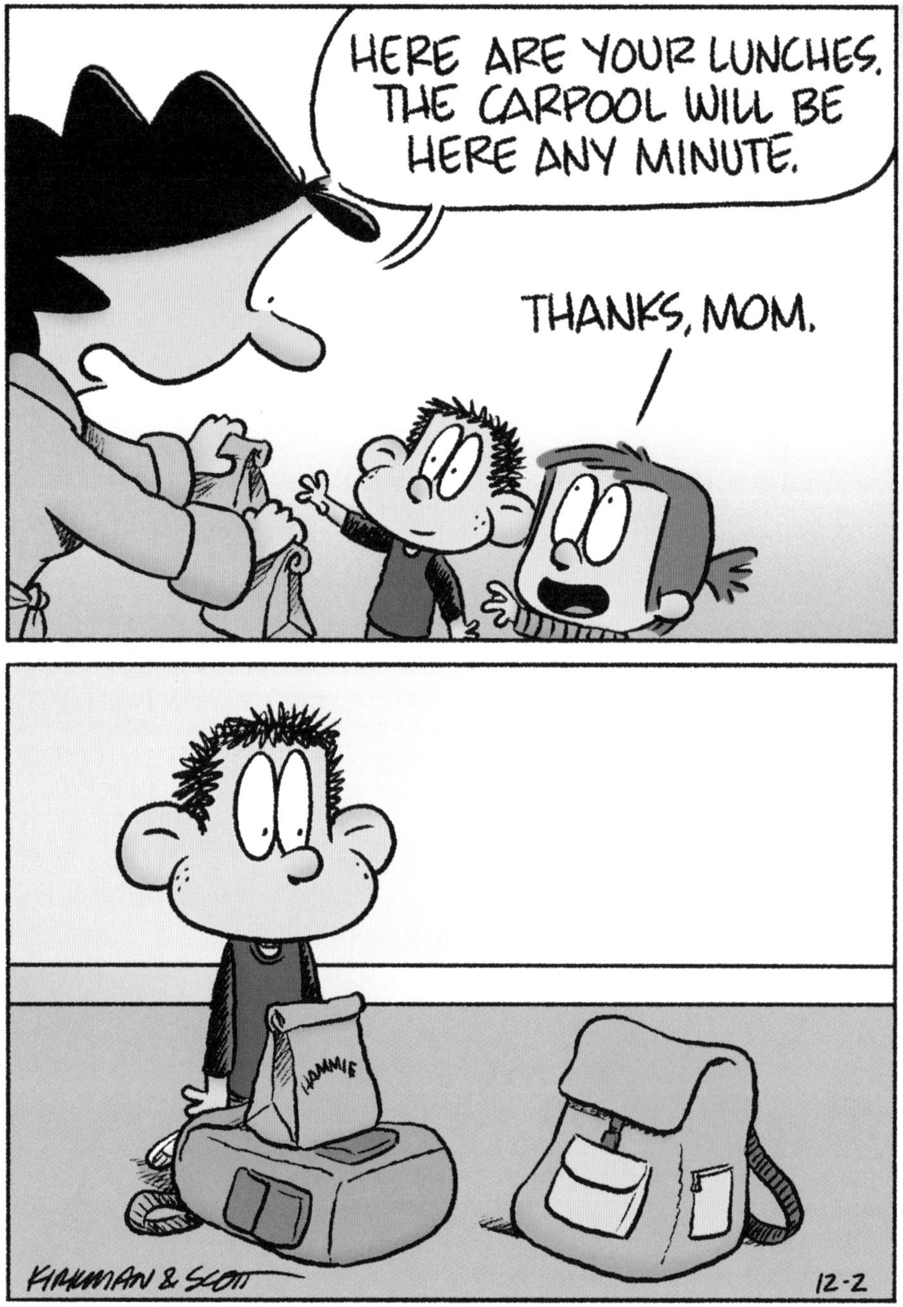
HERE ARE YOUR LUNCHES. THE CARPOOL WILL BE HERE ANY MINUTE.
THANKS, MOM.
HAMMIE
KIRKMAN & SCOTT
12-2

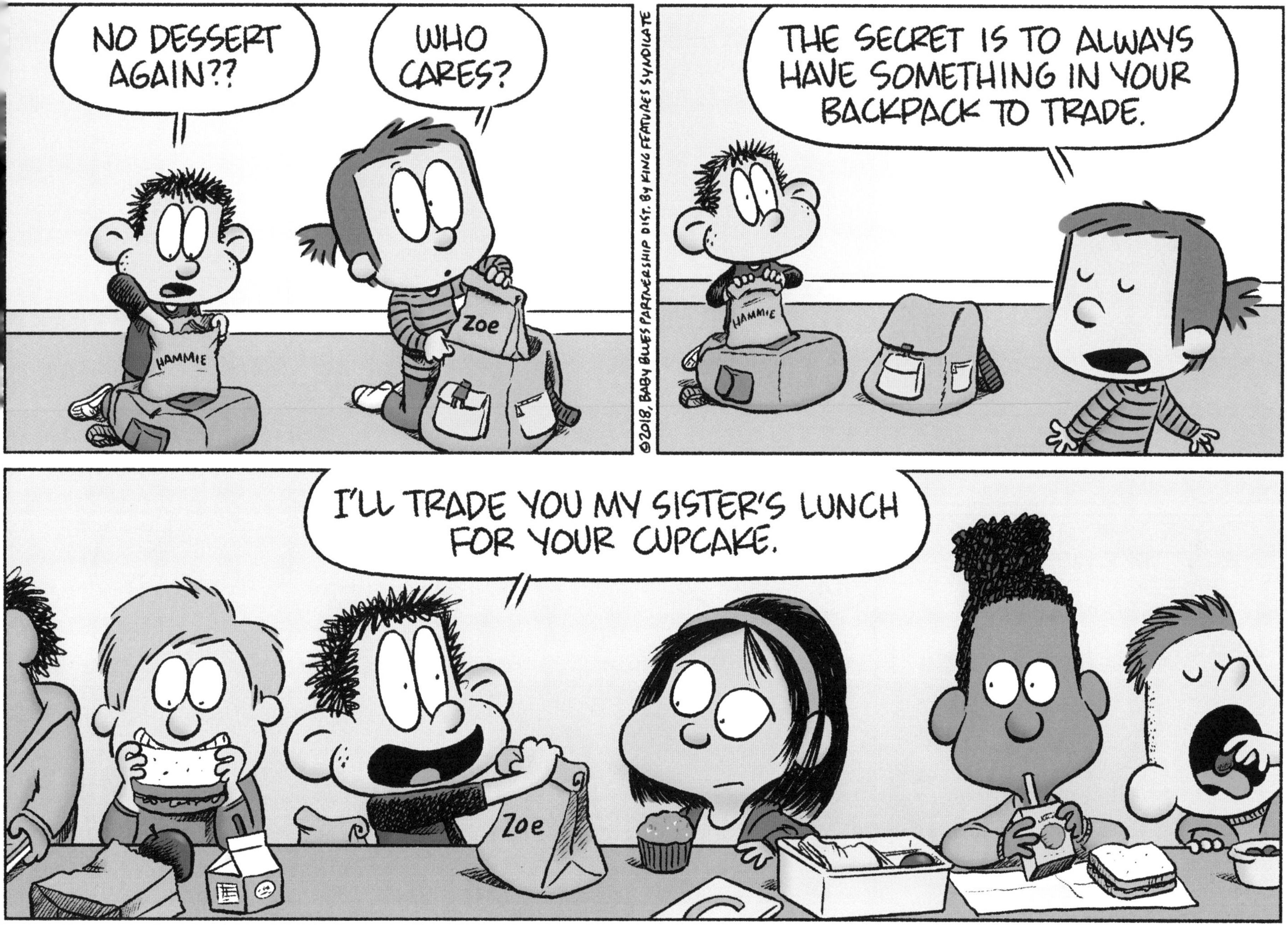
NO DESSERT AGAIN??
WHO CARES?
©2018, BABY BLUES PARTNERSHIP DIST. BY KING FEATURES SYNDICATE
HAMMIE
ZOE
THE SECRET IS TO ALWAYS HAVE SOMETHING IN YOUR BACKPACK TO TRADE.
HAMMIE
I'LL TRADE YOU MY SISTER'S LUNCH FOR YOUR CUPCAKE.
ZOE

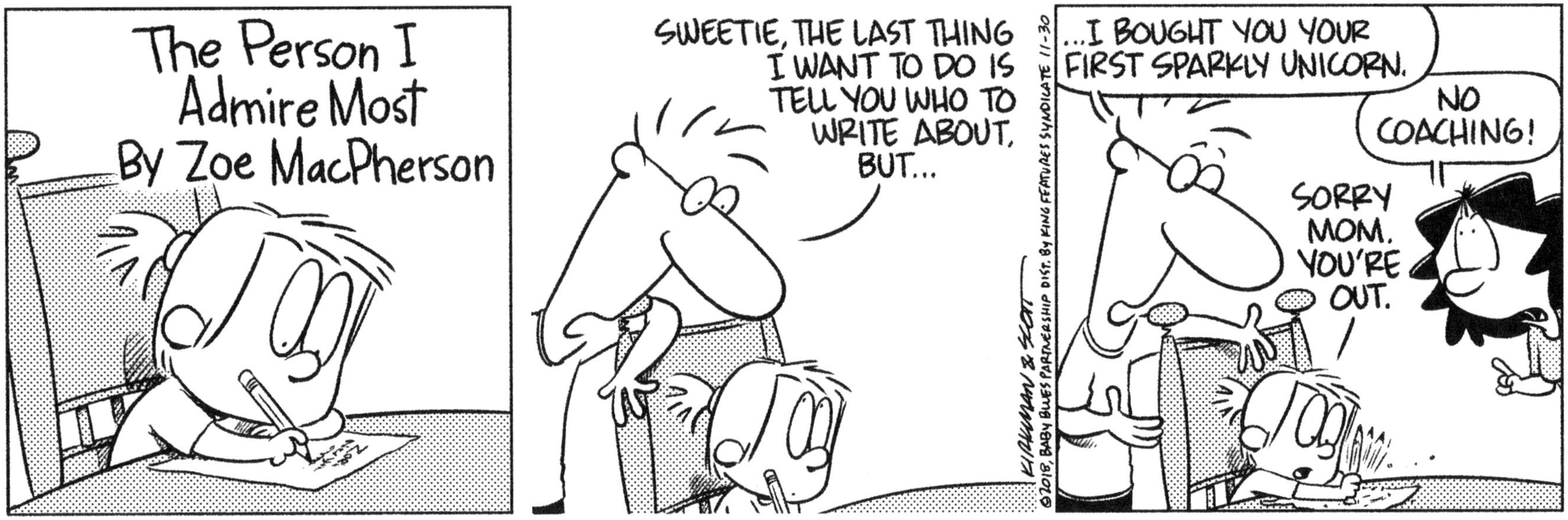
The Person I Admire Most By Zoe MacPherson
SWEETIE, THE LAST THING I WANT TO DO IS TELL YOU WHO TO WRITE ABOUT, BUT...
KIRKMAN & SCOTT
©2018, BABY BLUES PARTNERSHIP DIST. BY KING FEATURES SYNDICATE 11-30
...I BOUGHT YOU YOUR FIRST SPARKLY UNICORN.
NO COACHING!
SORRY MOM. YOU'RE OUT.

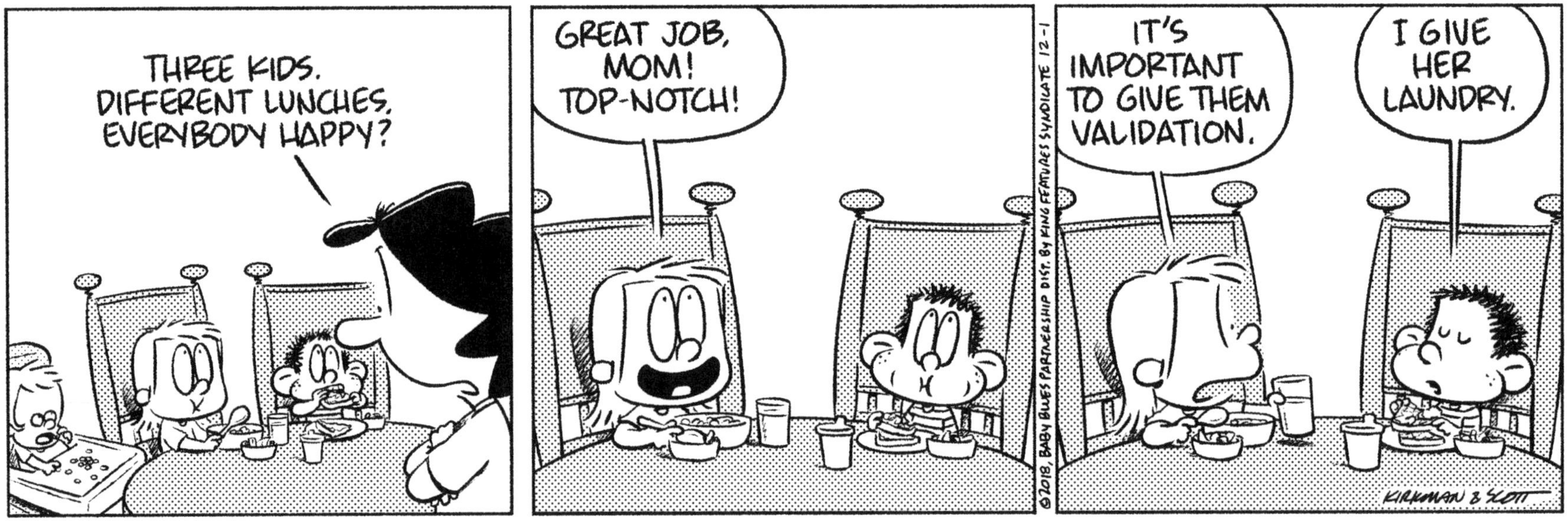
THREE KIDS. DIFFERENT LUNCHES. EVERYBODY HAPPY?
GREAT JOB, MOM! TOP-NOTCH!
©2018, BABY BLUES PARTNERSHIP DIST. BY KING FEATURES SYNDICATE 12-1
IT'S IMPORTANT TO GIVE THEM VALIDATION.
I GIVE HER LAUNDRY.
KIRKMAN & SCOTT

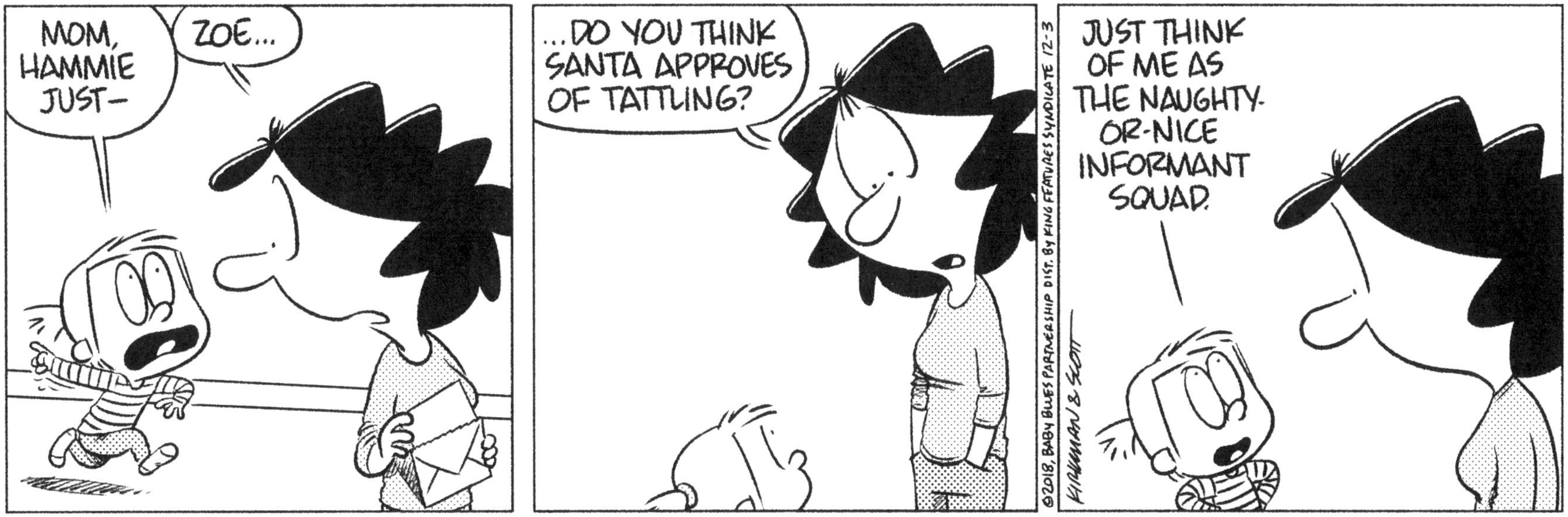
MOM, HAMMIE JUST–
ZOE...
...DO YOU THINK SANTA APPROVES OF TATTLING?
©2018, BABY BLUES PARTNERSHIP DIST. BY KING FEATURES SYNDICATE 12-3
KIRKMAN & SCOTT
JUST THINK OF ME AS THE NAUGHTY-OR-NICE INFORMANT SQUAD.

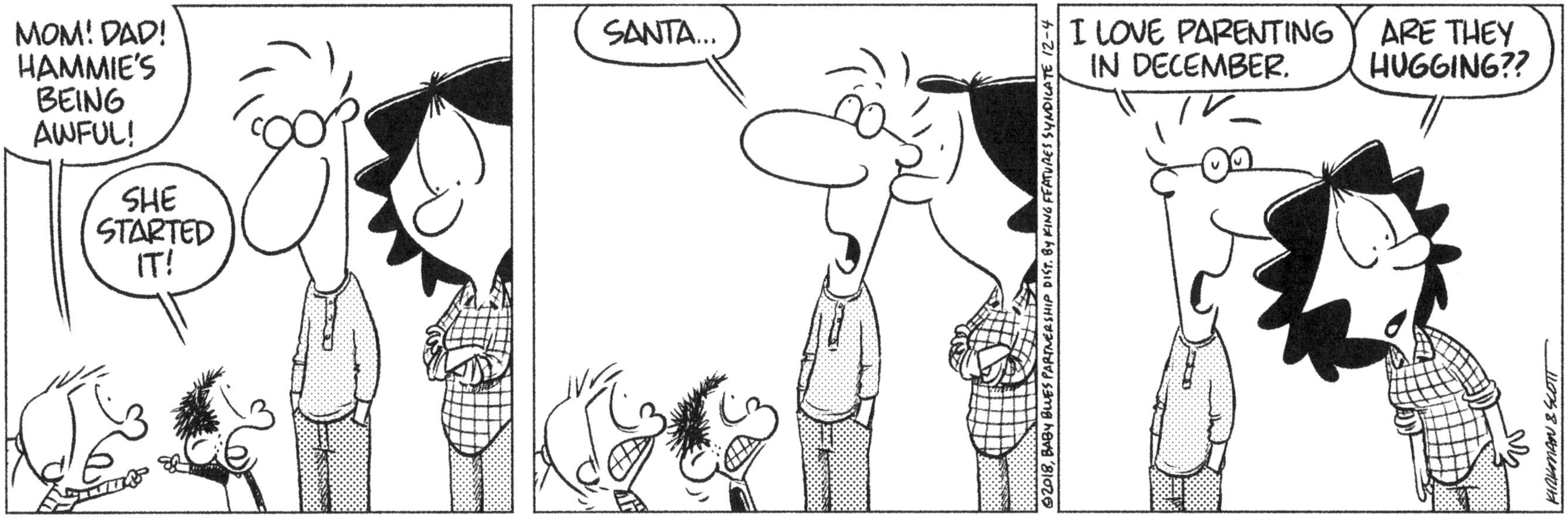
MOM! DAD! HAMMIE'S BEING AWFUL!
SHE STARTED IT!
SANTA...
©2018, BABY BLUES PARTNERSHIP DIST. BY KING FEATURES SYNDICATE 12-4
I LOVE PARENTING IN DECEMBER.
ARE THEY HUGGING??
KIRKMAN & SCOTT

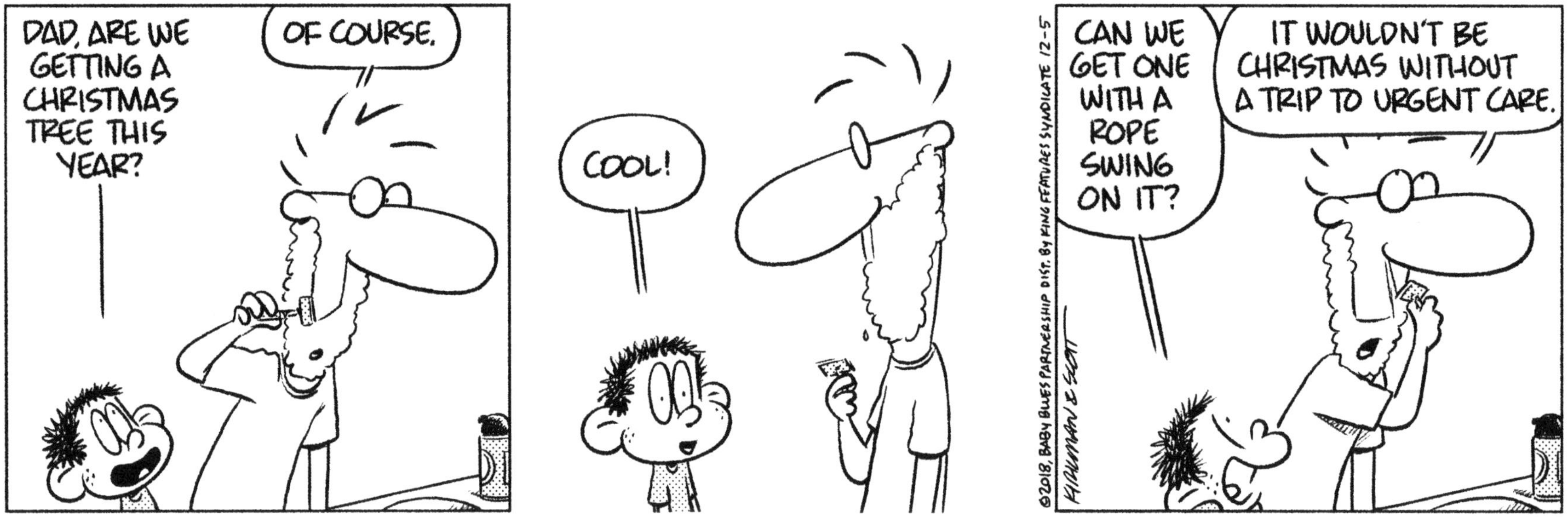
DAD, ARE WE GETTING A CHRISTMAS TREE THIS YEAR?
OF COURSE.
COOL!
CAN WE GET ONE WITH A ROPE SWING ON IT?
IT WOULDN'T BE CHRISTMAS WITHOUT A TRIP TO URGENT CARE.
©2018, BABY BLUES PARTNERSHIP DIST. BY KING FEATURES SYNDICATE 12-5
KIRKMAN & SCOTT

Jerry: Always ask for the peppermint-scented stitches.

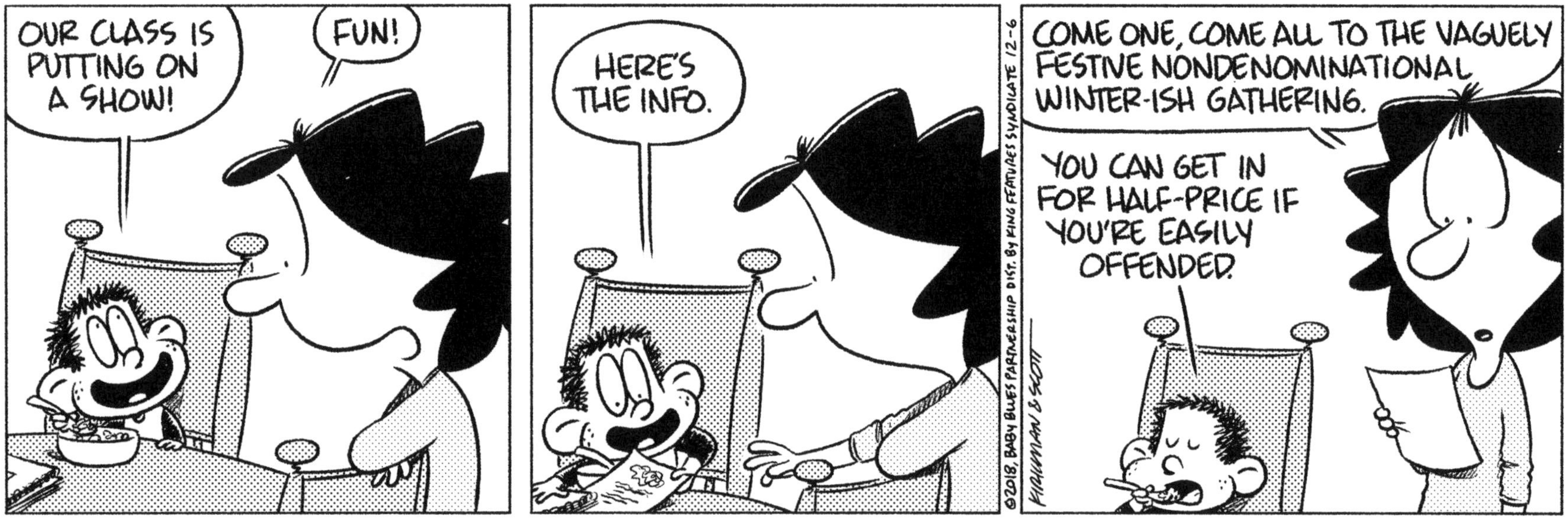
OUR CLASS IS PUTTING ON A SHOW!
FUN!
HERE'S THE INFO.
COME ONE, COME ALL TO THE VAGUELY FESTIVE NONDENOMINATIONAL WINTER-ISH GATHERING.
YOU CAN GET IN FOR HALF-PRICE IF YOU'RE EASILY OFFENDED.
©2018, BABY BLUES PARTNERSHIP DIST. BY KING FEATURES SYNDICATE 12-6
KIRKMAN & SCOTT

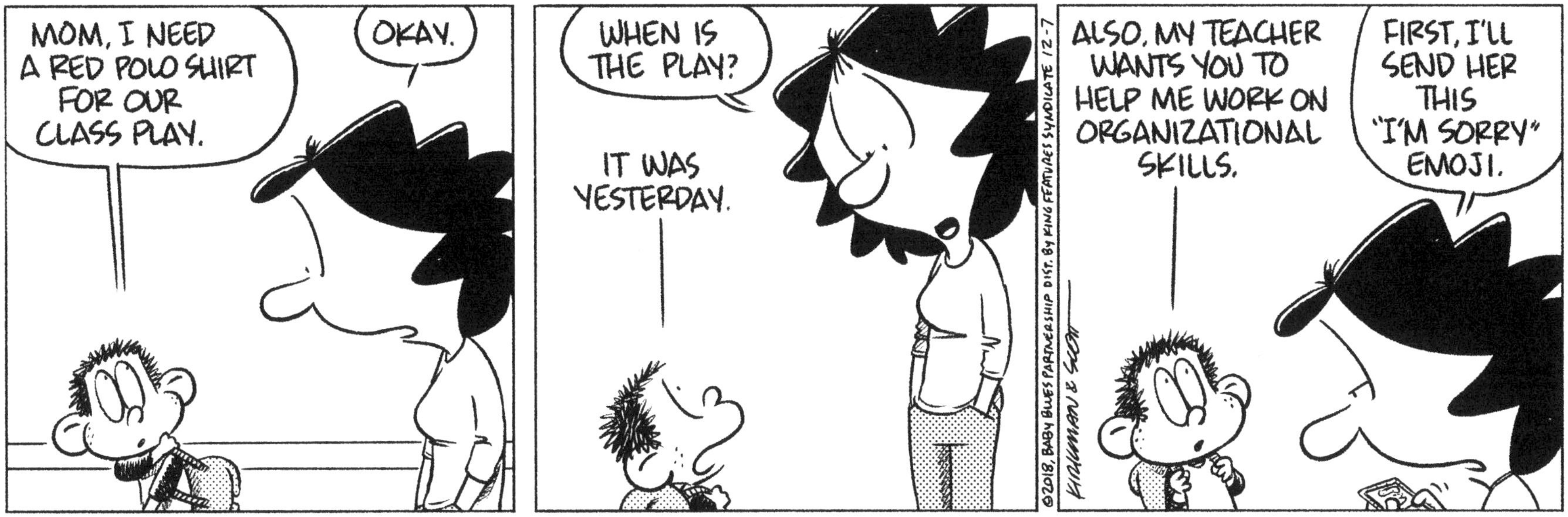
MOM, I NEED A RED POLO SHIRT FOR OUR CLASS PLAY.
OKAY.
WHEN IS THE PLAY?
IT WAS YESTERDAY.
©2018, BABY BLUES PARTNERSHIP DIST. BY KING FEATURES SYNDICATE 12-7
KIRKMAN & SCOTT
ALSO, MY TEACHER WANTS YOU TO HELP ME WORK ON ORGANIZATIONAL SKILLS.
FIRST, I'LL SEND HER THIS "I'M SORRY" EMOJI.

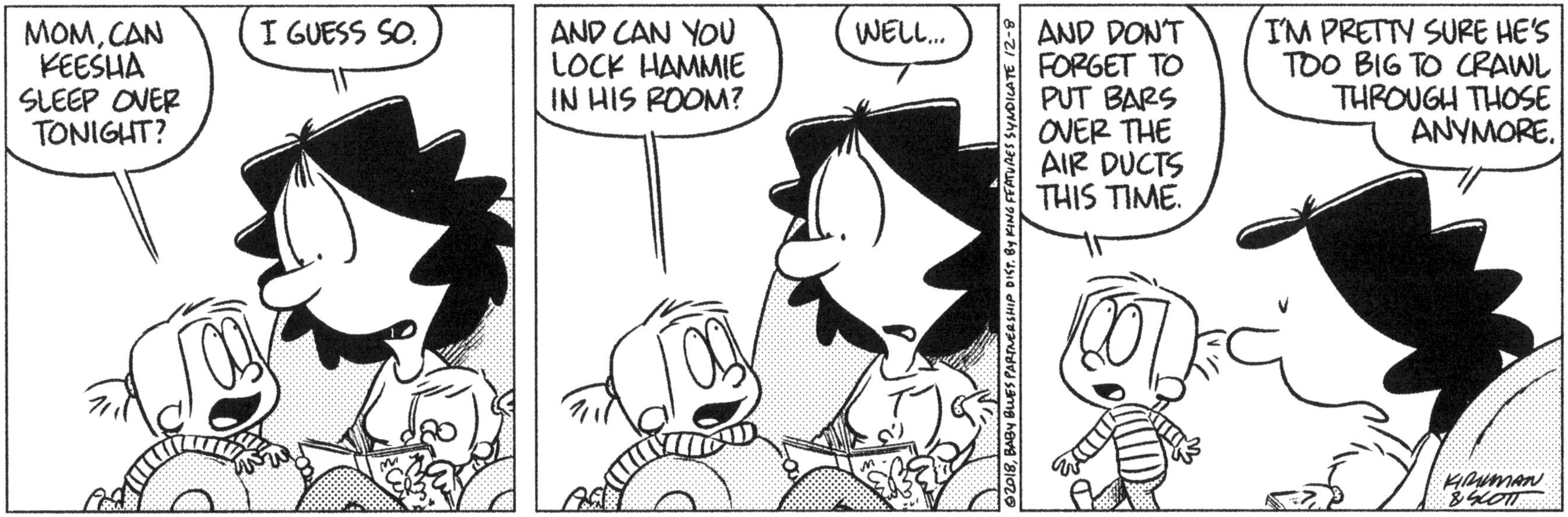
MOM, CAN KEESHA SLEEP OVER TONIGHT?
I GUESS SO.
AND CAN YOU LOCK HAMMIE IN HIS ROOM?
WELL...
©2018, BABY BLUES PARTNERSHIP DIST. BY KING FEATURES SYNDICATE 12-8
AND DON'T FORGET TO PUT BARS OVER THE AIR DUCTS THIS TIME.
I'M PRETTY SURE HE'S TOO BIG TO CRAWL THROUGH THOSE ANYMORE.
KIRKMAN & SCOTT

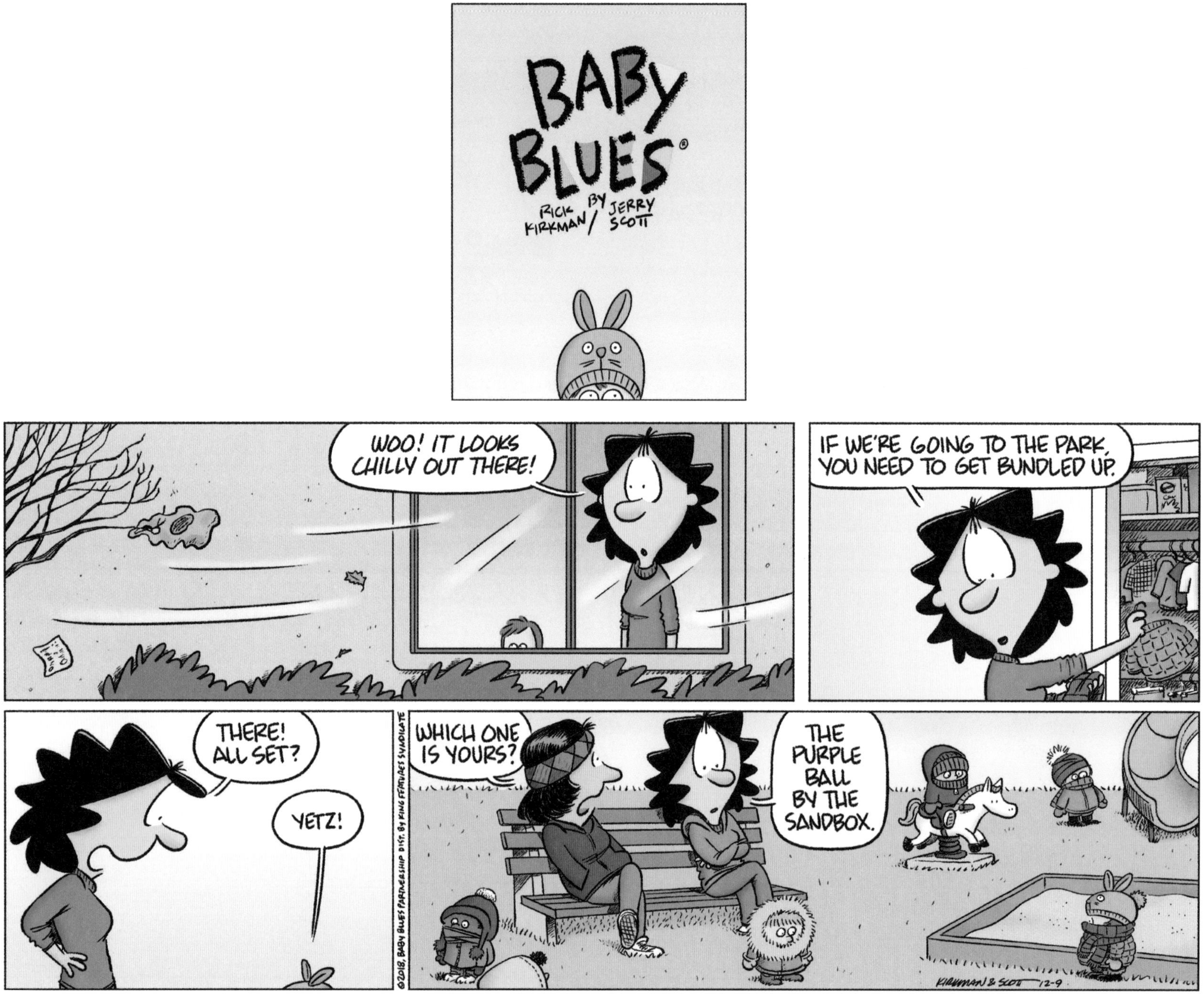
BABY BLUES®
BY RICK KIRKMAN / JERRY SCOTT
WOO! IT LOOKS CHILLY OUT THERE!
IF WE'RE GOING TO THE PARK, YOU NEED TO GET BUNDLED UP.
THERE! ALL SET?
YETZ!
©2018, BABY BLUES PARTNERSHIP DIST. BY KING FEATURES SYNDICATE
WHICH ONE IS YOURS?
THE PURPLE BALL BY THE SANDBOX.
KIRKMAN & SCOTT 12-9

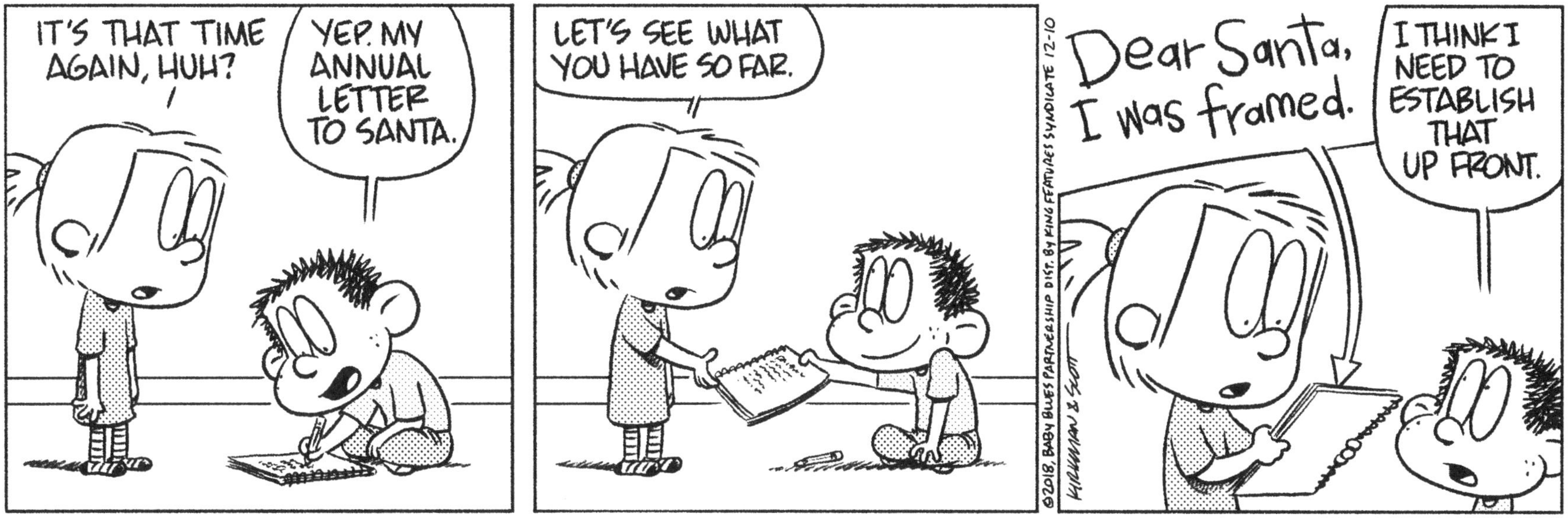
IT'S THAT TIME AGAIN, HUH?
YEP. MY ANNUAL LETTER TO SANTA.
LET'S SEE WHAT YOU HAVE SO FAR.
Dear Santa, I was framed.
I THINK I NEED TO ESTABLISH THAT UP FRONT.
©2018, BABY BLUES PARTNERSHIP DIST. BY KING FEATURES SYNDICATE 12-10
KIRKMAN & SCOTT

Jerry: The best defense is a good offense.

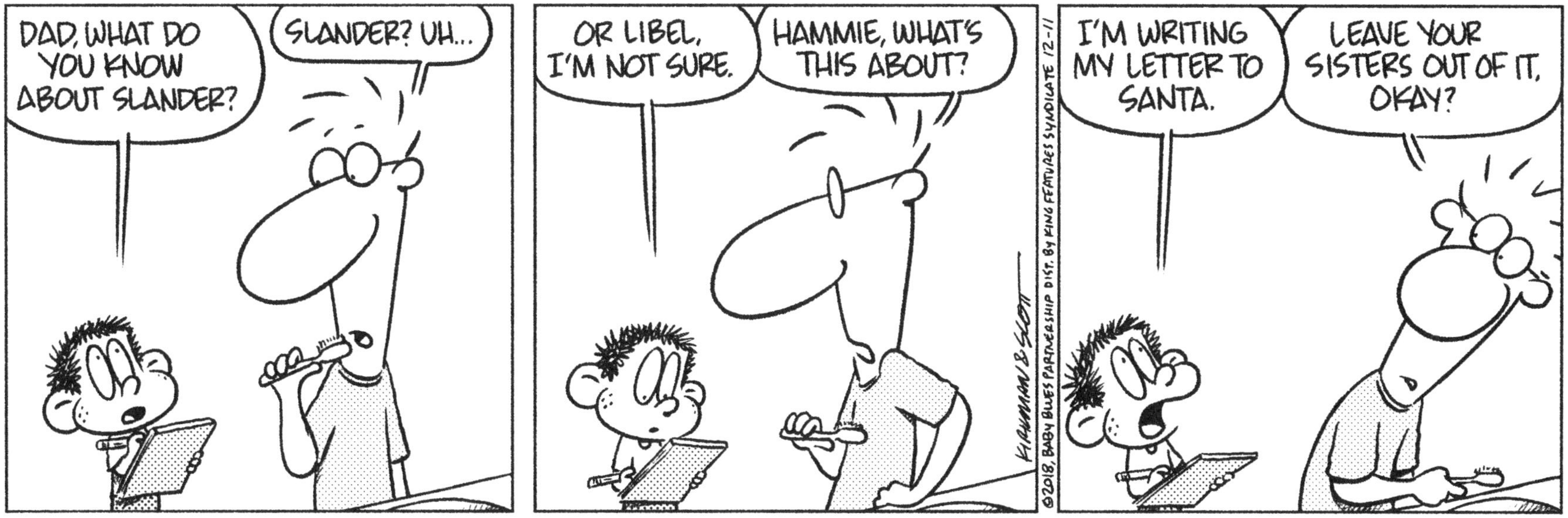
DAD, WHAT DO YOU KNOW ABOUT SLANDER?
SLANDER? UH...
OR LIBEL, I'M NOT SURE.
HAMMIE, WHAT'S THIS ABOUT?
I'M WRITING MY LETTER TO SANTA.
LEAVE YOUR SISTERS OUT OF IT, OKAY?
©2018, BABY BLUES PARTNERSHIP DIST. BY KING FEATURES SYNDICATE 12-11
KIRKMAN & SCOTT

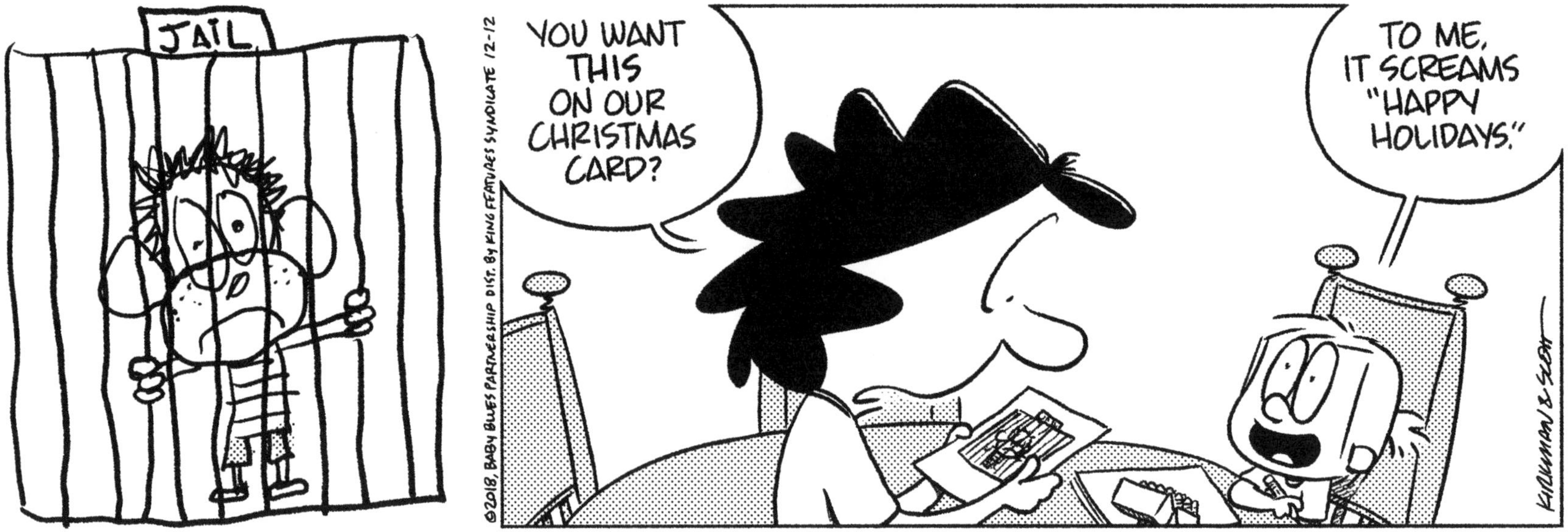
JAIL
©2018, BABY BLUES PARTNERSHIP DIST. BY KING FEATURES SYNDICATE 12-12
YOU WANT THIS ON OUR CHRISTMAS CARD?
TO ME, IT SCREAMS "HAPPY HOLIDAYS."
KIRKMAN & SCOTT

Rick: I was pretty pleased at how I channeled Zoe's drawing. There's a reason beyond sentiment that I keep my kids' drawings around. They're great reference material.

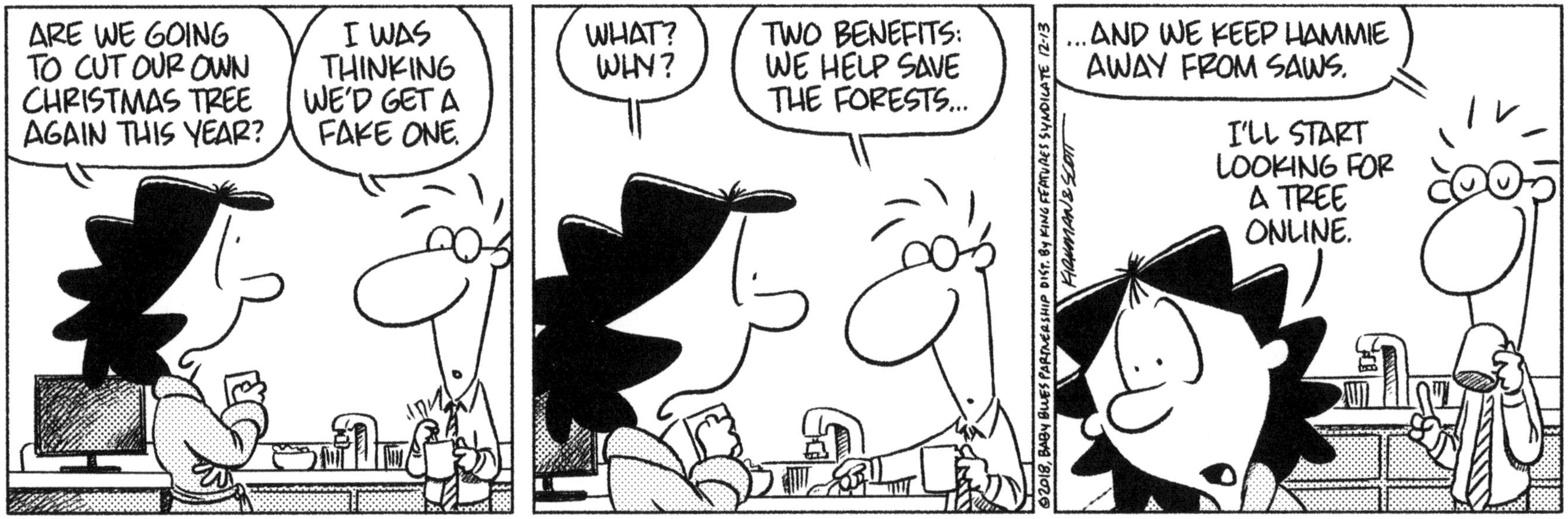
ARE WE GOING TO CUT OUR OWN CHRISTMAS TREE AGAIN THIS YEAR?
I WAS THINKING WE'D GET A FAKE ONE.
WHAT? WHY?
TWO BENEFITS: WE HELP SAVE THE FORESTS...
©2018, BABY BLUES PARTNERSHIP DIST. BY KING FEATURES SYNDICATE 12-13
KIRKMAN & SCOTT
...AND WE KEEP HAMMIE AWAY FROM SAWS.
I'LL START LOOKING FOR A TREE ONLINE.

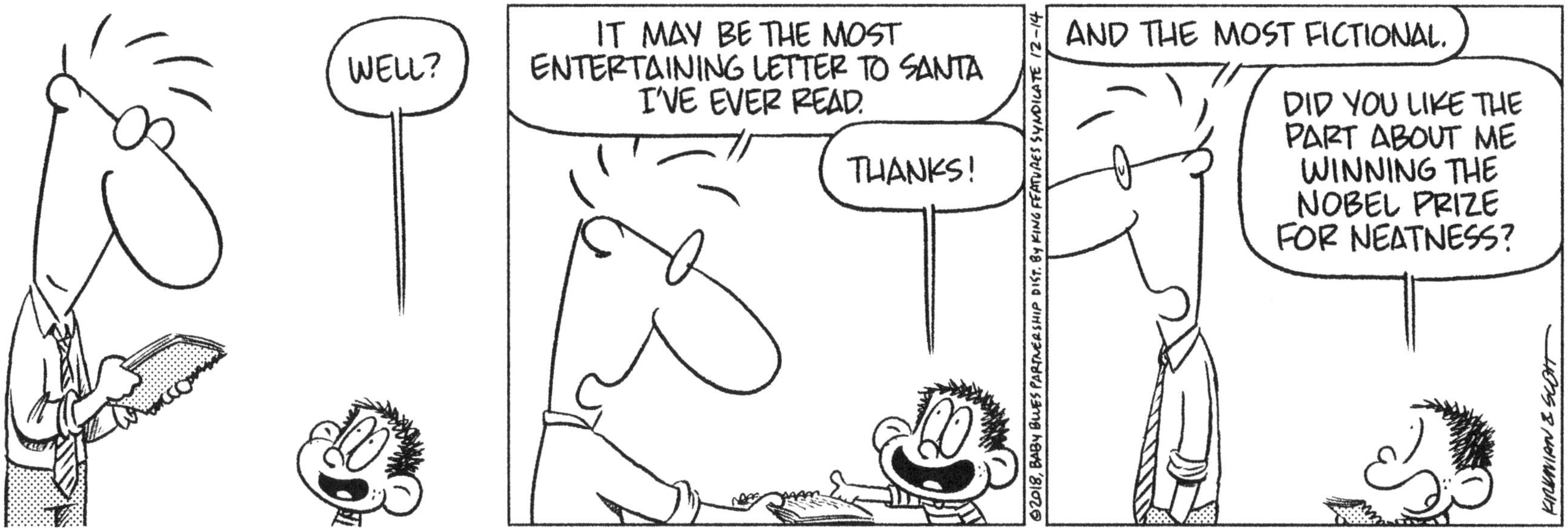
WELL?
IT MAY BE THE MOST ENTERTAINING LETTER TO SANTA I'VE EVER READ.
THANKS!
©2018, BABY BLUES PARTNERSHIP DIST. BY KING FEATURES SYNDICATE 12-14
AND THE MOST FICTIONAL.
DID YOU LIKE THE PART ABOUT ME WINNING THE NOBEL PRIZE FOR NEATNESS?
KIRKMAN & SCOTT

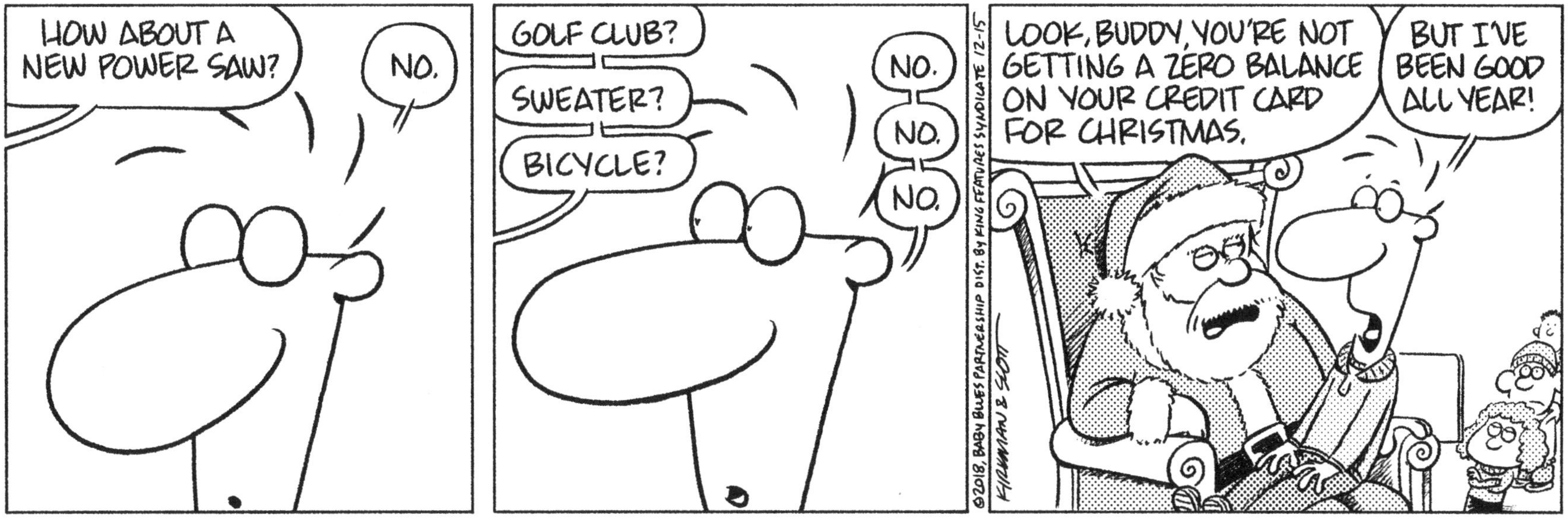
HOW ABOUT A NEW POWER SAW?
NO.
GOLF CLUB?
NO.
SWEATER?
NO.
BICYCLE?
NO.
©2018, BABY BLUES PARTNERSHIP DIST. BY KING FEATURES SYNDICATE 12-15
KIRKMAN & SCOTT
LOOK, BUDDY, YOU'RE NOT GETTING A ZERO BALANCE ON YOUR CREDIT CARD FOR CHRISTMAS.
BUT I'VE BEEN GOOD ALL YEAR!

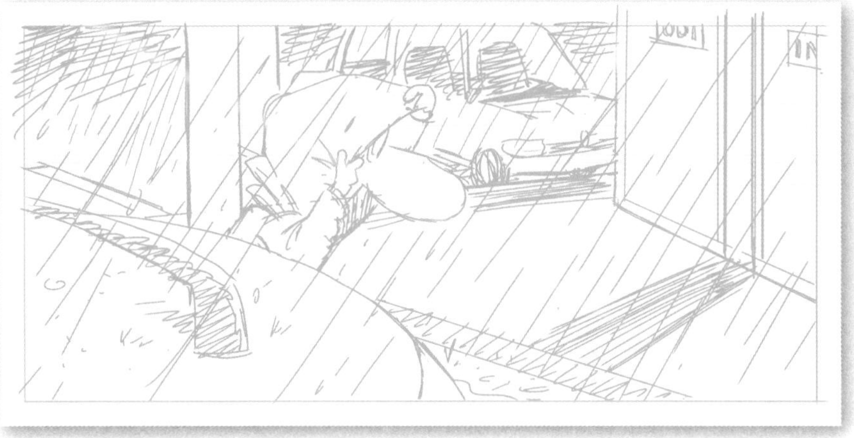

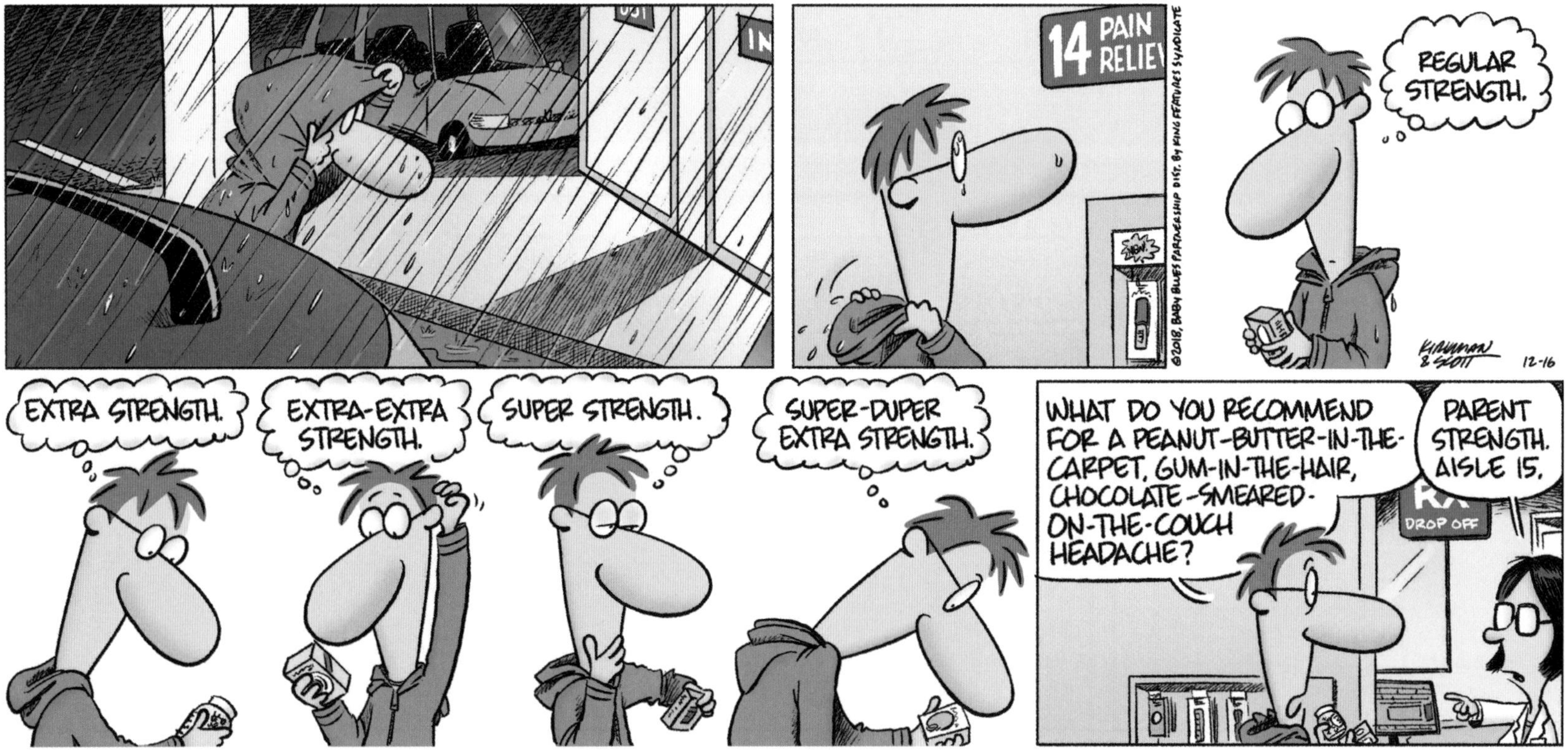
14 PAIN RELIEV
©2018, BABY BLUES PARTNERSHIP DIST. BY KING FEATURES SYNDICATE
REGULAR STRENGTH.
KIRKMAN & SCOTT
12-16
EXTRA STRENGTH.
EXTRA-EXTRA STRENGTH.
SUPER STRENGTH.
SUPER-DUPER EXTRA STRENGTH.
WHAT DO YOU RECOMMEND FOR A PEANUT-BUTTER-IN-THE-CARPET, GUM-IN-THE-HAIR, CHOCOLATE-SMEARED-ON-THE-COUCH HEADACHE?
PARENT STRENGTH. AISLE 15.
RX
DROP OFF

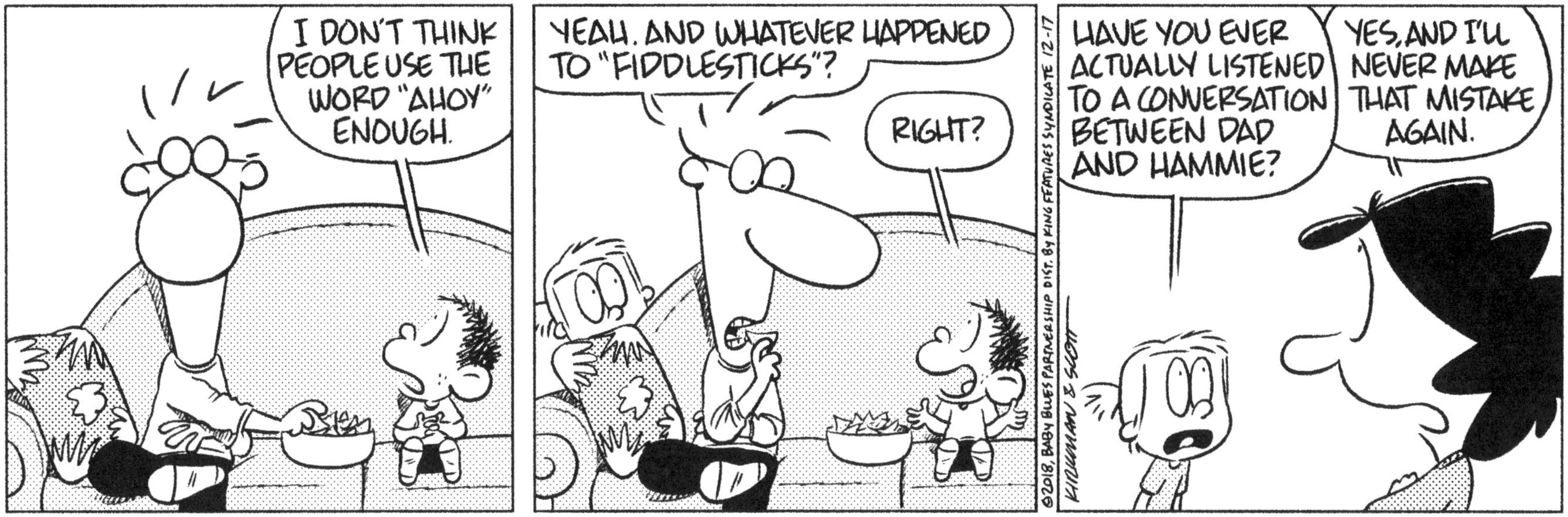
I DON'T THINK PEOPLE USE THE WORD "AHOY" ENOUGH.
YEAH. AND WHATEVER HAPPENED TO "FIDDLESTICKS"?
RIGHT?
©2018, BABY BLUES PARTNERSHIP DIST. BY KING FEATURES SYNDICATE 12-17
KIRKMAN & SCOTT
HAVE YOU EVER ACTUALLY LISTENED TO A CONVERSATION BETWEEN DAD AND HAMMIE?
YES, AND I'LL NEVER MAKE THAT MISTAKE AGAIN.

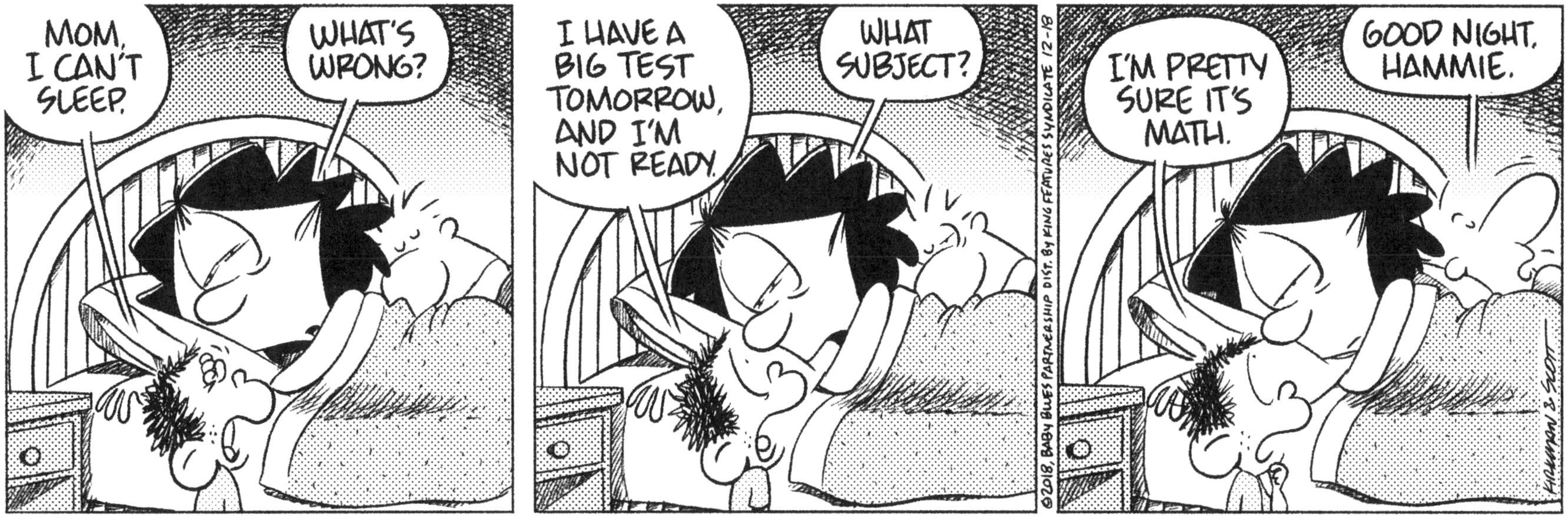
MOM, I CAN'T SLEEP.
WHAT'S WRONG?
I HAVE A BIG TEST TOMORROW, AND I'M NOT READY.
WHAT SUBJECT?
©2018, BABY BLUES PARTNERSHIP DIST. BY KING FEATURES SYNDICATE 12-18
I'M PRETTY SURE IT'S MATH.
GOOD NIGHT, HAMMIE.
KIRKMAN & SCOTT

Jerry: I don't remember school being especially tough for me, but these strips about Hammie's classroom troubles sure seem familiar.

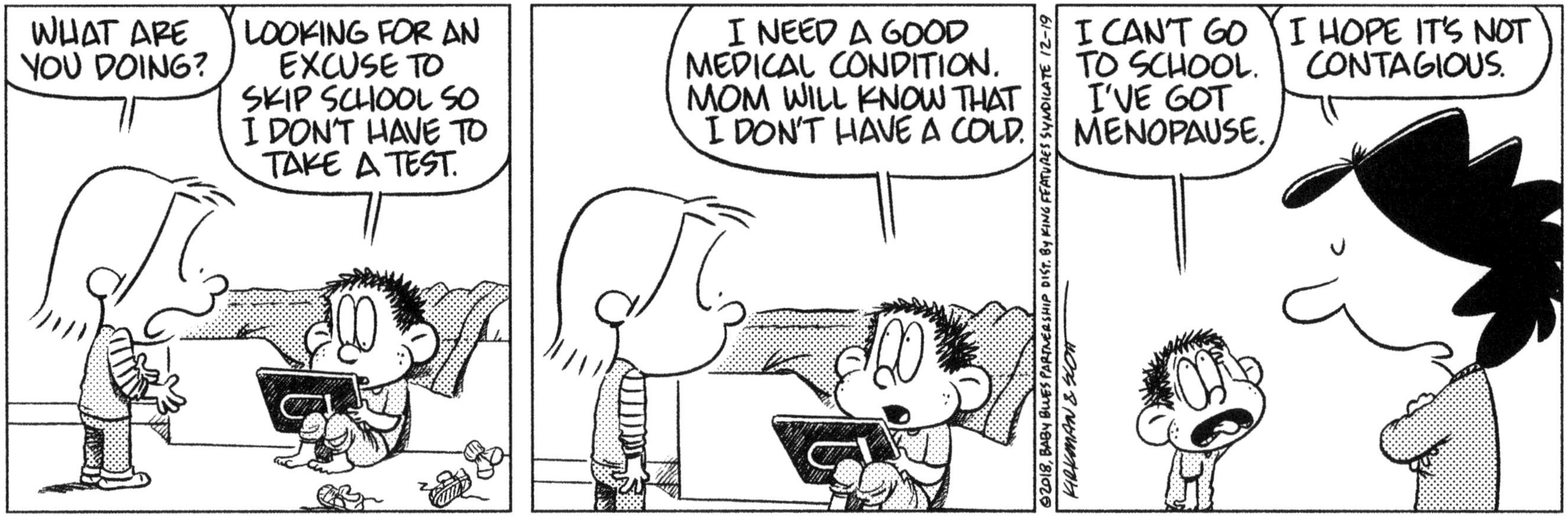
WHAT ARE YOU DOING?
LOOKING FOR AN EXCUSE TO SKIP SCHOOL SO I DON'T HAVE TO TAKE A TEST.
I NEED A GOOD MEDICAL CONDITION. MOM WILL KNOW THAT I DON'T HAVE A COLD.
©2018, BABY BLUES PARTNERSHIP DIST. BY KING FEATURES SYNDICATE 12-19
KIRKMAN & SCOTT
I CAN'T GO TO SCHOOL. I'VE GOT MENOPAUSE.
I HOPE IT'S NOT CONTAGIOUS.

Rick: Great choice.

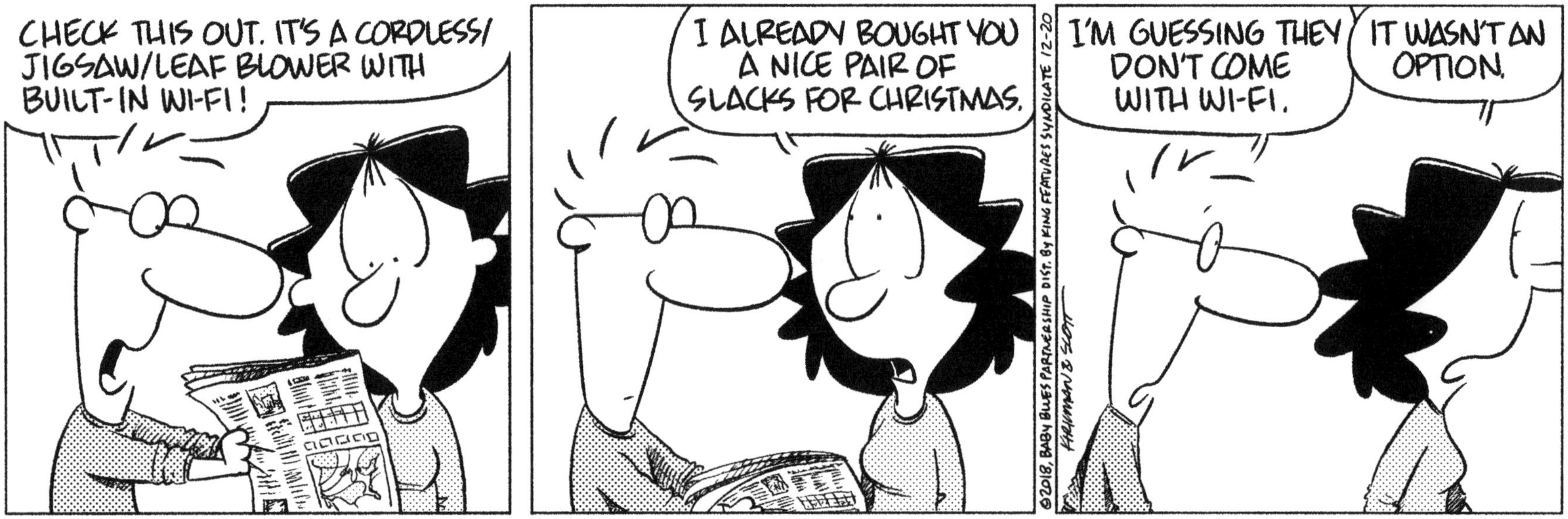
CHECK THIS OUT. IT'S A CORDLESS/ JIGSAW/LEAF BLOWER WITH BUILT-IN WI-FI!
I ALREADY BOUGHT YOU A NICE PAIR OF SLACKS FOR CHRISTMAS.
©2018, BABY BLUES PARTNERSHIP DIST. BY KING FEATURES SYNDICATE 12-20
KIRKMAN & SCOTT
I'M GUESSING THEY DON'T COME WITH WI-FI.
IT WASN'T AN OPTION.

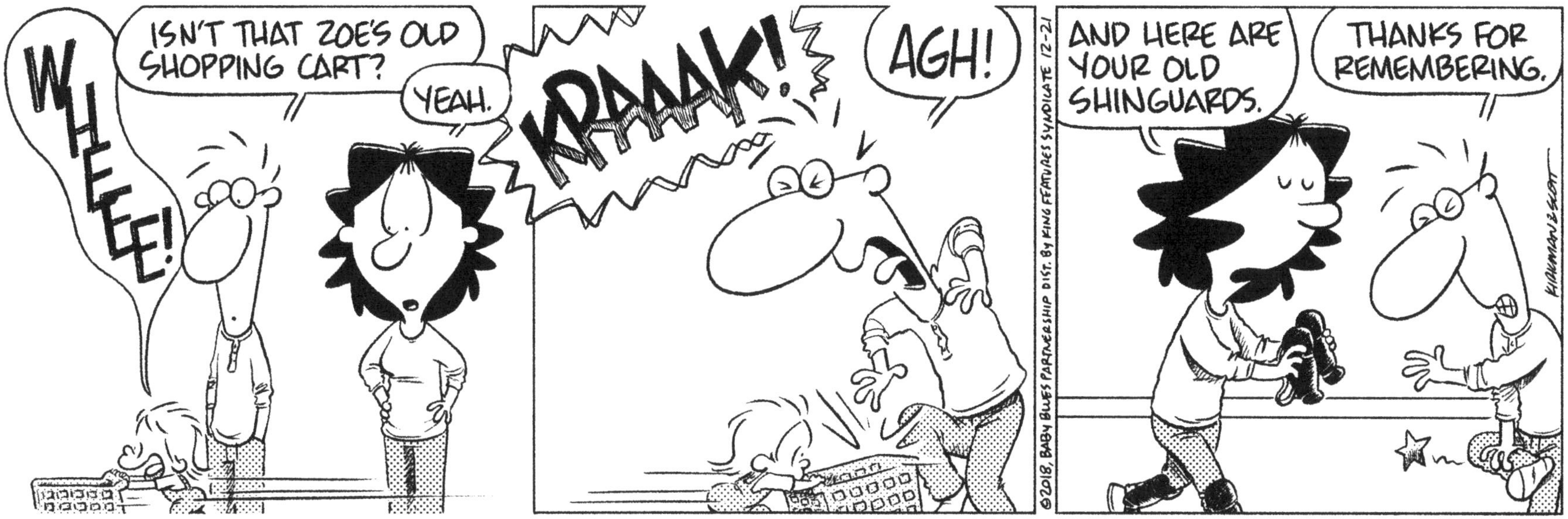
WHEEEE!
ISN'T THAT ZOE'S OLD SHOPPING CART?
YEAH.
KRAAAK!
AGH!
©2018, BABY BLUES PARTNERSHIP DIST. BY KING FEATURES SYNDICATE 12-21
AND HERE ARE YOUR OLD SHINGUARDS.
THANKS FOR REMEMBERING.
KIRKMAN & SCOTT

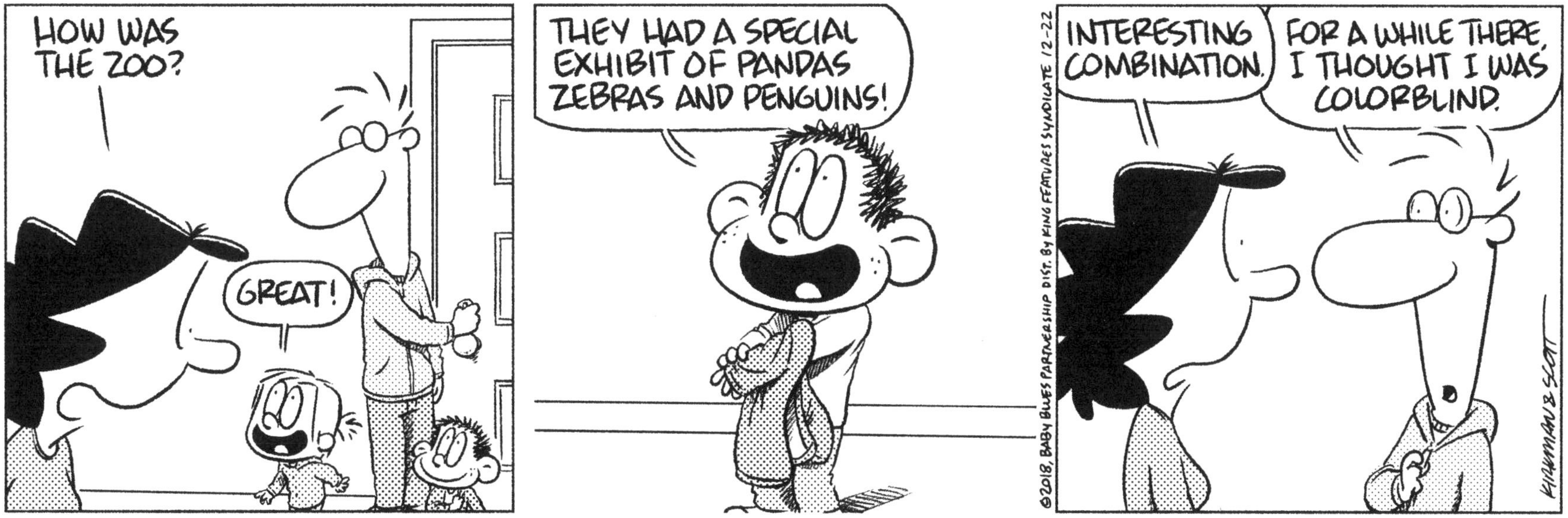
HOW WAS THE ZOO?
GREAT!
THEY HAD A SPECIAL EXHIBIT OF PANDAS ZEBRAS AND PENGUINS!
©2018, BABY BLUES PARTNERSHIP DIST. BY KING FEATURES SYNDICATE 12-22
INTERESTING COMBINATION.
FOR A WHILE THERE, I THOUGHT I WAS COLORBLIND.
KIRKMAN & SCOTT

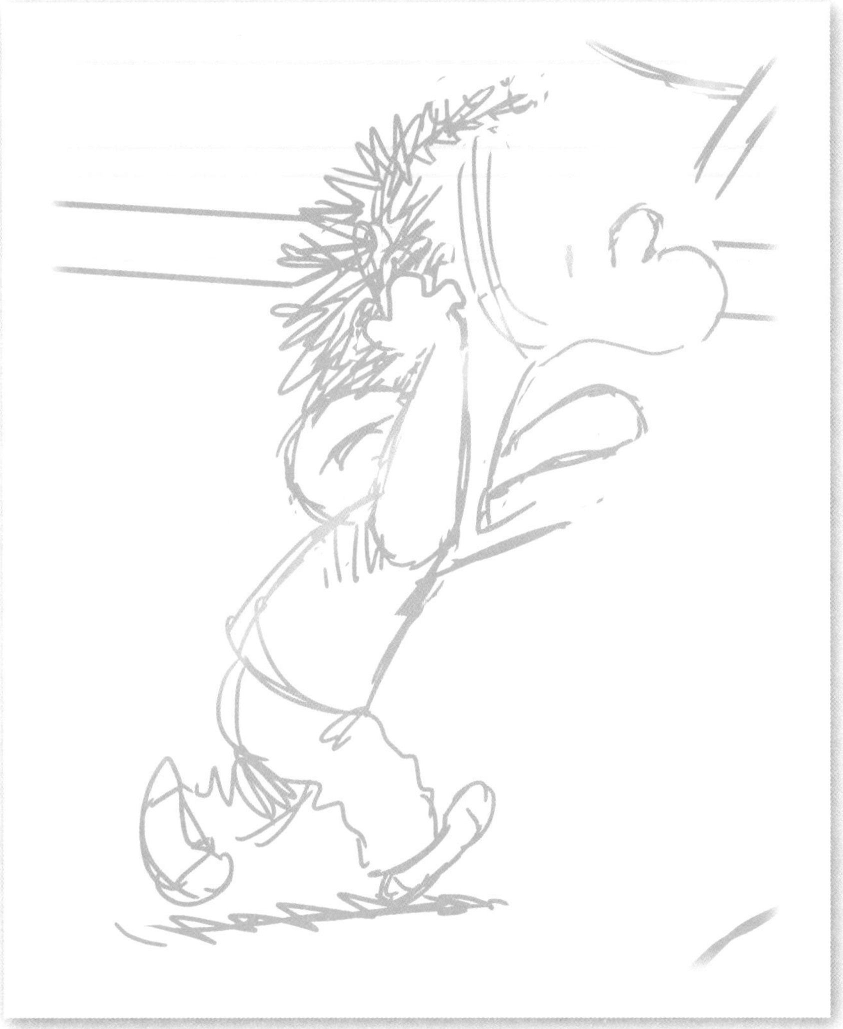

Rick: Just when you think they're not paying attention, they get it. Only not enough.

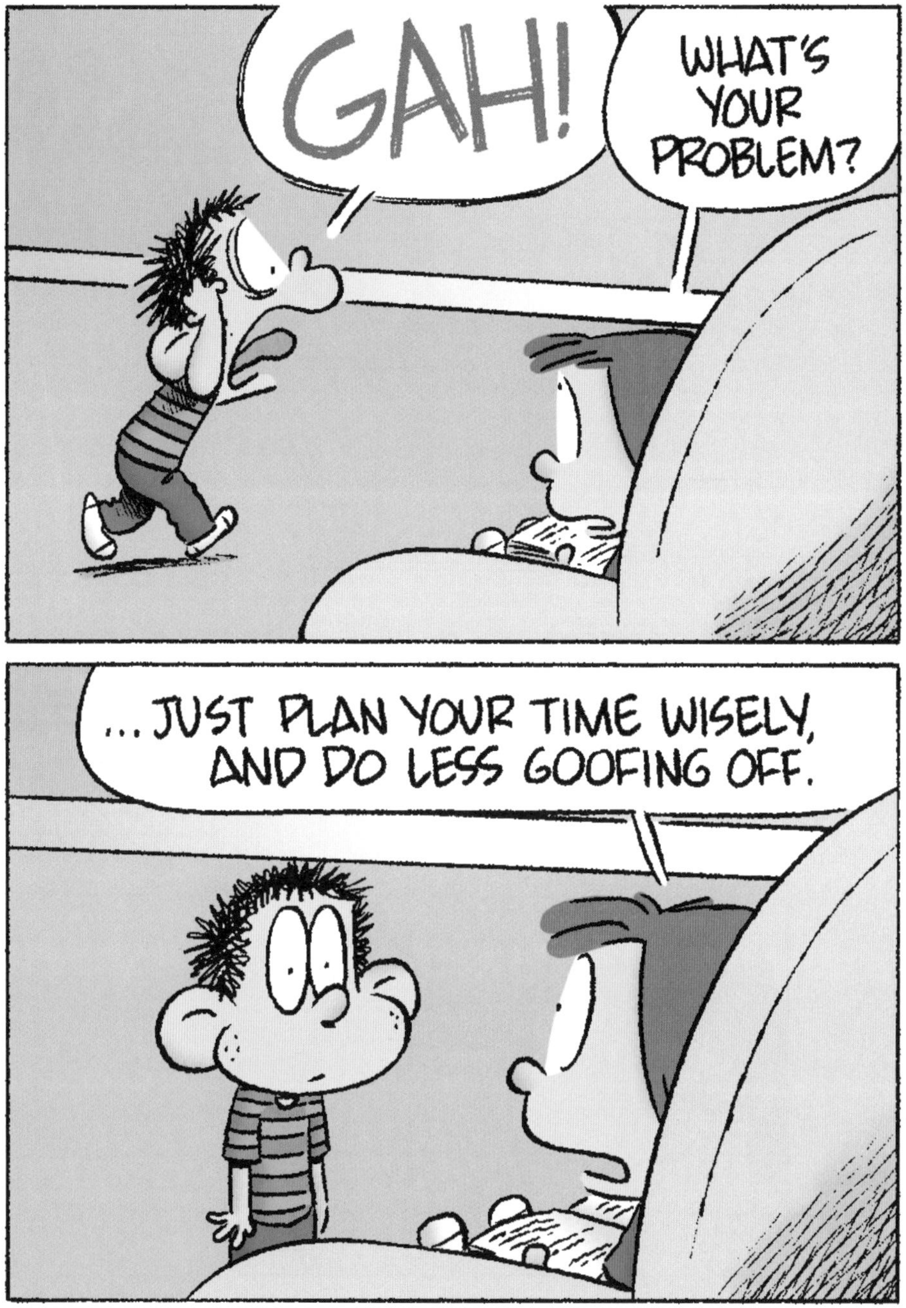

GAH!
WHAT'S YOUR PROBLEM?
...JUST PLAN YOUR TIME WISELY, AND DO LESS GOOFING OFF.

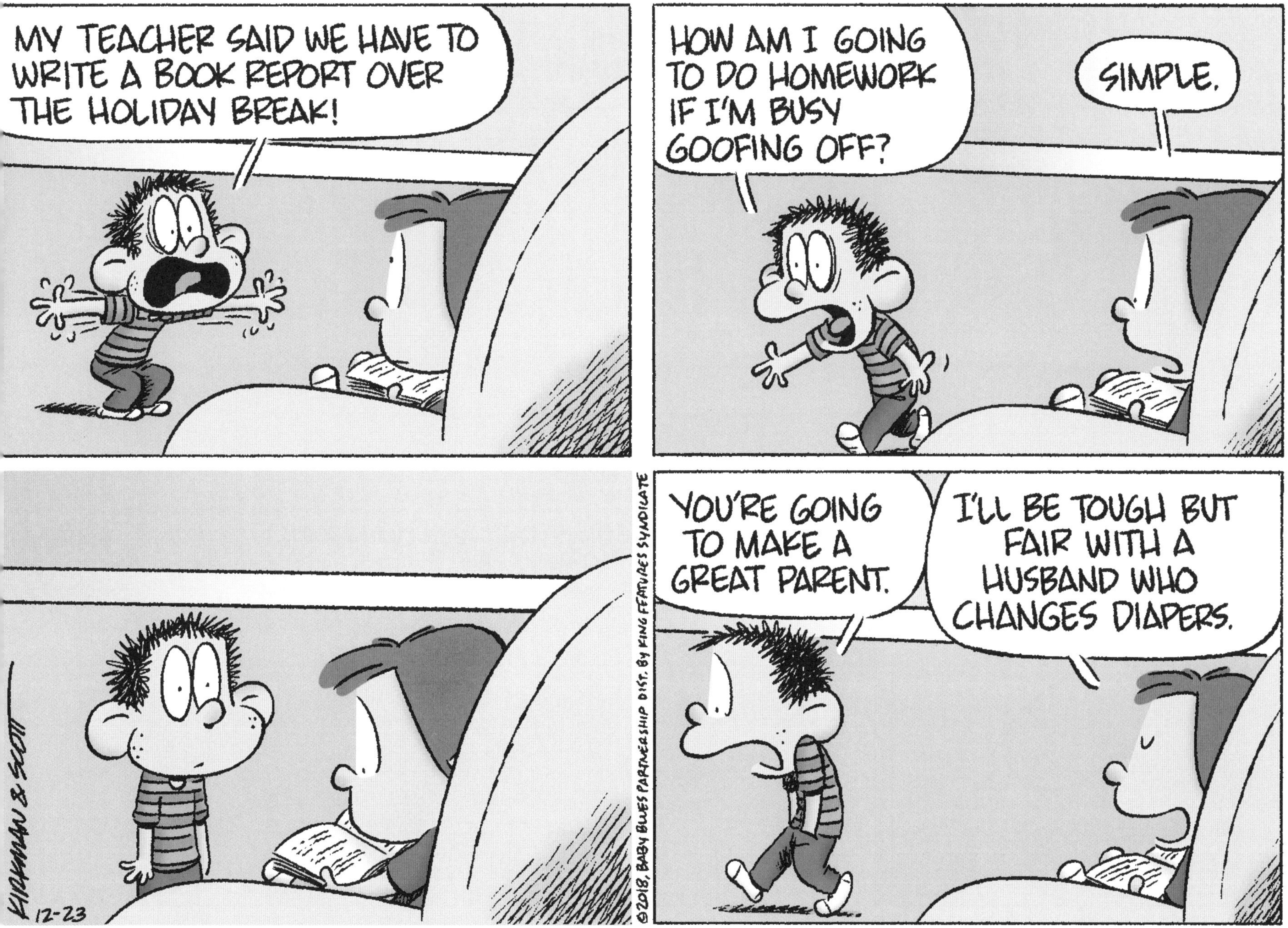
MY TEACHER SAID WE HAVE TO WRITE A BOOK REPORT OVER THE HOLIDAY BREAK!
HOW AM I GOING TO DO HOMEWORK IF I'M BUSY GOOFING OFF?
SIMPLE.
KIRKMAN & SCOTT
12-23
©2018, BABY BLUES PARTNERSHIP DIST. BY KING FEATURES SYNDICATE
YOU'RE GOING TO MAKE A GREAT PARENT.
I'LL BE TOUGH BUT FAIR WITH A HUSBAND WHO CHANGES DIAPERS.

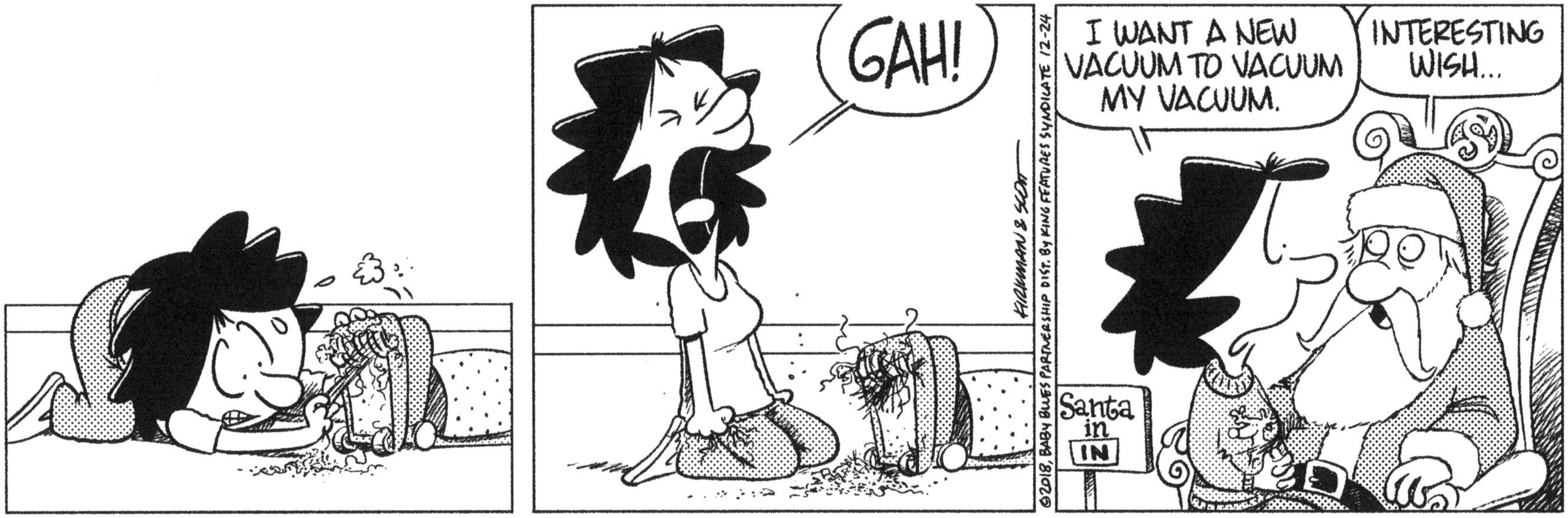
GAH!
KIRKMAN & SCOTT
©2018, BABY BLUES PARTNERSHIP DIST. BY KING FEATURES SYNDICATE 12-24
I WANT A NEW VACUUM TO VACUUM MY VACUUM.
INTERESTING WISH...
Santa in
IN

Rick: True story.

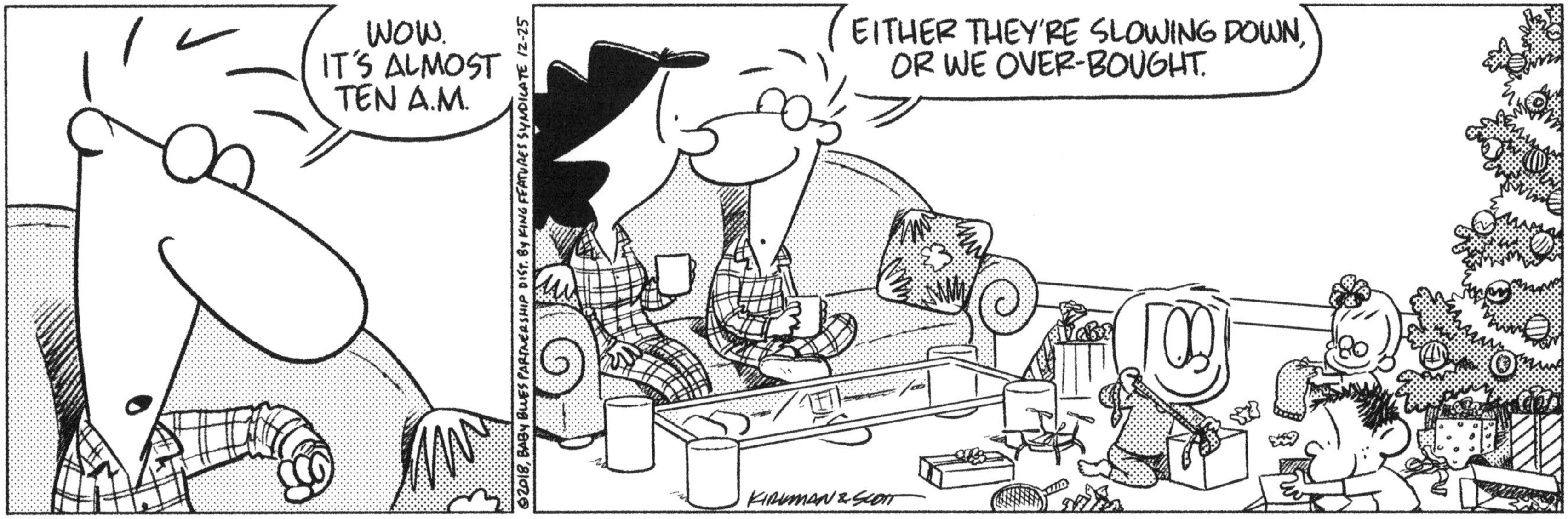
WOW. IT'S ALMOST TEN A.M.
©2018, BABY BLUES PARTNERSHIP DIST. BY KING FEATURES SYNDICATE 12-25
EITHER THEY'RE SLOWING DOWN, OR WE OVER-BOUGHT.
KIRKMAN & SCOTT

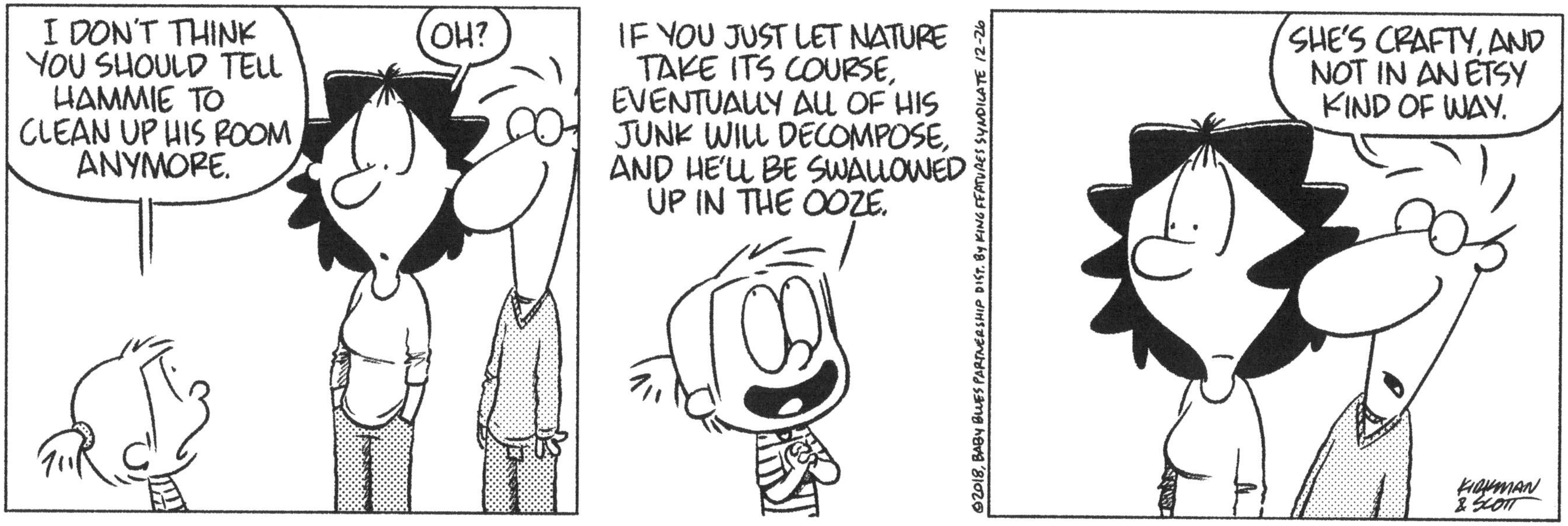
I DON'T THINK YOU SHOULD TELL HAMMIE TO CLEAN UP HIS ROOM ANYMORE.
OH?
IF YOU JUST LET NATURE TAKE ITS COURSE, EVENTUALLY ALL OF HIS JUNK WILL DECOMPOSE, AND HE'LL BE SWALLOWED UP IN THE OOZE.
©2018, BABY BLUES PARTNERSHIP DIST. BY KING FEATURES SYNDICATE 12-26
SHE'S CRAFTY, AND NOT IN AN ETSY KIND OF WAY.
KIRKMAN & SCOTT

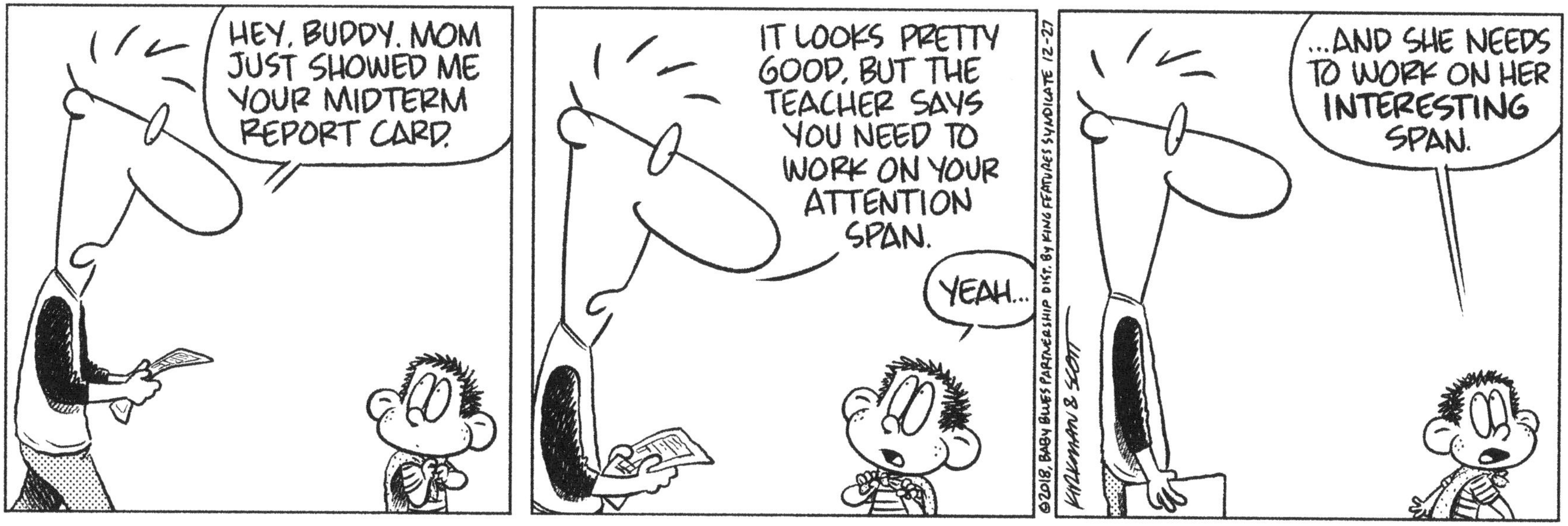
HEY, BUDDY. MOM JUST SHOWED ME YOUR MIDTERM REPORT CARD.
IT LOOKS PRETTY GOOD, BUT THE TEACHER SAYS YOU NEED TO WORK ON YOUR ATTENTION SPAN.
YEAH...
©2018, BABY BLUES PARTNERSHIP DIST. BY KING FEATURES SYNDICATE 12-27
KIRKMAN & SCOTT
...AND SHE NEEDS TO WORK ON HER INTERESTING SPAN.

Rick: Man, that would make a great workshop.

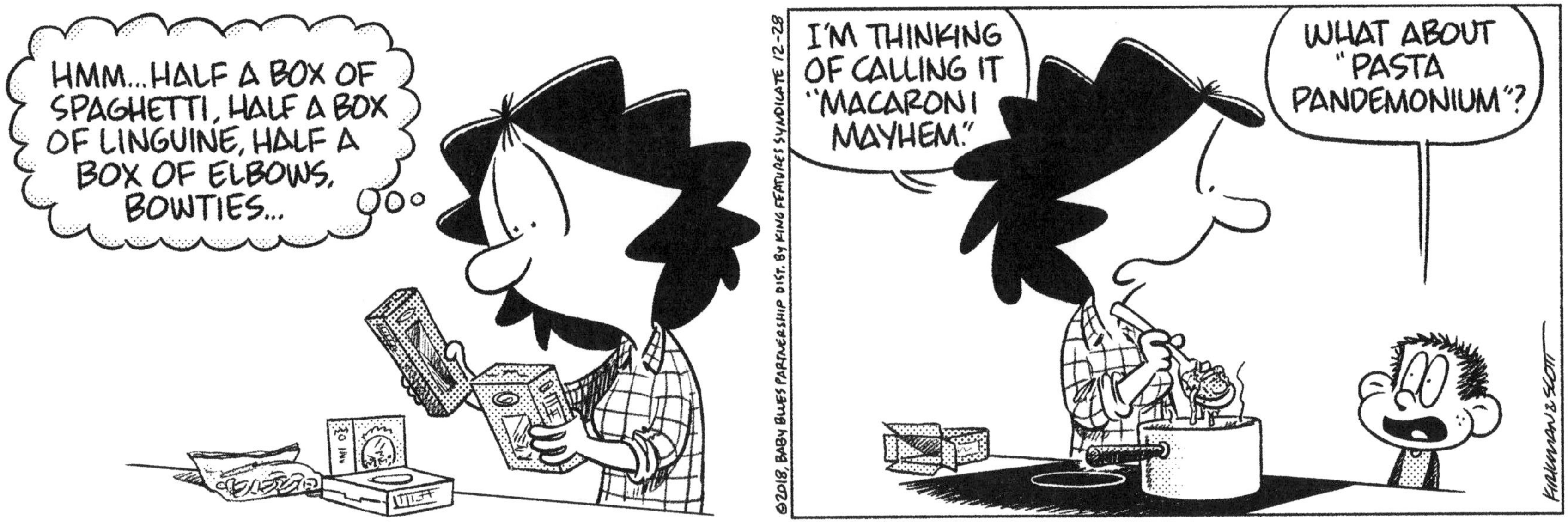
HMM...HALF A BOX OF SPAGHETTI, HALF A BOX OF LINGUINE, HALF A BOX OF ELBOWS, BOWTIES...
©2018, BABY BLUES PARTNERSHIP DIST. BY KING FEATURES SYNDICATE 12-28
I'M THINKING OF CALLING IT "MACARONI MAYHEM."
WHAT ABOUT "PASTA PANDEMONIUM"?
KIRKMAN & SCOTT

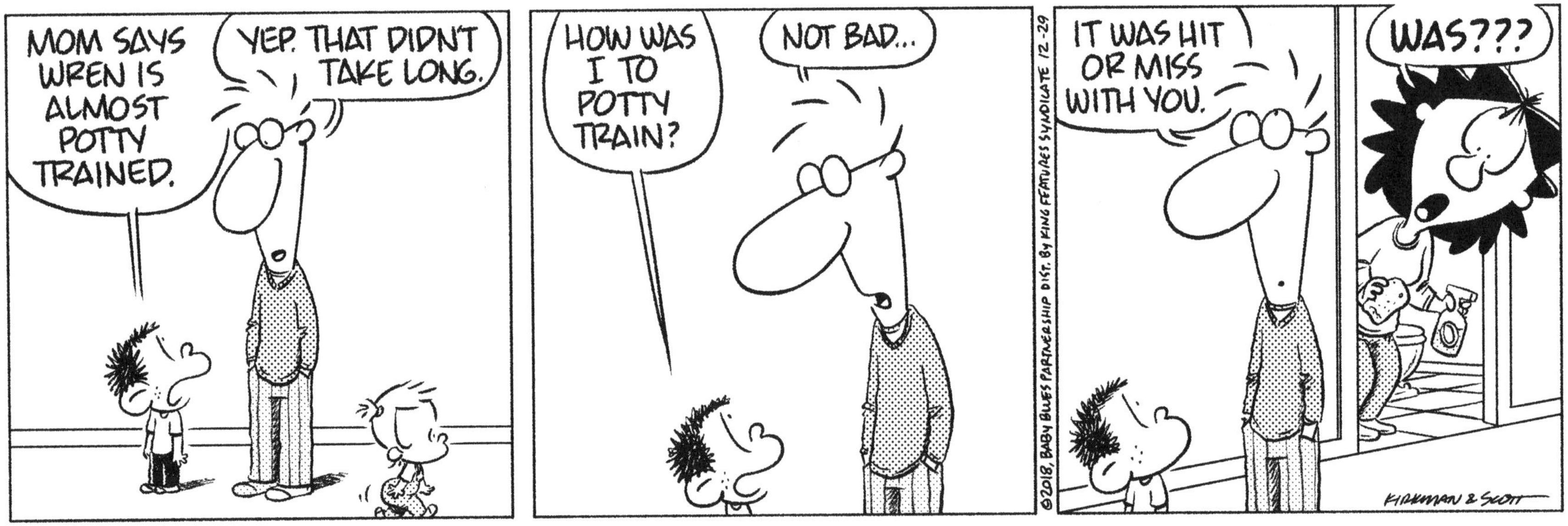
MOM SAYS WREN IS ALMOST POTTY TRAINED.
YEP. THAT DIDN'T TAKE LONG.
HOW WAS I TO POTTY TRAIN?
NOT BAD...
©2018, BABY BLUES PARTNERSHIP DIST. BY KING FEATURES SYNDICATE 12-29
IT WAS HIT OR MISS WITH YOU.
WAS???
KIRKMAN & SCOTT

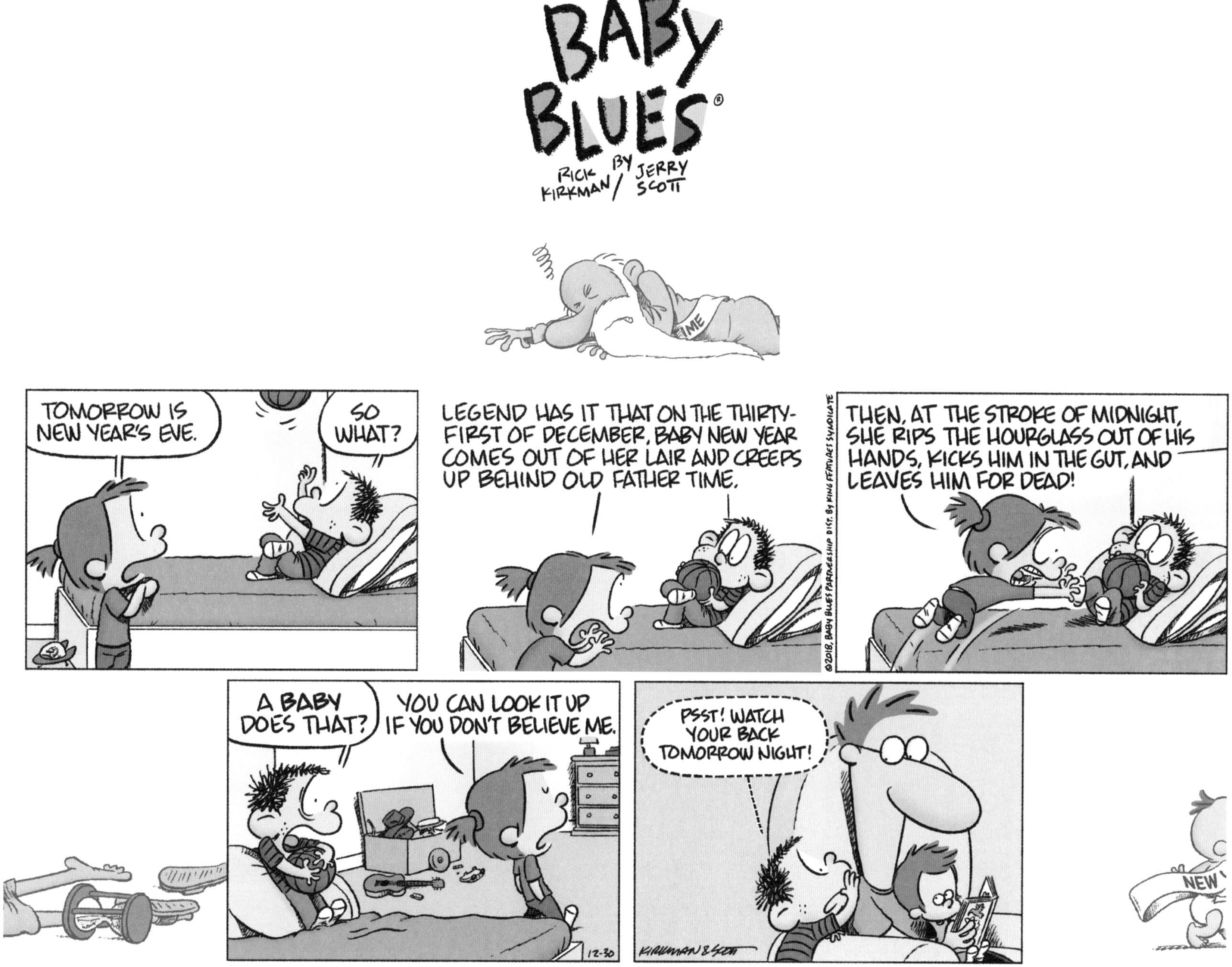
BABY BLUES®
BY RICK KIRKMAN / JERRY SCOTT
TIME
TOMORROW IS NEW YEAR'S EVE.
SO WHAT?
LEGEND HAS IT THAT ON THE THIRTY-FIRST OF DECEMBER, BABY NEW YEAR COMES OUT OF HER LAIR AND CREEPS UP BEHIND OLD FATHER TIME.
©2018, BABY BLUES PARTNERSHIP DIST. BY KING FEATURES SYNDICATE
THEN, AT THE STROKE OF MIDNIGHT, SHE RIPS THE HOURGLASS OUT OF HIS HANDS, KICKS HIM IN THE GUT, AND LEAVES HIM FOR DEAD!
A BABY DOES THAT?
YOU CAN LOOK IT UP IF YOU DON'T BELIEVE ME.
12-30
PSST! WATCH YOUR BACK TOMORROW NIGHT!
KIRKMAN & SCOTT
NEW

Rick: I admire Zoe's imagination. And Hammie's gullibility. We can't show the title panel the way it was intended here, but Father Time and Baby New Year bookend the bottom panels.

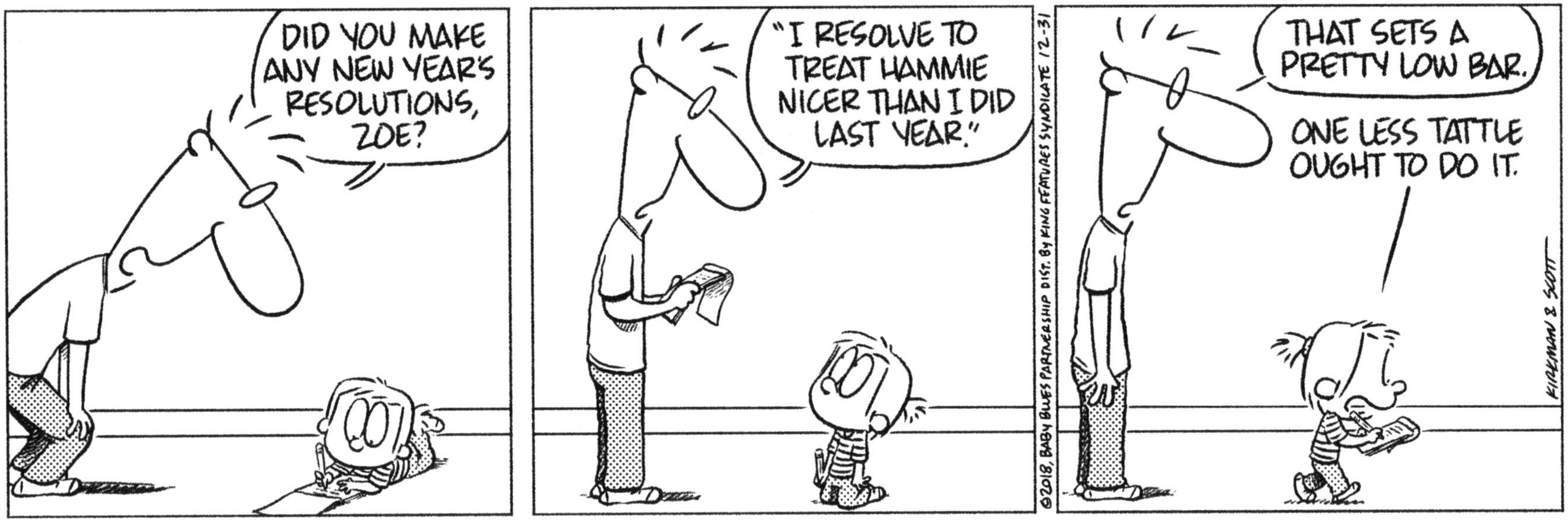
DID YOU MAKE ANY NEW YEAR'S RESOLUTIONS, ZOE?
"I RESOLVE TO TREAT HAMMIE NICER THAN I DID LAST YEAR."
©2018, BABY BLUES PARTNERSHIP DIST. BY KING FEATURES SYNDICATE 12-31
THAT SETS A PRETTY LOW BAR.
ONE LESS TATTLE OUGHT TO DO IT.
KIRKMAN & SCOTT

Rick: Ugh.

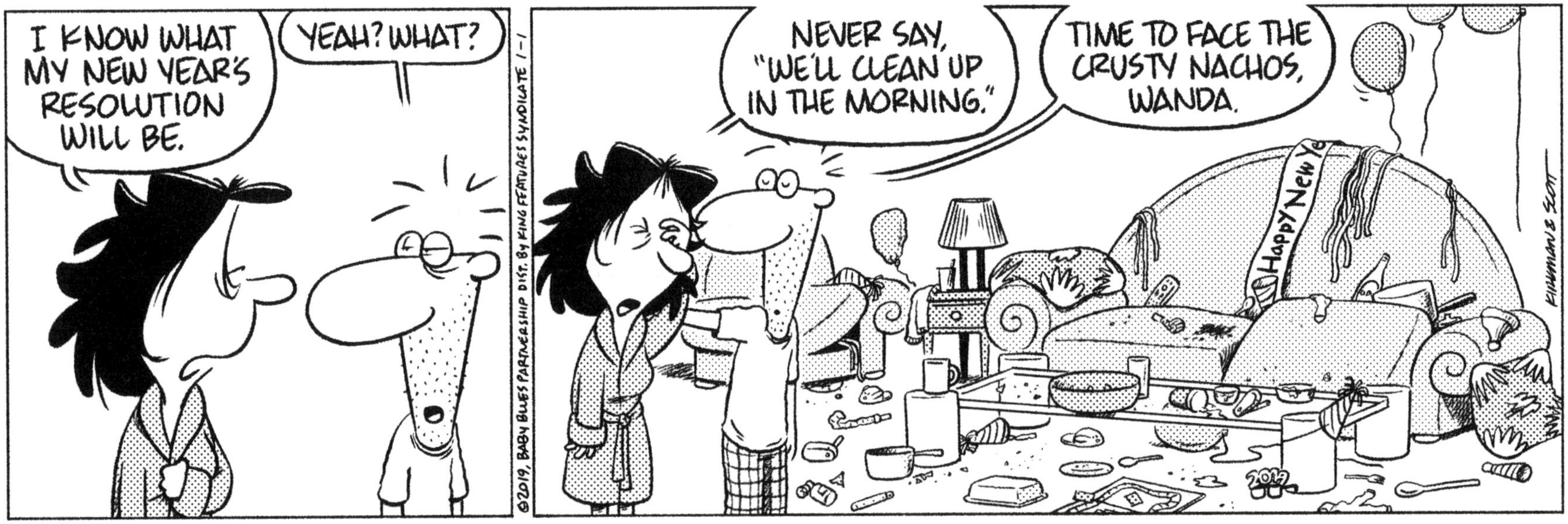
I KNOW WHAT MY NEW YEAR'S RESOLUTION WILL BE.
YEAH? WHAT?
©2019, BABY BLUES PARTNERSHIP DIST. BY KING FEATURES SYNDICATE 1-1
NEVER SAY, "WE'LL CLEAN UP IN THE MORNING."
TIME TO FACE THE CRUSTY NACHOS, WANDA.
Happy New Ye
2019
KIRKMAN & SCOTT

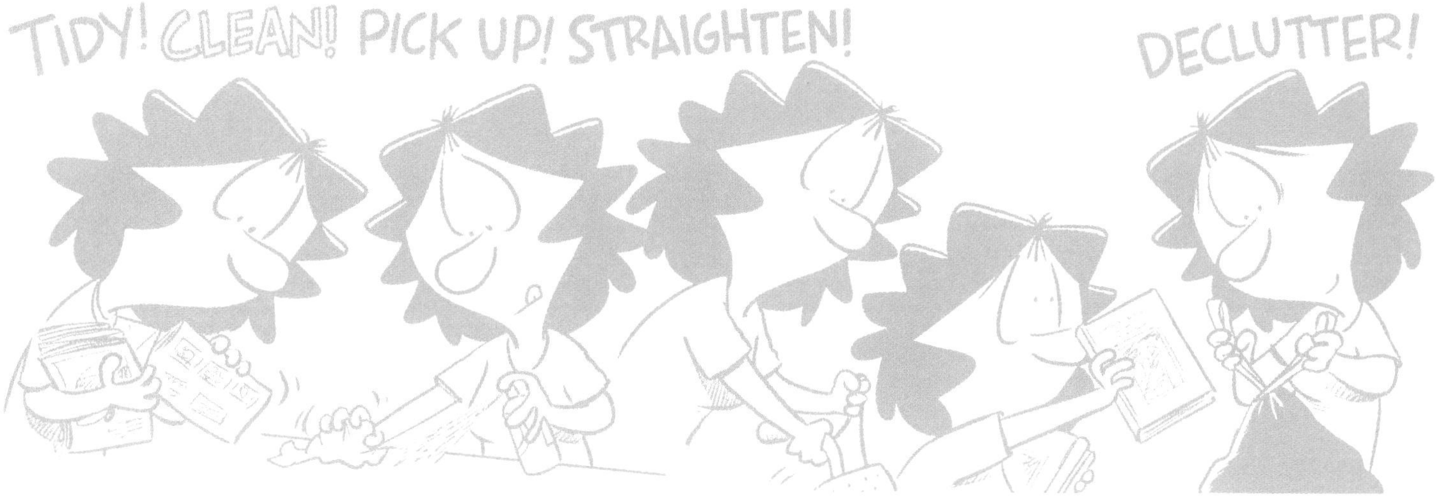
TIDY! CLEAN! PICK UP! STRAIGHTEN!
DECLUTTER!

Baby Blues® is syndicated internationally by King Features Syndicate, Inc.
For information, write King Features Syndicate, Inc.,
300 West Fifty-Seventh Street, New York, New York 10019.

Andrews McMeel Publishing
a division of Andrews McMeel Universal
1130 Walnut Street, Kansas City, Missouri 64106
www.andrewsmcmeel.com

19 20 21 22 23 SDB 10 9 8 7 6 5 4 3 2 1

ISBN: 978-1-5248-5175-0

Library of Congress Control Number: 2019935717

Editor: Lucas Wetzel
Designer/Art Director: Julie Barnes
Production Manager: Chuck Harper
Production Editor: Amy Strassner
Demand Planner: Sue Eikos

Find *Baby Blues*® on the Web at www.babyblues.com.

ATTENTION: SCHOOLS AND BUSINESSES
Andrews McMeel books are available at quantity discounts with bulk purchase for educational,
business, or sales promotional use. For information, please e-mail the Andrews McMeel Publishing
Special Sales Department: specialsales@amuniversal.com.